Data and Analytics in Accounting

INTERNATIONAL ADAPTATION

Data and Analytics in Accounting

An Integrated Approach

INTERNATIONAL ADAPTATION

Ann Dzuranin, PhD, CPA
Northern Illinois University
Chicago, USA

Guido Geerts, PhD
University of Delaware
Newark, USA

Margarita Lenk, PhD, CMA
Colorado State University
Fort Collins, USA

WILEY

Data and Analytics in Accounting

An Integrated Approach

INTERNATIONAL ADAPTATION

Copyright © 2024 The content provided in this textbook is based on Data and Analytics in Accounting: An Integrated Approach, by Ann Dzuranin, Guido Geerts, and Margarita Lenk, 1st edition [2023]. John Wiley & Sons Singapore Pte. Ltd

Cover image: © Adobe Stock

Contributing Subject Matter Expert: Dr K Lubza Nihar, Associate Professor, GITAM School of Business, India

Founded in 1807, John Wiley & Sons, Inc. has been a valued source of knowledge and understanding for more than 200 years, helping people around the world meet their needs and fulfill their aspirations. Our company is built on a foundation of principles that include responsibility to the communities we serve and where we live and work. In 2008, we launched a Corporate Citizenship Initiative, a global effort to address the environmental, social, economic, and ethical challenges we face in our business. Among the issues we are addressing are carbon impact, paper specifications and procurement, ethical conduct within our business and among our vendors, and community and charitable support. For more information, please visit our website: www.wiley.com/go/citizenship.

C9781119889120 _050724

ISBN: 978-1-119-88913-7 (ePub)

ISBN: 978-1-119-88914-4 (ePdf)

Printed and bound by CPI Group (UK) Ltd, Croydon CR0 4YY

About the Authors

© Nick Porcaro

© Guido Geerts

© Margarita Maria Lenk

ANN C. DZURANIN is the KPMG Endowed Professor of Accountancy at Northern Illinois University. She earned her BS from Fairleigh Dickinson University, her MBA from New York University, and her PhD from the University of South Florida. Ann is a CPA (NJ) with 15 years of experience in both public and corporate accounting.

Ann conducts behavioral research in managerial accounting decision-making and the ways in which accounting information systems interact with those decisions. Her publications include *Issues in Accounting Education, Journal of Information Systems, Journal of Business Ethics, Strategic Finance, Management Accounting Quarterly, IMA Statement on Management Accounting, Journal of Corporate Accounting and Finance,* and *Journal of Accounting Education.*

Ann received the 2018 American Accounting Association's Innovation in Accounting Education Award for her work in data analytics curriculum development. Ann's work in data analytics has resulted in invitations to present on Data Analytics and Accounting curriculum at both academic and professional conferences. Her presentations have reached over 3,000 people and her materials have been shared with more than 75 universities.

Ann served on the AICPA CPA Evolution Taskforce and currently serves as a BEC subcommittee member and a member of the CPA exam Content Committee.

GUIDO L. GEERTS is a professor of accounting and EY Faculty Scholar at the Lerner College of Business, University of Delaware, where he teaches accounting information systems and data analytics. He received a PhD in accounting information systems from the Free University of Brussels, Belgium, in 1993.

Guido's research has been published in journals such as *Accounting Horizons, Decision Support Systems, IEEE Intelligent Systems, International Journal of Accounting Information Systems, Journal of Accountancy, Journal of Emerging Technologies in Accounting,* and *Journal of Information Systems.* He has also co-authored a research monograph published by the American Accounting Association titled *The REA Accounting Model as an Accounting and Economic Ontology.*

Guido has received numerous research, teaching, and service awards, including the 2012 American Accounting Association Strategic and Emerging Technologies Section Outstanding Contribution to Research Award, the 2015 University of Delaware's Excellence in Teaching Award, the 2018 American Accounting Association Outstanding Service Award, and the 2022 American Accounting Association/J. Michael and Mary Anne Cook/Deloitte Foundation Prize for undergraduate teaching.

Guido is the former chair of the Technology Task Force for the Pathways Commission Recommendation 4 (Curriculum and Pedagogy) and currently serves as a Trustee on the AICPA Foundation Board.

MARGARITA MARIA LENK'S signature sincere enthusiasm, caring ethic, integrity, inclusion values, and her intellectual curiosity have served the accounting profession and students for decades in her roles as a national and international accounting professional, instructor, author, mentor, coach, consultant, presenter, and researcher. Margarita studied accounting, computer science, psychology, and economics, with degrees and teaching awards from the University of Central Florida, the University of North Carolina at Chapel Hill, and the University of South Carolina. She is a Colorado State University faculty emeritus.

Margarita integrates ethics, critical thinking, risk management, and data-driven decision-making perspectives in all her work. Her expertise includes data analytics, artificial intelligence, AIS security, governance and internal controls, sustainability accounting, social media risk management, service-learning, and university-community engagement and research partnerships. Her native Argentine innovative nature, strong service ethic and belief in our potential and responsibility to improve the world have always informed her accounting perspective and instructional philosophies toward developing future leaders.

Margarita has published over 50 interdisciplinary research articles in journals such as *Journal of Information Systems, Strategic Finance, Review of Accounting Information Systems, Journal of Production Planning and Control, Issues in Accounting Education, Journal of Information Systems Education, The Michigan Journal of Community Service Learning,* and *Business Communication Quarterly.* She has won over 30 instruction and mentoring related awards, including the 2019 Michael J. and Mary Ann Cook/Deloitte Foundation/AAA Prize for Outstanding Accounting Undergraduate Professor, the 2009 Outstanding Accounting Professor in the state of Colorado, the CSU System Board of Governors Outstanding Undergraduate Professor, and the 2006 Best Information Systems Professor from the Strategic and Emerging Technologies of the American Accounting Association. In 2021, she was inducted into the PhD Project Hall of Fame for mentoring and coaching three decades of diverse accounting faculty and students.

From the Authors

Dear Students,

The accounting profession is in a transformative time with data and analytics at its center. The accountants of the future will be agile, creative, data literate professionals who use critical thinking and problem-solving to drive business and professional value. The materials presented within this course will help you become a successful accountant in this new data and analytics environment.

Our author team is passionate about your success, and we have each applied unique skillsets and expertise to the resources created for this course. Our critical thinking framework and data analysis process model will help you develop the professional skills you need to plan data analysis projects, perform analyses, and report their results. Our pattern-based approach to analysis skills will help you effectively prepare data, calculate the information needed for analytical purposes, and explore data from a variety of perspectives. This approach has a hands-on emphasis that provides plenty of opportunities to learn new technology skills.

The course has several distinguishing features that will help you develop your critical thinking, data analysis, and communication skills:

- A critical thinking framework with six elements that can be applied to any data analysis process (SPARKS).
- A data analysis process model with three stages that reflects the process used in the accounting profession (Plan, Analyze, Report).
- A model for planning data analysis projects.
- A pattern-based approach to profiling, cleaning, and transforming data, calculating information for analytical purposes, and exploring key data relationships.
- Applications to five accounting areas: accounting information systems, auditing, financial, managerial, and tax accounting.
- Theories and tools to help you interpret the results of data analyses.
- Best practices for creating data visualizations and telling a compelling story with data.
- Exposure to emerging technologies and how they are changing accounting data analysis projects.

We believe that knowing how to use data to improve processes, enhance efficiencies and accuracy, assess and reduce risks, and evaluate issues and opportunities will maximize your professional and societal impacts and the effectiveness of your organizations. We also want you to develop the technical skills to accomplish these goals.

This course and its accompanying learning resources will help you:

- Develop a data analytics mindset.
- Follow sustainable, documented, and defendable data analysis processes.
- Integrate critical thinking into the data analysis process by understanding the stakeholders, purpose, analysis alternatives, risks, and knowledge needed to prepare, interpret, and communicate data analysis results.
- Develop foundational, professionally relevant technical skills you can apply across tools and accounting areas.
- Develop the technical agility and data acumen needed to create data analytics solutions for accounting problems.

We are excited you are using these resources and wish you tremendous success in your accounting career.

ANN DZURANIN, PhD, CPA
GUIDO GEERTS, PhD
MARGARITA LENK, PhD, CMA

About This International Adaptation

Pedagogical Framework

This edition uses a process-based approach to data analysis by systematically introducing, explaining, and applying key concepts at each stage of the data analysis process.

Laying the Foundation

Chapter 1 provides an overview of how data and analytics are being used in the accounting profession, the data analysis process, and the benefits of integrating critical thinking into that process. The visual of the Chapter Roadmap feature summarizes the topics covered in Chapter 2, which is a review of foundational data analysis skills to prepare the student for the rest of the course.

Chapter Roadmap

LEARNING OBJECTIVES	TOPICS	APPLY IT
LO 2.1 Describe how data is stored in and extracted from relational databases.	• Relational Databases • Joining Tables	**Identify Primary and Foreign Keys** (Example: Accounting Information Systems)
LO 2.2 Explain how functions help answer data analysis questions.	• Basic Functions for Data Analysis • Applying Excel Basic Functions	**Analyze Sales Transactions with Excel Functions** (Example: Financial and Managerial Accounting)
LO 2.3 Illustrate how pivottables organize and filter data.	• Using PivotTables • Filtering PivotTables	**Analyze Sales with Excel PivotTables** (Example: Financial and Managerial Accounting)
LO 2.4 Identify descriptive measures used to perform data analysis.	• Measures of Location • Measures of Dispersion • Measures of Shape • Correlation Analysis	**Use Descriptive Statistics to Audit Warranty Expense** (Example: Auditing)
LO 2.5 Summarize how data visualization explores and explains data.	• Making Sense of Large Data Sets • Visualizations and When to Use Them • Microsoft Excel Visualizations	**Analyze Product Costs with Data Visualization** (Example: Managerial Accounting)

Integrating Critical Thinking into the Data Analysis Process

Chapters 3 through 9 focus on the three stages of the data analysis process—Plan, Analyze, and Report.

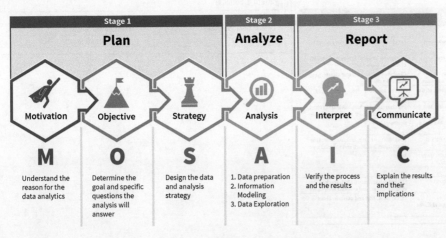

- Chapter 3 develops the first two steps of the planning stage by explaining how motivation, or the "why" behind the project, influences the project's objective. This objective is the foundation for developing the specific analysis questions that must be answered. How to design data and analysis strategies to answer these questions and achieve the project's objective is covered in Chapter 4.

- Chapters 5 through 7 describe the analysis stage, demonstrating how patterns can be used to prepare data for analysis, build information models, and explore data.

- Chapters 8 and 9 detail how to report analysis results by accurately interpreting and effectively communicating them.

Finally, Chapter 10 discusses how changing data characteristics and recently developed technologies and tools are impacting how accounting professionals are performing data analysis. This edition also discusses how Generative AI has the power to transform accounting and financial reporting.

Six essential elements of critical thinking are integrated into each chapter. By consistently applying the SPARKS critical thinking framework to data analysis topics, students refine their ability to think critically as they develop their data analysis skills.

Using a Pattern-Based Approach

The three analysis chapters use a unique approach to learning data analytics—patterns, which the student can leverage across data analytics projects. Each pattern represents a real-world scenario commonly encountered during data analysis and presents best practices and techniques to address such a scenario.

Patterns are introduced, explained, and summarized at key points, including at the conclusion of discussions and as part of the chapter summaries. This diverse set of patterns provide the foundational knowledge needed to be a successful data analyst.

ILLUSTRATION 7.46 Overview of Data Exploration Patterns

Id	Data Relationship	Description	Visualization Examples (Bold Indicates Chapter Example)
Foundational Data Relationships			
1	Nominal Comparison	Compares the values of a nominal variable based on the values of a second, numeric variable.	Bar chart, **column chart**, dot plot, and lollipop chart
2	Distribution	Shows how the values of a numeric variable are distributed, or spread.	Histogram, **box-and-whisker (boxplot) chart**, and violin plot
3	Deviation	Shows how a set of actual values deviate from their reference values such as budgeted or forecasted values.	**Clustered bar** and column **charts**, gauge, and bullet chart
4	Ranking	Orders the values of a variable sequentially based on the values of a second variable.	Defined as part of a table, bar chart, or **column chart**.
5	Part-to-Whole	Shows how each part compares to the whole and how the parts compare to one another.	**Pie chart**, donut chart, stacked bar chart, stacked column chart, and tree map chart
6	Correlation	Indicates the degree to which two variables move in the same or the opposite direction.	**Scatterplot**
7	Time Series	Shows the values of a variable at sequential points in time.	Area chart, bar chart, column chart, **line chart**, sparkline chart, and waterfall chart
8	Geospatial	Assigns numeric values to locations and encodes them through coloring (shade) and size (bubble size).	**Maps**
Integrated Data Relationships			
9	Composite Trends	Shows how a composite structure (part-to-whole) changes over time (time series).	Stacked column chart, **100% stacked column chart, and stacked area chart**
10	Pareto Analysis	Illustrates the importance of different categories (nominal comparison), ranks them (ranking), and shows their cumulative percentage (part-to-whole).	Pareto chart, **line and column chart**

Pattern 1 Summary

Problem	All the data did not transfer.
Detect (Data Profiling)	Compare row counts.
Correct (ETL)	Add the missing rows.

Connecting to the Profession

Chapter features, examples, questions, and cases present a mix of accounting examples so students can see how topics can be applied in different accounting contexts.

Insights from Accounting Professionals

Each chapter opens with an insight from an accounting professional introducing key topics covered in the chapter. These engaging insights are a window into how data analysis is being used in the accounting profession.

PROFESSIONAL INSIGHT — **How Can You Approach the Challenges of Data Preparation?**

Bill is a director in the audit data analytics practice at one of the large public accounting firms.

After graduating with an accounting degree, I gradually moved to our data analytics practice. **I love how accounting and technology blend together in our audit engagements and that there are always new opportunities and challenges to work on.**

A key challenge in working with data at a public accounting firm is that our clients come in all shapes and sizes, with ERP systems ranging from legacy proprietary systems to increasingly modern, cloud-based integrated systems with sophisticated reporting and analytics capabilities. This means that **the cleanliness, quality, granularity, volume, and structure of the data can vary significantly. This increases the importance of ETL (Extract-Transform-Load) solutions to help our professionals efficiently extract data from client systems, transform that data into a common format, and ultimately load the data into our analytics platform.**

To be successful, the data professionals at my firm must be able to understand and evaluate our clients' data to ensure that they are relevant and reliable. This includes knowing how to have the right conversations with our clients, often including representatives from the client's IT department and our internal data extraction specialists, in order to effectively communicate our data requirements. The skills you are building in this chapter are all highly relevant to a successful career as a data analyst in today's public accounting profession.

Accounting Area Examples

Chapter topics are consistently applied to accounting areas such as financial, managerial, and tax accounting, as well as AIS and auditing. Application opportunities and end-of-chapter assessment are also tagged by accounting areas to help students practice applying data analysis to these respective accounting areas.

BE 8.11 (LO 5) Tax Accounting One consideration of tax planning is understanding and projecting the amount of net revenue that a company expects for the upcoming year. Your team has created a what-if analysis to predict Super Scooters' net revenue for next year. Based on current year data, the team has performed three sensitivity analyses:

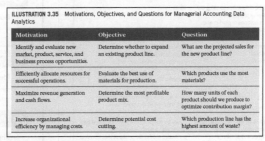

ILLUSTRATION 3.35 Motivations, Objectives, and Questions for Managerial Accounting Data Analytics

Motivation	Objective	Question
Identify and evaluate new market, product, service, and business process opportunities.	Determine whether to expand an existing product line.	What are the projected sales for the new product line?
Efficiently allocate resources for successful operations.	Evaluate the best use of materials for production.	Which products use the most materials?
Maximize revenue generation and cash flows.	Determine the most profitable product mix.	How many units of each product should we produce to optimize contribution margin?
Increase organizational efficiency by managing costs.	Determine potential cost cutting.	Which production line has the highest amount of waste?

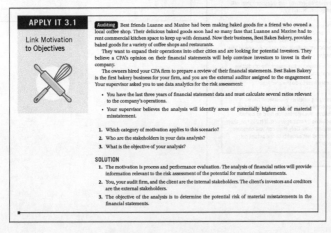

APPLY IT 3.1

Link Motivation to Objectives

Auditing Best friends Luanne and Maxine had been making baked goods for a friend who owned a local coffee shop. Their delicious baked goods soon had so many fans that Luanne and Maxine had to rent commercial kitchen space to keep up with demand. Now their business, Best Bakes Bakery, provides baked goods for a variety of coffee shops and restaurants.

They want to expand their operations into other cities and are looking for potential investors. They believe a CPA's opinion on their financial statements will help convince investors to invest in their company.

The owners hired your CPA firm to prepare a review of their financial statements. Best Bakes Bakery is the first bakery business for your firm, and you are the external auditor assigned to the engagement. Your supervisor asked you to use data analytics for the risk assessment.

- You have the last three years of financial statement data and must calculate several ratios relevant to the company's operations.
- Your supervisor believes the analysis will identify areas of potentially higher risk of material misstatement.

1. Which category of motivation applies to this scenario?
2. Who are the stakeholders in your data analysis?
3. What is the objective of your analysis?

SOLUTION

1. The motivation is process and performance evaluation. The analysis of financial ratios will provide information relevant to the risk assessment of the potential for material misstatements.
2. You, your audit firm, and the client are the internal stakeholders. The client's investors and creditors are the external stakeholders.
3. The objective of the analysis is to determine the potential risk of material misstatements in the financial statements.

Developing In-Demand Skills

Chapter features help students develop the skills employers are demanding from accounting professionals today.

Critical Thinking

In each chapter, Applying Critical Thinking feature boxes illustrate how a disciplined, reasoned approach to data analysis is the foundation of a data analytics mindset.

Applying Critical Thinking 4.4

Threats to Data Strategy

Data risks can impact the accuracy and validity of analysis results. These risks must be evaluated so appropriate controls can be added to the project plan. Data strategy risks can include **(Risks)**:

- Dirty data such as incomplete data, inaccurate data, and incorrectly formatted data fields.
- Data irrelevant to the objective of the project.
- Insufficient data for the analysis to be reliable.
- Data that is an unrepresentative sample of the underlying population.
- Errors in management estimates and assumptions about the data.

Chapters also demonstrate critical thinking application at key points and emphasize the benefits of evaluating a data analysis project from multiple angles at each process stage.

ILLUSTRATION 3.5 Thinking Critically About Motivations and Objectives

Critical Thinking Element		Why It Matters	Super Scooters Example
S	**Stakeholders**	Considering the perspectives of stakeholders helps identify the objective and develop good questions.	The internal stakeholders are Lyla and Calvin. Their motivation is to better understand company performance. The objective is to describe current performance, diagnose issues related to poor performance, predict future sales, and make recommendations for improvements.
P	**Purpose**	Critically thinking through the purpose of data analyses is the link between a defined objective and specific questions: • A purpose is the reason something is done or created. • An objective is something we plan to do, or a goal. The questions will be different depending on whether the purpose is to describe and diagnose current conditions or predict and prescribe future outcomes.	Based on the objectives, the purpose is to: • Describe what is happening now and diagnose issues related to poor performance. • Predict future sales. • Prescribe a profitable sales mix.
A	**Alternatives**	Evaluating different methods of analysis increases the likelihood of selecting the best option for the project's purpose.	Develop several alternative methods for performing the analysis to describe performance over the past year. Consider how likely each option is to provide valuable information. Rank the alternatives and choose the one with the highest expected value.
R	**Risks**	Being aware of potential risks makes it possible to also mitigate them when evaluating motivation, objectives, and questions.	It may be tempting to make Calvin and Lyla happy with a positive outlook in the predictive model. Be aware of that bias and develop objectives and questions that will not be influenced by it.
K	**Knowledge**	Successfully completing a project requires confirming we have the necessary knowledge to do so or doing additional research to obtain that knowledge.	One purpose of the Super Scooters analysis is to predict future sales and expenses. If you do not know how to prepare a predictive analysis, you must do one of two things: • Hire someone to prepare the predictive analysis. • Learn how to do the analysis.
S	**Self-Reflection**	Understanding the purpose of the analysis makes it easier to apply the experience of performing it to future data analytics contexts and tasks. Similarly, considering past experiences can help identify objectives and develop questions.	Assessing whether you should have performed the analyses may depend on whether the information lead to better decisions by management. If it did not, then consider why. Only then can you compare expected net benefits to the actual net benefits.

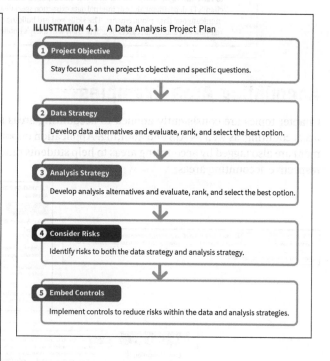

ILLUSTRATION 4.1 A Data Analysis Project Plan

1 Project Objective
Stay focused on the project's objective and specific questions.

2 Data Strategy
Develop data alternatives and evaluate, rank, and select the best option.

3 Analysis Strategy
Develop analysis alternatives and evaluate, rank, and select the best option.

4 Consider Risks
Identify risks to both the data strategy and analysis strategy.

5 Embed Controls
Implement controls to reduce risks within the data and analysis strategies.

How To Walk-Throughs

How To Walk-Throughs appear at the end of each chapter. They are step-by-step guides for recreating chapter illustrations or examples using a technology tool covered in the course— Power BI, Alteryx, Tableau, or Excel. When possible, alternative technology options are also presented. (For example, a How To in Chapter 8 details how to create a frequency table using Power BI, but Excel and Tableau are also highlighted as alternatives).

Chapter How To

HOW TO 8.1   Create a Frequency Distribution with Power BI

Illustration 8.14 is a frequency distribution for Super Scooters' different models. It was created in Excel, but other tools, such as Power BI, can also create frequency distributions.

What You Need: Data The How To 8.1 data file.

STEP 1: Extract the data. Open Power BI and select the **Home** tab on the top horizontal menu (**Illustration 8.37**).

- Select the Excel icon below.
- When the file dialog box opens, navigate to the Super Scooters Excel file and select **Open** in the bottom-right corner.

Apply It Features

A hands-on feature at the end of each learning objective, Apply Its offer regular opportunities for students to practice what they have learned.

Data Managerial Accounting DHI would like to understand what is driving total expenses for the hotel chain. Luciana feels strongly that the following variables have the most influence on expenses:

- Age of the hotel
- The number of maintenance employees
- Total housekeeping hours
- Total rooms rented

She has asked you to prepare a regression model using those variables to predict expenses. The following illustration is the result of that model:

APPLY IT 8.5

Interpret Regression Results

Housekeeping Hours and Rooms Rented by Location Regression Model

Regression Statistics	
Multiple R	0.7215151
R Square	0.520584
Adjusted R Square	0.4714132
Standard Error	93,901.466
Observations	44

ANOVA					
	df	SS	MS	F	Significance F
Regression	4	3.73412E+11	9.3353E+10	10.58724498	6.62556E-06
Residual	39	3.43882E+11	8,817,485,253		
Total	43	7.17293E+11			

	Coefficients	Standard Error	t Stat	P-value
Intercept	413,314.47	107,148.5543	3.85739665	0.000418405
Room Rentals	11.015461	2.918679199	3.77412543	0.000534577
Hours Worked, Housekeeping	6.0934507	5.531393108	1.1016123	0.277382666
Age	−3,565.695	1,674.938087	−2.12885155	0.039637083
Employees, Maintenance	16,762.392	6,906.902129	2.42690446	0.019949355

1. What does the adjusted R square reveal about the model?
2. Is the model better than not having a model?
3. Are there any variables you would recommend Luciana remove from the model? Why?

SOLUTION

1. The adjusted R square is 0.471, meaning that room rentals, housekeeping hours worked, the age of the hotel, and the number of maintenance employees can explain 47.1% of total expenses.
2. The model is significant—Significance F is less than 0.05—so, it is better than no model at all.
3. The p-value for Hours Worked, Housekeeping is greater than 0.05, so it should be removed from the model.

Robust Data Sets

Becoming technically agile requires working with data, so we offer over 125 unique data sets that include examples from small businesses, manufacturing, hotels, restaurants, services, hospitals, municipalities, state taxes, retail, financial services, and wholesale companies. Data tags attached to chapter examples and end-of-chapter material indicate when students can access related data in the book's product page on www.wiley.com.

Data Let's use a case to illustrate how to apply data preparation patterns in a real-world scenario. You can also use the available data to work through each pattern yourself.

EX 9.6 (LO 5) Data Financial Accounting **Create Interactive Visualizations** U.S. Outdoor Adventures would like to use an interactive dashboard to evaluate product sales and profits. Review the static visualizations in one of the Excel, Power BI, or Tableau files prepared by the accounting department at U.S. Outdoor Adventures. Convert the static visualizations into interactive visualizations that management can use to monitor the profitability of products by sub-category and location.

Data Literacy and Communication Skills

The ability to work and communicate with data is one of the top skills demanded by employers. Learning to communicate with data can be challenging. We demystify creating effective data visualizations by providing easy-to-understand decision trees, best practice summaries, and data story guidelines. After completing the course, students will be able to identify misleading visualizations and tell an accurate and engaging data story.

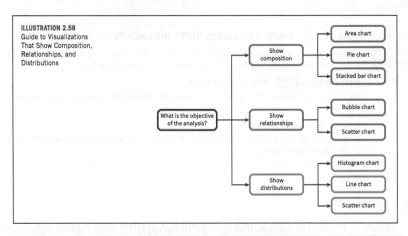

ILLUSTRATION 2.58
Guide to Visualizations That Show Composition, Relationships, and Distributions

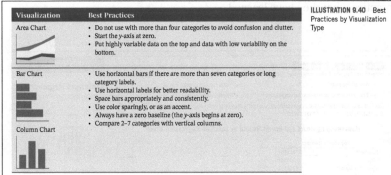

ILLUSTRATION 9.40 Best Practices by Visualization Type

Each chapter helps students develop data literacy by giving them both opportunities to work with data and offering guidelines for doing so.

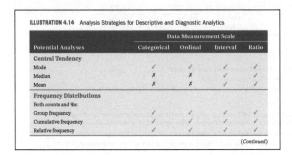

ILLUSTRATION 4.14 Analysis Strategies for Descriptive and Diagnostic Analytics

End-of-Chapter Assessment

In addition to a chapter summary organized by learning objective and a list of key terms, the end-of-chapter material offers a variety of assessment opportunities.

Questions, Exercises, and Cases

A number of questions are available at the end of each chapter, including multiple choice, review questions, brief exercises, exercises, problems, and professional application cases to help students practice and assess their understanding of data concepts and application.

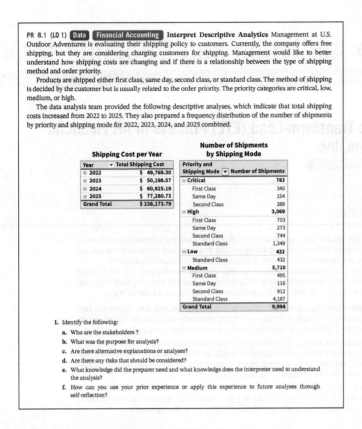

PR 8.1 (LO 1) `Data` `Financial Accounting` **Interpret Descriptive Analytics** Management at U.S. Outdoor Adventures is evaluating their shipping policy to customers. Currently, the company offers free shipping, but they are considering charging customers for shipping. Management would like to better understand how shipping costs are changing and if there is a relationship between the type of shipping method and order priority.

Products are shipped either first class, same day, second class, or standard class. The method of shipping is decided by the customer but is usually related to the order priority. The priority categories are critical, low, medium, or high.

The data analysis team provided the following descriptive analyses, which indicate that total shipping costs increased from 2022 to 2025. They also prepared a frequency distribution of the number of shipments by priority and shipping mode for 2022, 2023, 2024, and 2025 combined.

Shipping Cost per Year

Year	Total Shipping Cost
⊞ 2022	$ 49,769.30
⊞ 2023	$ 50,198.57
⊞ 2024	$ 60,925.19
⊞ 2025	$ 77,280.73
Grand Total	**$ 238,173.79**

Number of Shipments by Shipping Mode

Priority and Shipping Mode	Number of Shipments
⊟ Critical	783
First Class	340
Same Day	154
Second Class	289
⊟ High	3,069
First Class	703
Same Day	273
Second Class	744
Standard Class	1,349
⊟ Low	432
Standard Class	432
⊟ Medium	5,710
First Class	495
Same Day	116
Second Class	912
Standard Class	4,187
Grand Total	**9,994**

1. Identify the following:
   a. Who are the stakeholders?
   b. What was the purpose for analysis?
   c. Are there alternative explanations or analyses?
   d. Are there any risks that should be considered?
   e. What knowledge did the preparer need and what knowledge does the interpreter need to understand the analysis?
   f. How can you use your prior experience or apply this experience to future analyses through self-reflection?

Professional Application Case

Every chapter concludes with a Professional Application Case. The case provides data for one company that can be used to perform analyses in each area of accounting. By focusing on one company, students can see how data analysis can be applied across accounting areas within one organization.

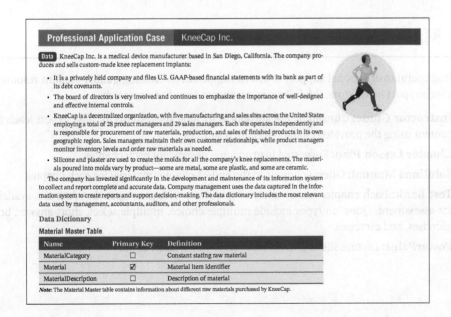

Professional Application Case   KneeCap Inc.

`Data` KneeCap Inc. is a medical device manufacturer based in San Diego, California. The company produces and sells custom-made knee replacement implants:

- It is a privately held company and files U.S. GAAP-based financial statements with its bank as part of its debt covenants.
- The board of directors is very involved and continues to emphasize the importance of well-designed and effective internal controls.
- KneeCap is a decentralized organization, with five manufacturing and sales sites across the United States employing a total of 28 product managers and 29 sales managers. Each site operates independently and is responsible for procurement of raw materials, production, and sales of finished products in its own geographic region. Sales managers maintain their own customer relationships, while product managers monitor inventory levels and order raw materials as needed.
- Silicone and plaster are used to create the molds for all the company's knee replacements. The materials poured into molds vary by product—some are metal, some are plastic, and some are ceramic.

The company has invested significantly in the development and maintenance of its information system to collect and report complete and accurate data. Company management uses the data captured in the information system to create reports and support decision-making. The data dictionary includes the most relevant data used by management, accountants, auditors, and other professionals.

Data Dictionary

Material Master Table

Name	Primary Key	Definition
MaterialCategory	☐	Constant stating raw material
Material	☑	Material item identifier
MaterialDescription	☐	Description of material

Note: The Material Master table contains information about different raw materials purchased by KneeCap.

Data Analytics and Decision-Making

This edition introduces a new feature "Data Analytics and Decision-Making" at the end of the book, which offers students the opportunity to see how they can use data analytics to help solve realistic business problems.

Data Analytics and Decision-Making

Extract-Transform-Load (ETL) Process in AR Financial Services, Inc.

Introduction

AR Financial Services, Inc. operates across multiple geographies, offering a diverse range of financial products and services. With operations spanning banking, insurance, and investment management, the company generates substantial volumes of transactional and analytical data every day.

To streamline data management and mostly spreadsheet-based reporting processes, AR Financial Services adopted the extract-transform-load (ETL) framework powered by cutting-edge technology using SQL databases and data lakes. The ETL process involves the following three key stages:

1. **Extraction:** Raw data is sourced from various internal systems, including transaction databases, customer relationship management (CRM) platforms, and financial reporting tools. This data encompasses customer transactions, account balances, market data, and more.

2. **Transformation:** Extracted data undergoes rigorous transformation to ensure consistency, accuracy, and compliance with regulatory standards. This phase involves data cleansing, validation, normalization, and enrichment. Additionally, complex algorithms are applied for risk analysis, fraud detection, and performance measurement.

3. **Loading:** Transformed data is loaded into a centralized data warehouse or data lake, where it is organized into structured data sets for reporting and analysis purposes. This repository serves as a single source of truth for decision-making across the organization.

Data Extracts

Here are the partial data extracts from the customer transactions database of AR Financial Services, following both the extraction and transformation stages:

Online Supplementary Material

Providing useful instructional support is just as important as creating quality student resources. To further support instructors, the following resources have been created:

- **Instructor Guide:** Curated by the authors to include suggestions for how to best teach the content using the provided chapter-specific resources.
- **Chapter Lesson Plan:** Suggested instructional designs for each chapter.
- **Solutions Manual:** Offers solutions to the end-of-chapter material for each chapter.
- **Test Bank:** Each chapter has a variety of questions with accompanying data sets available for assessment. Question types include multiple choice, multiple select, short answer, brief exercises, and exercises.
- **PowerPoint:** Lecture slides provide an overview of chapter content.

Acknowledgments

We would not have been able to publish *Data and Analytics in Accounting* without the tremendous contributions of our advisory board members, reviewers, accuracy checkers, class testers, and the students who provided feedback during the creation of this product. We appreciate the recommendations and constructive comments from everyone. We also thank the instructors who participated in development and authoring activities for this edition. Diane Janvrin, Jennifer Riley, and Juergen Sidgman read and commented on every chapter. Matt Pickard and Vincent Shea provided helpful feedback on the continuing case. Special thanks goes to Renee Olvera for her valuable contributions to the end-of-chapter content and her thoughtful review of our online material.

Advisory Board Members

Tom Aleman	Wake Forest University
Xu Cheng	Auburn University
Kimberly Church	Missouri State University
Gregory Dawson	Arizona State University
Diane Janvrin	Ivy College of Business
Pablo Machado	San Diego State University
Uday Murthy	University of South Florida
Jennifer Riley	University of Nebraska at Omaha
Weiwei Wang	Weber State University

Reviewers

Angela Seidel	Saint Francis University
Billy Morehead	Mississippi College
Bradley Winton	The University of Southern Mississippi
Cherie Henderson	University of Texas - Arlington
Dave Henderson	University of Mary Washington
Diane Janvrin	Ivy College of Business
Eric Bostwick	The University of West Florida
Fangjun Sang	St. Bonaventure University
Jennifer Riley	University of Nebraska - Omaha
Joseph Zhang	The University of Memphis
Juergen Sidgman	University of Alaska - Anchorage
Julia Kokina	Babson College
Kathleen Bakarich	Hofstra University
Kevin Agnew	Elon University
Lin Wang	Midwestern State University - Texas
Matt Pickard	Northern Illinois University
Matthew Sargent	The University of Texas at Arlington
Meiying Hua	University of Wisconsin - River Falls
Michael Flores	Wichita State University
Michael Luehlfing	Louisiana Tech University
Pablo Machado	San Diego State University
Phil Larprom	University of Toronto
Robert Lin	California State University - East Bay
Sang-Kyu Lee	Endicott College

Steven Johnson	Minnesota State University
Tillie Parmer	Trinity Western University
Uday Murthy	University of South Florida
Vince Shea	St. Johns University
Weiwei Wang	Weber State University
Xu Cheng	Auburn University

Accuracy Checkers

Laura De Luca	Fanshawe College
Christopher Nogot	Sienna College of Taytay, IQEQ
Renee Olvera	Texas Christian University
Ronald Premuroso	Western Governor University
Matt Pickard	Northern Illinois University
Allison Richardson	College of the Holy Cross
Angela Seidel	Saint Francis University
Vincent Shea	St. Johns University
Melanie Yon	

Student Reviewers

Mykala Birch	Northern Illinois University
Joanna Coveyou	Northern Illinois University
Kaitong Feng	University of Delaware
Luis Garcia	Colorado State University
Krystal Hegg	Northern Illinois University
Nick Iscra	Northern Illinois University
Megan Johnson	Colorado State University
Noah Kim	Colorado State University
Lori Neff	Northern Illinois University
Riddhi Patel	University of Delaware
Siddhi Patel	University of Delaware
Melissa Saputo	Northern Illinois University

This product would not have been possible without the guidance, support, and hard work of so many people behind the scenes. Our editors, Emily Marcoux and Veronica Schram, provided a constant source of encouragement, guidance, and leadership. Jessica Carlisle, our developmental content editor, spent countless hours helping us shape the product into the amazing resource that it will be for students. Jodie Bernard was our fabulous art lead and helped create the wonderful chapter illustrations. We also need to thank Ed Brislin, Kali Ridley, Tim Lindner, and Nicole Repasky for all the work they have done to create a collection of amazing resources for both students and instructors. Thank you also to our Lumina partners and specifically our project manager, Vimal Shanmugavelu. We also want to thank Maureen Shelburn, Christina Koop, and Karolina Zarychta for helping bring the product to the market. Thank you to all the people at Wiley who have helped us realize our dream of bringing this product to life. We could not have done it without you.

Brief Contents

Plan

Analyze

Report

Contents

5   Analysis: Data Preparation   229

6 Analysis: Information Modeling 299

7 Analysis: Data Exploration 363

8 Interpreting Data Analysis Results   423

9 Communicating Data Analysis Results   483

CHAPTER 1

Data and Analytics in the Accounting Profession

Changes in data and technology are impacting the role of accountants in all areas of accounting. The accountants of the future must be agile, creative, data and technology literate professionals. They will be critically thinking problem-solvers who can use technology and data to drive business understanding and change. They need to "think outside the box" to create value using data and analyses. This chapter is an overview of how these changes are happening, the types of data and analytics new graduates are likely to encounter, and the skills they need to be successful in this changing environment.

PROFESSIONAL INSIGHT **Why Does Data Analytics Matter for Your Career?**

This chapter previews data and analytics in the accounting profession and the related skills needed for your future accounting career. Some quotes from leaders at two of the world's largest accounting firms puts the importance of these skills into perspective.

Roger O'Donnell, Global Head of Data and Analytics, in KPMG's auditing practice:

> Technology is not displacing accountants; rather, it is augmenting their technical proficiency as well as their **critical thinking and problem-solving skills** to make more insightful decisions, reducing the risks and increasing the efficiency of producing financial statements and tax filings... **But there's a growing need for accounting students to learn how to harness and analyze financial and accounting data, as it can greatly enhance their abilities.**[1]

Patty Pogemiller, Managing Director of Global Talent Experience for Deloitte:

> **Problem-solving skills are essential in a client business like professional services. Employers are looking for people who demonstrate an ability to think analytically and approach a problem in a structured and methodical way. Can they objectively analyze and solve an issue? And once they have a solution, they must have the ability to communicate it to others—their clients, managers and fellow team members.**[2]

---

[1]Forbes. (2019). The Next Generation Accountant. https://www.forbes.com/sites/insights-kpmg/2019/04/29/the-next-generation-accountant/?sh=57090091ae67 (accessed April 2022).

[2]U.S. News & World Report. What Is an Accountant? https://money.usnews.com/careers/best-jobs/accountant (accessed April 2022).

Chapter Roadmap

LEARNING OBJECTIVES	TOPICS	APPLY IT
LO 1.1 Summarize how advances in data and technology are impacting accounting professionals.	• Data and Technology • Analytics and Accounting Professional Practice	**Match Data Analytics to Accounting Areas**
LO 1.2 Describe the stages of the data analysis process.	• Stage 1: Plan • Stage 2: Analyze • Stage 3: Report • MOSAIC: Putting It All Together	**Explain the Data Analysis Process for a Fraud Risk Assessment** (Example: Auditing)
LO 1.3 Identify the skills necessary to perform data analyses.	• Critical Thinking • Data Literacy • Technology Skills • Communication Skills	**Evaluate the Relationships Between Skills and Tasks** (Example: Tax Accounting)
LO 1.4 Explain how to apply a data analytics mindset to the data analysis process.	• Understand the Stakeholders • Identify the Purpose • Consider Alternatives • Assess Risks • Identify Knowledge • Perform Self-Reflection • SPARKS: A Critical Thinking Toolkit	**Integrate Critical Thinking with the Data Analysis Process** (Example: Auditing)

Data The Data tag appears in the chapter when the data for an example, illustration, or application are available in the book's product page on www.wiley.com.

Data analytics software is continuously changing, and there may be more recent versions of the software referenced in this chapter.

1.1 How Are Data and Analytics Transforming the Accounting Profession?

LEARNING OBJECTIVE ❶
Summarize how advances in data and technology are impacting accounting professionals.

This is an exciting time to enter the accounting profession! New, user-friendly technology allows accountants to complete accounting functions, such as creating journal entries and preparing financial statements and reports, in a fraction of the time they used to take. Because these repetitive accounting functions can be automated, accountants can focus on activities that add value to their organizations, such as evaluating controls, providing financial insights, and performing analyses to aid in business decision-making.

This evolution of the accounting profession is also reflected in the professional certification exams required to practice in the field:

- The Certified Public Accountant (CPA) and the Certified Management Accountant (CMA) exams now include the topic of data analytics.
- Beginning in 2020, the Institute of Management Accountants (IMA) added a "Technology and Analytics" section to the CMA exam. The IMA stated that the changes were implemented to "make the exam more relevant to the current job market."
- The American Institute of Certified Public Accountants (AICPA), in a joint effort with the National Association of the State Boards of Accountancy (NASBA), launched the CPA Evolution in 2021. The CPA Evolution is a change in the CPA licensure model to "recognize the rapidly changing skills and competencies the practice of accounting requires today and will require in the future."[3] While the current CPA exam already includes data analytics, the new exam format, which will be implemented in 2024, will include more technology and data analytics in both the core and the discipline exams.

Data and Technology

As these changes to accounting professional exams show, data, analytics, and technology are changing the accounting profession. But what *are* data and analytics? Note the separation of the words "data" and "analytics." While it is often referred to simply as "data analytics," each is its own element, and it is important to think about them separately. Performing data analytics includes identifying both the data necessary for the analysis and the appropriate analysis method.

Data are raw figures and facts. Technology helps convert that data to **information**, which is the knowledge gained from the data. For example, sales transaction data will include the date sold, the product purchased, quantity sold, and price for each sale. We can get information such as the total sales by product by summarizing the data (multiplying quantity sold by price) by product. **Data analytics** is the process of analyzing raw data to answer questions or provide insights.

The emergence of **self-service business intelligence (SSBI) software** has fostered the increased use of data and analytics. SSBI is now readily available and accessible by all business users. There are two key features of SSBI software:

- It provides extended data processing capabilities for preparing data, analyzing data, and reporting data analysis results.
- It is easy to use. No degree in computer science is required!

Several excellent SSBI tools are available, including Alteryx, Microsoft Excel, Power BI, and Tableau. These tools allow all businesses to be successful in the new data environment. **Illustration 1.1** is an example of the SSBI software Alteryx. Alteryx lets users quickly design workflows that access, manipulate, analyze, and output data. Like all SSBI software, the interface is user-friendly and does not require knowing how to program.

The workflow in Illustration 1.1 imports, cleans, filters, and exports results. In this example, the user wants to do an analysis of U.S. transactions for a company. The workflow begins with an import of an Excel spreadsheet of all transactions. Next, the data is cleaned to remove null values and leading and trailing spaces. A **null value** indicates an unknown or missing value. (Later in the course you will learn the importance of cleaning data prior to analysis.) Once the data are cleaned, they are filtered to separate transactions made in the United States from transactions made in other countries. **Illustration 1.2** shows how long (run time) it took for the software to complete the workflow.

It took only 0.5 seconds to import, clean, filter, and export over 2,000 rows of data. Software such as Alteryx can save accountants countless hours of tedious work.

The growing availability of data, the techniques and tools used to create value from them, and the ease with which these tools can be used have impacted how accountants, from auditors to financial accountants, do their jobs every day.

---

[3]CPA Evolution. http://www.evolutionofcpa.org

ILLUSTRATION 1.1 Alteryx Software Workflow Example

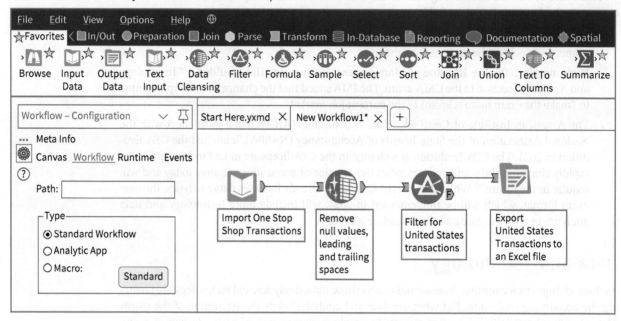

ILLUSTRATION 1.2 Alteryx Workflow Run Time

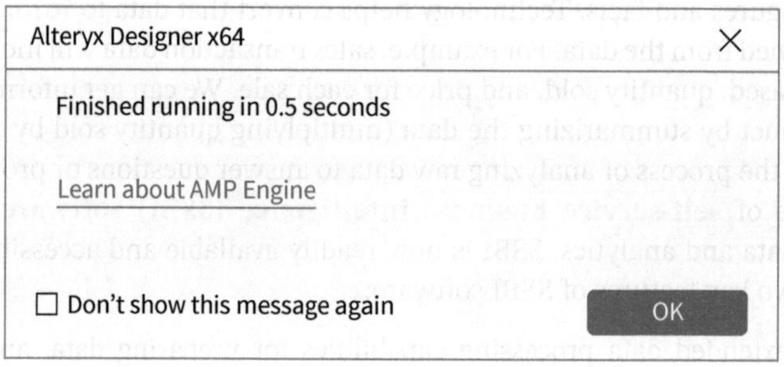

Analytics and Accounting Professional Practice

Using self-service business intelligence tools has empowered accountants in different practice areas to use data and analytics to provide value-added services to their clients and employers.

Auditing

The use of analytics in the audit profession is growing:

- Audits have expanded beyond sample-based testing to include analyses of entire populations of audit-relevant data.
- Auditors can review entire data sets to identify all exceptions, anomalies, and outliers.
- Data-driven audits reduce the time the client spends gathering information for the auditor and allows more time for the analysis, making audits a better experience for everyone involved.

Both internal and external auditors use analytics to perform risk assessment and substantive procedures. **Illustration 1.3** is an example of how analytics are used to perform risk assessment by showing the increase or decrease in each general ledger account for the current and prior year. Notice that the visual includes prior year amounts by showing them enclosed in a black border. The green bars represent current year amounts that are less than $3 million. The orange bars represent the current year amounts that are more than $3 million and should be investigated further. This type of analysis helps the auditor quickly identify the accounts that appear to have a higher risk of misstatement, so they can investigate further.

ILLUSTRATION 1.3 Audit Risk Assessment Example

Financial Statement Line Items Compared with Previous Year

Net Assets 5,100–7,120 Increase/(Decrease); Net Income 8,100–8,510 Increase/(Decrease)

Balance Sheet	5,100 Cash — 3.0
	5,200 Investments
	5,300 Accounts Receivable — 12.6
	5,350 Other Receivables—Short-term — 1.5
	5,500 Prepaid Expenses — 0.8
	5,560 Other Receivables—Long-term — 3.4
	5,600 Property, Plant, and Equipment — 0.3
	5,700 Other Assets — 7.5
	5,710 Goodwill — 1.6
	6,100 Accounts Payable and Accrued Liabilities — (4.2)
	6,140 Income Taxes Payable — (1.0)
	6,300 Long-term Liabilities — (7.0)
	6,400 Income Taxes — 1.7
	6,500 Deferred Revenues — (3.1)
	7,100 Share Capital (Note 7) — (5.0)
	7,110 Contributed Surplus — (0.5)
	7,120 Retained Earnings—Beginning of Year — (5.8)

Prior Year Amounts

Income Statement	8,100 Sales/Revenue — 39.0
	8,200 Operating Expenses — (13.3)
	8,300 Research and Development — (6.9)
	8,340 General and Administrative — (5.0)
	8,350 Sales and Marketing — (7.7)
	8,360 Fixed Asset—Depreciation and Amortization — (0.2)
	8,365 Intangible—Depreciation and Amortization — (0.2)
	8,370 Foreign Exchange Gain/Loss — 0.4
	8,400 Provision For Income Taxes — -
	8,500 Interest Income — (0.1)
	8,510 Other Expense — -

$Millions

■ Current Year, Pass (Changes of Less than $3 Million) ■ Current Year, Investigate (Changes of $3 Million or More)

Source: AICPA Guide to Audit Data Analytics (page 39). Reproduced with permission from AICPA.

In addition to risk assessment, auditors can use data analytics to perform substantive analytical procedures that support the assertion that the financial records of an entity are complete, valid, and accurate. **Illustration 1.4** is an example of this using **data visualization**, which is the graphical representation of information and data.

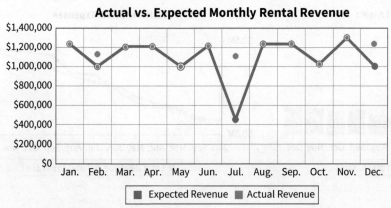

Actual vs. Expected Monthly Rental Revenue

■ Expected Revenue ■ Actual Revenue

ILLUSTRATION 1.4
Substantive Analytical
Procedure Example

Source: AICPA Guide to Audit Data Analytics (page 80).

The example in Illustration 1.4 used data visualization to compare expected and actual revenue to identify if any months require additional analysis. It shows that actual revenue was higher than expected in February, July, and December, so the auditor may decide to focus on those three months for additional testing.

Auditing procedures are also changing. Since many firms are investing in robotic process automation software (RPA) and analytics automation software to automate manual audit tasks, auditors can focus on analysis and providing valuable insights.

Financial Accounting

The role of financial accountants is also shifting. As in auditing, changes are related to both automation software (RPA and analytics automation software) and SSBI software. Using automation software to perform routine financial accounting functions such as recording journal entries, creating trial balances, doing preliminary account analyses, and creating financial statements lets accountants spend more time analyzing data for insights.

SSBI software lets financial accountants perform analytics and create financial dashboards to support decision-making. A **dashboard** is a graphical user interface that shows key performance indicators for an organization. **Illustration 1.5** is an example of the types of insights

ILLUSTRATION 1.5 Financial Statement Analysis Dashboard

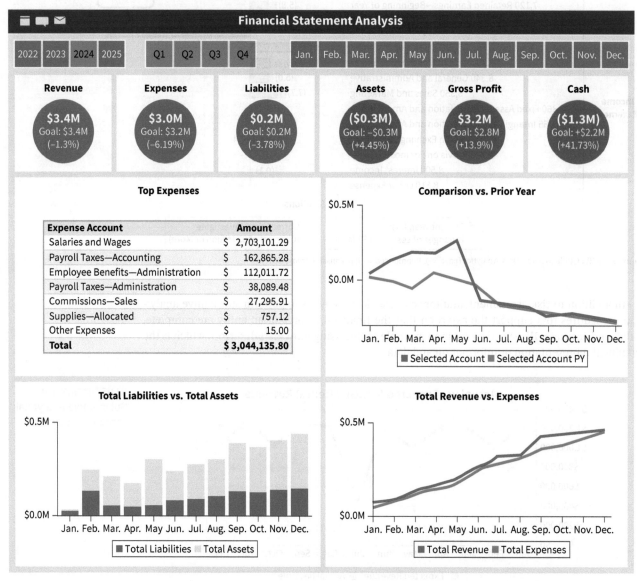

financial accountants can find using data—in this case, a dashboard that can monitor financial performance.

This dashboard brings together analyses of different elements of the financial statements. Users can quickly see key performance indicators that provide insight into overall business performance:

- The dashboard information can be viewed by year, quarter, or month using the tabs across the top.
- The top row is a snapshot of how revenue, expenses, liabilities, assets, gross profit, and cash compare to goals.
- The visualizations in the dashboard provide an analysis of revenue and expenses, total assets and total liabilities, and a visualization that allows the user to choose an account to view compared to the prior year.
- Finally, the table in the top left of the dashboard provides the top expenses incurred by the company.

Frequently used in business, dashboards are a useful tool to communicate key information to everyone who needs it.

Managerial Accounting

While financial accountants analyze financial statements for external reporting, managerial accountants deal with internal reporting and performance analysis. With SSBI software, management accountants can more easily use data to help identify and manage risks, improve budgeting and forecasting (by using more data), and automate internal reporting. SSBI software can also help to identify operational improvements and create dashboards of key performance indicators (KPI).

Illustration 1.6 is a dashboard that provides analysis of product sales and profit for an office supply company:

- The top visualization in the dashboard is called a highlight table. The colors are on a scale from light to dark. Darker colors indicate higher sales and lighter colors indicate lower sales. User can quickly locate high-performing and low-performing products. For example, the darkest color is technology sales in 2021 in the month of November.
- The bottom visualization in the dashboard provides both sales and profit margin information by product and subcategory. The colored dots represent individual sales to customers by total amount. The color of the dots indicates the profit ratio on each sale. The color scale of profit ratio ranges from negative 50% (dark red) and positive profit ratios up to 50% (dark black).

This product dashboard provides management with real-time updates of sales and profit information, enabling management to identify and respond to possible issues quickly. For example, customers with negative profit ratios can be investigated immediately.

ILLUSTRATION 1.6 Product Performance Dashboard

Product Drilldown
Sales by Product Category

		Jul.	Aug.	Sep.	Oct.	Nov.	Dec.
Furniture	2018	$10,821	$ 7,320	$23,816	$12,304	$21,565	$30,646
	2019	$13,674	$ 9,639	$26,273	$12,027	$30,881	$23,086
	2020	$13,069	$ 12,483	$27,263	$11,873	$31,784	$36,679
	2021	$11,813	$ 15,442	$29,028	$21,884	$37,057	$31,407
Office Supplies	2018	$15,121	$ 11,379	$27,423	$ 7,211	$26,862	$18,006
	2019	$ 4,720	$ 11,735	$19,306	$ 8,673	$21,218	$16,202
	2020	$12,924	$ 8,960	$23,264	$16,282	$20,487	$37,998
	2021	$10,241	$ 30,060	$31,896	$23,037	$31,472	$30,437
Technology	2018	$ 8,004	$ 9,210	$30,538	$11,938	$30,201	$20,893
	2019	$10,371	$ 15,525	$19,017	$10,705	$23,874	$35,632
	2020	$13,269	$ 9,672	$22,883	$31,533	$27,141	$22,323
	2021	$23,210	$ 17,619	$26,943	$32,856	$49,919	$21,985

Sales

$1,072 $49,919

Sales and Profit by Product Names
Year: All, Month: All, Product Category: Furniture

		Consumer	Corporate	Home Office
Furniture	Bookcases			
	Chairs			
	Furnishings			
	Tables			

$0 $5k $10k $15k $0 $5k $10k $15k $0 $5k $10k $15k

Region All

Profit Ratio

–50.0%   50.0%

Tax Accounting

Data analytics can also be used to analyze tax efficiency of business units, identify tax opportunities, and aid in evaluating global opportunities:

- Data analytics is used to help with tax compliance.
- Automation of data gathering for tax compliance can help speed the process, leaving the tax accountant with more time to do tax analysis and planning.
- Tax dashboards can help organizations monitor real-time tax positions.

Illustration 1.7 is a tax dashboard that uses data visualization to dynamically portray state tax information to help tax professionals monitor the organization's tax position. The menus at the top left let the user interact with the data to drill down to the supporting detail. Users can pick the corporate entity, the type of taxes, the jurisdiction (state), and how many entities to show. The visualization on the top of the dashboard is an overview of payroll taxes by state for the chosen entity. The bottom visualization shows the total amount of payroll taxes.

ILLUSTRATION 1.7 State Income Tax Dashboard

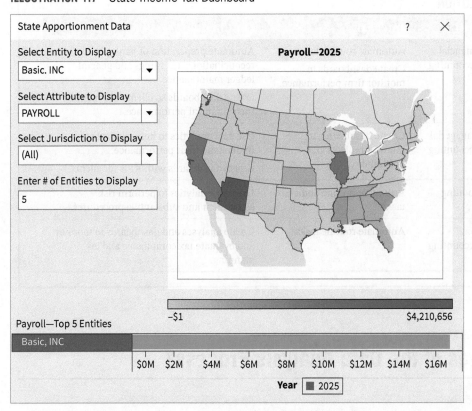

Of course, these examples/analytics being used in the accounting profession are dependent upon the accountant not only understanding the relevant accounting knowledge, but also having the ability to use the available tools.

You are a new hire at a large regional CPA firm called Castillo, Flowers, & Welch (CFW). With approximately $94 million in annual revenue, the firm has 16 offices, 83 partners, and 484 employees. CFW provides accounting, advisory, assurance, and tax services:

- Accounting services include financial statement preparation and services such as bank account reconciliation, payroll tax filings, and maintenance of general ledgers (financial accounting).

- The advisory group specializes in helping clients understand their financial position so they can better manage their business. Services include cash flow analysis, budgeting, industry benchmarking, and key performance indicator reporting (managerial accounting).

- The assurance services include audit services and fraud risk assessment (auditing).

- Tax services provided by CFW include tax preparation, estate planning, state and local tax consulting, and sales and use tax consulting (tax accounting).

CFW is considering increasing their use of data analytics. They want to use data analytics both within the firm and to provide value-added services to their clients. Identify how CFW can apply data analytics in their accounting, advisory, assurance, and tax services areas, both internally and for their clients.

Area	Internal	For Clients
Financial Accounting		
Managerial Accounting		
Auditing		
Tax Accounting		

SOLUTION

Area	Internal	For Clients
Financial Accounting	Automate routine tasks. Create dashboards to monitor firm performance.	Automate preparation of bank reconciliations, tax filings and general ledger maintenance. Create dashboards so clients can monitor their financial performance.
Managerial Accounting	Create dashboards to monitor projects and profitability.	Use data analytics to help clients better understand their performance. Create dashboards with KPIs for clients.
Auditing	Automate routine audit tasks.	Use data analytics to perform risk assessment and substantive procedures.
Tax Accounting	Automate routine tasks.	Create analyses and dashboards to monitor and evaluate tax compliance and tax planning.

1.2 What Are the Stages of the Data Analysis Process?

Regardless of the area of accounting, accountants follow a data analysis process comprised of three equally important stages (**Illustration 1.8**).

ILLUSTRATION 1.8   The Data Analysis Process

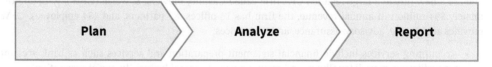

| Plan | Analyze | Report |

Following a data analysis process helps assure that data analyses are performed efficiently and effectively. There are specific chapters devoted to each stage, but we use a high-level example here to introduce the process.

One Stop Shop (OSS) is a wholesale distributor for convenience stores. A wholesale distributor buys products from suppliers in large quantities and then sells the products to retailers for a slightly higher price, keeping the difference as profit. Since its humble beginnings in 1888 in San Francisco, California, as a general store, OSS has grown into one of the largest distributors of consumer goods in North America. OSS has the same goal today as it did over one hundred and thirty years ago—to provide customers with quality goods and fast service.

Today, OSS operates in Canada, Mexico, and the United States. The company has 15 regions (five regions in each country) and 30 distribution centers. OSS distributes products from the following categories:

- Baby food
- Beverages
- Cereal
- Clothes
- Cosmetics
- Fruits

- Household
- Meat
- Office supplies

- Personal care
- Snacks
- Vegetables

Imagine you are an accountant at OSS and your manager has asked you to use data analytics to evaluate performance. Let's apply the data analysis process to this task.

Stage 1: Plan

The first stage of the data analysis process is planning. This includes identifying the motivation for the analysis, determining the objective and questions to answer, and devising a strategy to perform the analysis.

Understand Motivation

Motivation is the reason the analysis is being performed. It is why we are doing the analysis. The "why" behind a project can vary from taking advantage of opportunities to solving problems, and its source can be external or internal:

- **External motivation:** The project originates from a request or requirement by another party, such as external stakeholders. These external stakeholders could be investors, creditors, supply chain partners, industry regulators, or government agencies. Another example of external motivation is when someone internal to the organization, but on a different team, assigns the project.
- **Internal motivation:** The project is motivated by a desire to better serve a client, better understand phenomena to gain business intelligence, or to perform job responsibilities. Projects are motivated internally when the incremental information gained is believed to outweigh potential costs involved with performing the data analyses.

Illustration 1.9 is an analysis of sales and profit for the last four years at OSS.

ILLUSTRATION 1.9 One Stop Shop Sales and Profit: 2022–2025

Year	SumofTotalSales	SumofTotalProfit	ProfitPercent Increase/(Decrease)
2022	$ 628,166,810	$ 182,498,922	
2023	$ 650,651,094	$ 185,587,854	1.7%
2024	$ 779,599,949	$ 229,372,260	23.6%
2025	$ 727,151,326	$ 207,834,052	(9.4%)

The analysis reveals that total sales and total profit increased from 2023 to 2024, but decreased from 2024 to 2025 by 9.4%. OSS is concerned about the decrease, so their motivation for performing the analysis is to understand why revenue decreased from 2024 to 2025. This type of motivation would be considered internal motivation. Once the motivation for the data analysis is established, it is time to move from the big picture to specific objectives.

Determine the Objective

Every data analysis project begins with setting an **objective**, which is the project's goal. A clear objective narrows the analysis' focus, and specific questions that guide the analysis can be developed based on it.

For example, the objective of the OSS analysis is to determine what factors are driving the decrease in sales and profits. Based on that, you could develop these specific questions:

- Is there a single product category that has experienced a decrease in sales and profit?
- Has there been a decrease in all the countries and regions?

Design the Data and Analysis Strategy

Developing a strategy for the project is the final step in the planning stage. There are two aspects to this—determining the data necessary to answer questions and deciding what type of analysis is appropriate considering both the data and those questions.

Designing a strategy for the data involves identifying the specific data needed and knowing how to access it. There are two categories of data:

- **Internal data** are found within the organization. This includes transaction data, general ledger data, sales data, customer data, vendor data, internal documents, and internal email.

- **External data** are acquired from outside the organization. Data like this might come from social media, websites, weather data, government data, and maps.

Understanding the potential source of data is critical. For example, performing an analysis of accounts payable requires access to internal data sources for general ledger data and vendor data. If a company sells beverages and the objective of the analysis is to predict the sales of hot chocolate, then both internal data (transactions) and external data (weather data) would be used.

As to analysis strategy, there are four types of data analysis methods, each of which is discussed in future chapters. **Illustration 1.10** offers some brief examples and definitions for them.

ILLUSTRATION 1.10 Types of Data Analytics

Method	Objective	Sample Question
Descriptive	Investigates *what* is happening currently or has occurred in the past.	What were gross sales by region for the past two years?
Diagnostic	Helps understand *why* something happened.	Why did sales decrease in Region 1 in the prior year?
Predictive	Forecasts *what might happen* in the future.	What will sales be next year if we increase market share by 10%?
Prescriptive	Helps understand *what should happen* to meet goals and objectives.	What is the most cost-effective way to ship our products?

The most common and easily understood analytics, **descriptive analytics** reveal what is currently happening or what has happened in the past. They are the first analytics performed to help understand data. Sum, count, average, median, standard deviation, and proportions are examples.

Instead of telling us that something happened, **diagnostic analytics** reveal *why* something has happened. The information gained from descriptive analytics about what happened lets us drill down further to understand why. The results of these analyses inform decision-making about actions in the future. Examples include anomaly and outlier detection, trend analysis, and pattern recognition.

Predictive analytics also help to understand and predict what might happen in the future. Predictive analytics use data, statistical algorithms, and machine learning to identify the likelihood of future outcomes based on historical data. The goal is to use what is known about the past to make a better assessment of what might happen in the future. Forecasting, regression analysis, and time-series analysis are a few examples.

Finally, **prescriptive analytics** help determine the best course of action to achieve a goal in a given scenario. These analyses go beyond descriptive and predictive analyses by recommending one or more possible courses of action. Prescriptive analytics include optimization and what-if analyses.

Illustration 1.11 summarizes the planning stage for OSS, including the data analysis method that should be used to perform the analyses.

ILLUSTRATION 1.11 Applying the Planning Stage to the One Stop Shop Data Scenario

Planning Stage	Explanation
Motivation	**Understand the reason for the data analysis.** One Stop Shop Example: • Management wants to understand why profit decreased from 2024 to 2025.
Objective	**Articulate the goal, or objective, and develop a specific question(s).** One Stop Shop Example: • Objective: What is driving the decrease in sales and profit from 2024 to 2025? • Specific question: Which product categories have experienced a decrease in sales and profits from 2024 to 2025?
Strategy	**Identify the necessary data and analysis methods to answer questions.** One Stop Shop Example: • Use transaction data from 2022 to 2025. This is internal data. • The data analysis method would include descriptive and diagnostic analyses.

Stage 2: Analyze

After careful planning, it is time to begin the analysis. This stage includes data preparation, building information models, and exploring the data. Each is covered in detail later in this course, but they are briefly described here and applied to the OSS scenario.

Prepare Data

Good quality data result in good quality analyses, so preparing the data for analysis is a critical step in this stage. This process is often referred to as **extract-transform-load (ETL)**.

- Extracting is the process by which data are retrieved from a source. This could be downloading an Excel file or extracting data from a database or a data warehouse.

- Transforming the data occurs when data are cleaned, restructured, and/or integrated with other data prior to using it for analysis.

- Loading is the process of importing transformed data into the software used to perform analyses. There are many types of analysis software available, including Excel, Power BI, and Tableau.

In the OSS example, the company has extracted a file of thousands of transactions and a file with the region numbers and names. Both files must be prepared for analysis. The first step is determining if data needs to be cleaned. The process of reviewing the data for possible issues is called **data profiling**. To verify all the data have been extracted, you can compare the row counts of the data extracted to the total number of rows that should be in the data. To ensure that the data were transferred correctly, compare the amounts transferred to control amounts. The OSS data could be prepared like this:

- **Extract:** Compare the data to the total sales and revenue numbers provided to be sure all the transactions are there.

- **Transform:** Integrate the file with the OSS Regions Excel file to get the region names for the analysis by region.

- **Load:** Once cleaned and transformed, the files can be loaded into the analysis software.

Once the data are loaded, the analysis can begin by building information models and exploring the data.

Build Information Models

Information modeling is the creation of information needed for analysis purposes, starting from the data collected. Examples are calculations such as net income, profit margin, total assets, or even break-even point in sales dollars.

Let's build the information model using the OSS example to diagnose if one or more products or regions are driving the decline in profit. To analyze profit by product and region, use the cleaned and transformed OSS data:

- Create a model that calculates profit margin by product and region.
- Create a model that calculates the profit margin ratio.

Illustration 1.12 is an analysis of profit by country.

ILLUSTRATION 1.12   Analysis of Profit by Country for One Stop Shop

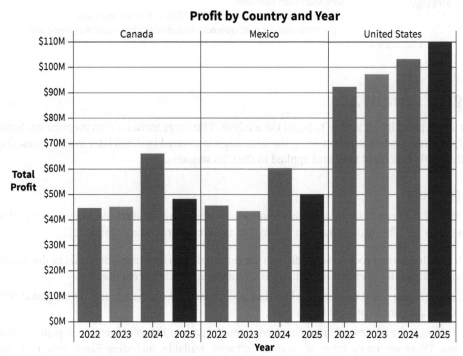

It shows that profits are only decreasing for Canada and Mexico. Exploring further could identify specific regions in Canada and Mexico that may be contributing to the decline.

Explore Data

The core goal of data analysis is to explore data to identify patterns, trends, or unusual observations. Exploring data lets us discover, question, and investigate data relationships to successfully execute data analysis objectives. The combined OSS data set and data generated by the profit margin analysis can be explored to find relationships, patterns, or insights that help explain why profit has decreased from 2024 to 2025. Sales is a significant driver of profit, so the sales data for Canada and Mexico can be explored for insights. **Illustration 1.13** is an analysis of sales by country and region for Canada and Mexico.

ILLUSTRATION 1.13   Change in Sales by Country and Region for One Stop Shop

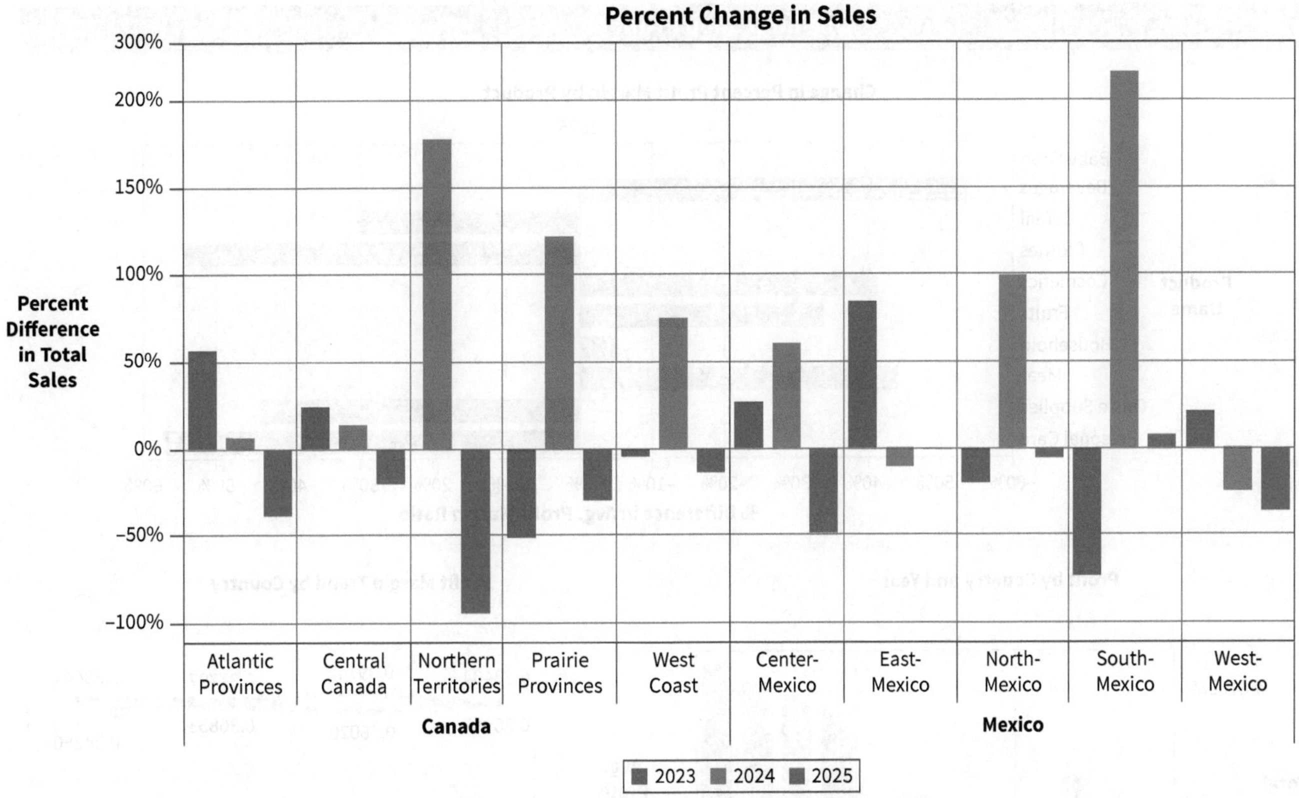

Percent Change in Sales

This analysis shows there are many regions in both countries where sales are declining.
Data You can explore the OSS data yourself using Excel, Tableau, or Power BI.

Stage 3: Report

The goal of this stage is to determine if the analyses met the project's objectives and then to
share the results. Interpreting the analyses and communicating the results is a crucial stage—an
amazing analysis that does not meet the project's objectives is useless. Moreover, if the results
are not communicated effectively, then the analyses and recommendations cannot be acted on.

Interpret Results

Data analysis interpretation is the process of reviewing analyses to be sure they make sense
based on the project's objective and that the results are valid and reliable. Imagine that you
or someone else prepared the analysis of profit for OSS shown in Illustration 1.12. Recall that
OSS's objective is to determine what is driving the decrease in profit from 2024 to 2025. Does the
analysis meet the objective?

- It is a good start. The visualization in Illustration 1.12 shows that Canada and Mexico had
  declines in profit, whereas the United States had a small increase in profit.
- However, the analysis is not finished. The next step is to dig deeper into the decreases to find
  out *why* Canada and Mexico had such large declines.

Communicate Results

The results of a data analysis project can be communicated orally, with visuals, or in writing.
Typically, data analysis communication will include data visualizations (Illustrations 1.12 and
1.13). Communication can also include dashboards (**Illustration 1.14**).

ILLUSTRATION 1.14 Communicating Using Dashboards: One Stop Shop Profit Analysis

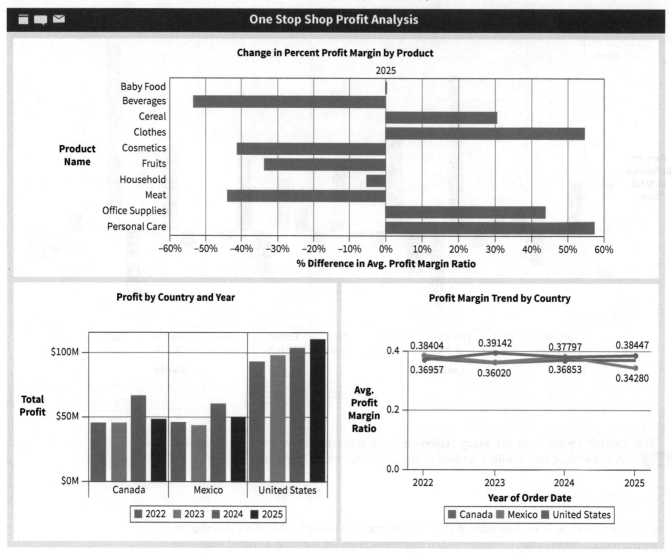

The dashboard in Illustration 1.14 communicates changes in profit to OSS's management:

- The percent change in profit by country from prior year (2024–2025).
- Total profit by country (2022–2025).
- How profit for each country has changed from the prior year.

Management can use this analysis to monitor profit. For example, it seems like OSS's profits have decreased in all products except cereal, clothes, office supplies, and personal care. Like the other steps in the data analysis process, communication is also discussed in more detail later in the course.

MOSAIC: Putting It All Together

Created by arranging tiny pieces of different colored tiles into patterns, mosaics are visual art forms that evoke meaning and emotion. To easily remember the steps in the data analysis process, imagine using data to create a mosaic that will tell a story. Like the artists who use creative and logical processes to reveal meaning about the world around them through art, accountants use data analytics to interpret the meaning of data and reveal business insights to help organizations meet their goals. **Illustration 1.15** provides a visual representation of the MOSAIC data analysis process.

ILLUSTRATION 1.15 The Data Analysis Process

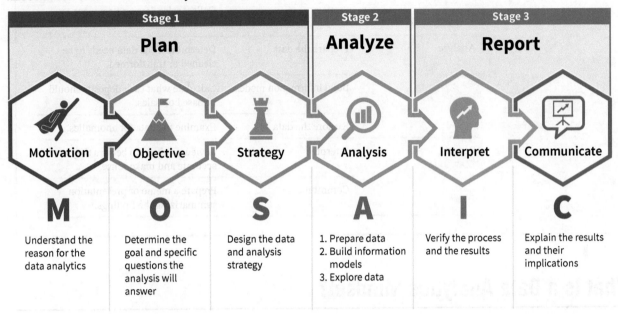

This course will cover each aspect of MOSAIC.

Auditing LocalPics (LP) is a busy movie theater chain with hundreds of sales each day and thousands on the weekends. LocalPics was tipped off by an employee that some workers were stealing the cash from ticket sales. Unfortunately, the anonymous person did not identify in which of the seven theaters the theft was happening. The CPA firm, CFW, has been hired to perform a fraud risk assessment for the company.

Identify the steps in the data analysis process for the fraud risk assessment, and provide a brief explanation of each.

Data Analysis Stage	Step	Explanation
Plan		
Analyze		
Report		

SOLUTION

Data Analysis Stage	Step	Explanation
Plan	Motivation	Discover if theft is occurring.
	Objective	Determine if any employees are stealing cash.
	Strategy	Collect sales data and compare to bank deposits.
Analyze	Prepare the data	Determine if the data needs to be cleaned or transformed.
	Build information models	Calculate what cash deposits should be based on sales.
	Explore the data	Examine the data for anomalies.
Report	Interpret	Review analyses to be sure they are accurate and make sense.
	Communicate	Prepare a memo or presentation summarizing the findings.

1.3 What Is a Data Analytics Mindset?

LEARNING OBJECTIVE ❸
Identify the skills necessary to perform data analyses.

A **data analytics mindset** is the professional habit of critically thinking through the planning, analysis, and reporting of data analysis results before making and communicating a professional choice or decision. Individuals with a data analytics mindset are inquisitive. They always ask "why" when interpreting results, they are open to learning new technologies, and they evaluate their own thinking. How can you develop a data analytics mindset? Focus on developing skills such as critical thinking, data literacy, technological agility, and communication skills.

The shortage of employees with these data analytics skills has led to increased demand for data and analytics education in all business programs, and there are many available degree and certificate programs for data analytics. While all accounting professionals do not need a specialized degree or certificate, they do need to develop the skill set needed to effectively work with data.

 **What Skills Are Employers Looking For?**

The following are excerpts from the EY Careers webpage:[4]

It's clear that many of us will be working with technology that hasn't yet been invented, solving problems that haven't yet been identified. **So, while technical skill sets are evolving faster than ever, many are becoming irrelevant or obsolete just as quickly. That's why we recruit people today based on their mindset—not just their skillset.** When you join us, we invest in your development, so you can continue to build the mindset and technology skillset to thrive.

---
[4]https://www.ey.com/en_us/careers/what-we-look-for

What is an analytics mindset? **You'll understand the importance of analytics and data to your profession, with the ability to extract, transform and interpret the relevant data.** You'll be a natural **problem-solver**, able to **translate complex data into simple and useful insights**. You'll be comfortable **sharing these results with both internal and external stakeholders.** You'll also **be committed to asking better questions** to get relevant data and understand how to use it.

These are the "preferred knowledge skills" from a tax associate job posting for PwC:

- Innovating through **new** and **existing technologies**, along with experimenting with **digitization solutions**; and
- Working with large, complex data sets to **build models and leverage data visualization tools**.

Critical Thinking

Critical thinking is disciplined reasoning used to investigate, understand, and evaluate an event, opportunity, or an issue. **Reasoning** is the human process of logically forming conclusions, judgments, or inferences from facts. Not only do employers want critical thinkers, but professional certification exams such as the CPA exam and the CMA exam also include assessment questions that test critical thinking skills. Critical thinking is the foundation of a data analytics mindset and should be integrated throughout the data analysis process. (Critical thinking will be explored and applied to the data analysis process at the end of the chapter.)

Data Literacy

Data literacy is the ability to understand and communicate data. Gartner, Inc., a world leading research and advisory company, defines it in more detail, stating that data literacy is "the ability to read, write and communicate data in context, including an understanding of data sources and constructs, analytical methods and techniques applied, and the ability to describe the use of case application and resulting value."[5]

Why is data literacy so important?

- A study by the data visualization software company Qlik and the consulting firm Accenture found that 63% of employees use data for decision-making at least once a week.[6]
- Further, a study by the consulting firm McKinsey & Company found that companies where employees consistently use data in decision-making are more likely to report revenue growth of more than 10% in the past three years.[7]

These examples show that the ability to read, write, and communicate with data is a skill that is critical for success.

Technology Skills

Along with data literacy skills, accountants must know how to use technology to work with data. An analysis of over 500 entry-level accounting job postings for graduates with a bachelor of science

---

[5]Logan, V. (2018). Information as a Second Language: Enabling Data Literacy for a Digital Society. Gartner, Inc. ID: G00365697.

[6]Qlik and Accenture. (2020). The Human Impact of Data Literacy. Data Literacy Project. https://thedataliteracyproject. org/humanimpact (accessed July 2022).

[7]McKinsey. (2019). Catch Them If You Can: How Leaders in Data and Analytics Have Pulled Ahead. https://www. mckinsey.com/business-functions/mckinsey-analytics/our-insights/catch-them-if-you-can-how-leaders-in-data-and-analytics-have-pulled-ahead (accessed July 2022).

degree in accounting confirms these skills are highly sought by employers.[8] **Illustration 1.16** shows an analysis of the technology skills listed in the Robert Half July 2022 postings. Notice that most of the job postings required that applicants have strong Excel skills and more than half the postings are looking for ERP and database skills.

ILLUSTRATION 1.16 Technology Skill Requirements in Entry-Level Accounting Job Postings

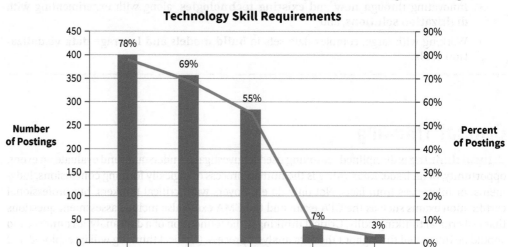

We have emphasized the influence of technology on the accounting profession, the demand for technology skills, and that technology changes rapidly. But how do you develop technology skills if technology is always changing?

If mental agility is the ability to think and understand quickly, then **technological agility** is an awareness of the latest technological developments and a willingness to try new things. We can become technologically agile by learning new technology and developing the skills that help us to do so. In fact, being comfortable learning new technology leads to more agility. This "learn to learn" mindset is what employers are looking for in new employees.

While the ability to learn and use new technology is important, so is in-depth knowledge of specific software packages essential to accountants. Microsoft Excel is a perfect example of an essential skill, which Illustration 1.16 demonstrates is one desired by most employers.

Finally, tools are just that–tools. They help accountants do their jobs more effectively, but they do not replace professional judgment or critical thinking, and they do not make decisions. In-depth accounting and business knowledge are what differentiates accountants from machines. Technology has just become an important part of that knowledge.

Communication Skills

Further evaluation of the Robert Half job postings reveals more skills required for entry-level accounting positions (**Illustration 1.17**). Critical thinking skills are mentioned in 73% of the postings, closely followed by communication skills at 66%.

The ability to communicate is important for all aspects of your accounting career. Recall that the managing director for Deloitte stated staff members must be able to communicate solutions to others. The Professional Insight feature at the beginning of this chapter also emphasized the need for strong communication skills. The EY careers website post mentions "sharing these results with both internal and external stakeholders" which clearly indicates that communicating the results of data analyses is a critical skill for new graduates.

---

[8]This data was collected by the authors from roberthalf.com in July 2022.

ILLUSTRATION 1.17 More Skill Requirements in Entry-Level Accounting Job Postings

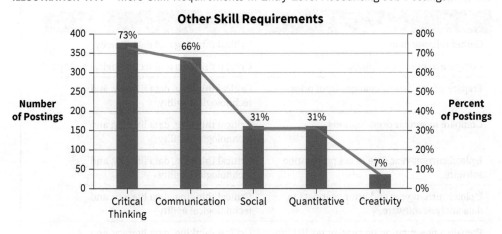

Communicating data analysis results requires specific skills:

- Writing clear and effective memos and reports.
- Preparing successful presentations.
- Creating meaningful data visualizations.
- Telling compelling data stories.

Data visualization is particularly important because it is used to perform data analysis and to communicate the results of data analysis. Data visualization is introduced in Chapter 2, and those skills are used throughout the course. Chapter 9 also explores data visualization best practices, as well as how to communicate data analysis results.

APPLY IT 1.3

Evaluate the Relationships Between Skills and Tasks

Tax Accounting You are a new tax associate at CFW assigned to work on the LocalPics corporate tax preparation. Match the following skills with the tasks that you will be performing. Skills can be used once, more than once, or not at all. Each task will require at least two skills and often more than two.

- Critical thinking
- Data literacy
- Technological agility
- Communication skills

Task	Skill
Gather relevant data.	
Compare to prior year filings.	
Prepare an analysis of changes from prior year.	
Compare to similar organizations.	
Upload current year data to tax preparation software.	
Upload current year and prior year data to data analysis software.	
Prepare a presentation on current tax liability for LocalPics senior management.	

SOLUTION

Task	Skill
Gather relevant data.	Critical thinking and data literacy
Compare to prior year filings.	Critical thinking and technological agility
Prepare an analysis of changes from prior year.	Critical thinking, data literacy, and technological agility
Compare to similar organizations.	Critical thinking, data literacy, and technological agility
Upload current year data to tax preparation software.	Critical thinking, data literacy, and technological agility
Upload current year and prior year data to data analysis software.	Critical thinking, data literacy, and technological agility
Prepare a presentation on current tax liability for LocalPics senior management.	Critical thinking, data literacy, and technological agility, and communication

1.4 How Is a Data Analytics Mindset Applied?

LEARNING OBJECTIVE ❹
Explain how to apply a data analytics mindset to the data analysis process.

You have learned that a data analytics mindset is the professional habit of critically thinking through the planning, analysis, and interpretation of data results before making and communicating a professional choice or decision. The data analysis process requires applying critical thinking skills at each stage:

- **Stage 1:** Taking the time to critically create and evaluate a data analysis plan will ensure you have considered all possible aspects of the analysis.
- **Stage 2:** Preparing data, building information models, and exploring data also require thinking critically as you move through the analyze stage of the project.
- **Stage 3:** Finally, critical thinking will help you interpret and communicate findings in the results stage.

There are six elements of critical thinking to consider when performing data analytics: stakeholders, purpose, alternatives, risks, knowledge, and self-reflection (**Illustration 1.18**). Keep in mind that these elements are not sequential, rather they are recursive. In other words, the order in which you consider the elements is not as important as continually thinking through them.

Understand the Stakeholders

Stakeholders are those individuals or groups with an interest in the outcome of a data analysis project. Stakeholders can be internal or external to an organization (**Illustration 1.19**).

- **Internal stakeholders** are individuals or groups involved in a business's operations. They include an organization's managers and employees.
- **External stakeholders** are individuals or groups outside the company. Examples include investors and creditors, regulators, organizational partners (clients or customers, suppliers, outsource partners, and donors), and community leaders and members.

ILLUSTRATION 1.18 SPARKS: The Six Elements of Critical Thinking

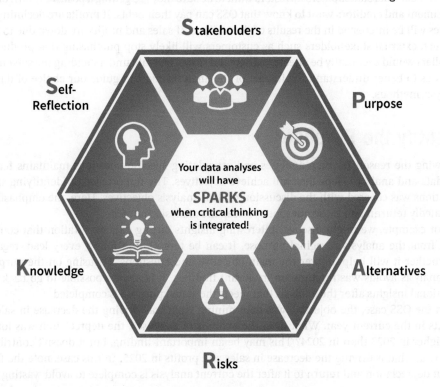

ILLUSTRATION 1.19 Internal and External Stakeholders

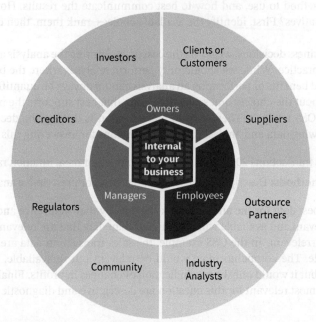

Let's go back to the One Stop Shop (OSS) analysis. Who are the relevant stakeholders in the analysis of OSS performance? Internal stakeholders would include the person performing the analysis, the supervisor, and the employees affected by the outcome of the analysis. If the analysis showed that the decrease in sales and profit was primarily driven by one region, internal stakeholders such as the employees in the region would have an interest in the analysis.

As for external stakeholders, investors want to be sure they are getting a positive return on their investment and creditors want to know that OSS can pay their debts. If profits are declining, both parties will be interested in the results of the analysis. If sales and profits are down due to a poor product, external stakeholders such as customers will likely stop purchasing that product, and suppliers would eventually be affected as demand slows. Overall, understanding the stakeholders helps us to better understand the impact of the analysis and can guide our choice of data and analysis methods.

Identify the Purpose

Knowing the reason for data analyses and articulating specific questions maintains focus on the data and analyses steps that will achieve objectives. The importance of identifying specific questions was covered with the discussion of data analysis objectives. Here, the emphasis is on repeatedly returning to those questions to keep the analysis on track.

For example, we might discover interesting insights during data exploration that could distract from the analysis's original purpose. It can be tempting to follow every lead, regardless of whether it will help answer the main objective and questions. Focusing on the purpose of the analysis avoids wasting time on irrelevant findings. It is always possible to go back to the additional insights after the analysis that meets the stated purpose is completed.

In the OSS case, the objective was determining what was driving the decrease in sales and profits in the current year. What if, in the analysis of expenses, the depreciation was found to be higher in 2023 than in 2024? This may be an important finding, but it doesn't contribute to knowing what is driving the decrease in sales and profits in 2025. In this case, note the finding about depreciation and return to it after the current analysis is complete to avoid wasting time.

Consider Alternatives

Performing data analyses involves many choices—which questions to evaluate, what data are needed, which method to use, and how to best communicate the results. How should we consider these alternatives? First, identify the available choices, rank them, then choose the highest ranked option.

As with all business decisions, weighing the cost of performing the analysis against its expected benefits is good practice. While we should only perform analyses where the benefits exceed the cost, the costs and benefits of performing an analysis cannot always be quantified. In these cases, think critically about the choices and select the option that best supports the purpose.

Consider the OSS analysis. They want to identify what is driving the decrease in sales and profits. The following data and analysis choices are options for answering this question:

- **Data:** Sales transactions 2022–2025 by region, competitor data, inflation rate.
- **Analysis methods:** Descriptive, diagnostic, predictive, or prescriptive analytics.

To select the best data for the analysis, rank the data by their relevance and availability. Data that are both relevant and available will rank higher than data that are relevant but not available or data that are irrelevant. In the OSS example, the sales transaction data are the most relevant and also available. The competitor data would be relevant but unavailable. The inflation rate might be useful, but it would only be one indication of changes in profits. Finally, the methods of analysis that are most relevant for this question are descriptive and diagnostic methods.

Assess Risks

There are many risks to consider when performing data analyses, and it's important to examine all aspects of the analysis to identify them. This begins with the data and extends to potential biases, including our own, that may be held by the stakeholders. Potential risks in four areas—data, analyses, assumptions, and biases—can affect decisions. These risks are illustrated with the OSS example in **Illustration 1.20**.

A habit of critically considering inherent risks in the data analyses work performed by ourselves or others avoids unintentionally creating or using incorrect data.

ILLUSTRATION 1.20 Types of Risks

Risk	Description	OSS Example
Data	Choosing inappropriate data, or data that are incomplete or incorrect.	Are the transaction data we plan to analyze complete and accurate?
Analysis	Choosing an inappropriate method, or applying a data analysis method incorrectly.	Are the descriptive and diagnostic analysis methods the correct methods? Were the analyses performed correctly?
Assumptions	Not understanding or evaluating assumptions about the data or the results.	What assumptions were made when collecting data, and are they correct? For example, are we assuming that we have all the data? Are we assuming that the 2023–2024 results are as expected? Perhaps they were higher than expected, and the 2024–2025 results did not decline as we initially thought.
Biases	Mental shortcuts that can affect decisions.	Do we have biases that could influence the data analysis? For example, assumptions about the cause of the sales decline could bias the preparation for the analysis or interpretation of the results.

Identify Knowledge

The next element of critical thinking in data analytics includes identifying knowledge gaps:

- Recognizing when more knowledge is necessary to complete the analysis.
- Acquiring knowledge from a reliable source.
- Learning how to correctly apply it to the data analysis.

Performing the analysis for the OSS case requires understanding how wholesale distributors operate, how profit is calculated, and how to perform descriptive and diagnostic data analyses. There is also a technology component, as it is necessary to know how to use the available technology to download the data and perform the descriptive and diagnostic analyses.

Perform Self-Reflection

The final critical thinking element is investing in a "post-project audit" habit honestly and without self-criticism. A start-to-finish project review connects and synthesizes what happened and why. The professional development we gain by this practice, whether the project was a success, a struggle, or a failure, can be valuable for both individuals and teams.

When the analysis of the decline in sales and profit for OSS is complete, reflect on what worked well and what did not. For example, if you had difficultly downloading the data but eventually figured it out, then use that experience in future projects to avoid similar issues.

SPARKS: A Critical Thinking Toolkit

The mnemonic SPARKS represents the six elements of critical thinking. Considering each will help you continue to develop your critical thinking skills. **Illustration 1.21** provides a summary of the elements of critical thinking in the SPARKS framework.

Critical thinking in accounting data analytics projects is essential because it forces us to anticipate impacts and issues and evaluate our choices. The results are better processes, improved judgments, and the ability to more provide value for our organizations, clients, and stakeholders. As you work through the data analysis process, apply SPARKS continuously. Doing so helps ensure you are performing the individual steps of the data analysis process (MOSAIC) effectively.

ILLUSTRATION 1.21 The Six Elements of Critical Thinking

Critical Thinking		Definition	Why It Matters
S	Stakeholders	Parties impacted by the data analysis results.	The potential impacts guide analysis and communication choices.
P	Purpose	The reason driving the questions for the analysis.	Focusing on the purpose helps select the best data, analysis, interpretation, and communication options.
A	Alternatives	Every choice should be the best option available.	Generating and ranking alternatives helps us make good choices.
R	Risks	Consider all risks related to data, strategy, biases, and assumptions.	Anticipating risks improves data and analysis choices.
K	Knowledge	Proper analysis strategy and interpretation of results often depends on accounting, economics, industry, statistics, and technology knowledge.	Applying knowledge provides meaning to the data and to the results.
S	Self-Reflection	Reviewing each choice throughout the data analysis process (MOSAIC) reveals what worked best.	Reflecting on lessons learned helps improve future analyses.

APPLY IT 1.4

Integrate Critical Thinking with the Data Analysis Process

Auditing Consider CFW's fraud risk assessment for LocalPics from Apply It 1.3. You were asked to identify and explain the data analysis steps you would perform during the risk assessment. Now, apply the six elements of critical thinking to each of those steps. Complete the last column in the table. Note that two elements are listed in each step, but it is possible that more elements could apply.

Data Analysis			Critical Thinking	
Stage	**Step**	**Explanation**	**Element**	**Application**
Plan	Motivation	Determine if theft is occurring.	Stakeholders Purpose	
	Objective	Identify if employees are stealing cash.	Purpose Risks	
	Strategy	Collect sales data and compare it to bank deposits.	Risks Knowledge	
Analyze	Prepare the data	Determine if the data needs to be cleaned or transformed.	Risks Self-Reflection	
	Build information models	Calculate what cash deposits should be based on sales.	Purpose Alternatives	
	Explore the data	Examine the data for anomalies.	Alternatives Knowledge	
Report	Interpret the results	Review analyses to ensure they are accurate and make sense.	Stakeholders Purpose	
	Communicate the results	Prepare a memo or presentation summarizing the findings.	Stakeholders Risks	

SOLUTION

Data Analysis Stage	Step	Explanation	Critical Thinking Element	Application
Plan	**M** Motivation	Determine if theft is occurring.	Stakeholders	The stakeholders are LocalPics management and employees, as well as the accounting firm.
			Purpose	The motivation is to determine if fraud is occurring for the client, LocalPics. It is also to do a good job for the firm you work for. The purpose of the analysis is to determine if theft is occurring. You must stay focused on that purpose throughout the analyses.
	O Objective	Identify if any employees are stealing cash.	Purpose	Articulating objective questions requires staying focused on the purpose.
			Risks	Risks to consider include not asking the correct questions and not asking enough questions.
	S Strategy	Collect sales data and compare to bank deposits.	Risks	When choosing data and an analysis strategy, consider risks related to the data, methods, and your thinking.
			Knowledge	Identify the specific knowledge needed to perform the analyses. For example, understanding the operating process for ticket sales and bank deposits is necessary.
Analyze	Prepare the Data	Determine if the data needs to be cleaned or transformed.	Risks	Risks to consider during data preparation include data completeness and data integrity.
			Self-Reflection	Reflect on past experiences with preparing data for analysis, and apply lessons learned to the current analysis.
	A Build Information Models	Calculate what cash deposits should be based on sales.	Purpose	Stay focused on the purpose, which is to identify theft, when building analysis models. The best way to do this is to calculate what the daily deposits should be based on sales and compare that to the actual deposits.
			Alternatives	Consider alternative models. Instead of total daily deposits, break that down into cash and credit card deposits, which is an alternative that will let you focus on cash theft.
	Explore the Data	Examine the data for anomalies.	Alternatives	You could use a visualization of cash receipts and cash deposits by day and employee to look for anomalies. Consider alternative visualizations to determine which will best answer the questions.
			Knowledge	Necessary knowledge for data exploration includes understanding the visualization software as well as the underlying data. You also must understand what would be considered an anomaly.
Report	**I** Interpret the Results	Review analyses to ensure they are accurate and make sense.	Purpose	Losing sight of the purpose of the analysis could lead to interpreting the results incorrectly. In this example, the purpose is to determine if theft occurred, so ensure that the results make sense in that context.
			Risks	Results could be misinterpreted when risks are not considered. If the data is incorrect or incomplete, the wrong employee could be identified in the theft, or the involved employee might not be found at all.
	C Communicate the Results	Prepare a memo or presentation summarizing the findings.	Stakeholders	Before communicating the results, understand the audience for the presentation and the information they need. Identifying the stakeholders in the analysis is the best way to do this.
			Risks	Using the correct visualizations and following best practices will reduce the risk of someone misinterpreting the results.

Chapter Review and Practice

Learning Objectives Review

❶ Summarize how advances in data and technology are impacting accounting professionals.

Data and technology are driving major changes in the accounting profession:

- The increased availability of data and easy-to-use technologies are changing the accounting profession and consequently accounting professional exams like the CPA and CMA. Data are raw figures and facts, which technology helps convert into information. Information is the knowledge gained from the data.
- Data analytics is the process of analyzing raw data to answer questions or provide insights. Self-service business intelligence tools have empowered accountants to use data and analytics to provide value-added services to their clients and employers. SSBI software has extended processing capabilities for preparing data, analyzing data, and reporting data analysis results and does not require programming knowledge or skills.
- Auditors use data analytics for risk assessment and substantive procedures. Financial accountants use technology to automate account analyses and routine tasks. They also use dashboards to monitor performance and enable decision-making. Managerial accountants use automation for variance analyses, budgeting, and performance dashboards. Tax accountants use data analytics to help with tax compliance, and dashboards can monitor real-time tax positions.

❷ Describe the stages of the data analysis process.

Stage 1: Plan:

- Motivation is the reason the analysis is performed.
- The objective is the goal of the project. To address the objective, form specific questions to guide the analysis.
- Strategy is the final step in the planning stage. There are two aspects: a data strategy and an analysis strategy. There are four types of data analysis methods:
  - Descriptive analytics are used to understand what is currently happening or has happened in the past.
  - Diagnostic analytics help reveal why something has happened.
  - Predictive analytics help predict what might happen in the future.
  - Prescriptive analytics can tell us what we should do to meet a specific objective.

Stage 2: Analyze:

- Data preparation is a critical step in the data analysis stage, and the process is often referred to as extract-transform-load (ETL). Data are extracted from a source and transformed by cleaning, restructuring, or integrating with other data prior to analysis. Loading is the process of uploading transformed data into analysis software.
- Information modeling refers to creating the information needed for analysis purposes. Examples of information models in accounting are models to calculate net income, profit margin, total assets, etc.

- The final step is exploring the data to derive insights occurs once the data and information models are prepared.

Stage 3: Report:

- Interpreting the results requires confirming the results address the objective of the analysis and make sense.
- Communicate the results by choosing the best presentation and method of communication.

The three stages of the data analysis process and the steps within them can be remembered by the mnemonic MOSAIC.

❸ Identify the skills necessary to perform data analyses.

A data analytics mindset is the professional habit of critically thinking through the planning, analysis, and interpretation of data results before communicating a professional choice or decision. Data analysis skills that are in demand from employers include critical thinking, data literacy, technology agility, and communication:

- Practice critical thinking skills in every stage of the data analysis process. Critical thinking is disciplined reasoning used to investigate, understand, and evaluate an event, opportunity, or issue.
- Accounting graduates also need to be data literate. They should be the able to read, write, and communicate about data in context.
- Accounting graduates must be technologically agile. They should be comfortable learning new technology and be ready to use new technology.
- Finally, accounting graduates must have strong written, oral, and visual communication skills to effectively communicate the results of data analyses.

❹ Explain how to apply a data analytics mindset to the data analysis process.

To apply a data analytics mindset to the data analysis process, continuously apply the six elements of critical thinking:

- Identify and consider stakeholders. Stakeholders are individuals or groups with an interest in the outcome of a data analysis project. They can be internal or external to the organization.
- Identify the purpose of the analysis and stay focused on it throughout the process.
- Determine and evaluate data and analysis possibilities and choose the best data and method to achieve the project's objective. Alternatives are determined and evaluated.
- Identify risk to mitigate problems that may occur due to data risks, analysis risks, incorrect assumptions, and biases.
- Acquire and apply the knowledge that is necessary for project success.
- Self-reflection on the planning, processes, and outcomes from prior projects can be applied to future projects.

The mnemonic SPARKS is a tool to remember the six critical thinking elements.

Key Terms Review

Critical thinking   19
Dashboard   6
Data   3
Data analytics   3
Data analytics mindset   18
Data literacy   19
Data profiling   13
Data visualization   5
Descriptive analytics   12

Diagnostic analytics   12
External data   12
External stakeholders   22
Extract-transform-load (ETL)   13
Information   3
Internal data   12
Internal stakeholders   22
Motivation   11
Null value   3

Objective   11
Predictive analytics   12
Prescriptive analytics   12
Reasoning   19
Self-service business intelligence software (SSBI)   3
Stakeholders   22
Technological agility   20

Data The Data tag appears when the data required to answer a question or complete an exercise are available in the book's product page on www.wiley.com.

Multiple Choice Questions

1. (LO 1) Data differs from information because

  a. data are raw figures and facts whereas information is the knowledge we gain from the data.

  b. data are larger than information.

  c. information is raw figures and facts whereas data are the knowledge we gain from the information.

  d. information is larger than data.

2. (LO 1) One key feature of self-service business intelligence (SSBI) software is that

  a. it is easy to use.

  b. it costs less to implement.

  c. it connects to multiple data sources.

  d. it provides dashboarding capabilities.

3. (LO 2) Predictive analytics

  a. assesses what is happening currently and in the past.

  b. identifies a problem to understand why an outcome occurred.

  c. forecasts what might happen in the future.

  d. helps determine what should happen to meet goals or objectives.

4. (LO 2) The question "Why are costs rising in business unit A?" would be answered using which type of data analysis method?

  a. Descriptive   **c.** Predictive

  b. Diagnostic   **d.** Prescriptive

5. (LO 2) The stages in the data analysis process are

  a. analyze, report, and reflection.

  b. strategize, plan, and analyze.

  c. plan, analyze, and report.

  d. plan, report, and reflection.

6. (LO 2) The data analysis process stage in which information models are built is the

  a. extraction stage.   **c.** analyze stage.

  b. plan stage.   **d.** report stage.

7. (LO 2) Which activities are performed during the reporting stage of data analysis?

  a. Data cleaning and analysis

  b. Data preparation and communication

  c. Data analysis and interpretation

  d. Data interpretation and communication

8. (LO 2) The analyze stage of the data analysis process includes which of the following tasks?

  a. Interpreting the analysis findings

  b. Communicating the analysis results

  c. Cleaning the data set to remove errors and omissions

  d. Planning the data analysis strategy

9. (LO 3) Accountants with critical thinking skills will

  a. use professional judgment to investigate, understand, and evaluate an event, opportunity, or issue.

  b. use best practices to investigate, understand, and evaluate an event, opportunity, or issue.

  c. use disciplined reasoning to investigate, understand, and evaluate an event, opportunity, or issue.

  d. seek expert advice to investigate, understand, and evaluate an event, opportunity, or issue.

10. (LO 3) A mindset of being aware of the newest technology and a willingness to try new things is referred to as

  a. analytical thinking.   **c.** data literacy.

  b. critical thinking.   **d.** technological agility.

11. (LO 3) The ability to prepare effective data visualizations for the results of an analysis is part of which skill set?

  a. Analytical thinking   **c.** Statistical ability

  b. Communication   **d.** Logical thinking

12. (LO 4) Professional critical thinking elements in data analysis include

  a. understanding stakeholders, identifying the purpose, considering alternatives, assessing risks, identifying knowledge needed, and self-reflecting.

  b. understanding stakeholders, considering alternatives, and understanding the desired results of analysis and actively pursuing that outcome.

c. understanding stakeholders, assessing risks, identifying knowledge needed, and following instructions without questioning them.

d. understanding stakeholders, identifying the purpose, and following data analysis best practices to achieve the desired result.

13. (LO 4) You are a tax accountant who prepares corporate tax returns. An example of an internal stakeholder and an external stakeholder are

a. tax clients and the Securities and Exchange Commission (SEC), respectively.

b. partners of the tax firm and competing tax firms, respectively.

c. partners of the tax firm and tax regulators, respectively.

d. tax clients and investors of the tax clients, respectively.

14. (LO 4) Which of these is a risk in data analysis?

a. A client that wants a particular outcome.

b. Data that is current and relevant.

c. You have performed this analysis before.

d. You have used the analysis software before.

15. (LO 4) Which element of critical thinking helps avoid wasting time on irrelevant analyses or findings?

a. Understanding the stakeholders

b. Identifying the purpose

c. Considering alternatives

d. Identifying the knowledge necessary for the analysis

Review Questions

1. (LO 1) How are the CPA exam and CMA exam changing due to shifts in the accounting profession?

2. (LO 1) Match the practice area of accounting to the changes driven by data and technology. You may use more than one accounting area.

a. Auditing   c. Managerial accounting

b. Financial accounting   d. Tax accounting

Changes	Accounting Practice Area
1. Ability to use entire data sets to identify exceptions, anomalies, and outliers	
2. Automation of manual processes	
3. Automation of journal entries	
4. Risk identification	
5. Forecasting	
6. Compliance reporting	

3. (LO 1) Discuss the difference between data and information.

4. (LO 2) Match the type of data analytics method with the purpose for the analysis.

a. Descriptive   c. Predictive

b. Diagnostic   d. Prescriptive

Purpose	Method
1. Understanding what is happening currently and what has happened in the past.	
2. Understanding what should happen to meet goals and objectives.	
3. Understanding what might happen in the future.	
4. Understanding why something happened.	

5. (LO 2) Discuss the three steps in the planning stage of the data analysis process.

6. (LO 2) Preparing data for analysis is often referred to as ETL (extract-transform-load). Describe each aspect of the ETL process.

7. (LO 2) Match the data analysis process stages to the examples.

a. Plan   b. Analyze   c. Report

Example	Data Analysis Process Stage
1. Develop a model to calculate contribution margin.	
2. Get data from a database.	
3. Upload data into analysis software.	
4. Determine the objective of the analysis.	
5. Create a forecast of net income.	
6. Identify the data needed for analysis.	
7. Identify relationships within the data.	
8. Create a visualization to show the results of the analyses.	
9. Identify sales patterns.	

8. (LO 3) Discuss the meaning of having a data analytics mindset.

9. (LO 3) Explain the importance of communication skills when reporting the results of data analysis.

10. (LO 3) Match the data analysis skill to its definition.

a. Critical thinking   c. Technology agility

b. Data literacy   d. Communication

Definition	Skill
1. Willingness to try new technology.	
2. The ability to read, write, and communicate data in context.	
3. Ability to create effective data visualizations.	
4. Disciplined reasoning used to investigate, understand, and evaluate an event, opportunity, or issue.	

11. (LO 4) List and describe the six elements of critical thinking.

12. (LO 4) Give an example and explain how one of the elements of critical thinking can be applied to the planning stage of the data analysis process.

13. (LO 4) Give an example and explain how one of the elements of critical thinking can be applied to the analyzing stage of the data analysis process.

14. (LO 4) Give an example and explain how one of the elements of critical thinking can be applied to the reporting stage of the data analysis process.

Brief Exercises

BE 1.1 (LO 1) `Auditing` The following analysis of sales by month and quarter for 2025 has been prepared for One Stop Shop:

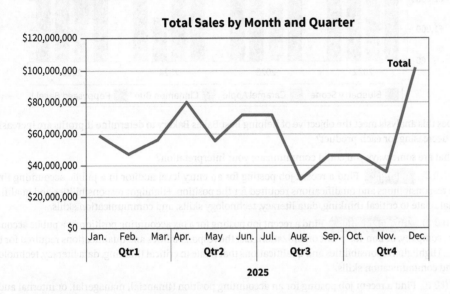

Total Sales by Month and Quarter

1. How might an auditor use this analysis?
2. Identify any months that might warrant additional investigation.

BE 1.2 (LO 1) `Data` `Financial Accounting` Examine the available data to do the following:

1. Identify total sales, total costs, and total profit.
2. Discuss how a financial accountant might use this information to create a dashboard.
3. What additional information would a financial accountant find useful in a dashboard?

BE 1.3 (LO 2) `Managerial Accounting` Denton Hospitality is a hotel chain located in Singapore. Denton wants to know following four things:

1. Which hotels have the highest revenue?
2. Are there any hotels that have unusual revenue?
3. Can we estimate expenses for the next year?
4. How long does it take, on average, to clean a room?

For each request, identify the appropriate data analysis method to answer the question.

BE 1.4 (LO 2) `Managerial Accounting` A television manufacturing company manufactures and sells three variants of television sets. The company wants to evaluate each variant and decide whether any variant production can be discontinued.

1. List the financial data that will be useful for your analysis.
2. Is the financial data listed by you internal or external?

(*Note:* Student answers will vary.)

BE 1.5 (LO 2) `Financial Accounting` A car rental company rents its cars to hotels regularly. The company wants to maintain an average profit margin of 30%. For the past three years, it has seen a decline in average profits and wants to find the customer(s) affecting the target profit margin.

What analysis should be performed to identify the customer pulling down average profit margins?

BE 1.6 (LO 2) [Financial Accounting] You are a financial accountant for Best Bakes Bakery asked to interpret an analysis of sales by product. The objective is to determine which products are increasing and decreasing in profit. You were given the following visualization:

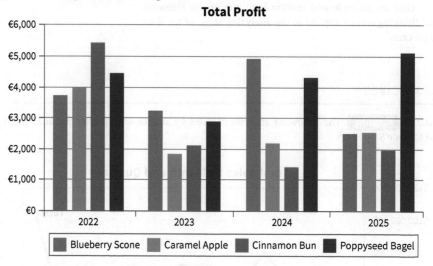

1. Does this analysis meet the objective of helping Best Bakes Bakery to determine if profits are increasing or decreasing for each product?
2. What are some ways you could communicate your interpretation?

BE 1.7 (LO 3) [Auditing] Find a recent job posting for an entry-level auditor in a public accounting firm. List the responsibilities and qualifications required for the position. Highlight responsibilities and qualifications that relate to critical thinking, data literacy, technology skills, and communication skills.

BE 1.8 (LO 3) [Tax Accounting] Find a recent job posting for a tax accounting position in a public accounting firm, company, or non-for-profit organization. List the responsibilities and qualifications required for the position. Highlight responsibilities and qualifications that relate to critical thinking, data literacy, technology skills and communication skills.

BE 1.9 (LO 3) Find a recent job posting for an accounting position (financial, managerial, or internal audit) in a company or not-for-profit organization. List the responsibilities and qualifications required for the position. Highlight responsibilities and qualifications that relate to critical thinking, data literacy, technology skills, and communication skills.

BE 1.10 (LO 4) Indicate whether the party is an internal (I) or an external (E) stakeholder:

1. CEO, CFO, or sales manager
2. Clients or customers
3. Employees
4. Suppliers
5. Outsource partners
6. Investors
7. Creditors and lenders
8. Regulators at state and federal agencies

BE 1.11 (LO 4) Crispy Buds is a startup bakery that specializes in warm cookies. They have expanded to multiple locations. Their data volume has increased, and their current in-house data infrastructure is not scalable, so cloud data services are being investigated. A data analysis is required to project their data needs and help determine the type of cloud data service that is required.

For each step in the data analysis (MOSAIC) process, apply the critical thinking framework by describing at least two critical thinking considerations.

Data Analysis Process (MOSAIC)	Critical Thinking Elements (SPARKS)
Stage 1: Plan	
Motivation	
Objective	
Strategy	
Stage 2: Analyze	
Prepare data	
Build models	
Explore data	
Stage 3: Report	
Interpret	
Communicate	

Exercises

EX 1.1 (LO 2, 4) [Managerial Accounting] **Apply Critical Thinking** A bank branch located inside a large university has salary accounts of the staff of the university, vehicle loan accounts, education loan accounts, and personal loan accounts too. The branch manager wants to understand the mix of vehicle loan accounts, education loan accounts, and personal loan accounts that would result in the highest interest income for the bank branch.

1. Can you guess who would be the users of this bank branch?
2. The objective is to determine which combination of loan accounts could result in the best net interest income maximization. What specific questions will address this objective?
3. What are the data alternatives that can be used to answer the objective?
4. How would you compare and analyze any two options that you have created? Explain why you selected the data and the analysis options.
5. List three accounting information/values that you will use in the data analysis.

(*Note:* Student answers will vary.)

EX 1.2 (LO 2, 4) [Auditing] **Identify Stakeholders, Objectives, and Risks** You are conducting an independent audit of the financial statements for a Sydney-based car dealer company. They have multiple locations in various cities across the state of New South Wales. You have been assigned the task of recalculating the company's payroll commission expense, which is reported as selling, general, and administrative expenses on the company's financial statements.

1. List two external stakeholders who may be impacted by the audit findings.
2. Your objective is to determine whether the financial statements are reasonable representations of the company's operations and financial position. Assume you were provided the company's monthly payroll commission payouts for the fiscal year under audit. Develop three specific questions you could ask to achieve your objective.
3. Discuss one risk to critical thinking related to your examination of payroll commission payout data.
4. Identify at least one useful insight to leverage when working with other audit clients.

EX 1.3 (LO 2, 4) [Financial Accounting] **Apply the Data Analysis Process** Boris, the CFO for a large retail company, has asked you to perform data analysis to identify obsolete inventory and to calculate an inventory obsolescence reserve for the year-end financial statements. Inventory is one of the largest assets on your balance sheet. Complete the chart.

Stage	Data Analysis Process	Response
Plan	1. What is your motivation for performing the analysis?	
	2. What is the objective of your data analysis project?	
	3. What is your strategy to achieve the objective?	
Analyze	4. What would you consider in the data set before you begin your analysis?	
	5. What information model might you use to satisfy the objective?	
	6. Assume your analysis identified several items in inventory that have not sold over the last year. How would you explore initial results?	
Report	7. Assume your analysis results in a calculation of inventory obsolescence as of year-end. What would you consider as you interpret these results?	
	8. How would you communicate your results to the CFO?	

EX 1.4 (LO 2, 4) `Accounting Information Systems` `Auditing` **Critical Thinking and the Data Analysis Process** You are working in the internal audit department of a publicly traded company. This is the first year the company must analyze and report on the operating effectiveness of internal controls over financial reporting.

Hito, the internal audit director, asks you to test controls associated with the authorization and authentication of users into the company's information system. Specifically, you are asked to identify whether any terminated employees continue to have access to login to the information system. You plan to request files from human resources and information technology groups. For each step in the data analysis (MOSAIC) process, use the critical thinking framework by applying at least two critical thinking elements.

Stage	Data Analysis Process	Critical Thinking
Plan	**1.** Motivation	
	2. Objective	
	3. Strategy	
Analyze	**4.** Prepare data	
	5. Build models	
	6. Explore data	
Report	**7.** Interpret	
	8. Communicate	

EX 1.5 (LO 2, 4) `Auditing` **Critical Thinking and the Data Analysis Process** You are a first-year external auditor assigned to a client whose primary business activity is breeding and raising bison. They sell the meat to grocery stores and distributors, who then sell to restaurants. You will audit the company's accounts receivable allowance for doubtful accounts. The client has prepared a schedule that indicates they have over 200 customers with outstanding receivables balances as of year-end. Your senior auditor indicated that the primary assertion on which you should focus is valuation of the allowance for doubtful accounts. You must perform an analysis to recalculate the company's recorded balance.

For each step in the data analysis process, use the critical thinking framework by applying at least two critical thinking elements.

Stage	Data Analysis Process	Critical Thinking
Plan	**1.** Motivation	
	2. Objective	
	3. Strategy	
Analyze	**4.** Prepare data	
	5. Build models	
	6. Explore data	
Report	**7.** Interpret	
	8. Communicate	

EX 1.6 (LO 2, 4) `Financial Accounting` **Critical Thinking and the Data Analysis Process** You are a financial analyst working for a major airline company's accounting department. The CFO wants to understand the company's debt solvency (meaning their ability to meet their debt obligations) compared to that of its primary competitors. You have been tasked with the calculation, interpretation, and evaluation of the following ratios:

Debt to equity: Total liabilities/Stockholders' equity

Debt to assets: Total liabilities/Total assets

Times interest earned: (Net income + Interest expense + Tax expense)/Interest expense

For each step in the data analysis process, use the critical thinking framework by applying at least two critical thinking elements.

Stage	Data Analysis Process	Critical Thinking
Plan	**1.** Motivation	
	2. Objective	
	3. Strategy	
Analyze	**4.** Prepare data	
	5. Build models	
	6. Explore data	
Report	**7.** Interpret	
	8. Communicate	

EX 1.7 (LO 2, 4) `Financial Accounting` `Managerial Accounting` **Critical Thinking and the Data Analysis Process** You are a financial analyst working for a manufacturing company that produces and sells two very different products. The vice president of operations, Juan, has asked you to prepare an analysis to explain why the company's total sales revenues decreased, while net income increased. He prepared the following preliminary analysis for you:

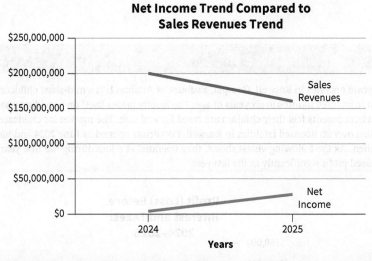

Briefly describe what you would suggest for each step in the data analysis process, then use critical thinking by describing at least two critical thinking elements for each step you listed.

Stage	Data Analysis Process	Brief Description	Critical Thinking
Plan	**1.** Motivation		
	2. Objective		
	3. Strategy		
Analyze	**4.** Prepare data		
	5. Build models		
	6. Explore data		
Report	**7.** Interpret		
	8. Communicate		

EX 1.8 (LO 2, 4) `Tax Accounting` **Critical Thinking and the Data Analysis Process** You work for a nonprofit in Washington D.C. whose mission is to understand and document how changes in the federal tax code cause changes in predicted federal tax revenues. Your group is currently considering several elements of the newly proposed tax reform bill. You and your team want to predict tax revenue changes if the tax rates were decreased by 1% for the middle brackets of taxable income for single filing individuals (not those who

file jointly as married, separately as married, or heads of households). The tax rates you are considering are as follows:

Tax Rate (%)	Taxable Income Bracket	Tax Owed
22	$40,126 to $85,525	$4,617.50 + 22% on income over $40,125
24	$85,526 to $163,300	$14,605.50 + 24% on income over $85,525
32	$163,301 to $207,350	$33,271.50 + 32% on income over $163,300

Briefly describe what you would suggest for each step in the data analysis process, then apply two critical thinking elements to each step listed.

Stage	Data Analysis Process	Brief Description	Critical Thinking
Plan	1. Motivation		
	2. Objective		
	3. Strategy		
Analyze	4. Prepare data		
	5. Build models		
	6. Explore data		
Report	7. Interpret		
	8. Communicate		

Professional Application Case   FootPrints Daycare

FootPrints Daycare operates in Roswell, Georgia, a suburb of Atlanta. It is a mid-sized childcare facility that serves children from three months to six years of age. The facility prides itself on providing a safe and secure environment where parents feel their children are cared for and safe. The market for childcare is very competitive, with just over 20 licensed facilities in Roswell. FootPrints opened in June 2024 and has seen steady growth since then. As the following visual shows, they operated at a loss during the first year they opened but have increased profit significantly in the last year.

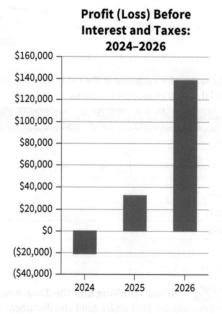

Profit (Loss) Before Interest and Taxes: 2024–2026

The income statement for the past three years shows that the first year ended with a loss of $21,579, but by 2026 they earned a profit, before interest and taxes, of $138,654.

Income Statement
Year Ended December 31

	2024	2025	2026
Income			
Sales	$287,787.50	$566,527.50	$742,214.00
Direct Cost of Sales	($8,586.60)	($17,600.00)	($23,760.00)
Gross Margin	**$279,200.90**	**$548,927.50**	**$718,454.00**
Expenses			
Payroll	$235,200.00	$371,840.00	$420,000.00
Sales and Marketing and Other Expenses	$5,000.00	$5,000.00	$5,000.00
Leased Equipment	$1,900.00	$2,100.00	$2,300.00
Certifications & Inspections	$2,500.00	$2,500.00	$2,500.00
Utilities	$1,900.00	$20,000.00	$22,000.00
Insurance	$3,000.00	$35,000.00	$40,000.00
Rent	$16,000.00	$25,000.00	$25,000.00
Payroll Taxes	$35,280.00	$55,776.00	$63,000.00
Other	$0.00	$0.00	$0.00
Total Operating Expenses	**$300,780.00**	**$517,216.00**	**$579,800.00**
Profit (Loss) Before Interest and Taxes	**($21,579.10)**	**$31,711.50**	**$138,654.00**

The balance sheet for FootPrints shows a steady growth in total assets. Total liabilities have remained relatively flat all three years.

Balance Sheet
December 31

	2024	2025	2026
Assets			
Current Assets			
Cash	$44,676	$45,065	$162,840
Other Current Assets	$0	$25,000	$150,000
Total Current Assets	$44,676	$70,065	$312,840
Long-term Assets			
Long-term Assets	$0	$0	$0
Total Assets	$44,676	$70,065	$312,840
Liabilities and Capital			
Current Liabilities			
Accounts Payable	$6,455	$10,133	$17,311
Current Borrowing	$0	$0	$0
Other Current Liabilities	$0	$0	$0
Subtotal Current Liabilities	$6,455	$10,133	$17,311
Long-term Liabilities	$22,800	$12,800	$2,800
Total Liabilities	$29,255	$22,933	$20,111
Paid-in Capital	$40,000	$40,000	$40,000
Retained Earnings	($3,000)	($24,579)	$114,075
Earnings	($21,579)	$31,711	$138,654
Total Capital	$15,421	$47,132	$292,729
Total Liabilities and Capital	$44,676	$70,065	$312,840

FootPrints provides two types of services: full-time and drop-in childcare. Full-time services are charged monthly and drop-in services are charged by the hour. The next visualization shows the number of children per year for each service.

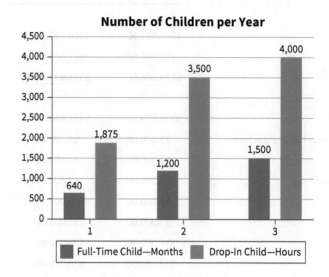

Consider how data analytics can be used at FootPrints Daycare in each of the following scenarios:

PAC 1.1 Auditing: Risk Assessment and Audit Procedures

Data **Auditing** Your audit team has been given a data set of all transactions for the year 2026. A sample of the file is provided.

	ReceiptNumber	Date	Service	CustomerFirstName	CustomerLastName	ChildsFirstName	ChildsLastName	Amount
1								
2	F-01251	1/15/2026	Full Time	Teri	Park	Nicholas	Park	$ 125.00
3	D-01251	1/16/2026	Drop in	Esther	Rodgers	Lucia	Salazar	$ 45.00
4	D-01252	1/17/2026	Drop in	Brandy	Morales	Krystal	Morales	$ 60.00
5	F-01252	1/18/2026	Full Time	Hubert	Roberts	Trevor	Roberts	$ 125.00
6	F-01253	1/19/2026	Full Time	Rebecca	Spencer	Patricia	Spencer	$ 125.00
7	D-01253	1/20/2026	Drop in	Eula	Pierce	Alec	Luciano	$ 30.00
8	D-01254	1/21/2026	Drop in	Alexander	Hoffman	Cassy	Hoffman	$ 55.00

Based on the sample data set, discuss how the audit team might use the data provided to perform each of the following procedures:

1. Audit risk assessment
2. Substantive analytical procedures

PAC 1.2 Financial Accounting: Understand Financial Performance

Data **Financial Accounting** You have been asked to suggest how data analytics can be used to help better understand the financial position of the company.

1. Discuss how FootPrints can use SSBI software to provide information about company performance.
2. What are some financial statement analysis items that FootPrints should consider for a financial dashboard?
3. Sketch a sample of what a financial dashboard might look like for FootPrints. Consider the data that is available when determining what to include in your dashboard.

PAC 1.3 Managerial Accounting: Understand Operational Performance

Data **Managerial Accounting** You are preparing the next year budget plan, as well as an analysis to determine which city FootPrints should consider for expansion.

City	State	Country	Population	Percentage of Five Years Old and Under	Number of Children Five Yrs or Under	MedianIncome
Atlanta	Georgia	USA	498,715	5.4	26,931	$ 59,948
Columbus	Georgia	USA	206,922	7.2	14,898	$ 46,408
Augusta	Georgia	USA	202,081	6.9	13,944	$ 42,592
Macon	Georgia	USA	157,346	5.0	7,867	$ 32,161
Savannah	Georgia	USA	147,780	6.4	9,458	$ 43,307
Athens	Georgia	USA	127,315	5.3	6,748	$ 38,311
Sandy Springs	Georgia	USA	108,080	5.9	6,377	$ 78,613
South Fulton	Georgia	USA	107,436	7.1	7,628	$ 65,919
Roswell	Georgia	USA	92,833	7.1	6,591	$ 99,726
Johns Creek	Georgia	USA	82,453	4.7	3,875	$ 122,514

1. Discuss how the managerial accounting team might use the data provided to determine a city in which they could open another daycare location.

2. Identify data that would be useful for a management accounting dashboard.

3. What type of data analytics method would you use to prepare the budget for the next year?

PAC 1.4 Tax Accounting: Use Tax Data for Decision-Making

You are helping the management accounting department with their analysis to determine a potential city for opening another location. You have gathered data from the IRS that shows information about tax returns filed in each zip code in the state of Georgia. A list of the data available for analysis follows. If an item would be useful for your analysis, indicate whether you would use the number of returns or the dollar amount in your analysis. Then, explain why you chose that specific item.

Data Available	Number of Returns	Dollar Amount	Reason
Zip Code			
Size of Adjusted Gross Income: $1 under $25,000 $25,000 under $50,000 $50,000 under $75,000 $75,000 under $100,000 $100,000 under $200,000 $200,000 or more			
Number of Single Returns			
Number of Joint Returns			
Number of Head of Household Returns			
Total Income			
Salaries and Wages in AGI			
Taxable Interest			
State and Local Income Tax Refunds			
Business or Professional Net Income			
Unemployment Compensation			
Student Loan Interest			
Total Standard Deduction			
Total Itemized Deduction			
State and Local Taxes			
Total Taxes Paid			
Income Before Tax Credits			
Earned Income Credit			
Additional Child Tax Credit			

Foundational Data Analysis Skills

CHAPTER PREVIEW   You will be working with data and data analysis software throughout your career, and one of the most common software tools used in accounting is Microsoft Excel. As you will see in the Professional Insight feature, the ability to use Microsoft Excel to manipulate large data sets is a tremendous asset for newly hired professional accountants. While Microsoft Excel skills are important, the software is not powerful enough to analyze extremely large data sets, so it is not the only tool used to analyze data. This chapter introduces some skills that, regardless of the technology used, are fundamental to performing data analytics. Microsoft Excel is used to demonstrate many of the core data analysis skills, but subsequent chapters also introduce data analysis software such as Power BI and Tableau. A combination of a core understanding of data, data visualization, and descriptive analysis skills are the foundation for performing more advanced data analytics.

PROFESSIONAL INSIGHT   **How Can PivotTables Help Make Sense of Large Data Sets?**

Josh, a senior accounting student, explains how learning Microsoft Excel helped him in his internship.

My first assignment was to create an Excel PivotTable to manipulate a huge data file of approximately 450,000 records. I had just obtained my Microsoft Office Specialist Basic Excel certification when I began my internship at PwC. It feels great to apply what I learned in the classroom in the business world. **This experience gave me confidence interacting with my superiors and helped me build a reputation of reliability at my firm.** My director on the client was thoroughly impressed with my work, and my senior associate was surprised that I was able to put together such a comprehensive table with so little experience.

Chapter Roadmap

LEARNING OBJECTIVES	TOPICS	APPLY IT
LO 2.1 Describe how data is stored in and extracted from relational databases.	• Relational Databases • Joining Tables	**Identify Primary and Foreign Keys** (Example: Accounting Information Systems)
LO 2.2 Explain how functions help answer data analysis questions.	• Basic Functions for Data Analysis • Applying Excel Basic Functions	**Analyze Sales Transactions with Excel Functions** (Example: Financial and Managerial Accounting)
LO 2.3 Illustrate how pivottables organize and filter data.	• Using PivotTables • Filtering PivotTables	**Analyze Sales with Excel PivotTables** (Example: Financial and Managerial Accounting)
LO 2.4 Identify descriptive measures used to perform data analysis.	• Measures of Location • Measures of Dispersion • Measures of Shape • Correlation Analysis	**Use Descriptive Statistics to Audit Warranty Expense** (Example: Auditing)
LO 2.5 Summarize how data visualization explores and explains data.	• Making Sense of Large Data Sets • Visualizations and When to Use Them • Microsoft Excel Visualizations	**Analyze Product Costs with Data Visualization** (Example: Managerial Accounting)

Data The Data tag appears in the chapter when the data for an example, illustration, or application are available in the book's product page on www.wiley.com.

Data analytics software is continuously changing, and there may be more recent versions of the software referenced in this chapter.

2.1 How Does Understanding Data Storage Help Answer Questions?

LEARNING OBJECTIVE ❶
Describe how data is stored in and extracted from relational databases.

Understanding how data is stored is critical for data analysis. This is because the kind of analysis that can be performed depends on the data being used, and identifying and extracting the data we need requires knowing how it is stored.

Relational Databases

Data, regardless of type or format, needs to be stored somewhere. One way to do that is in a **relational database,** which is a collection of logically related data that can be retrieved, manipulated, and updated to meet users' needs. Most data you will work with in your accounting career will come from relational databases, where data are stored in individual tables that can be linked together.

Once the tables are linked, data from multiple tables can be accessed. A **table** in a relational database stores valuable data related to an object of interest, such as a business resource, event, or agent. Tables are comprised of rows and columns:

- Each row represents one record or instance of the table's object.
- The columns reflect the **attributes,** which are the data fields that describe different aspects of the records (**Illustration 2.1**).

ILLUSTRATION 2.1 Database Elements and Examples of Tables and Attributes

Database Elements	Table Examples	Examples of Attributes
Resources: Identifiable objects that have economic value to the business entity.	Inventory items	• Inventory item's code number • Description • Cost • Quantity on hand
Events: An organization's business activities.	Sales orders	• Sales order number • The date of a sales order • Customer ID of the purchaser
Agents: Represent people or organizations about which data are collected.	Employees	• Employee number • Name • Address • Phone number

Illustration 2.2 is the database view of a university's asset data table that contains data for the inventory of its assets.

ILLUSTRATION 2.2 University Database

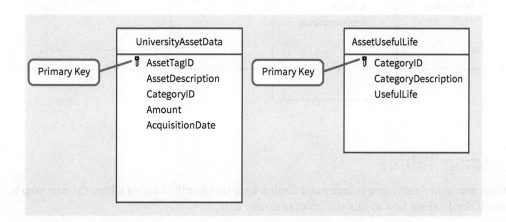

Each row in the table shows a uniquely identifiable asset. Its associated attributes are organized in each vertical column listed below the table name:

- AssetTagID: Tag identification number
- AssetDescription: Description of asset
- CategoryID: Category identification number
- Amount: Cost of asset
- AcquisitionDate: Date asset was acquired

The AssetUsefulLife table contains information related to the asset categories. Each row is a unique category, and the columns are the attributes of that category:

- CategoryID: Identification number for each category of assets
- CategoryDescription: Category description
- UsefulLife: Useful life in years of assets in each category

There is a symbol for a key next to the AssetTagID attribute in the first table and the CategoryID in the second table. This symbol identifies the **primary key,** which is the column that must have a unique value for each row in the table. In the UniversityAssetData table, every asset is uniquely identified by the primary key column AssetTagID. In the AssetUsefulLife table, the primary key is CategoryID. Each row in the AssetUsefulLife table will have a unique CategoryID number.

To calculate depreciation on assets, we need cost information, useful life information, and the age of the asset. However, that information appears in two different tables. Linking them requires a common field in both:

- The CategoryID field is in both tables.
- CategoryID is the primary key column in the AssetUsefulLife table.
- In the UniversityAssetData table, CategoryID is a **foreign key** column. A foreign key column contains the same data as a primary key from another table. It has been repeated in the second table so the tables can be linked in relationship to each other. **Illustration 2.3** shows the relationship linking the two tables using the CategoryID attribute.

Why does this matter? Linking tables creates a relationship that makes it possible to pull information from both tables and create calculations of depreciation for every asset in the asset data table.

ILLUSTRATION 2.3 Creating a Relationship Between Tables

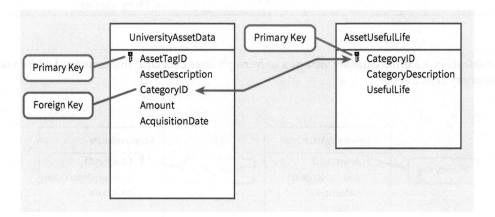

Joining Tables

Once common fields using primary and foreign keys are identified across tables, the next step is to tell the database how to link the tables to extract data:

- A **query** is an action request made to a database. It provides the computer instructions for joining, adding, updating, deleting, retrieving, or manipulating the data in its tables. Queries can be created and used once or stored for later reuse.
- The standard query command language used for database management is **Structured Query Language (SQL).** Writing SQL code is beyond the scope of this chapter, but fortunately, many software programs have built-in applications that automatically create the SQL code needed to query the database.

Retrieving all the data fields necessary to complete a particular task requires understanding how to join tables based on columns they have in common. Tables are linked by creating a **join** that combines rows from two or more tables based on a related column between them. Joins are also used in visualization software and other data analysis software when there is more than one table of data being used in an analysis. (We discuss data visualization in more detail both at the end of this chapter and in later chapters.)

The most common joins are inner, left, right, and full joins. **Illustration 2.4** summarizes the different joins and provides a visual representation. The blue shading represents the results of the join. Note that a null value is not the same as a value of zero. A **null value** is when a value is unknown or missing.

ILLUSTRATION 2.4 Types of Joins

Join	Description	Visual Representation
Inner	• Selects all rows from both tables with matching values. • The results will not have null values in any key column.	Table 1 Table 2
Left	• Returns all records from the left table and the matching records from the right table. • There could be null values if there is no matching value in the right table to a left table record.	Table 1 Table 2
Right	• Returns all records from the right table and the matched records from the left table. • Could return null values if there is not a matching value in the left table to the record in the right table.	Table 1 Table 2
Full	• Returns all records when there is a match in either the left or right table. • Nulls could be present in this result if there are no matching records between the tables.	Table 1 Table 2

We can illustrate how these joins work with an example. Bikes R Us is a bicycle wholesale dealer. **Illustration 2.5** shows two tables from their database:

- The left table is the Customer table, and the Order table is on the right.
- CustomerID is the primary key in the Customer table.
- OrderID is the primary key in the Order table. CustomerID is a foreign key.

ILLUSTRATION 2.5 Bikes R Us Database Tables

Customer Table

CustomerID	CompanyName	ContactLastName	State
1001	Cycle Nation	Creebo	NY
1002	Spins	Geck	NC
1003	Little Town Bike Stores	Blunsom	TX
1004	Triathletes Store	Rings	CA

Order Table

OrderID	OrderDate	Amount	CustomerID
50012	2/1/2025	$ 578.23	1001
50013	2/2/2025	$ 982.99	1002
50014	2/3/2025	$ 1,563.32	1004
50015	2/4/2025	$ 300.12	1001
50016	2/5/2025	$ 639.99	102

An inner join on these two tables will result in a table with all the data from the tables that match on the CustomerID field (**Illustration 2.6**).

ILLUSTRATION 2.6 Results from an Inner Join for Bikes R Us

Inner Join

CustomerID	CompanyName	ContactLastName	State	OrderID	OrderDate	Amount
1001	Cycle Nation	Creebo	NY	50012	2/1/2025	$ 578.23
1001	Cycle Nation	Creebo	NY	50015	2/4/2025	$ 300.12
1002	Spins	Geck	NC	50013	2/2/2025	$ 982.99
1004	Triathletes Store	Rings	CA	50014	2/3/2025	$ 1,563.32

The inner join shows the customer and order information for each customer that has placed an order:

- These results reveal that the customer with CustomerID = 1003, Little Town Bike Stores, has not made any purchases.
- OrderID 50016 does not have a match in the customer table for CustomerID = 102, so that order is not reflected in the joined tables.

A left join returns all the rows from the left table and will show any matching data from the right table. If there are no matching rows in the right table, then the fields without matches will be null (**Illustration 2.7**).

ILLUSTRATION 2.7   Results from a Left Join for Bikes R Us

Left Join

CustomerID	CompanyName	ContactLastName	State	OrderID	OrderDate	Amount	CustomerID
1001	Cycle Nation	Creebo	NY	50012	2/1/2025	$ 578.23	1001
1001	Cycle Nation	Creebo	NY	50015	2/4/2025	$ 300.12	1001
1002	Spins	Geck	NC	50013	2/2/2025	$ 982.99	1002
1003	Little Town Bike Stores	Blunsom	TX	**NULL**	**NULL**	**NULL**	**NULL**
1004	Triathletes Store	Rings	CA	50014	2/3/2025	$ 1,563.32	1004

The left join in Illustration 2.7 shows all the customers from the Customer table and matching information from the Order table:

- CustomerID = 1003 is listed in this join, but because there is not a matching order, the results for the order fields are null.
- OrderID = 50016 is not reflected in the joined table results. There is no CustomerID = 102 in the Customer table, so that record is not picked up in the join.

A right join returns all the rows from the right table and will show any matching data from the left table (**Illustration 2.8**).

ILLUSTRATION 2.8   Results from a Right Join for Bikes R Us

Right Join

CustomerID	CompanyName	ContactLastName	State	OrderID	OrderDate	Amount	CustomerID
1001	Cycle Nation	Creebo	NY	50012	2/1/2025	$ 578.23	1001
1001	Cycle Nation	Creebo	NY	50015	2/4/2025	$ 300.12	1001
1002	Spins	Geck	NC	50013	2/2/2025	$ 982.99	1002
1004	Triathletes Store	Rings	CA	50014	2/3/2025	$ 1,563.32	1004
NULL	**NULL**	**NULL**	**NULL**	50016	2/5/2025	$ 639.99	102

The right join in Illustration 2.8 shows all orders from the Order table and any matching customers from the Customer table:

- There is not a matching customer record for CustomerID = 102, so the fields from the Customer table will have null values for that record.
- If there are no matching rows in the left table, then the fields will have null values.

A full join will return all the rows from both tables (**Illustration 2.9**).

ILLUSTRATION 2.9   Results from a Full Join for Bikes R Us

Full Join

CustomerID	CompanyName	ContactLastName	State	OrderID	OrderDate	Amount	CustomerID
1001	Cycle Nation	Creebo	NY	50012	2/1/2025	$ 578.23	1001
1001	Cycle Nation	Creebo	NY	50015	2/4/2025	$ 300.12	1001
1002	Spins	Geck	NC	50013	2/2/2025	$ 982.99	1002
1003	Little Town Bike Stores	Blunsom	TX	**NULL**	**NULL**	**NULL**	**NULL**
1004	Triathletes Store	Rings	CA	50014	2/3/2025	$ 1,563.32	1004
NULL	**NULL**	**NULL**	**NULL**	50016	2/5/2025	$ 639.99	102

The full join shown in Illustration 2.9 shows all the records from both tables:

- Note the null values for the Order table fields for CustomerID = 1003 and the null values for the Customer table fields for OrderID = 50016.
- Any unmatched fields will have null values.

Joins are essential when analyzing data from multiple sources. **Illustration 2.10** shows examples of some questions accountants may need to ask of the data and the type of join that will answer them.

ILLUSTRATION 2.10 Sample Data Analysis Questions and Appropriate Join

Questions	Join
Are there any customer invoices without receipts?	Left join
Have any transactions been charged to accounts that do not exist?	Left join
Have any payroll checks been issued to false employees?	Left join
Are there any sales returns to customers that do not exist?	Left join
Are there any inventory items that have not been sold? (Orders table on left)	Right join
Are there any customers that have not made a purchase? (Orders table on left)	Right join
Are there any vendors that have not been sent a purchase order? (PurchaseOrder table on left)	Right join
Are there any vendor invoices that have not been paid? (Payments table on left)	Right join
Do any employee addresses match vendor addresses?	Inner join
Do any employee phone numbers match vendor phone numbers?	Inner join
Have sales been made in a specific region?	Inner join

Accounting Information Systems Super Scooters, a manufacturer of motorized scooters, has just converted to a relational database system. You work in the accounting information systems area of the company and have been helping with the conversion to the new database system. The following tables have been established:

APPLY IT 2.1

Identify Primary and Foreign Keys

Locations
- 🔑 LocationNumber
- LocationDescription

SalesOrders
- 🔑 SalesOrderNumber
- OrderNumber
- Model
- SoldDate
- SalesVolume
- Color
- LocationNumber
- RegionNumber
- State
- Country
- UnitSalePrice
- ItemNumber
- CustomerNumber
- EmployeeNumber

Employee
- 🔑 EmployeeNumber
- FirstName
- LastName
- Address
- City
- State
- ZipCode
- RegionNumber

Regions
- 🔑 RegionNumber
- RegionDescription

SalesOrderExpenses
- 🔑 OrderNumber
- VariableMarketing
- Labor
- Materials
- Overhead
- TotalWarranty
- TotalDepreciation
- SalesTax

Customer
- 🔑 CustomerNumber
- CustomerName
- CustomerAddress
- CustomerCity
- CustomerState
- CustomerZipCode
- ContactFirstName
- ContactLastName
- PhoneNumber

Inventory
- 🔑 ItemNumber
- ItemDescription
- Color
- QuantityOnHand

Your boss asks you to identify all primary and foreign keys for the tables in the database so joins can be created. For each table, list the primary key and any foreign keys.

SOLUTION

Table	Primary Key	Foreign Key
SalesOrders	SalesOrderNumber	OrderNumber LocationNumber RegionNumber CustomerNumber EmployeeNumber
Locations	LocationNumber	None
Region	RegionNumber	None
Inventory	ItemNumber	None
SalesOrderExpenses	OrderNumber	None
Employee	EmployeeNumber	RegionNumber
Customer	CustomerNumber	None

2.2 How Do Spreadsheet Functions Analyze Large Amounts of Data?

LEARNING OBJECTIVE ❷
Explain how functions help answer data analysis questions.

Data analysis usually includes performing calculations such as adding amounts, counting data entries, and calculating averages. Frequently used calculations are often built into analysis software as **functions,** which are predefined formulas that perform calculations. One example is the SUM function in Microsoft Excel that adds a range of numbers in rows or columns.

Functions make it possible to quickly analyze large amounts of data without writing complex formulas. In fact, some of the most powerful attributes of Microsoft Excel are the built-in functions that perform calculations. Keep in mind that the most common functions and the logic behind them also apply to software other than Microsoft Excel. For example, functions can be used in analysis and visualization tools like Power BI and in Tableau. Understanding how these functions work, and more importantly, when to use them is a core data analysis skill.

Basic Functions for Data Analysis

Illustration 2.11 describes some basic Excel functions used in data analysis:

- The function name appears in the first column.
- The second column shows the function argument, which is the syntax necessary to invoke the function and the range and criteria to apply to it. All Excel functions begin with an equal sign, followed by the type of function being performed, and then parentheses that specify the arguments for the function. For example, to sum a column of numbers in column C and rows 2 through 245, the function would be: =SUM(C2:C245).
- The function calculation is described in the third column.

Returning to the university data example, **Illustration 2.12** shows the function arguments box for a COUNTIF function used to determine how many pumps the university owns. There are two input options to execute the functions illustrated:

- Type the function argument directly into a cell on the spreadsheet, or
- Use the Function Arguments box.

ILLUSTRATION 2.11 Basic Microsoft Excel Functions

Function	Function Arguments	Function Calculation
IF	=IF(logic test, value if true, value if false)	Returns one value if the condition is true and another one if it is false.
AVERAGE	=AVERAGE(*Range*)	Returns the arithmetic mean of the range, array, or numbers.
AVERAGEIF	=AVERAGEIF(*Range, Criteria, AverageRange*)	Finds the arithmetic mean for the cells specified by a given condition or criteria.
AVERAGEIFS	=AVERAGEIFS(*SumRange, CriteriaRange1, Criteria1, CriteriaRange2, Criteria2*)	Finds the arithmetic mean for the cells specified by a given set of conditions or criteria. Additional ranges, criteria ranges, and criteria can be added.
COUNT	=COUNT(*Range*)	Counts the number of cells in a range that contain numbers.
COUNTIF	=COUNTIF(*Range, Criteria*)	Counts the number of cells within a range that meet the given criteria.
COUNTIFS	=COUNTIFS(*Range1, Criteria1, Range2, Criteria2*)	Counts the number of cells specified by a given set of criteria. Additional ranges, criteria ranges, and criteria can be added.
COUNTA	=COUNTA(*Range*)	Counts the number of cells containing text in a range.
COUNTBLANK	=COUNTBLANK(*Range*)	Counts the number of blank cells in a range.
SUM	=SUM(*Range*)	Adds the cells in a range.
SUMIF	=SUMIF(*Range, Criteria, SumRange*)	Adds the cells specified by a specified condition or criteria.
SUMIFS	=SUMIFS(*SumRange, CriteriaRange1, Criteria1, CriteriaRange2, Criteria2*)	Adds the cells specified by a given set of conditions or criteria. Additional ranges, criteria ranges, and criteria can be added.

ILLUSTRATION 2.12 University Asset Data COUNTIF Function Arguments Box

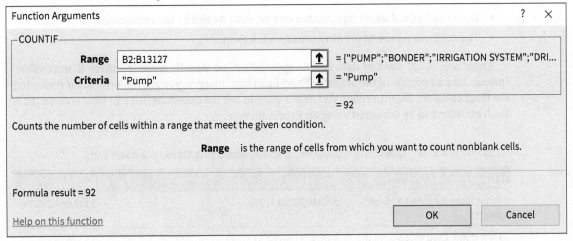

To open:

- Click on the *fx* next to the cell formula, which is above the spreadsheet (see the green *fx* in **Illustration 2.13**).
- Next, the **Function Arguments** input box in Illustration 2.12 appears on the screen.
- Fill in the range and criteria, and select **OK**. The formula for the function then appears (Illustration 2.13). Note that the criteria (in this example "Pump") must be typed in quotations. This is true for any criteria that is not a cell reference or a number.

ILLUSTRATION 2.13 Finding the Function Arguments Symbol

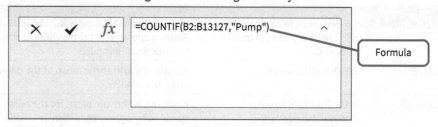

These Excel functions can help quickly analyze data sets, especially when they are very large. Let's now apply these functions to answer questions from a data set about fixed assets.

Applying Excel Basic Functions

Data We will use the university's assets data set (**Illustration 2.14**) to illustrate how functions can help make sense of data.

ILLUSTRATION 2.14 University Asset Data

University Asset Data

	A	B	C	D	E	F
1	**AssetTagID**	**AssetDescription**	**CategoryID**	**Category**	**Amount**	**AcquisitionDate**
2	U000009	Pump	15	Laboratory Equipment	$ 7,826.00	9/2/2021
3	U000010	Bonder	15	Laboratory Equipment	$ 28,628.01	9/11/2021
4	U000015	Irrigation System	1	Agricultural and Farm Machinery	$ 17,068.00	9/29/2020
5	U000016	Drill	1	Agricultural and Farm Machinery	$ 28,344.00	10/27/2019
13126	U102879	Server	7	Computer Equipment	$ 53,008.90	10/9/2021
13127	U204391	Oven	11	Food Preparation & Serving Equipment	$ 7,255.53	5/6/2023

The data set was created from the University Asset Data file:

- Each row in the data set represents a unique asset owned by the university.
- The columns represent the attributes for each asset.

There are 13,127 rows of data in this spreadsheet, so visually scanning them is impossible. Instead, take advantage of the available Excel functions. Imagine you are responsible for reviewing the fixed assets for the university. You might want to ask the questions listed in **Illustration 2.15**. Each question can be answered using an Excel function.

ILLUSTRATION 2.15 Questions, Functions, and Answers Using University Asset Data

Question	Function	Answer
What is the total cost of fixed assets?	=SUM(E2:E13127)	$225,069,282.74
How many fixed assets does the university have in total?	=COUNTA(A2:A13127)	13,126
How many assets were acquired after 2022?	=COUNTIF(F2:F13127,">12/31/2022")	1,388
What is the total cost of assets acquired after 2022?	=SUMIF(F2:F13127,">12/31/2022",E2:E13127)	$27,653,067.52
Are any descriptions missing?	=COUNTBLANK(D2:D13127)	0

Illustration 2.15 uses the SUM, COUNTA, COUNTIF, SUMIF, and COUNTBLANK functions. Could a SUMIFS or a COUNTIFS also be used?

If the question was how many computers the university purchased in 2023, then use the COUNTIFS function because there are two criteria. Recall that the COUNTIFS function requires specifying the range of cells to apply to the first criteria (computer equipment). The next criteria are purchases made in 2023, and the range will be the column with the dates acquired. **Illustration 2.16** shows the Function Arguments box for the COUNTIFS function and the result.

ILLUSTRATION 2.16   Function Arguments for COUNTIFS Function

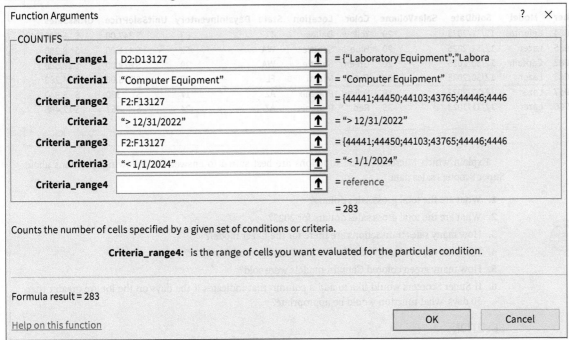

The function box creates a formula:

=COUNTIFS(D2:D13127,"Computer Equipment",F2:F13127,">12/31/2022",
F2:F13127,"<1/1/2024")

To retrieve only the year 2023 data, create two criteria in the function argument:

- First, the date must be greater than December 31, 2022 (Criteria2).
- Second, the date must be less than January 1, 2024 (Criteria3).

By including those criteria in the argument, only results for the year 2023 are displayed.

Basic Excel functions are useful for answering questions with a single answer or an answer with one dimension. **Dimensions** are the variables or other fields that can be used to drill down or disaggregate the analysis measures. In other words, dimensions are used when there is a specific question about a specific aspect of the data.

For example, a question about how many computers were purchased in 2023 has only one dimension—computers in 2023. What about a question with more than one dimension? What if we want to know the sum of costs for each of the asset categories rather than just computers in a specific year? That question has more than one dimension because it involves every asset category and all years. We discuss how to address multi-dimension questions next.

APPLY IT 2.2

Analyze Sales Transactions with Excel Functions

Data **Financial Accounting** **Managerial Accounting** Super Scooters manufactures and sells four models of stand-on scooters: Celeritas, Captain, Lazer, and Kicks. Their customers range from large scooter-sharing companies to small retailers. Your supervisor has given you, an accountant for the company, a list of questions to answer using the Super Scooters data set. What follows is a portion of the Super Scooters Sales Transactions for the years 2023–2025. There are 3,645 transactions in the sales database.

	A	B	C	D	E	F	G	H	I	J
1	OrderNumber	Model	SoldDate	SalesVolume	Color	Location	State	DaysInInventory	UnitSalePrice	GrossSales
2	13684	Celeritas	12/31/2025	20	Yellow	Dallas	TX	83	$ 342.00	$ 6,840
3	13685	Lazer	12/31/2025	20	Blue	Seattle	WA	52	$ 414.00	$ 8,280
4	13682	Captain	12/30/2025	20	Green	Seattle	WA	29	$ 679.00	$ 13,580
5	13683	Lazer	12/30/2025	38	Green	Miami	FL	22	$ 376.00	$ 14,288
3645	10957	Lazer	12/22/2023	18	Yellow	Phoenix	AZ	17	$ 330	$ 5,940
3646	10960	Lazer	12/31/2023	35	Red	Phoenix	AZ	24	$ 357	$ 12,495
3647										

Explain which Microsoft Excel functions are best suited to answer the following questions about Super Scooters sales data:

1. What are the total gross sales dollars?
2. What are the total gross sales dollars for 2023?
3. How many sales transactions are there for the Lazer model?
4. What are the average gross sales for the Celeritas model in 2023?
5. How many green colored Captain models were sold?
6. If Super Scooters would like to add a column that indicates if the days on the lot are greater than 50 days, what function would be appropriate?

SOLUTION

1. SUM
2. SUMIF
3. CountIF
4. AverageIFS
5. CountIFS
6. IF

2.3 How Do We Organize Data Sets for Analysis?

LEARNING OBJECTIVE ❸
Illustrate how pivottables organize and filter data.

You have just learned how to use functions to answer questions with a single dimension. While you could use several functions to answer questions that involve multiple dimensions, it is more efficient to first use a data organization technique on the data set.

Data organization is the process of rearranging data to make it easier to understand. A **pivottable** is a tool that summarizes and reorganizes selected columns and rows of data in a spreadsheet, database, or business intelligence program. Pivottables can quickly rearrange data to help answer many important business questions. Recall from the chapter-opening professional insight that Josh needed to use one to reorganize a spreadsheet with 450,000 rows of data. It is unlikely Josh could have analyzed the spreadsheet data efficiently without a pivottable.

The examples here use Microsoft Excel to demonstrate how to create and filter a pivottable. (Note that pivottables created in this software are generally labeled as PivotTables.) Although the demonstrations use Excel PivotTables, these techniques are also used in other data analysis software. For example, they are useful when creating visualizations. Whichever data analysis tool you use, understanding the basic functionality of creating useful pivottables and how to filter them is essential.

Using PivotTables

Both powerful and easy to use, a pivottable is also one of the most common tools you will use in your accounting career. It has five main components:

1. **Fields:** The data elements available for use in the pivottable.

2. **Columns:** When a field is chosen for a column area, only the unique values of the field are listed across the top.

3. **Rows:** When a field is chosen for the row area, it populates it as the first column. All row values are unique values and duplicates are removed.

4. **Values:** Each value is kept in a pivottable cell and displays the summarized information. Examples are sum, average, or count.

5. **Filters:** Apply a restriction to the entire table.

Once you know the basics of creating a pivottable in Microsoft Excel, you can use this tool to answer accounting questions.

Create a Microsoft Excel PivotTable

Follow these steps:

1. Open the spreadsheet with the data to summarize.

2. Click any cell within the data (the first cell in row A in **Illustration 2.17**).

3. Click the **Insert** option on the top menu ribbon.

4. A **PivotTable** input box option will appear at the top left of the screen (Illustration 2.17).

   When this option is selected a new dialogue box opens called **PivotTable from table or range** (**Illustration 2.18**).

5. Ensure the Table/Range in the **Select a table or range** box reflects all data that should be included. (Remember to include the column headings.) Choose **New Worksheet** and click **OK** (Illustration 2.18).

6. This will open a new spreadsheet. A blank PivotTable canvas will appear on the left, and the PivotTable Fields box that creates the PivotTable will be on the right (**Illustration 2.19**).

ILLUSTRATION 2.17 University Assets Data Excel Spreadsheet

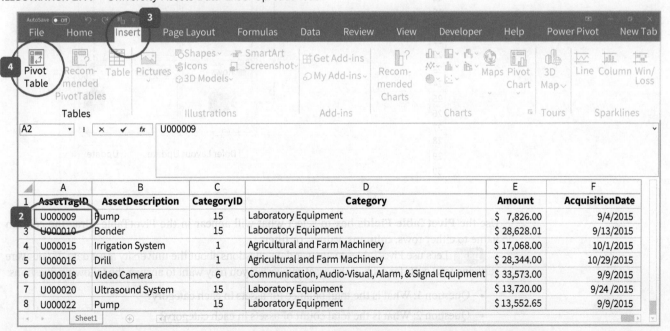

	A	B	C	D	E	F
1	AssetTagID	AssetDescription	CategoryID	Category	Amount	AcquisitionDate
2	U000009	Pump	15	Laboratory Equipment	$ 7,826.00	9/4/2015
3	U000010	Bonder	15	Laboratory Equipment	$ 28,628.01	9/13/2015
4	U000015	Irrigation System	1	Agricultural and Farm Machinery	$ 17,068.00	10/1/2015
5	U000016	Drill	1	Agricultural and Farm Machinery	$ 28,344.00	10/29/2015
6	U000018	Video Camera	6	Communication, Audio-Visual, Alarm, & Signal Equipment	$ 33,573.00	9/9/2015
7	U000020	Ultrasound System	15	Laboratory Equipment	$ 13,720.00	9/24/2015
8	U000022	Pump	15	Laboratory Equipment	$ 13,552.65	9/9/2015

ILLUSTRATION 2.18 Excel
Create PivotTable Dialog Box

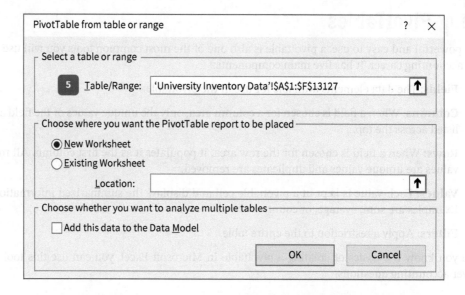

ILLUSTRATION 2.19 Blank
PivotTable Canvas

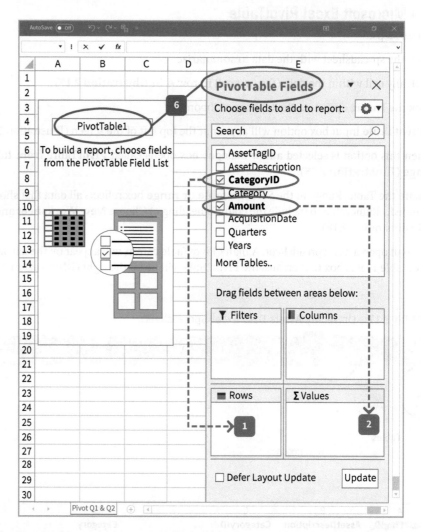

Use the **PivotTable Fields** box to select what will appear in the PivotTable. Drag the column name to either rows, columns, values, or filters.

Data Let's use PivotTables to answer data questions about the university asset data. If you were verifying total costs for each of the asset categories, you may want to answer the following questions:

- Question 1: What is the total balance for assets in each category?
- Question 2: What is the total count of assets in each category?

Find the Total Balance by Category

Answer the first question by finding the total balance by category.

1. Drag **Category** to the **Rows** area.

2. Drag **Amount** to the **Values** area. The Σ Values in Columns is then automatically generated by Excel.

3. Excel will fill in the values for each category in the second column of the spreadsheet.

    Illustration 2.20 shows the resulting PivotTable.

ILLUSTRATION 2.20 Excel PivotTable for Question 1: What Is the Total Balance by Category?

Row Labels	Question 1 Sum of Amount
Agricultural and Farm Machinery	$ 3,838,203.58
Art Equipment	$ 129,924.35
Athletic and Recreational Equipment	$ 1,047,971.77
Boats, Boat Motors, and Marine Equipment	$ 530,673.88
Cleaning and Maintenance Equipment	$ 2,458,319.00
Communication, Audio-Visual, Alarm, and Signal Equipment	$ 4,242,923.45
Computer Equipment	$ 43,294,238.92
Drafting and Surveying Equipment	$ 18,033.00
Electrical Appliances and Equipment	$ 51,825.00
Electronic Equipment	$ 278,233.02
Food Preparation and Serving Equipment	$ 1,210,703.93
Furniture and Furnishings	$ 3,060,781.37
Hand and Power Tools (Portable)	$ 90,332.00
Industrial, Shop, and Construction Equipment	$ 2,287,996.49
Laboratory Equipment	$ 147,343,867.13
Material Handling Equipment	$ 650,212.23
Medical Equipment	$ 2,449,781.57
Miscellaneous Equipment	$ 47,239.00
Motor Vehicles and Transportation Equipment	$ 1,270,121.50
Musical Instruments	$ 88,248.00
Office and Business Machines and Nonconsumable Supplies	$ 1,587,495.45
Parking Control Equipment	$ 230,506.72
Photographic Equipment	$ 1,865,573.30
Plumbing, Heating, Air Conditioning, and Ventilating Equipment	$ 146,953.15
Police, Fire Fighting, and Safety Equipment	$ 102,458.55
Printing and Bookbinding Equipment	$ 279,665.97
Refrigeration Equipment	$ 6,467,000.41
Grand Total	**$ 225,069,282.74**

4. Excel will default to a sum of the value. The type of measurement can be changed by clicking the down arrow in the **Sum of Amount** field and choosing the desired measure (**Illustration 2.21**).

Another useful feature of the Value Field Settings dialog box is the ability to change the number format in the PivotTable. (**Data** How To 2.1 at the end of this chapter explains the Show Values capability with pre-built calculations.)

How To

Determine Total Count of Assets

To determine the total count of assets in each category (question 2), use the first Excel PivotTable:

1. Drag **AssetTagID** to the **Values** area.

2. Click the down arrow, choose **Value Field Settings**, and choose **Count**.

    The data can be summarized with several different calculations. The question asks about the number of assets per category, so choose **Count**.

3. Excel populates the next table column with the count by asset category.

The result is shown in **Illustration 2.22**.

ILLUSTRATION 2.21 Excel PivotTable Value Field Settings Dialog Box

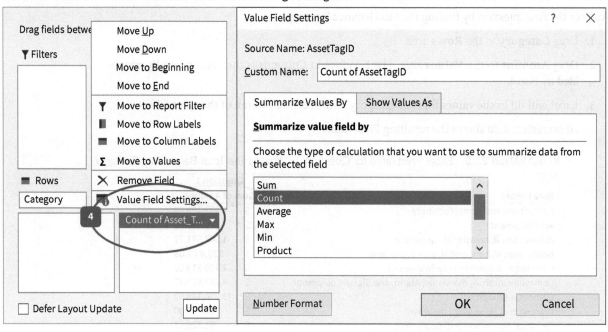

ILLUSTRATION 2.22 Excel PivotTable for Question 2: What Is the Total Count of Assets in Each Category?

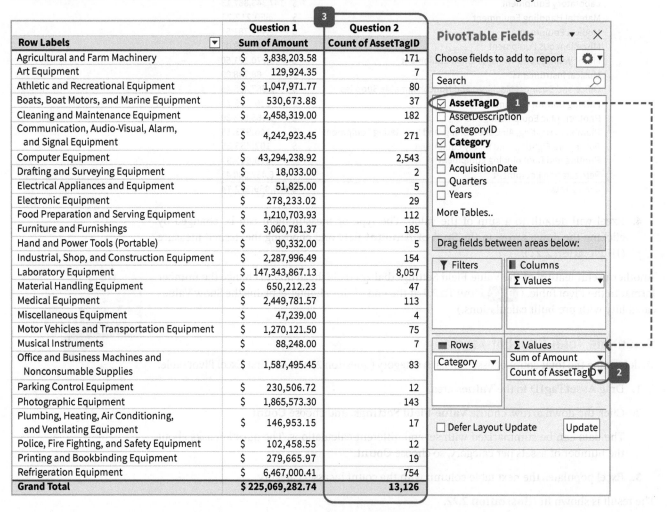

Row Labels	Question 1 Sum of Amount	Question 2 Count of AssetTagID
Agricultural and Farm Machinery	$ 3,838,203.58	171
Art Equipment	$ 129,924.35	7
Athletic and Recreational Equipment	$ 1,047,971.77	80
Boats, Boat Motors, and Marine Equipment	$ 530,673.88	37
Cleaning and Maintenance Equipment	$ 2,458,319.00	182
Communication, Audio-Visual, Alarm, and Signal Equipment	$ 4,242,923.45	271
Computer Equipment	$ 43,294,238.92	2,543
Drafting and Surveying Equipment	$ 18,033.00	2
Electrical Appliances and Equipment	$ 51,825.00	5
Electronic Equipment	$ 278,233.02	29
Food Preparation and Serving Equipment	$ 1,210,703.93	112
Furniture and Furnishings	$ 3,060,781.37	185
Hand and Power Tools (Portable)	$ 90,332.00	5
Industrial, Shop, and Construction Equipment	$ 2,287,996.49	154
Laboratory Equipment	$ 147,343,867.13	8,057
Material Handling Equipment	$ 650,212.23	47
Medical Equipment	$ 2,449,781.57	113
Miscellaneous Equipment	$ 47,239.00	4
Motor Vehicles and Transportation Equipment	$ 1,270,121.50	75
Musical Instruments	$ 88,248.00	7
Office and Business Machines and Nonconsumable Supplies	$ 1,587,495.45	83
Parking Control Equipment	$ 230,506.72	12
Photographic Equipment	$ 1,865,573.30	143
Plumbing, Heating, Air Conditioning, and Ventilating Equipment	$ 146,953.15	17
Police, Fire Fighting, and Safety Equipment	$ 102,458.55	12
Printing and Bookbinding Equipment	$ 279,665.97	19
Refrigeration Equipment	$ 6,467,000.41	754
Grand Total	**$ 225,069,282.74**	**13,126**

Filtering PivotTables

One way to focus on a specific aspect of the data in a PivotTable is to use a filter. Applying a filter means that only data that fits its criteria will be displayed. There are three ways to filter in Excel:

- Apply the filter criteria to the Filter field area.
- Use AutoFilter in the PivotTable's Row field.
- Insert one or more slicers.

Data Answering a third assets data question will demonstrate each filtering option:

Question 3: What is the total amount of purchases by category made in 2022?

Apply Filter Criteria to the Filter Field Box

To discover the total amount of purchases by category for the year 2022, create a PivotTable that shows assets purchased in 2022 by category:

1. Drag **Category** to **Rows,** and drag **Amount** to **Values**.

2. The focus is on assets purchased in 2022, so bring **Years** to the **Filters** area.

3. The word **Years** in the first column and the word **ALL** in the second column will now appear at the top of the PivotTable.

4. Clicking the down arrow next to **ALL** results in a dropdown box to select years to filter (**Illustration 2.23**).

ILLUSTRATION 2.23 How to Filter in an Excel PivotTable

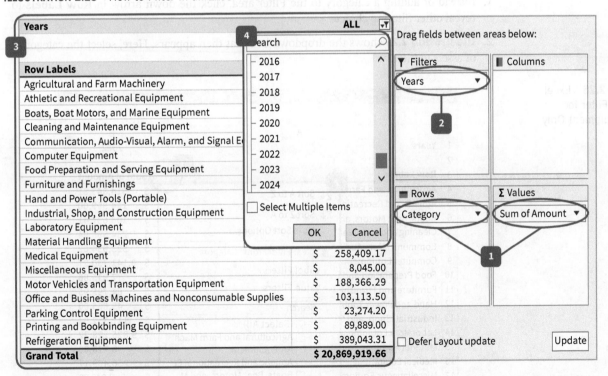

Illustration 2.24 shows the result of filtering for assets purchased in 2022.

ILLUSTRATION 2.24 PivotTable Answer to Question 3: What Is the Total Cost of Assets Purchased in 2022?

Years	2022
Row Labels	**Sum of Amount**
Agricultural and Farm Machinery	$ 514,343.81
Athletic and Recreational Equipment	$ 144,999.00
Boats, Boat Motors, and Marine Equipment	$ 108,637.41
Cleaning and Maintenance Equipment	$ 234,398.94
Communication, Audio-Visual, Alarm, and Signal Equipment	$ 523,934.69
Computer Equipment	$ 8,141,730.27
Food Preparation and Serving Equipment	$ 77,915.86
Furniture and Furnishings	$ 64,795.95
Hand and Power Tools (Portable)	$ 49,665.00
Industrial, Shop, and Construction Equipment	$ 117,352.04
Laboratory Equipment	$ 9,825,228.22
Material Handling Equipment	$ 6,778.00
Medical Equipment	$ 258,409.17
Miscellaneous Equipment	$ 8,045.00
Motor Vehicles and Transportation Equipment	$ 188,366.29
Office and Business Machines and Nonconsumable Supplies	$ 103,113.50
Parking Control Equipment	$ 23,274.20
Printing and Bookbinding Equipment	$ 89,889.00
Refrigeration Equipment	$ 389,043.31
Grand Total	**$ 20,869,919.66**

Use a Row Auto Filter

Filters can also be created in an Excel PivotTable with the Auto Filter functionality for rows. In this example, the question is how much was spent on computer equipment in 2022.

1. Instead of adding a category to the Filter area, click the down arrow in **Row Labels** to reveal other filtering choices.

2. **Illustration 2.25** shows the dropdown box that then appears. Here, select the categories of assets to filter.

ILLUSTRATION 2.25 Excel PivotTable to Filter for Computer Equipment Only

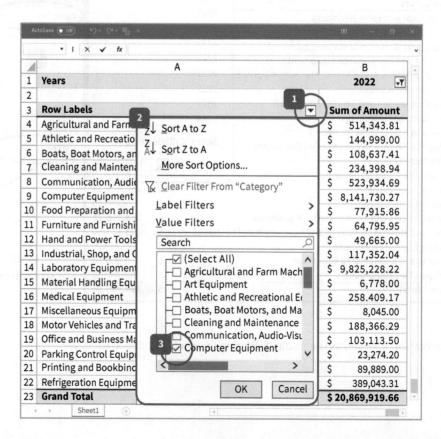

3. In this example, only Computer Equipment is selected. The resulting PivotTable is shown in **Illustration 2.26**

ILLUSTRATION 2.26 Excel PivotTable Showing Just Computer Equipment Purchased in 2022

Years	2022	▼
Row Labels ▼	**Sum of Amount**	
Computer Equipment	$ 8,141,730.27	
Grand Total	**$ 8,141,730.27**	

The auto filter option quickly isolates a specific item. Two more auto filters are Label Filters and Value Filters. **Illustration 2.27** shows the options available after choosing Label Filters.

ILLUSTRATION 2.27 Excel PivotTables Label Filters

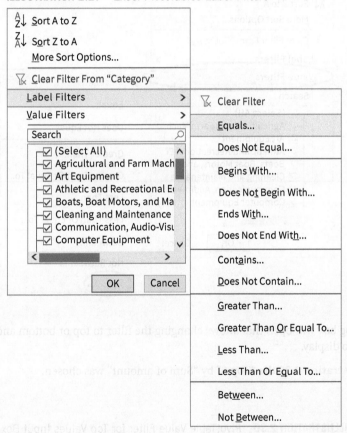

Highlighting and clicking one of the options under **Label Filters** opens a dialog box to insert the filter's parameter. For example, choosing **Equals** and entering "Computer Equipment" in the dialog box (**Illustration 2.28**) achieves the same results as Illustration 2.26.

ILLUSTRATION 2.28 Excel PivotTable Label Filter Equals Dialog Box

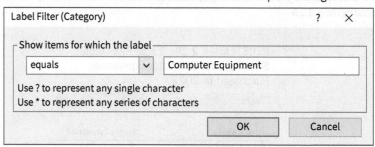

What if the goal was to filter the data so only the top five asset categories appear?

1. Use the **Value Filters** and pick the option for **Top 10...** (**Illustration 2.29**).

ILLUSTRATION 2.29 PivotTable Value Filter Options

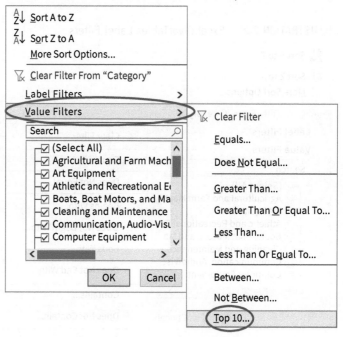

2. A dialog box will open that allows changing the filter to top or bottom and the number of items to display.

   In **Illustration 2.30** the "Top 5" by "Sum of amount" was chosen.

ILLUSTRATION 2.30 PivotTable Value Filter for Top Values Input Box

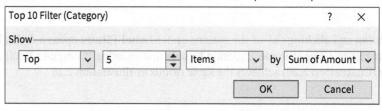

The resulting Excel PivotTable is shown in **Illustration 2.31**.

ILLUSTRATION 2.31   PivotTable Value Filter Results for Top Five Amounts

Years	2022
Row Labels	**Sum of Amount**
Agricultural and Farm Machinery	$ 514,343.81
Communication, Audio-Visual, Alarm, and Signal Equipment	$ 523,934.69
Computer Equipment	$ 8,141,730.27
Laboratory Equipment	$ 9,825,228.22
Refrigeration Equipment	$ 389,043.31
Grand Total	**$ 19,394,280.30**

What about filtering for multiple dimensions at the same time?

Use Slicers to Filter Data

Simultaneously filtering for multiple dimensions is often referred to as **slicing**, or slice and dice, which is the process of breaking the data down into smaller parts or examining it from different viewpoints. **Slicers** are an analysis tool that separate the resulting analysis measures per the selected dimensions. All data analysis software has slicing capabilities:

- Microsoft Excel and Power BI use slicers.
- In Tableau, it is accomplished with interactive filters.

In all types of software, slicers customize interaction with a data set by providing a visual display of available filters. **Illustration 2.32** shows where the option to add slicers can be found in Microsoft Excel.

ILLUSTRATION 2.32   Adding Slicers to PivotTables

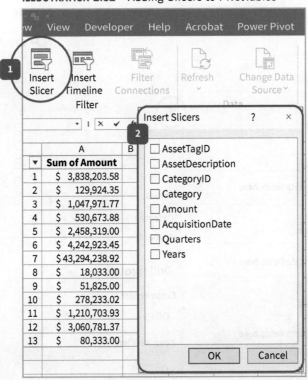

1. Click in the PivotTable and choose **Insert Slicer** from the menu. This will open a box with all the PivotTable fields.

2. Select the fields for the slicers. If the goal is to determine how much was spent on each category of assets by year, then slice data by asset category and year. To do this, select **Category** and **AcquisitionDate**.

Illustration 2.33 shows the resulting slicers. One is for category and the other is for year.

ILLUSTRATION 2.33 PivotTable Slicers Discovering the Total Amount by Category and Year

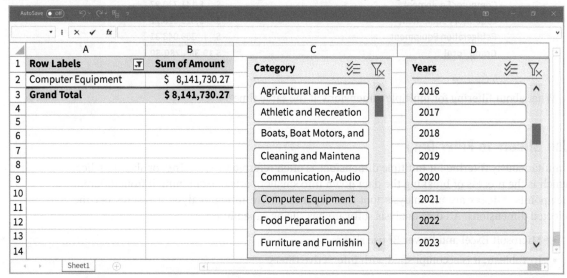

In Illustration 2.33, clicking **Computer Equipment** in the **Category** slicer and **2022** in the **Years** slicer results in a PivotTable with the sum of computer equipment purchased in 2022. Slicers can be added to Power BI by choosing the slicer tool in **Visualizations** (**Illustration 2.34**).

ILLUSTRATION 2.34 PivotTable Slicers Using Power BI

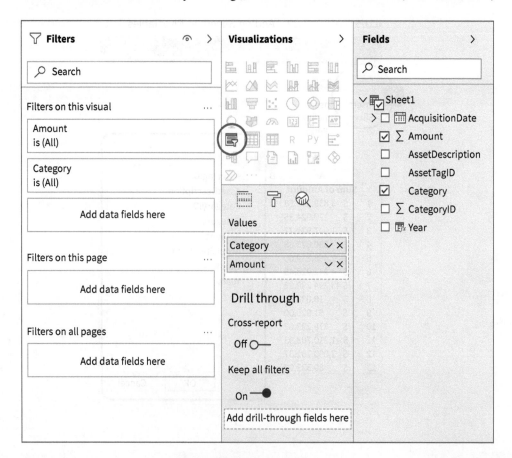

Next, select **Category** to create category slicers and repeat for the AcquisitionDate slicers. **Illustration 2.35** shows the result.

ILLUSTRATION 2.35 Power BI Slicers for Category and Year

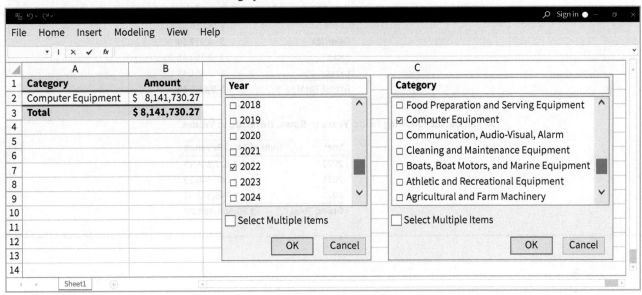

Because pivottable functions summarize data to quickly find answers to our questions, creating pivottables is a core data analysis skill you will use frequently in your career.

Data Financial Accounting Managerial Accounting Your supervisor at Super Scooters has asked you to analyze sales for 2025 and revenue for all years. Create an Excel PivotTable to determine the following:

1. What are the total gross sales for each location in 2025?
2. What is the average gross sales amount for each model in 2025?
3. What is total revenue per year?

SOLUTION

1. Choose (or drag) the fields: **Location** for **Rows**, **Gross Sales** for **Values**, and **Year** for **Filters**. In the year filter pick 2025.

Year	2025
Row Labels	**Sum of Gross Sales**
Boston	$ 1,433,578.00
Charlotte	$ 1,653,506.00
Chicago	$ 1,624,719.00
Dallas	$ 1,134,785.00
Miami	$ 1,606,576.00
Phoenix	$ 1,376,503.00
Salt Lake City	$ 1,593,184.00
Seattle	$ 1,742,311.00
Grand Total	**$ 12,165,162.00**

APPLY IT 2.3

Analyze Sales with Excel PivotTables

2. Begin by dragging the fields: **Model** to **Rows**, **Gross Sales** to **Values**, and **Year** to **Filters**. Change the Sum of Gross Sales to Average by opening **Value Field Settings** and choosing **Average**. In the year filter, select 2025.

Year	2025	

Row Labels	Average of Gross Sales
Captain	$ 15,855.84
Celeritas	$ 4,977.54
Kicks	$ 2,760.45
Lazer	$ 7,981.45
Grand Total	**$ 9,098.85**

3. Choose the following fields: **Years** to **Rows**, **Revenue** to **Values**.

Year	Sum of Total Revenue
2023	$ 1,827,384.78
2024	$ 4,086,546.19
2025	$ 4,745,563.32
Grand Total	**$ 10,659,494.29**

2.4 Which Descriptive Measures Help Us Understand Data?

LEARNING OBJECTIVE ❹

Identify descriptive measures used to perform data analysis.

You have learned how to identify and retrieve data and some basic approaches to analyzing it. Earlier in the course, you also learned that there are four types of data analytics:

- Descriptive
- Diagnostic
- Predictive
- Prescriptive

Recall that descriptive analytics help reveal what has happened or is currently happening in the data. Why are descriptive analytics considered central to data analytics? Without that basic understanding of the data, advancing to more sophisticated data analysis methods is impossible. Sometimes descriptive analyses are all that are necessary, but more often this method is the precursor for diagnostic, predictive, and prescriptive analyses. The core data analysis skill for descriptive analytics is understanding descriptive statistics and correlation analysis.

Descriptive statistics reveal average observations in the data, the data's shape, and the distribution of the data. In addition, correlation analysis can show relationships in the data. Together, these statistics provide data insights.

Measures of Location

Measures of location determine the average, or typical, observation in the data set.

Mean, Median, and Mode

A **measure of central tendency** is a single value that describes a set of data by identifying the central position within that data set. There are three measures of central tendency:

- **Mean:** The sum of all observations in a data set divided by the total number of observations.
- **Median:** The middle value when the data is arranged from smallest to largest.
- **Mode:** The observation that occurs most frequently.

Determining the mean and median is the first step for understanding data during descriptive analysis. The two measures are often similar, but because the mean can be influenced by outliers (extreme values in the data set), there may be a large difference between them. If there are outliers in the data, then the median is a better representation of the central value in the data set.

Mode is useful in data sets with a small number of unique values. For example, an accounts receivable aging report may have values of 30, 60, and 90 days. A mode of the aging report data would reveal which category has the most observations. If there are few repeating values, then mode is not a useful measure of central tendency.

Excel is used here to calculate mean and median and interpret the results, but many tools can calculate mean and median values. In fact, all data visualization software can calculate mean and median. Regardless of how it is calculated, two things are important:

- Understanding how to *calculate* the measures.
- Knowing how to *interpret* the results.

Calculate Measures of Location

We will use the university example again to illustrate how to calculate the mean, median, and mode. Instead of assets, however, we will perform a descriptive analysis of the university payroll.

Data Illustration 2.36 is an excerpt from the university payroll data set. The data set shows the employee titles column and the annual salaries for all university employees (10,789 employees).

University Payroll Data

ILLUSTRATION 2.36   University Payroll Data

	B	C
1	**Title**	**AnnualSalary**
2	Program Coordinator	$ 57,633.00
3	Eminent Scholar	$ 94,626.00
4	Eminent Scholar	$ 141,939.00
5	Assistant Professor	$ 87,454.00
6	Network Administrator	$ 48,874.00
10789	Associate Professor	$ 23,998.00
10790	Professor	$ 59,196.00
10791		

The first two steps involve Excel functions:

1. Calculate the mean using the Excel function AVERAGE. The formula is =*AVERAGE (C2:C10790)*. The result is $40,065.88.

2. Calculate the median using the Excel function MEDIAN. The formula is =*MEDIAN (C2:C10790)*. The result is $28,276.00.

Comparing the two measures shows a large difference between the mean and the median annual salary for an employee ($11,789.88). What could cause this? Remember, mean can be affected by outliers. The data can be further examined to determine if there are extremely high or low salary amounts.

3. Finally, use the Excel filter option in the data file to filter the salaries from highest to lowest.

Illustration 2.37 shows the top five salaries and the bottom five salaries.

ILLUSTRATION 2.37 University Salaries Highest to Lowest

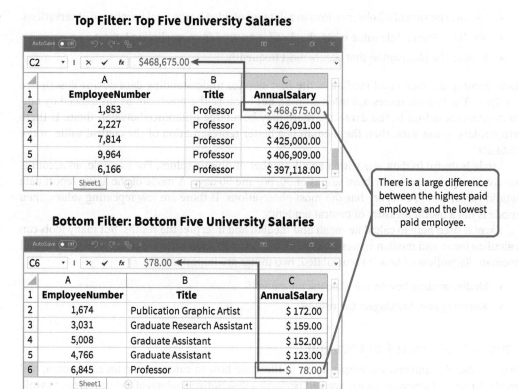

Top Filter: Top Five University Salaries

Bottom Filter: Bottom Five University Salaries

> There is a large difference between the highest paid employee and the lowest paid employee.

Given how much higher the mean salary is compared to the median, it is likely there are more salaries at lower amounts than at higher amounts. We can better understand the difference between the mean and median salary amounts by considering how much variation is in the data.

Measures of Dispersion

In the salary example there was a large difference between the mean and median annual salary amounts. **Measures of dispersion,** which describe the amount of variation in the data, can help find the cause of this disparity. Are the data spread out or are they compact? In other words, how far apart are all the observations, or data points, from the mean?

Variance and Standard Deviation

There are two widely-used measures of dispersion:

- **Variance** is the average squared distance between the data points in the data set and the mean.
- **Standard deviation** is the square root of the variance.

Although variance is necessary to calculate standard deviation, only standard deviation is usually reported because it is easier to interpret than variance. It is easier to understand because it is in the same units as the mean. In the university payroll example, standard deviation would be in dollars of annual salary.

Calculate Measures of Dispersion

Data Measures of dispersion can be calculated using Microsoft Excel (**Illustration 2.38**). Again, calculate these measures by performing calculations in Excel:

1. Calculate the variance using the Excel function VAR. The formula is =*VAR(C2:C10790)*. The result is $1,939,797,496.92.

2. Next, calculate the standard deviation using the Excel function STDEV. The formula is =*STDEV(C2:C10790)*. The result is $44,043.13.

University Payroll Data

	B	C
1	**Title**	**AnnualSalary**
2	Program Coordinator	$ 57,633.00
3	Eminent Scholar	$ 94,626.00
4	Eminent Scholar	$ 141,939.00
5	Assistant Professor	$ 87,454.00
6	Network Administrator	$ 48,874.00
10789	Associate Professor	$ 23,998.00
10790	Professor	$ 59,196.00
10791		
10792	Variance	=VAR(C2:C10790)
10793	Standard Deviation	=STDEV(C2:C10790)

ILLUSTRATION 2.38
University Payroll Data

While there is not a practical interpretation of the variance number, there is for standard deviation:

- A low standard deviation indicates the observations in the data set tend to be close to the mean of the data set.
- A high standard deviation indicates the values are spread out over a wider range.

In this example a standard deviation of $44,043.14 indicates that an observation, in this case an employee's annual salary, in the data set could vary by $44,043.14 from the mean. Recall that the mean is $40,068.88, so $44,043.14 would be considered a high standard deviation.

Another way to evaluate dispersion is to use a scatterplot (also called a scatter chart) to visualize the data (**Illustration 2.39**).

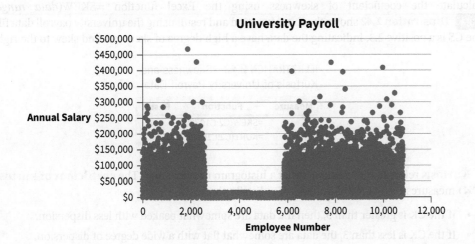

ILLUSTRATION 2.39 University Payroll Scatterplot

Salaries are widely dispersed between $0 and a little over $450,000. This visualization of the data coincides with the large standard deviation of $44,043.14.

Measures of Shape

Besides understanding the dispersion of data, it is also important to understand its distribution, or shape. **Measures of shape** describe the distribution of the data in the data set. How a data set is shaped can reveal the best measure of central tendency to use, or it can show patterns in the data.

Skewness and Kurtosis

Data sets are either symmetrical or asymmetrical in shape. In a symmetrical distribution, the mean, median, and mode are equal and the data distribution to the right of the mean mirrors the data to the left of the mean. A symmetrical distribution will look like a bell curve in a graph (**Illustration 2.40**).

ILLUSTRATION 2.40
Symmetrical Distribution

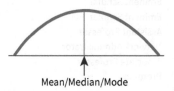

Mean/Median/Mode

The distribution's shape can be determined by graphing the data or by using two statistical measures. Often, both are appropriate. Two measures of shape are skewness and kurtosis.

Skewness describes the lack of symmetry of data:

- Distributions that tail off to the right of the mean are considered positively skewed.
- Distributions that tail to the left of the mean are negatively skewed.

ILLUSTRATION 2.41   Skewness Examples

Positive Skew

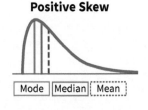

Mode   Median   Mean

Symmetrical Distribution

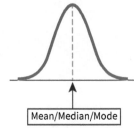

Mean/Median/Mode

Negative Skew

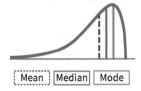

Mean   Median   Mode

Illustration 2.41 shows a positive, symmetrical, and negative skewed distribution.

The **coefficient of skewness (CS)** measures the skewness of a distribution. If the CS is negative, then the data are left skewed (tails off to the left). If the CS is positive, the data are right skewed (tails off to the right). The degree of skewness can be interpreted by the absolute value of the CS:

- $|CS| > 1$, high degree of skewness
- $0.5 \le |CS| \ge 1$, moderate skewness
- $|CS| < 0.5$, relative symmetry

Calculate the coefficient of skewness using the Excel function =SKEW(*data range*). **Data** **Illustration 2.42** shows the Excel function and result using the university payroll data file. The CS is a positive 2.3, indicating the data have a high degree of skewness and skew to the right.

ILLUSTRATION 2.42   Skewness and Kurtosis of University Payroll Data

Measure	Function	Result
CS	=SKEW(C2:C10790)	2.3
CK	=KURT(C2:C10790)	8.2

Kurtosis refers to how peaked or flat a histogram of the data is. The **coefficient of kurtosis (CK)** measures the degree of kurtosis of a distribution:

- If the CK is greater than 3, then the data are somewhat peaked with less dispersion.
- If the CK is less than 3, the data are somewhat flat with a wide degree of dispersion.

The coefficient of kurtosis can be calculated in Excel using the function =KURT(*data range*). Illustration 2.42 shows the CK of the university salary data is 8.2. This indicates the data are peaked with less dispersion.

Frequency Distributions and Histograms

Along with the CS and CK measures, the shape of a distribution can be visualized with two other measures:

- A **frequency distribution** is a representation of the data that summarizes the number of observations within a given interval. For example, the number of employees by salary dollar groupings.

- A **histogram** is a bar chart of a frequency distribution in which the height of the bar reflects the frequency within the interval. For example, we may want to group salaries by dollar amounts of $10,000, $20,000, and $30,000 and then count how many employees are in each category.

These measures can be created in data visualization software such as Power BI, Tableau, and in Microsoft Excel using the Analysis Toolpak. Analysis Toolpak is a free add-on for Excel. Once added, it will be under the **Data** tab. **Illustration 2.43** shows where to find the Data Analysis tool and the corresponding box that opens after clicking **Data Analysis**.

ILLUSTRATION 2.43 Excel Data Analysis Tool

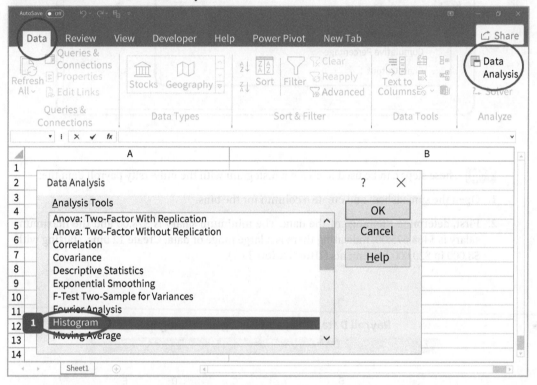

1. To prepare a histogram and frequency distribution, choose **Histogram** and click **OK**.

2. A dialog box opens (**Illustration 2.44**).

3. There are two input boxes:
   - The **Input Range** is the data that will be visualized. It is helpful to select the column title and check the **Labels** box so the histogram is labeled with the title of the data being visualized (Illustration 2.44).
   - The next input box is **Bin Range**, which defines the groups used for the frequency distribution and histogram bars. These must be established before opening the dialog box. Create the Bin Range by setting up a column of the values in which the data should be grouped. In general, the values should be in equal increments and the number of groups should be between five and fifteen.

4. Finally, choose where the outputs should go. Be sure to check the **Chart Output** box before clicking **OK**.

How do you know how many groups to create? The best way is to experiment with the data to find the number that will create a useful visualization. For example, using fewer groups means the group widths will be wider and the visualization may provide less detailed insight. It is often helpful to divide the range (maximum observation – minimum observation) by the number of groups you would like display as a starting point.

ILLUSTRATION 2.44 Histogram Dialog Box

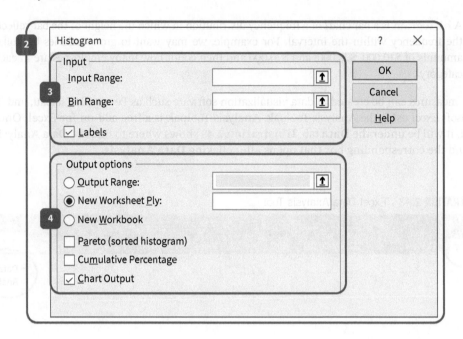

Data These steps can be used to create a histogram with the university payroll data file:

1. Open the spreadsheet and create a column for the bins.

2. First, determine the range of the data. The minimum salary is $78.00 and the maximum salary is $468,675.00, indicating there is a large range of data. Create 12 bins, starting with $8,000 in $20,000 increments (**Illustration 2.45**).

ILLUSTRATION 2.45 Payroll Data, Bins, and Histogram Dialog Box

Payroll Data, Bins, and Histogram Dialog Box

	B	C	D	E
1	**Title**	**Annual Salary**		**Bins**
2	Program Coordinator	$ 57,633.00		8,000
3	Eminent Scholar	$ 94,626.00		28,000
4	Eminent Scholar	$ 141,939.00		48,000
5	Assistant Professor	$ 87,454.00		68,000
6	Network Administrator	$ 48,874.00		88,000
7	Student Program Coordinator	$ 42,630.00		108,000
8	Professor	$ 113,736.00		128,000
9	Professor	$ 2,170.00		148,000
10	Professor	$ 115,228.00		168,000
11	Research Assistant	$ 6,700.00		188,000
12	Research Assistant	$ 6,700.00		208,000
13	Research Assistant	$ 20,100.00		228,000
14	Professor	$ 119,900.00		
10789	Associate Professor	$ 23,998.00		
10790	Professor	$ 59,196.00		

ILLUSTRATION 2.45 (*Continued*)

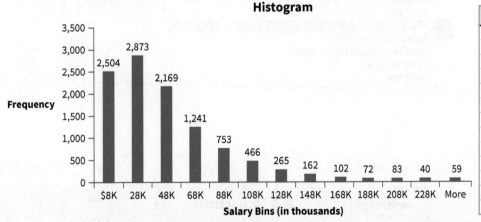

The results from the histogram dialog box are presented in **Illustration 2.46**.

ILLUSTRATION 2.46 University Payroll Data Histogram and Frequency Distribution

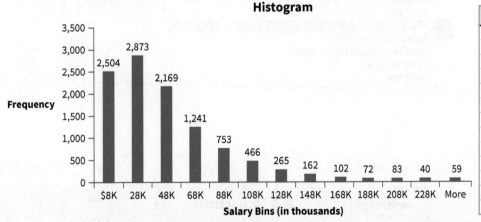

Bins	Frequency	Frequency %
8,000	2,504	23.21
28,000	2,873	26.63
48,000	2,169	20.10
68,000	1,241	11.50
88,000	753	6.98
108,000	466	4.32
128,000	265	2.46
148,000	162	1.50
168,000	102	0.95
188,000	72	0.67
208,000	83	0.77
228,000	40	0.37
More	59	0.55

Note that the *Bins* and *Frequency* are generated by Excel when the histogram is created. The column for Frequency % was calculated by dividing the *Frequency* for each bin by the total number of observations (10,789).

The histogram reveals some information about the shape of the data set, including that most of the data is grouped between $8,000 and $48,000:

- The data then trails off to the right. This supports the results of the measures of location and shape. Recall the median for the data is $28,276.00, and the mean is $40,065.88. The data peaks at the mode.
- The data then tails off to the right, which supports the result for the coefficient of skewness of a positive 2.3.
- Finally, the data are highly peaked. The majority (69%) are within the first three bars on the histogram. This supports the result for the coefficient of kurtosis of 8.2 that indicates highly peaked data with less dispersion.

Descriptive Statistics Tools

You have now learned how to calculate measures of location, dispersion, and shape using single Excel functions. There is another Excel tool, Descriptive Statistics, that calculates all these measures at once (**Illustration 2.47**):

1. Choose **Descriptive Statistics** from the **Analysis Tools** list.

2. Use the dialog box for **Descriptive Statistics** to input the data range to analyze.

3. Once the data range is entered, select labels (if you chose the row with the column title), choose where the output will go, select **Summary statistics**, and click **OK**.

Excel will then calculate the descriptive statistics and print the results on a new worksheet (**Illustration 2.48**).

Statistical software packages typically have a similar feature to calculate multiple descriptive statistics simultaneously. Whether we use multiple single Excel functions or just one to calculate it, revealing the shape of a data set helps us better understand the data. There is also another important component—understanding relationships within a data set.

ILLUSTRATION 2.47
Descriptive Statistics Excel
Tool and Dialog Box

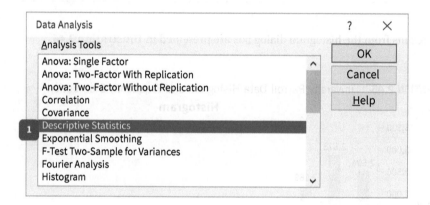

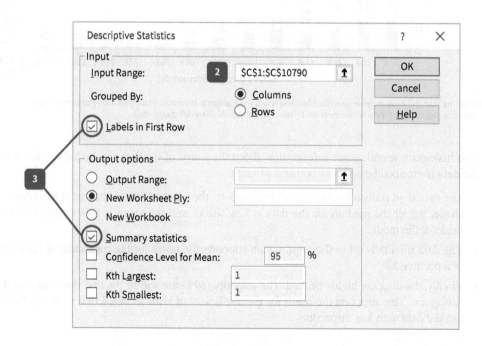

Annual Salary	
Mean	$ 40,065.88
Standard Error	$ 424.02
Median	$ 28,276.00
Mode	$ 3,269.00
Standard Deviation	$ 44,043.13
Sample Variance	$ 1,939,797,496.92
Kurtosis	$ 8.19
Skewness	$ 2.30
Range	$ 468,597.00
Minimum	$ 78.00
Maximum	$ 468,675.00
Sum	$ 432,270,823.00
Count	10,789.00

ILLUSTRATION 2.48 University Salary Data Descriptive Statistics

Correlation Analysis

Correlation analysis can reveal relationships in data by measuring the linear relationship between two variables. The first step is understanding how variables are correlated, and the second step involves calculating the correlation.

Interpret Correlation Coefficients

Linear correlation of continuous variables is measured by the **correlation coefficient**, also known as the Pearson Product Moment Correlation Coefficient. This measure is a numerical value between −1 and +1. The higher the absolute number, the greater the strength of the relationship.

A correlation can be negative, zero, or positive (**Illustration 2.49**):

- A negative correlation is an inverse relationship. As one variable increases, the other decreases. There is a negative relationship between soup sales and temperature because as temperatures decrease, the soup sales increase.

- No correlation indicates no relationship between the variables. We would not expect the outdoor temperature to have an impact on the sale of cereal, for example.

- A positive correlation coefficient indicates that as one variable increases, so does the other variable. We would expect a positive relationship between ice cream sales and outdoor temperature. As the temperature rises, ice cream sales tend to rise as well.

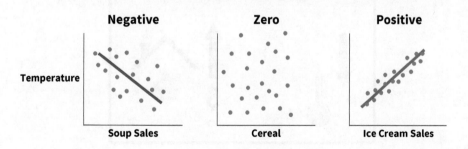

ILLUSTRATION 2.49 Correlation Examples

We can also consider the strength of a relationship. The higher the correlation coefficient, between a negative 1 and a positive 1, the stronger the correlation. **Illustration 2.50** is a guide to determining if a correlation coefficient indicates a weak, moderate, or strong relationship.

ILLUSTRATION 2.50
Interpreting Correlation
Coefficients

Correlation *r*	Interpretation
Exactly −1	A perfect negative linear relationship
−0.70	A strong negative linear relationship
−0.50	A moderate negative linear relationship
−0.30	A weak negative linear relationship
0	No linear relationship
+0.30	A weak positive linear relationship
+0.50	A moderate positive linear relationship
+0.70	A strong positive linear relationship
Exactly +1	A perfect positive linear relationship

Imagine examining the relationship between ice cream sales and the outdoor temperature. If the correlation coefficient of sales and temperature was positive 0.75, then there is a strong positive relationship between sales and temperature. As temperatures rise, sales of ice cream increase and vice versa (**Illustration 2.51**).

ILLUSTRATION 2.51 Positive
Correlation Example

Correlation Coefficient of Ice Cream Sales and Temperature

Suppose instead we are examining the relationship between heating costs and temperature, and the correlation coefficient is a negative 0.70 (**Illustration 2.52**).

ILLUSTRATION 2.52 Negative
Correlation Example

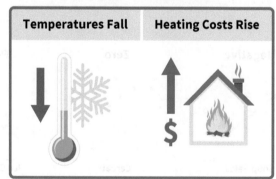

Correlation Coefficient of Heating Costs and Temperature

In this case, there is a strong negative correlation between heating costs and temperature. As the temperature decreases, the cost of heating a home increases and vice versa.

Perform Correlation Analysis

Correlation can be visually assessed by preparing a scatterplot, like those in Illustration 2.49, and then plotting a line. This will indicate if a correlation exists and whether it is positive or negative.

The correlation coefficient can be calculated by hand with a formula or with software. All statistical software can calculate a correlation coefficient, including Microsoft Excel, which is used in this example. Regardless of the software used, the interpretation of the results is the same. There are two ways to perform correlation analysis in Excel:

- Using the CORREL function.
- Using the Correlation option in the Data Analysis tool.

The benefit of using the Correlation option in the Data Analysis tool is that a correlation table for more than one variable can be created at the same time. **Data** We use the university payroll data to illustrate the correlation option in Excel and then interpret the results.

In the Salary Hours tab in the data file (**Illustration 2.53**), perform a correlation analysis to see if there is a correlation between annual salary and hours worked.

University Salary and Hours Data

	Title	AnnualSalary	HoursWorked
1	**Title**	**AnnualSalary**	**HoursWorked**
2	Program Coordinator	$ 57,633.00	2,040
3	Eminent Scholar	$ 94,626.00	612
4	Eminent Scholar	$ 141,939.00	918
5	Assistant Professor	$ 87,454.00	1,530
6	Network Administrator	$ 48,874.00	2,040
7	Student Program Coordinator	$ 42,630.00	2,040
10789	Associate Professor	$ 23,998.00	387.6
10790	Professor	$ 59,196.00	306

ILLUSTRATION 2.53
University Salary and Hours Data

Illustration 2.54 shows the correlation dialog box that opens after clicking **Correlation** and selecting **OK** in the **Data Analysis Tools** dropdown menu. The input range in the dialog box contains the columns being tested for correlation. This example is testing for correlation between column G (Annual Salary) rows 1–10,790, and column H (Hours Worked) rows 1–10,790.

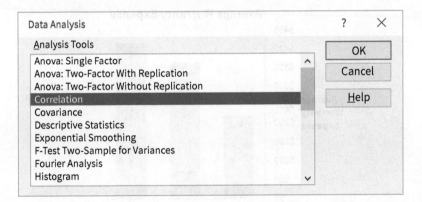

ILLUSTRATION 2.54 Data Analysis Tool and Correlation Dialog Box

The dialog box in Illustration 2.54 shows the inputs necessary to run the correlation analysis. The result of the correlation analysis is shown in **Illustration 2.55**:

- The correlation coefficient is 0.552.
- There is a moderate positive correlation between annual salary and hours worked.

In other words, as hours worked increases so does annual salary.

ILLUSTRATION 2.55 University Salary Correlation Analysis

	Annual Salary	Hours Worked
Annual Salary	1	
Hours Worked	0.552	1

Why is there not a stronger correlation? A strong correlation between the hours worked and the amount of annual salary paid seems to make sense. However, if employees are paid a fixed annual salary rather than hourly that would reduce the correlation to hours.

Correlation analysis can help uncover relationships in the data and understand their strength. But never assume that one variable causes a change in the other because there is correlation between the two. It is possible to find a correlation between two variables that have nothing to do with one another. This is a spurious correlation, which occurs when there is a mathematical, but not a logical, relationship between two variables. Always ensure correlations make sense before using one to make decisions.

APPLY IT 2.4

Use Descriptive Statistics to Audit Warranty Expense

Data **Auditing** As an external auditor, you have been assigned to the audit engagement for Super Scooters. One of your responsibilities is to review warranty expense. As the illustration shows, average warranty expense for Super Scooters has been rising over the last three years.

To analyze the warranty expense, you have decided to use descriptive statistics. Perform the following analyses and interpret your results:

1. Use the Descriptive Statistics option in the Data Analysis tool to calculate the descriptive statistics for warranty expense from 2023 to 2025. Interpret the following measures:

   - Mean
   - Median
   - Standard deviation
   - Kurtosis
   - Skewness

2. Perform descriptive statistics for warranty expense in 2025. Interpret the following measures:

   - Mean
   - Median
   - Kurtosis
   - Skewness

3. Prepare a histogram of 2025 Warranty Expense with the following bins: 200, 400, 600, 800, 1,000, 1,200, and 1,400.

   - Chart the data.
   - Does the shape and distribution of your histogram support the kurtosis and skewness measures?

SOLUTION

1. Descriptive statistics for warranty expense from 2023 to 2025:

Total Warranty	
Mean	343.57
Standard Error	4.06
Median	300
Mode	240
Standard Deviation	244.90
Sample Variance	59,977.92
Kurtosis	1.54
Skewness	1.23
Range	1,493
Minimum	7
Maximum	1,500
Sum	1,252,326
Count	3,645

Measure Interpretation:

Measure	Result	Interpretation
Mean	The mean warranty cost for the 3-year period was $343.57.	The average warranty cost for all 3,645 sales over the 3-year period is $343.57.
Median	The median warranty cost for the 3-year period was $300.00.	The middle value of warranty expense for the 3-year period, when ranking warranty expense from high to low, is $300.
Standard deviation	The standard deviation over the 3-year period was $244.90.	This is a high standard deviation compared to the mean and median. It indicates a wide dispersion of the warranty costs. For any given sale, the warranty cost could be + or − $244.90 from the mean.
Kurtosis	The coefficient of kurtosis is 1.54.	This is less than 3, indicating that the shape of the distribution is somewhat flat with a wide degree of dispersion.
Skewness	The coefficient of skewness is a positive 1.23.	This is greater than 1, indicating that the data peaks around the mean and then tails off to the right.

2. Descriptive statistics for warranty expense in 2025:

Total Warranty—2025	
Mean	414.18
Standard Error	7.551634
Median	330
Mode	330
Standard Deviation	276.13
Sample Variance	76,245.34
Kurtosis	0.93
Skewness	1.18
Range	1,460
Minimum	40
Maximum	1,500
Sum	553,759
Count	1,337

Measure Interpretation:

Measure	Result	Interpretation
Mean	The mean warranty cost for 2025 was $414.18.	This is higher than the three year average found in question 1.
Median	The median warranty cost for 2025 was $330.00.	This represents the exact middle of the distribution if the data is arranged from lowest to highest.
Kurtosis	The coefficient of kurtosis is 0.93.	This is less than 3, indicating that the shape of the distribution is somewhat flat with a wide degree of dispersion.
Skewness	The coefficient of skewness is a positive 1.18.	This is greater than 1, indicating the data peaks around the mean and then tails off to the right.

3. Histogram:

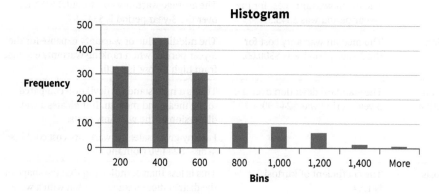

Yes, the kurtosis indicates a wide dispersion. The warranty expense is spread out from $200 to $1,200:

- There are three peaks versus one high peak. The skewness indicates the data peaks around the mean and then tails off to the right.
- The highest peak is around the mean of $414 and then tails off to the right.

2.5 How Is Visualization Used in Data Analysis?

LEARNING OBJECTIVE ⑤
Summarize how data visualization explores and explains data.

Data visualization is the graphical presentation of data and information. Businesses are increasingly focused on data visualization due to the combination of increased data availability and easy-to-use software tools. In today's workplace, employers expect accounting graduates to know how to use data visualization to understand, explain, and communicate answers to data questions.

There are two types of data visualization:

- **Exploratory data visualization** uses data visualization tools and techniques to explore data to find insights. Exploratory data visualization helps to understand the data and identify underlying patterns, trends, or anomalies.

- **Explanatory data visualization** uses data visualization tools and techniques to communicate the results of an analysis. It is used to explain the results of an analysis, show relationships in the data, and communicate insights.

This course will eventually cover both in greater detail. This discussion introduces how visualizations make sense of large data sets, identifies common visualizations and when to use them, and explains how to create them in Microsoft Excel. Many accounting professionals prefer more powerful visualization software such as Power BI and Tableau because Microsoft Excel has limited data visualization capabilities. However, creating visualizations in Excel is an efficient and simple introduction.

Making Sense of Large Data Sets

Visualization is powerful because it can quickly and efficiently reveal insights buried in raw data. **Illustration 2.56** is a tabular summary of sales for an electronics store for the years 2023–2025. Compare the table to its visualization in column chart.

Annual Sales

Product Category	FY 2023	FY 2024	FY 2025	Grand Total
Appliances	$ 434,363,120	$ 434,358,182	$ 486,955,296	$ 1,355,676,598
Cameras	$ 217,276,947	$ 217,491,906	$ 192,648,723	$ 627,417,576
Computers	$ 327,140,700	$ 323,513,274	$ 281,322,005	$ 931,975,979
Computer Accessories	$ 216,412,502	$ 215,524,232	$ 157,419,883	$ 589,356,617
TVs	$ 432,403,786	$ 434,187,852	$ 389,195,034	$ 1,255,786,672
Grand Total	**$ 1,627,597,055**	**$ 1,625,075,446**	**$ 1,507,540,941**	**$ 4,760,213,442**

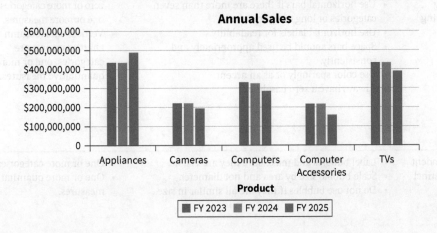

ILLUSTRATION 2.56
Visualizing Sales Data

The graph of sales is easier to interpret:

- It is immediately clear that appliances and TVs have the highest sales in all three years, and only appliances had an increase in sales in 2025.
- All other product categories had lower sales in 2025 than the prior two years.

While it is possible to come to the same conclusions using the table, it is not as easy to detect the differences or make comparisons. The ability to quickly see patterns and relationships in large data sets are why data visualizations skills are so important.

Visualizations and When to Use Them

There are many types of visualizations available. Determining which to use is driven by the type of data available and what you are trying to show in the visualization. Data visualizations are covered in more detail in the analysis, interpretation, and communication chapters, but next is a summary of some common visualizations and how to select them.

Common Visualizations

Categorical data are labeled or named data that can be sorted into groups according to specific characteristics. The data do not have a quantitative value. Categorical data are used in visualizations to portray groups of data. The visualization in Illustration 2.56 is an example using categorical data. The product types are the groups that summarize sales. The same visualization also includes quantitative data in the form of the sales amounts. Putting them together shows the relationship between product categories and sales. Notice the graph also has years. The bars represent the years 2023–2025.

Always consider whether the data being analyzed can be used in a particular visualization. For example, showing a relationship in the data using a scatterplot requires at least one quantitative measure. Showing trends over time requires a time measure (dates) plus a quantitative measure.

Illustration 2.57 lists some common data visualizations along with a description, best practices, and the types of data needed to create the visualization.

ILLUSTRATION 2.57 Common Data Visualizations

Visualization	Use	Best Practices	Data Required
Area Chart	Representing changes in volume over time.	• Do not use if data has more than four categories to avoid confusion and clutter. • Start the y-axis at zero or above. • Put highly variable data on the top and data with low variability on the bottom.	• Date field. • At least one quantitative measure.
Bar and Column Chart	Comparing parts to a whole, highlighting categories, or showing changes over time.	• Compare two to seven categories with vertical bars. • Use horizontal bars if there are more than seven categories or long category labels. • Use horizontal labels for readability. • Space bars should be used appropriately and consistently. • Use color sparingly or as an accent. • Always have a zero baseline.	• Horizontal bars (bar chart): zero or more categories, one or more measures. • Vertical bars (column chart): one or more categories, one or more quantitative measures.
Bubble Chart	Comparing independent values that have distinct gaps or outliers.	• Label bubbles and make sure they are visible. • Scale bubble size by area and not diameter. • Do not use bubbles if they are all similar in size.	• One or more categories. • One or more quantitative measures.

ILLUSTRATION 2.57 (*Continued*)

Visualization	Use	Best Practices	Data Required

Histogram Chart	Showing frequency distributions.	• Use a zero baseline.
		• Choose an appropriate number of bins:
		  • Bins are numbers that represent the intervals into which the data will be grouped.
		  • Bins define the groups used for the frequency distribution.
		  • Use between 5 and 15 bins.
			• Numerical data

Line Graph	Displaying one or more series of data. Allows for the use of multiple data series and data points.	• Time runs from left to right. • Be consistent plotting time points. • Use solid lines, not dotted. • Use a zero baseline. • Do not plot more than four lines. Use multiple charts instead.	• Continuous lines require one date, zero or more categories, and one or more quantitative measure.
Pie Chart	Illustrating simple part-to-whole relationships. Not suited for making precise comparisons.	• Most impactful with small data sets. • Best for showing differences within groups based on one variable. • Make sure the data adds up to 100%. • Limit to a max of five segments. • Start first segment at 12 o'clock position.	• One or more categories. • One or two quantitative measures.
Stacked Bar Chart	Comparing multiple part-to-whole relationships.	• Can be vertical or horizontal. • Follow same best practices as bar charts.	• One or more categories. • One or more quantitative measures.
Scatterplot (Scatter Chart)	Highlighting correlation and distribution of large amounts of data.	• Data set should be in pairs with an independent variable (*x*-axis) and a dependent variable (*y*-axis). • Use if order is not relevant—otherwise use a line graph. • Do not use if there are only a few pieces of data or if there is no correlation.	• Zero or more categories. • One or more quantitative measures.
Tree Map	Visualizing a part-to-whole relationship among many categories.	• Appropriate when precise comparisons are not important. • Use bright, contrasting colors so each box is easily defined. • Label boxes with text or numbers.	• One or more categories. • One or two quantitative measures.

As you develop your data analysis skills, you will be working with large sets of data and will need to use data visualization to analyze them and communicate findings. This chart can be a useful reference as you explore data and communicate your findings.

Choosing Visualizations

How do you know which visualization is best for an analysis? Start by considering the project's objective. There are some common analysis objectives:

- Showing composition
- Indicating relationships
- Displaying distributions
- Finding trends
- Making comparisons

Illustration 2.58 breaks down visualization choices if the goal is to show composition, relationships, or distributions.

ILLUSTRATION 2.58
Guide to Visualizations That Show Composition, Relationships, and Distributions

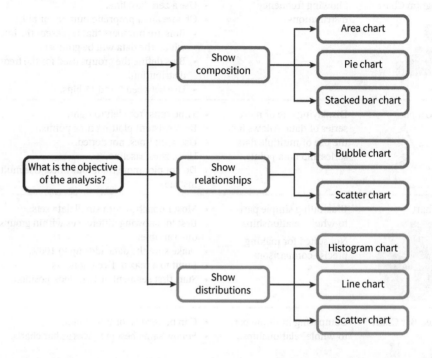

Illustration 2.59 identifies useful visualizations for showing trends or making comparisons.

ILLUSTRATION 2.59 Guide to Visualizations Showing Trends or Comparisons

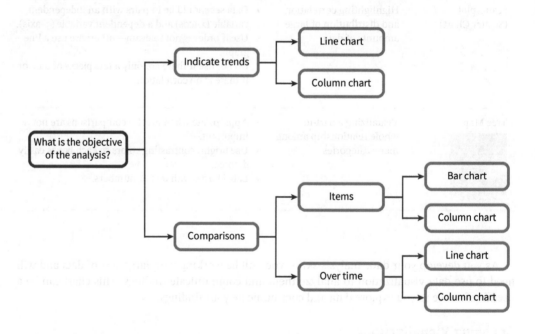

You can use both visualization guides, along with the descriptions and best practices in Illustration 2.57, to create the best visualization to address the purpose of the analysis.

Microsoft Excel Visualizations

Many tools can create visualizations. This course focuses on a trio of software, Tableau, Power BI, and Microsoft Excel, which are the most common (but certainly not only) tools used in business today.

Microsoft Excel can create basic data visualizations. The visualization tools in Microsoft Excel are in the **Insert** ribbon (**Illustration 2.60**).

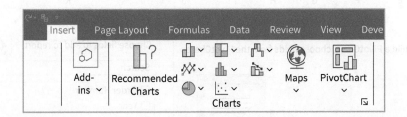

ILLUSTRATION 2.60   Insert a Visualization in Excel

To use the Charts tool:

- Highlight the data to chart.
- Choose a specific chart, or click on **Recommended Charts** to see suggestions.

A chart can also be created from an Excel PivotTable. Either create the PivotTable first or create the PivotTable and chart at the same time by using PivotChart. **Illustration 2.61** shows the dialog box when **Create PivotChart** is chosen. Notice that it is the same as the PivotTable dialog box.

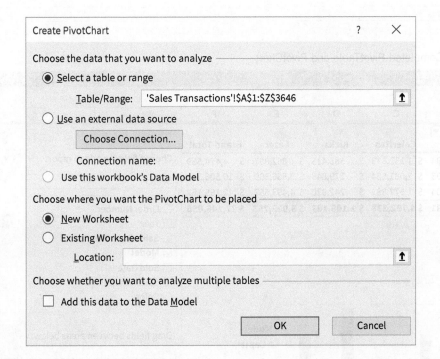

ILLUSTRATION 2.61   PivotChart Dialog Box

Data This example uses the Super Scooters data file to create a PivotTable and PivotChart of gross sales by year and model simultaneously (**Illustration 2.62**). To do this, select:

- The field **Model** for **Legend** (Series).
- The **Year** for **Axis** (Categories).
- **Sum of Gross Sales** for **Values**.

Illustration 2.63 shows the resulting PivotTable and PivotChart, which is a bar chart in which the bar colors represent the models.

ILLUSTRATION 2.62 PivotTable and PivotChart Canvas

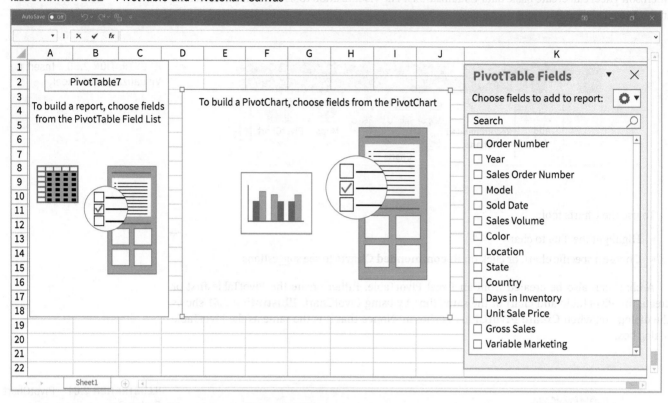

ILLUSTRATION 2.63 Super Scooters Completed PivotTable and PivotChart

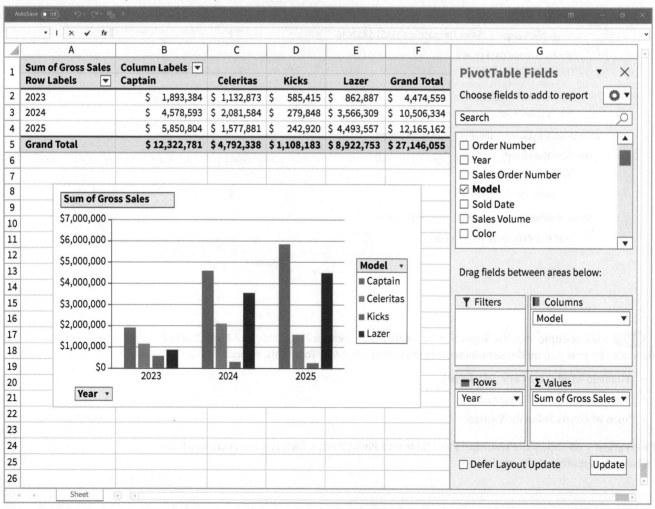

During your accounting career, you will encounter many types of data visualization software programs. However, learning how to use any of these software programs helps prepare you to use and learn new technology. (**Data** **How To 2.2** is a walk-through for how to create a bar chart using Tableau.)

How To

APPLY IT 2.5

Analyze Product Costs with Data Visualization

Managerial Accounting The controller at Super Scooters has asked you to prepare an analysis of product costs. Specifically, the controller would like answers to four questions:

1. What is the total cost per model each year?
2. Which variable costs are the highest?
3. Have labor, materials, and overhead costs been increasing or decreasing over time?
4. Are total costs related to sales volume?

For each question:

- Identify an appropriate visualization and explain your reasoning.
- List best practices for the visualization.
- Determine the type of data needed for the visualization.

SOLUTION

1. An area chart is the best choice because it represents changes in volume over time. For this question, it would show changes in total costs over time.

   Best Practices:
   - Do not use for data with more than four categories to avoid confusion and clutter. There are four models, so this requirement is met.
   - Start the y-axis at zero or above.
   - Place highly variable data on the top and data with low variability on the bottom.

   Data:
   - Date field (use year)
   - At least one quantitative measure (use total costs)

2. A bar chart is the most appropriate visualization because it compares parts to a whole, highlights categories, or shows changes over time.

   Best Practices:
   - Compare two to seven categories with vertical bars.
   - Use horizontal bars if there are more than seven categories or long category labels.
   - Use horizontal labels for better readability.
   - Space bars appropriately and consistently.
   - Use color sparingly or as an accent.
   - Always have a zero baseline.

   Data:
   - One or more categories (labor costs, materials, overhead)
   - One or more quantitative measures (costs)

3. A line chart is appropriate because it displays one or more series of data and allows the use of multiple data series and data points.

   Best Practices:
   - Time runs from left to right.
   - Be consistent plotting time points.
   - Use solid lines, not dotted.
   - Use a zero baseline.
   - Do not plot more than four lines. Instead, use multiple charts.

Data:

- Continuous lines need one date, zero or more categories, and one or more quantitative measures.
- For this question, there are years, three categories of expenses, and the costs of those expenses.

4. A scatterplot is the best choice because it highlights correlation and distribution of large amounts of data.

Best Practices:

- Data set should be in pairs with an independent variable (*x*-axis) and a dependent variable (*y*-axis).
- Use only if order is irrelevant, otherwise use a line graph.
- Avoid if there are only a few pieces of data or if there is no correlation.

Data:

- Zero or more categories
- One or more quantitative measures

Chapter Review and Practice

Learning Objectives Review

❶ Describe how data is stored in and extracted from relational databases.

Data used in accounting data analyses is often stored in a relational database. Retrieving data from a database requires understanding how tables in a relational database are structured:

- Data is stored in tables, which are comprised of fields and records. Fields are the columns representing the characteristics about each record stored in the columns of the data set. Records are data in the rows representing instances of the phenomena being captured in the data set.
- Tables have a primary key, which is a unique value for each row in the table. Often, a table will have a foreign key. A foreign key is a primary key column repeated from another table. Foreign keys make it possible to join the data stored in different tables.
- To analyze data stored in more than one table, join the data from multiple tables. There are inner joins, right joins, left joins, or full joins, each of which retrieves data in different ways. The join selected should be appropriate for the data analysis question being asked.

❷ Explain how functions help answer data analysis questions.

Data analysis includes performing calculations:

- Functions are predefined formulas that perform frequently used calculations.

- The most common functions include AVERAGE, AVERAGEIF, AVERAGEIFS, COUNT, COUNTIF, COUNTIFS, SUM, SUMIF, and SUMIFS.

❸ Illustrate how pivottables organize and filter data.

Data organization is the process of rearranging data to make it easier to understand or to answer a specific question:

- Sort, filter, and slice are common tools for reorganizing data in a spreadsheet to answer questions.
- Pivottables efficiently reorganize data in a spreadsheet to create custom summaries of key information.

❹ Identify descriptive measures used to perform data analysis.

The core data analysis skills for descriptive analytics are descriptive statistics and correlation analysis:

- Measures of location include the mean, median, and mode.
- Measures of distribution include variance and standard deviation.
- Measures of shape include skewness and kurtosis.
- Correlation measures can help identify relationships among the data. Correlation for continuous variables is measured using the correlation coefficient. This measure is a numerical value between −1 and +1. The closer the value is to the absolute value of 1, the stronger the correlation.

❺ Summarize how data visualization explores and explains data.

Data visualization is one of the fastest growing areas of data analysis in the accounting profession:

- Data visualization is the graphical presentation of data and information. Visualizing data can help quickly understand large sets of data.

- Exploratory data visualization examines data to uncover patterns, trends, or anomalies. Explanatory data visualization uses data visualization tools and techniques to communicate the results of data analysis.

- Choosing the right visualization is a combination of considering the purpose of the analysis and deciding whether the goal is to show composition, relationships, distributions, trends, or comparisons.

Key Terms Review

Attributes 43
Categorical data 80
Coefficient of kurtosis (CK) 68
Coefficient of skewness (CS) 68
Correlation analysis 73
Correlation coefficient 73
Data organization 52
Data visualization 79
Dimensions 51
Explanatory data visualization 79
Foreign key 44
Frequency distribution 68

Functions 48
Histogram 69
Join 44
Kurtosis 68
Mean 65
Measures of central tendency 64
Measures of dispersion 66
Measures of location 64
Measures of shape 67
Median 65
Mode 65
Null value 44

Pivottable 52
Primary key 44
Query 44
Relational database 42
Skewness 68
Slicers 61
Slicing 61
Standard deviation 66
Structured Query Language (SQL) 44
Table 43
Variance 66

How To Walk-Throughs

HOW TO 2.1   Format and Show Values As Options in PivotTables

How To

Values in an Excel PivotTable can be formatted with the Value Field Settings dialog box.

What You Need: **Data** The How To 2.1 data file.

STEP 1: Click **Number Format.** The same **Format Cells** dialog available in the Home tool ribbon will appear (**Illustration 2.64**).

ILLUSTRATION 2.64   Format Values in a PivotTable

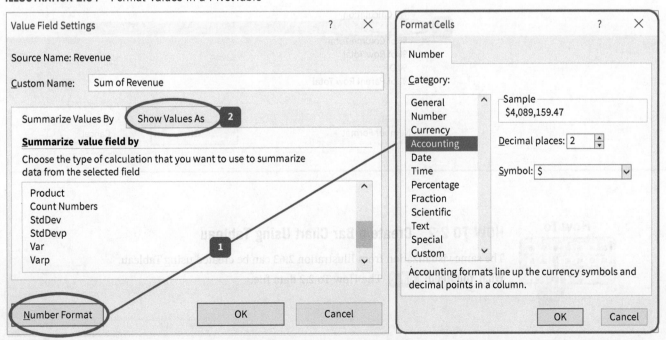

STEP 2: It is also possible to use the **Show Values As** option in the **Value Field Settings** dialog box to add a quick calculation of the values:

- Clicking on **Show Values As** reveals a dropdown list of built-in calculations.
- **Illustration 2.65** displays values as a percentage of a grand total.

ILLUSTRATION 2.65 Show Values As Options

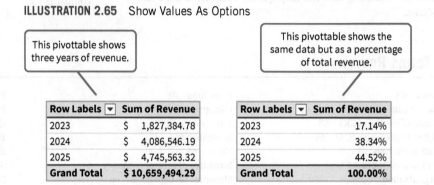

This pivottable shows three years of revenue.

Row Labels ▼	Sum of Revenue
2023	$ 1,827,384.78
2024	$ 4,086,546.19
2025	$ 4,745,563.32
Grand Total	**$ 10,659,494.29**

This pivottable shows the same data but as a percentage of total revenue.

Row Labels ▼	Sum of Revenue
2023	17.14%
2024	38.34%
2025	44.52%
Grand Total	**100.00%**

STEP 3: The **Sum of Revenue** can quickly be changed to the **Percent of Total Revenue** by selecting **% of Grand Total** in the dialog box (**Illustration 2.66**).

ILLUSTRATION 2.66 Show Values As Options

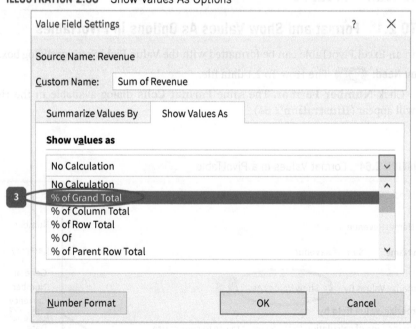

HOW TO 2.2 **Create a Bar Chart Using Tableau**

The same visualization from Illustration 2.63 can be created using Tableau.

What You Need: Data The How To 2.2 data file.

STEP 1: Add the fields for the visualization to the canvas:

- Open the file and click **Sheet 1** along the bottom of the screen (**Illustration 2.67**).
- This will open a new worksheet for a visualization. Click on the field to visualize and drag it to the column or row line:
  - Drag **Sold Date** to **Columns**, **Model** to **Rows**, and **Gross Sales** to **Text**.
  - You could also drag it to the desired spot in the canvas in the area labeled **Drop field here**.

ILLUSTRATION 2.67   Tableau Visualization Canvas

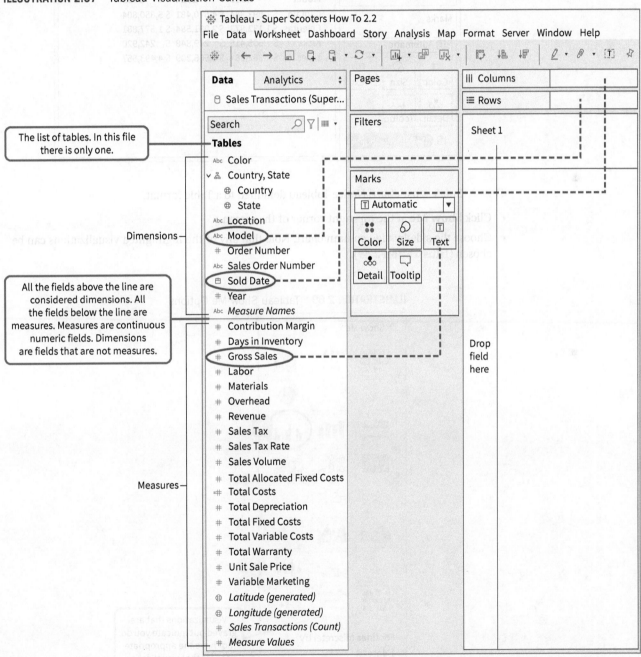

Illustration 2.68 shows the result when **Year** is dragged to **Columns**, **Model** to **Rows**, and **Gross Sales** to **Text**.

ILLUSTRATION 2.68   Tableau Visualization Canvas: Step 1

Pages			⫶⫶⫶ Columns	⊞ Year(Sold Date)	
			≡ Rows	Model	

Filters	**Gross Sales by Model**			
	Sold Date			
	Model	**2023**	**2024**	**2025**
Marks	Captain	$ 1,893,384	$ 4,570,481	$ 5,850,804
	Celeritas	$ 1,132,873	$ 2,081,584	$ 1,577,881
Ⓣ Automatic ▾	Kicks	$ 585,415	$ 279,848	$ 242,920
	Lazer	$ 862,887	$ 3,566,309	$ 4,493,557

Marks:
- ∷ Color
- ⬡ Size
- Ⓣ Text
- ⚬⚬⚬ Detail
- ⌗ Tooltip
- Ⓣ SUM(Gross Sale)

STEP 2: Create a bar chart. Notice Tableau defaulted to a Table format.

- Click **Show Me** at the top-right corner of the screen.
- Choose the side-by-side column chart. Note that any of the highlighted visualizations can be chosen (**Illustration 2.69**).

ILLUSTRATION 2.69   Tableau Show Me Options

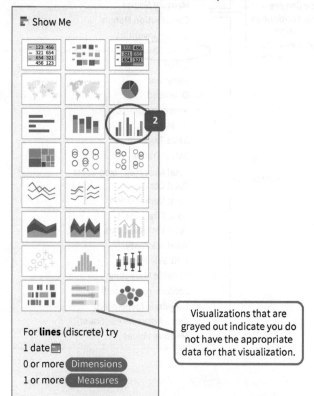

⊩ Show Me

For **lines** (discrete) try
1 date 🗓
0 or more Dimensions
1 or more Measures

> Visualizations that are grayed out indicate you do not have the appropriate data for that visualization.

Illustration 2.70 is the result of selecting the column bar chart visualization option.

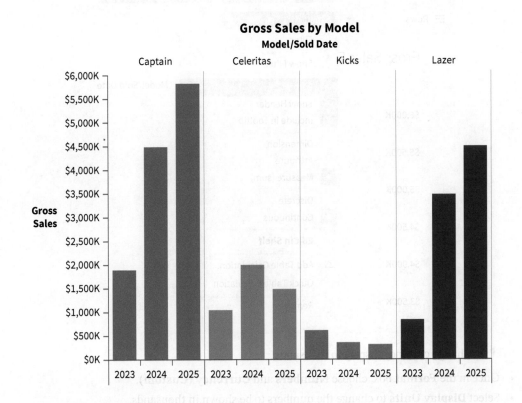

ILLUSTRATION 2.70 Tableau Bar Chart Visualization

STEP 3: Title the visualization:

- Double-click on the **Sheet 1** title and choose **Edit Title**.
- Change the title by typing "Gross Sales by Model" (**Illustration 2.71**).

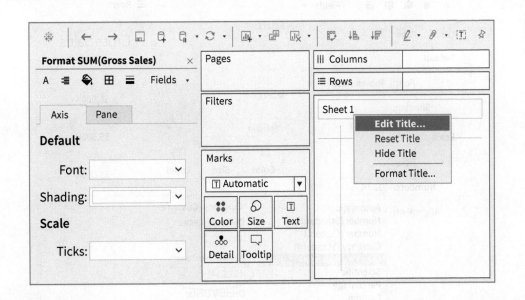

ILLUSTRATION 2.71 Tableau Bar Chart: Add a Title

STEP 4: Format the axis:

- To format the Gross sales axis and dollars in thousands, click the down arrow in the **SUM** (Gross Sales).
- Choose **Format** and click the **Axis Tab** (**Illustration 2.72**).

ILLUSTRATION 2.72 Tableau
Bar Chart: Format the Axis

STEP 5: Change currency display to thousands:

- Once in the **Format** box, choose **Numbers** and **Currency (Custom)**.
- Select **Display Units** to change the numbers to be shown in thousands.
- Note that we have also changed the decimal places to zero (**Illustration 2.73**).

ILLUSTRATION 2.73 Tableau
Bar Chart: Change Currency
Display

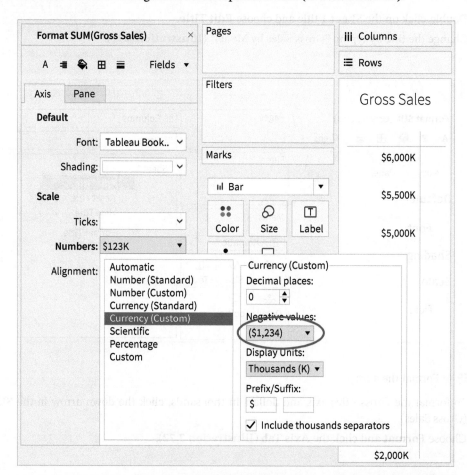

> **Data** The Data tag appears when the data required to answer a question or complete an exercise are available in the book's product page on www.wiley.com.

Multiple Choice Questions

1. (LO 1) A collection of logically related data that can be retrieved, manipulated, and updated to meet users' needs is called a

   a. table.   **c.** data set.

   b. relational database.   **d.** data warehouse.

2. (LO 1) Bridgeport University is designing a new information system to track purchasing activity. The following database tables have been created. What are the primary keys to each of the tables? Select the right option.

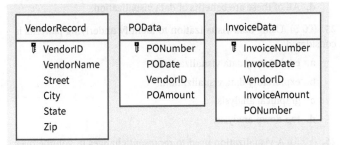

   a. VendorName is the primary key for VendorRecord; PONumber is the primary key for POData; and PONumber is the primary key for InvoiceData.

   b. VendorID is the primary key for VendorRecord; PONumber is the primary key for POData; and InvoiceNumber is the primary key for InvoiceData.

   c. VendorName is the primary key for VendorRecord; PONumber is the primary key for POData; and VendorID is the primary key for InvoiceData.

   d. VendorID is the primary key for VendorRecord; VendorID is the primary key for POData; and InvoiceDate is the primary key for InvoiceData.

3. (LO 1) Tables in a database may be in which of the following elements?

   a. Assets, liabilities, and expenses

   b. Resources, expenses, and employees

   c. Revenue, events, and agents

   d. Resources, events, and agents

4. (LO 1) Columns in a database reflect

   a. attributes.   **c.** resources.

   b. events.   **d.** agents.

5. (LO 1) A request for data from a database in order to retrieve or manipulate it is called

   a. data analysis.   **c.** a question.

   b. a query.   **d.** a join.

6. (LO 1) When performing a join between two tables, if a null value is returned, that indicates

   a. a value of zero.

   b. the join was incorrect.

   c. a value does not exist in the database.

   d. an inner join was performed.

7. (LO 1) What join type would be used to determine if there are matching data in the rows of left and right tables?

   a. Left join   **c.** Inner join

   b. Right join   **d.** Full join

8. (LO 1) A join that returns all rows from both tables that have matching values is which type of join?

   a. Inner   **c.** Right

   b. Left   **d.** Full

9. (LO 1) A join that returns all the records from the right table as well as all the matched records from the left table is which type of join?

   a. Inner   **c.** Right

   b. Left   **d.** Full

10. (LO 1) A join that returns all records when there is a match in either the left or right table is which type of join?

   a. Inner   **c.** Right

   b. Left   **d.** Full

11. (LO 2) Which of the following Microsoft Excel functions returns the arithmetic mean for a range or array of numbers?

   a. AVERAGE   **c.** AVERAGEIF

   b. MEAN   **d.** SUM

12. (LO 2) Which of the following Microsoft Excel functions counts the number of cells that meet one or more conditions?

   a. COUNT   **c.** COUNTA

   b. COUNTIF   **d.** COUNTIFS

13. (LO 2) This function adds the cells specified by a given set of conditions or criteria.

   a. SUM   **c.** SUMIFS

   b. SUMIF   **d.** SUMPRODUCT

14. (LO 3) This function adds the cells specified by a condition or criteria.

   a. SUM   **c.** SUMIFS

   b. SUMIF   **d.** SUMPRODUCT

15. (LO 3) Which tool in Microsoft Excel will reorganize spreadsheet data into custom summaries of key information?

   a. Sort   **c.** PivotTable

   b. Filter   **d.** Developer

16. (LO 3) You have an extract of the payroll data for the last fiscal year. Payroll runs twice a month. The spreadsheet has the following columns: Pay Date, Employee, Department, and Payment Amount. How do you summarize the data as a pivottable to show the total payroll payments by department?

a. Set Department as dimensions and set Sum of Payment Amount as values.

b. Set Department as rows and set Payment Amount as columns.

c. Set Department as columns and set Sum of Payment Amount as measures.

d. Set Department as rows and set Sum of Payment Amount as values.

17. **(LO 3)** Auto filter functionality in a PivotTable can be accessed by

a. using the filter box in the PivotTable fields.

b. clicking on the dropdown arrow in the row labels.

c. clicking on the dropdown arrow in the filter box.

d. dragging a field to the field filter box.

18. **(LO 3)** Slicing refers to

a. removing decimal places.

b. eliminating data.

c. sorting data.

d. breaking down the data into smaller parts.

19. **(LO 4)** The sum of all observations in a data set divided by the total number of observations is called the

a. mean.   c. mode.

b. median.   d. range.

20. **(LO 4)** The middle value when the data in a data set are arranged from smallest to largest is called the

a. mean.   c. mode.

b. median.   d. range.

21. **(LO 4)** You are analyzing employee salaries. If the salary values are spread out evenly, then

a. the mode and median should be similar.

b. the mean and median should be similar.

c. the mode and mean should be similar.

d. the mean and median should be very different.

22. **(LO 4)** If the coefficient of skewness is –1.5, the data distribution will have a

a. high degree of skewness and tail to the right.

b. high degree of skewness and tail to the left.

c. moderate degree of skewness and tail the right.

d. moderate degree of skewness and tail to the left.

23. **(LO 4)** A negative correlation means

a. as one variable decreases, the other variable decreases.

b. as one variable increases, the other variable increases.

c. as one variable increases, the other variable decreases.

d. as one variable decreases, the other variable remains unchanged.

24. **(LO 5)** Which of the following are benefits of data visualization?

a. Visualizing helps to quickly understand large data sets.

b. Data visualization can be used to explore data.

c. Data visualization can be used to explain data analysis.

d. All of these are benefits of data visualization.

25. **(LO 5)** Using data visualization to identify underlying patterns is considered

a. explanatory data visualization.

b. exploratory data visualization.

c. graphical analysis.

d. top-down analysis.

26. **(LO 5)** A visualization used to represent changes in volume over time is a/an

a. area chart.   c. line graph.

b. bar chart.   d. pie chart.

27. **(LO 5)** Your company produces 25 different product categories. To compare the total value of sales for each product category, what data visualization would be the most appropriate to use?

a. Area charts   c. Pie charts

b. Line charts   d. Tree maps

28. **(LO 5)** A visualization used to show frequency distributions is a

a. pie chart.   c. histogram chart.

b. line chart.   d. bubble chart.

Review Questions

1. **(LO 1)** Identify and describe the four types of joins that can query a data set.

2. **(LO 2)** For each scenario, match the best basic Excel function that could be used to address it. Each function can be used once, more than once, or not at all.

a. AVERAGE   e. COUNTA

b. AVERAGEIF   f. COUNTBLANK

c. COUNT   g. SUM

d. COUNTIF   h. SUMIF

Scenario	Function
1. Count the number of cells in an Excel file that have inventory quantities.	
2. Count the number of cells in an Excel file that have an inventory quantity of 1,150 items.	

Scenario	Function
3. Calculate the arithmetic mean of the commission amounts paid to sales personnel during the fourth quarter.	
4. Calculate the total sales amount for the period, which is listed in column K of your Excel spreadsheet.	
5. Calculate the total sales amount for the period for customer #4920 only. The sales amounts are listed in column K in your Excel spreadsheet and customer numbers are listed in column A of your Excel spreadsheet.	
6. Count the number of inventory items listed on the spreadsheet with no inventory quantities.	

3. (LO 2) Give an example of when you should use a COUNTIFS function.

4. (LO 2) Give an example of when you might use a COUNTBLANK function.

5. (LO 3) Describe the five components of an Excel PivotTable.

6. (LO 3) Describe how an Excel PivotTable can be filtered.

7. (LO 4) Provide an example of when the median of a distribution might be more meaningful to interpret than the mean.

8. (LO 4) Define standard deviation and give an example of how to interpret it.

9. (LO 4) Define negative correlation and positive correlation. Provide an example of each.

10. (LO 5) Describe exploratory data visualization and explanatory data visualization. How are they the same? How are they different?

11. (LO 5) For each scenario identify whether you would perform exploratory data visualization or explanatory data visualization.

Scenario	Visualization Type
1. Your manager provides you with all the sales data by product line for the last two years and asks you to identify sales trends between years.	
2. You have analyzed data related to sales trends by country over the past three years and will present that data using a tree map.	

Scenario	Visualization Type
3. Your manager provides you with all the payments made to approved vendors in the past six months and asks you to identify if any payments are outside of expected payment amounts.	
4. Your manager provides you with analysis of maintenance expenses for the year and asks you to prepare a pie chart to illustrate the categories of expenses.	

12. (LO 5) As a tax professional for an online retailer, you have been asked to create a line graph visualization depicting the increase in sales tax collected and remitted each month this year compared to last year. Using the line graph best practices outlined in the chapter, describe how you would set up the visualization. Identify the data points on the x-axis, y-axis, and series of data.

13. (LO 5) Describe the best practices for bar charts and area charts.

14. (LO 5) You are a financial analyst in the operations division of a manufacturing company. As part of quality control metrics, your company tracks rework expenses for goods that were not manufactured to meet quality standards. Your manager has asked you to prepare a line chart illustrating the trend of rework expenses by reason code category. You note that there are five different reason codes for why rework may be required. Using the best practices outlined in this chapter, describe how you would set up the line chart to depict rework expense trends by category.

Brief Exercises

BE 2.1 (LO 1) 〔 Managerial Accounting 〕 You are a financial analyst for PizzaNow! The corporate controller wants you to perform an analysis using three tables in the relational database.

For each item, identify whether it is a primary key, foreign key, or neither.

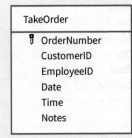
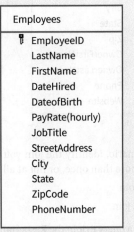

TakeOrder
⚷ OrderNumber
CustomerID
EmployeeID
Date
Time
Notes

Customers
⚷ CustomerID
LastName
FirstName
StreetAddress
City
State
ZipCode
PhoneNumber

Employees
⚷ EmployeeID
LastName
FirstName
DateHired
DateofBirth
PayRate(hourly)
JobTitle
StreetAddress
City
State
ZipCode
PhoneNumber

1. OrderNumber in the TakeOrder table
2. EmployeeID in the TakeOrder table
3. CustomerID in the Customers table
4. EmployeeID in the Employees table
5. Date in the TakeOrder table
6. ZipCode in the Employees table

BE 2.2 (LO 1) **Accounting Information Systems** Flower Special provides home delivery of floral bouquets and other flower decorations ordered from various local florists in the area. You are the liaison between the company's information technology group and the accounting group. You are asked to explain the relationship among these tables to the accounting group. The tables are from the Flower Special database.

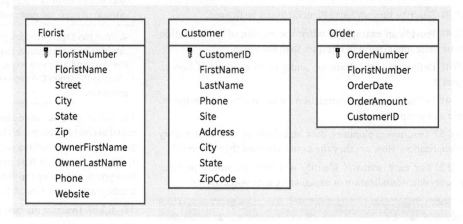

1. Is there a foreign key for each table given above?
2. Which two tables will be used to get the name of the florist for a specific order?

BE 2.3 (LO 1) **Financial Accounting** Assume you are a financial analyst in the finance team of a university. You have been asked to identify all student numbers who have not paid their tuition fees in the last 12 months. The IT team has given you the Student file and Fees Collected file for the past 12 months. You have identified the Student file as the left table and the Fees Collected file as the right table. What join type will help you in your analysis and why do you think that the join type that you have selected will give the right result?

BE 2.4 (LO 1) **Financial Accounting** You are a financial analyst for Dine At Home who has been asked to analyze the data in the following three tables:

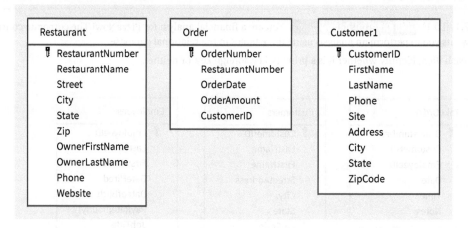

For each scenario, identify the join you would most likely use to query the data. Each join type can be used once, more than once, or not at all.

   a. Left join   **c.** Inner join

   b. Right join   **d.** Full join

1. Execute a query to join the Restaurant table (left table) and the Order table (right table), but only return the rows from both tables that have matching values.
2. Execute a query to join the Restaurant table (left table) and the Customer1 (right table) table, and return all records from the Restaurant table, but only those matching records from the Customer1 table.
3. Execute a query to join the Order table (left table) and the Customer1 table (right table), and return all records from both tables. Match the records that can be matched in both tables.

4. Execute a query to join the Order table (left table) and the Customer1 table (right table), and only return all the records from the Order table and the matching records from the Customer1 table.

BE 2.5 (LO 2) `Data` `Managerial Accounting` The controller at ThisBigCity has asked that you perform an analysis on the city's employee reimbursement expenses over the past 15 years. The IT group has provided a download of all the employee reimbursement data since 2005.

1. Use the AVERAGE function. What was the average reimbursement amount paid from July 2005 to November 2020?

2. Use the AVERAGEIF function. What was the average reimbursement amount paid in 2019?

3. Use the AVERAGEIFS function. What was the average reimbursement amount paid in the fire department during 2019?

BE 2.6 (LO 2) `Data` `Accounting Information Systems` As an internal auditor at ThisBigCity, you have been asked to test internal controls over the employee reimbursement process for the city. The IT group provided a download of all the employee reimbursement data since 2005. Your manager suggested performing descriptive statistics on this file to determine if you have a complete population of data, and to start the process of identifying a sample size for internal control testing.

1. Use the COUNT function. How many reimbursements were paid from July 2005 to November 2020?

2. Use the COUNTIF function. How many reimbursements were paid in 2019?

3. Use the COUNTIFS function. How many reimbursements were paid in 2019 to firefighters?

BE 2.7 (LO 3) `Data` `Auditing` Use PivotTables and the available data to answer the following questions:

1. Which customer has the highest accounts receivable balance?

2. Which customer has the highest accounts receivable balance that is more than 150 days past due?

BE 2.8 (LO 3) `Data` `Financial Accounting` Use PivotTables and the available data to answer the following questions:

1. What is the total of accounts receivable?

2. What are the totals by region?

BE 2.9 (LO 3) `Data` `Financial Accounting` `Managerial Accounting` Use PivotTables and the Super Scooters data to answer the following questions:

1. What are the total gross sales for each scooter model by year?

2. Which color scooter had the highest sales volume in 2023?

3. What was the total variable marketing expense for 2023 by model?

BE 2.10 (LO 4) `Data` `Managerial Accounting` As a financial analyst working for an investment company, you want to understand the prices of bitcoin from July 2010 to January 2024. Find the following statistics for price:

1. Mean

2. Median

3. Mode

BE 2.11 (LO 4) `Data` `Financial Accounting` You are preparing the management's discussion and analysis (MD&A) regarding the city of Chicago's fire department. One of the most important expenses for the fire department is overtime. Therefore, you would like to understand the overtime data before you write the MD&A.

1. Calculate the coefficient of skewness for overtime pay.

2. Calculate the coefficient of kurtosis for overtime pay.

3. Prepare a histogram with these groupings: $500, $1,000, $2,000, $3,000, $4,000, $5,000, and $6,000.

BE 2.12 (LO 5) `Data` `Financial Accounting` Your company, Loans Are US, provides loans to small to medium-sized businesses. The company has loan offices in four regions. You are asked to prepare a visualization that illustrates the total amount of loans by region and by the age of receivables. Prepare a stacked column chart that does this.

BE 2.13 (LO 5) `Data` Loans Are US keeps track of credit ratings for all customer accounts. You must prepare a visualization that illustrates the total number of loans by credit rating. Prepare a bar chart visualizing the number of accounts in each of the three credit ratings: AAA, BBB, and CCC.

BE 2.14 (LO 5) `Data` Your supervisor at Loans Are US has asked you to prepare a visualization that illustrates the total dollar amount of loans past due by more than 150 days by credit rating. Prepare a bar chart visualizing the number of accounts in each of the three credit ratings: AAA, BBB, and CCC.

Exercises

EX 2.1 (LO 1) **Auditing** **Identify Data and Joins Needed to Verify Data** You are an internal auditor for Way Cool Stuff. You must verify that no employees are also customers. The following tables are in the database:

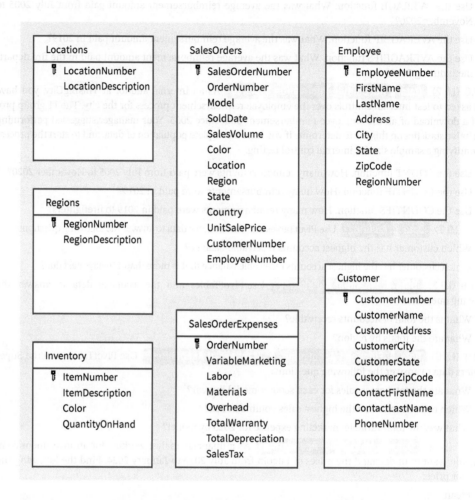

Locations	SalesOrders	Employee
⌗ LocationNumber	⌗ SalesOrderNumber	⌗ EmployeeNumber
LocationDescription	OrderNumber	FirstName
	Model	LastName
	SoldDate	Address
	SalesVolume	City
	Color	State
	Location	ZipCode
	Region	RegionNumber
	State	
Regions	Country	
⌗ RegionNumber	UnitSalePrice	
RegionDescription	CustomerNumber	**Customer**
	EmployeeNumber	⌗ CustomerNumber
		CustomerName
		CustomerAddress
	SalesOrderExpenses	CustomerCity
Inventory	⌗ OrderNumber	CustomerState
⌗ ItemNumber	VariableMarketing	CustomerZipCode
ItemDescription	Labor	ContactFirstName
Color	Materials	ContactLastName
QuantityOnHand	Overhead	PhoneNumber
	TotalWarranty	
	TotalDepreciation	
	SalesTax	

1. What table(s) will you need to be able to complete this test?
2. What fields will you use to join the tables, if necessary?
3. What fields do you need from the table(s) to complete this test?

EX 2.2 (LO 1) `Financial Accounting` **Identify Data and Joins Needed to Summarize Data** You are a financial accountant at Wax Company. What follows are the database tables available for Wax Company.

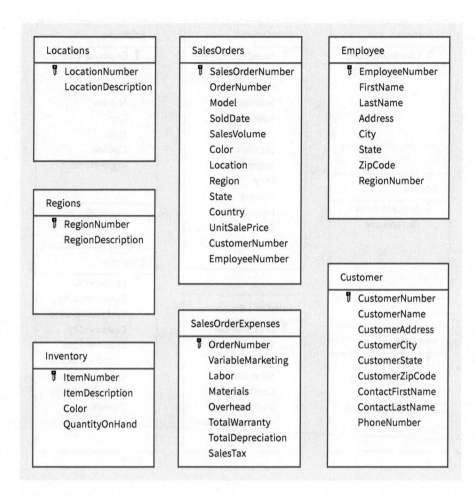

1. What are the tables that you will use to find the excess sales amount over sales order expenses, including details of the customer and employee who sold it?

   SalesOrders table and SalesOrderExpenses table

2. What fields would you use to join the tables to identify sales by employee?

3. Using a join type, capture the customer data with their order. Assume the customer table is on the left and the sales order table is on the right.

EX 2.3 (LO 1) Managerial Accounting **Apply Joins to Answer Questions** You are analyzing sales at Way Cool Stuff by region for the years 2024 and 2025. The following database tables are available:

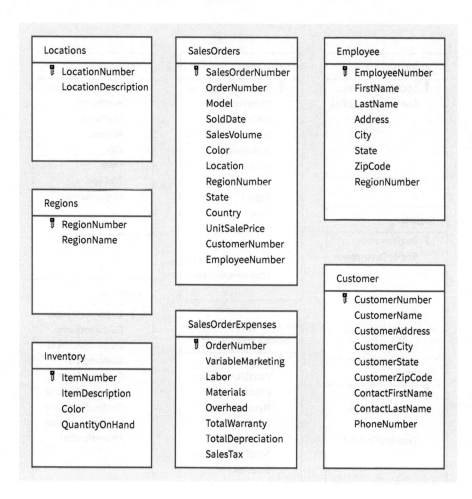

1. Which table(s) do you need to gather the data necessary to analyze gross sales by region for 2024 and 2025?

2. What fields will you use to join the tables?

3. Which fields will you need to perform your analysis?

EX 2.4 (LO 1) Tax Accounting **Identify Data and Joins Needed for Tax Compliance** You are filing Way Cool Stuff's state sales tax returns for the month ended December 31, 2025 for all locations in which sales tax was collected. Use the available database tables to answer the following questions:

1. Which table(s) do you need to be able to gather the data needed to calculate sales tax remittance for December 2025?

2. What fields will you use to join the tables?

3. Which fields will you need to gather the information necessary to submit sales tax 2025?

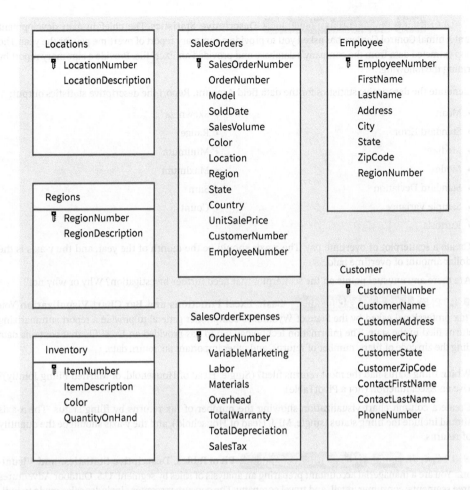

Locations
- LocationNumber
- LocationDescription

Regions
- RegionNumber
- RegionDescription

Inventory
- ItemNumber
- ItemDescription
- Color
- QuantityOnHand

SalesOrders
- SalesOrderNumber
- OrderNumber
- Model
- SoldDate
- SalesVolume
- Color
- Location
- Region
- State
- Country
- UnitSalePrice
- CustomerNumber
- EmployeeNumber

SalesOrderExpenses
- OrderNumber
- VariableMarketing
- Labor
- Materials
- Overhead
- TotalWarranty
- TotalDepreciation
- SalesTax

Employee
- EmployeeNumber
- FirstName
- LastName
- Address
- City
- State
- ZipCode
- RegionNumber

Customer
- CustomerNumber
- CustomerName
- CustomerAddress
- CustomerCity
- CustomerState
- CustomerZipCode
- ContactFirstName
- ContactLastName
- PhoneNumber

EX 2.5 (LO 3) `Data` `Managerial Accounting` **Scholarship Data Given** Apply the pivottable and create a table to show the number of scholarship categories given across institutions and campuses of a university. This will help the management accountant to prepare budgets for the upcoming academic year. Keep the amount of scholarship as a filter.

EX 2.6 (LO 4) `Data` `Managerial Accounting` **Descriptive Statistics** You are a financial analyst at Animal Control Centers of America tasked with understanding the overtime pay for the year. Your IT group has provided a file that includes overtime pay per employee per month. The spreadsheet also includes the average monthly temperature. Perform a correlation analysis between the amount of overtime incurred and the temperature for each month.

1. What is the correlation coefficient for the amount and temperature variables?
2. Is the correlation between amount and temperature strong, moderate, or weak? Explain your answer.

EX 2.7 (LO 4) `Data` `Managerial Accounting` **Descriptive Statistics** The chief human development officer at Animal Control Centers has asked you to provide a summary report of overtime pay for the year. The IT group extracted data from the company's database and provided an Excel file. Provide a summary report by performing the following:

1. Generate the descriptive statistics for the data field Amount. Report the descriptive statistics output:

   - Mean
   - Standard Error
   - Median
   - Mode
   - Standard Deviation
   - Sample Variance
   - Kurtosis
   - Skewness
   - Range
   - Minimum
   - Maximum
   - Sum
   - Count

2. Create a scatterplot of overtime pay. The *x*-axis should be the month of the year, and the *y*-axis is the dollar amount of overtime paid.

3. Are there any unusual points on the scatterplot that need further investigation? Why or why not?

EX 2.8 (LO 2, 5) `Data` `Tax Accounting` **Basic Excel Functions and Bar Chart Visualization** You are a tax professional asked by the State of Wyoming's comptroller general to provide a report summarizing tax returns filed in the state. The information technology group has provided an Excel file that contains data regarding the zip code of filers, number of returns, and other important tax return data.

1. Which filing status had the most returns filed? (Single, Head of Household, or Married Filing Jointly)? Use an Excel function (not a PivotTable).

2. Create a column chart visualization showing the number of tax returns by filing status. The *x*-axis should include the filing status (single, MFJ, Head of Household), and the *y*-axis should be the quantity of returns.

EX 2.9 (LO 2, 4, 5) `Data` `Managerial Accounting` **PivotTables, Descriptive Statistics, and Visualizations** You are a managerial accountant preparing an analysis of sales by segment. U.S. Outdoor Adventures has three segments: consumer, retail, and travel company. The consumer segment includes sales made to individual customers via the U.S. Outdoor Adventures website. The retail segment are those sales made to retail stores. The travel company segment are sales made to travel companies that organize and run camping trips.

1. Create an Excel PivotTable summarizing sales by segment from 2022 to 2025. Show each segment and the total sales by year.

2. Create a bar chart for sales by segment from 2022 to 2025. Which segments are increasing, and which segments are decreasing?

3. Create a PivotTable to analyze average sales by segment from 2022 to 2025. Show each segment and the average sales by year.

4. Create a line chart for average sales by segment from 2022 to 2025. Are average sales increasing or decreasing from 2024 to 2025?

5. **Dig Deeper:** Examine the variation in sales by segment using a PivotTable and line chart that displays standard deviation. Which segment has the most variation in sales? How did you determine your answer?

EX 2.10 (LO 2, 5) `Data` `Auditing` **PivotTables and Line Graphs** You are working on the U.S. Outdoor Adventure Company financial statement audit for the year ended December 31, 2023. Your senior has asked you to understand the sales data and identify significant customers on which to perform detail testing. The client has provided the sales data. According to the general ledger, total sales for the years ended 2025 and 2024 are $273,323 and $269,196, respectively.

1. Create an Excel PivotTable depicting sum of sales by year using the variable ShipDate. Verify the reported total sales for the year agrees with the client's general ledger balances as presented.

2. Create a PivotTable that presents sales for 2024 and 2025 by product category.

3. Using the best practices outlined in Illustration 2.57, create a line graph that shows sales for 2024 and 2025 by category. The *x*-axis should include the years 2024 and 2025, and the *y*-axis should have the dollar amount of sales. There should be three lines, one for each category of sales, camping gear, paddles, and tents.

4. **Dig Deeper:** Modify the line graph so the *x*-axis has quarterly sales information for 2024 compared to 2025 for each category of sales.

Problems

PR 2.1 (LO 3) `Data` `Auditing` **Applying Filtering in PivotTables** Your firm has been hired to perform an audit for Best Bakes Bakery. You must perform an analysis of profit by customer to determine if there are any unusual changes.

1. Create an Excel PivotTable that displays all customers and profit for 2024 in one column and 2025 in another column.

2. Use the Value Field Settings to show the percent difference from 2024.

3. How many customers have a percent changes in profit that is greater than ±30% from the prior year?

PR 2.2 (LO 2, 4) `Data` `Auditing` **Excel Functions and Descriptive Statistics** You are an auditor working on the financial statement audit of ThisBigCity asked to perform analytical procedures to understand the city's reimbursement expenses for the year ended December 31, 2025. The client provided a download of all the employee reimbursement data since 2010. To answer the following questions, use Excel functions, *not* PivotTables:

1. What is the total dollar amount of reimbursements paid in 2025?

2. Calculate the total dollar amount of reimbursements paid in 2025 to the following departments:

Department	Reimbursement paid in 2025
Department of Buildings	
Department of Health	
Department of Water Management	

3. What is the mean, median, and mode of the reimbursement amount in 2025?

4. What is the standard deviation of the reimbursement amount in 2025?

5. Generate a scatterplot depicting the reimbursement amounts in 2025. On the *x*-axis, show the date, and on the *y*-axis, show the amount. The *y*-axis range should be between $500 and $3,500.

6. Use the following descriptive statistics and the scatterplot to identify any anomalies in the city's reimbursements during 2025:

   - Mean
   - Median
   - Mode
   - Standard deviation

7. **Dig Deeper:** Expand on this analyses to include a discussion of reimbursement amounts by department or by job title.

PR 2.3 (LO 2, 5) `Data` `Auditing` **Basic Excel Functions and Pie Chart** You are an auditor assigned to the Outdoor Adventure Company financial statement audit for the year ended December 31, 2025. Your senior wants to understand the sales data and identify significant customers on which to perform detail testing. Total sales for the year ended December 31, 2025, according to the company's general ledger, is $273,323. (*Note*: Sales are recognized when the product shipped to the customer.) Using the client-provided Excel file, perform the following:

1. Verify the data set is complete by summing the sales column and agreeing to the sales figure recorded in the client's general ledger. Write a sentence that indicates you have agreed the sales amount to the amount in the client's general ledger.

2. Using the best practices outlined in Illustration 2.57, create a pie chart that depicts sales by region for 2025 and identify the region with the largest sales. Is a pie chart the best visual for this question? Why or why not?

3. **Dig Deeper:** Analyze the data set to understand the company's largest customers. Present your analysis in the form of a visualization.

PR 2.4 (LO 2, 5) 〔 Data 〕 〔 Financial Accounting 〕 〔 Managerial Accounting 〕 **PivotTables and Bar Charts**
You are an accountant for U.S. Outdoor Adventures preparing an analysis of sales for the monthly internal sales analysis report.

1. Create an Excel PivotTable to identify if there is a monthly sales pattern for total sales or from 2024 to 2025. Format the PivotTable so the sales amounts are in currency with zero decimal places.

2. Create a bar chart of monthly sales from 2024 to 2025. Does this chart help determine if there is a monthly sales pattern? Why or why not?

3. **Dig Deeper:** Create a PivotTable and a line chart to illustrate monthly sales patterns by product category in 2024 and 2025. What does the line chart reveal about product category sales patterns?

Professional Application Case   PizzaGotTaste, Inc.

In 2020, Antonio Ricci started PizzaGotTaste, Inc. with an old family recipe and one food truck in Fort Lauderdale, Florida. PizzaGotTaste serves 11 types of pizzas, as well as breadsticks and chicken wings. They operate at local breweries in the Fort Lauderdale and Orlando areas. In 2021, Antonio purchased a second food truck that his son, Enzo, operates in Orlando, FL.

Antonio and Enzo believe their business is doing well and are considering expanding to other Florida cities. This is the income statement for the last two years.

PizzaGotTaste Income Statement 2024 and 2025

		2024	2025
Revenues			
	Truck 1	$151,200	$333,396
	Truck 2	$100,800	$222,264
	Total Revenues	$252,000	$555,660
Expenses and Costs			
	Cost of Goods Sold	$138,600	$305,613
	Marketing	$ 2,000	$ 2,000
	Salaries	$133,890	$155,600
	Other Expenses	$ 3,500	$ 4,000
	Total Expenses and Costs	$277,990	$467,213
EBITDA		($25,990)	$ 88,447
	Depreciation—Trucks	$43,750	$ 43,750
EBIT		($69,740)	$ 44,697
	Interest—Truck Loan	$25,856	$ 20,506
Pretax Income		($95,596)	$ 24,191
	Income Tax Expense	$ 0	$ 0
Net Income		($95,596)	$ 24,191
	Net Operating Loss Carryforward	($95,596)	($71,405)

- The business was operating at loss in 2024. This was largely due to the start-up costs of the second truck and because Antonio and Enzo were still searching for the best locations in Fort Lauderdale and Orlando for their trucks.
- The company began to turn a profit in 2025. Sales nearly doubled for the Fort Lauderdale truck and more than doubled for the Orlando truck.
- With the rapid increase in sales, Antonio and Enzo needed a better way to capture their financial and nonfinancial data.

They hired the accounting firm DGJ, LLC to create a database for them. The fields in each table are shown in the diagram. Primary keys are identified with a key symbol preceding the field name.

PizzaGotTaste Database

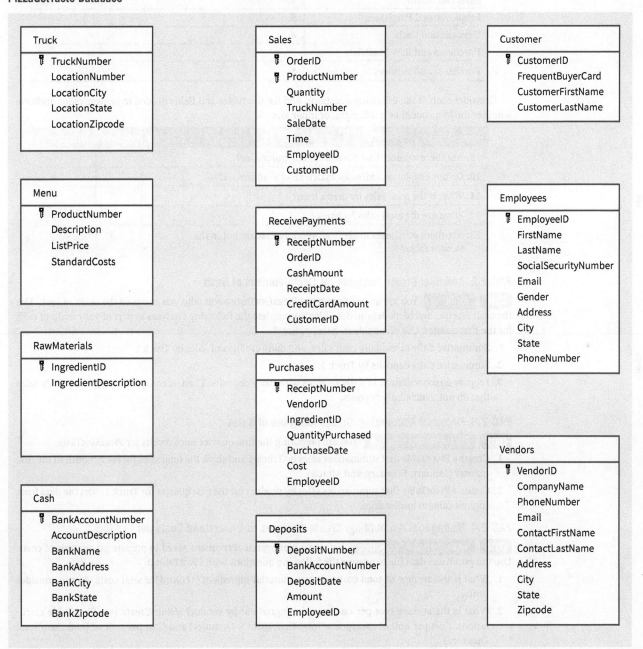

Truck
- 🔑 TruckNumber
- LocationNumber
- LocationCity
- LocationState
- LocationZipcode

Menu
- 🔑 ProductNumber
- Description
- ListPrice
- StandardCosts

RawMaterials
- 🔑 IngredientID
- IngredientDescription

Cash
- 🔑 BankAccountNumber
- AccountDescription
- BankName
- BankAddress
- BankCity
- BankState
- BankZipcode

Sales
- 🔑 OrderID
- 🔑 ProductNumber
- Quantity
- TruckNumber
- SaleDate
- Time
- EmployeeID
- CustomerID

ReceivePayments
- 🔑 ReceiptNumber
- OrderID
- CashAmount
- ReceiptDate
- CreditCardAmount
- CustomerID

Purchases
- 🔑 ReceiptNumber
- VendorID
- IngredientID
- QuantityPurchased
- PurchaseDate
- Cost
- EmployeeID

Deposits
- 🔑 DepositNumber
- BankAccountNumber
- DepositDate
- Amount
- EmployeeID

Customer
- 🔑 CustomerID
- FrequentBuyerCard
- CustomerFirstName
- CustomerLastName

Employees
- 🔑 EmployeeID
- FirstName
- LastName
- SocialSecurityNumber
- Email
- Gender
- Address
- City
- State
- PhoneNumber

Vendors
- 🔑 VendorID
- CompanyName
- PhoneNumber
- Email
- ContactFirstName
- ContactLastName
- Address
- City
- State
- Zipcode

PAC 2.1 Accounting Information Systems: Understand Relational Database Structure

[Accounting Information Systems] You are an accountant at the accounting firm, DGJ, that is helping PizzaGotTaste create a relational database for their business. You have already created the tables shown previously. Now, you must create joins between the tables.

Identify the fields that would create a join between the following tables:

Tables	Fields
Sales and Customer	1.
Sales and Employee	2.
Sales and Truck	3.
Sales and Menu	4.
Employee and Purchases	5.
Deposits and Cash	6.
Purchases and Raw Materials	7.
Purchases and Vendors	8.

Consider each of the following questions, and list the tables and fields needed to answer them. Indicate whether the join should be a left, right, or inner join.

Question	Table	Fields	Join type
9. Are there vendors that have not made purchases?			
10. Do any employee addresses match vendor addresses?			
11. What is the total sales by menu item?			
12. What are the total sales by truck?			
13. Are there purchases made from vendors that are not in the Vendor table?			

PAC 2.2 Auditing: Create Analyses for Completeness of Cash

[Data] [Auditing] You are an auditor on the PizzaGotTaste audit who was assigned the audit of cash. Use the cash receipts and bank deposit data files to complete the following analyses as part of your audit of cash for the first quarter. Use pivottables where applicable.

1. Summarize daily sales, daily cash sales, and daily credit card sales by Truck 1.
2. Summarize daily deposits by Truck 1.
3. Prepare a reconciliation of daily receipts with daily deposits. Then, identify if there are any daily sales that do not match daily deposits.

PAC 2.3 Financial Accounting: Create Analyses of Sales

[Data] [Financial Accounting] You are preparing the first quarter sales results for PizzaGotTaste.

1. Create a PivotTable that summarizes sales by Truck 1 and show the total sales for each month in the first quarter (January, February, and March).
2. Create a PivotTable that summarizes sales by product for the first quarter for Truck 1. Sort the data from highest sales to lowest sales.

PAC 2.4 Managerial Accounting: Create Analyses to Understand Costs per Product

[Data] [Managerial Accounting] You are a managerial accountant asked to prepare an analysis of costs. Use the purchases data file to answer the following questions with PivotTables:

1. What is the average of total costs per raw material ingredient? (*Hint*: Use total costs, do not consider units).
2. What is the average cost per raw material ingredient by vendor? (*Hint*: Create two PivotTable calculations. Cost per unit of measure = Total Cost/(Size × Quantity) and Cost per unit = Total Cost/Total Quantity)
3. Are there vendors that are charging higher than average costs for ingredients?

PAC 2.5 Tax Accounting: Create Analyses to Plan for Expansion

[Data] [Tax Accounting] PizzaGotTaste is considering purchasing another food truck, and Florida charges sales tax on food truck sales. Antonio wants to choose the best location, not only for sales, but also for sales tax. Use the Florida population and sales tax by city data files to create a visualization that shows which cities have the largest populations and which also shows the tax rates by city.

1. What are the top 10 most populated cities in Florida?

2. Use a PivotTable to determine the cities with the 10 lowest tax rates.

3. PizzaGotTaste is considering Tallahassee as a potential city for a new truck. Antonio estimates that sales in the first year will be $150,000. How much sales tax will be collected?

Motivations and Objectives for Data Analysis

CHAPTER PREVIEW

Data analytics is a rapidly evolving and exciting field, and there is a demand within it for accounting professionals who can use new tools to analyze large amounts of data. Analyzing data and extracting information from it leads to informed decisions, and businesses today want people with these skills.

But a data analytics project does not start with a deep dive into the data. Planning the project, including understanding the motivation for performing it and developing its specific goals, is equally important. Data analytics can be costly, complex, and time consuming. A detailed plan links the project's motivation with its objective and key questions, which helps us select the best analysis method. Without a plan, it is possible to overlook important information or critical questions, which could make the analysis less effective or even useless.

The first stage of the data analytics process is planning. It includes identifying the motivation for the project, which helps determine the objective. A project's objective drives everything from the questions asked to the analysis choices we make to find the answers to them. This chapter examines the link between understanding why the project is necessary and developing a focused project objective.

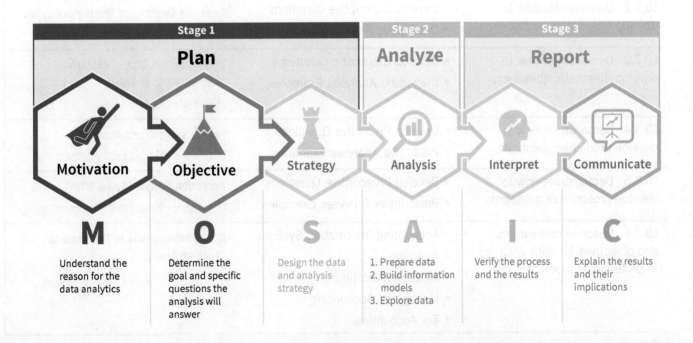

	Stage 1			Stage 2	Stage 3	
	Plan			**Analyze**	**Report**	
M Motivation	**O** Objective	**S** Strategy		**A** Analysis	**I** Interpret	**C** Communicate
Understand the reason for the data analytics	Determine the goal and specific questions the analysis will answer	Design the data and analysis strategy		1. Prepare data 2. Build information models 3. Explore data	Verify the process and the results	Explain the results and their implications

 **Why Do Motivations and Objectives Matter for Data Analysis Projects?**

Georgia lived with her parents while earning an undergraduate accounting degree at the local university. Immediately after graduation, she completed an auditing internship during busy season. She is entering a master's program of accounting in the fall semester.

On the first day of my internship, I learned professional accountants follow a process each time they work on a data analyses project. **First, they understand the motivation for their projects, which in turn influences their specific work objectives. When they are clear about their motivation and objectives, they can plan a successful strategy for their data analyses projects.**

I also learned that professional accountants are motivated by more than personal career goals. Auditors want to add value to their firms and clients by assuring them that their financial statements are reliable and accurate. After all, good information means better capital markets, lending decisions, government relationships, and business partnerships.

This helped me realize that I was also motivated by more than just getting that great job after college. I want to make a difference in the world, and I want to honor my parents' hard work raising me to be successful. This awareness of my motivations has helped me become more committed to my objective and my studies!

Chapter Roadmap

LEARNING OBJECTIVES	TOPICS	APPLY IT
LO 3.1 Summarize the relationship between motivations, objectives, and data analysis questions.	• Understanding Motivation • Clear Objectives Lead to Focused Data Analysis Questions	**Link Motivation to Objectives** (Example: Auditing)
LO 3.2 Demonstrate how to develop descriptive questions.	• Develop Descriptive Questions • Descriptive Analyses Examples	**Describe Customers' Buying Behaviors** (Example: Financial Accounting)
LO 3.3 Demonstrate how to develop diagnostic questions.	• Develop Diagnostic Questions • Diagnostic Analyses Examples	**Determine the Risk of Material Misstatement of Sales** (Example: Auditing)
LO 3.4 Demonstrate how to develop predictive questions.	• Develop Predictive Questions • Predictive Analyses Examples	**Plan a Sales Trend Analysis** (Example: Managerial Accounting)
LO 3.5 Demonstrate how to develop prescriptive questions.	• Develop Prescriptive Questions • Prescriptive Analyses Examples	**Prescribe Optimal Sales Mix** (Example: Managerial Accounting)
LO 3.6 Describe motivations and objectives for data analytics in professional practice.	• Accounting Information Systems • Auditing • Financial Accounting • Managerial Accounting • Tax Accounting	**Match Motivations to Professional Practice Areas**

Data The Data tag appears in the chapter when the data for an example, illustration, or application are available in the book's product page on www.wiley.com.

Data analytics software is continuously changing, and there may be more recent versions of the software referenced in this chapter.

3.1 How Does Motivation Inform Objective-Based Data Analysis Questions?

It is easier to stay focused on a task's objective when we know why we are performing it in the first place. Understanding the motivation to perform an analysis and identifying its objective also helps create specific, objective-based questions. After all, it is impossible to get the right answers if we do not know what to ask.

Understanding Motivation

Motivation in data analytics in accounting is the reason the analysis is being performed. The "why" behind a project can vary, but data analysis projects are typically motivated by four forces:

- **Opportunity:** Evaluating new opportunities that will benefit the organization.
- **Professional issues:** Evaluating changes due to new laws, regulations, or changes in accounting practices.
- **Problem-solving:** Solving a problem or issue that the organization is facing.
- **Process and performance assessment:** Understanding and improving the processes and performance of the organization.

Illustration 3.1 describes some common motivations and includes an example from a company called Super Scooters, which manufactures and sells a variety of scooters.

In each Super Scooters example, the motivation for the analysis is to either describe the situation's potential, diagnose the causal factors or determine operational change, predict sales revenues or net income, or prescribe the best course of action. Regardless of the motivation's source,

ILLUSTRATION 3.1 Motivation for Data Analytics in Accounting

Motivation	Description	Role of Data Analysis	Super Scooters Example
Opportunities	New, potentially advantageous occasions or channels.	Reliable evidence justifies new products and services. Evidence to justify changing resource allocations and capital sourcing.	• New scooter models. • New services, such as scooter training classes. • Store expansions.
Professional Issues and Requirements	Compliance with new or upcoming regulations, laws, or changes in practices.	Understanding changes improves responses. Evaluating new accounting regulations can positively impact client financial statements.	The local government may have recently allowed scooters, unmotorized and motorized, on all paved bicycle paths and road lanes in the city.
Problem-Solving	Solving problems related to risks and issues around clients, technologies, employees, operations, and supply chains.	Solving problems to minimize productivity losses.	Super Scooters may need to investigate why a particular scooter is no longer selling as well as it did, or why it is not selling as well as their other scooter products.
Process and Performance Assessment	Evaluating financial statements for material misstatements or risks of material misstatement. Inspecting operational efficiency and effectiveness at the individual, functional, unit, and business levels.	Audit data analytics can provide risk assessment and substantive audit evidence. Evaluating the success of a new strategy helps management make future decisions.	Super Scooters may need to evaluate the contribution margin and inventory turnover for each product line, or the performance of each salesperson.

the data analyses choices we make depend on what can be gained from the analysis. If its potential benefits outweigh the costs of doing it, then stakeholders will consider it a valuable analysis.

Clear Objectives Lead to Focused Data Analysis Questions

You just learned that the four common motivators for data analytics in accounting are opportunities, regulatory changes, solving problems, and process and performance evaluation. For example, a company with an underperforming business unit will evaluate its performance to understand why. A successful data analytics project depends on a more specific statement, which will then inform the questions that will be asked in the analysis.

Determine the Objective

The objective of a data analysis project naturally follows the motivation. Let's go back to that common motivation for data analysis, an underperforming business unit:

- The motivation is to solve a problem by evaluating the unit's performance to discover why it is underperforming.
- It is necessary to be more specific because poor performance could have several causes.
- The first step is to specify the areas of performance to investigate and articulate what those investigations should accomplish.

In other words, it is important to clarify the goal of the data analysis.

Every data analysis project begins with setting an **objective,** which is the project's goal. It is a statement that details what the project will accomplish. A new example can illustrate how to determine a project's objective. Omni Restaurants owns restaurants across five regions in the United States. The financial information for the current year by region is shown in **Illustration 3.2**.

ILLUSTRATION 3.2   Omni Restaurants Financial Performance by Region

	Region 1	Region 2	Region 3	Region 4	Region 5	Total
Dine in Sales	$226,800	$333,396	$367,569	$405,245	$446,783	$1,779,793
Takeout Sales	$151,200	$222,264	$245,046	$270,163	$297,855	$1,186,528
Total Revenues	$378,000	$555,660	$612,615	$675,408	$744,638	$2,966,321
Cost of Goods Sold	$ 86,940	$122,245	$122,523	$128,328	$134,035	$ 594,071
Gross Profit	$291,060	$433,415	$490,092	$547,080	$610,603	$2,372,250
Lease	$ 90,000	$ 61,500	$ 63,038	$ 64,613	$ 66,229	$ 345,380
Marketing	$ 30,000	$ 25,000	$ 25,000	$ 25,000	$ 25,000	$ 130,000
Salaries	$200,835	$204,030	$224,943	$236,190	$248,000	$1,113,998
Other Expenses	$ 5,250	$ 4,000	$ 4,500	$ 5,000	$ 5,500	$ 24,250
Total S G & A Expenses	$326,085	$294,530	$317,481	$330,803	$344,729	$1,613,628
Depreciation	$ 36,960	$ 36,960	$ 36,960	$ 36,960	$ 36,960	$ 184,800
Interest	$ 23,621	$ 20,668	$ 17,716	$ 14,763	$ 11,810	$ 88,578
Earnings Before Tax	($95,606)	$ 81,257	$117,935	$164,554	$217,104	$ 485,244
Income Tax Expenses	0	$ 29,526	$ 42,853	$ 59,344	$ 77,911	$ 209,634
Net Income (Loss)	($95,606)	$ 51,731	$ 75,082	$105,210	$139,193	$ 275,610

Illustration 3.2 shows that Omni is losing money in one region:

- **Motivation:** They are concerned about the losses in Region 1 and want to understand what is driving them.
- **General objective:** Eliminate those financial losses.

Now we have moved from motivation to objective. But the objective is so general that it is difficult to decide where to begin the analysis. A specific objective would narrow the analysis' focus. In the Omni case, only one region is experiencing losses:

- **Specific objective:** Identify the factors driving the losses in Region 1.

After the objective is clear and specific, formulate the questions that will achieve that objective once they are addressed.

Articulate Questions

Asking the wrong questions leads to answers that do not address the objective. Good questions are clear, concise, and measurable. So, how are good questions developed? Evaluate each question as to whether it addresses the objective, focuses on a single issue, is measurable, and if the data necessary to answer it are available. If the question does not meet this criteria, then either revise it, break it down, or drop it. Use the flowchart in **Illustration 3.3** to develop specific data analysis questions.

ILLUSTRATION 3.3   Flowchart for Developing Data Analysis Questions

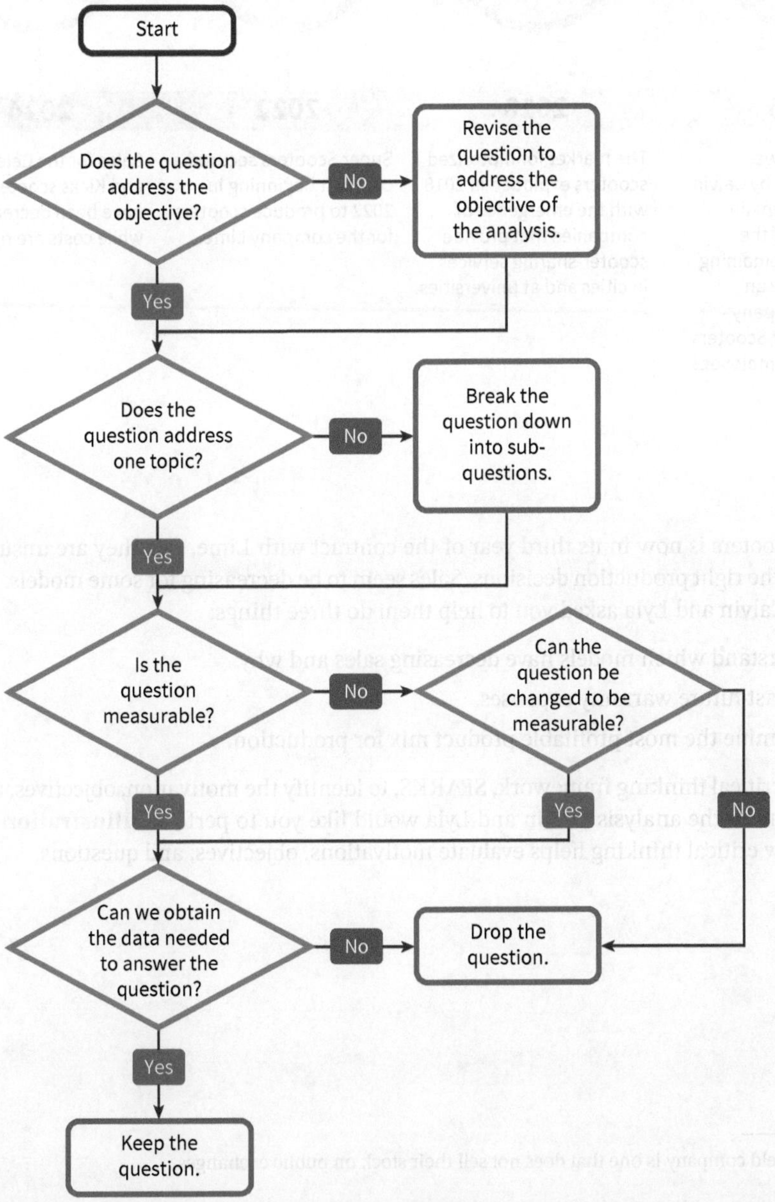

A critical thinking approach to question development can help with this process. Recall that thinking critically when performing data analytics involves considering those who are impacted by the analysis, its purpose, considering a variety of alternatives at each step, controlling for risks, acquiring the right information or knowledge, and reflecting on past and current projects.

The Role of Critical Thinking

Let's use the Super Scooters example to show the importance of critically evaluating motivation, objectives, and questions at this stage of the data analysis process. Assume you are an accountant for the company Super Scooters. Super Scooters is a privately held company[1] that produces three models of motorized scooters (two electric and one gas-powered) and one nonmotorized scooter (**Illustration 3.4**).

ILLUSTRATION 3.4 Super Scooters Company Timeline

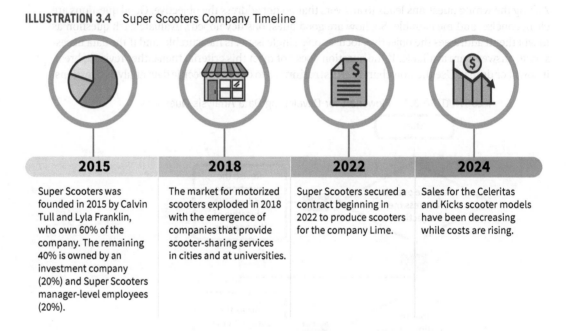

2015	2018	2022	2024
Super Scooters was founded in 2015 by Calvin Tull and Lyla Franklin, who own 60% of the company. The remaining 40% is owned by an investment company (20%) and Super Scooters manager-level employees (20%).	The market for motorized scooters exploded in 2018 with the emergence of companies that provide scooter-sharing services in cities and at universities.	Super Scooters secured a contract beginning in 2022 to produce scooters for the company Lime.	Sales for the Celeritas and Kicks scooter models have been decreasing while costs are rising.

Super Scooters is now in its third year of the contract with Lime, and they are unsure if they have made the right production decisions. Sales seem to be decreasing for some models, and costs are rising. Calvin and Lyla asked you to help them do three things:

1. Understand which models have decreasing sales and why.
2. Forecast future warranty expenses.
3. Determine the most profitable product mix for production.

Use the critical thinking framework, SPARKS, to identify the motivation, objectives, and questions relevant to the analysis Calvin and Lyla would like you to perform. **Illustration 3.5** summarizes how critical thinking helps evaluate motivations, objectives, and questions.

---

[1]A privately held company is one that does not sell their stock on public exchanges.

ILLUSTRATION 3.5 Thinking Critically About Motivations and Objectives

Critical Thinking Element	Why It Matters	Super Scooters Example
S Stakeholders	Considering the perspectives of stakeholders helps identify the objective and develop good questions.	The internal stakeholders are Lyla and Calvin. Their motivation is to better understand company performance. The objective is to describe current performance, diagnose issues related to poor performance, predict future sales, and make recommendations for improvements.
P Purpose	Critically thinking through the purpose of data analyses is the link between a defined objective and specific questions: • A purpose is the reason something is done or created. • An objective is something we plan to do, or a goal. The questions will be different depending on whether the purpose is to describe and diagnose current conditions or predict and prescribe future outcomes.	Based on the objectives, the purpose is to: • Describe what is happening now and diagnose issues related to poor performance. • Predict future sales. • Prescribe a profitable sales mix.
A Alternatives	Evaluating different methods of analysis increases the likelihood of selecting the best option for the project's purpose.	Develop several alternative methods for performing the analysis to describe performance over the past year. Consider how likely each option is to provide valuable information. Rank the alternatives and choose the one with the highest expected value.
R Risks	Being aware of potential risks makes it possible to also mitigate them when evaluating motivation, objectives, and questions.	It may be tempting to make Calvin and Lyla happy with a positive outlook in the predictive model. Be aware of that bias and develop objectives and questions that will not be influenced by it.
K Knowledge	Successfully completing a project requires confirming we have the necessary knowledge to do so or doing additional research to obtain that knowledge.	One purpose of the Super Scooters analysis is to predict future sales and expenses. If you do not know how to prepare a predictive analysis, you must do one of two things: • Hire someone to prepare the predictive analysis. • Learn how to do the analysis.
S Self-Reflection	Understanding the purpose of the analysis makes it easier to apply the experience of performing it to future data analytics contexts and tasks. Similarly, considering past experiences can help identify objectives and develop questions.	Assessing whether you should have performed the analyses may depend on whether the information lead to better decisions by management. If it did not, then consider why. Only then can you compare expected net benefits to the actual net benefits.

Auditing Best friends Luanne and Maxine had been making baked goods for a friend who owned a local coffee shop. Their delicious baked goods soon had so many fans that Luanne and Maxine had to rent commercial kitchen space to keep up with demand. Now their business, Best Bakes Bakery, provides baked goods for a variety of coffee shops and restaurants.

They want to expand their operations into other cities and are looking for potential investors. They believe a CPA's opinion on their financial statements will help convince investors to invest in their company.

The owners hired your CPA firm to prepare a review of their financial statements. Best Bakes Bakery is the first bakery business for your firm, and you are the external auditor assigned to the engagement. Your supervisor asked you to use data analytics for the risk assessment:

- You have the last three years of financial statement data and must calculate several ratios relevant to the company's operations.
- Your supervisor believes the analysis will identify areas of potentially higher risk of material misstatement.

1. Which category of motivation applies to this scenario?
2. Who are the stakeholders in your data analysis?
3. What is the objective of your analysis?

SOLUTION
1. The motivation is process and performance evaluation. The analysis of financial ratios will provide information relevant to the risk assessment of the potential for material misstatements.
2. You, your audit firm, and the client are the internal stakeholders. The client's investors and creditors are the external stakeholders.
3. The objective of the analysis is to determine the potential risk of material misstatements in the financial statements.

3.2 What Are Descriptive Objectives?

LEARNING OBJECTIVE ❷
Demonstrate how to develop descriptive questions.

A data analysis project with the objective to understand something that is currently happening or that has happened requires descriptive questions. These types of questions are answered using descriptive analytics. Descriptive questions are often the first asked in any analysis because understanding the data is necessary before beginning more advanced analyses.

Develop Descriptive Questions

Descriptive questions are designed to better understand data to answer business questions. To develop good descriptive questions, first identify the objective of the analysis, then break that down into questions. Remember, a good question is one that relates to the objective, is specific, measurable, and can be answered with the available data.

Let's continue with the Super Scooters example to illustrate. **Illustration 3.6** provides the financial information for the years 2023 through 2025.

ILLUSTRATION 3.6   Super Scooters' Income Statements: 2023–2025

	Year Ended December 31		
	2023	2024	2025
Gross Sales	$4,924,816	$10,506,334	$11,378,847
Total Variable Costs	$2,190,588	$ 4,922,488	$ 5,416,827
Contribution Margin	$2,734,228	$ 5,583,846	$ 5,962,020
Total Fixed Costs	$ 579,988	$ 1,027,391	$ 1,042,201
Net Income	$2,154,240	$ 4,556,455	$ 4,919,819

While sales and net revenue have increased, two of the models have decreasing net revenue (**Illustration 3.7**).

ILLUSTRATION 3.7   Scooter Model Revenue: 2023–2025

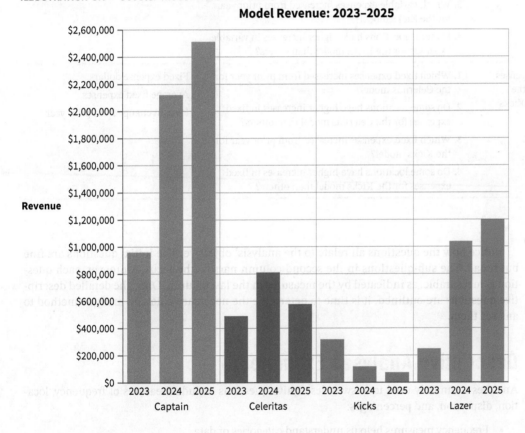

Super Scooters wants to understand the decreases in net revenue for the Celeritas and Kicks models. What questions should they ask of the data? What possible measure(s) can be used to answer the questions?

Illustration 3.8 provides examples of both initial questions and sub-questions (in other words, more detailed questions).

ILLUSTRATION 3.8 Descriptive Questions to Understand Decreases in Revenue at Super Scooters

Objective	Initial Questions	Sub-Questions	Possible Measures
Understand decreases in net revenue for the Celeritas and Kicks models.	Have sales decreased for the Celeritas and Kicks models?	**1.** Have sales decreased for the Celeritas model? **2.** Have sales decreased in all locations for the Celeritas model? **3.** Have sales decreased for the Kicks model? **4.** Have sales decreased in all locations for the Kicks model?	Gross sales dollars Average gross sales dollars Sales volume
	Have expenses increased for the Celeritas and Kicks models?	**1.** Have expenses increased in all locations for the Celeritas model? **2.** Have expenses increased in all locations for the Kicks model?	Total expense dollars Average total expense dollars Percent change from prior year
	Have variable expenses increased for the Celeritas and Kicks models?	**1.** Which variable expenses increased from prior year for the Celeritas model? **2.** Do some locations have higher increases in variable expenses for the Celeritas model than others? **3.** Which variable expenses increased from prior year for the Kicks model? **4.** Do some locations have higher increases in variable expenses for the Kicks model than others?	Variable expense dollars Average variable expenses Percent change from prior year
	Have fixed expenses increased for the Celeritas and Kicks models?	**1.** Which fixed expenses increased from prior year for the Celeritas model? **2.** Do some locations have higher increases in fixed expenses for the Celeritas model than others? **3.** Which fixed expenses increased from prior year for the Kicks model? **4.** Do some locations have higher increases in fixed expenses for the Kicks model than others?	Fixed expense dollars Average fixed expenses Percent change from prior year

Notice how the questions all relate to the analysis' objective. The initial questions are fine but broad. The sub-questions in the second column narrow the focus. Moreover, each question is measurable, as indicated by the measures in the last column. Once the detailed descriptive questions are outlined, it is time to determine the necessary data and analysis method to answer them.

Descriptive Analyses Examples

Analyses commonly used to answer descriptive questions include measures of frequency, location, dispersion, and percentages:

- Frequency measures help us understand categories of data.
- Measures of location (mean, median, and mode) reveal average observations in a data set.
- Measures of dispersion (minimum, maximum, range, variance, and standard deviation) show how much variance there is among the observations in the data set.
- Measures of percentage change compare results to prior periods and the percent of total.

Data Let's demonstrate an example using the questions identified in Illustration 3.8.

It is possible to discover if gross sales have decreased for the Celeritas model by using the measure gross sales. Several different analyses can determine if gross sales have decreased:

- Gross sales dollars: total measure
- Sales volume: total measure
- Average unit sales price

A PivotTable in Microsoft Excel created with the Super Scooter data prepares a descriptive analysis for this question (**Illustration 3.9**).

Model	Total Gross Sales	Total Sales Volume	Average of Unit Sale Price
⊟ Celeritas			
⊞ 2023	$ 1,256,478.00	3,595	$ 350.25
⊞ 2024	$ 2,081,584.00	5,932	$ 350.57
⊞ 2025	$ 1,488,293.00	4,258	$ 347.92
⊟ Kicks			
⊞ 2023	$ 628,271.00	3,385	$ 187.88
⊞ 2024	$ 279,848.00	1,816	$ 148.37
⊞ 2025	$ 221,134.00	1,695	$ 136.21

ILLUSTRATION 3.9 Descriptive Analysis of Celeritas and Kicks Sales

The sales data confirms the Celeritas and Kicks models each declined from 2024 to 2025. Interestingly, both sales volume and average price decreased, so the decline is a combination of both volume and price. The next step is answering the next sub-question: Did sales decrease in all locations?

Illustration 3.10 shows the change in average gross sales dollars, which is a measure of location. It is the result of a descriptive analysis in Tableau that shows the change in gross sales from 2023 to 2025 by location for the Celeritas model. This is a highlight table where the darker color signals a larger decrease. (**Data** See **How To 3.1** at the end of this chapter to learn how to create this table in Tableau.)

How To

Change in Gross Sales from 2024—Celeritas

	2025
Seattle	$ (140,206)
Dallas	$ (106,783)
Charlotte	$ (94,794)
Boston	$ (88,837)
Chicago	$ (58,619)
Miami	$ (57,786)
Salt Lake City	$ (46,867)
Phoenix	$ (20,787)

Difference in Gross Sales

−140K $ (20,787)

ILLUSTRATION 3.10 Descriptive Analysis of Celeritas' Change in Gross Sales by Location

The Seattle location had the largest total gross sales decrease from 2024 at $140,206. Dallas had the second largest decrease at $106,783. However, it is also clear that sales have dropped in all locations. The next step is to determine why sales have decreased, which will require diagnostic analytics.

APPLY IT 3.2

Describe Customers' Buying Behaviors

Data   Financial Accounting   Best Bakes Bakery would like to better understand their top customers' buying behavior. You have been given sales transactions for the years 2022 to 2025. An excerpt from the file follows:

SalesOrder Number	Customer Number	Customer Name	Customer Address	Customer City	Customer ZipCode	Customer State	Customer Phone
101	521121	Bluebird Cafe	524 W Laurel St	Fort Collins	80521	CO	(720) 296-2323
101	521121	Bluebird Cafe	524 W Laurel St	Fort Collins	80521	CO	(720) 296-2323
101	521121	Bluebird Cafe	524 W Laurel St	Fort Collins	80521	CO	(720) 296-2323
101	521121	Bluebird Cafe	524 W Laurel St	Fort Collins	80521	CO	(720) 296-2323
101	521121	Bluebird Cafe	524 W Laurel St	Fort Collins	80521	CO	(720) 296-2323
101	521121	Bluebird Cafe	524 W Laurel St	Fort Collins	80521	CO	(720) 296-2323
102	521425	Walrus Ice Cream	125 W Mountain Ave	Fort Collins	80521	CO	(303) 674-0930

Inventory Code	Inventory Description	SalesOrder Date	SalesOrder Quantity	Inventory Price	Gross Sales	Inventory Cost	Costof GoodsSold	Profit
853200	Caramel Apple	2/19/2022	36	$ 3.45	$ 124.20	$ 1.85	$ 66.60	$ 57.60
853300	Poppyseed Bagel	2/19/2022	24	$ 4.85	$ 116.40	$ 2.00	$ 48.00	$ 68.40
853500	Cheesecake Bite	2/19/2022	25	$ 3.40	$ 85.00	$ 1.60	$ 40.00	$ 45.00
853600	Chocolate Chip Cookie	2/19/2022	30	$ 3.20	$ 96.00	$ 2.05	$ 61.50	$ 34.50
853800	Blueberry Scone	2/19/2022	24	$ 4.10	$ 98.40	$ 1.45	$ 34.80	$ 63.60
853900	Raspberry Scone	2/19/2022	10	$ 4.05	$ 40.50	$ 3.40	$ 34.00	$ 6.50
853100	Cinnamon Bun	3/10/2022	24	$ 4.35	$ 104.40	$ 2.90	$ 69.60	$ 34.80

1. What is the objective of the analysis?
2. Develop three questions relevant to the objective, and describe the measures necessary to answer the questions.
3. What analyses will you use to answer these questions?

SOLUTION

1. The objective of the analysis is to identify the top customers and evaluate what products they purchase.

2.
Questions	Measures
1. Who are the top five customers?	Gross sales, sales volume, and profit margin
2. What are the top five products sold?	Sales volume and gross sales
3. What are the spending patterns for the top five customers?	Sales volume and gross sales

3. Analyses for the three questions:
   - Descriptive analysis: Top five customers by year for each of the measures compared to average for all customers.
   - Descriptive analysis: Five highest selling products by year for each of the measures compared to average for all products.
   - Descriptive analysis: Analysis showing sales by month or quarter for each year for the top five customers. A bar chart or a line chart could be used.

3.3 What Are Diagnostic Objectives?

LEARNING OBJECTIVE ❸

Demonstrate how to develop diagnostic questions.

Once we know what has happened, the next step is to determine *why*. Diagnostic questions build on descriptive analyses and further explore the data to find the outcome's cause. Diagnostic analytics do this by looking for anomalies, correlations, patterns, or trends.

Develop Diagnostic Questions

Diagnostic questions identify a problem or issue to understand why an outcome occurred. **Illustration 3.11** shows diagnostic questions based on the results of the descriptive analysis of Super Scooters' sales in the previous section.

ILLUSTRATION 3.11 Diagnostic Questions About Super Scooters' Sales Decline

Objective	Initial Question	Sub-Questions	Possible Measures
Determine why sales are decreasing for the Celeritas and Kicks models.	What is driving the sales volume decrease?	1. Are there anomalies in sales volume for the Celeritas model? 2. Are there anomalies in sales volume for the Kicks model? 3. Are there identifiable patterns in sales volume for the Celeritas model? 4. Are there identifiable patterns in sales volume for the Kicks model?	Sales volume
Understand the large decrease in sales at the Seattle location.	What factors are driving the decrease in sales at the Seattle locations?	1. Are there unusual patterns in the Seattle location sales of Celeritas models? 2. Are there unusual patterns in the Seattle location sales of the Kicks model?	Gross sales dollars Average gross sales dollars Sales volume

Why are sales decreasing, and specifically, why did the Seattle location have the largest decrease? The questions and sub-questions dive deeper into the sales decrease by asking about anomalies and unusual patterns. Now, identify the data and analyses that will answer these questions.

Diagnostic Analyses Examples

There are four common types of diagnostic analyses: anomaly detection, correlation, pattern detection, and trend analysis.

Using the Super Scooters questions in Illustration 3.11, let's examine these sub-questions:

1. Are there identifiable patterns in sales volume for the Celeritas model?
2. Are there unusual patterns in the Seattle location's Celeritas model sales?

Line charts can identify patterns by revealing repeating patterns in the data. **Illustration 3.12** shows Celeritas sales by month for each year.

ILLUSTRATION 3.12 Celeritas Sales Volume Patterns

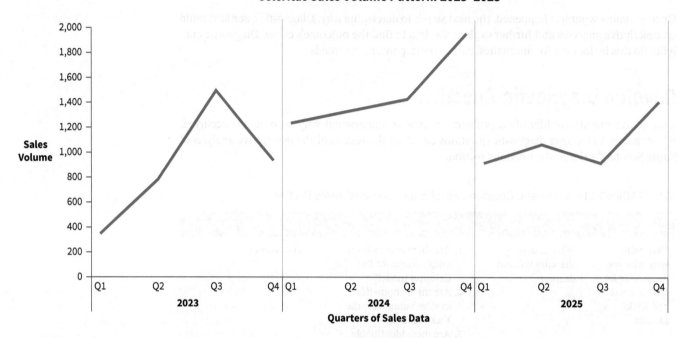

The line charts in Illustration 3.12 do not appear to show a pattern in sales volume for the Celeritas model. However, the line chart shows all locations, and previous analyses revealed the Seattle location had a drop in Celeritas sales.

The sales pattern in years 2023 and 2025 indicate that sales generally increase from the first quarter to the third quarter:

- In 2023 there is a drop in sales in the fourth quarter, but 2024 and 2025 saw an increase in fourth quarter sales.
- However, 2025 sales are below 2024 sales, and there was a large drop in the third quarter.

To understand why sales are lower in 2025 and why there was a drop in the the third quarter of 2025, we must further analyze sales volume by location.

Illustration 3.13 shows an analysis examining monthly sales of the Celeritas at the Seattle location.

The column chart of Celeritas sales over 2025 shows one thing and suggests another:

- In 2025, there are several months with no sales.
- This could be a contributing factor to the decline in overall Celeritas sales in 2025.

The next step would be asking management what happened in March 2025 that led to six months without any sales of the Celeritas model. This also raises additional questions to investigate:

- Did sales drop at the Seattle location only?
- Was the Celeritas model the only product with declining sales?

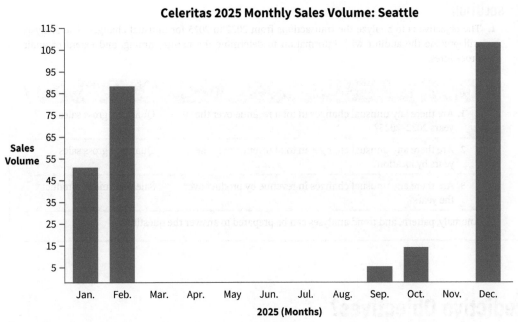

Celeritas 2025 Monthly Sales Volume: Seattle

ILLUSTRATION 3.13 Seattle Location's Monthly Celeritas Sales—2025

This investigative process is called exploratory data analysis, which you learn about later in this course.

During the Best Bakes Bakery financial statement audit, you have been asked to determine if there are unusual changes in sales from prior years that might affect risks of material misstatement. You have been given an excerpt of the transactions in an Excel file so that you know the data available.

APPLY IT 3.3

Determine the Risk of Material Misstatement of Sales

SalesOrder Number	Customer Number	Customer Name	Customer Address	Customer City	Customer ZipCode	Customer State	Customer Phone
101	521121	Bluebird Cafe	524 W Laurel St	Fort Collins	80521	CO	(720) 296-2323
101	521121	Bluebird Cafe	524 W Laurel St	Fort Collins	80521	CO	(720) 296-2323
101	521121	Bluebird Cafe	524 W Laurel St	Fort Collins	80521	CO	(720) 296-2323
101	521121	Bluebird Cafe	524 W Laurel St	Fort Collins	80521	CO	(720) 296-2323
101	521121	Bluebird Cafe	524 W Laurel St	Fort Collins	80521	CO	(720) 296-2323
101	521121	Bluebird Cafe	524 W Laurel St	Fort Collins	80521	CO	(720) 296-2323
102	521425	Walrus Ice Cream	125 W Mountain Ave	Fort Collins	80521	CO	(303) 674-0930

Inventory Code	Inventory Description	SalesOrder Date	SalesOrder Quantity	Inventory Price	Gross Sales	Inventory Cost	Costof GoodsSold	Profit	Profit Margin
853200	Caramel Apple	2/19/2022	36	$ 3.45	$ 124.20	$ 1.85	$ 66.60	$ 57.60	0.463768
853300	Poppyseed Bagel	2/19/2022	24	$ 4.85	$ 116.40	$ 2.00	$ 48.00	$ 68.40	0.587629
853500	Cheesecake Bite	2/19/2022	25	$ 3.40	$ 85.00	$ 1.60	$ 40.00	$ 45.00	0.529412
853600	Chocolate Chip Cookie	2/19/2022	30	$ 3.20	$ 96.00	$ 2.05	$ 61.50	$ 34.50	0.359375
853800	Blueberry Scone	2/19/2022	24	$ 4.10	$ 98.40	$ 1.45	$ 34.80	$ 63.60	0.646341
853900	Raspberry Scone	2/19/2022	10	$ 4.05	$ 40.50	$ 3.40	$ 34.00	$ 6.50	0.160193
853100	Cinnamon Bun	3/10/2022	24	$ 4.35	$ 104.40	$ 2.90	$ 69.60	$ 34.80	0.333333

1. What is the objective of the analysis?
2. Develop three questions relevant to the objective, and state the measures necessary to answer them.
3. What analyses will you use to answer these three questions?

SOLUTION

1. The objective is to analyze the transactions from 2022 to 2025 for unusual changes. The analysis will provide the auditor with information to determine the nature, timing, and extent of audit procedures.

2.

Questions	Measures
1. Are there any unusual changes in total revenue over the years 2022–2025?	Quarterly gross sales
2. Are there any unusual changes in total revenue over the years by location?	Quarterly gross sales
3. Are there any unusual changes in revenue by product over the years?	Sales volume by product

3. Anomaly, pattern, and trend analyses can be prepared to answer the questions.

3.4 What Are Predictive Objectives?

LEARNING OBJECTIVE ❹

Demonstrate how to develop predictive questions.

So far, you have learned how to develop descriptive questions to find out what happened in the past and diagnostic questions to understand why. What if you want to know what may happen in the future? In this case, you would ask **predictive questions**.

Develop Predictive Questions

When making loan decisions, banks use historical information about whether a potential borrower pays bills consistently and on time to predict if they will continue to do so. In the same way, predictive analytics use past and present data to create models so businesses can make predictions.

The use of predictive analytics is not new in the accounting profession, but as the availability of data and software tools to perform predictive analytics has increased, so has performing these analytics in all areas of accounting:

- Financial accountants can identify trends in sales or expenses.
- Cost accountants can predict costs, create forecasts, and evaluate cost drivers.
- Auditors identify potential material misstatements using predictive analytics.
- Tax accountants may use predictive analytics for tax planning.

Suppose Super Scooters is preparing their budget for the next year:

- They want to predict revenue for 2026 assuming a 10% increase in sales volume.
- They also believe there will be a 10% increase in warranty costs.
- Finally, they are considering discontinuing the Celeritas model and want to know if that will change predicted revenue.

What is the overall objective of the data analysis? What questions should Super Scooters ask to meet that objective?

When determining predictive questions, it is helpful to ask, "What do I want to do with the answer?" **Illustration 3.14** shows the overall objective of predicting revenue for 2026, the initial question, plus specific sub-questions.

ILLUSTRATION 3.14
Predictive Questions to
Forecast Super Scooters'
Revenue

Objective	Initial Question	Sub-Questions
Predict revenue for 2026.	How much will revenue change with a 10% increase in sales volume?	How much will revenue change for each model?
		How much will revenue change at each location?
	How will revenue be affected with a 10% increase in warranty costs?	What factors influence warranty expense?
	How will revenue be affected by discontinuing the Celeritas and/or the Kicks model?	How much will revenue at each location be affected by discontinuing the Celeritas and/or the Kicks model?

Like all questions, predictive questions should be related to the objective, specific, measurable, and the appropriate data and analytics should be used to answer them.

Predictive Analyses Examples

Two common analyses that answer predictive questions are trendlines and regression analysis.[2]

Trendlines

Trendlines show the underlying functional relationship of data:

- A **functional relationship** is the effect of an independent variable on a dependent variable.
- A **linear function** shows steady increases or decreases over the range of the independent variable.

The Excel Trendline tool can help determine if the data follow a linear function. Remember that Super Scooters believes warranty costs will rise by 10%. Further, warranty costs are believed to be driven by sales.

Illustration 3.15 shows a trendline created in Excel to determine if there is a linear relationship between sales and warranty expense for Super Scooters.

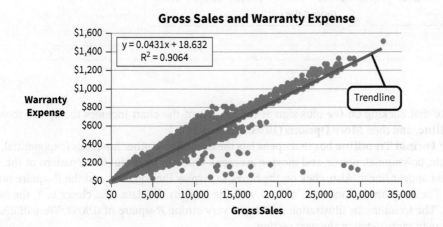

Gross Sales and Warranty Expense

$y = 0.0431x + 18.632$
$R^2 = 0.9064$

ILLUSTRATION 3.15 Trendline
Using Sales and Warranty
Expense

---

[2]There are many other predictive analytical methods, such as artificial intelligence, which are beyond the scope of this chapter.

The trendline supports a linear relationship:

- As gross sale amounts increase, warranty expense also increases.
- The equation for the trendline is shown in the chart: ($y = 0.0431x + 18.632$, $R^2 = 0.9064$).

That equation can be used to predict future warranty expense based on expected sales where y is the amount of warranty expense and x is the amount of the gross sale. For example, if a gross sale was $2,000, then the expected warranty expense would be:

$$(0.0431 \times 2{,}000) + 18.632 = \$104.83$$

If warranty costs increase by 10% as Super Scooters expects, the prediction model can be adjusted by increasing 0.0431 by 10%. Find the trendline tool **Chart Elements** in Excel by clicking on the graph and then the plus sign (**Illustration 3.16**).

ILLUSTRATION 3.16 Trendline Choice in Chart Elements

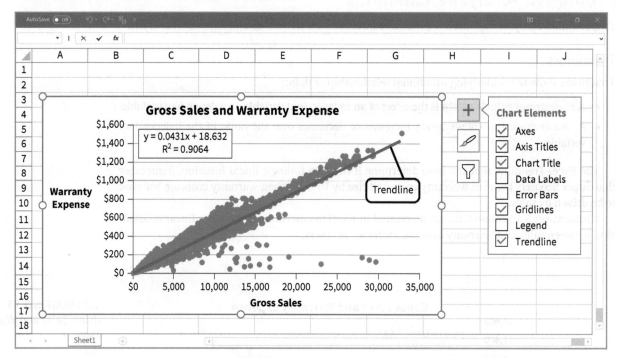

Note that clicking on the plus sign at the top left of the chart includes the option to select **Trendline**, and then **More Options** (**Illustration 3.17**).

The **Format Trendline** box that opens lets the user choose other functions (exponential, logarithmic, polynomial, power, and moving average). This can be useful if the pattern of the data does not appear linear. Also, click on the boxes to display the equation and the R-square on the chart. The R-square is a measure of how well the line fits the data. The closer to 1, the better the fit. The trendline in Illustration 3.16 has a very strong R-square of 0.9064. We will discuss R-square in more detail in the next section.

Linear Regression

While you may not prepare a predictive model during your career, you will likely use predictive models or need to interpret their output. **Linear regression** is a tool for building

ILLUSTRATION 3.17   Trendline Options in Microsoft Excel

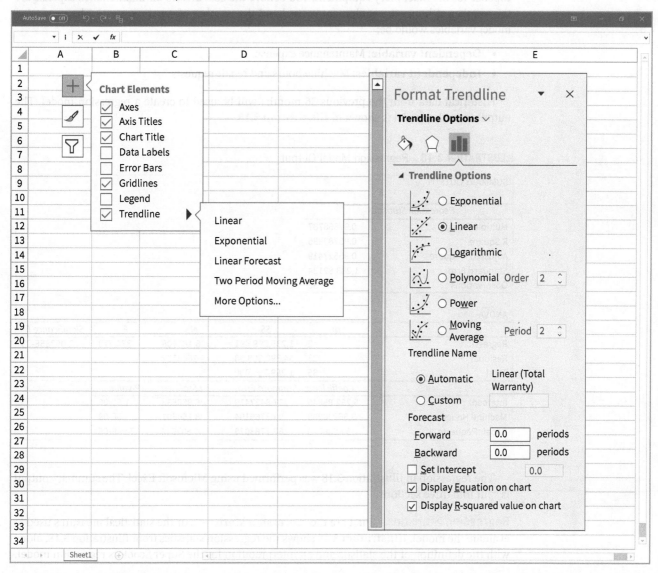

mathematical and statistical models to explain the relationship between a dependent variable and one or more independent variables.

Predictive analytics build models to predict or better understand a phenomenon. To find out what factors influence warranty expense, we would build a model that predicts warranty expense.

Building a model requires identifying the variables that will be included in it:

- A **variable** is a data field used for analysis.
- A **dependent variable** is the outcome measure (warranty expense).
- **Independent variables** are the variables that influence the dependent variable (specific variables that we believe influence warranty expense, such as sales or number of warranty claims).

Simple linear regression involves a single independent variable, while multiple regression involves two or more independent variables. The goal of a regression model is finding the equation of the line that best fits the data.

Let's examine the output of a regression model to understand how they help answer questions. As an accountant at Super Scooters, you are trying to estimate next year's maintenance expense for the machinery equipment. You believe the cost drivers for maintenance expense are the number of hours the equipment is used and the number of repair requests. The regression model variables would be:

- **Dependent variable:** Maintenance expense
- **Independent variables:** Machine hours and repair requests

Historical data from the previous 36 months will be used to create a regression model. The output from the model is shown in **Illustration 3.18**.

ILLUSTRATION 3.18 Regression Model Output

SUMMARY OUTPUT

Regression Statistics					
Multiple R	0.97868787				
R Square	0.95782995				
Adjusted R Square	0.95527419				
Standard Error	1,283.82134				
Observations	36				

ANOVA

	df	SS	MS	F	Significance F
Regression	2	1,235,399,491	6.18E+08	374.773	2.05385E-23
Residual	33	54,390,508.88	1648197		
Total	35	1,289,790,000			

	Coefficients	Standard Error	t Stat	P-value	
Intercept	5,252.85845	897.8427419	5.850533	1.5E-06	
Machine Hours	3.56920298	0.43769194	8.154601	2.05E-09	
Repair Requests	759.836675	168.7763028	4.502034	7.94E-05	

The regression in Illustration 3.18 was performed using Microsoft Excel. The summary output is split into three sections.

Regression Statistics   First are the **regression statistics,** or the statistical measures used to evaluate the model. **Illustration 3.19** shows the regression statistics from Illustration 3.18, along with the definition of the statistic and an interpretation for the Super Scooters regression model.

ILLUSTRATION 3.19 Regression Statistics

Regression Statistics	Definition	Output	Interpretation
Multiple R	• Also called the **correlation coefficient,** it measures the strength of the relationship between the dependent and independent variables. • It is a measure from −1 to 1. A positive number equals a positive correlation, so the variables move in the same direction. A negative number equals a negative correlation, where the variables move in opposite directions.	0.97868787	• Multiple R is 0.978. This is a positive correlation between total expenses and the independent variables in the model (machine hours, repair requests). • As the variables in the model increase, total maintenance expenses will also increase.
R Square (R^2)	• Also called the **coefficient of determination,** it is a measure of how well the regression line fits the data. • R^2 gives the proportion of the variation in the dependent variable that is explained by the independent variables. • The closer the R^2 is to 1, the better the regression line fits to the data.	0.95782995	This shows that 95.8% (0.9578) of the change in total maintenance expense is explained by how many hours the equipment is used (machine hours) and how many repair requests are made.

ILLUSTRATION 3.19   (*Continued*)

Regression Statistics	Definition	Output	Interpretation
Adjusted R^2	• Explains how well the regression line fits the data. • Modifies the value of R^2 by incorporating the sample size and the number of independent variables. • Generally used to evaluate a multiple regression model. • The closer the adjusted R^2 is to 1, the better the fit of the regression line to the data.	0.95527419	Adjusted R^2 is interpreted in the same way as R^2. This shows that 95.5% of total expenses can be explained by how many hours the equipment is used and the number of repair requests made.

Standard Error	• Represents the variability of the observed dependent variable values from the values predicted by the model.
	• If the data are clustered close to the regression line, then the standard error is small (optimal).
	• If the data are more scattered, then it is larger.
		1,283.82134	• The standard error is $1,283.82.
			• To determine if standard error is large or small, compare it to the standard deviation of the dependent variable.
			• In this example, compare the standard error to the standard deviation of total expenses. If the standard error is smaller than the standard deviation, the standard error is acceptable.
			• The mean and standard deviation for total expenses is:
			  • Mean: $27,450
			  • Standard deviation: $6,070

Observations	• The number of observations included in the data set.	36	In the Super Scooters example, it is 36 months of data.

Analysis of Variance (ANOVA)

The next section of the regression output is the ANOVA (analysis of variance). **Illustration 3.20** is the ANOVA section from the regression model.

ILLUSTRATION 3.20   ANOVA Regression Statistics

ANOVA	df	SS	MS	F	Significance F
Regression	2	1,235,399,491	6.18E+08	374.773	2.05385E-23
Residual	33	54,390,508.88	1,648,197		
Total	35	1,289,790,000			

In a multiple linear regression such as this, significance is a hypothesis test of whether the regression model is better than a model with no independent variables. In other words, is the model better than no model at all?

Generally, a model is considered significant if the *F* statistic (*Significance F* in Illustration 3.20) is less than 0.05:

• If *F* is significant, then the model can explain some of the variation of the dependent variable. In other words, it is better than no model at all.

• The ANOVA in Illustration 3.20 has a significance *F* of 2.05385E-23. The notation "E-23" after 2.05385 represents scientific notation, also known as exponential notation. 2.05385E-23 is the same as 0.0000000000000000000000205385. It is clearly a number well below 0.05, so the model is significant.

In other words, the independent variables can explain some of the variation of total expenses, so the model is better than no model at all.

Regression Equation   The last section of the regression summary output provides the information to create the equation to predict the dependent variable:

- The intercept and coefficients of the model represent the equation of the line that best fits the data.
- The key statistic to analyze in this section is the *p*-value for each of the independent variables. Like the *F* statistic, the *p*-value provides a test of significance. In the case of *p*-value, it is a test as to whether the independent variable improves the ability of the model to better predict the dependent variable. A *p*-value of 0.05 or less is generally considered significant.

Let's use the output in **Illustration 3.21** to identify the prediction model for machine maintenance costs and interpret the coefficients.

ILLUSTRATION 3.21   Regression Model

	Coefficients	Standard Error	t Stat	P-value
Intercept	5,252.85845	897.8427419	5.850533	1.5E-06
Machine Hours	3.56920298	0.43769194	8.154601	2.05E-09
Repair Requests	759.836675	168.7763028	4.502034	7.94E-05

Notice that the *p*-values for the independent variables meet the test of being less than 0.05 and are therefore significant. The prediction model will be equal to the intercept plus (or minus if the number is negative) the coefficients of the independent variables times the predicted values for those variables. Based on the regression model in Illustration 3.21, the equation to predict total purchasing department costs is:

$5,252.86 + $3.57 (number of Machine Hours) + $759.84 (number of repair requests)

The calculation of predicted total expenses if there are 2,250 machine hours in one month and 8 repair requests is shown in **Illustration 3.22**. Start with the intercept and add the product of each independent variable coefficient and variable predicted value for a prediction of $19,364.08 of total maintenance costs for the year.

ILLUSTRATION 3.22
Prediction Model Example

	Model Coefficient	Variable Values	Prediction
Intercept	$ 5,252.86	1	$ 5,252.86
Machine Hours	$ 3.57	2,250	$ 8,032.50
Repair Requests	$ 759.84	8	$ 6,078.72
			$ 19,364.08

The model could be interpreted as follows:

- **Intercept:** The intercept does not always have a practical interpretation. It is a result of the model that represents the mean for the response when all the independent variables are zero. It is where the equation function crosses the *y*-axis. However, here the intercept represents the amount of fixed costs that exist regardless of machine hours and repair requests.
- **Machine hours:** Each hour machine equipment is used adds $3.57 to total costs.
- **Repair requests:** Each request adds $759.84 to total costs.

Using a model like the one in Illustration 3.22 helps businesses predict future outcomes. (Data See **How To 3.2** to learn how to perform this regression in Microsoft Excel.)

How To

APPLY IT 3.4

Plan a Sales Trend Analysis

`Data` `Managerial Accounting` As a managerial accountant for Best Bakes Bakery, you are preparing an analysis of sales trends to help create the 2026 operating budget. You have been given sales transactions for the years 2022–2025. Following is an excerpt from the file:

SalesOrder Number	Customer Number	Customer Name	Customer Address	Customer City	Customer ZipCode	Customer State	Customer Phone
101	521121	Bluebird Cafe	524 W Laurel St	Fort Collins	80521	CO	(720) 296-2323
101	521121	Bluebird Cafe	524 W Laurel St	Fort Collins	80521	CO	(720) 296-2323
101	521121	Bluebird Cafe	524 W Laurel St	Fort Collins	80521	CO	(720) 296-2323
101	521121	Bluebird Cafe	524 W Laurel St	Fort Collins	80521	CO	(720) 296-2323
101	521121	Bluebird Cafe	524 W Laurel St	Fort Collins	80521	CO	(720) 296-2323
101	521121	Bluebird Cafe	524 W Laurel St	Fort Collins	80521	CO	(720) 296-2323
102	521425	Walrus Ice Cream	125 W Mountain Ave	Fort Collins	80521	CO	(303) 674-0930

Inventory Code	Inventory Description	SalesOrder Date	SalesOrder Quantity	Inventory Price	Gross Sales	Inventory Cost	Costof GoodsSold	Profit	Profit Margin
853200	Caramel Apple	2/19/2022	36	$ 3.45	$ 124.20	$ 1.85	$ 66.60	$ 57.60	0.463768
853300	Poppyseed Bagel	2/19/2022	24	$ 4.85	$ 116.40	$ 2.00	$ 48.00	$ 68.40	0.587629
853500	Cheesecake Bite	2/19/2022	25	$ 3.40	$ 85.00	$ 1.60	$ 40.00	$ 45.00	0.529412
853600	Chocolate Chip Cookie	2/19/2022	30	$ 3.20	$ 96.00	$ 2.05	$ 61.50	$ 34.50	0.359375
853800	Blueberry Scone	2/19/2022	24	$ 4.10	$ 98.40	$ 1.45	$ 34.80	$ 63.60	0.646341
853900	Raspberry Scone	2/19/2022	10	$ 4.05	$ 40.50	$ 3.40	$ 34.00	$ 6.50	0.160193
853100	Cinnamon Bun	3/10/2022	24	$ 4.35	$ 104.40	$ 2.90	$ 69.60	$ 34.80	0.333333

1. What is the objective of the analysis?
2. Develop three questions relevant to the objective, and state the measures necessary to answer them.
3. What analyses will you use to answer these three questions?

SOLUTION

1. The objective of the analysis is to predict sales for the next year's operating budget.

2.

Questions	Measures
How are sales trending from 2022 to 2025?	Sales volume and average sales price
How are sales trending by product from 2022 to 2025?	Sales volume and average sales price
How are sales trending by location from 2022 to 2025?	Sales volume and average sales price

3. Trendline analysis will provide an estimate of sales trends that can then be applied to the budget for 2026.

3.5 What Are Prescriptive Objectives?

LEARNING OBJECTIVE ❺

Demonstrate how to develop prescriptive questions.

You have learned about questions that help describe what happened, investigate why, and forecast what will happen next. Next, let's examine the questions we ask when we want to know what *should* happen.

Develop Prescriptive Questions

Prescriptive objectives build on descriptions of the present and predictions about the future to determine the best action. **Prescriptive questions** investigate how to take advantage of future opportunities or mitigate a future risk outcome. The analyses specify the actions necessary to achieve the desired outcomes.

In the Super Scooters example, we answered the previous predictive question regarding warranty expenses for 2026. Now, we can address the third analysis requested by Super Scooters—deciding how many units of each model should be produced to meet the 2026 revenue goal. The first step is to clearly articulate the questions.

Illustration 3.23 starts with the objective of determining the most profitable product mix:

- The initial question is more specific. How many scooters should be produced and sold to maximize contribution margin?
- Next, dig deeper by asking about potential constraints that should be considered and how many units of each model should be produced.

ILLUSTRATION 3.23
Prescriptive Question to Determine Super Scooters' Product Mix

Objective	Initial Question	Sub-Questions
Identify the most profitable product mix.	How many scooters should we produce and sell to maximize contribution margin?	Are there constraints that should be included in the optimization model?
		How many units of each model scooter should be produced to maximize contribution margin and satisfy any constraints?

Prescriptive analyses are performed with specific analysis methods and data.

Prescriptive Analyses Examples

The two most common methods of analysis used to answer prescriptive questions are optimization models and what-if analyses.

Linear Optimization

Optimization is the process of selecting values of variables that minimize or maximize some quantity of interest. Optimization modeling helps managers allocate resources more efficiently and make cost/profit decisions. The most common optimization model used in accounting is **linear optimization**. In linear optimization, the model is comprised of:

- **Decision variables:** The unknown values the model seeks to determine.
- **Objective function:** The mathematical equation that describes the output target to minimize or maximize.
- **Constraints:** The limitations, requirements, or other restrictions that must be imposed on any solution, such as demand, material, or labor constraints.

The output from a linear optimization model will show the optimal solution.

Super Scooters' management has decided to continue producing both the Celeritas and the Kicks models for at least one more year. They want to know how many of each model should be produced to maximize contribution margin. They have forecasted demand for each model:

- Captain: 18,000 units
- Celeritas: 10,000 units
- Kicks: 7,000 units
- Lazer: 24,000 units

Because they want to avoid excess inventory, they do not want to produce more than they expect to sell. There is also a limit to the number of machine hours available for the year.

Illustration 3.24 shows information needed to create an optimization model for Super Scooters.

ILLUSTRATION 3.24 Contribution Margin and Resource Requirements

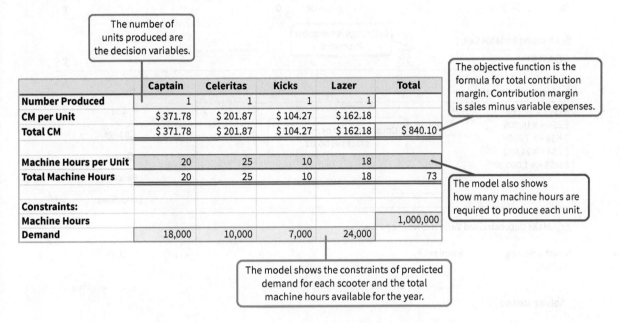

	Captain	Celeritas	Kicks	Lazer	Total
Number Produced	1	1	1	1	
CM per Unit	$ 371.78	$ 201.87	$ 104.27	$ 162.18	
Total CM	$ 371.78	$ 201.87	$ 104.27	$ 162.18	$ 840.10
Machine Hours per Unit	20	25	10	18	
Total Machine Hours	20	25	10	18	73
Constraints:					
Machine Hours					1,000,000
Demand	18,000	10,000	7,000	24,000	

The number of units produced are the decision variables.

The objective function is the formula for total contribution margin. Contribution margin is sales minus variable expenses.

The model also shows how many machine hours are required to produce each unit.

The model shows the constraints of predicted demand for each scooter and the total machine hours available for the year.

The linear optimization program will use this data to solve for the optimal number of each model that should be produced where contribution margin (objective function) is maximized subject to the constraints. Note that we started with an arbitrary number of one in the number of units produced cells. This could also be zero to start; however, using the number one makes it possible to confirm the formulas. The linear optimization available in Microsoft Excel Solver can illustrate how optimization models work. The Solver program is accessed via the **Data** tab in the toolbar ribbon (**Illustration 3.25**).

ILLUSTRATION 3.25 Accessing Microsoft Excel Solver

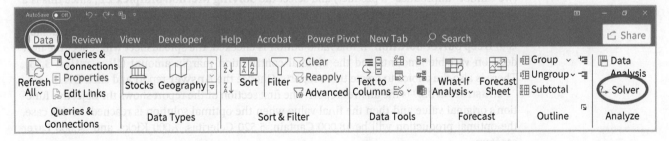

Clicking on **Solver** opens a dialog box to input the objective function cell, decision variable cell, and create any relevant constraints. **Illustration 3.26** is the Solver dialog box used to create the optimization program for Super Scooters.

ILLUSTRATION 3.26 Solver Dialog Box Inputs for Super Scooters Contribution Margin Optimization

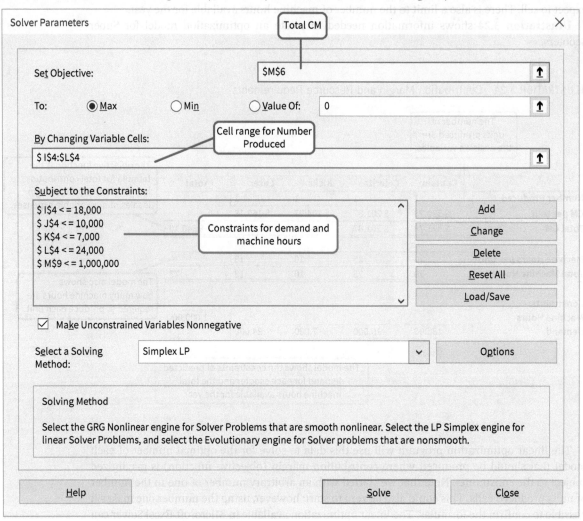

Once all the constraints are input, check the box to ensure the Solver results are not negative (we cannot "unproduce" a product) and select the **Solving Method Simplex LP**, since this is a linear optimization. Clicking **Solve** produces the box in **Illustration 3.27**.

This shows that Solver found an optimal solution that satisfied the constraints. The default is to **Keep Solver Solution**. If this radio button is checked, the spreadsheet will reflect the new decision variable amounts and the optimal contribution margin amount (**Illustration 3.28**). There is also the choice to create three reports. Choose the **Answer** report and click **OK**.

Illustration 3.29 is the answer report. The first section of the report shows the objective function's original value and then the final value when the optimal solution is reached. In this case, the optimal production will be 18,000 Captain, 5,520 Celeritas, 7,000 Kicks, and 24,000 Lazer scooters.

ILLUSTRATION 3.27 Solver Results Choice Box

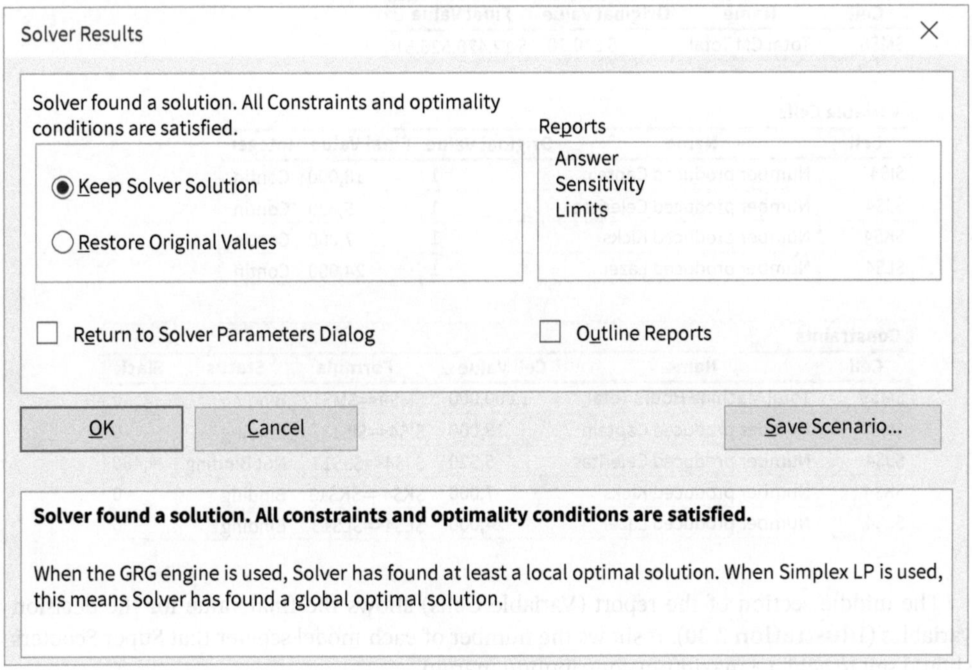

Solver Results   ✕

Solver found a solution. All Constraints and optimality conditions are satisfied.

Re**p**orts

Answer
Sensitivity
Limits

● **K**eep Solver Solution

○ **R**estore Original Values

☐ Re**t**urn to Solver Parameters Dialog

☐ **O**utline Reports

| **O**K | **C**ancel | | **S**ave Scenario... |

Solver found a solution. All constraints and optimality conditions are satisfied.

When the GRG engine is used, Solver has found at least a local optimal solution. When Simplex LP is used, this means Solver has found a global optimal solution.

ILLUSTRATION 3.28 Optimization Model After Running Solver

The number of units produced are the decision variables.

The objective function is the formula for total contribution margin. Contribution margin is sales minus variable expenses.

	Captain	Celeritas	Kicks	Lazer	Total
Number Produced	18,000	5,520	7,000	24,000	
CM per Unit	$ 371.78	$ 201.87	$ 104.27	$ 162.18	
Total CM	$ 6,692,106.26	$ 1,114,328.39	$ 729,872.21	$ 3,892,219.65	$ 12,428,526.51
Machine Hours per Unit	20	25	10	18	
Total Machine Hours	360,000	138,000	70,000	432,000	1,000,000
Constraints:					
Machine Hours					1,000,000
Demand	18,000	10,000	7,000	24,000	

The model also shows how many machine hours are required to produce each unit.

The model shows the constraints of predicted demand for each scooter and the total machine hours available for the year.

ILLUSTRATION 3.29 Solver
Results Output

Objective Cell (Max)

Cell	Name	Original Value	Final Value
$M$6	Total CM Total	$ 840.10	$ 12,428,526.51

Variable Cells

Cell	Name	Original Value	Final Value	Integer
$I$4	Number produced Captain	1	18,000	Contin
$J$4	Number produced Celeritas	1	5,520	Contin
$K$4	Number produced Kicks	1	7,000	Contin
$L$4	Number produced Lazer	1	24,000	Contin

Constraints

Cell	Name	Cell Value	Formula	Status	Slack
$M$9	Total Machine Hours Total	1,000,000	$M$9<=$M$12	Binding	0
$I$4	Number produced Captain	18,000	$I$4<=$I$13	Binding	0
$J$4	Number produced Celeritas	5,520	$J$4<=$J$13	Not Binding	4,480
$K$4	Number produced Kicks	7,000	$K$4<=$K$13	Binding	0
$L$4	Number produced Lazer	24,000	$L$4<=$L$13	Binding	0

The middle section of the report (Variable Cells) shows the final value for the decision variables (**Illustration 3.30**). It shows the number of each model scooter that Super Scooters should sell to achieve maximum contribution margin.

ILLUSTRATION 3.30 Solver
Results Output—Variable
Cells Report

Variable Cells

Cell	Name	Original Value	Final Value	Integer
$I$4	Number produced Captain	1	18,000	Contin
$J$4	Number produced Celeritas	1	5,520	Contin
$K$4	Number produced Kicks	1	7,000	Contin
$L$4	Number produced Lazer	1	24,000	Contin

Finally, the last section of the report shows how much of the constraints were used in the optimal solution (**Illustration 3.31**). The Status column indicates whether the constraint is binding or not binding. In other words, additional production is not possible without an increase in the constraint. The amount shown in the Slack column represents the amount of the constraint that is remaining after the optimal solution.

ILLUSTRATION 3.31 Solver
Results Output—Constraints
Report

Constraints

Name	Cell Value	Formula	Status	Slack
Total Machine Hours Total	1,000,000	$M$9<=$M$12	Binding	0
Number produced Captain	18,000	$I$4<=$I$13	Binding	0
Number produced Celeritas	5,520	$J$4<=$J$13	Not Binding	4,480
Number produced Kicks	7,000	$K$4<=$K$13	Binding	0
Number produced Lazer	24,000	$L$4<=$L$13	Binding	0

Since machine hours are limited, the optimal model prescribes the best use of those hours to maximize contribution margin is to produce all the Captain, Kicks, and Lazer models and 4,480 less than demand of the Celeritas model. Any other mix will result in less contribution margin than the optimal model.

What-If Analyses

A spreadsheet model that evaluates changes and specific combinations of model inputs and assumptions is called a **what-if analysis**. A what-if analysis is an easy way to change values in a spreadsheet and recalculate the outputs. Microsoft Excel has three tools built into the Data tab under What-if Analyses. Two of these tools—Scenario Manager and Goal Seek—are useful tools to facilitate what-if analyses. We will discuss each tool in a later chapter, but here is a short explanation:

- Scenario Manager in Excel allows changing or substituting input values for multiple cells (maximum 32). Therefore, the results of different input values or scenarios can be viewed at the same time.
- Goal Seek is used when the desired result is already known but the input value to achieve that result is not. Goal Seek is limited because it can only use one input variable. If the analysis being performed requires more than one variable to change, then an optimization model using Excel Solver is necessary. For example, the Super Scooters optimization model had more than one variable because it was necessary to consider the demand and machine hours constraints.

APPLY IT 3.5

Prescribe Optimal Sales Mix

`Data` `Managerial Accounting` You are a managerial accountant for Best Bakes Bakery asked to prepare an analysis to determine the optimal mix of products to maximize profit. You have been given sales transactions for the years 2022–2025. Besides prior sales data, you know there are some resource constraints (such as supplies or labor hours) that should be included in the analysis.

1. What is the objective of the analysis?
2. Develop three questions that will be relevant to the objective.
3. What analyses will you use to answer these three questions?

SOLUTION
1. The objective is to determine the optimal sales mix of products given the resources available.
2. Three questions:
   - What resource constraints should be included in the decision?
   - What are the resource requirements for each product?
   - What is the expected profit per product?
3. Linear optimization can be used to determine the best mix of products for maximum profit.

3.6 What Are Data Analytics Motivations and Objectives in Professional Practice?

LEARNING OBJECTIVE ❻
Describe motivations and objectives for data analytics in professional practice.

While the methods of analysis—descriptive, diagnostic, predictive, and prescriptive—are the same across accounting areas, project objectives and what motivates them can be different given the variety of purposes and stakeholders. In auditing, stakeholders are largely external (e.g., shareholders, regulatory agencies), whereas stakeholders in managerial accounting are primarily internal (e.g., management, employees). Their perspectives help identify the objective and develop good questions.

Accounting Information Systems

Motivations for data analyses in AIS can range widely in scope. **Illustration 3.32** provides a summary of typical AIS data analysis motivations, objectives, and questions.

ILLUSTRATION 3.32 Motivations, Objectives, and Questions for AIS Data Analytics

Motivation	Objective	Question
Investing in new technologies.	Determine the technology with the highest return on investment.	What are the labor cost savings if we adopt a new technology?
Increasing security of AIS assets, including data.	Determine how many security breaches or attempted breaches have occurred.	What is the total number of attempted security breaches per day?
Innovations in operational processes, either human or computer, to improve processes.	Identify inefficient processes.	Which processes take the longest?
Improving system performance, such as processing time, reliability, and availability.	Evaluate processing time for monthly financial statement reporting.	How many hours does it take to process financial statements each month?
Improvements in AIS system maintenance.	Evaluate how long it takes to address system maintenance issues.	How long does it take to resolve maintenance requests?
Improvements in data integrity.	Determine how often data must be corrected.	How many corrections were made to data in the last month?

Although the list of questions in Illustration 3.32 is not exhaustive, the questions are a starting point for conducting analyses to address them.

Applying Critical Thinking 3.1

Understand AIS Stakeholders

Understanding the stakeholders' motivations helps accurately identify the objectives of analyses. Stakeholders in AIS data analysis projects can be internal or external to the organization (Stakeholders):

- Internal stakeholders include the chief financial officer, internal auditors, managers, chief information officer, and employees. They want to understand and improve processes, so objectives focus on specific aspects of internal processes and how to improve them.

- External stakeholders may include investors, external auditors, customers, and vendors. These stakeholders are motivated by increased return on investment, so the projects with the greatest potential to offer a return on any investment are usually prioritized.

Auditing

Auditors perform data analyses to verify financial statement information is not materially misstated. Their purpose is providing a professional opinion about whether the financial statements provide reliable, accurate information for the client's primary stakeholders, which include company owners and investors and creditors in the capital markets and financial institutions.

Illustration 3.33 includes examples of motivations, objectives, and questions in auditing data analytics.

Note that the motivation identifies a specific aspect of the audit. The objective states the goal of the analysis. The third column in the illustration provides an example of a specific question the auditor can address with the analysis. Audit analytics are used to perform risk assessment, substantive analytical procedures, and to perform tests of detail.

ILLUSTRATION 3.33 Motivations, Objectives, and Questions for Auditing Data Analytics

Motivation	Objective	Question
Evaluate the risk of material misstatement of revenue.	Determine if there are any unusual changes in revenue compared to prior years.	Are there any unusual trends or changes in sales from prior years?
Evaluate the risk of material misstatement in the company's general ledger accounts.	Analyze balances in the company's general ledger to identify unusual changes from prior year.	Are any changes in general ledger balances higher than our specified material amount?
Evaluate the risk of fraudulent payments.	Verify employees are not receiving unauthorized payments.	Are there any vendors in the vendor file with the same address as an employee?
Verify physical inventory and fixed asset counts.	Test for existence of assets.	Do inventory counts match amounts on the balance sheet?

Applying Critical Thinking 3.2

Acquire Auditing Knowledge and Avoid Biases

Auditors acquire and apply certain types of information when performing audit data analytics (**Knowledge**):

- Client's industry, governance, policies, and procedures.
- Relevant accounting and auditing standards, and SEC regulations.
- Risk assessment and statistical and sampling techniques.

Auditors can be biased when they make assumptions about what they expect to find during an audit engagement. They must be vigilantly skeptical of all information they are given (**Risks**).

Financial Accounting

There are a few typical motivations for financial accountants to perform data analyses:

- Ensuring economic transactions, value changes, and period closing entries have been properly captured by the accounting system, valued in the appropriate account, and in the correct accounting period.
- Predicting future net income and cash flows for top management.
- Identifying, evaluating, and securing alternative capital sources.

Illustration 3.34 shows examples of objectives for these motivations and possible questions to address them.

ILLUSTRATION 3.34 Motivations, Objectives, and Questions for Financial Accounting Data Analytics

Motivation	Objective	Question
Ensure the financial statements reflect all transactions.	Verify transactions are not missing.	Does the sales transaction file agree to the financial statements?
Predict cashflows.	Determine expected cash inflow from sales.	Based on prior year sales and expected growth, what are predicted sales for the next year?
Evaluate alternative capital sources.	Decide whether to issue stock or bonds to raise capital.	What is the expected value of issuing more stock based on current market prices?

Managerial Accounting

Managerial accountants perform data analyses to improve management decision-making and operational performance.

Applying Critical Thinking 3.3

Consider Alternative Methods

If the objective of an analysis is to predict future income, then managerial accountants may use regression, trendlines, or a what-if analysis. Always choose the method that can answer the questions most effectively and efficiently (**Alternatives**).

Illustration 3.35 shows some typical motivations, objectives, and questions for the projects managerial accountants work on.

ILLUSTRATION 3.35 Motivations, Objectives, and Questions for Managerial Accounting Data Analytics

Motivation	Objective	Question
Identify and evaluate new market, product, service, and business process opportunities.	Determine whether to expand an existing product line.	What are the projected sales for the new product line?
Efficiently allocate resources for successful operations.	Evaluate the best use of materials for production.	Which products use the most materials?
Maximize revenue generation and cash flows.	Determine the most profitable product mix.	How many units of each product should we produce to optimize contribution margin?
Increase organizational efficiency by managing costs.	Determine potential cost cutting.	Which production line has the highest amount of waste?

Tax Accounting

Tax accountants perform data analytics to enhance the quality of their professional advice and decisions, as well as to meet compliance requirements for their organization or clients. Typical motivations for tax analytics include:

- Performing tax research.
- Designing tax plans.
- Correctly calculating tax liability and completing applicable tax returns.

Illustration 3.36 summarizes examples of the objectives related to these motivations and some specific questions.

Although general motivations in tax analytics may be similar, objectives and questions will be specific to individual clients. For example, tax planning is a common motivation, but a client may have differing objectives for their tax plan, such as saving for retirement or estate planning. The objective of the client will determine the type of analysis.

As this chapter has emphasized, accounting professionals are increasingly performing data analysis to provide value to their organizations and clients. Wherever your career takes you, thinking critically about what is motivating a project will help you ask the best objective-based data questions to achieve your goals. These are the first two steps of successful data analysis projects across professional practice areas.

ILLUSTRATION 3.36 Motivations, Objectives, and Questions for Tax Accounting Data Analytics

Motivation	Objective	Question
A new tax law has been passed that potentially changes a client's tax liability.	Identify relevant tax law changes.	Based on last year's tax return, how will the change in tax law affect the client's tax liability?
A client requested tax planning for the next three years.	Prepare a tax plan to minimize tax liability.	Based on the client's past tax returns and current business projections, how much tax will they owe next year?
Analyzing a client's tax liability after preparing their tax return.	Identify unusual deductions.	How do the client's deductions compare to their prior year return and to national averages?

Match at least one professional practice area's acronym to the following motivations to perform data analyses:

a. Accounting information systems
b. Auditing
c. Financial Accounting
d. Managerial Accounting
e. Tax Accounting

Motivation	Practice Area
Performing tax research.	
Investing in new technologies.	
Performing analytical procedures on variances in account balances and on classes of transactions.	
Ensuring all economic transactions have been recorded.	
Investing in business intelligence tools.	
Increasing security of AIS assets, including data.	
Innovations in operational processes, either human or computer, to increase process effectiveness.	
Designing defendable tax plans.	
Learning if all adjusting entries at the end of the period have been recorded.	
Improving system performance, such as processing time and availability.	
Reviewing and evaluating the internal control system.	
Increasing security of AIS assets, including data.	
Computing tax liability and completing tax forms.	
Performing physical inventory and fixed asset counts at the fiscal year end.	
Testing documentation to determine if account balances are supported.	

SOLUTION

Motivation	Practice Area
Performing tax research.	Tax accounting
Investing in new technologies.	AIS
Performing analytical procedures on variances in account balances and on classes of transactions.	Auditing
Ensuring all economic transactions have been recorded.	Financial accounting

(Continued)

Motivation	Practice Area
Investing in business intelligence tools.	AIS
Increasing security of AIS assets, including data.	AIS
Innovations in operational processes, either human or computer, to increase process effectiveness.	Managerial accounting
Designing defendable tax plans.	Tax accounting
Learning if all adjusting entries at the end of the period have been recorded.	Financial accounting
Improving system performance, such as processing time and availability.	AIS
Reviewing and evaluating the internal control system.	Auditing
Increasing security of AIS assets, including data.	AIS
Computing tax liability and completing tax forms.	Tax accounting
Performing physical inventory and fixed asset counts at the fiscal year end.	Financial accounting
Testing documentation to determine if account balances are supported.	Auditing

Chapter Review and Practice

Learning Objectives Review

❶ Summarize the relationship between motivations, objectives, and data analysis questions.

Accountants generally perform data analyses for four reasons:

- Opportunities within their organizations and in the marketplace.
- Professional issues and requirements from regulations and laws.
- Solving problems within their organizations or for clients.
- Process and performance evaluation of their own work, or work performed within their organizations.

First, identify the objective, which is the goal of the data analysis. Then, develop questions designed to achieve the project's goal. Data analysis questions can be evaluated for clarity, conciseness, and measurability:

- Will the answer address the objective of the analysis?
- Does the question address a single topic? If not, break it down into sub-questions.
- Is the question measurable?
- Are the data needed to answer it available?

If the answer to any of these questions is no, then either revise the question or drop it.

The six elements of critical thinking can help us think about what is motivating data analyses and how to develop objectives and questions:

- Understanding the stakeholders and their perspectives helps identify the project's motivation and develop specific objectives and questions.

- Critically thinking through the purpose of data analyses supports moving from objective to specific questions.
- Considering several alternative methods of analyses increases the likelihood of selecting the best option for the purpose.
- Being aware of potential risks makes it possible to mitigate them when evaluating motivation, determining objectives, and developing questions.
- Considering what knowledge is necessary to successfully complete the project involves either confirming we already have that knowledge or doing additional research.
- Understanding why we are performing data analyses lets us leverage the experience to future data analytics contexts and tasks. Considering past experiences can speed up the process of identifying objectives and developing questions.

❷ Demonstrate how to develop descriptive questions.

Descriptive questions focus on understanding what is currently happening or what has happened in the past. They are developed by identifying the objective of the analysis and then formulating sub-questions that narrow the focus. The next step is identifying the data and the method of analysis to answer those questions. Common descriptive methods:

- Frequency measures help understand categories of data.
- Measures of location (mean, median, and mode) reveal average observations in a data set.
- Measures of dispersion (minimum, maximum, range, variance, and standard deviation) show how much variance there is among the observations in the data set.

- Measures of percentage change show percentage increases and decreases as compared to prior periods and the percent of total.

❸ Demonstrate how to develop diagnostic questions.

Diagnostic questions build on what was learned in descriptive analysis and explore the data to find the cause of the outcome. Diagnostic analytics determine why an outcome occurred by looking for anomalies, correlations, patterns, or trends. Common diagnostic analyses:

- Anomaly detection: Scatterplots and bar charts.
- Correlation (linear): Scatterplots and correlation.
- Pattern detection: Line graphs and bar charts.
- Trend analysis: Bar charts, line charts, and trendlines.

❹ Demonstrate how to develop predictive questions.

Predictive analytics use past and present data to forecast and create models so businesses can make predictions about the future. The increased availability of data and software tools to perform predictive analytics means it is now used in all areas of accounting. To determine a predictive question, ask, "What do I want to do with the answer?" Common analyses used to answer predictive questions:

- Trendlines: Show the underlying functional relationships of the data.
- Regression analysis: Linear regression builds mathematical and statistical models to explain the relationship between a dependent variable and one or more independent variables.

❺ Demonstrate how to develop prescriptive questions.

Prescriptive objectives build on predictions about the future and descriptions of the present to determine the best course of action. The objectives for prescriptive analytics focus on what should happen. There are two common methods of prescriptive analysis:

- Optimization is the process of selecting values of variables that *minimize* or *maximize* some quantity of interest. Optimization modeling helps managers allocate resources more efficiently and make cost/profit decisions.
- A spreadsheet model that evaluates how changes and specific combinations of model inputs and assumptions is called a what-if analysis. A what-if analysis is an easy way to change values in a spreadsheet and recalculate the outputs.

❻ Describe motivations and objectives for data analytics in professional practice.

The primary professional accounting practice areas have both common and unique motivations to perform data analyses:

- Accounting information systems professionals have governance, strategic, operational, and compliance motivations.
- Auditors have professional compliance, quality, firm, and market motivations.
- Financial accountants have both internal and external stakeholder motivations.
- Managerial accountants have internal governance, strategic, and operational motivations.
- Tax accountants have professional compliance, client, firm, and market motivations.

Key Terms Review

How To Walk-Throughs

HOW TO 3.1   Create a Highlight Table in Tableau

How To

The table shown in Illustration 3.10 was created in Tableau version 2021.1.2. Create it yourself by following these steps:

What You Need: `Data` The How To 3.1 data file.

STEP 1: Open a new worksheet and drag the **Sold Date** to **Columns** and **Location** to **Rows**. Drag **Gross Sales** to the open area under years, or to the Text symbol under **Marks** (**Illustration 3.37**).

ILLUSTRATION 3.37   Tableau Worksheet

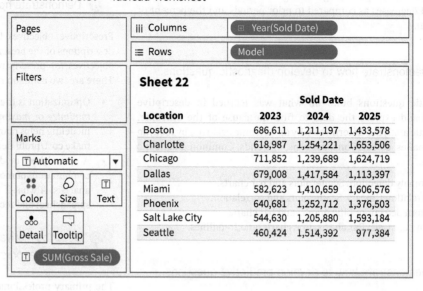

			Sold Date	
Location	2023	2024	2025
Boston	686,611	1,211,197	1,433,578
Charlotte	618,987	1,254,221	1,653,506
Chicago	711,852	1,239,689	1,624,719
Dallas	679,008	1,417,584	1,113,397
Miami	582,623	1,410,659	1,606,576
Phoenix	640,681	1,252,712	1,376,503
Salt Lake City	544,630	1,205,880	1,593,184
Seattle	460,424	1,514,392	977,384

STEP 2: Create a calculation that will calculate the change in sales from 2024 to 2025. Because data from 2023 is unnecessary and we are only interested in the Celeritas model, create two filters. First, drag **Model** to the **Filters** box. This opens an input box (**Illustration 3.38**).

ILLUSTRATION 3.38   Filter Input Box

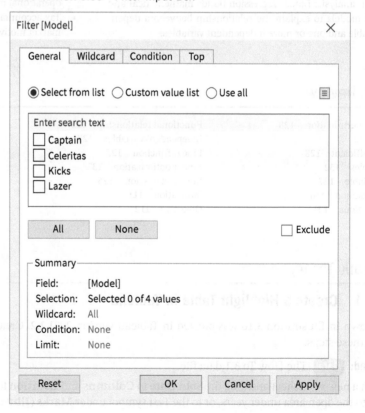

Check the box for Celeritas and click **OK**. Next, drag **Sold Date** to **Filter** and select **Years** from the input box (**Illustration 3.39**).

ILLUSTRATION 3.39   Filter Field Choices

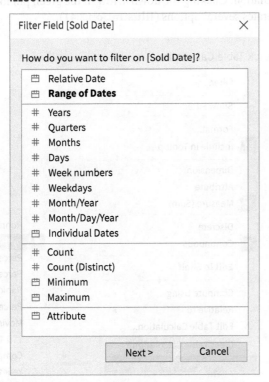

Click **Next** to see the following input box choices (**Illustration 3.40**):

ILLUSTRATION 3.40   Filter Choices

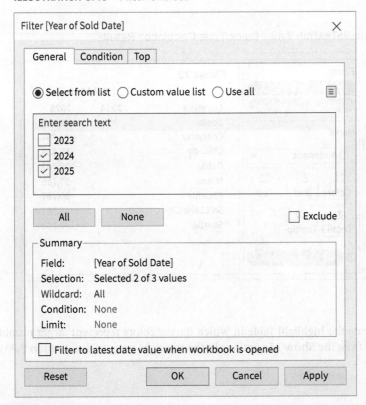

Select 2024 and 2025 and click **OK.**

STEP 3: Create the calculation. Clicking the down arrow in the green pill for **Sum(Gross Sales)** in the **Marks** area generates several options (**Illustration 3.41**).

ILLUSTRATION 3.41 Creating a Quick Table Calculation

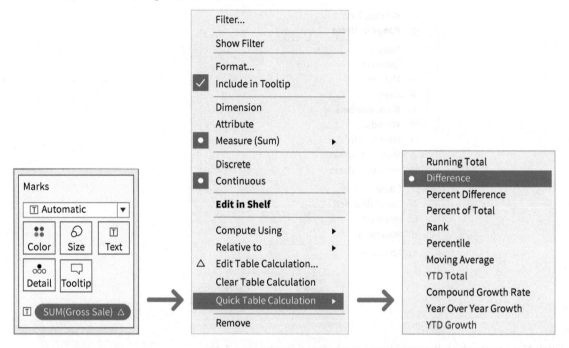

Select the **Quick Table Calculation** option, then select **Difference**. This will change the columns in the table to differences (**Illustration 3.42**).

ILLUSTRATION 3.42 Quick Table Calculation Results

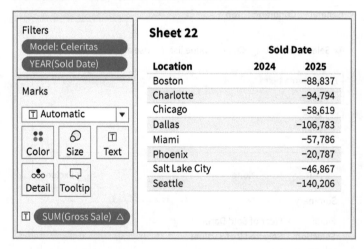

ILLUSTRATION 3.43
Choosing a Highlight Table

STEP 4: To create the highlight table in which darker colors represent larger numbers, choose that chart type from the **Show Me** options in the top-right corner (**Illustration 3.43**).

Now the table looks like the table in **Illustration 3.44**.

ILLUSTRATION 3.44   Highlight Table Results

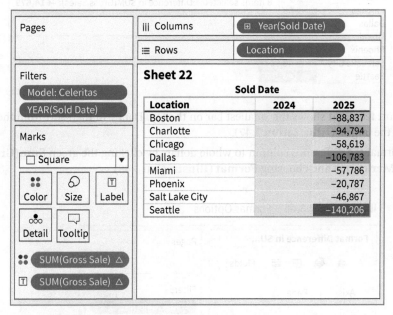

STEP 5: To only show the column for 2025, right click on 2024 in the column and choose **Hide** (**Illustration 3.45**).

ILLUSTRATION 3.45   Hide Column Feature

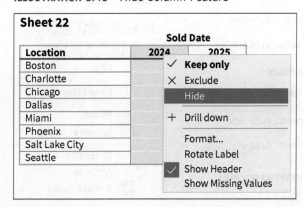

Click on **Hide** and *not* **Exclude**. (Selecting **Exclude** means that the calculation will no longer work because the 2024 data would be removed.)

STEP 6: Order the locations by the largest loss to the smallest loss. To do that, click 2025 at the top of the column. The box will appear as shown in **Illustration 3.46**.

ILLUSTRATION 3.46 Sorting Data from Smallest to Largest

Location	Sold Date 2025
Boston	−88,
Charlotte	−94,
Chicago	−58,
Dallas	−106,
Miami	−57,786
Phoenix	−20,787
Salt Lake City	−46,867
Seattle	−140,206

✓ Keep Only   ✕ Exclude   ⊞ ⊛ ⇲   ✏ ▾   ▥

8 items selected   Difference in SUM(Gross Sales): **−614,679**

2025

ILLUSTRATION 3.47
Sorted Highlight Table

Location	Sold Date 2025
Seattle	−140,206
Dallas	−106,783
Charlotte	−94,794
Boston	−88,837
Chicago	−58,619
Miami	−57,786
Salt Lake City	−46,867
Phoenix	−20,787

Click the sort icon that shows the smallest bar on the top. Data will then sort from the smallest number to the largest (**Illustration 3.47**).

STEP 7: Format the difference column to whole dollars by clicking the green **Sum(Gross Sale)** pill in the **Marks** area and choosing **Format** (**Illustration 3.48**).

ILLUSTRATION 3.48 Format Options

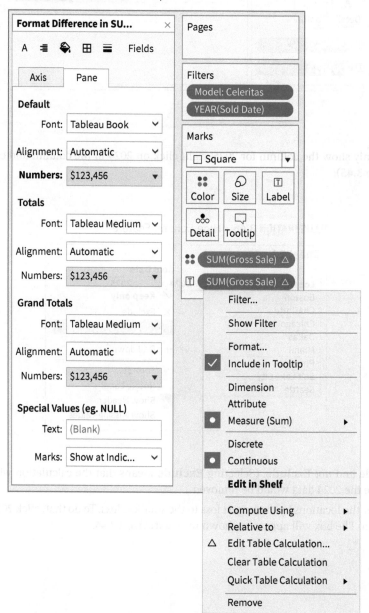

Here, the default format can be changed to currency.

STEP 8: Create a title for the visualization. Tableau will name the visualization by the sheet number by default. To change that, right click in the sheet title area and then choose **Edit Title** (**Illustration 3.49**).

ILLUSTRATION 3.49   Editing a Worksheet Title

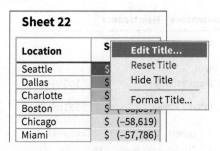

Enter a title in the box that appears (**Illustration 3.50**).

ILLUSTRATION 3.50   Editing a Worksheet Title

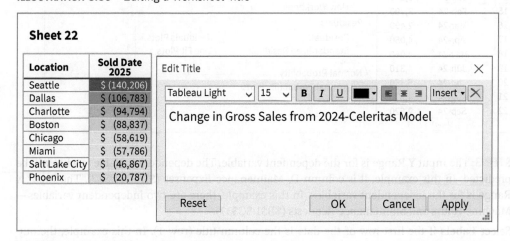

HOW TO 3.2   Perform a Regression in Microsoft Excel

How To

Illustration 3.18 is regression performed in Excel. You can create it by following these steps:

What You Need: **Data**   The How To 3.2 data file.

STEP 1: The Data Analysis tool in the **Data** ribbon has an option for regression. **Illustration 3.51** shows the dialog box that opens when **Data Analysis** is selected.

ILLUSTRATION 3.51   Excel Data Analysis Tool—Regression

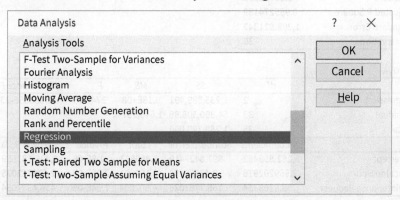

STEP 2: Click on **Regression**, then **OK**. A Regression dialog box will appear (**Illustration 3.52**).

ILLUSTRATION 3.52   Regression Dialog Box

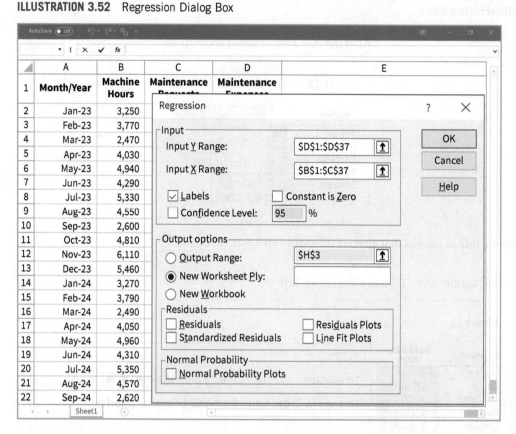

STEP 3: The Input Y Range is for the dependent variable. The dependent variable is what will be predicted. In this example, it is column D, Maintenance Expenses ($D$1:$D$37). The Input X Range is for the independent variables. In this example, there are two independent variables—Machine Hours and Maintenance Requests ($B$1:$C$37).

Select **Labels** if the first row of the data is the column title (row 1). In this example, the output will be in a new worksheet. Finally, **Residuals**, **Standardized Residuals**, **Residual Plots**, and **Normal Probability Plots** are selected. These residuals options will be used to evaluate the regression assumptions.

STEP 4: Click **OK** for the regression results (**Illustration 3.53**).

ILLUSTRATION 3.53   Regression Output

SUMMARY OUTPUT					
Regression Statistics					
Multiple R	0.978687872				
R Square	0.95782995				
Adjusted R Square	0.955274189				
Standard Error	1,283.821342				
Observations	36				
ANOVA					
	df	*SS*	*MS*	*F*	*Significance F*
Regression	2	1,235,399,491	6.18E+08	374.773	2.05385E-23
Residual	33	54,390,508.88	1,648,197		
Total	35	1,289,790,000			
	Coefficients	*Standard Error*	*t Stat*	*P-value*	*Lower 95%*
Intercept	5,252.858452	897.8427419	5.850533	1.5E-06	3,426.183659
Machine Hours	3.569202976	0.43769194	8.154601	2.05E-09	2.678712028
Maintenance Request	759.8366754	168.7763028	4.502034	7.94E-05	416.4587054

> **Data** The Data tag appears when the data required to answer a question or complete an exercise are available in the book's product page on www.wiley.com.

Multiple Choice Questions

1. (LO 1) Motivation in data analytics in accounting is

   a. the reason why the analysis is being performed.

   b. the interpretation of results of analysis.

   c. based only on factors outside analysis.

   d. based only on whether your career will benefit from performing the analysis.

2. (LO 1) What would be an example of motivation for professional issues and requirements?

   a. Analyzing how new proposed capital gain tax rates will affect financial statements

   b. Determining the appropriate calculation for the allowance of doubtful accounts

   c. Analyzing whether to outsource its IT functions or keep these functions in-house

   d. Analyzing your company's stock prices in comparison to other competitors in the industry

3. (LO 1) There are different types of motivations in data analytics projects. An example of an opportunity motivation would be

   a. analyzing how new proposed capital gain tax rates will affect financial statements.

   b. determining the appropriate calculation for allowance of doubtful accounts.

   c. analyzing whether to outsource its IT functions or keep the function in-house.

   d. analyzing your stock prices and comparing them to those of other competitors in the industry.

4. (LO 1) Critically thinking through the motivation to perform data analyses includes considering

   a. stakeholders, purpose, alternatives, risks, knowledge, and self-reflection.

   b. stakeholders and purpose.

   c. stakeholders, purpose, risk management, and alternatives.

   d. stakeholders, acquiring knowledge, alternatives, and self-reflection.

   e. stakeholders, risk management, alternatives, and self-reflection.

5. (LO 1) Analyses of the stakeholders and their perspectives help to critically think through motivation to perform data analyses because

   a. it reminds you who pays your salary.

   b. some may be external to your organization.

   c. considering the perspectives of stakeholders helps identify the objective and develop good questions.

   d. internal stakeholders should never be considered.

   e. All of these are reasons for considering stakeholders in your critical thinking.

6. (LO 1) Critically considering the purpose for performing data analyses

   a. keeps us focused on the reason why something is done or created.

   b. provides free data for analyses.

   c. reveals the stakeholders' perspectives.

   d. helps avoid biases and assumptions.

   e. None of these list the critical thinking benefits of considering the purpose of data analyses.

7. (LO 1) Performing the most appropriate data analyses is more likely if you critically think through issues by

   a. using bar charts from last year's operational results.

   b. starting with the results you want to achieve.

   c. paying others to help you.

   d. acquiring and applying new knowledge.

   e. None of these help you perform better data analyses.

8. (LO 1) Critically thinking through the risks to your perspective as you determine your motivation to perform data analyses helps you minimize

   a. errors from biases.

   b. errors from lack of experience.

   c. errors from your assumptions.

   d. faulty conclusions from errors or omissions in your data.

   e. All of these are benefits of considering the risks to your data analyses choices.

9. (LO 1) Considering several alternative methods of analysis helps you

   a. go with the first alternative that comes to mind.

   b. select the option that is best for the project's purpose.

   c. pick the alternative with the highest incremental cost.

   d. pick the alternative with the lowest likelihood of informative results.

10. (LO 2) If the objective of data analysis is to understand what is currently happening or has happened in the past, then what type of question are you asking?

   a. Descriptive   **c.** Predictive

   b. Diagnostic   **d.** Prescriptive

11. (LO 2) Once you have articulated a descriptive question, what type of analysis is necessary to understand the dispersion of the data?

   a. Median   **c.** Standard deviation

   b. Frequency   **d.** Percent change

12. (LO 2) To answer descriptive questions in a data analysis project, possible measures include

   a. the calculation of median, the calculation of variance, and projected percentage changes in future periods.

   b. the calculation of frequency measures, the calculation of mode, and what-if scenarios.

c. the calculation of mode, the calculation of variance, and the calculation of correlation coefficients.

d. the calculation of mean, the calculation of standard deviation, and percentage changes compared to the prior period.

13. **(LO 3)** A diagnostic question

a. identifies a problem or issue to understand why an outcome occurred.

b. is designed to gain a better understanding of data to answer business questions.

c. asks what you want to know about what may happen in the future.

d. investigates how to take advantage of future opportunities or mitigate a future risk outcome.

14. **(LO 3)** The sub-question "Are there any unusual sales transactions in 2023?" is best associated with which of the following objectives of data analysis?

a. What is the average dollar amount of sales in 2023?

b. What is the best predictor of increased sales for future periods?

c. Why are sales decreasing during 2023?

d. What are the minimum and maximum dollar amount of sales during 2023?

15. **(LO 4)** A predictive question

a. identifies a problem or issue to understand why an outcome occurred.

b. is designed to gain a better understanding of data to answer business questions.

c. asks what you want to know about what may happen in the future.

d. investigates how to take advantage of future opportunities or mitigate a future risk outcome.

16. **(LO 4)** Which of the following is a question asked in predictive analysis?

a. Are there any unusual changes in total revenue from 2021 to 2024?

b. What is the average sales amount for online customers each year?

c. How will revenue be affected if we have a 5% decrease in variable costs?

d. How much revenue is categorized as business-to-business sales?

17. **(LO 5)** What type of question is "How many units of product should we buy each month to minimize inventory holding costs but still meet demand?"

a. Descriptive

b. Diagnostic

c. Predictive

d. Prescriptive

18. **(LO 5)** A linear optimization model is comprised of

a. decision variables, an objective function, and constraints.

b. dependent and independent variables, an objective function, and constraints.

c. dependent and independent variables and constraints.

d. dependent and independent variables, a regression equation, and constraints.

19. **(LO 6)** AIS accountants are most likely to be motivated to perform data analyses for which of the following opportunities?

a. New technologies that can provide cost savings for operational processes

b. New customers in the marketplace

c. Turnover in the regulatory body leadership

d. Changes to the footnote disclosures required by generally accepted accounting rules

e. Changes in tax rules

20. **(LO 6)** What would be a typical objective in an audit performed in accordance with generally accepted auditing standards to perform data analysis? Select all that apply.

a. Determine whether physical inventory exists and whether the total inventory value matches the balance sheet amount.

b. Determine the risk of fraudulent sales transactions.

c. Determine if the tax liability is correctly calculated in accordance with new tax laws.

d. Determine the return on investment on a new capital project.

21. **(LO 6)** Financial accountants would be most likely motivated to perform data analyses for which of the following?

a. Changes to the management team

b. New competitors in the marketplace

c. Identifying and supporting assumptions and estimates for end of period adjusting entries

d. Changes to the tax rates applicable to their organization

e. None of these would motivate data analyses by financial accountants

22. **(LO 6)** Managerial accountants would most likely be motivated to perform data analyses for which of the following?

a. Changes to the tax code

b. Changes to the financial statement footnote disclosure rules

c. Changes to reporting rules by the Securities and Exchange Commission

d. Changes to their organization's strategies, performance, and resource costs

e. None of these would motivate data analyses by managerial accountants

Review Questions

1. **(LO 1)** Discuss the following motivations for data analyses in accounting by providing an example for each:

1. Opportunities

2. Professional issues and requirements

3. Problem-solving

4. Process and performance assessment

2. **(LO 1, 6)** Compare and contrast the professional considerations and requirements that motivate financial and managerial accountants to perform data analyses.

3. **(LO 2, 4)** Assume you are a financial analyst at a nonpublic entity. Your supervisor has asked you to calculate and analyze debt solvency ratios over the last five years. You note that there are several stakeholders associated with this analysis, including your manager and the

bank that holds your entity's debt. Provide an example of how these two stakeholders may be impacted differently by the results of your data analyses.

4. (LO 1, 4) As an auditor assigned to a public company audit in the manufacturing industry, you have been asked to analyze the company's inventory to understand the types of products in inventory and the mix of raw materials, work-in-process, and finished goods. You receive the inventory on hand file from the information technology department. Identify the knowledge you might need to acquire or apply to this analysis that may contribute to your motivation to perform it.

5. (LO 2) Assume you are performing a descriptive analysis of the employee expense reimbursement data for your company's current fiscal year compared to the prior fiscal year. Give an example of an initial question related to this analysis.

6. (LO 2) As an auditor working in the internal audit group, you are asked to perform a descriptive analysis of the employee login attempts during business hours and nonbusiness hours. Your objective is to understand whether the quantity of failed login attempts has increased or decreased. Your initial question is "Have login attempts increased?" Provide an example of a sub-question that would address that objective and initial question for descriptive analysis.

7. (LO 3) Explain how accountants can use diagnostic analytics to determine why an outcome occurred.

8. (LO 3) Your company controller asked you to perform diagnostic analysis on the company's product sales to understand why sales increased compared to the prior year. Your initial question is "What is driving sales volume increase?" Identify two sub-questions to consider as you plan your analysis.

9. (LO 2, 4) Describe the difference between predictive objectives and descriptive objectives in accounting analytics.

10. (LO 4) Define the terms dependent variable and independent variable. How are these variables used in predictive analytics?

11. (LO 5) Define and explain optimization and what-if analyses. Why are these two types of analyses considered prescriptive analytics?

12. (LO 5) Assume you are a financial analyst working for a manufacturing company. Your company manufactures and sells a variety of component parts for high-end remote-controlled cars. Your product mix includes three popular products:

Metal Gear

High-Torque 330

High-Torque 400

Your controller has asked you to identify the most profitable product mix. Give an example of an initial question and sub-question that may drive your analysis plan.

13. (LO 6) As an accounting information systems accountant, identify the primary stakeholders you prioritize when performing data analyses.

14. (LO 6) What are external auditors' primary motivations to perform data analyses?

15. (LO 6) Your controller has asked you to prepare adjusting journal entries for the month-end close. Discuss why a financial reporting accountant may engage in data analysis as they prepare adjusting journal entries.

16. (LO 6) Tax accountants often consider alternatives when deciding whether they are motivated to perform data analyses. Discuss some alternatives that could improve their decisions.

Brief Exercises

BE 3.1 (LO 1) Identify the motivation for data analysis for the following scenarios:

Scenario	Motivation Solutions
1. In 2022, taxpayers saw increases in the cost of living. The inflation rate increased as a result, and the Revenue and Customs Authority provided tax inflation adjustments for tax rate schedules. Your tax firm would like data analysis on how these changes will affect its tax clients.	
2. North Star Industries manufactures steel bearings for the automotive sector. Data analysis is needed to investigate if investing in a new machine will yield a good return on investment (ROI).	
3. Bid and Buy is an online platform that allows users to bid on customer products. Bid and Buy require users to add their shipping information. Data analysis of users' shipping information revealed incomplete and incorrect addresses.	

BE 3.2 (LO 1–6) [Accounting Information Systems] Assume you are an accounting information system professional tasked with performing several analyses related to your company's information security controls. Match the analytics area to the motivation scenario (analytics areas can be used more than once).

a. Descriptive analysis

c. Predictive analysis

b. Diagnostic analysis

d. Prescriptive analysis

Motivation to Perform Analyses	Analytics Area
1. Analyze the mean, median, and mode number of failed login attempts after the company changed password requirements to understand if the benefits of enhanced password requirements outweigh the costs.	

(Continued)

(Continued)

Motivation to Perform Analyses	Analytics Area
2. Analyze the correlation between the quantity of phishing attempts reported and employee attendance at cybersecurity training to determine if training is related to reporting of phishing attempts.	
3. Analyze trends of failed login attempts over time to determine if employees are complying with company policy regarding login credentials.	
4. Perform a linear regression analysis to consider the likelihood of future information security breaches based on the independent variables of dollars spent on cybersecurity training and encryption software.	
5. Perform a what-if analysis to identify the appropriate dollar amount of spending that is necessary to meet the entity's goals for information security.	

BE 3.3 (LO 1, 6) Match the motivation source for data analytics in professional accounting to the appropriate scenario. Each source may be used once, more than once, or not at all.

a. Opportunities

b. Process and performance assessment

c. Regulatory changes

d. Problem-solving

Scenario	Motivation Source
1. You are a tax accountant working at a large London-based multi-national company. Executive management is trying to decide the best country in which to expand operations. You have been tasked with identifying independent variables and performing regression analysis to predict potential revenue from this expansion.	
2. Your company has several key performance indicators (KPIs) associated with its manufacturing process—especially quality control. You have been tasked with performing an analysis to identify whether quality control benchmarks are being accurately recorded in the information system.	
3. You are an external auditor working on a public company manufacturing client. You have been asked to test the operating effectiveness of internal controls associated with the purchasing groups' compliance with the internal control that all purchase orders above £10,000 are approved by a purchasing supervisor.	
4. You are a financial analyst working for a company that distributes consumer products to retailers across the United Kingdom. You must find out why sales of your historically most popular product, the electric grill, have been declining.	

BE 3.4 (LO 2) OfficePlus sells office furniture to businesses. They want to understand if accounts receivable collections are a problem for the company. The following spreadsheet is provided, and it shows invoices by customers and which invoices have been paid:

Customer ID	Invoice ID	Invoice Date	Invoice Amount	Payment Amount
203211	INV204312	2021-02-02	$15,110	$0
203212	INV204333	2022-01-07	$25,200	$25,200
203213	INV204345	2022-03-14	$76,000	$70,000
203211	INV206311	2022-03-16	$76,900	$0
…	…	…	…	…

1. What would be the objective of the analysis? Select the right one from the following choices:

- Who are the customers that have the highest invoice totals?
- Who are the customers that have the highest overdue accounts receivable dollar amounts?
- Who are the customers that have the highest invoice counts?
- Who are the customers that have the highest average days' delinquent?

2. If the descriptive question is "Have overdue accounts receivable balances increased for each month?" what analysis can be used to answer this question? Select one from the given choices.

- Line or Bar Chart
- PivotTable
- Pie Chart

BE 3.5 (LO 2) `Financial Accounting` You are a financial accountant working for the city. Your controller would like to better understand vendor payments made by the city. You have downloaded the Vendor Payment file for fiscal years 2024 and 2025 from the city's database. An excerpt of the data set is provided.

FY	Activity	Department	Check Date	Vendor	Check Total
2024	Landfill Management	Sanitation Svcs	8/22/2024	Smith Temporaries, Inc	$ 570.24
2025	Service Maintenance Centers	Public Works and Transportation	8/14/2025	Ferrell Gas, LP	$ 32.22
2023	Water Treatment	Water Utilities	10/30/2023	Custom-Crete Redi-Mix, LLC	$ 100.00
2023	Inventory	Inventory Purchase	11/21/2023	Installer Sales and Service	$ 8.76
2024	Fleet Replacement	Equipment and Fleet Management	6/28/2024	Sam Pack's Five Star Ford	$ 22,155.00
2024	Homeless Housing Services	Housing/Community Services	6/26/2024	Saint Augustine Estates	$ 614.00
2024	Complete Street	Public Works and Transportation	3/11/2024	HERC Rentals Inc	$ 4,236.00
2023	Nondepartmental	Office of Budget	12/24/2023	William H Bancroft Jr.	$ 2,000.34

1. What is the objective of the analysis?
2. Develop three questions relevant to the objective, and determine what measures you will use to answer the questions.
3. What analyses will you use to answer these three questions?

BE 3.6 (LO 2, 6) `Managerial Accounting` Match the appropriate analysis that can be used to answer descriptive questions or sub-questions. Each analysis choice can be used once, more than once, or not at all.

a. Filter the data to only analyze the machine of interest and use the maximum function.

b. Use the minimum and maximum functions to identify the smallest number of units produced and the largest number of units produced.

c. Filter the data to only analyze the unit of interest and machine of interest and calculate the mean number of units produced for each shift.

d. Create a linear equation to estimate the number of machine hours needed to produce a unit.

e. Use the optimization model function in Excel to identify the maximum number of units that can be produced given the constraint of time during shift.

f. Create a frequency distribution table to categorize product category.

Initial Descriptive Analysis Questions or Sub-Questions	Analysis Choice
1. How many units were produced for each product category in the facility?	
2. What is the average number of units produced by machine #1065 during first shift, second shift, and third shift?	
3. What is the greatest number of units that machine #1810 produced?	
4. What is the range of units produced during the period?	

BE 3.7 (LO 3) `Managerial Accounting` Vista Education is an educational publisher of college textbooks. A visualization was created to show sales and sales returns trends for the year 2025 as follows:

Sales vs. Sales Returns

■ Sales   ■ Sales Returns

The question that the publisher wants to answer is whether there are any identifiable trends in monthly sales returns. Do you have the answer in the above visualization? What is the type of question?

BE 3.8 (LO 3) `Auditing` As an auditor for a private entity, your senior has asked you to examine your client's sales returns in the first 30 days after year-end. The descriptive analysis revealed sales returns dramatically decreased compared to the prior year. Further, you noted that the largest decrease related to sales returns was in the northwest region. You must perform diagnostic analyses to understand why there was a decrease in sales returns.

Next is an outline of the data analysis objective, initial question, sub-questions, and possible measures. Complete the outline by matching the appropriate statement to the corresponding blank square. Statement choices may be used once, more than once, or not at all.

a. What is driving the sales return decrease?

b. Are there unusual patterns in the northwest region sales returns for certain product lines?

c. Create a trend analysis showing returns by date for each product line for the current year compared to the prior year.

d. Filter data to isolate the northwest region sales returns and examine total sales returns, average sales returns, and sales return quantity.

e. Create an optimization model to identify the most appropriate number of sales returns given the constraint of sales and quantity manufactured.

f. Calculate the standard deviation of sales and compare to the standard deviation of employee expenses for the period.

g. Calculate the overall spending by the company in customer services to determine if sales returns are related to manufacturing quality.

Objective	Initial Question	Sub-Questions	Possible Measures
Why did sales returns decrease from prior year?	**1.**	Are there anomalies in sales returns for any specific product the company sells?	Create a scatterplot comparing quantity returned to sales price for items to identify anomalies in returns. Create a scatterplot comparing sales dollars to sales returns for items to identify anomalies in returns.
		Are there identifiable trends in sales returns for any specific product?	**2.**
Why is there a large decrease in sales returns in the northwest region?	What factors are driving the decrease in sales returns in the northwest region?	**3.**	**4.**

BE 3.9 (LO 4) Match the analysis to its description. Each term may be used once, more than once, or not at all.

Analyses:

a. Independent variable

b. Linear function

c. Regression statistics

d. Correlation coefficient

e. Dependent variable

f. Adjusted R^2

Description	Analysis
1. The statistical measures used to evaluate a regression model.	
2. The outcome variable in a regression model.	
3. The variable or variables that influence the outcome variable.	
4. This type of relationship shows steady increases or decreases over the range of the independent variable.	
5. This statistic measures the strength of the relationship between the dependent and independent variables.	
6. This statistic explains how well the regression line fits the data.	

BE 3.10 (LO 4) The objective is to engage in predictive analyses. For each of the following initial or sub-question, identify the independent variable and the dependent variable:

1. How much will electricity costs change with a 10% increase in production hours?
2. How much will be the tax liability with the applicable tax rates?
3. How much will maintenance expenses change if we increase production volume by 5%?
4. How much is the change in investment value with the changes in the S&P 500 Index?
5. What is the strength of the relationship between income and happiness?

BE 3.11 (LO 4, 6) Accounting Information Systems Assume you are an accounting information systems accountant asked to consider the success of your company's cyber training program. You collected data on the monthly number of cybersecurity training hours provided to employees and the number of cyberthreats reported. You created the following trendline line graph:

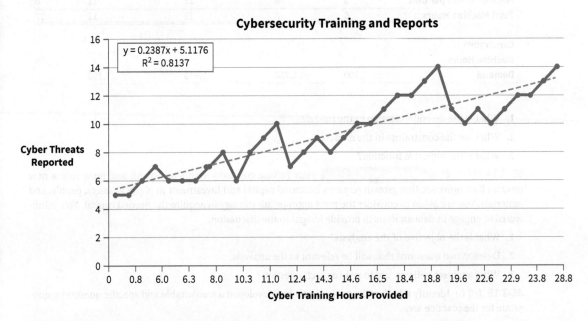

Cybersecurity Training and Reports

$y = 0.2387x + 5.1176$
$R^2 = 0.8137$

Use the information provided in the line graph and the equation to answer the following questions:

1. If the company offered 9 hours of cyber training during a period, what is the expected number of cyber-security threats reported by employees?
2. If the company offered 35 hours of cyber training during a period, what is the expected number of cybersecurity threats reported by employees?

BE 3.12 (LO 5) Match the appropriate term to each definition. Terms can be used once, more than once, or not at all.

a. Constraints
b. Objective function
c. Decision variable
d. Optimization

e. Linear regression
f. Dependent variable
g. Independent variable

Definition	Term
1. The process of selecting values of variables that minimize or maximize some quantity of interest.	
2. The unknown values a model seeks to determine.	
3. The mathematical equation that describes the output target that we seek to minimize or maximize.	
4. The limitations, requirements, or other restrictions that must be imposed on any solution.	

BE 3.13 (LO 5, 6) **Managerial Accounting** As a managerial accountant for a manufacturing company, you are asked to identify the optimal number of units that must be produced in order to maximize the company's contribution margin (CM). Your company manufactures four different types of units:

- Standard widgets
- Blue flying widgets
- Red swimming widgets
- Yellow hopping widgets

To perform prescriptive analysis, your manager has built a spreadsheet for you to execute a Microsoft Excel Solver function.

	Standard	Blue Flying	Red Swimming	Yellow Hopping	Total
Number Produced	1	1	1	1	
CM per unit	17.87	15.20	21.00	19.87	
Total CM	17.87	15.20	21.00	19.87	73.94
Machine Hours per Unit	6	8	12	11	0
Total Machine Hours	6	8	12	11	37
Constraints					
Machine Hours					50,000
Demand	1,200	1,750	1,670	1,250	

1. What is the decision variable in the model?
2. What are the constraints in the model?
3. What is the objective function?

BE 3.14 (LO 5, 6) **Financial Accounting** Your private company wants to expand and grow into a new product line; however, that growth requires increased capital and investment in physical assets, people, and materials. You are asked to consider the most appropriate strategy to acquire the needed capital. You volunteered to engage in data analysis to provide insight to the discussion.

1. What is the objective of the analysis?
2. Develop two questions that will be relevant to the analysis.
3. What analyses will you use to answer each question?

BE 3.15 (LO 6) Identify whether the professional has developed a measurable and specific question appropriate for the practice area.

1. A financial statement auditor asks, "What is the expected value of the client issuing stock based on current market prices?"
2. An accounting information systems accountant asks, "How many units should the company produce to optimize the company's contribution margin?"
3. A tax accountant poses the question, "Based on last year's tax return, how will the current year changes in tax law impact the client's tax liability?"
4. A managerial accountant considers "Which products use the highest amount of raw materials in production?"
5. A financial accountant ponders "What dollar amount of accounts receivable are classified in the over 90 days outstanding category?"

BE 3.16 (LO 6) For each area of professional practice, identify an internal stakeholder and an external stakeholder.

Professional Practice	Internal Stakeholder	External Stakeholder
Accounting information systems		
Auditors		
Financial accountants		
Managerial accountants		
Tax accountants		

Exercises

EX 3.1 (LO 2, 6) `Data` `Financial Accounting` **Analysis of Measures** As the company controller for a yarn manufacturing supply company, you are asked to investigate sales by customer for the month of June 2025. You have critically assessed the objective and questions of your analysis and documented them as follows:

Objective	Initial Question	Sub-Questions	Possible Measures
Understand sales by customer for the month of June.	What happened to sales in the month of June?	What was total sales? What was the average sales amount? What was total sales by customer? Which customers had the highest sales?	**1.** Sum of sales amount (total measure). **2.** Average of sales amount (measure of location). **3.** Total sales separated by customer. **4.** Total sales separated by customer using a highlight table.

Use the available data to perform the analyses proposed in the possible measures section of the analysis plan.

EX 3.2 (LO 2, 6) `Data` `Managerial Accounting` **Analysis of Measures** Your company manufactures high-quality yarn for sale at craft stores and yarn and specialty shops across the country. Specifically, your facility manufactures merino wool yarn in a variety of colors and in two weights: chunky and DK weight. The product manager wants to understand differences in production quantities by product between 2025 and 2024 in the July manufacturing period, and has provided you with production data for select products. Use the spreadsheet to identify the available data and complete the following:

1. What is the objective of the analysis?

2. What are two initial questions you can ask about the data?

3. Create a column chart depicting the production quantity by ProductDescription and Year.

4. Calculate and identify several descriptive measures:

   a. Calculate the Average ProductionQuantity by ProductDescription in 2024 compared to 2025.

   b. Identify the lowest number of units produced by ProductionDescription in 2024 compared to 2025.

   c. Identify the highest number of units produced by ProductionDescription in 2024 compared to 2025.

EX 3.3 (LO 2, 6) `Data` `Financial Accounting` **Tableau Highlight Table** Your controller would like to better understand changes in specific vendor payments between 2024 and 2025 that were made by the city you work for. The controller is specifically interested in understanding the payments made to the following vendors:

- 4-Star Hose & Supply
- Aecom Technical Services, Inc.
- WRG, LLC
- Winston Water Cooler Ltd.
- Zoetis Inc.

You have downloaded the Vendor Payment file and uploaded it into Tableau for analysis. Create a highlight table in Tableau to identify changes in payments to each of these five vendors between 2024 and 2025.

EX 3.4 (LO 1, 2, 3, 4, 5) [Managerial Accounting] Vista Education is an educational publisher of college textbooks. There are some concerns that textbooks are being sold to increase bonuses at year-end. Subsequently, textbooks are being returned at the beginning of the new year for credit. The controller has asked you to perform data analysis of the issue so that they can understand the problem better. A visualization was created below to show sales and sales returns trends for the period from November 2024 to February 2026.

Complete the chart below for descriptive, diagnostic, predictive, and prescriptive analytics.

Objective	Initial Question	Sub-Question	Measures	Analyses
Descriptive Analysis: Understand total sales and sales returns.				
Diagnostic Analysis: Understand if there are patterns to sales and sales returns by the salesperson.				
Predictive Analysis: Can sales returns be predicted using historic values?				
Prescriptive Analysis: Understand the impacts on bonuses if the bonus calculation is changed.				

EX 3.5 (LO 3, 6) [Data] [Auditing] **Diagnostic Measures** Assume you are an audit staff assigned to audit the financial statements of a private entity distribution client for the year ended December 31, 2025. The client does not manufacture items, but acquires finished products and sells to a variety of retailers. The senior on the engagement team asked you to perform analytical procedures on sales returns. Your descriptive analysis revealed that sales returns increased as a percentage of sales. Use the spreadsheet to perform the following:

1. Calculate total sales dollars, returns dollars, sales quantity, and returns quantity for each year 2024 and 2025.
2. Calculate the percentage change in sales dollars, returns dollars, sales quantity, and returns quantity between 2024 and 2025.
3. Create a scatterplot whereby sales dollars are on the *x*-axis and the sales returns are on the *y*-axis.
4. Which months in 2025 have sales returns that you may consider as anomalies?

EX 3.6 (LO 3, 6) [Managerial Accounting] Glassworks is a supplier of office windows. The company has had a problem with debt collection, and bad debt write-offs have been increasing. They want to predict bad debt write-off amounts based on the dollar amounts of the accounts receivable. Historic data of bad debt write-off amounts have been plotted against its related accounts receivable dollar balances.

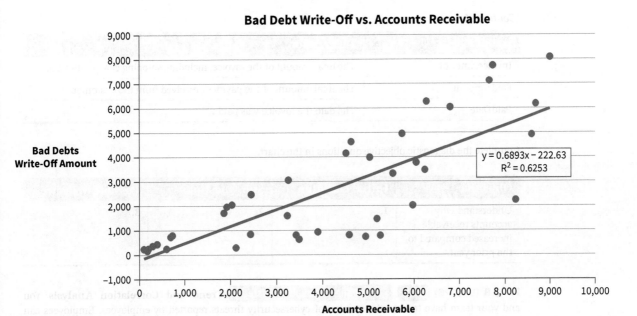

Bad Debt Write-Off vs. Accounts Receivable

$y = 0.6893x - 222.63$
$R^2 = 0.6253$

1. Identify the main stakeholder and their motivation for the data analysis.
2. What is the objective?
3. What kind of analysis is this (e.g., diagnostic, prescriptive, predictive, or descriptive)? Explain why.
4. What is the area of accounting practice in this data analysis?
5. How would you interpret the trendline being shown?
6. How would you interpret the value of the R^2 value?
7. What is the predicted bad debt write-off value if the accounts receivable value is $10,000?

EX 3.7 (LO 3, 6) ⬛ Financial Accounting ⬛ **Trend and Correlation Analysis** The corporate controller asked the team to analyze accounts receivable and the aging of accounts receivable compared to prior year. Your descriptive analysis indicates accounts receivable increased over prior year, while sales have remained steady. Since you are the intern on the job, your colleagues have asked you to consider the diagnostic analysis questions that you must ask to plan your analysis. You were provided with the data dictionary.

Data Field	Description
SalesOrderNumber	Uniquely assigned sales order number.
CustomerID	Uniquely assigned customer number.
CustomerName	A customers name.
CustomerCredit	Customer's credit limit.
CustomerAddress	U.S. Postal mailing address and street name.
CustomerCity	Mailing address city.
CustomerState	Mailing address state.
CustomerZipcode	Mailing address zip.
CustomerPayTerms	Payment terms negotiated with the customer.
SalesOrderDate	Sales order date.
SalesOrderID	Uniquely identifiable item number.
SalesOrderDescription	Description of item.
ItemPrice	Sales price of the item per negotiated terms with the customer.
ItemQuantity	Total quantity of items sold to the customer.
InvoiceNumber	Uniquely assigned invoice number.

(Continued)

(*Continued*)

Data Field	Description
InvoiceAmount	The total amount of the invoice, including shipping charges and tax.
PaidAmount	The total amount of the payment received from the customer.
PaidDate	The date the invoice was paid.

Complete the diagnostic objective questions in the chart.

Objective	Initial Question	Sub-Questions	Possible Measures
Understand why accounts receivable increased compared to the prior year.	1.	2.	3.

EX 3.8 (LO 3, 6) `Data` `Accounting Information Systems` **Trend and Correlation Analysis** You and your team have tracked the number of cybersecurity threats reported by employees. Employees can report cybersecurity threats such as phishing attempts, and IT specialists can report threats through examination of the monthly login report.

Your initial descriptive analysis revealed that in the last three years, 313 cyber incidents were reported. There were 73 reports in 2023, 111 in 2024, and 129 in 2025. Your manager would like to understand why cyber incident reports have increased. You have started to identify initial questions, sub-questions, and possible measures for your analysis in the following chart. Complete the chart.

Objective	Initial Questions	Sub-Questions	Possible Measures
Determine why cyber incident reports are increasing.	1.	Are there more cyber incidents reporting during a specific period of time?	Create a line chart of cyber incident reports over time and review for a trend or pattern.
	2.	3.	Perform a correlation between training expenses and cyber incidents reported by using the CORREL function in Excel.

4. Perform the possible analyses.

EX 3.9 (LO 4, 6) `Data` `Accounting Information Systems` **Trendlines** Your controller has asked you to demonstrate the relationship between cybersecurity training expenses and the number of valid cybersecurity threats reported by employees. You have collected monthly data reporting the monthly cybersecurity training expense and the number of valid cybersecurity threats reported by employees. Create a line graph showing the relationship between these two variables. Include the trendline, equation, and *R*-square of your analysis.

EX 3.10 (LO 5, 6) `Data` `Auditing` **Sales Returns Analytical Procedures** You are the audit intern staffed on the fiscal year ended December 31, 2025 financial statement audit of a private company. Your senior auditor is thrilled that you have just completed a data analytics in accounting course and wants you to use your knowledge of predictive analytics to develop an expectation of sales returns based on sales quantity to perform analytical procedures. You have engaged in critical thinking and developed the partial chart.

1. Complete the chart:

Objective	Initial Question	Sub-Question	Possible Measures
Predict sales returns.	How much will sales returns change if we have a 10% increase in sales quantity?	1.	Regression analysis

2. Perform the regression analysis to predict sales return dollars using sales quantity.

3. Write the regression equation.

4. What is the R^2 for the regression model?

EX 3.11 (LO 5, 6) `Data` `Financial Accounting` **Estimate Warranty Expense for Accruals** As a financial accountant for a public widget manufacturing company, you are given a data file and asked to calculate and record month-end adjusting journal entries. You must calculate the warranty expense amount for January 2025.

1. Perform a regression to predict warranty expense using sales quantity.

2. Write the regression equation.

3. You just performed a query of your company's accounting information system and determined that January 2026 sales quantity is 10,385. Write the journal entry to record warranty expense.

EX 3.12 (LO 5, 6) `Data` `Managerial Accounting` **Trend Analysis** You are a financial analyst supporting the control in a private company that manufactures paper plates, trays, and other disposable paper products. The company is owned by a private equity (PE) investment group. The PE board is interested in cost savings and identifying efficiencies within the company's processes. You collected monthly data on the number of die-cut changes and the monthly maintenance expenses. The goal is to predict the cost of maintenance expenses for the next period.

1. Run a regression analysis using die-cut changes to predict maintenance expenses.

2. Write the regression equation.

3. If the company plans to have 650 die-cut changes during the month of January 2024, what is the company's expected maintenance expense?

EX 3.13 (LO 4, 6) Collins Realtors would like to predict home sales using a regression model. The regression model is based on historic values for certain variables. The regression statistics from Excel are provided below.

SUMMARY OUTPUT					
Regression Statistics					
Multiple R	0.992439				
R Square	0.984935				
Adjusted R Square	0.983523				
Standard Error	1.641107				
Observations	36				
ANOVA					
	df	*SS*	*MS*	*F*	*Significance F*
Regression	2	5,634.567	1,878.189	697.3737	3.23E-29
Residual	32	86.18341	2.693232		
Total	35	5,720.75			
	Coefficients	*Standard Error*	*t Stat*	*P-value*	
Intercept	−45.5369	2.340635	−19.4549	2.7E-19	
Inventory Count	0.005637	0.00037	15.22256	3.28E-16	
Unemployment Rate	443.7485	77.97933	5.690592	2.66E-06	
Mortgage Rate	1,060.542	205.0054	5.173237	1.2E-05	

1. What are the dependent variables and independent values in the regression model?

2. What does the ANOVA statistic show?

3. What can be interpreted from the multiple R-value?

4. What can be interpreted from the R-squared value?

5. The mean for home sales count is 26.5 and the standard deviation is 12.78. What can be interpreted from the standard error value?

6. What can be interpreted from the p-values for inventory count, unemployment, and mortgage rate?

EX 3.14 (LO 5, 6) `Data` `Managerial Accounting` **Optimization** Your production manager has asked you to identify the quantity of items that should be produced to maximize the company's contribution margin for the period. Your company has four products:

- Standard widgets
- Blue flying widgets
- Red swimming widgets
- Yellow hopping widgets

You have created a spreadsheet outlining the demand, machine hours per unit, contribution margin per unit, and overall machine hours. Use Microsoft Solver to identify the number of units to be produced for each product and the maximum contribution margin.

EX 3.15 (LO 5) `Data` `Managerial Accounting` **Use Linear Optimization to Determine Product Mix and Profit** You and your college roommates open a business designing and crafting dog and cat leashes with your college logo and colors. You have decided to offer leashes in three lengths: 6, 8, and 12 feet.

Further, you have two types of leash: "standard" or "decorative." While the decorative leashes take longer to create, they have a large profit margin per each. However, the standard leashes are in higher demand. You and your two roommates have put a schedule together so that you can fit everything into your week—this includes classes, social events, and crafting time. Since you are enrolled in the data analytics in accounting course, you have volunteered to calculate how many of each type of leash you should produce weekly based on demand, gross profit for each product, and the constraint of work hours.

1. Perform a linear optimization using Excel Solver.
2. How many of each unit should you and your two roommates produce each week?
3. What is the total gross profit you should expect to earn based on the weekly production of dog leashes?
4. Are there any constraints identified in the answer report that are nonbinding?

EX 3.16 (LO 4, 5) `Data` **Build the Spreadsheet and Identify Constraints** Along with your college roommates, you are opening a business to make decorative hats, T-shirts, and socks with your college colors. You have decided to start with five core products:

- Decorative ball cap
- Decorative "GO Team" t-shirt
- Decorative "Defense Wins Championships" t-shirt
- Decorative socks
- Decorative knee-high socks

As part of your business plan, you want to calculate the total number of each product to create each week. You plan to use Microsoft Solver to identify the maximum number of units to produce given your constraints. You want to maximize your company's profit given the constraints of work hours per person. The table outlines the gross profit and crafting hours per unit for each item.

Product	Gross Profit per Item	Crafting Hours per Item
Ball cap	5.00	4
GO Team t-shirt	7.50	2.5
Defense Wins Championships t-shirt	7.50	3
Socks	3.30	6
Knee-high socks	4.50	3.5

In addition, you and your roommates have committed to working the following hours each week:

- You: 20
- Roommate 1: 20
- Roommate 2: 15
- Roommate 3: 10

1. Build a linear optimization model spreadsheet.
2. Calculate the total number of units for each product that should be produced each week.
3. What is the total gross profit you should expect to earn based on the weekly production?
4. Are there any constraints identified in the answer report that are nonbinding?

EX 3.17 (LO 5, 6) `Data` `Managerial Accounting` **Linear Optimization** Tiana's Jewel Design, Inc. designs and manufactures mass-produced metal jewelry and custom-designed silver-plated jewelry.

Currently, the owner designs and produces three lines of custom jewelry: necklaces, bracelets, and earrings (decision variables). The contribution margin and the resource requirements for each product follows:

	Necklaces	Bracelets	Earrings
Contribution Margin per unit	$ 12.00	$ 8.00	$ 14.00
Resource Requirements:			
Direct Materials, ounces per unit	22	8	13
Design Hours per unit	4	1	5
Machining Hours per unit	2	1	2

They would like to maximize the contribution margin (objective function). However, the owner has these constraints:

- A contract to produce at least 10 pairs of custom earrings a month.
- They can sell all the custom necklaces and custom earrings that are produced.
- Demand for custom bracelets is only 30 a month.
- Each month 800 ounces of silver plate can be purchased.
- Two designers work a total of 120 hours a month.
- An estimated 80 hours of machining time are available each month.

1. Use Microsoft Excel Solver to create a linear optimization model.
2. How many of each product should be produced to maximize the contribution margin?
3. Are any of the constraints binding?
4. Based on the output from the answer report, what advice would you give the owner?

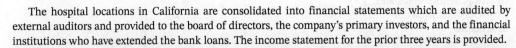

Professional Application Case   Healthcare Service Company

Kindred Healthcare is a post-acute healthcare service company that operates long-term acute care and rehabilitation services across the United States. Kindred's hospitals offer the same in-depth care that a patient would receive at a traditional hospital, but for an extended recovery period. The data used in this case is based on actual data from the California Health and Human Services Open Data Portal.

Kindred has 13 long-term acute care hospitals in California:

- Baldwin Park
- Brea
- La Mirada
- Los Angeles
- Ontario
- Paramount
- Rancho

- Riverside
- Sacramento
- San Diego
- San Francisco Bay Area
- South Bay
- Westminster

The hospital locations in California are consolidated into financial statements which are audited by external auditors and provided to the board of directors, the company's primary investors, and the financial institutions who have extended the bank loans. The income statement for the prior three years is provided.

	2019 (unaudited)	2018 (audited)	2017 (audited)
Gross Patient Revenue	$2,802,211,999	$2,515,881,547	$2,423,431,540
Deductions from Revenue	$2,206,888,182	$1,940,233,238	$1,869,518,824
Net Patient Revenue	$ 595,323,817	$ 575,648,309	$ 553,912,716
Other Operating Revenue	$ 2,262,385	$ 2,367,007	$ 2,663,316

(Continued)

(*Continued*)

	2019 (unaudited)	2018 (audited)	2017 (audited)
Operating Expenses	$ 579,928,100	$ 523,090,033	$ 506,521,633
Net Revenue from Operations	$ 17,658,102	$ 54,925,283	$ 50,054,399
Nonoperating Revenue	$ 1,237,718	$ 970,497	$ 763,174
Nonoperating Expense	$ 110,477	$ 200,367	$ 385,724
Income Tax	$ 86,442	$ 73,200	$ 25,176
Net Income	$ 18,698,901	$ 55,622,213	$ 50,406,673

The financial statements are prepared based on annual amounts from each of the California locations. The consolidated entity has provided a data file that contains annual data by location for a variety of data fields.

PAC 3.1 Auditing: Develop Objectives and Questions for an Audit Plan

Data **Auditing** You are a second-year staff member at a public accounting firm who is assigned to the Kindred Hospitals engagement, which is a new engagement for the firm. You have been asked to perform descriptive, diagnostic, and predictive analytics for your engagement team.

The senior auditor provided you with an Excel file that includes gross patient revenue by hospital location from 2013 to 2019. The senior asked you to perform exploratory data analytics and outline an audit plan, which you recognize is similar to outlining objectives, questions, and sub-questions for data analysis. Before you can fully explore the data, you must understand it, so you begin with descriptive statistics.

Complete the chart.

Objective	Initial Question	Sub-Questions	Possible Measures
Descriptive Analysis: Understand gross patient revenue (GrossPatientRevenue) for the year 2019, which is the year under audit.	What happened to gross patient revenue during 2019?	1.	2.
Diagnostic Analysis: Understand what happened to gross patient revenue for the year 2019 compared to 2018, specifically, GrossPatientRevenue, GrossInpatientRevenue, and GrossOutpatientRevenue data points.	Which locations had changes in revenue from 2018 to 2019?	3.	4.
Predictive Analysis: Develop an expectation for gross patient revenue in 2019 based on the components patient days, out patient visits, and average length of stay.	What factors drive changes in gross revenue?	5.	6.

7. Perform the possible analytics as described for each measure.

PAC 3.2 Managerial Accounting: Evaluate Labor Costs and Productivity

Data **Managerial Accounting**   Assume you are a managerial accountant for the consolidated California group of Kindred Hospitals. The director of operations has asked that you analyze the annual data associated with hospital labor. Specifically, the director of operations is interested in the following variables:

Variables	Definition per Data Dictionary
HopsitalFTE	Number of hospital full-time employees
NurseFTE	Average number of nursing personnel
ProductiveHours	Total productive hours
NonproductiveHours	Total nonproductive hours
PaidHours	Total paid hours
MedicalStaff	Number of active medical staff

Complete the chart.

Objective	Initial Question	Sub-Questions	Possible Measures
Descriptive Analysis: Understand labor information for 2018–2019.	What happened to labor hours during 2018 and 2019?	1.	2.
Diagnostic Analysis: Determine why variables changed between 2018 and 2019.	Which hospitals have increasing salary expenses from 2018 to 2019?	3.	4.
Predictive Analysis: Identify if there is relationship between total productive hours and gross patient revenue.	Can productive hours predict gross patient revenue?	5.	6.

7. Use the data to calculate the measures.

PAC 3.3 Financial Accounting: Understand Patient Revenue

Data **Financial Accounting**   You are a financial analyst working for the controller's group for the California location of Kindred Hospital group. Your controller has highlighted the fact that gross revenue consists of both inpatient revenue and outpatient revenue. However, only one facility—Kindred Hospital-Rancho—has outpatient revenue. Therefore, the controller wants a full understanding of inpatient revenue by facility for 2019. Specifically, you are asked to understand the dollar amount of inpatient revenue contributed by each facility in 2019, and how inpatient revenue has changed since 2018. Finally, the controller is creating a financial forecast for inpatient revenue for 2020 and wants to understand the utilization data that may contribute to the generation of this forecast. To satisfy your company controller, you are planning your analysis and have started the chart which follows. The controller has also provided you with a data dictionary for the data relevant to this analysis.

Variables	Definition per Data Dictionary
DayTotal	Patient Days Total
OccupancyLicensed	Occupancy rate—Licensed beds
OccupancyAvailable	Occupancy rate—Available beds
AverageLengthStayAll	Average Length of Stay—Including Long Term Care
AverageLengthStayNoLTC	Average Length of Stay—Excluding Long Term Care
GrossInpatientRevenue	Gross Inpatient Revenue

Complete the chart for descriptive, diagnostic, and predictive analytics.

Objective	Initial Question	Sub-Questions	Possible Measures
Descriptive Analysis: Understand gross inpatient revenue for the year 2019, which is the year under audit.	What happened to gross patient revenue during 2019?	1.	2.
Diagnostic Analysis: Understand what happened to gross inpatient revenue for the year 2019 compared to 2018.	How has revenue changed at the locations?	3.	4.
Predictive Analysis: Identify the utilization measures that are related to in-patient revenue.	Are there any measures correlated to inpatient revenue?	5.	6.

7. Use the data available to calculate the measures.

PAC 3.4 Tax Accounting: Evaluate Nonprofit and For-Profit Tax Return Data

Data **Tax Accounting** As a tax accountant at Kindred you have been asked to analyze the nonprofit and for-profit hospital data. Kindred Hospitals has three hospitals in California that are tax-exempt organizations. These three hospitals must be separated from the for-profit hospitals for tax purposes. In addition, you have been asked to do an analysis of a sample of nonprofit tax filings and compare those filings to the amounts that Kindred's nonprofit hospitals filed for 2019. The variables and data definitions for both files are included in the following tables:

IRS 990 Data:

Variables	Definition per Data Dictionary
Assets	Total asset book value at year-end
Income	Net Income
Revenue	Revenue reported on line 12 of Form 990

Kindred 2013–2019 Financial Data

Variables	Definition per Data Dictionary
TotalAssets	Total Assets
TotalRevenue	Net patient revenue plus other operating revenue
NetIncome	Net Income

Complete the chart.

Objective	Initial Question	Sub-Questions	Possible Measures
Descriptive Analysis: Understand assets, revenue, and income information for Kindred's nonprofit and for-profit hospitals.	Which hospitals have the highest income?	1.	2.
Descriptive Analysis: Understand how IRS 990 data for nonprofit hospitals compares to the Kindred nonprofit hospitals.	Are the Kindred Hospitals comparable to the sample of IRS 990 filings?	3.	4.

(Continued)

Objective	Initial Question	Sub-Questions	Possible Measures
Diagnostic Analysis: Identify trends in assets, revenue, and income for Kindred hospitals.	5.	6.	7.
Diagnostic Analysis: Compare Kindred data to IRS 990 data.	8.	9.	10.

11. Use the data to calculate the measures.

Planning Data and Analysis Strategies

Armed with an understanding of the motivations and objectives for the data analysis project and after formulating the necessary objective questions, it is time for the final step in the planning stage—designing the data and analysis strategies. You will soon be expected to apply your knowledge, common sense, and problem-solving skills to design a variety of accounting, audit, and tax-related data and analysis strategies. This chapter will help you develop the skills necessary to create effective data analysis project plans.

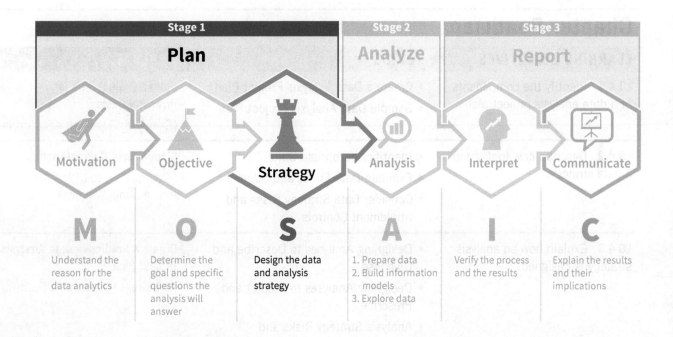

Stage 1			Stage 2	Stage 3	
Plan			Analyze	Report	
Motivation	Objective	Strategy	Analysis	Interpret	Communicate
M	**O**	**S**	**A**	**I**	**C**
Understand the reason for the data analytics	Determine the goal and specific questions the analysis will answer	Design the data and analysis strategy	1. Prepare data 2. Build information models 3. Explore data	Verify the process and the results	Explain the results and their implications

PROFESSIONAL INSIGHT   **Why Should You Plan Data and Analysis Strategies?**

Taylor was excited to begin her career in auditing after interning at a Big Four accounting firm during the last busy season.

My audit team had me design my own data and analysis strategies and document each step I performed. While I lacked confidence at first, I felt very supported. I learned so much, even when I made mistakes and had to pivot my strategies.

I was more successful when I understood the motivation for and the objective of my tasks. I was able to formulate better questions, which resulted in better data choices. The measurement scales of my selected data also pointed me toward the appropriate analyses.

My first task was a descriptive analysis. I had to determine if the year-end accounts receivable subsidiary ledger and general ledger balances reconciled. After checking if any credit customer's activities were excluded from the general ledger accounts receivable balance, I created an accounts receivable aging report listing each credit customer's outstanding balances from the subsidiary ledger. I compared the aging reports' items to the general ledger accounts receivable postings and noted each unmatched item. If there were no unmatched items, the accounts receivable balance in the general ledger was successfully reconciled and verified.

I then designed a diagnostic analysis strategy to determine which receivable activities were causing any unmatched items I had found. My strategy began with gathering the client's accounts receivable process documentation. For each unmatched item, I identified which process caused the items to be included in both ledgers. Documenting my work helped me explain what, how, and why I performed each step. This record will be helpful when we repeat this verification in next year's audit. **Designing my own data and analysis strategies helped me gain relevant skills and the confidence to start my auditing career.**

Chapter Roadmap

LEARNING OBJECTIVES	TOPICS	APPLY IT
LO 4.1 Identify the components of a data analysis project plan.	• Create a Data Analysis Project Plan • Sample Data Analysis Project Plan	**Build a Project Plan for Inventory Costs** (Example: Financial Accounting)
LO 4.2 Describe how to develop a data strategy.	• Identify Appropriate Data • Evaluate Data Fields and Sources • Consider Data Strategy Risks and Implement Controls	**Identify Data Characteristics** (Example: Accounting Information Systems)
LO 4.3 Explain how an analysis strategy is designed.	• Designing Analyses to Describe and Diagnose • Designing Analyses to Predict and Prescribe • Analysis Strategy Risks and Suggested Controls	**Create a Predictive Data Analysis Project Plan** (Example: Financial Accounting)
LO 4.4 Summarize data and analysis strategies in professional practice areas.	• Accounting Information Systems • Auditing • Financial Accounting • Managerial Accounting • Tax Accounting	**Match Strategies with Professional Practice Areas**

Data   The Data tag appears in the chapter when the data for an example, illustration, or application are available in the book's product page on www.wiley.com.

Data analytics software is continuously changing, and there may be more recent versions of the software referenced in this chapter.

4.1 How Do Accountants Design Data Analysis Projects?

LEARNING OBJECTIVE ❶
Identify the components of a data analysis project plan.

Recall that the first step in planning a data analysis project is understanding the motivations for the project, such as identifying problems, evaluating patterns and opportunities, measuring performance, and regulatory compliance. Considering the perspectives of the project's primary stakeholders is an important part of that understanding. Next, thinking critically about a project's purpose helps define the objective and articulate the project's specific questions. Common objectives and questions can be grouped by whether the analysis results describe, diagnose, or predict an outcome, or if the analysis results should prescribe future organizational strategy.

The final step of the data analysis planning stage is designing a professional plan for the data analysis project. Critical thinking continues to play a vital role, from selecting a strategy for the data and the analysis, to identifying inherent risks to both and embedding internal controls to reduce them. A data and analysis strategy plan is an organized and deliberate blueprint for the project. It also allows someone other than its creator to perform the analysis, which can free accountants to perform other valuable services with their business and regulatory expertise.

Create a Data Analysis Project Plan

Many of us use planning tools every day, such as relying on navigation applications to plan travel time and how to get to new destinations. Planning tools make tasks more efficient and the results more effective. They also often provide logical explanations for the necessity of certain steps or why they should be performed in a particular order.

This chapter summarizes a tool for data analysis project planning that provides similar benefits for accountants (**Illustration 4.1**). The order of the components is intentional:

Step 1: Focus on the Objective

- Keep the project's objective and specific questions in mind to select the best data and analysis strategies to fulfill the objective and answer those questions. Simply remembering to ask how the plan's proposed data and analysis strategy decisions relate to the objective helps us make better choices.

Step 2: Select a Data Strategy

- Use critical thinking to develop and rank a few data alternatives. This ensures that we choose the data option most appropriate for the objective.

Step 3: Select an Analysis Strategy

- Use what was learned from selecting the data strategy and apply that same development and ranking process to analysis alternatives. Following this step increases the likelihood of selecting the best analysis option.

Step 4: Consider Risks

- Considering and prioritizing critical risks to both the data and the analysis strategies reveals how these risks can create misleading and invalid results.

Step 5: Embed Controls

- Designing and implementing preventative and detective controls into the analysis process leads to results that are accurate, valid, and reliable.

A data analysis plan increases the likelihood that analysis results accurately describe what happened, diagnose why it happened, predict what is likely to happen, or prescribe the best

ILLUSTRATION 4.1   A Data Analysis Project Plan

❶ Project Objective

Stay focused on the project's objective and specific questions.

❷ Data Strategy

Develop data alternatives and evaluate, rank, and select the best option.

❸ Analysis Strategy

Develop analysis alternatives and evaluate, rank, and select the best option.

❹ Consider Risks

Identify risks to both the data strategy and analysis strategy.

❺ Embed Controls

Implement controls to reduce risks within the data and analysis strategies.

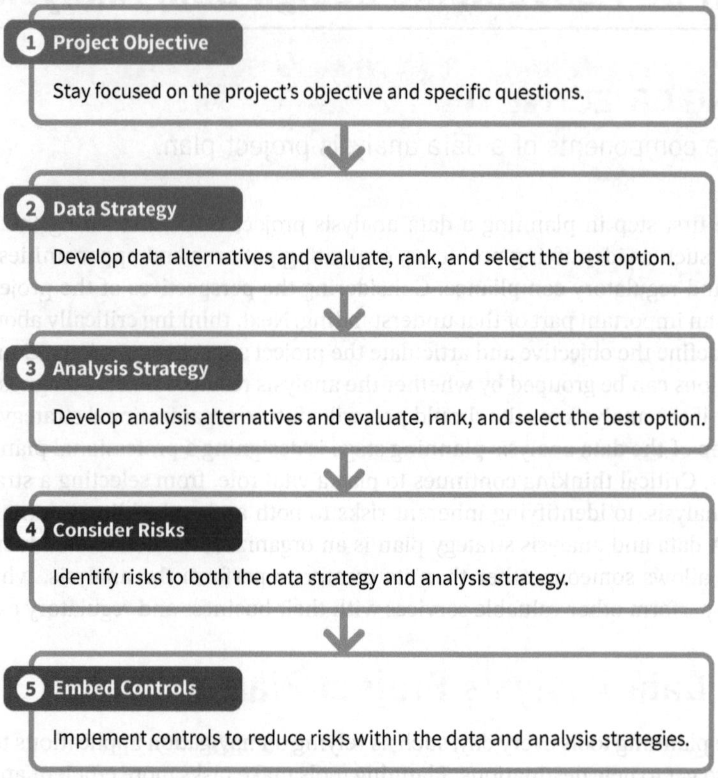

course forward. When the project plan is complete, so is the data analysis process planning stage, and it is time to move to the analysis stage. Chapter 5 describes how to properly prepare data for analysis. But first, practice using this project planning tool in an accounting context.

Sample Data Analysis Project Plan

Imagine you are a financial accountant for WeMakeIt, Inc., which is an employee-owned 3D printing corporation in Phoenix, Arizona. They sell superhero figurines, mechanical shop tools, and medical prostheses that are manufactured with 3D printing technologies. Founded five years ago by a local college student, Marisabel Cordoba, WeMakeIt, Inc. grew quickly to fill their production capacities and has maintained a stable size for the last three years.

Step 1: Focus on the Objective

The project in this example is to estimate the bad debts in the 2025 year-end accounts receivable balance. The result will be the value estimate for the 2025 year-end adjusting journal entry that debits bad debts expense and credits the allowance for uncollectible accounts contra-asset.

Applying Critical Thinking 4.1

Estimate Bad Debts

The U.S. GAAP ending accounts receivable method requires the following:

- The year-end accounts receivable balance can be considered in total or in age group subtotals. Age grouping rules for manufacturing companies are typically less than 30 days, 30 to 60 days, and greater than 60 days outstanding, but these vary by industry.

- Reviewing regulatory guidance, industry practices, business policies and processes, and past bad debt estimation percentages is the professional approach for selecting bad debt estimation percentages. Typically, as the age of the accounts receivable increases, the percentage uncollectible applied to that age also increases **(Knowledge)**.

Assume the following for this example:

- The company offers its credit customers payment terms of 30 days.
- The 2025 year-end accounts receivable balance in the general ledger is $83,734.30.
- The 2025 year-end unadjusted allowance for uncollectible accounts has a credit balance of $3,000.
- WeMakeIt, Inc. decided to use the percentage of year-end accounts receivable method to estimate bad debts expense each year. They have authorized a 2% bad debts assumption for invoices that are 30 to 60 days outstanding and 30% for invoices that are outstanding for more than 60 days.

This data analysis project has the following objective and related questions:

- **Objective:** Accurately estimate bad debts within the year-end accounts receivable balance in accordance with U.S. GAAP.
- **Specific questions:**
  1. What is a reasonable estimate of the uncollectible receivables in the 2025 year-end outstanding accounts receivables?
  2. What amount should be used in the adjusting journal entry for bad debts expense?

With the objective defined and the questions articulated, it is time to develop the data strategy.

Step 2: Select the Data Strategy

Develop several data alternatives that could help answer the objective question. Then, to select the most useful data alternative for the project plan, identify the factors you want to use to rank these alternatives, and assign values to each alternative's factors. The best data strategy alternative is the one with the highest overall factor ratings.

Applying Critical Thinking 4.2

Consider Different Perspectives

The net realizable value of accounts receivable (accounts receivable minus the allowance for uncollectible accounts) is reported on the balance sheet as a current asset. The bad debts expense reduces net income reported on the income statement. Keep in mind that parties with very different perspectives use this information for decision-making (**Stakeholders**):

- Creditors, who want to be repaid, are interested in the liquidity of the assets.
- Shareholders, who predict future stock values as well as dividend expectations, must understand the expected future cash inflows from operations.
- Managers want to earn bonuses that are determined by growth in net income and total assets. The change in the allowance for uncollectible accounts will influence both amounts.

There are a few data strategy alternatives that could be considered either individually or in combination for this project:

- All credit sales invoices and collections data that pertain to the accounting period.
- All outstanding invoices included in the year-end accounts receivable balance.
- The prior year-end's adjusted account balance and the current year-end's unadjusted account balance in the allowance for uncollectible accounts.
- Current year's total accounts receivable write-offs.
- Authorized bad debt estimation percentages for accounts receivable age categories.

Recall that the objective question for this analysis project asks for a reasonable estimate of the year-end uncollectible accounts receivables. Because WeMakeIt, Inc. uses the GAAP percentage of ending accounts receivables method with the three age categories typical for manufacturing companies, the data that would be most useful considering the objectives would include:

- The outstanding invoices in the year-end accounts receivable balance.
- This year's unadjusted allowance for uncollectible account balance.
- Authorized bad debt estimation percentages for each accounts receivable age group.

Applying Critical Thinking 4.3

Choose the Data Strategy That Fits Your Objective

Both data and analysis strategies are improved when they are developed, evaluated, and ranked by the factor values placed on each potential data strategy:

- Factors that value data relevance, such as expected future collections, prior estimation errors, and expected risk of uncollectibility, should be used to select the best data strategy for WeMakeIt, Inc's analysis plan (**Alternatives**).
- Using the data from outstanding invoices, the unadjusted allowance for uncollectible accounts receivable, and authorized bad debt estimation percentages was the best choice for WeMakeIt, Inc's analysis. These data choices best match the objective of the analysis, which is to calculate a reasonable estimate for the year-end uncollectible accounts receivable (**Purpose**).
- For a personal example, if your objective was to dress successfully for an interview, then you could develop, evaluate, and rank the alternatives of wearing something you already own, borrowing from a friend, or buying something new to wear to the interview. Using clothes you already own would rank higher than buying new clothes if you were ranking options based on lowest costs and time factors.

Step 3: Select the Analysis Strategy

For any project plan, choosing the best analysis strategy involves considering and evaluating several possible alternative analyses given the objective questions and the already selected strategy for the data. The analysis alternatives in this bad debt estimation example involve different methods for determining the age of an outstanding invoice:

- Days outstanding from the invoice date forward.
- Days outstanding from the due date forward.

The first analysis alternative is preferable because WeMakeIt, Inc.'s policy is to allow customers 30 days to pay their invoices and because they estimate bad debts only when an invoice is past its due date, which is equal to or more than 30 days outstanding.

How To

Therefore, the first question, what is a reasonable estimate of the uncollectible receivables in the 2025 year-end outstanding accounts receivables, will be answered by summing each age group's estimated bad debts value. This is a measure estimating the uncollectible portion of the year-end accounts receivable balance (**Illustration 4.2**). (**Data** See **How To 4.1** at the end of the chapter to learn how to calculate the figures in this illustration.)

ILLUSTRATION 4.2   WeMakeIt, Inc.: Estimated Value of Uncollectible Receivables

	< 30 days	30–60 days	> 60 days	Total
Total accounts receivable value	$ 30,099.29	$ 20,441.46	$ 33,193.55	$ 83,734.30
x % uncollectible	0%	2%	30%	
$ Estimated as uncollectible	$ 0	$ 408.83	$ 9,958.07	$ 10,366.89

The second question, what value should be used in the adjusting journal entry at year-end for bad debts expense, will be answered when this total of $10,366.89 is reduced by the unadjusted year-end allowance for uncollectible accounts balance ($3,000). The resulting calculated value is the year-end adjusting journal entry debiting bad debt expense and crediting allowance for uncollectible accounts:

	Debit	Credit
Bad debts expense	$7,366.89	
Allowance for uncollectible accounts		$7,366.89

Increasing the allowance account's $3,000 unadjusted balance by $7,366.89 will result in an adjusted balance of $10,366.89, equal to the estimated uncollectible amounts in accounts receivable at the 2025 year-end. **Illustration 4.3** summarizes the first three steps of this project's plan.

ILLUSTRATION 4.3　In-Progress Project Plan for Estimating Year-End Bad Debts: Steps 1–3

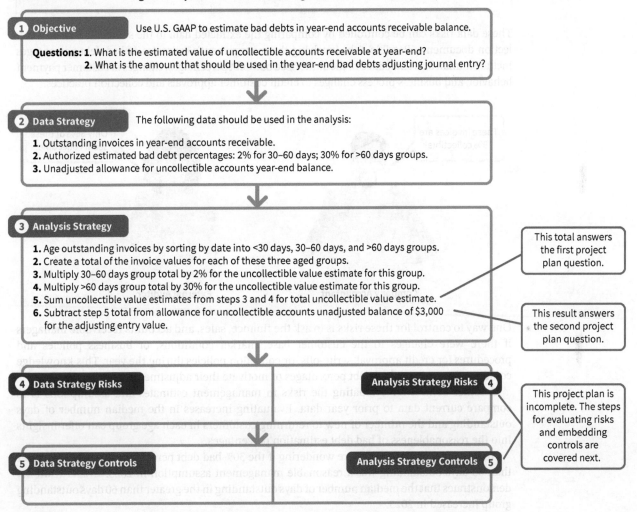

The last two steps are considering risks and controls for both the data strategy and the analysis strategy. First we will evaluate the data strategy's risks and controls, and then the analysis strategy risks and controls.

Steps 4 and 5: Data Strategy Risks and Controls

While organizations invest in processes and controls designed to capture accounting data correctly, accounting databases inevitably have some data issues. In this example, the data include the 2025 year-end accounts receivable outstanding invoices and the authorized bad debt estimation percentages. There could be some risks to using this accounts receivable data:

- Missing or incorrectly included invoices in the general or the subsidiary ledger.
- Errors in the invoice due date fields or the invoice total amounts.
- Errors created when the data are exported from the AIS system into the analysis tool.

Applying Critical Thinking 4.4

Threats to Data Strategy

Data risks can impact the accuracy and validity of analysis results. These risks must be evaluated so appropriate controls can be added to the project plan. Data strategy risks can include (**Risks**):

- Dirty data such as incomplete data, inaccurate data, and incorrectly formatted data fields.
- Data irrelevant to the objective of the project.
- Insufficient data for the analysis to be reliable.
- Data that is an unrepresentative sample of the underlying population.
- Errors in management estimates and assumptions about the data.

These data risks can be controlled by comparing the extracted data to the source invoice and collection documents. Possible risks involving the management's estimates of bad debt percentages include human bias embedded in the authorized bad debt percentages, changes in customer payment behavior, and business process changes to credit customer approvals and collection practices.

Company Accountant — These invoices are 99% collectible!

External Auditor — Only 86% of these seem collectible...

One way to control for these risks is to ask the finance, sales, and accounts receivable managers if there were changes to the customer base, market conditions, or business policies and procedures for credit approval, write-offs, or collection policies during the year. This knowledge could confirm existing bad debt percentages or motivate their adjustment.

Another control for evaluating the risks in management estimates and assumptions is to compare current data to prior year data. Evaluating increases in the median number of days outstanding and the number of new to returning customers in each age group can offer insights into the reasonableness of bad debt estimation percentages.

To illustrate, imagine you were wondering if the 30% bad debt percentage for invoices greater than 60 days outstanding was a reasonable management assumption in 2025. **Illustration 4.4** demonstrates that the median number of days outstanding in the greater than 60 days outstanding group increased in 2025.

ILLUSTRATION 4.4 Data Risk in Bad Debt Percentages: Median Days Outstanding

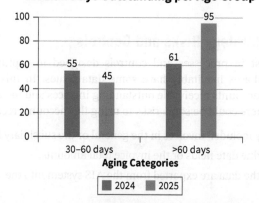

2024 and 2025 Past-Due Accounts Receivable Median Days Outstanding per Age Group

Aging Categories	2024	2025
30–60 days	55	45
>60 days	61	95

Additionally, you might wonder if this increase was caused by new customers, as the payment habits of new customers are more uncertain than those of continuing customers. **Illustration 4.5** shows that the >60 days age group has many outstanding invoices from new customers.

Comparing Past-Due Invoices for New Customers vs. Returning Customers by Age Group

ILLUSTRATION 4.5 Data Risk in Bad Debt Percentages: Risks from New Customers

The results of these control tests indicate that if the 2024 bad debt percentage for this age group was used in 2025, it may not accurately measure the bad debts expected in the 2025 accounts receivable balance. These visualizations show that implementing controls, such as data reasonableness tests, before performing an analysis can result in better business and professional intelligence.

Steps 4 and 5: Analysis Strategy Risks and Controls

Common analysis risks include errors in data manipulation, calculation, or using technology, as well as human biases and ethical violations when using sensitive data. Here are some examples of analysis risks when estimating bad debts:

- Errors in age group categorization and age total calculations.
- Incorrect application of bad debt estimation percentages to age group totals.
- Erroneous summing of estimated bad debts across age groups.
- Mistakes in the calculation of the value to use for bad debts expense.

Verifying the accuracy of the age group categorizations and each sum and multiplication performed on age group data items and totals would control for these risks.

Another control is to use common sense when reviewing the results for reasonableness. **Illustration 4.6** uses an example from the 30–60 days age group estimation to show how a common sense check helps catch large errors. The total outstanding accounts receivable for that age group was $20,441.46, and the uncollectible percentage for that group was 2%. The estimated uncollectible value for that age group was calculated as the product of those two numbers, resulting in $408.83. This control has verified our calculation.

ILLUSTRATION 4.6 Common Sense Check for the 30–60 Days Group Results

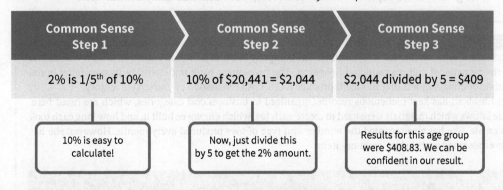

Analysis results that significantly vary from common sense checks should be verified.

The project plan design for this example is now complete (**Illustration 4.7**).

ILLUSTRATION 4.7 Complete Project Plan for Estimating Bad Debts

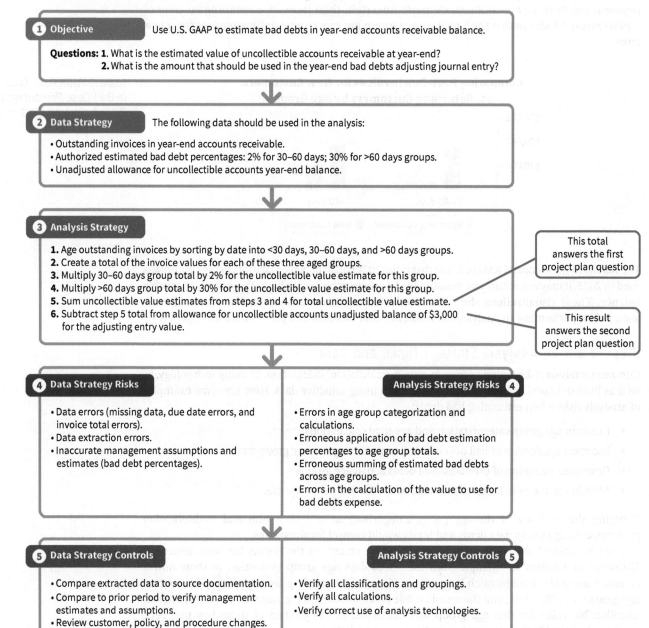

① Objective — Use U.S. GAAP to estimate bad debts in year-end accounts receivable balance.

Questions: 1. What is the estimated value of uncollectible accounts receivable at year-end?
2. What is the amount that should be used in the year-end bad debts adjusting journal entry?

② Data Strategy — The following data should be used in the analysis:

- Outstanding invoices in year-end accounts receivable.
- Authorized estimated bad debt percentages: 2% for 30–60 days; 30% for >60 days groups.
- Unadjusted allowance for uncollectible accounts year-end balance.

③ Analysis Strategy

1. Age outstanding invoices by sorting by date into <30 days, 30–60 days, and >60 days groups.
2. Create a total of the invoice values for each of these three aged groups.
3. Multiply 30–60 days group total by 2% for the uncollectible value estimate for this group.
4. Multiply >60 days group total by 30% for the uncollectible value estimate for this group.
5. Sum uncollectible value estimates from steps 3 and 4 for total uncollectible value estimate.
6. Subtract step 5 total from allowance for uncollectible accounts unadjusted balance of $3,000 for the adjusting entry value.

> This total answers the first project plan question

> This result answers the second project plan question

④ Data Strategy Risks

- Data errors (missing data, due date errors, and invoice total errors).
- Data extraction errors.
- Inaccurate management assumptions and estimates (bad debt percentages).

④ Analysis Strategy Risks

- Errors in age group categorization and calculations.
- Erroneous application of bad debt estimation percentages to age group totals.
- Erroneous summing of estimated bad debts across age groups.
- Errors in the calculation of the value to use for bad debts expense.

⑤ Data Strategy Controls

- Compare extracted data to source documentation.
- Compare to prior period to verify management estimates and assumptions.
- Review customer, policy, and procedure changes.

⑤ Analysis Strategy Controls

- Verify all classifications and groupings.
- Verify all calculations.
- Verify correct use of analysis technologies.

Next, we go into more depth about how to develop both data and analysis strategies.

APPLY IT 4.1

Build a Project Plan for Inventory Costs

Financial Accounting Founded by Elisabeth Hess and based in Wisconsin, Tremendous Toys produces and sells unique animal-form toys online. The company has over a million dollars in sales revenues and a strong national and international following. The investment bank underwriting its upcoming initial public offering requires that Elisabeth produce a U.S. GAAP valuation of year-end inventory.

Elisabeth has kept meticulous records, organized in business cost categories, which are listed here. She knows which materials were used to create each toy, which employee built it, and how long each took to create. She has also recorded the number and type of toys produced every month. However, she has never assigned costs to her inventory items.

Materials	Labor	Overhead
Plastic for 3D printers	Production workers' time	3D printer costs
Wood	Production workers' pay rate	Production tools costs

(*Continued*)

Materials	Labor	Overhead
Resin		Computer (peripherals and internet) costs
Fiber and fabric		Shipping costs
Paints, varnishes, and dyes		Factory rent, utilities, and storage
Toy clothing		Production supplies
Glues and epoxies		Tax and legal fees
Bling and other accessories		Donations to charities
Eyes and body parts		Advertising costs

Prepare a data analysis project plan to help Elisabeth develop her inventoriable costs. Use the following structure for your answer:

1. Project objective and specific question
2. Data strategy
3. Analysis strategy
4. Data and analysis strategy risks
5. Data and analysis strategy controls

SOLUTION

1. Project objective Specific question	Prepare a U.S. GAAP compliant full costing valuation for Tremendous Toys' current inventory. What is the U.S. GAAP year-end value of inventory?
2. Data strategy	• Collect all costs and raw measures of consumption of resources related to production (direct materials, direct labor, and manufacturing overhead costs) for the last three years. • Collect records of how many units were produced for each month of cost data received. • Take a physical count of the current inventory by product.
3. Analysis strategy	• Aggregate cost data by monthly production of figurines. • Estimate cost behavior using regression to find variable costs per figurine and total fixed production costs per month. • Apply results to year-end inventory.
4. Risks to data strategy Risks to analysis strategy	• Missing data. • Including personal expenses. • Material costs and worker costs may not be representative of true replacement costs of future material and labor costs. • Potential bias for minimizing cost information to make business seem more profitable. • Averaging costs across figurines may not be accurate if true costs of different figurines vary significantly. • Regression may not have strong explanatory power (*R*-square). • Costs may have seasonality differences (due to scarcity of materials or heating and cooling costs). • Cost formula may need to be recalculated annually to capture cost changes.
5. Data strategy controls Analysis strategy controls	• Interview Elisabeth with a typical list of inventory costs to catch omitted costs. • Inquire about the seasonal or economic trends of materials, labor and production overhead costs, and use the average of the highest and lowest points. • Use median tendencies rather than means. • Run sensitivity models with future replacement cost values to note potential risk in final product cost estimations and possible data bias.

4.2 What Should We Consider When Selecting Data for Analysis?

LEARNING OBJECTIVE ❷
Describe how to develop a data strategy.

It's easier to make better decisions when we have the necessary information. Each semester, students who know their educational and career goals can select the courses that will prepare them to graduate and begin their careers. For example, accounting majors do not need to take the same courses as education majors. The same idea applies when developing a strategy for selecting data in data analysis. A successful data analysis project hinges on selecting data that are relevant and appropriate for the objective of the project, respecting the data's characteristics and measurement scales, and controlling for inherent data risks.

Identify Appropriate Data

Data can be considered appropriate for analysis when they are relevant, available, and the characteristics match the analysis method requirements. Appropriate data can be internal, external, or a combination of both:

- Internal data are generated within the organization, such as sales data, purchase data, inventory data, customer data, and vendor data. Internal data can typically be more easily controlled and verified by an organization.

- External data are obtained from sources outside of an organization. This data can include weather data, geographic data, and publicly available competitor data. External data are somewhat riskier to use since we often cannot know if the data are accurate or complete. External data can, however, provide insights that internal data alone cannot provide.

After identifying the available and relevant data alternatives, the characteristics of the possible data sets need to be verified as suitable for the planned analysis.

Evaluate Data Fields and Sources

A **data set** is a collection of data columns and rows available for analysis. Understanding the characteristics of a data set is important because, for example, statistical measures and tests often require certain data characteristics or a minimum of data points. Violating the data requirements for these measures and tests can threaten the accuracy, reliability, and significance of the analysis results.

Let's use an example to evaluate the impact data can have on analysis. **Illustration 4.8** shows the inventory data set for the 3D manufacturing company WeMakeIt, Inc.

ILLUSTRATION 4.8 Typical Elements in a Data Set from WeMakeIt, Inc.'s Inventory

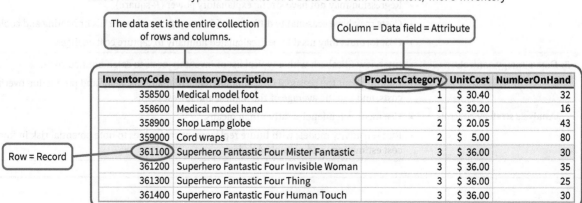

The data set is the entire collection of rows and columns.

Column = Data field = Attribute

Row = Record

InventoryCode	InventoryDescription	ProductCategory	UnitCost	NumberOnHand
358500	Medical model foot	1	$ 30.40	32
358600	Medical model hand	1	$ 30.20	16
358900	Shop Lamp globe	2	$ 20.05	43
359000	Cord wraps	2	$ 5.00	80
361100	Superhero Fantastic Four Mister Fantastic	3	$ 36.00	30
361200	Superhero Fantastic Four Invisible Woman	3	$ 36.00	35
361300	Superhero Fantastic Four Thing	3	$ 36.00	25
361400	Superhero Fantastic Four Human Touch	3	$ 36.00	30

The individual columns in a data set are called **fields**, and if the source of the data was a database, the columns are called **attributes**. Each column describes and represents one unique characteristic, a description, or aspect of the phenomena captured in the data set. Rows in a data set from a database are **records**, which represent the collection of columns that hold the descriptions of a single occurrence of the data set's purpose. In Illustration 4.8, the highlighted row contains all the information about the inventory item Superhero Fantastic Four Mister Fantastic–inventory code, the description, product category, unit cost, and the number of items on hand. This inventory item belongs to the ProductCategory group #3, indicating that it is a superhero figurine.

The records, or rows, in this inventory data set represent the different products manufactured in each product line. The columns that describe each inventory product for the WeMakeIt, Inc. inventory data set are listed in **Illustration 4.9**.

ILLUSTRATION 4.9   Data Dictionary for the WeMakeIt, Inc. Inventory Data Set

Field Name	Description
InventoryCode	Unique numerical code to identify inventory (primary key)
InventoryDescription	Text that describes the inventory product
ProductCategory	The type of product (1 = medical, 2 = tool, 3 = toy)
UnitCost	Currency value assigned to each unit's cost
NumberOnHand	Quantity of items in inventory

In addition to understanding the content of data fields in accounting databases, considering the source of the data is important because the quality of the data in the fields impact the quality of the analysis. Were the data created by an external party on a web page, entered internally by an employee, or automatically assigned by the computer? Do the data refer to a category, a measurement, or a calculation? For example, in the WeMakeIt, Inc. inventory data in Illustration 4.9, the InventoryCode field's data are probably automatic sequential numbers assigned by the AIS system whenever a new inventory product is added. Since a human is not creating that field's value when a new row is added, we can be confident that the InventoryCode data are consistently correct. **Illustration 4.10** summarizes the typical internal data field sources often used by accountants.

ILLUSTRATION 4.10   Common Data Field Sources and Examples

Source	Description	WeMakeIt Inc. Examples
Raw Data Fields		
Measured Raw Data	• Data created or captured by a controlled process capturing the value of the data. Examples include price, cost, number on hand, weight, date, hours worked, temperature, sensor readings, human observation, or economic value. • Their format can be discrete or continuous data.	InventoryCost NumberOnHand UnitCost
Nonmeasured Raw Data	• Data often created automatically by the computer or company policy for control. Examples include identification codes, chart of account numbers, standard descriptions, product category codes, or location codes such as city. • These fields are typically formatted as discrete data.	InventoryCode ProductCategory
Calculated Data Fields		
Calculated Data	• Data created when one or more fields in a particular record (row) have any number of mathematical operators (such as +, −, ×, %) applied, and often are derived from using the data in another field or fields within the same record (never across different rows). • These fields can be formatted as discrete or continuous data.	TotalCost (=UnitCost × NumberOnHand)

In the WeMakeIt, Inc. data set example, both the InventoryCode and ProductCategory fields' data are **nonmeasured raw data** that have been formatted as numeric and discrete, meaning that they are noncontinuous and will never have partial unit values. These fields cannot be used in analysis for mathematical calculations because they refer to unique identifiers for inventory items and their product category group. The InventoryDescription field's data source is also a nonmeasured raw data field formatted as a text field, which cannot be used in numeric calculations during the analysis.

The sources for data fields like UnitCost and NumberOnHand are different because they are **measured raw numeric data**, which can be used in mathematical calculations.

Finally, UnitCost and NumberOnHand can be multiplied in an expression to calculate a new field within a query called TotalCost. This new field source is **calculated data** that is also numeric and likely to be used in a variety of different mathematical calculations in accounting.

A data field's **measurement scale** refers to the type of information provided by the data. Data measurement scales should be considered when designing the data strategy, as they impact which analyses can be performed on the data. Data measurement scales are grouped into four categories: categorical, ordinal, interval, or ratio (**Illustration 4.11**).

ILLUSTRATION 4.11 Measurement Scale Descriptions and Examples

Measurement Scale Classification	Description	Example
Categorical (nominal) data	Labeled or named data that can be sorted into groups according to specific characteristics. The data do not have a quantitative value.	Regions, product type, account numbers, account category, and locations.
Ordinal data	Ordered or ranked categorical data. Distance between the categories does not need to be known or equal.	A survey question inquiring about customer service may ask customers to rate their experience from 1 to 10.
Interval data	Ordinal data that have equal and constant differences between observations and an arbitrary zero point.	Temperature, time, and credit scores.
Ratio data	Interval data with a natural zero point. A natural zero point means that it is not arbitrary.	Economic data, such as dollars or euros.

We discuss how data measurement scales influence analysis strategy options later in this chapter. Next, let's examine the risks and controls related to our data strategy.

 **PROFESSIONAL INSIGHT** **How Do You Select Financial Data for Analysis?**

Jadon is an accounting and finance major, student athlete, and president of the first-generation student organization on campus. During his internship, he realized how much his career would involve data analysis of financial statement information.

On the first day of my summer internship, I was tasked with calculating 10 financial ratios for five companies in the same industry for the most recent three years. I was left to figure out how to get the data and perform the calculations on my own. I reached into my sports experience to gather my courage by creating a game plan. **First, I had to select and set up my analysis tool.**

I chose Excel with the Analysis ToolPak and made a raw data template based on the totals I would need for the ratios in the first worksheet. I copied it five times for each company's raw data. I made another worksheet for all the ratio calculations as the rows, and the companies would be the columns, grouped by each year. I organized the ratios into profitability, liquidity, and solvency groups. I entered ratio formulas that tied back to the raw data worksheet cells and documented my steps on another sheet to remember my choices.

Next, I had to find out where to get the data. I went to the SEC's xBRL data and downloaded the financial statement information and entered what I needed into Excel. An unexpected benefit of having my ratios all in one sheet was that it was easy to make visualizations of my results. I was amazed by how clear the best and worst performing companies were from these visualizations. I saved my file and emailed it to my boss.

Consider Data Strategy Risks and Implement Controls

Another benefit of documenting data strategy in a project plan is that examining each choice can help identify three common data risks that might affect an analysis's validity, accuracy, and reliability (**Illustration 4.12**).

ILLUSTRATION 4.12   Common Data Risks and Recommended Controls

	Risks	Controls
Data	Nonrepresentative sample selections	Verify representativeness of sample.
	Outlier data points	Perform a histogram or quartile analysis to identify outliers, then explain or justify the rule used for outlier adjustment or removal.
	Dirty data	Verify integrity of data set and clean up dirty data issues.

The first risk is that a sample extracted from a larger population of data are a poor representation of the underlying population. For example, a random selection of different colored marbles might not be a sample that accurately represents the characteristics of the marble population (**Illustration 4.13**).

ILLUSTRATION 4.13   Representative Sampling Risks

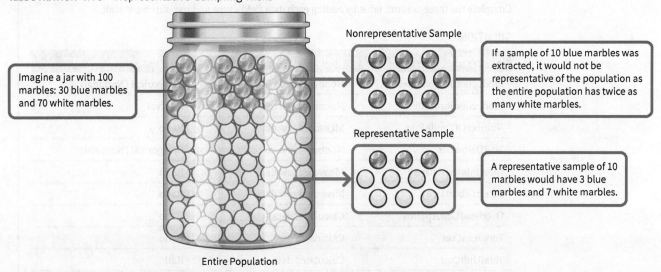

Imagine a jar with 100 marbles: 30 blue marbles and 70 white marbles.

Nonrepresentative Sample

If a sample of 10 blue marbles was extracted, it would not be representative of the population as the entire population has twice as many white marbles.

Representative Sample

A representative sample of 10 marbles would have 3 blue marbles and 7 white marbles.

Entire Population

That is why performing tests on the sample's representativeness can either verify its validity or detect its significant weakness in representing the underlying marble populations.

The second risk is potentially including unusual data points in an analysis. Outlier data points are unusual data points compared to the rest of the data in either an activity point (x-axis or the independent variable), such as number of units produced, or an unusual level of the economic value (y-axis or the dependent variable), such as total costs or total sales. The best control for identifying outliers is to visualize the data in a graph to check if the measure is very different than the rest of the data. Identified outliers can either be remeasured (if possible) or removed with a logical and documented rule.

The final data risk is that a variety of data errors, or **dirty data**, are problematic for data analysis. Dirty data include missing, invalid, duplicate, and incorrectly formatted data. For example, the purchase orders, invoices, or checks written by the company should be sequentially accounted for, with no missing numbers or two with the same identifying number. Controls should always test for dirty data before the analysis is performed. Data can be compared to its source documents, or if that is not possible, tested for reasonableness. Testing for reasonableness can include checking for missing sequence numbers or duplicate numbers, or verifying the data have the expected format or acceptable characters.

Once data have been selected, evaluated, and any risks identified and controlled, the next step is to develop an analysis strategy appropriate for the objective of the project.

APPLY IT 4.2

Identify Data Characteristics

Accounting Information Systems Tremendous Toys has recently developed a database to capture inventoriable costs from their production each week.

Data has been extracted from the following data fields:

Field Name	Field Type	Field Measurement Scale
ProductionRunNumber		
ProductionRunDate		
NumberOfToysinRun		
ToyIDNumber		
DirectMaterialsUsed		
DirectLaborUsed		
OverheadCostApplied		
TotalRunCost		
TotalUnitCost		

Complete the three-column table by adding each data field's type and measurement scale.

SOLUTION

Field Name	Field Type	Field Measurement Scale
ProductionRunNumber	Nonmeasured raw data	Categorical (Nominal)
ProductionRunDate	Nonmeasured raw data	Interval
NumberOfToysinRun	Measured raw data	Ratio
ToyIDNumber	Nonmeasured raw data	Categorical (Nominal)
DirectMaterialsUsed	Measured raw data	Ratio
DirectLaborUsed	Measured raw data	Ratio
OverheadCostApplied	Calculated data	Ratio
TotalRunCost	Calculated data	Ratio
TotalUnitCost	Calculated data	Ratio

4.3 What Should We Consider When Selecting an Analysis?

> **LEARNING OBJECTIVE ❸**
> Explain how an analysis strategy is designed.

Consider these two questions when designing a data analysis strategy:

1. Can the chosen analysis strategy answer the specific objective questions?
2. Is the measurement scale of the data appropriate for the selected analysis strategy?

Earlier in this course you learned that there are four types of data analysis objectives: descriptive, diagnostic, predictive, and prescriptive. Each asks different questions of the data. We perform analyses to answer those questions. The specific analysis that can be performed on the data is influenced by the data's measurement scales. Next, we summarize what to consider when designing analyses for projects with descriptive and diagnostic objectives.

Designing Analyses to Describe and Diagnose

Because understanding the phenomena captured by the data is essential, many data analysis projects begin with descriptive analyses. Diagnostic analytics involve many of the same analyses as descriptive, but the focus is on explaining why something happened. Because many types of analyses can be both descriptive and diagnostic, it makes sense to discuss these two analysis strategies together.

The specific type of descriptive and diagnostic analysis used depends on the measurement scale of the data. For example, calculating the median observation in the data requires using either interval or ratio measures. **Illustration 4.14** shows some analysis strategies for descriptive and diagnostic objectives (checkmarks indicate appropriate analyses, and X's indicate analyses that are inappropriate for the measurement scale).

ILLUSTRATION 4.14   Analysis Strategies for Descriptive and Diagnostic Analytics

	Data Measurement Scale			
Potential Analyses	**Categorical**	**Ordinal**	**Interval**	**Ratio**
Central Tendency				
Mode	✓	✓	✓	✓
Median	✗	✗	✓	✓
Mean	✗	✗	✓	✓
Frequency Distributions				
Both counts and %s:				
Group frequency	✓	✓	✓	✓
Cumulative frequency	✓	✓	✓	✓
Relative frequency	✓	✓	✓	✓
Data Dispersion				
Minimum, maximum, range, and quartiles	✗	✓	✓	✓
Variance and standard deviation	✗	✗	✓	✓
Normality, skewness, and kurtosis tests	✗	✗	✓	✓
Visualizations				
Only bar and pie chart	✓	✓	✓	✓
Many other trends options	✗	✗	✓	✓
Histograms/box plots	✗	✓	✓	✓

(Continued)

ILLUSTRATION 4.14 (*Continued*)

Potential Analyses	Data Measurement Scale			
	Categorical	Ordinal	Interval	Ratio
Correlation				
Scatterplots and Pearson's *R*	✗	✓	✓	✓
Cross tabulation analysis	✓	✓	✓	✓
Calculations				
Totals and subtotals	✗	✗	✓	✓
Percent change	✗	✗	✓	✓
Percent of total	✗	✗	✓	✓
Regression	✗	✗	✓	✓

Descriptive Analysis Strategies

Recall that accounting data are historic economic transaction and valuation data. Accountants, business managers, and regulators all want to know more about what happened and whether the data signals good or concerning news, so descriptive analyses are the most common analysis strategies using accounting data. It is useful for evaluating strategy performance because it provides more meaning and business intelligence than from just looking, for example, at the totals reported on one year's financial statements.

Let's work through an example using the WeMakeIt Inc. accounts receivable data set to illustrate the explanatory power of descriptive analysis even when using categorical data. Recall that the objective for this analysis was to become more confident in the percentages used for estimating bad debts. The initial descriptive analysis results indicated a large increase in the number of customers with open invoices at the 2025 year-end compared to the 2024 year-end. This analysis had been designed to answer two descriptive questions:

- **Objective question 1:** How many customers had outstanding invoices at the end of 2024?

- **Objective question 2:** How many customers had outstanding invoices at the end of 2025?

A data strategy and an analysis strategy were developed:

- **Data strategy:** Use the categorical variable of CustomerNumber to identify customers with outstanding balances.

- **Analysis strategy:** Count and compare the frequency of unique customer numbers with outstanding invoices at the year-end of 2024, and then repeat the analysis for the 2025 year-end. Note that both count and frequency are analyses that can be performed on categorical data.

Illustration 4.15 reports the results of this analysis.

ILLUSTRATION 4.15
Outstanding Invoices by
Customer Number

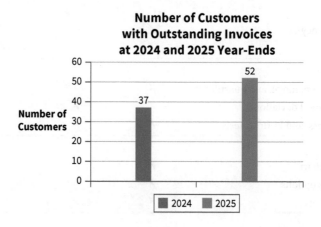

The results indicated that in 2024 there were 37 unique customer numbers with outstanding invoices, and in 2025 there were 52 unique customers numbers with outstanding invoices. Next, we discuss diagnostic analysis strategies.

Applying Critical Thinking 4.5

Be Careful Interpreting Initial Results

You might initially conclude that accounts receivable in 2025 has the potential for higher collectability risk simply because there were more customers with outstanding invoices in 2025 than in 2024. However, this initial judgment may be affected by internal assumptions and biases (**Risks**):

- The 2025 increase in the number of customers with outstanding balances may not be a negative result, as the company grew and added new customers in 2025.
- These results may motivate you to evaluate alternative explanations and perform new analyses, such as determining if the 2025 customer numbers with outstanding invoices at year-end had more invoices owed in 2025 than in 2024, or if the value of their outstanding balances were higher in 2025, possibly signaling a cash liquidity concern This result is more closely relevant to our company's accounts receivable risks of uncollectability (**Alternatives**).

Diagnostic Analysis Strategies

Diagnostic analysis strategies can be compared to detective work. Accountants can use these analysis strategies to identify and discover the most likely causes of accounting phenomena. While both descriptive and diagnostic analysis strategies are descriptive techniques, diagnostic analysis strategies also identify what factors have caused the lower sales revenues or the higher costs, for example. Diagnostic strategies always require applying critical thinking skills.

Stakeholders rely on accountants across accounting practice areas to diagnose what is happening and explain, typically in nonaccounting terms, why it is happening. For instance, systems accountants often use error dispersion data to identify system performance issues or unusual activity data that may indicate unauthorized party access.

Let's use the WeMakeIt Inc. accounts receivable data set again, this time to illustrate diagnostic analysis:

- **New objective question:** Do the returning credit customers have more outstanding invoices at the 2025 year-end than they had outstanding at the 2024 year-end?
- **Data strategy:** Once again, use the data set for the 2024 and 2025 year-end accounts receivable open invoices.
- **Analysis strategy:** Group the data by CustomerNumber for this question.

To answer this question, we may choose to create a new, calculated ordinal variable (recall that a **variable** is a data item that will be used in the analysis). This variable will group credit customers into increasing ranges based on the number of invoices they have outstanding at year-end. There are some benefits to this strategy:

- Changing a continuous variable into ordinal ranges results in meaningful groupings rather than a simple count of the number of invoices outstanding per customer.
- The new ordinal variable allows a better understanding of the overall results of the number of outstanding invoices in total.

Let's create three levels for outstanding invoices: ranges of 1–3 invoices, 4–6 invoices, and 7–9 invoices as the new ordinal variable levels. **Illustration 4.16** provides a visualization of the results of this analysis strategy. (Data **How To 4.2** describes how to recreate this visualization with a different tool.)

How To

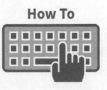

ILLUSTRATION 4.16
Frequency of Customers with
Outstanding Balances

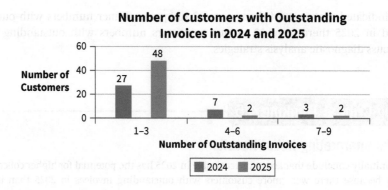

The results of this second analysis show that the number of customers with 4–6 and 7–9 outstanding invoices had decreased in 2025 compared to 2024. However, there are almost twice as many customers with 1–3 past due invoices in 2025 compared to 2024. These results are mixed news for concerns about future accounts receivable collectability risks.

This surprise finding is a good reminder about the importance of critical thinking and deliberation about the initial analysis results. Thinking critically when interpreting analysis results involves evaluating both the analysis strategies performed and not performed. Skeptically questioning data analysis strategies can provide valuable insights, as this final analysis did.

Applying Critical Thinking 4.6

Controls for Risks to Analysis Strategies

Depending on the objective of the project, analysis strategies can involve a diverse mix of variables with different sources and measurement scales. Simply adding variables and complexities to analysis choices without justification can lead to information overload, which can impair your judgement. For example, sales forecasts might involve fewer variables in industries such as agriculture, as food demand is more stable, than for airlines, as travel is more discretionary. Professional risk-reducing habits include (**Risks**):

- Keeping analysis as simple as possible by including the fewest yet most relevant variables.
- Documenting each step, especially the benefits and drawbacks of each choice as you develop, evaluate, and choose an analysis strategy (**Alternatives**).

The process for analyzing WeMakeIt, Inc.'s accounts receivable, whether descriptive or diagnostic, involves an approach that can be used for most analysis strategies in accounting:

- Start with a clear objective and specific questions that should be answered.
- Develop data alternatives, evaluate each on factors related to the objective, and select the best data strategy. Filter the data set down to the variables and ranges of interest necessary for the objective.
- The best analysis strategies typically create new calculated within-row variables necessary for the analysis. These new calculated variables can be categorical groupings, ordinal rankings, interval measures, and ratio variables. Remember that relevant groupings can make it easier to interpret results.
- Calculate any vertical analysis measures necessary, such as totals, frequencies, averages, and measures of dispersion across the rows in the data set.
- Finally, the analysis variables can be correlated or sliced by dimension variables to add insights from disaggregating the vertical measure total.

Descriptive and diagnostic analyses help to better understand what happened and why it happened. What if the objective is to predict a future outcome or determine what strategies might achieve a specific outcome? In those cases, we need to use predictive or prescriptive analyses, which are explained next.

Designing Analyses to Predict and Prescribe

Predictive analysis strategies use historical data to create models that estimate a future value or outcome. Prescriptive analysis strategies, on the other hand, help determine which option is most likely to produce the best outcome given the objective. Predictive and prescriptive analysis strategies can determine the best use of resources, improve performance, anticipate market reactions and movements, and avoid process breakdowns:

- Accountants commonly use these analysis strategies to evaluate tax planning options, operational and marketing strategy options, financing options, investment options, and exit strategy options.
- Industries with these analysis objectives include lending institutions that want to avoid bad credit decisions and insurance companies that must anticipate natural disasters and disease onset so they can adjust business models before crises that cause their businesses to suffer happen.

Illustration 4.17 summarizes the most common predictive and prescriptive analysis strategies used by accountants that do not involve advanced technology tools. The green checkmarks indicate appropriate analyses, and the red X's indicate inappropriate analyses. As the illustration shows, there are not many predictive or prescriptive models for categorical and ordinal scale variables unless they are used in models in which interval or ratio scale variables are desired for the prediction.

ILLUSTRATION 4.17 Analysis Strategies for Predictive and Prescriptive Analytics

Potential Analyses	Data Measurement Scale			
	Categorical	Ordinal	Interval	Ratio
Trendlines	X	X	✓	✓
Regression analysis (linear)	✓	X	✓	✓
Optimization models	X	X	✓	✓
What-if analyses	X	X	✓	✓

X = inappropriate analysis for the scale

Both predictive and prescriptive analysis strategies often use statistics and sophisticated modeling techniques for their algorithms:

- Common tools for this include statistical regression, time series analyses, process mining and mapping, text analysis, artificial intelligence models, data mining, mathematical modeling, complex simulations, and what-if sensitivity analysis modeling.
- These models train themselves by leveraging patterns, relationships, and structures within the existing data to accurately anticipate future conditions and outcomes.

The key to designing predictive or prescriptive strategies is to select data that will have the best potential to inform the predictive or prescriptive objective questions:

- If the goal is to predict next year's production equipment maintenance expense, data that helps explain the expected amount or increases or decreases in maintenance expenses are necessary. In other words, what variables drive changes in maintenance expense? Once those variables are identified, the related data can be selected and prepared for analysis.
- If we believe production level impacts maintenance expense, then include a data variable for the number of products produced, a measure of the most common levels of production, or a measure of whether production is expected to increase or decrease from current levels.

Suppose the WeMakeIt's auditors are testing the assumptions used to create the balance in the the company's allowance for doubtful accounts. The auditors developed a model that included three variables that might impact whether the invoices would be collected on time. The model predicts how many days outstanding an invoice may be based on the invoice amount, if they are a new (1) or existing customer (0), and the credit period allowed on their invoice. The result of the regression model is provided in **Illustration 4.18**.

ILLUSTRATION 4.18   Prediction Model for Accounts Receivable Days Outstanding

Regression Statistics					
Multiple R	0.825790307				
R Square	0.681929631				
Adjusted R Square	0.681542056				
Standard Error	3.549920129				
Observations	2466				
ANOVA					
	df	SS	MS	F	Significance F
Regression	3	66,518.36434	22,172.78811	1,759.475173	0.0000
Residual	2,462	31,025.95885	12.60193292		
Total	2,465	97,544.3232			
	Coefficients	Standard Error	t Stat	P-value	
Intercept	−7.961650225	0.670515711	−11.87392047	1.16228E-31	
InvoiceAmount	0.000829906	0.000903172	0.918879698	0.358248513	
New or Existing Customer	1.535043063	0.189912705	8.082887691	9.81036E-16	
Credit Period in Days	0.395420024	0.006452145	61.28504622	0.000	

This model reveals that these variables (invoice amount, new or existing customer, and credit period) explain about 68% of the change in days outstanding for a customer (adjusted R-square). The model is significant with a Significance F of less than 0.05. The negative intercept corrects the model's predictions by almost eight days because customers rarely pay within the first week when they are offered an interest-free period of time to pay their invoices. The significance of the intercept indicates that the mere existence of a credit period is a variable that impacts the number of days customers take to pay their invoices. With this model, the auditors can now predict that a new customer with a $900 invoice and 60 days to settle will take about 16.5 days to make their payment:

$$-7.9617 + \$900\ (0.0008) + 1(1.5350) + 60(0.3954) = 16.48\ \text{days}$$

Analysis Strategy Risks and Suggested Controls

The last two steps of a data analysis plan are to consider risks inherent to the data and analysis strategies and to put in place controls to reduce those risks. **Illustration 4.19** captures the most common risks that accountants face when analyzing data.

It is critical to consider these risks during analysis strategy planning and to add controls to help mitigate them. Without those controls we risk preparing, interpreting, and reporting incorrect analysis results, possibly causing ourselves or our stakeholders to make harmful decisions. Now that we have worked through the process of choosing the best data and analysis strategies, let's examine how accountants do this in professional practice.

ILLUSTRATION 4.19 Common Analysis Risks and Recommended Controls

	Risk	Control
Analysis	The analysis is not appropriate for the variable's measurement scales.	Review whether the analysis is appropriate for variables' measure scales. Change analysis strategy if needed.
	The sample size is too small to allow for accurate inferences.	Gather more data to meet the model's minimum data points and assumptions, or select data analyses that do not require large samples.
	The sample is not representative.	Test the reasonableness of sample with descriptive analyses.
	Confounding variables are interfering with the reliability of the information models.	Perform the analysis with and without the confounding variable to test for explanatory power differences.
	The omission of relevant variables, or variables that are unknown and not controlled for, resulting in less reliable modeling.	Add available proxies for the missing variables to see if the model's explanatory power increases.
	Uncorrected and uncontrolled dirty data issues, such as errors, empty fields, outlier data points, and data from different levels of quality sources.	Properly prepare the data before starting the analysis. (Data preparation is explained in Chapter 5.)
	Insufficient knowledge about or experience in performing the analysis strategy or interpreting the results.	Acquire proper training or work with a team that has more collective knowledge.
	Poorly made or misleading visualizations.	Perform descriptive analyses to compare and augment the visualization. Use visualization best practices.
	Failing to address the underlying uncertainties in the context.	Perform sensitivity analysis on all assumptions used in the analysis decisions.
	Insufficiently trained prediction and classification models.	Include more data to train the models and fully verify their accuracy before using them on the test data.

APPLY IT 4.3

Create a Predictive Data Analysis Project Plan

Financial Accounting Tremendous Toys has implemented a database to capture inventoriable costs from their production each week. Data from the following data fields have been extracted, noting each field's data type and measurement scale:

Field Name	Field Type	Field Measurement Scale
ProductionRunNumber	Nonmeasured raw data	Categorical (Nominal)
ProductionRunDate	Nonmeasured raw data	Interval
NumberOfToysinRun	Measured raw data	Ratio
ToyIDNumber	Nonmeasured raw data	Categorical (Nominal)
DirectMaterialsUsed	Measured raw data	Ratio
DirectLaborUsed	Measured raw data	Ratio
OverheadCostApplied	Calculated data	Ratio
TotalRunCost	Calculated data	Ratio
TotalUnitCost	Calculated data	Ratio

Using this production data, as well as the sales data for how many toys of each type were sold each month for the last three years, create a predictive data analysis project plan that will estimate Tremendous Toy's year-end inventory valuation at the end of the next fiscal year. Your project plan should address the following:

1. Project objective and specific questions
2. Data strategy
3. Analysis strategy
4. Risks in data and analysis strategies
5. Controls for data and analysis strategies

SOLUTION

1. Project objective Specific questions	• Accurately predict the next year-end's inventory value. • How many units are predicted to be in inventory at the next year-end? What is the predicted unit cost for each toy type at the end of next year?
2. Data strategy	• Data from the last three years of Tremendous Toys' production records will be extracted and prepared for analysis regarding materials costs, labor costs, and overhead charges. • The sales units data by toy type for the last three years will be extracted, cleaned for missing, duplicate, and outlier data errors, and aggregated by month. This results in 36 data points for the monthly unit sales of each toy type. • A calculated variable for average monthly cost for each toy type will need to be created using the NumberofToysinRun and TotalRunCost fields. First, this data must be aggregated by month. Then, for each toy in each month, the total monthly production cost should be divided by the total number of toys produced to calculate the average toy cost per month for each toy type. The result will be 36 data points for the monthly average cost for each type of toy.
3. Analysis strategy	• The December sales in units can be estimated by running a regression on each month's unit sales. • A calculated variable must be created for each month's ending inventory units for each toy type, resulting in 36 data points for each toy. This variable's formula is: beginning inventory units + monthly toys produced – monthly units sold. (You can assume that this business started three years ago with no beginning inventory.) • The December year-end ending inventory in units can be estimated by running a regression on the monthly ending inventory units for each toy type. • The December year-end average cost per toy can be estimated by running a regression on the average monthly costs per toy. • To calculate the total December ending inventory valuation, the December ending inventory units for each toy should be multiplied by its corresponding estimated December average cost. Then these total costs per toy must be added for the total December year-end inventory value.
4. Risks to data strategy Risks to analysis strategy	• There may be missing, duplicated, or erroneous data in the fields selected for analysis. • Costs may have changed over the three years due to seasonality, changes in vendors, and inflation. • Calculations may contain errors.
5. Data strategy controls Analysis strategy controls	• Perform data cleaning tests to find and correct missing data, duplicates, and errors that result in outlier data points. • Compare the unit cost and sales per month to determine if an inflation factor, seasonality, or other changes have occurred. If data shifts are noticed, their cause and permanence should be verified by speaking with the employees who would know the answers. • Each of the calculations performed should be verified, as well as the averaging calculations. • Regression analyses can be verified by making visualizations of the three years of monthly data points and visually inspected for agreement with the regression estimations.

4.4 How Do Data and Analysis Strategies Differ Across Practice Areas?

LEARNING OBJECTIVE ❹

Summarize data and analysis strategies in professional practice areas.

As the last step of the data analysis planning stage, accounting professionals across practice areas design data and analysis strategies based on their project objectives. Here, we offer examples of common data and analytics strategies for the accounting information systems (AIS), auditing, financial accounting, managerial accounting, and tax accounting professional practice areas.

Accounting Information Systems

Because a company's accounting information system is involved in planning, executing, controlling, and reporting the business' operations, data analysis projects in this area often involve interdisciplinary data and knowledge. These project objectives can range in scope from impacting just one or two employees to involving most of the organization. All four types of analytics objectives (descriptive, diagnostic, predictive, and prescriptive) are commonly used.

The data analyzed in these projects can include a variety of IT operational data with different levels of data integrity and control documentation. More traditional accounting data are often analyzed with qualitative categorical and ordinal data:

- Counts of help tickets and incidents.
- Error counts and delay times.
- Login issues.
- System satisfaction and IT service satisfaction.

Illustration 4.20 is an example of a visualization of the number of monthly service requests related to the accounting information system of a company. The objective was to identify how many and which months experienced more than the IT staff's capacity of 90 service requests.

ILLUSTRATION 4.20   Number of Service Requests Each Month

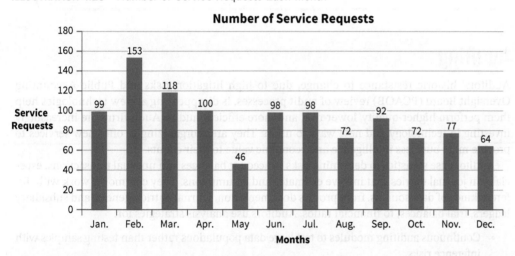

AIS data analysis projects may also choose data strategies which use quantitative interval and ratio data:

- Costs such as equipment and software installations and updates, and IT staff labor.
- Budget variances for any of these costs.

It is important to select data that captures the AIS system's performance, vulnerabilities, and errors. For example, to analyze performance we could analyze the number of spam emails (ratio data) before and after investment in a new firewall.

Accountants designing analysis strategies for AIS projects are focused on increasing competitive advantage and improving the organization's operations. They often use statistics to understand which element of the accounting system they should focus on. The mathematical formality of statistical tools can help to persuade management to make the necessary investments.

There are risks involved with AIS data choice and analysis choices. Some common strategic and critical risks and suggested controls for AIS data and analysis are listed in Illustration 4.21.

ILLUSTRATION 4.21 Risks and Controls for AIS Data and Analysis Strategies

	Risks	Controls
Data	• Human behavior is not captured. • Data manipulation from unauthorized access or untrained employees. • Loss of data due to security breaches, ransomware, or natural disasters. • Difficulties capturing high velocity data. • Difficulties measuring interdepartmental dependencies on process software. • Dirty data and outliers.	• Strong logs and segregation of duties in IT. • Strong access controls. • Effective backups and graceful degradation. • Clear procedures. • Thorough data cleaning and triangulation to verify data capture. • Strong audit trails. • Data and change management controls. • Data retention and destruction policies.
Analysis	• Errors in variable transformations. • Errors in calculations. • Data availability windows are too short to capture more strategic trends and issues.	• Verifying analysis steps and calculations. • Performing sensitivity analyses for critical results. • Creating effective visualizations and explanations.

Auditing

Auditors' historic resistance to change, due to high litigation risks and Public Accounting Oversight Board (PCAOB) review of audit processes, is disappearing as new technologies help them perform higher-quality, lower-risk, and more efficient audits. Audit firms are increasingly investing in technology and new ways to use it. They are reorganizing to offer new services to provide more business intelligence and economic value to their clients.

Auditors use statistics to determine risks to account balances and unusual transactions, especially in journal entries that involve estimates and assumptions. They commonly work with different kinds of data sources, from process documentation, journal entries, general and subsidiary ledgers, trial balances, to financial ratios. Auditors use analysis strategies for:

- Continuous auditing modules to test large data populations rather than testing samples with inference risks.

- Automated identification of dirty data, unusual transactions, and pattern anomalies to better reduce audit risk and fraud risks.

- Testing entire transaction cycles' internal controls with process mining and tracing purchasing to payment flows, P-cards (purchasing credit cards) usage and payroll documentation. Testing the revenue cycle from order to collection.

- Using robotic process automation (RPA) to remove the human (and often inconsistent) element of repetitive audit tasks, freeing auditors to focus on areas that require thoughtful critical thinking and judgments. (RPA applications and benefits to accountants are explained in Chapter 10.)

- Testing hypotheses about inventory and fixed assets with sampling, statistical tests, and inferences for the population of these assets.

Illustration 4.22 is an example of auditors using a process mining analysis strategy to learn whether all purchases followed the correct process from requisition to the recording of the invoice for the purchase. The visualization indicates that more than expected purchases (308 purchases) skip the authorized purchase requisition process step as well as the authorized order confirmation, goods receipt, and vendor invoice steps. These deviations from the authorized process are concerning to an auditor. The blue boxes indicate where the process is letting in purchase orders without purchase requisitions and letting out purchase orders without the subsequent required steps. An auditor will then want to follow up on these exceptions to the authorized process.

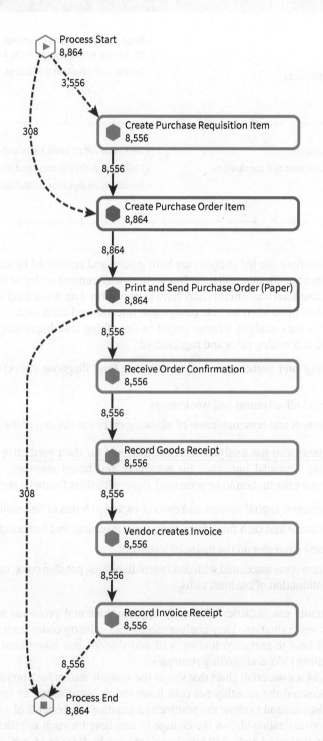

ILLUSTRATION 4.22 Process Mining Results for Purchases Analysis

Regardless of the data and analysis strategies used, auditors must identify the risks and controls necessary to assure they can rely on the results of their analyses (**Illustration 4.23**).

Financial Accounting

Financial accountants are primarily responsible for capturing, recording, processing, storing, and reporting accounting information. Accuracy, thoroughness, and documentation are essential.

ILLUSTRATION 4.23   Risks and Controls for Auditing Data and Analysis Strategies

	Risks	Controls
Data	• Missing data. • Dirty data. • Fake transaction data.	• Strong audit trail tests of internal controls for data entry, storage, processing, and reporting. • Testing authorization and access controls.
Analysis	• Errors in assumptions. • Errors in calculations and conclusions.	• Verification of all audit steps and calculations. • Checks on authentication and approvals. • Sensitivity analysis for critical results.

The accounting data they use for analyses are both guided and restrained by accounting regulations and government agency compliance. Due to the measurement scales of the variables they need for analysis, financial accountants may have to transform data depending on their objective questions. These data most often include categorical, interval, and ratio data.

The purpose of a data analysis strategy might be describing and diagnosing based on corresponding financial accounting rules and regulations:

- Nature, timing, and authorization of transactions (and diagnose issues) charged to each account.

- Internal control effectiveness and weaknesses.

- The completeness and reasonableness of adjusting entries at the end of the period.

Financial accountants also use analysis strategies designed for their predictive and prescriptive objectives regarding financial outcomes for managers and board members. One example is estimating additional information to be presented along with their financial statements, such as:

- Ranking alternative capital sources and costs of capital in terms of favorability.

- Future net income and cash flows from operations, investing, and financing activities.

- Impacts of new strategies on the financial statement.

- Expected future costs associated with contingent liabilities, pension costs, new business units or the discontinuation of business units.

Financial accountants use statistics to identify opportunities and problems with profitability, liquidity, and business valuation. They analyze categorical industry codes from their client's categorical groups of held to maturity, trading, and available for sale investment assets to ensure desired diversification risks and holding strategies.

Illustration 4.24 is a waterfall chart that shows the analysis results for a project with the objective to better understand the monthly net cash flows for an organization by month. A waterfall chart is a useful visualization to show the positive and negative components of a change.

This waterfall visualization shows the change in cashflow for each month. For instance, in February cashflow increased by $2,350 but then decreased by $900 in March. The net of all the monthly changes agrees to the total. Like other accountants, financial accountants must identify potential risks in their data and analysis strategies (**Illustration 4.25**).

Managerial Accounting

Managerial accountants add value to their organization with different data analysis strategies. The purpose of most managerial accounting data analyses is to improve planning, operational control, and decision-making to support an organization's mission and strategies.

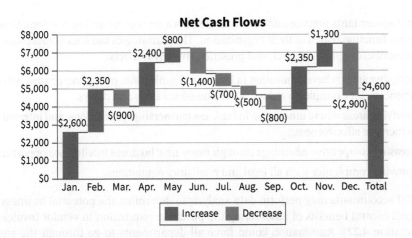

ILLUSTRATION 4.24 Net Cash Flow Visualization

ILLUSTRATION 4.25 Risks and Controls for Financial Accounting Data and Analysis Strategies

	Risks	Controls
Data	• Missing operational and adjusting entries. • Dirty data. • Fake transaction data. • Incorrect valuation. • Incorrect account. • Incorrect time period. • Missing data.	• Strong accounting cycle steps. • Strong internal controls for data entry, storage, processing, and reporting. • Authorization and access controls. • Testing for and correcting missing, duplicate, and outlier data.
Analysis	• Calculation errors. • Biases and self-interests. • Incorrect calculations. • Not following GAAP analysis guidance.	• Verifying all cycle steps and calculations. • Checking authentication and approvals. • Sensitivity analysis for critical results. • Verify applicable GAAP guidance.

This type of data analysis is valuable for improving the selection, execution, and evaluation of organizational strategy. These kinds of analyses can also lead to decisions that give employees more access to information, which improves performance and, eventually, organizational culture and operations.

Managerial accountants prepare analysis strategies, both for routine and ad hoc (one-time) objectives for each functional area of their organization. These strategies use data across measurement scales to describe, diagnose, predict, and prescribe strategy impacts:

- Identifying areas where innovation in business organization, policy and process will increase efficiencies, for example, to reduce non-value-added steps and delays.
- Identifying areas where innovation in business partnerships, operations, and internal controls will increase effectiveness.
- Increasing competitive advantage through many new business intelligence opportunities.
- Improving compliance with all legal and regulatory regulations.

Managerial accountants may perform data analysis to determine the potential business process and internal control benefits of automating the purchase requisition to vendor invoice process (see Illustration 4.22). Automation could force all departments to go through the authorized business process rather than going around it. Identifying risks to the data and analyses used in managerial accounting is important to ensure analysis results are accurate and reliable (**Illustration 4.26**).

ILLUSTRATION 4.26   Risks and Controls for Managerial Accounting Data and Analysis Strategies

	Risks	Control Choices
Data	• Dirty data. • Missing data. • Irrelevant data.	• Independent verification. • Segregation of duties. • Sound personnel governance. • Verify authorization. • Considering the purpose when making data choices.
Analysis	• Errors in calculations. • Errors in attributions. • Biases and self-interests.	• Verifying all steps and calculations.

Tax Accounting

Thanks to data analytics, tax accountants have more information for their tax planning and compliance services, which improves their judgments and how they document defend their positions to both clients and regulators. Recent surveys show that over 58% of tax accountants are using data and analytics strategies for many areas of their professional practice,[1] including:

- Sales and use taxes and local taxes (SALT)
- Value added taxes (VAT)
- Goods and services taxes (GST)
- Customs duties

---

[1]International Tax Review. (2019). Preparing for the Future of Tax. https://www.internationaltaxreview.com/article/2a6a41udxe4e2kuc8zoqo/preparing-for-the-future-of-tax (accessed July 13, 2022).

- Transfer pricing and intercompany transactions
- Tax compliance
- Tax provisions

Perhaps the biggest effect of data analysis strategies on tax practice is the movement away from a dependency on historic data and toward a forward-looking, value-adding service perspective by using predicting and prescribing analytics strategies. Examples of these predictive and prescriptive analytics include using complex data modeling to evaluate decision and position alternatives, which improves the value and accuracy of advice. **Illustration 4.27** is a live dashboard that shows current year medical expenses compared to the level needed for itemized deductions for five of their individual clients. This would help the tax accountant provide advice to these clients.

ILLUSTRATION 4.27   Medical Expenses Itemized Deduction Threshold Assessment by Client

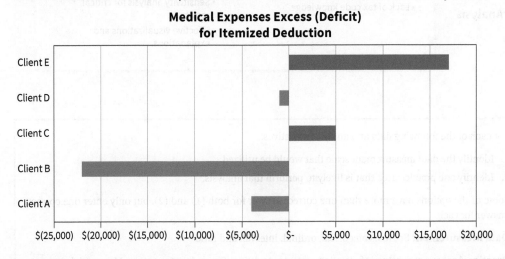

Another example is sophisticated querying of clients' accounting data to better identify opportunities, such as when to buy or sell assets, and understanding the operational decisions driving tax liabilities.

Applying Critical Thinking 4.8

Think Critically in Tax Accounting

- Tax accountants consider their clients, tax authorities, and their tax firm partners when they plan different data analyses. Each of these stakeholders may have different objectives and priorities. For example, clients may prioritize minimizing their tax obligations, so that would be the objective of your tax planning services **(Stakeholders)**.
- Strong research and analysis skills are necessary, such as when performing tax research, developing tax strategies, and estimating tax liabilities. For example, state laws are different than the national and international laws for every type of tax category **(Knowledge)**.
- Clients, both individuals and organizations, may have incentives to omit taxable revenues and include irrelevant and inappropriate expenses. These data risks should be controlled, perhaps with interview questions as well as verifying the records provided through indirect tests of reasonableness **(Risks)**.

Identifying risks and assuring that proper controls are in place to mitigate risks are also critical (**Illustration 4.28**).

ILLUSTRATION 4.28 Risks and Controls for Tax Accounting Data and Analysis Strategies

	Risks	Control Choices
Data	• Dirty data and outliers. • Missing data.	• Implement backups. • Strong audit trails. • Tax management controls. • Data retention and destruction policies. • Data authenticity and dirty data verification and correction.
Analysis	• Errors in data evaluations and tests. • Errors in calculations and forms. • Lack of tax code knowledge.	• Verification of all tax rules' liability steps and calculations. • Sensitivity analysis for critical results. • Effective visualizations and explanations.

APPLY IT 4.4

Match Strategies with Professional Practice Areas

For each of the following data and analysis objectives:

1. Identify the data measurement scale that would be utilized.
2. Identify one practice area that is likely to perform that analysis.

Some of the options have more than one correct answer for both (1) and (2), but only enter one correct answer for each.

Data Measurement Scales: categorical, ordinal, interval, and ratio

Practice Areas: Accounting information systems, Auditing, Financial accounting, Managerial accounting, and Tax accounting

Objective	Measurement Scale	Practice Area
Aging of accounts receivable's year-end open invoices on days outstanding.		
Predicting cost savings and productivity increases from new AIS investments.		
Creating dollar value stratified sampling plans for investment asset accounts.		
Evaluating web server security incidents by type of incident.		
Prescribing product revenue increases by product from marketing campaigns.		
Predicting future cash flows from operations.		
Calculating before and after process improvements from system investments.		
Testing different tax planning strategies by evaluating future cash savings.		
Estimating inventory counts at year-end by sampling a few of the stores and making population inferences.		
Testing approvals and documentation for transaction authorization.		

SOLUTION

Objective	Measurement Scale	Practice Area
Aging of accounts receivable's year-end open invoices on days outstanding.	Interval	Financial and managerial accounting
Predicting cost savings and productivity increases from new AIS investments.	Ratio	Managerial accounting
Creating dollar value stratified sampling plans for investment asset accounts.	Interval	Auditing
Evaluating web server security incidents by type of incident.	Categorical	Accounting information systems
Prescribing product revenue increases by product from marketing campaigns.	Ratio	Managerial accounting
Predicting future cash flows from operations.	Ratio	Managerial accounting
Calculating before and after process improvements from system investments.	Interval	Accounting information systems
Testing different tax planning strategies by evaluating future cash savings.	Ratio	Tax accounting
Estimating inventory counts at year-end by sampling a few of the stores and making population inferences.	Ratio	Auditing
Testing approvals and documentation for transaction authorization.	Categorical	Financial accounting

Chapter Review and Practice

Learning Objectives Review

❶ Identify the components of a data analysis project plan.

A data analysis project plan is a blueprint to follow for the project. Using a planning tool can help choose the best data and analysis strategies for the project objectives. There are five steps:

- Step 1: Focus on the project's objective and the specific questions that must be answered.
- Step 2: Decide which data are needed to answer the questions, develop alternatives, evaluate, and rank the best option.
- Step 3: Consider the methods available to do the analysis and rank the alternatives. Evaluate and choose the best strategy option.
- Steps 4 and 5: Consider critical risks inherent to both the data strategy and analysis strategy.
- Steps 4 and 5: Embed controls to reduce these risks in data strategy and analysis strategy.

❷ Describe how to develop a data strategy.

A successful project hinges on using the appropriate data and evaluating its characteristics. Considering the data's potential impact on the

analysis and any risks makes it easier to select the most suitable data for a project's goals:

- The first step is selecting the most appropriate data. Appropriate data are data that are available and relevant to the data analysis objective questions.
- The data's measurement scales must also be suitable for use with the chosen data analysis method, as not all analyses are valid for every measure scale. Data can have categorical, interval, ordinal, or ratio scales.
- Data can be either internal (generated within the organization), external (obtained from a source outside of the organization), or a combination of both. Data can be raw measures or assigned nonmeasures, and can also be calculated fields.
- Consider potential risks related to the data chosen for the analysis and put controls in place to mitigate those risks. Three common data risks (and controls) include: nonrepresentative samples (verify representativeness of the sample), outlier data points (identify outliers and then justify or remove), and dirty data (verify integrity of the data set and clean).

❸ Explain how an analysis strategy is designed.

There are two things to consider when designing a data analysis strategy: (1) the objective questions and (2) the measurement scale of the data. There are four data analysis objectives: descriptive, diagnostic, predictive, and prescriptive. The questions we design are based on the objective:

- When designing any type of analysis, the appropriate analysis is dependent on the measurement scale of the data. Typical descriptive and diagnostic analysis methods include measure of central tendency (mean and median), frequency distributions, measures of data dispersion (e.g., range, quartiles, and standard deviation), visualizations, correlation, and calculations (e.g., totals, percent change).
- Typical analyses used for predictive and prescriptive analyses include trendlines, regression analysis, optimization models, and what-if analyses.
- There are many common risks inherent in descriptive, diagnostic, predictive, and prescriptive analyses that can be identified and controlled. Some of these risks include performing an analysis with dirty data, or analysis not appropriate for the variable's measure scales, using too small a sample, or a nonrepresentative sample, or including (or omitting) variables from the analysis.

❹ Summarize data and analysis strategies in professional practice areas.

Each professional accounting practice area plans different data and analysis strategies for varying objectives, using data with a range of measurement scales to describe, diagnose, predict, and prescribe results for their stakeholders and objectives. The risks inherent to their data and analysis choices, as well as the controls they implement are a function of their roles, responsibilities, and project objectives:

- Accounting information systems professionals plan data and analysis strategies for AIS governance, strategic planning and evaluation, operational performance, and compliance objectives. Their projects typically involve business process functionality, business intelligence, and cybersecurity purposes.
- Auditors plan data and analyses that have professional audit process compliance and audit quality objectives to verify the representativeness of their clients' financial statement balances or their organization's accounting systems. External auditors have the additional data risks of using data that has been captured and extracted by their clients, oftentimes not able to verify the data completeness or accuracy.
- Financial accountants focus on regulatory compliance regarding transaction capturing, recording, processing, storing, and reporting objectives.
- Managerial accountants have a wide variety of internal governance, strategic, financing, investing, and operational objectives for their data and analysis plans.
- Tax accountants focus on both compliance and more forward-facing tax planning opportunities to serve their clients and organizations with their data analysis strategy plans. Similar to external auditors, tax accountants often must use data sets prepared by their clients, which may have greater risks of inaccuracy and incompleteness.

Key Terms Review

Attributes 183	Fields 183	Records 183
Calculated data 184	Measured raw numeric data 184	Variable 189
Data set 182	Measurement scale 184	
Dirty data 186	Nonmeasured raw data 184	

How To Walk-Throughs

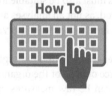

How To

HOW TO 4.1 Calculate Year-End Bad Debts Estimation Using Excel

The figures shown in the table in Illustration 4.2 were calculated in Excel. Recall a few facts about this example:

- WeMakeIt, Inc. estimates that 2% of its 30 to 60 days outstanding receivables will be uncollectible, and that 30% of outstanding receivables older than 60 days will be uncollectible.
- The 2025 year-end allowance for uncollectible accounts unadjusted balance is $3,000.

What You Need: Data The How To 4.1 data file.

STEP 1: Select the entire data set, but not the labels, and sort the outstanding invoice data by invoice date. The **Sort** option appears in the **Data** tab (**Illustration 4.29**).

ILLUSTRATION 4.29   Sort Outstanding Invoices by Date

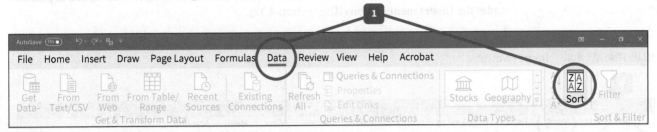

STEP 2: Create a new column to the right of the data for the year-end date of 12/31/2025:

- Add a label name for this column in row 1: "Analysis Date."
- In row 2, enter "12/31/2025" and copy this date to the bottom row of data. This can be easily done by clicking on the bottom corner of the cell where "12/31/2025" was entered and dragging the cursor down to the last row of data (**Illustration 4.30**).

ILLUSTRATION 4.30   Add Analysis Date Column

	A	B	C	D	E	F	G
1	CustID	InvoiceNumber	InvoiceDate	DueDate	InvoiceAmount	AnalysisDate	
2	121054	1405	1/8/2025	2/7/2025	$ 1,169.74	12/31/2025	
3	121054	1501	2/6/2025	3/8/2025	$ 286.00		
4	121050	1551	2/18/2025	3/20/2025	$ 760.89		
5	121053	1651	3/22/2025	4/21/2025	$ 298.09		

Sheet1

STEP 3: Create a new column to the right of the 12/31/2025 date column:

- Add a label name for this column in row 1: "Days Outstanding."
- Calculate the days outstanding by creating a formula in cell G2 which subtracts the invoice date (Cell C2) from 12/31/2025 cell (F2) for the Analysis Date. The formula is =F2-C2.
- Copy this formula through all the data rows in Column G. Copying can be done by clicking on the bottom corner of the cell where the formula was entered and dragging in down to the last row of data (**Illustration 4.31**).

ILLUSTRATION 4.31   Data Set with Analysis Date and Days Outstanding Columns

	A	B	C	D	E	F	G
1	CustID	InvoiceNumber	InvoiceDate	DueDate	InvoiceAmount	AnalysisDate	DaysOutstanding
2	121054	1405	1/8/2025	2/7/2025	$ 1,169.74	12/31/2025	357
3	121054	1501	2/6/2025	3/8/2025	$ 286.00	12/31/2025	328
4	121050	1551	2/18/2025	3/20/2025	$ 760.89	12/31/2025	316
5	121053	1651	3/22/2025	4/21/2025	$ 298.09	12/31/2025	284
6	121050	1724	4/11/2025	5/11/2025	$ 572.78	12/31/2025	264
7	121049	1999	6/22/2025	7/22/2025	$ 795.60	12/31/2025	192
8	121050	2033	7/3/2025	8/2/2025	$ 819.39	12/31/2025	181

Sheet1

STEP 4: Select the data field titles and data rows and create a PivotTable. This option is located under the **Insert** menu option (**Illustration 4.32**).

ILLUSTRATION 4.32 Insert PivotTable

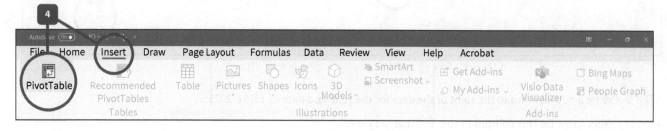

Select **New Worksheet**. Your screen will automatically move to the new worksheet. Name this table "BadDebts2025." The name appears at the top left of your screen.

STEP 5: Select any place in the PivotTable so the **PivotTable Fields** appears on the right of your screen:

- Drag **Invoice Amount** to the **Values** area.
- Drag **Days Outstanding** to **Rows**. The new PivotTable solution should appear (**Illustration 4.33**).

ILLUSTRATION 4.33 Unpaid Invoices by Days Outstanding

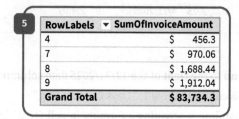

RowLabels	▾	SumOfInvoiceAmount
4		$ 456.3
7		$ 970.06
8		$ 1,688.44
9		$ 1,912.04
Grand Total		**$ 83,734.3**

STEP 6: Next, select any row in the **Days Outstanding** column:

- Right click and select **Group**.
- In the dialog box that opens (**Illustration 4.34**), enter a zero (0) in the starting point, 60 in the ending point, and then enter 30 for the **By** option. Select **OK**.

ILLUSTRATION 4.34 Dialog Box to Group by Days Outstanding

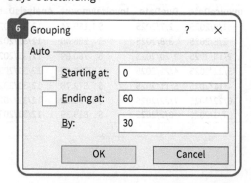

Now the PivotTable has become three rows for the three desired age categories, with the subtotals already calculated for the **Sum of InvoiceAmount** column. Format the **Sum column** as currency (**Illustration 4.35**). Format the amounts as currency.

ILLUSTRATION 4.35   Age Group Totals for Accounts Receivable Invoice Values

	A	B
1	**RowLabels** ▼	**SumOfInvoiceAmount**
2	0–29	$ 30,099.29
3	30–60	$ 20,441.46
4	>60	$ 33,193.55
5	**Grand Total**	**$ 83,734.30**

STEP 7: In the cell to the right of the SumofInvoiceAmount title, enter "Estimation %." In the cell to the right, enter "$ Uncollectible." Adjust column widths:

- In the cell to the right of the $20,441.46, enter "0.02," and in the cell below enter "0.3" for the uncollectible percentages.

- Format the **$ Uncollectible** column as currency.

STEP 8: In the cells to the right of each of these percentages, enter the following formulas using cell references:

- For the 30–60 day group, the formula is:

    =(click on cell with 20,441.46)*(click on the cell with the 0.02)

- And for the >60 days group:

    =(click on the cell with 33,193.55)*(click on cell with the 0.3)

- An example of the formula and totals that result is shown in **Illustration 4.36**. Add an underline to the cell containing the last formula.

ILLUSTRATION 4.36   Age Group Totals for Bad Debt Estimations

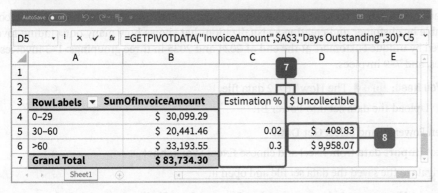

D5 — fx =GETPIVOTDATA("InvoiceAmount",$A$3,"Days Outstanding",30)*C5

	A	B	C	D	E
1					
2					
3	**RowLabels** ▼	**SumOfInvoiceAmount**	Estimation %	$ Uncollectible	
4	0–29	$ 30,099.29			
5	30–60	$ 20,441.46	0.02	$ 408.83	
6	>60	$ 33,193.55	0.3	$ 9,958.07	
7	**Grand Total**	**$ 83,734.30**			

STEP 9: Enter the sum formula in the next cell (D7 in this example solution):

    =sum(D5:D6)

This sum is the desired adjusted year-end credit balance of allowance for uncollectible accounts. This total is $10,366.89 (also shown in Illustration 4.37).

STEP 10: Compare the 2025 unadjusted allowance account balance, a $3,000 credit balance, to the calculated desired ending balance to calculate the amount needed for the adjusting entry to ensure the allowance for uncollectible accounts has that desired credit balance:

- Enter the unadjusted balance in cell D8 and the formula for the calculation in cell D10 (**Illustration 4.37**):

$$=D7-D8$$

- You are now ready to make your adjusting entry:

	Debit	Credit
Bad debt expense	7,366.89	
Allowance for uncollectible accounts		7,366.89

ILLUSTRATION 4.37 Completed Analysis of Bad Debts Expense Calculation

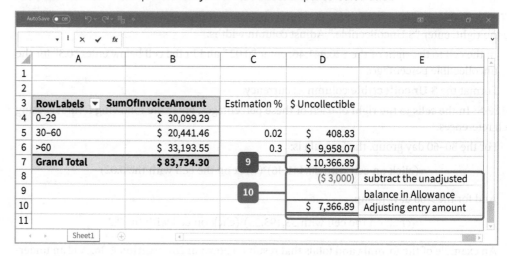

HOW TO 4.2 Create a Frequency Bar Chart in Power BI

Illustration 4.16 can be recreated in Power BI by analyzing the outstanding invoices in accounts receivable by customer and creating a visualization that shows how many outstanding invoices are owed by unique customers at the end of 2024 and 2025 in three groupings: 1–3 invoices, 4–6 invoices, and 7–9 invoices.

What You Need: **Data** The How To 4.2 data file.

STEP 1: Upload the data set into Power BI:

- Open Power BI and Select **Get Data**.
- Select **Import data** from Excel and choose **Excel Worksheet**.
- Navigate to the saved the data set file and open it.

Once the Navigator window opens, select Sheet 1 of the file listed on the left, then select **Load** (**Illustration 4.38**).

ILLUSTRATION 4.38 Load Data into Power BI

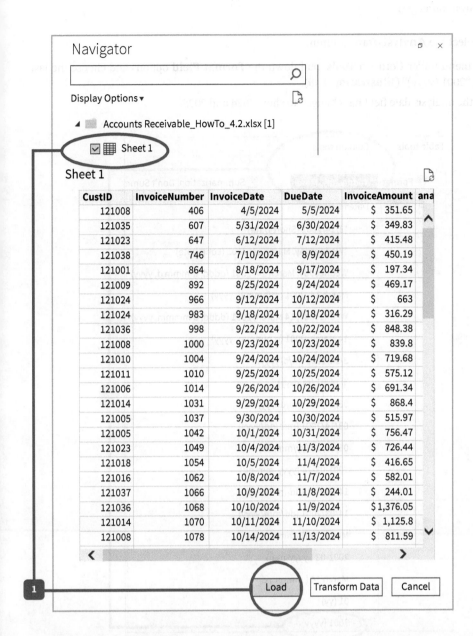

- Verify this import by double-clicking on the data sheet icon on the left side of the screen. Look at the bottom-left corner to verify that you have successfully loaded all 201 records of the data set (**Illustration 4.39**).

ILLUSTRATION 4.39 Verify Excel Import

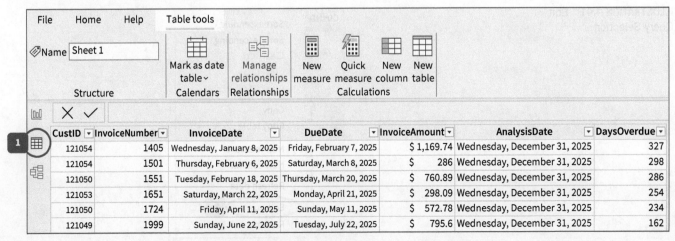

STEP 2: Select the **AnalysisDate** column.

- In the menu under **Column Tools**, pull down the **Format Field** options and choose the last option "2001 (yyyy)" (**Illustration 4.40**).
- Verify the analysis date field has changed to show 2024 and 2025.

ILLUSTRATION 4.40 Change the AnalysisDate Column Format

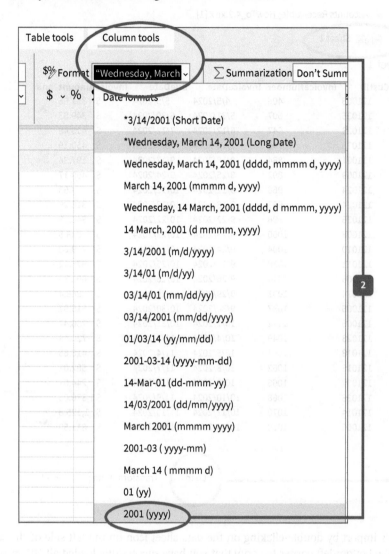

STEP 3: Select the **CustID** column by clicking on the column header. Right click and select **Edit Query** (**Illustration 4.41**).

ILLUSTRATION 4.41 Edit Query Selection

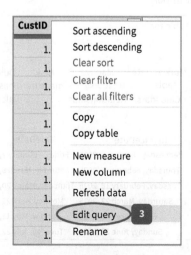

- This will open the Power Query Editor window. In this window, the **CustID column** will also be selected.
- Select **Group By** from the top menu, and it will open.
- Select **Advanced**. Right below the CustID field you will see the Add grouping button. Select this to add a second grouping for the field AnalysisDate. Then, below the new grouping box, in the New column name box, enter "CountInvoices" (do not enter the quotes).
- In the pull down menu for **Operation**, select **Count Distinct Rows** and select **OK**. Close and Apply the Power Query Editor (**Illustration 4.42**).

ILLUSTRATION 4.42   Group By Customer ID and Count Distinct Invoices

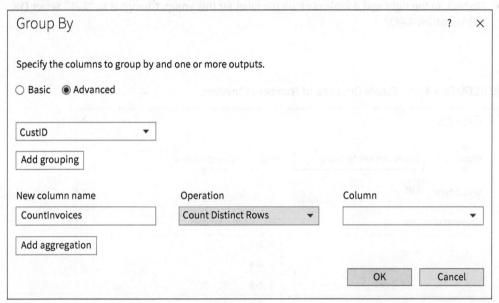

STEP 4: Select the **Count Invoices** column. Select **Data Groups** from the top column, then select **New Data Group** (**Illustration 4.43**).

ILLUSTRATION 4.43   Select Data Groups

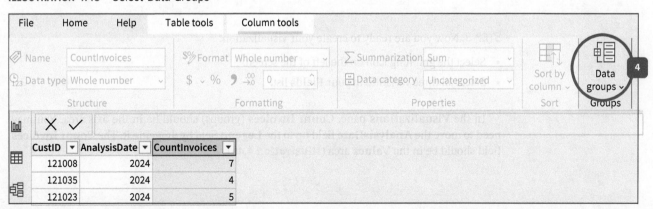

Illustration 4.43 shows the dialog box that opens once you select **Data Groups**:

- In the dialog box select **List** (not bins) for the Group Type.
- Under **Ungrouped values**, hold the shift key down to select values 1, 2, and 3.
- Select **Group**. Double click the new group that appears on the right window and change the label to "1–3."
- Select the **Other** group, and move to the ungrouped left side. Select 4 and 5 together by again holding down the shift key. Select **Group** and move over to the right window. Double click on the label for this field, and type "4–6" (it happens that there are no customers with six outstanding invoices, but the range will be 4–6 regardless).
- Once again, select **Other** and move to the **Ungrouped values** window. Select 7, 8, and 9 by holding down the shift key and selecting **GROUP**.
- Go back to the right and double click on the label for this group. Change it to "7–9." Select **OK** (**Illustration 4.44**).

ILLUSTRATION 4.44   Create Grouping of Number of Invoices

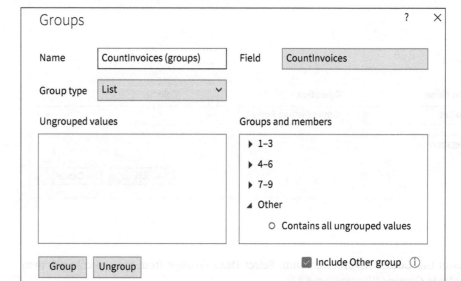

STEP 5: Now you are ready to create your visualization:

- Select the graphing icon on the left of the screen.
- Select all three variables in your **Fields** list.

In the **Visualizations** pane, **Count Invoices** (groups) should be in the axis area. You may need to move the **AnalysisDate** field up to the **Legend** field by dragging it. The **Count Invoices** field should be in the **Values** area (**Illustration 4.45**).

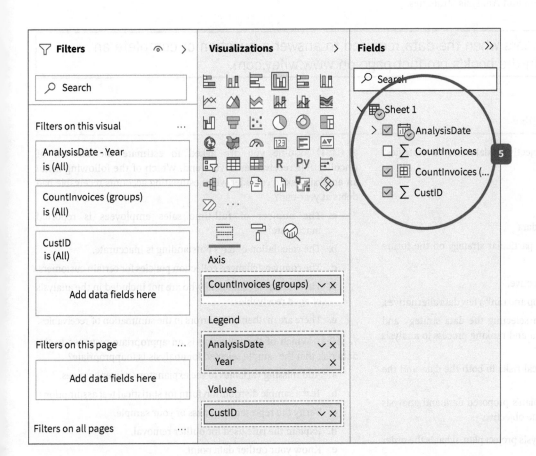

ILLUSTRATION 4.45 Create the Visualization

Your visualization is complete (**Illustration 4.46**)!

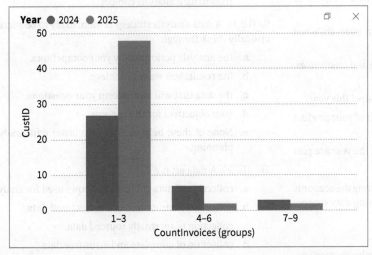

ILLUSTRATION 4.46
WeMakeIt, Inc. Accounts
Receivable

> **Data** The Data tag appears when the data required to answer a question or complete an exercise are available in the book's product page on www.wiley.com.

Multiple Choice Questions

1. (LO 1) Which of these is *not* an objective of data analysis strategies?

   a. Collecting data

   b. Describing data

   c. Diagnosing data

   d. Predicting a future value of data

   e. Prescribing the impact of a particular strategy on the future value of the data

2. (LO 1) When focusing on the objective,

   a. use critical thinking to develop and rank a few data alternatives.

   b. use what was learned from selecting the data strategy and apply that same development and ranking process to analysis alternatives.

   c. consider and prioritize critical risks to both the data and the analysis strategies.

   d. remember to ask how the plan's proposed data and analysis strategy decisions relate to the objective.

3. (LO 1) When creating a data analysis project plan, what is the order of steps?

   a. Focus on the objective, select a data strategy, select an analysis strategy, consider risks, and embed controls.

   b. Select a data strategy, focus on the objective, select an analysis strategy, embed controls, and consider risks.

   c. Select an analysis strategy, select a data strategy, focus on the objective, embed controls, and consider risks.

4. (LO 1) Which of the following specific questions depicts a descriptive analysis objective for accounts receivable balance at year-end?

   a. How many invoices from the current year were collected during the year?

   b. What was the total of all sales revenues, cash and credit sales, for the year?

   c. How many salespersons were employed in Taipei this year?

   d. What is the average days in inventory for each of your product lines?

   e. How many of the open invoices at the end of the year are past due?

5. (LO 1) You are asked to perform an analysis predicting the accounts payable balance at the year-end. Which of the following data sources are best to analyze for this objective?

   a. A list of authorized new vendors for the year.

   b. Open vendor invoices that refer to purchases already received.

   c. A list of checks paid to accounts payable vendors during the year.

   d. A list of purchase orders issued during the month of December.

   e. None of these data resources are useful to predict the accounts payable year-end balance.

6. (LO 1) Assume you are asked to estimate the amount of uncollectible receivables at year-end. Which of the following is *not* an analysis risk to consider when estimating accounts receivable bad debts at year-end?

   a. The number of full-time sales employees is reported inaccurately.

   b. The calculation of days outstanding is inaccurate.

   c. The company changed collection policies for certain customers.

   d. There are new customers who are not included in the analysis of aged receivables.

   e. There are mathematical errors in the summation of receivables.

7. (LO 1) Which of the following is an appropriate response to the data risk that the sample selected for analysis is inappropriate?

   a. Add missing variables to see explanatory power changes.

   b. Test a sample distribution form for statistical test assumptions.

   c. Verify the representativeness of your sample.

   d. Explain the rule used for outlier removal.

   e. Know your outlier data point.

8. (LO 1) Critically thinking through the risks to a data analysis strategy during planning will help avoid

   a. data selection biases.

   b. judgment errors from lack of experience.

   c. interpretation errors from dirty data sets.

   d. incorrect applications of statistical tests.

   e. All of the these are possible costs from not considering the risks to data analysis choices.

9. (LO 1) A data analysis strategy is more likely to be successful if you critically think through

   a. the analysis performed by your competitors.

   b. the results you want to achieve.

   c. the data that will best inform your questions.

   d. your objectives for the analysis.

   e. None of these help you perform better data analysis strategy planning.

10. (LO 2) A data set is a

   a. collection of data columns and rows used for analysis.

   b. collection of structured or unstructured data.

   c. collection of internally sourced data.

   d. collection of complete and error-free data.

11. (LO 2) Attributes are

   a. columns in the data only if the source is from a database.

   b. columns in a data set.

   c. a row in a data set.

   d. rows in a data set only if the source is from a database.

12. (LO 2) Which of the following is an example of knowledge you might need to acquire for data analysis strategy planning?

   a. The analysis is appropriate for your data measurement scales.

   b. An understanding of your biases.

   c. Identifying the key stakeholders.

   d. Analysis resources that are available for your compensation.

   e. Compensation correlation with results.

13. (LO 2) Which of the following is *not* a data measure scale that can be used in designing your data analysis strategy?

   a. Optimal data

   b. Ordinal data

   c. Interval data

   d. Ratio data

   e. All of these are data measure scales.

14. (LO 2) Which of the following data measure scales allows for meaningful multiplication of data points?

   a. Interval data

   b. Categorical data

   c. Ordinal data

   d. Ratio data

   e. Group data

15. (LO 3) Descriptive analyses that include median central tendency measures are appropriate for which data measurement scale?

   a. Categorical

   b. Ordinal

   c. Nominal

   d. Interval

   e. All these measurement scales support the median central tendency measure.

16. (LO 3) Diagnostic analyses that include data dispersion measures such as variance and standard deviation are appropriate for which data measurement scale?

   a. Categorical

   b. Ordinal

   c. Ratio

   d. Nominal

   e. All measurement scales are appropriate for variance analysis.

17. (LO 3) A scatterplot chart was created to show the correlation between employee salaries and their tenure at the company. The scatterplot chart has a data measurement scale(s) of

   a. categorical, ordinal, interval, and ratio.

   b. ordinal, interval, and ratio.

   c. interval and ratio.

   d. ratio.

18. (LO 3) Pooch Wear is an online retailer of pet clothing and accessories. A data visualization has been created to show sales revenue and marketing costs for each month. Diagnosing objectives in data analysis strategies involves which of the following?

   a. Determining the period that had the highest marketing costs

   b. Determining if there is a relationship between marketing costs and sales revenue

   c. Determining the factors that caused lower sales revenues at the beginning of the year

   d. Determining if marketing costs can be a predictor of sales revenue

19. (LO 3) Predictive and prescriptive analyses that include creating trendline visualizations are appropriate for which data measurement scale?

   a. Categorical

   b. Ordinal

   c. Nominal

   d. Interval

   e. All of these measurement scales support using trendline visualizations.

20. (LO 2, LO 3) Which of these analysis strategies involve categorical and ratio data measurement scales?

   a. Reconciliations of subsidiary ledger balances to the general ledger balance

   b. Depreciation schedules for all real estate assets

   c. Which types of capital sourcing have the highest cost of capital

   d. Changes to the tax rates applicable to their organization

21. (LO 4) Managerial accountants would most likely plan data analyses when which of the following occur?

   a. Changes to the tax rates

   b. Elimination of the financial statement footnote disclosure requirements

   c. Changes to Securities and Exchange Commission website

   d. Changes to their organization's performance

22. (LO 4) Information systems accountants would most likely plan data analyses when which of the following occur?

   a. A proposal of tax incentives for investments in green technologies

   b. Internal controls were implemented to improve segregation of duties

   c. A new product launch increased sales revenue for the company

   d. An audit of financial statements is taking place

23. (LO 4) Auditors plan data analysis strategies for which of the following situations?

   a. Evaluating the effectiveness of internal controls in their client's accounting system.

   b. Evaluating the representativeness of an account balance on their client's balance sheet or income statement.

   c. Considering the risk involved in providing an audit opinion for a client.

   d. Investigating whether a client's assumptions for recording their lease liabilities is consistent with other companies in their industry.

   e. All of these are examples of situations where auditors plan their data analysis strategies.

24. (LO 4) Financial accountants would most likely plan data analysis strategies for which of the following?

   a. Changes to the management team.

   b. New competitors in the marketplace.

   c. Changes to their assumptions and estimates for end of period adjusting entries.

d. Changes to the tax rates applicable to their organization.

e. None of these would motivate data analyses by financial accountants.

25. (LO 4) Tax accountants would most likely plan data analyses when which of the following occur?

a. A tax rebate is being proposed for lower-income individuals.

b. Cryptocurrency tax rules have changed.

c. The tax rate has increased for the high-income bracket.

d. All of the answer choices are correct.

Review Questions

1. (LO 1) Describe the five components in a data analysis project plan.

2. (LO 1) Discuss why it is important for accounting professionals to focus on the objective and questions to generate data and analysis alternatives.

3. (LO 1) Describe data and analysis risks that should be considered when planning a data analysis project.

4. (LO 2) Define and describe the four measurement scales used as accounting data variables.

5. (LO 2) Explain how selecting certain data fields could be inappropriate for your project plan.

6. (LO 2) Provide examples of two common data risks and a control for each that would reduce the risk.

7. (LO 3) Discuss why it is important to know the measurement scales of variables used in the analysis when determining whether to design a descriptive, diagnostic, predictive or prescriptive data analysis strategy.

8. (LO 3) Discuss why it is important to match the type of analysis performed with the measurement scale of the data.

9. (LO 3) Explain a trend analysis strategy, and provide an example of how an accountant may analyze sales using a trend analysis.

10. (LO 4) Assume you are a systems accountant working in the accounting information systems group at your company. You have been asked to perform data analysis to analyze the number of spam emails that pass through to employees before and after the company's investment in a new firewall. Discuss data risks and identify related controls to minimize those risks in your analysis.

11. (LO 4) Assume you are an auditor working to test internal controls regarding p-card usage at a company. You have the following data fields:

> EmployeeNumber
>
> EmployeeName
>
> P-cardTransactionDate
>
> P-cardTransaction vendor
>
> P-cardTransactionAmount

Describe a descriptive analysis strategy you can perform using the data strategy of the p-card transaction amount and any one of the other data fields.

12. (LO 4) Assume you are a tax accountant evaluating an individual's financial records for their federal tax compliance. What data risks should be considered?

Brief Exercises

BE 4.1 (LO 1) Put the data analysis project plan components in their proper sequential order, starting with number 1 for the first step.

___ **1.** Embed controls.

___ **2.** Identify project objective and specific questions.

___ **3.** Design data strategy.

___ **4.** Consider risks.

___ **5.** Design analysis strategy.

BE 4.2 (LO 1) Identify measured (M) and nonmeasured (NM) raw data in the table given below:

Raw Data Information
Product description
Sensor readings
Hours worked
Employee state of residence
Product category
Sales region
Economic value
Cash on hand

BE 4.3 (LO 1) Financial Accounting For each of the following, list which critical thinking element is most clearly involved (S = Stakeholders; P = Purpose; A = Alternatives; R = Risks; K = Knowledge):

___ **1.** Knowing what valuation procedure to use for U.S. GAAP.

___ **2.** Considering the impact of the analysis results.

___ **3.** The basis for the appropriateness of your data selections.

___ **4.** Not just going with the first idea that you think of for your data and your analysis.

___ **5.** Performing an analysis that is not appropriate for the measurement scale of your data.

BE 4.4 (LO 2) Cougar Motors manufactures electric vehicles globally. A visualization was created to show the number of orders for each sales region. This visualization has data measurement scales of

   a. categorical and ratio.   **c.** categorical and ordinal.

   b. categorical.   **d.** ratio.

BE 4.5 (LO 2) Auditing Assume you are a senior auditor responsible for supervising this year's intern on a data analysis project related to the client's purchases. You provided the intern with a data set and requested that the intern review the data set and be prepared to discuss. An excerpt of the data follows:

PONo	VendID	VendorName	Vendor Quality	Vendor Payterms	PODate	PO ItemNo	ItemCost	ItemQty
2001	783	Pep N Supply	3	1/10 net 30	12/1/2023	23568	41.99	12
2002	783	Pep N Supply	3	1/10 net 30	12/2/2023	23567	31.99	12
2003	784	Playtime Toys	4	1/15 net 30		32425	15.99	11
2004	784	Playtime Toys	4	1/15 net 30	12/4/2023	32426	15.99	10
2005	784	Playtime Toys	4	1/15 net 30	12/5/2023	32427	15.99	25
2006	258	Snappy Supplies	5	net 45	12/6/2023	11246	3.25	26
2007	153		2	2/10 net 60	12/7/2023	11258	333.25	35
	153	Production	2	2/10 net 60	12/8/2023	11259	6.75	45
2009	783	Pep N Supply	3	1/10 net 30	12/9/2023	23566	22.99	100

1. The intern stated, "Reviewing the data set, I classified VendorID as a measured raw data field source." Explain why VendorID should be considered nonmeasured raw data.

2. The intern stated, "The VendorQuality data field must be considered ratio data because we can analyze this as a variable in our analysis." Explain why the VendorQuality data field should not be considered ratio data.

3. The intern said, "The ItemCost and ItemQty data fields can be combined to create a calculated data field." Explain why this is correct.

4. Based on your review of the excerpt of the data set, what data risks would you expect the intern to identify?

5. Assume you asked the intern to verify the accuracy of the PO number 2006. What would the intern review to determine if the data in the database is accurate?

BE 4.6 (LO 2) For each of the following, identify if the data field is a (MRD) measured raw data field, a (NRD) nonmeasured raw data field, or a (CAL) calculated field:

___ **1.** ProductIdentificationCode

___ **2.** UnitCost for each inventory item

___ **3.** TotalCost

___ **4.** GrossProfit

___ **5.** ProductCategory

___ **6.** NumberOnHand in the warehouse of each product

BE 4.7 (LO 3) Identify the objective of each of the following analysis strategies as descriptive, diagnostic, predictive, or prescriptive:

Eco Clean is a manufacturer of eco-friendly products.

Wants Answer to the Questions	Objective
Finance has implemented a 2% discount on advance payments and wants to determine if the company increased the discount to 3%; how would that affect the accounts receivable amounts?	
A data visualization has been created to show sales revenue and marketing costs for each month, and the sales head wants to know the factors that caused lower sales revenues at the beginning of the year.	
The sales head wants to know the monthly average sales revenue.	
The finance head wants to know how much of a discount is required to reduce accounts receivable by 10%.	

BE 4.8 (LO 3) For each data structure and analysis listed for descriptive and diagnostic objectives, indicate whether the analysis can be performed with a "Yes" or "No."

___ **1.** The calculation of the mode on categorical data.

___ **2.** The variance dispersion of ordinal data.

___ **3.** The calculation of median on interval data.

___ **4.** Cumulative frequency distributions on categorical data.

___ **5.** A visualization of categorical data trends.

___ **6.** Cross tabulation correlations of ratio data.

BE 4.9 (LO 3) For each data structure and analysis listed for predictive and prescriptive objectives, indicate whether the analysis can be performed with a "Yes" or "No."

___ **1.** Trendlines on categorical data.

___ **2.** Regression analysis of ordinal data.

___ **3.** Optimization modeling of interval data.

___ **4.** Regression analysis of categorical data.

___ **5.** What-if analysis of ratio data.

___ **6.** Trendlines on ratio data.

BE 4.10 (LO 4) OneSun is a manufacturer of roof solar panels. The production manager provided you with a scatterplot chart showing material costs against production units. You are reviewing the analysis report to ensure that all steps of the data strategy have been completed.

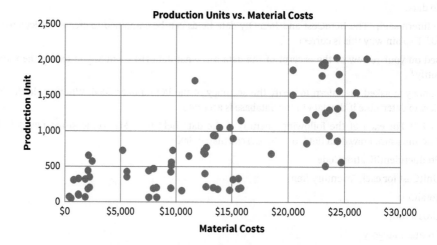

1. What type of analysis is being accomplished using the scatterplot chart? Explain why.

2. What could be a specific objective question being asked in this analysis?

3. What data risk and analysis risk should be considered in the data analysis strategy? How can the identified risks be controlled?

BE 4.11 (LO 4) [Accounting Information Systems] For each of the following analysis strategies for AIS projects, identify whether the project's objective is descriptive or diagnostic (D) or predictive or prescriptive (P):

Strategy	Objective
1. Calculating the average amount of time each department in the revenue cycle takes to perform its function per order.	
2. Calculating the cost savings expected from moving to RFID (radio frequency identification) technologies for inventory identification, pricing, and costing.	
3. Estimating how much server space would be needed for the AIS if sales revenues were to increase by 10% each year for the next five years.	
4. Detecting at which times of day and by which channel the unauthorized access is occurring to the customer relationship management module.	

BE 4.12 (LO 4) [Managerial Accounting] Mama's Pies is a pizza producer. They are looking to maximize the contribution margin on their pizza. As shown in the visualization, raw materials have been affected by inflation, which is reducing their contribution margin. You are a management accountant, and you need to conduct a data analysis to determine what price should be charged for each pizza to maintain a contribution of 15%.

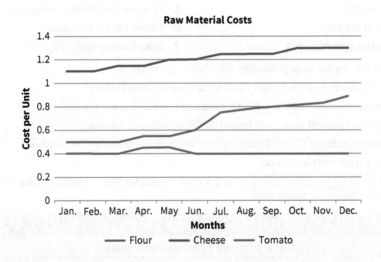

Create a prescriptive data analysis project plan for this analysis. Fill in the table below:

Data Analysis Project Plan
1. Project objective and specific question
2. Data strategy
3. Analysis strategy
4. Risks in data and analysis strategies
a. Data risk
b. Analysis risk
5. Controls for data and analysis strategies
a. Data strategy controls
b. Analysis strategy controls

Exercises

EX 4.1 (LO 1) Match Project Plan Components Match the data analysis project plan component to each of the following statements:

a. Project objectives and questions

b. Data strategy

c. Analysis strategy

d. Critical risks

e. Embedded controls

___ **1.** Verifying data values for reasonableness.

___ **2.** Data formatting that must be transformed before analysis.

___ **3.** Predicting next year's sales volume.

___ **4.** Sales volume data.

___ **5.** Using regression analysis to predict next year's sales volume.

___ **6.** Diagnosing what is causing the cost overruns in the production process.

___ **7.** Use of different scales on the y-axis and x-axis across visualizations.

EX 4.2 (LO 1) `Managerial Accounting` `Financial Accounting` **Design a Data Strategy and an Analysis Strategy** Assume your motivation for performing data analysis is to minimize cost. Your specific objective questions are to determine whether costs are increasing, stable, or dropping for each of your company's product lines this year compared to last year. Describe one possible data strategy and analysis strategy for this objective.

EX 4.3 (LO 1) `Managerial Accounting` `Accounting Information Systems` **Match Data Strategy Choices** Match each objective to the following data selections:

a. Labor cost data

b. Production run data

c. Past marketing strategy data

d. IT service satisfaction survey data

e. Online market sales data

f. Sales contract data

___ **1.** What is causing our large production materials usage variance?

___ **2.** Which marketing strategy is most likely to increase our market share?

___ **3.** Are we in compliance with U.S. GAAP procedures for revenue recognition?

___ **4.** Which of our product lines could be sold online as well as in the store?

___ **5.** Is the turnover in our IT staff impacting their service to the other functional areas?

___ **6.** Are our payroll costs increasing?

EX 4.4 (LO 2) `Managerial Accounting` **Design Data Strategies** The following is a list of the available fields in a data set from a pet supply store:

Data Field	Description
1. PONo	Uniquely assigned purchase order number
2. VendorID	Uniquely assigned vendor number
3. VendorName	Vendor name
4. VendorQuality	Quality rating ranging from 1–6 where 1 = poor and 6 = exceptional
5. VendorAddress	Postal mailing address and street name
6. VendorCity	Mailing address city
7. VendorState	Mailing address state
8. VendorZip	Mailing address zip
9. VendorPayterms	Payment terms negotiated with the vendor
10. PODate	Purchase order date
11. POItemID	Uniquely identifiable item number
12. POItemDescription	Description of item
13. ItemCost	Cost of the inventory item per negotiated terms with vendor
14. ItemQty	Total quantity of items purchased

For each of the following objectives (a, b, and c), identify the minimum data fields (1–14) you would select for your data strategy:

a. Your objective is to reduce the carbon footprint of your purchases, so you want to identify which vendor transported your purchases across the most miles last year.

b. Your objective is to determine which inventory items have the greatest cost increases over the past five years.

c. Your objective is to identify the five vendors from whom you made the highest value of purchases last year.

EX 4.5 (LO 2) Prepare a Project Plan You are a sales manager and will have a regional sales meeting a month from now. Your objective is to showcase the sales targets your team met successfully. You want to show how your sales improved month-on-month. Describe your data strategy, your analysis strategy, and three possible risks you need to control by providing control suggestions.

(*Note*: Students' answers will vary.)

EX 4.6 (LO 2) [Managerial Accounting] **Data Strategy Risks and Controls** Assume your data analysis objective is to reduce the carbon footprint of your purchases from vendors. Your analysis strategy is to identify which vendor transported your purchases across the most miles last year. You have selected the following data fields for your data strategy:

Data Field	Description
PONo	Uniquely assigned purchase order number
VendorID	Uniquely assigned vendor number
VendorName	Vendor name
VendorAddress	Postal mailing address and street name
VendorCity	Mailing address city
VendorState	Mailing address state
VendorZip	Mailing address zip
PODate	Purchase order date

Identify three data risks and data controls you could use for those risks.

EX 4.7 (LO 3) [Auditing] [Managerial Accounting] **Prepare a Project Plan** You are an internal auditor working with your company's outdoor gear sales department to devise a new strategy for sales commissions that incentivizes higher profits than your current flat commission strategy. Describe a data strategy, an analysis strategy and three possible risks you need to control by providing control suggestions.

EX 4.8 (LO 3) [Managerial Accounting] **Prepare a Project Plan** You are a managerial accountant for Techie Doll manufacturing company. You have been asked to predict next year's contribution margin and sales value if the targeted profit is 1/10th of the contribution margin. A sample of the available data for your analysis is included here:

Field Label	Field Name in Database
Receipt Number	SaleReceiptNo
Sales Date	Saledate
Inventory Code	InvCode
Number Sold	NoSold
Inventory Description	InvDesc
Inventory Price	InvPrice
Inventory Cost	InvCost
Fixed Cost	FXDCost

Describe a data strategy, an analysis strategy, and three possible risks you need to control by providing control suggestions.

(*Note*: Students' answers will vary.)

EX 4.9 (LO 3) **Financial Accounting** **Managerial Accounting** **Prepare a Project Plan** You work as a financial analyst for a large coffee shop chain, such as Costa Coffee. Your objective is to diagnose which stores have increasing sales. Your data strategy is to use the store sales monthly data from the past two years. Design an analysis strategy, including which risks you should consider and controls that would help mitigate those risks.

EX 4.10 (LO 1–4) **Auditing** **Accounting Information Systems** **Prepare a Project Plan** You are working in the accounting information systems group at your company. You have been asked to evaluate the internal controls associated with authentication of users into the information system. Your manager has asked you to perform a descriptive analysis of failed login attempts. Your manager has provided you with the analysis objective and question. Using the chart, document your data and analysis choices and risks and controls for each.

Objective and Questions	Data and Analysis Strategies	Risks	Controls
Objective: Evaluate internal controls associated with authentication of users.	**1.** Data:	**3.** Data:	**5.** Data:
Questions: What are the mean, median, standard deviation, and distribution of failed login attempts during the current year?	**2.** Analysis:	**4.** Analysis:	**6.** Analysis:

EX 4.11 (LO 1–4) **Financial Accounting** **Managerial Accounting** **Prepare a Project Plan** You are a financial analyst at Sihrya's Beauty Salon. The company owner has asked you to perform data analyses to understand the products that contribute to the salon's retail store's profitability. The owner provided you a data dictionary, presented here, describing data that you may consider using in your analysis.

Field Label	Field Name in Database	Field Description
Receipt Number	ReceiptNo	POS assigned receipt number uniquely identifying each sale.
Sales Date	SaleDate	Date of sale per the POS.
Inventory Code	InvCode	Unique inventory identification number for each product in the salon's retail store.
Number Sold	NoSold	Quantity of items sold.
Inventory Description	InvDesc	Description of the inventory item.
Inventory Price	InvPrice	Gross sales price of the inventory item.
Inventory Cost	InvCost	Weighted average cost of the inventory item.

1. State the owner's objective for your data analysis project.
2. Assume your analysis question is to identify the products that have the highest gross profit. Identify the data fields you should include in your analysis. Identify the data analysis choices to answer this analysis question.
3. Identify risks and the related control choices related to the analysis question.

EX 4.12 (LO 1–4) **Data** **Managerial Accounting** **Select a Data Strategy and Perform an Analysis** You are a managerial accountant working at a multi-location pet care retail company. Your supervisor has asked you to compare the dollar amount of purchases made from each vendor in December 2024 compared to December 2025. After discussing with your supervisor, you have identified the following:

Objective: Compare total purchases by vendor in December 2024 and December 2025.

Question: In 2024 and 2025, from which vendors were the most purchases (in dollars) made?

Data: You have access to the following data:

Data Field	Description
PONo	Uniquely assigned purchase order number.
VendorID	Uniquely assigned vendor number.
VendorName	Vendor name.
VendorQuality	Quality rating ranging from 1–6 where 1 = poor and 6 = exceptional.
VendorAddress	Postal mailing address and street name.
VendorCity	Mailing address city.
VendorState	Mailing address state.
VendorZip	Mailing address zip.
VendorPayterms	Payment terms negotiated with the vendor.
PODate	Purchase order date.
POItemID	Uniquely identifiable item number.
POItemDescription	Description of item.
ItemCost	Cost of the item per negotiated terms with vendor.
ItemQty	Total quantity of items purchased.

1. Which data items would you use in your data strategy?

2. Design an analysis strategy to identify the vendor or vendors in which the company had a higher dollar amount of purchases in 2025 compared to 2024.

3. Perform the analysis per your analysis strategy. Identify the vendors in which the company had a higher dollar amount of purchases in 2025 compared to 2024.

Problems

PR 4.1 (LO 1–4) Data Auditing Managerial Accounting **Complete Project Plan** You work in the internal audit group in your organization, and your supervisor has asked you to analyze p-card data. The objective of the analysis is to understand p-card spending in the current year. The questions associated with the objective include:

- With which three vendors does the company spend the most money using p-cards?
- Which employee spends the highest dollar amount of money using the p-card?

Review the data and complete the chart to document your data and analysis strategy choices.

Objective and Questions	Data and Analysis Strategies	Risks	Controls
Objective: Understand p-card spending in the current year. **Questions:** • What are the three vendors where the company spends the most money using p-cards? • Which employee spends the highest dollar amount of money using the p-card?	**Data:** Use the data provided in the Excel file. **Analysis:** Use Excel to create a PivotTable that allows grouping of the p-card spending data by vendor and sort by the highest vendor. Use Excel to create a PivotTable to group p-card spending amount by employee and sort by the highest dollar amount by employee.	**1.** Data: **2.** Analysis:	**3.** Data: **4.** Analysis:

5. Perform the analyses suggested in the chart. Summarize your results.

PR 4.2 (LO 1, 2, 3) `Data` `Financial Accounting` `Managerial Accounting` **Complete Steps 2 and 3 of a Project Plan and Perform Analysis.** You are a financial analyst at Sihrya's Beauty Salon. The owner has asked you to perform data analyses to understand the products that contribute to the salon's retail store's profitability. The owner gave you a data dictionary, which is presented here, describing data that you may consider using in your analysis.

Field Label	Field Name in Database	Field Description
Receipt Number	ReceiptNo	POS assigned receipt number uniquely identifying each sale.
Sales Date	Saledate	Date of sale per the POS.
Inventory Code	InvCode	Unique inventory identification number for each product in the salon's retail store.
Number Sold	NoSold	Quantity of items sold.
Inventory Description	InvDesc	Description of the inventory item.
Inventory Price	InvPrice	Gross sales price of the inventory item.
Inventory Cost	InvCost	Weighted average cost of the inventory item.

Assume your analysis objective is to identify the products that contribute the most to the salon's retail store profitability. Your specific questions are: Which products have the highest units sold? Which products have a positive gross profit margin? Use the information provided to answer the following questions:

1. Identify the data fields to include in your data strategy.
2. Identify a data strategy that could be used to answer the objective questions.
3. Identify an analysis strategy that could be used to answer the objective questions.
4. Review the data provided to perform the analysis. After performing the analysis, identify the top two products that contribute to the salon's profitability.

PR 4.3 (LO 1–4) `Data` `Managerial Accounting` **Complete the Project Plan and Perform the Analysis** As a financial analyst at a hospitality industry company, you have been asked to design a data analysis strategy to understand the factors that influence a guest's quality rating. Your team administered a survey of guests staying at your properties during the month of June. The database team has linked the survey responses for quality rating of the stay to the guest's location, check-in and check-out date, and spending amounts. They indicated that they only included data related to surveys completed September 1 through September 10.

1. Which data measurement scales are included in the data fields labeled Location, QualityRating, and SpendingAmount?
2. Review the data set, identify data risks present in the data set, and suggest controls for these risks.
3. Assume a member of your team suggested that you use the data to predict the quality rating of future stays. To do this predictive analysis, you would have to use the quality rating data in a predictive analysis strategy. How would you respond to your team member about the appropriateness of using this type of analysis?
4. Use this data set to design and perform a different, original data strategy and an analysis strategy to satisfy the objective question. Document your data strategy, analysis strategy, risks, and controls and present your analysis results.

PR 4.4 (LO 1–4) `Data` `Tax Accounting` **Complete the Project Plan and Perform the Analysis** Beautiful Bites is a chain of bakeries located in Canberra, Australia. Its owners are committed to social sustainability values and want to focus their philanthropy in the municipalities where they are collecting the most sales tax. The objective of the data analysis is to determine where most of their customers live. The specific questions is: In which communities do most of our customers reside?

1. Prepare the data analysis project plan.
2. Perform the analysis and summarize the results.

Professional Application Case   Automated Transportation, Inc. (ATI)

Automated Transportation, Inc. is a medium-sized manufacturer of remote-controlled cars, boats, and drones. The company was established five years ago when two brothers decided to build and sell remote control cars to enthusiasts. As the company grew, they expanded their product offerings to include remote control cars, boats, and drones. The brothers serve as the president and CEO of the company, and they now have over 70 employees.

They have two key customer groups, hobbyists and businesses interested in incorporating drones into their business process and supply chain. These two customer bases provide a variety of opportunities for growth. Management values internal control, but since they are busy running the company they have employed accounting personnel to help design the company's processes, policies, and internal controls:

- The company is not required to have a report on internal controls and external auditors are not required to attest to the company's internal controls.

- However, the owners want to be sure the company employees are designing and following policies that will help them maintain efficient and effective operations.

- The owners are also very data-driven and make many of their business decisions only after considering the data collected and analyzed.

The following is an excerpt from the data dictionary designed by the company's information systems personnel and accounting information systems accountants:

Data Field Label	Field Name in Database	Field Description
Invoice number	InvoiceNO	The invoice number, which is hand-keyed into the AIS by the AP clerk from a manual invoice mailed to the company by the vendor.
Invoice amount	InvoiceAmt	The amount of the invoice, which is hand-keyed into the AIS by the AP clerk from a manual invoice mailed to the company by the vendor.
Shipment date	ShipDate	The date the product was shipped from the shipping location.
Invoice date	InvoiceDate	The date of the invoice, which is hand-keyed into the AIS by the AP clerk from a manual invoice mailed to the company by the vendor.
Vendor identification number	VendorID	Unique vendor identification number.
Vendor name	VendorName	Name of the vendor.
Product purchased	ProductID	Product code for the product purchased from the vendor. This product code is consistent with the catalog from the vendor.
Unit cost	UnitCost	The cost per unit of the product purchased from the vendor.
Shipping cost	ShipCost	Total shipping costs.
Flat duty	FlatDuty	The flat duty rate applies to article that are dutiable.
Tariff	TariffAmt	The total dollar amount of a tariff applied to the goods shipped.
Shipping location	ShipLocation	The country in which the goods are shipped from.
Receiving quality rating	QualityRate	This is a quality rating keyed into the AIS by the receiving team when they receive the goods. The scale is 1 = poor to 5 = excellent quality. The receiving team rates the shipment on packaging, quality of materials, and overall delivery.

(Continued)

(Continued)

Data Field Label	Field Name in Database	Field Description
Payment terms	PaymentTerms	The agreed-upon payment terms with the vendor. These terms are negotiated by the purchasing manager and keyed into the vendor master file by the purchasing supervisor.
Shipping terms	ShipTerms	Shipping terms—typically FOB destination or FOB shipping.
Payment address	PayAddress	The vendors address where payment is to be mailed.
Purchase order number	PONumber	The unique identifying number assigned to each purchase order issued by the company.
Purchase order date	PODate	The date the purchase order is issued by the company.
Receiving report number	ReceivingNumber	The unique identifying number assigned to each receiving report created by the company's receiving group.
Receiving report date	ReceivingDate	The date the product is received by the company's receiving department.
Quantity received	QtyReceived	The total quantity of items received.
Quantity purchased	QtyPurchased	The total quantity of items on the Purchase Order.
Invoiced quantity	QtyInvoice	The total quantity of items on the invoice, this amount is hand-keyed into the AIS by the AP clerk from the manual invoice mailed to the company by the vendor.
Treasurer approval	Approved	The initials of the Treasurer indicating their approval if the invoice was greater than $10,000.

PAC 4.1 Accounting Information Systems: Evaluate AIS Internal Controls

Accounting Information Systems As an information systems accountant, the owners have asked to you to design internal controls related to the company's vendor payment system. Remember from your accounting information systems course that there are several important controls in the order-to-pay cycle, including approval of purchases and approval of vendor invoices. You have implemented the following control:

- The accounting clerk prepares a voucher package containing a disbursement voucher, vendor invoice, purchase order, and receiving document for each payment to be made.

- Invoices where payment exceeds $10,000 have a second level of approval, which is noted in the information system by the treasurer's initials.

You want to test the operational effectiveness of this control by analyzing data captured by the accounting information system during this process. Assume the objective of your analysis is to understand whether the internal control is operating as designed. Design your data analysis strategy to address this objective. Be sure to document the following components:

1. What is the question your data analysis should address?
2. Using the data dictionary, what measured raw data and nonmeasured raw data fields should you request?
3. What analysis choices will you make to analyze the data? Specifically, what calculated data fields would you create in your analysis?
4. What are the data risks to your data analysis strategy?
5. What are the analysis risks in your strategy?
6. What controls should you include in your data and analysis strategies to minimize the risks you outlined?

PAC 4.2 Auditing: Select Large and Unusual Purchases

Data **Auditing** You are a second-year staff working at a public accounting firm assigned to the ATI engagement, which is a new engagement for the firm. Your senior auditor has provided you with a transaction file that contains all the company's payments to vendors for the month of January. You have been asked to determine if the company is accurately recording invoice information by designing a data analysis strategy to select purchase transactions for further testing. You must design a data analysis strategy to select purchase transactions for further testing. Your senior asked you to identify transactions that may be outside the normal purchasing behavior. Therefore, you must perform descriptive analyses. Your senior provided you with this partial data analysis plan.

Complete the chart by identifying the risk and related controls for the data and analysis choices determined in the data analysis plan.

Objective and Questions	Data and Analysis Strategies	Risks	Controls
Objective: Identify purchase transactions for further testing. **Questions:** Are there purchase transactions that may be considered anomalies?	**Data strategy:** InvoiceNo, InvoiceDate, QtyInvoice, InvoiceAmt, VendorID, VendorDescription **Analysis strategy:** Perform descriptive statistics to understand total dollar amount and count of purchases made to each vendor. Perform diagnostic statistics and create a scatterplot whereby the InvoiceDate is on the x-axis and the InvoiceAmount is on the y-axis to identify any outlier purchases.	**1.** Data: **2.** Analysis:	**3.** Data: **4.** Analysis:

5. Perform descriptive statistical analysis to identify the total dollar amount and count of purchases made to each vendor.

6. Use the provided data set to perform the diagnostic statistical analysis to create a scatterplot where the InvoiceDate is on the x-axis and the InvoiceAmt is on the y-axis to identify outlier purchases.

PAC 4.3 Financial Accounting: Plan to Identify High Activity Vendors

Financial Accounting The owners of the company want to know which vendors the purchasing group are using and how much they are paying each to negotiate better contract terms with regular vendors. You are performing data analysis to identify the most used vendors. Answer each question with respect to your data analysis.

1. What is the question your data analysis should address?

2. Using the data dictionary, what measured raw data and nonmeasured raw data fields should you request?

3. What analysis choices will you make to analyze the data? Be specific, what calculated data fields would you create in your analysis?

4. What are the data risks to your data analysis strategy?

5. What are the analysis risks in your strategy?

6. What controls should you include in your analysis to minimize the risks you outlined?

PAC 4.4 Managerial Accounting: Rank Vendor Quality

Data **Managerial Accounting** Because the company is growing so fast, the owners want to be sure that they are partnering with the right vendors for raw materials. They have asked the receiving team to give each receipt a rating to document the quality of the packaging, the materials in appearance, and overall delivery. For each receipt the receiving group documents a quality rating in the accounting information system. The owners have asked you to determine how the quality rating by vendor has changed since the beginning of the year. Your manager has designed the following partial data analysis strategy. Complete the chart and document the risks and related controls to your analyses.

Objective and Questions	Data and Analysis Strategies	Risks	Controls
Objective: Understand the quality ratings of purchases. **Questions:** What is the average quality rating by vendor? What is the highest and lowest quality rating by vendor? How has the quality rating by vendor changed over time?	**Data strategy:** VendorID, VendorName, ReceivingNo, ReceivingDate, QualityRate **Analysis strategy:** Calculate the average QualityRating by VendorName. Calculate the minimum and maximum QualityRating by VendorName. Visualize how QualityRating by VendorName has changed over time.	**1.** Data: **2.** Analysis:	**3.** Data: **4.** Analysis:

5. Perform the analyses suggested in the data analysis project plan.

PAC 4.5 Tax Accounting: Plan International Duty Cost Analysis

Tax Accounting The owners want to understand the total dollar amount of customs duty they will owe the U.S. government for the year. They have asked you to perform descriptive analytics to understand the purchases from vendors located in each country. Your company makes purchases from vendors located in several countries, such as China, Mexico, the United States, Japan, South Africa, Israel, Greece, and Egypt.

You and your team have designed a data analysis strategy. You have been asked to consider the risks and related controls in the development of that strategy. Complete the following chart:

Objective and Questions	Data and Analysis Strategies	Risks	Controls
Objective: Understand the purchases made from each country.	**Data strategy:** ShipLocation, InvoiceAmt, FlatDuty, TariffAmt, PONumber	**1.** Data:	**3.** Data:
Questions: What dollar amount of purchases are made from each country? How many purchases were made from vendors in each country?	**Analysis strategy:** Use a PivotTable to drop the ShipLocation into the rows and the sum of InvoiceAmt into values. Use a PivotTable to drop the ShipLocation into the rows and count of PONumber into values.	**2.** Analysis:	**4.** Analysis:

5

Analysis: Data Preparation

So far in this course, you have learned to plan a data analysis project by articulating what is motivating it, identifying its objectives, and designing a strategy to successfully complete it. Now that the plan is in place, it is time to move on to the data analysis stage. There are three tasks in this stage: preparing the data, building the information model, and exploring the data. Here, we will focus on the first task of preparing the data for analysis. Data preparation can be the most time-consuming activity in a data analytics project. You could spend over 75% of the project's total work time on this task alone! But there is a good reason for this, as data preparation involves multiple activities. There are two key factors to be aware of when preparing data for analysis:

1. The quality of the data will affect the quality of the insights and the decisions based on them. In other words, bad data leads to bad decisions.

2. The structure of the data will determine how effectively they can be analyzed.

First, we explore the two key data preparation processes in detail. Next, the chapter presents 20 data extraction, transformation, and loading patterns you can use to prepare data for analysis.

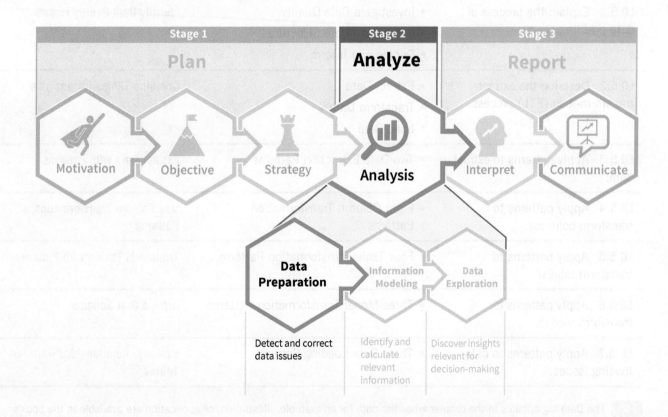

Stage 1	Stage 2	Stage 3
Plan	**Analyze**	**Report**
Motivation Objective Strategy	Analysis	Interpret Communicate

Data Preparation — Detect and correct data issues

Information Modeling — Identify and calculate relevant information

Data Exploration — Discover insights relevant for decision-making

How Can You Approach the Challenges of Data Preparation?

Bill is a director in the audit data analytics practice at one of the large public accounting firms.

After graduating with an accounting degree, I gradually moved to our data analytics practice. **I love how accounting and technology blend together in our audit engagements and that there are always new opportunities and challenges to work on.**

A key challenge in working with data at a public accounting firm is that our clients come in all shapes and sizes, with ERP systems ranging from legacy proprietary systems to increasingly modern, cloud-based integrated systems with sophisticated reporting and analytics capabilities. This means that **the cleanliness, quality, granularity, volume, and structure of the data can vary significantly. This increases the importance of ETL (Extract-Transform-Load) solutions to help our professionals efficiently extract data from client systems, transform that data into a common format, and ultimately load the data into our analytics platform.**

To be successful, the data professionals at my firm must be able to understand and evaluate our clients' data to ensure that they are relevant and reliable. This includes knowing how to have the right conversations with our clients, often including representatives from the client's IT department and our internal data extraction specialists, in order to effectively communicate our data requirements. The skills you are building in this chapter are all highly relevant to a successful career as a data analyst in today's public accounting profession.

Chapter Roadmap

LEARNING OBJECTIVES	TOPICS	APPLY IT
LO 5.1 Explain the process of data profiling.	• Investigate Data Quality • Investigate Data Structure • Decide and Inform	**Identify Data Quality Issues**
LO 5.2 Describe the extract-transform-load (ETL) process.	• Extract Data • Transform Data • Load Data	**Combine Tables for Analysis**
LO 5.3 Apply patterns to extract data.	• Two Data Extraction Patterns	**Extract Data with Patterns**
LO 5.4 Apply patterns to transform columns.	• Eight Column Transformation Patterns	**Use Column Transformation Patterns**
LO 5.5 Apply patterns to transform tables.	• Four Table Transformation Patterns	**Transform Tables with Patterns**
LO 5.6 Apply patterns to transform models.	• Three Model Transformation Patterns	**Draw a Star Schema**
LO 5.7 Apply patterns to data loading issues.	• Three Data Loading Patterns	**Evaluate Relationships Between Tables**

Data The Data tag appears in the chapter when the data for an example, illustration, or application are available in the book's product page on www.wiley.com.

Data analytics software is continuously changing, and there may be more recent versions of the software referenced in this chapter.

5.1 What Is Data Profiling?

Businesses lose billions of dollars every year due to **dirty data**, or data that provide inaccurate or incomplete descriptions of the economic activities of a business. Using dirty data can result in issues ranging from inaccurate pricing, to sending bills to the wrong customers (or not collecting them at all), to an inability to detect fraud. Data preparation helps avoid these issues and more.

Data preparation is the process of profiling, cleaning, restructuring, and integrating data prior to processing and analysis. It helps ensure high-quality data and, therefore, improved decision-making. **Data profiling** is the process of investigating data quality and structure. It has three parts:

1. **Investigating data quality:** Search for anomalies in the data. That is, are the data dirty?
2. **Investigating data structure:** Find the best way to organize the data and improve analytics.
3. **Deciding and informing:** Make decisions about whether it is possible to address the identified issues, what the cost of doing so would be, and consider the possible consequences if the issues are not addressed.

Decisions made in the final phase will guide the extract-transform-load (ETL) process by determining what must be changed. As **Illustration 5.1** shows, data preparation is an ongoing collaboration between the data profiling process, which is the subject of this discussion, and the ETL process, which is covered next. For now, keep in mind that data profiling detects data issues and ETL corrects them.

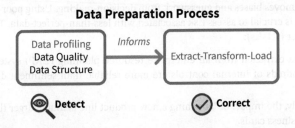

ILLUSTRATION 5.1 The Data Preparation Process

Investigate Data Quality

When discussing the "quality" of the data we work with, we are referring to the suitability of using the data for decision-making. Assessing data quality identifies flawed values in the data set, which reveals if there are data that must be cleaned. There are different methods for doing this:

- The rule-driven method is a top-down approach. A logical relationship, or rule, is defined among data and tested to determine if the data conform to it. The number of rules that can be specified is nearly unlimited. Examples include:
  - Segregation of duties.
  - Quantity on hand cannot be negative.
  - A car cannot be rented to someone who is younger than 16 years old.
  - Sales can only be executed with a valid order.
- The exploration and inference methods are bottom-up approaches. The goal is to find anomalies by examining the data from many different perspectives. Sorting, frequency distributions,

and outlier analysis are examples of powerful techniques for exploration purposes. The second bottom-up approach, inference, is a method that relies on computer algorithms to identify anomalies.

These different methods identify data anomalies, which occur when the data do not meet expectations of correctness, validity, consistency, and completeness.

Correctness

Data describe facts about entities, such as the name of a customer, the price of a product, or the date of a transaction. Data are incorrect when the value assigned to an entity's characteristic is wrong. For instance, a customer might live in New Jersey (NJ), but New York (NY) is recorded instead, or the price of a product is $252, but it is listed as $225.

Incorrect data are common, as these real-world examples of data glitches show. For the businesses involved, data mistakes can be significant:

- Delta Airlines sold a round trip plane ticket from mainland United States to Hawaii for less than $7. In a similar example, a United Airlines customer was able to purchase a first-class round-trip ticket from the United States to Hong Kong for just seven frequent flyer miles.
- A customer booked a luxury hotel room in Pasadena, California, for $10 a night.
- Walmart sold a treadmill for less than $35.

There are several ways to detect such errors. When pricing is incorrect, such as when a normally expensive airfare is available at a deep discount due to an error, then a sudden surge in demand might be an indication of a problem. Profiling techniques, such as exploring outliers, can also be useful. Regardless, always think critically about the data being analyzed and watch for anomalies.

Applying Critical Thinking 5.1

Assess Data Quality

Using sound data removes biases and guesswork from decision-making. Using poor data in the process increases risk. So, it is crucial to assess risk associated with less-than-perfect-data. There are two characteristics to consider (**Risks**):

- **Reliability:** Data extracted from an enterprise resource planning (ERP) system that have been subjected to hundreds of internal controls are more reliable than sentiment data extracted from Facebook.
- **Impact:** Similarly, the impact of launching a new product line is much larger than the decision to invest in new business cards.

The higher the impact, the more you should be willing to invest in improving the data's reliability.

Assessing Data Reliability and Impact

Validity

Another integral part of data profiling is designing **validation rules.** These rules define what values are and are not acceptable and they can take many shapes and forms. For example, an order should occur before a shipment, or an email address should contain the symbol @.

Validity and correctness are sometimes confused. Imagine that a business ships their items to the states in the Midwestern United States only: IL, IN, IA, KS, MI, MN, MO, NE, ND, OH, SD, and WI. Here are some scenarios:

- Goods are shipped to Ohio (OH), and OH is entered as the value for the state field in the system. The value is both *valid* and *correct*.
- Someone accidentally records Minnesota (MN) as the destination for a shipment that went to Michigan (MI). The value entered is *valid* (MN is an accepted state) but *incorrect*.
- The business receives an order from a customer in Pennsylvania (PA), and the goods are shipped. PA is entered into the system as the state. While the system will consider the value as *invalid*, it is *correct* (PA is the correct state, but the company cannot sell goods there).
- The same order from a customer in PA is received and the goods will be shipped there. NA—Not Applicable—is entered into the system as the state. In this case, the value entered is both *invalid* and *incorrect*.

An incorrect value means the wrong value is assigned, and an invalid value means an unacceptable value is assigned.

Consistency

In addition to being correct and valid, data should be consistent. Data inconsistency occurs when the same characteristic is represented multiple ways. Using both MI and Michigan to refer to the same state would create data inconsistency. Using mgr, mngr, and manager to describe the same job position would do the same. These inconsistencies create challenges during analysis. For example, it would be difficult to determine total revenues per state if there were separate totals for MI and Michigan.

How can we identify inconsistencies like these? Here are two profiling techniques:

- Create a list with all distinct values, then sort and review. The inconsistent values of mgr, mngr, and manager will likely be noticeable immediately.
- Build a frequency table, or a table that counts how many times a value occurs. Values with a low frequency might indicate inconsistent data.

Completeness

Data that are correct, valid, and consistent are only accurate if they are also complete, as noncomplete data might result in distorted insights. Data can be incomplete in two ways.

A missing instance is when a concept occurred but is not recorded, such as when goods were sold, but the sales transaction was not recorded. A missing instance such as a missing sales transaction can be identified with gap analysis. If there is a sequential number for each sales invoice, then a missing number might indicate a sale that occurred but was not recorded.

A missing value occurs when the transaction is recorded, but we do not have information for all characteristics. The result is empty cells. This might happen if a customer is recorded, but the record does not include the customer's email address. The term "null" typically indicates a missing or unknown value. It is important to assess how the missing information affects decision-making.

Investigate Data Structure

Along with their quality, data are investigated to assess whether they are structured in a way that makes data analytics easy and efficient.

Unambiguous Descriptions

During data exploration and interpretation, column names in tables become variables. We apply mathematical operations, such as sum, to them and use them as part of visualizations, such as pie charts. However, poorly named columns make it complicated to develop information models and to conduct analysis. Column names should also be correct, intuitive, and clear because they are part of the analytical database, which might have many different users. An **analytical database** is the integrated data set used for analysis purposes. Unambiguous descriptions should be a priority when developing an analytical database. Here are some examples of correct and clear column titles:

- An age column should contain numbers (e.g., 32) and not dates (e.g., 6/2/1990).
- CustomerID is more descriptive than ID.
- Birthday is easier to understand than bday.

Applying Critical Thinking 5.2

Create a Shared, Comprehensible Vocabulary

Creating a shared vocabulary requires identifying who is going to use the analytical database (Stakeholders):

- If you prepare the data for others, then make sure that you create a vocabulary for column and table names that is easy to understand and work with.
- For example, it is common for data scientists to use table names such as DCustomer and FSales with D and F referring to certain types of tables. However, such terms might be confusing to other stakeholders who are not data scientists!

Table Structures That Make Analysis Easier

Analysis includes aggregating, or grouping, data and then examining them from different viewpoints in many ways. This is known as **slicing**. Here is an example of slicing sales transaction data for a business with sales in multiple regions:

- **Aggregate:** Calculate the total sales amount.
- **Slice:** Break the total down by region to examine the regional sales in more detail.

Some data structures are a good fit for these aggregate and slice processes, while others are not, so learning best practices for structuring data is crucial. Two common best practices are single-valued columns and flat tables.

Single-Valued Columns For analytical purposes, each cell should contain one value describing one characteristic. That is, each column should be **single-valued**. Two or more values in the same cell makes analysis more challenging. Here are two scenarios that violate the single-valued rule:

A **composite column** combines values for two or more characteristics. The Name column in **Illustration 5.2**(A) combines last name, first name, and certification characteristics. Which data set would you prefer if you needed to generate a list with all employees who have a CPA—panel (A) or (B)? While the data are identical for both data sets, panel (B) makes it easier to answer this question.

ILLUSTRATION 5.2 Composite vs. Single-Valued Column

(A) Composite Column

Name
Cole, Lakeisha, NA
Lopez, Alejandro, CPA
Key, Kim, NA
David, Julie, CPA
Malone, Moses, NA
Buslepp, Bill, CPA
Potoms, Keme, NA
Despontin, Marc, CPA
Kaminski, Ivanka, NA

(B) Single-Valued Column

Name	Certification
Cole, Lakeisha	NA
Lopez, Alejandro	CPA
Key, Kim	NA
David, Julie	CPA
Malone, Moses	NA
Buslepp, Bill	CPA
Potoms, Keme	NA
Despontin, Marc	CPA
Kaminski, Ivanka	NA

In a **multi-valued column**, a cell contains multiple values of the same characteristic. The Certifications column in **Illustration 5.3**(A) lists all certifications for an employee. Again, which data set would you prefer if you needed to generate a list with all employees who have a CPA—panel (A) or (B)? While the data are identical for both data sets, it is easier to answer this question with the single-valued column in panel (B).

ILLUSTRATION 5.3   Multi-Valued vs. Single-Valued Column

(A) Multi-Valued Column

Name	Certifications
Cole, Lakeisha	CISA
Lopez, Alejandro	CPA, CISA
Key, Kim	CMA
David, Julie	CPA, CMA, CISA
Malone, Moses	CPA
Buslepp, Bill	CPA, CMA
Potoms, Keme	CMA
Despontin, Marc	CPA
Kaminski, Ivanka	CMA, CISA

(B) Single-Valued Column

Name	Certifications
Cole, Lakeisha	CISA
Lopez, Alejandro	CISA
Lopez, Alejandro	CPA
Key, Kim	CMA
David, Julie	CISA
David, Julie	CMA
David, Julie	CPA
Malone, Moses	CPA
Buslepp, Bill	CMA
Buslepp, Bill	CPA
Potoms, Keme	CMA
Despontin, Marc	CPA
Kaminski, Ivanka	CISA
Kaminski, Ivanka	CMA

Flat Tables   Another best practice for structuring data is using **flat tables**, in which column headers do not contain data values useful for analysis purposes. For data analysis, flat table structures are preferred over crosstabulation tables.

Illustration 5.4(A) shows a crosstabulation table representing a relationship between the two variables of car model and salesperson:

- In the first column are the values for the different car models: Focus, Mustang, Escape, and Explorer.
- The column headers in the top row show the values for salespeople.
- A cross-section cell shows how many units a salesperson has sold of a specific model. Salesperson Elodie has sold five units of the Focus model.

Crosstabulation tables have limitations for analysis. The names in the panel (A) column headers are examples of data values useful for data analysis. Column headers cannot be used for filter or group-by operations.

ILLUSTRATION 5.4   Crosstabulation Table Structure vs. Flat Table Structure

(A) Crosstabulation

	Jim	Jane	Elodie	Carlos
Focus	0	1	5	4
Mustang	1	2	3	3
Escape	4	1	0	2
Explorer	2	2	0	1

(B) Flat

Model	SalesPerson	UnitsSold
Focus	Carlos	4
Mustang	Carlos	3
Escape	Carlos	2
Explorer	Carlos	1
Focus	Elodie	5
Mustang	Elodie	3
Escape	Elodie	0
Explorer	Elodie	0
Focus	Jane	1
Mustang	Jane	2
Escape	Jane	1
Explorer	Jane	2
Focus	Jim	0
Mustang	Jim	1
Escape	Jim	4
Explorer	Jim	2

Illustration 5.4(B) shows the same data using a flat structure. Carlos, Elodie, Jane, and Jim have become values of the Salesperson column. They can be used for filter and group-by operations. Would you prefer the table in panel (A) or the table in panel (B) to answer a question like "How many Mustangs did Jane and Jim sell?" The flat structure in Illustration 5.4(B) makes analysis easier because we can filter by salesperson and then sum the values in the UnitsSold column.

Data Models That Make Analysis Easier

A **data model** defines how different tables relate to each other. Analytical data models should be easy to understand by business users such as accountants, and computers should be able to efficiently process them. The recommended structure for analytical data models is the **star schema**, which has both characteristics (**Illustration 5.5**). As the top of Illustration 5.5 shows, a star schema consists of two types of tables, fact tables and dimension tables, and the relationships between them.

ILLUSTRATION 5.5   Star Schema

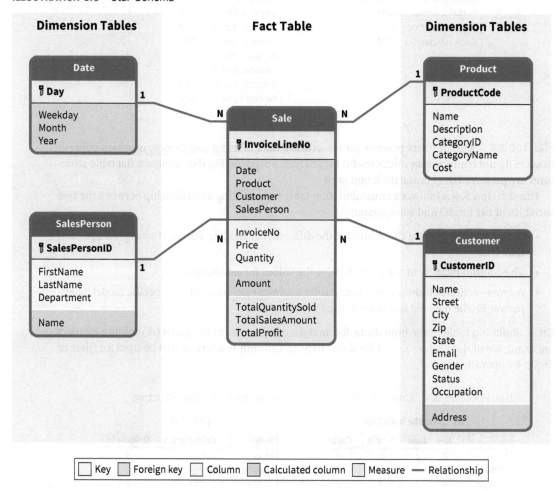

Fact Tables   In an accounting context, **facts** correspond to business transactions such as orders, sales, purchases, and payments. The fact table in the center of Illustration 5.5 contains sales data. Data in a fact table are captured at a high granularity level to avoid imposing additional constraints on the analysis. (The level of detail is known as the grain.) In Illustration 5.5 the grain is an invoice line, which is a specific product shipped to a specific customer, on a specific day, and involving a specific salesperson.

While the number of columns in a fact table is generally small, they usually have many rows. Companies often have thousands of sales on the same day, if not more—think of online retail giants such as Amazon. The columns in fact tables are also mostly quantitative, and more specifically, additive. The values in these columns can be easily aggregated, or grouped together, as measures. These measures can then be sliced using the columns in the next type of tables.

Dimension Tables **Dimensions** provide context to analysis and give meaning to facts. The dollar amount for a sale of $100 does not provide much information. Businesses want to know when the sales transaction occurred, who must pay the $100, and for what goods. The star schema in Illustration 5.5 has dimension tables for the date the sale occurred, the product that was sold, the customer, and the salesperson. Columns in dimension tables are variables that can be combined in multiple ways to slice the measures. **Illustration 5.6** demonstrates eight questions that can be answered by slicing a sale measure by one or more of the dimensions shown in Illustration 5.5.

ILLUSTRATION 5.6 Slicing Measures by Dimensions

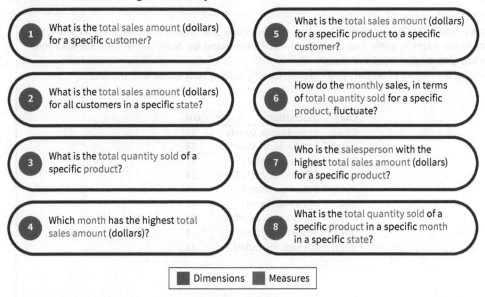

1. What is the total sales amount (dollars) for a specific customer?

2. What is the total sales amount (dollars) for all customers in a specific state?

3. What is the total quantity sold of a specific product?

4. Which month has the highest total sales amount (dollars)?

5. What is the total sales amount (dollars) for a specific product to a specific customer?

6. How do the monthly sales, in terms of total quantity sold for a specific product, fluctuate?

7. Who is the salesperson with the highest total sales amount (dollars) for a specific product?

8. What is the total quantity sold of a specific product in a specific month in a specific state?

■ Dimensions ■ Measures

While the number of rows in a dimension table is usually small, they often have many columns. The Customer dimension table in Illustration 5.5 has 10 columns but no measures. In practice, customer dimension tables often have more than 100 columns.

Relationships Relationships, the final element of data models, link tables and are represented by lines in Illustration 5.5. All relationships in a star schema have a one-to-many (1-N) cardinality pattern. A **cardinality** is a constraint that defines how many times an instance of an entity can participate in a relationship. It can take two possible values, N or 1:

- N: An instance can participate many times in the relationship. There is no restriction.

- 1: An instance can participate only one time in the relationship.

A 1-N cardinality pattern for a relationship between a dimension and a fact table can be interpreted as follows:

- 1: For every fact, there is just one corresponding value in each dimension table. For each instance of the Sale table (an invoice line), there is one date, product, customer, and salesperson.

- N: There can be many facts for each dimension. There can be many sales on the same day, and the same product type can be sold many times. Both customers and salespeople can be involved in many sales transactions.

Decide and Inform

After investigating the quality and structure of the data, it is time to take the next step:

- **Do not move forward:** If the data are unfit, such as the data having poor quality, then using the data for decision-making would be too risky. Similarly, if the data structure is poor, then restructuring and processing the data might be too complicated and economically unfeasible.

- **Redesign the source system:** This decision is usually made because errors generated by the source system need to be corrected. Once fixed, the data source should be profiled again.
- **Confirm the data's fitness for the analysis and move forward:** Moving forward with the data requires being risk-aware. That is, we can move forward with the data with an awareness of potential reliability issues and their impact on decisions.

If the decision is made to move forward, the next step in the process would be informed by any issues that must be addressed.

APPLY IT 5.1

Identify Data
Quality Issues

Stufan is a small store in Gumboro, Delaware, that buys and sells stuffed animals. Founder and CEO Shanice Parker wants to apply data analytics to better understand her business. To start, she asks your firm to help prepare the data for analysis.

The table is a sample of Stufan's product data. Identify three quality issues with the data.

Code	Description	QOH
BASHL	Bashful Large, Dwarfs	13
BASHS	Bashful Small, Dwarfs	67
BERL	Berlioz, Aristocats	23
CAPH	Captain Haddock, Tintin	14
DOCL	Doc Large, Dwarfs	23
DOCS	Doc Small, Dwarfs	45
DOPL	Dopey Large, Dwarfs	43
DOPS	Dopey Small, Dwarfs	−3
DUCH	Duchess, Aristocrats	44

SOLUTION

1. Description is not a single-valued column. It combines "description" and "category."
2. There is a consistency issue: "Aristocats" and "Aristocrats."
3. There is a validity issue: QOH (Quantity On Hand) cannot be negative.

5.2 What Does It Mean to Extract-Transform-Load (ETL) Data?

LEARNING OBJECTIVE ❷

Describe the extract-transform-load (ETL) process.

While the data profiling process you just learned about detects issues, the **extract-transform-load (ETL)** process corrects them. As **Illustration 5.7** shows, the ETL process builds an analytical database using one or more sources of raw data.

ILLUSTRATION 5.7   The Extract-Transform-Load (ETL) Process

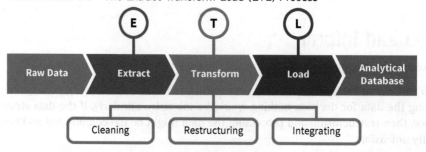

Extract Data

Data extraction, which involves transferring data, is the first step in the ETL process:

- Source data are moved to the platform where they will be transformed. This platform is normally a **data warehouse**, which is a software that stores and analyzes large data sets. Power BI and Tableau are examples of data warehouses.
- The process also includes data validation, or confirming that the data were transferred completely and correctly.

ETL tools make it easy to extract data from databases, spreadsheets, text files, and many other data sources by providing **data connectors** that are intuitive software programs designed to extract data. **Illustration 5.8**(A) shows some data connectors that are available in Excel, while panel (B) does the same for Power BI.

ILLUSTRATION 5.8 Data Extraction Using Data Connectors

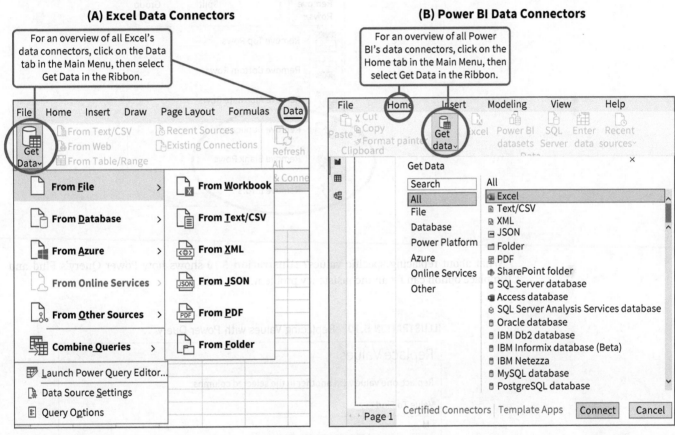

Transform Data

Raw data are rarely ready for analysis after they are extracted. **Data transformation** improves the raw data for analysis through cleaning, restructuring, and integration.

Cleaning Data

Data can be incorrect, invalid, inconsistent or incomplete. Cleaning data, one of the most important and time-consuming aspects of data transformation, is also known as data cleansing or data scrubbing. It involves adding, modifying, and deleting data:

- In the case of incomplete data, such as a missing sales transaction, data might need to be added. A specific strategy for dealing with incomplete data is imputation, which is when estimated values are substituted for missing data.

- Modifying data is necessary when a current value must be replaced with a new value if data are incorrect, invalid, inconsistent, or incomplete. Replacing the value NY with NJ in a column that records a customer's state is an example of this.
- Delete data that are not relevant for analysis. Redundant data, such as a duplicate sales transaction, should be removed.

ETL tools provide built-in functions for a range of data cleaning tasks. What if you wanted to remove rows from a table? **Illustration 5.9** shows that Excel's Power Query has commands for removing duplicate rows, blank rows, or rows containing errors. Power BI's ETL tool offers similar operations.

ILLUSTRATION 5.9 Removing Rows with Power Query

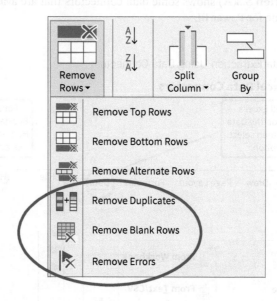

What about replacing specific values? **Illustration 5.10** shows how Power Query's Find and Replace option can fix an inconsistency problem.

ILLUSTRATION 5.10 Replacing Values with Power Query

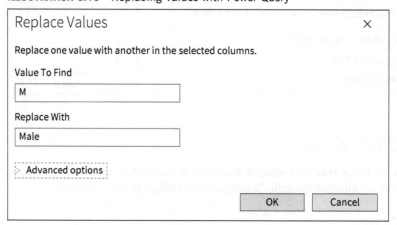

If "M" is sometimes used for "Male," and sometimes the word "Male" is used in the column for gender in the data set, then all M values in the Gender column can be replaced with "Male." Using this tool quickly resolves the inconsistent data by finding the inconsistent values and replacing them.

Applying Critical Thinking 5.3

Choose the Best Method

Data preparation is not an exact science. Judgment is an important part of building an analytical database. Always consider alternatives, examine their strengths and weaknesses, and rank them. In the following, panels (A) and (B) represent the same data but organize them differently (**Alternatives**):

- In panel (B), category becomes its own entity and the name of a category is recorded only once.
- On the other hand, adopting the data model in panel (A) means the category name is repeated for all products in the same category. The data model in panel (B) saves space at the price of complexity, given that there is an extra relationship that needs to be considered during analytics.

Alternative Data Models for the Same Data Set

Restructuring Data

Clean data are not necessarily structured in a way that makes analytics easy and efficient. **Data restructuring**, which is also known as data wrangling or data munging, does not change data values, but it does change how the data are organized.

ETL tools provide a variety of techniques to make restructuring easier:

- Adding and deleting columns.
- Renaming columns and tables.
- Splitting and merging columns.
- Splitting and combining tables.
- Transposing and unpivoting tables.

Integrating Data

Most data analytics projects involve multiple tables, often from different data sources, which must be integrated before performing analysis. **Data integration** is the process of connecting related data. There are two distinctive forms of integration:

- Linking two tables by defining a relationship between them. Relationships are created using primary and foreign keys. Other aspects of relationships that must be specified are cardinalities.

- Combining two or more tables unites information about the same entity. Tables can be combined two ways. A **union** combines different tables with the same data structure. The result is a table with more rows. Recall from Chapter 2 that a join, or **merge**, combines data elements or columns from different tables. The result is a table with more columns.

A challenge specific to integration is **data matching**, a process that compares data and determines whether they describe the same entity. Consider the two customer data sets shown in **Illustration 5.11**. Illustration 5.11(A) contains financial information, and panel (B) contains demographic information about customers. How would we reconcile, or match, the customer names? Specific issues to be addressed include:

- Nicknames: Jen Pollack versus Jenny Pollack.
- Typos: Carlos Panetta versus Carlos Paretta.
- Reversed names: Margarita David versus David Margo.

Panel (C) shows the merged table. Most ETL tools provide advanced support for data matching.

ILLUSTRATION 5.11 Data Matching Issues

(A) Customer Table: Financial Information

Names	Status	Discount
William McCarthy	A	5
Margarita David	C	1
Ann White	B	3
Carlos Panetta	A	5
Jen Pollack	B	3

(B) Customer Table: Demographic Information

Names	Gender	Age
Carlos Paretta	M	44
David Margo	M	22
Jenny Pollack	F	57
Bill McCarthy	M	38
Ann White	F	28

(C) Merged Customer Table

Names	Status	Discount	Gender	Age
Ann White	B	3	F	28
Carlos Panetta	A	5	M	44
Jen Pollack	B	3	F	57
Margarita David	C	1	M	22
William McCarthy	A	5	M	38

Load Data

Once the data are cleaned and transformed, they are loaded into the software for analysis. **Data loading** is the process of making the analytical database available for use. Analytical databases are often posted in the cloud where they can be used simultaneously by many users. Like extraction, part of transferring the data is validating whether all records were transferred and whether they were transferred correctly.

APPLY IT 5.2

Combine Tables for Analysis

Stufan CEO Shanice suggests organizing product data in three separate tables, with one table for each product category. She asks if there would be issues combining the three tables for analysis. How would you respond?

Aristocats		
Code	Description	QOH
BERL	Berlioz	23
DUCH	Duchess	44
MAR	Marie	34
THO	Thomas	19
TOU	Toulouse	32

Dwarfs	
Code	Description
BASHL	Bashful Large
BASHS	Bashful Small
DOCL	Doc Large
DOCS	Doc Small
DOPL	Dopey Large
DOPS	Dopey Small
GRUML	Grumpy Large
GRUMS	Grumpy Small
HAPL	Happy Large
HAPS	Happy Small
SLB	Sleepy Big
SLS	Sleepy Small
SNEL	Sneezy Large
SNES	Sneezy Small
SNOWL	Snow White Large
SNWS	Snow White Small

Tintin		
Code	Description	QOH
CAPH	Captain Haddock	14
SNO	Snowy	22
TINL	Tintin Large	23
TINS	Tintin Small	44

SOLUTION

- The three tables cannot be combined using a union since the table structure for the Dwarfs table is different from the table structures of the Aristocats and Tintin tables. The QOH column is missing.

- A product's category is determined by its table name and cannot be used for analysis purposes. A Category column needs to be added to each of the three tables.

5.3 Which Patterns Extract Data?

LEARNING OBJECTIVE ❸
Apply patterns to extract data.

Each data analytics project has unique data preparation challenges. While there is not a single, common approach for all projects, a structured set of data preparation patterns can address most challenges. These patterns signal potential problems and provide guidance for finding them within the data set and correcting them. Each pattern identifies a data issue, discusses how to detect it with a profiling method, and explains one or more ETL methods to correct it. Think of the patterns as a menu; you can select those which are most appropriate for your needs.

Data Let's use a case to illustrate how to apply data preparation patterns in a real-world scenario. You can also use the available data to work through each pattern yourself.

Beans is an accounting firm in Okemos, Michigan, providing accounting and tax services. Petra, their managing partner, has made improving analysis of their services a priority in the new year. Petra does not mind doing the analytics but struggles to integrate the different data sources. Imagine you are one of the staff accountants helping with the data preparation.

The data set for Beans consists of four worksheets in an Excel file (**Illustration 5.12**).

ILLUSTRATION 5.12 Worksheets in the Beans Data Set

Worksheet	Description
ClData	Information about Beans' clients.
Employee	General information about Beans' employees.
E-Dem	Demographic information about Beans' employees.
Service	Information about the services provided for the period January–July 2025.

The first step is identifying the available data and creating a **data dictionary**, a chart that indicates what data are available and where they can be found. A data dictionary records different pieces of information for each field, including a name, a brief description of content, the data type, whether the field is a primary or foreign key, and whether the field is mandatory or optional.

A data dictionary is often referred to as metadata—it is data about data. It is built gradually throughout the data preparation process, but creating column names and descriptions is a good starting point. **Illustration 5.13** shows the first draft of a data dictionary for the Beans data set. (See Illustration 5.44 at the end of the chapter for an example of the completed data dictionary.)

ILLUSTRATION 5.13 Beans Data Dictionary

ClData

Name	Description
ID	A client's unique ID.
Name	A client's name.
Industry Name	A client's industry.

(Continued)

ILLUSTRATION 5.13 (*Continued*)

Employee

Name	Description
ID	An employee's ID.
Name	An employee's name.
Job Title	An employee's job title.
Rate	An employee's hourly rate.
Office	An employee's office.
MS	An employee's marital status.

E-Dem

Name	Description
First	An employee's first name.
Last	An employee's last name.
Age	An employee's age.
CertList	List of an employee's certifications.
University	The university from which the employee received an undergraduate degree.

Service

Name	Description
ID	A unique ID for a service provided.
Date	The date the service occurred.
Actual Time	The actual time spent on a service provided.
Budgeted Time	The budgeted time for a service provided.
ID	The ID of the task performed.
Area	The task's area.
Task	The name of the task performed.
EmployeeID	The ID of the employee performing the task.

Starting from the data dictionary in Illustration 5.13, we are ready to prepare the data by applying 20 patterns. The first two are extraction patterns to determine if all data have been extracted and if they were transferred correctly.

Data Preparation Pattern 1: Incomplete Data Transfer

Extraction transfers data from the source files to the ETL tool for further processing. An incomplete transfer of data and missing data leads to unreliable results.

Compare Row Counts

Comparing row counts is one way to check completeness. Working with the Beans data set, test completeness by comparing the Excel worksheet's row count with the corresponding table's row count in the ETL tool. **Illustration 5.14** shows the Service Excel worksheet. When the ID column is selected, Excel's status bar shows that there are 4,632 rows in the worksheet.

Next, determine the row count for the Service table in the ETL tool used for extraction. **Illustration 5.15** shows that information as part of the ID column profile in Power Query. The matching numbers indicate that all rows have been transferred. If the numbers do not match, we must determine which data were not transferred and what caused the problem. Given the sequential nature of the IDs, gap analysis might be a useful tool to do this. In this case, there were no transfer issues when extracting the data from the Beans data set into Power Query.

ILLUSTRATION 5.14 Row Count for Excel Worksheet

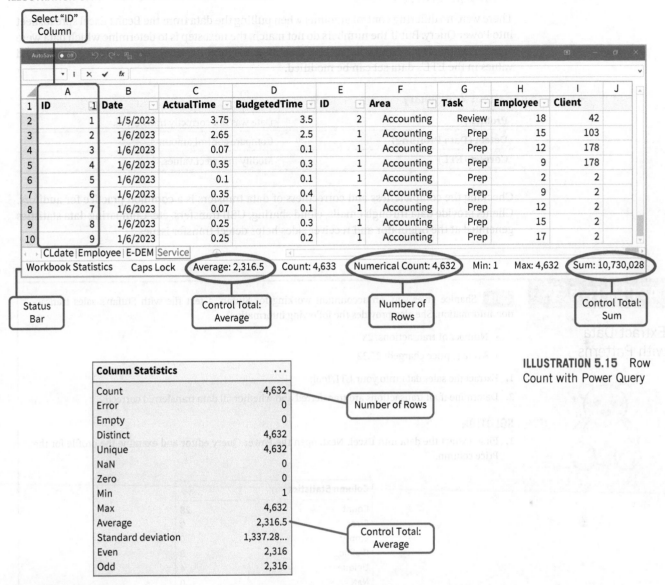

ILLUSTRATION 5.15 Row Count with Power Query

Add Missing Rows

If the row counts don't match, add the missing rows to the source data, the Service worksheet in the Beans data set file, or to the ETL's data set.

Pattern 1 Summary

Problem	All the data did not transfer.
Detect (Data Profiling)	Compare row counts.
Correct (ETL)	Add the missing rows.

Data Preparation Pattern 2: Incorrect Data Transfer

Even when all the rows have been transferred, the data might not have been transferred correctly. This is often caused by differences in data types.

Compare Control Amounts

This issue can be detected using control amounts. In the Beans data set, compare the Average in the Excel worksheet (Illustration 5.14) with the same number for the Service table in the ETL tool (Illustration 5.15). Matching numbers indicate a correct transfer of the values for the ID column in the Service table. Similar tests can be run for the other columns.

Modify Incorrect Values

There were no differing control amounts when pulling the data from the Beans Excel spreadsheet into Power Query. But if the numbers do not match, the next step is to determine which data were transferred incorrectly and what caused the problem. Once identified, the incorrectly transferred values in the ETL's data set can be modified.

Pattern 2 Summary

Problem	Data was not correctly transferred.
Detect (Data Profiling)	Compare control amounts.
Correct (ETL)	Modify incorrect values.

Checking the completeness and correctness of data transfers is a common practice for auditors. Clients provide data through emails, cloud sharing, USB transfers, etc. Comparing data statistics generated at the originator and receiver sides helps detect transfer issues.

APPLY IT 5.3

Extract Data with Patterns

Data Shanice gives you, an accountant working for Stufan, a text file with Stufan's sales transaction information. She also provides the following information:

- Number of transactions: 28
- Average price charged: 25.32

1. Extract the sales data into your ETL tool.
2. Determine if all transactions are transferred and whether all data transferred correctly.

SOLUTION

1. First, extract the data into Excel. Next, open the Power Query editor and examine the profile for the Price column.

Column Statistics	...
Count	28
Error	0
Empty	0
Distinct	8
Unique	4
NaN	0
Zero	0
Min	10
Max	40
Average	25.3214...

2. As the visual shows, the information provided indicates all transactions were transferred—Count: 28—and that they were transferred correctly—Average: 25.32.

5.4 Which Patterns Transform Columns?

LEARNING OBJECTIVE ❹

Apply patterns to transform columns.

Once all data are transferred to the ETL tool, it is time to transform them. Transformation has two purposes—cleaning the data by correcting values, and restructuring and integrating the data for analytics.

An analytical database consists of an integrated set of tables, which is a data model, and each table has several columns. This means that transformations can be conducted gradually at the column level, table level, and model level. This section focuses on transformation patterns at the column level. These patterns look for data problems in a single column, such as ambiguous names, data type issues, and incorrect, inconsistent, incomplete, or invalid values.

Data Preparation Pattern 3: Irrelevant and Unreliable Data

Data that are irrelevant for decisions bloat the data model. It is also important to avoid integrating unreliable data into the data model (recall the old adage, "garbage in, garbage out"). Keep in mind that excluding data from an analytical database is not the same as deleting the data. The raw data still exist and can be integrated if necessary.

Scan Columns for Irrelevant and Unreliable Data

Irrelevant columns can be identified primarily by scanning the data visually. The data dictionary can also be a helpful tool. For example, the Employee table contains information regarding offices. How would you use the data in this column for decision-making?

Scanning data can also determine whether a column contains unreliable data. In **Illustration 5.16** (A), the Age column in the E-Dem table mixes null values, numbers, dates, and text, which would

ILLUSTRATION 5.16   Detecting and Correcting Unreliable Data

(A) Column with Unreliable Data

Age
45
1998
thirty two
55
34
22
??
??
51
9/2/1998

(B) Removing a Column with Unreliable Data

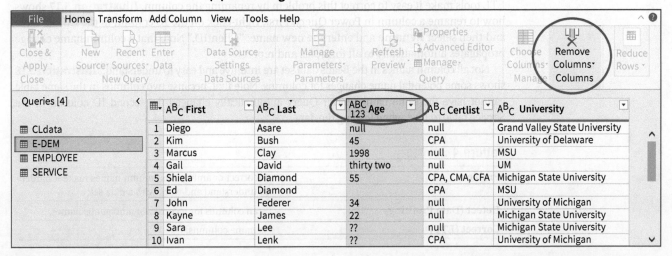

How To

make it challenging to generate reliable insights. Most ETL tools provide statistics about errors, null values, and more, that can help determine a column's reliability. (Data See **How to 5.1** at the end of the chapter to learn how to use Power Query to profile data.)

Remove Columns with Irrelevant or Unreliable Data

To correct the issue, delete the columns with irrelevant and unreliable data from the analytical database. Illustration 5.16(B) shows how to do this with Power Query. Select a column, such as Age, and then select Remove Columns. For the Beans data set, the irrelevant column, Office, and the unreliable column, Age, were deleted.

Pattern 3 Summary

Problem	Irrelevant data bloat a data set. Unreliable data increases the risk of making bad decisions.
Detect (Data Profiling)	Visually scan columns for irrelevant and unreliable data.
Correct (ETL)	Remove columns with irrelevant or unreliable data.

Data Preparation Pattern 4: Incorrect and Ambiguous Column Names

Column names become variables during data exploration and interpretation. Their names are important because other people might use the analytical database. Essentially, column names become part of the database's vocabulary. Recall that Beans' managing partner wants to perform the necessary analytics but struggles with the data preparation. Column names that are correct, intuitive, and unambiguous make it easier for other people to use a database and explore data.

Scan Columns for Incorrect or Ambiguous Names

Visually scanning a column's content and its data dictionary definition can reveal whether the column name accurately reflects its content. Here are four rules for naming columns:

1. Names should accurately describe the column's content.
2. They should be intuitive to businesspeople.
3. Use only common abbreviations that are understood by everyone, such as YTD.
4. Eliminate spaces, underscores, or other symbols. For example, use CustomerName instead of Customer_Name.

Rename Columns

ETL tools make it easy to correct this problem by renaming the column. **Illustration 5.17** shows how to rename a column in Power Query. First, right-click on the ID column in the ClData table and then select **Rename** and enter the new name: "ClientID." Note that a column name change propagates automatically to all formulas and reports.

Not all column names in the Beans data set are intuitive and easy to understand. **Illustration 5.18** shows some potential name changes for columns. Note that, because two columns in the same table cannot have the same name, Power Query automatically changed the second ID column in the Service table to ID-1 when loading the data.

Pattern 4 Summary

Problem	Incorrect or ambiguous column names make it harder to understand and work with a data set.
Detect (Data Profiling)	Scan columns for incorrect or ambiguous names.
Correct (ETL)	Rename columns.

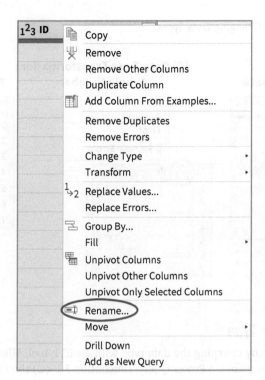

ILLUSTRATION 5.17 Modify Column Names

Table	ColumnName	RevisedColumnName
ClData	ID	ClientID
ClData	Industry Name	IndustryName
Employee	ID	EmployeeID
Employee	Job Title	JobTitle
Employee	MS	MaritalStatus
E-Dem	First	FirstName
E-Dem	Last	LastName
E-Dem	CertList	CertificationList
Service	ID	ServiceID
Service	Actual Time	ActualTime
Service	Budgeted Time	BudgetedTime
Service	ID-1	TaskID
Service	Task	TaskName

ILLUSTRATION 5.18 Column Name Suggestions for Beans

Data Preparation Pattern 5: Incorrect Data Types

Verifying data types is an essential part of data preparation. Data types are an integral part of column definitions because they determine what we can and cannot do with the data in a column. For example, mathematical operators such as SUM and AVERAGE require a numerical field, but time and date functions require a column with a date data type.

Inspect the Data Type

ETL tools automatically assign a data type to each column during extraction, but sometimes either the assignment is incorrect or the ETL tool is unable to determine a data type. Let's illustrate the last scenario with an example. **Illustration 5.19**(A) shows the raw spreadsheet data. Panel (B) shows the same data set after extraction in Power Query. Notice that the data type is $^{ABC}_{123}$, also known as the Any data type. It indicates that Power Query cannot identify the data type, which means calculations cannot be performed on the data in the column.

ILLUSTRATION 5.19 Inspecting and Changing Data Types

(A) Raw Spreadsheet Data

A
ID
1
2
A
4
5
B
6

(B) Extracted Data

ABC 123 ID ▼
1
2
A
4
5
B
6

(C) Data Type Transformation: Whole Number

ID
2 (28%)
Error
💡 Remove Errors   ⋯

1²3 ID ▼
1
2
3 Error
4
5
6 Error
7

1	1
2	2
3	Error
4	4
5	5
6	Error
7	6

(D) Data Type Transformation: Text

ABC ID ▼
1	1
2	2
3	A
4	4
5	5
6	B
7	6

Change the Data Type

Correct this problem by changing the data type with an ETL tool. **Illustration 5.20** shows the different data types available in Power Query. Illustration 5.19(C) shows what happens if Whole Number is selected for the data set in panel (B). Notice that some values are converted while other values generate an error. This is helpful because checking for errors should be part of data preparation. The red bar indicates there are errors, and clicking on it reveals the percentage of errors (28%). They can also be filtered out, which is useful for large data sets. Illustration 5.19(D) shows what happens when the Data Type is converted to Text. The errors disappear, but what can be done with the data is limited.

ILLUSTRATION 5.20 Power Query Data Types

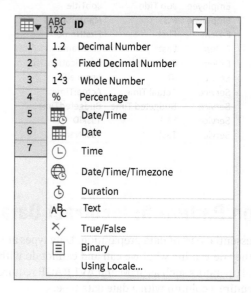

	ABC 123 ID	▼
1	1.2	Decimal Number
2	$	Fixed Decimal Number
3	1²3	Whole Number
4	%	Percentage
5	📅	Date/Time
6	🗓	Date
7	🕐	Time
	🌐	Date/Time/Timezone
	⏱	Duration
	ABC	Text
	✗✓	True/False
	☰	Binary
		Using Locale...

There are no issues with Beans' data types, so no changes must be made. However, make sure to add a column to the data dictionary that specifies the data types.

Pattern 5 Summary

Problem	An incorrect data type limits what can be done with the data in a column.
Detect (Data Profiling)	Inspect the data type.
Correct (ETL)	Change the data type.

Data Preparation Pattern 6: Composite and Multi-Valued Columns

Each cell should contain one value describing one characteristic because two or more values in the same cell makes analysis more challenging. Two specific scenarios that violate the single-valued rule and make analysis more complex are composite columns and multi-valued columns.

Scan for Composite and Multi-Valued Columns

The best method to detect composite or multi-valued columns is visual scanning. Examining the Beans data set this way would reveal:

- The Name column in the Employee table mixes an employee's first and last names. While this might not be an issue from an analytical perspective, it is an issue when matching them with the FirstName and LastName columns in the E-Dem table.
- The CertificationList column in the E-Dem table is multi-valued.

Restructure the Data

How a column is restructured depends on whether the column is composite or multi-valued. The solution for a composite column is to split it. In Power Query, click on the Name column. Then select the **Home** tab in the Main Menu. Click **Split Column** in the ribbon, and select **By Delimiter** (**Illustration 5.21**).

ILLUSTRATION 5.21 Power Query | Split Column | Setup

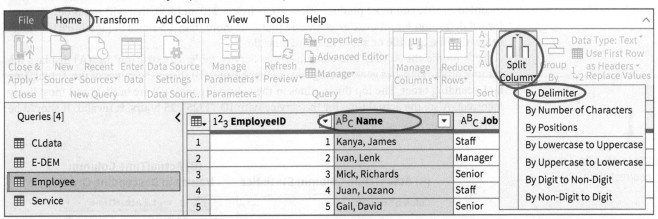

The window shown in **Illustration 5.22** will appear. Power Query already selected **Comma** as the delimiter, and since there is only one comma for each name, it does not matter which of the three **Split at** options is selected. In this example the **Left-most delimiter** option was selected. Once split, rename Name.1 as "FirstName" and Name.2 as "LastName."

On the other hand, the CertificationList column's multi-valued nature in the E-Dem table requires creating a new table. But because the employee data needs additional work, it makes sense to do that later. This example shows the nonsequential nature of applying the patterns—the order in which they are applied will depend on each project. The other columns in the Beans data set are single-valued, and this pattern does not apply to them.

Pattern 6 Summary

Problem	Columns that are not single-valued make analytics difficult.
Detect (Data Profiling)	Examine the values in the columns.
Correct (ETL)	Split combined columns.
	Create a separate table for multi-valued columns.

ILLUSTRATION 5.22   Power
Query I Split Column I Select
Delimiter

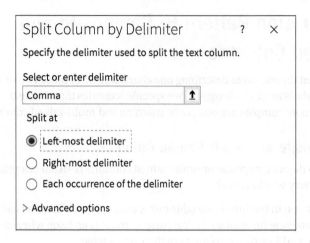

Data Preparation Pattern 7: Incorrect Values

At times the wrong value is assigned to one of the entities' characteristics. The certification for an employee could be recorded as CMA instead of CPA, which are both valid certifications. Incorrect values can have dramatic consequences, including shipping and billing errors.

Detect Incorrect Values with Outliers

Incorrect data are difficult to identify within the content of a single column, so it is helpful to look for outliers, values that stand out in numeric data. If a product with a price of $19 is instead recorded as $91, and most product prices are between $10 and $30, that will stand out. A more formal definition for an **outlier** is a value that falls more than 1.5 times the interquartile range below the first quartile or above the third quartile.

Let's profile the ActualTime column in the Service table. **Illustration 5.23**(A) displays the column profile statistics generated by Power Query. Panel (B) shows the values of the ActualTime in descending order. The top three values in the column [panel (B)] are outliers and most likely incorrect. Also, the actual time for the service with ID "1325", 25 hours, is invalid. It should be 2.5 hours.

ILLUSTRATION 5.23   Profiling
for Incorrect Data

(A) ActualTime Column: Statistics

Column Statistics	...
Count	4,632
Error	0
Empty	0
Distinct	190
Unique	48
NaN	0
Zero	0
Min	0.05
Max	25
Average	1.77672...
Standard deviation	2.03039...

(B) ActualTime Column: Values in Descending Order

123 ID ▼	1.2 ActualTime ▼
1325	25
3277	22.5
4387	20
2828	11.4
2452	10.75

Modify Incorrect Values

Once a questionable value is identified, there are a few options. The first is identifying the error's root cause and eliminating it. A user could be warned that an outlier is being entered into the system. This would significantly eliminate errors in the raw data. Another option is to correct the value in the source data. Finally, the value could be corrected in the analytical database, but not in the source data.

Illustration 5.24 shows the ActualTime values modified for the Beans example.

ID	IncorrectValue	CorrectValue
1325	25	2.5
3277	22.5	2.25
4387	20	2

ILLUSTRATION 5.24 Correcting the ActualTime Field in the Service Table

Pattern 7 Summary

Problem	Incorrect data might result in poor decision-making.
Detect (Data Profiling)	Detect incorrect values with outliers.
Correct (ETL)	Modify incorrect values.

Data Preparation Pattern 8: Inconsistent Values

The next pattern addresses data inconsistency, which occurs when two or more different representations of the same value are mixed in the same column. For example, determining the total sales amount in dollars for MI customers when both MI and Michigan are used as values could lead to an underestimation, which could in turn result in poor decisions.

Identify Inconsistent Values

Two profiling techniques are useful for detecting inconsistent values:

- **Distinct values:** Visually scanning the distinct values of a column is an effective way to identify inconsistent data.
- **Frequencies:** Values with a low frequency could indicate inconsistent data.

Illustration 5.25(A) shows the distinct values for the JobTitle column in the Employee table. This information is available for all columns in Power Query. The illustration shows that Sr. Manager is inconsistently represented. Low frequencies might also indicate a misspelling resulting in an inconsistency. As panel (B) shows, the frequency for Sr Manager is 1. The value distribution shown in panel (B) is part of a column's profile in Power Query. Another column with inconsistencies issues in the Beans data set is University.

ILLUSTRATION 5.25   Profiling for Inconsistent Data

(A) JobTitle Column: Distinct Values

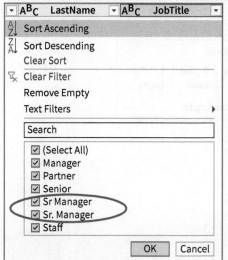

(B) JobTitle Column: Frequencies

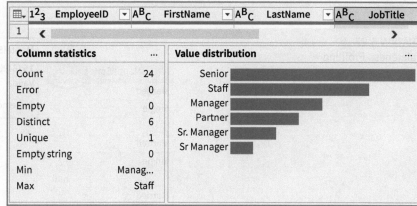

Modify Inconsistent Values

Correct the inconsistent data by identifying the root cause and eliminating it or modifying the values in either the source data or the analytical database. When modifying the values, first determine which representation to keep. For the JobTitle column, keep Sr. Manager. The changes shown in **Illustration 5.26** were made to the University column.

ILLUSTRATION 5.26 Changes to Address Inconsistencies in the University Column

Current Value	New Value
MSU	Michigan State University
UM	University of Michigan

Most ETL software, including Power Query, offer find and replace tools to modify values.

Pattern 8 Summary

Problem	Inconsistent data might result in poor decision-making.
Detect (Data Profiling)	Identify inconsistent values.
Correct (ETL)	Modify inconsistent values.

Data Preparation Pattern 9: Incomplete Values

This pattern addresses incompleteness that might make data unusable and unreliable. For example, without customers' addresses, a business cannot send them marketing materials. The different meanings given to null values might also result in unreliable data.

There are a few dimensions of incompleteness worth exploring:

- Should null values be allowed, and if not, are there any?
- If null values are allowed, what percentage of the values are null? If the percentage is high, should the column be loaded?
- How are incomplete values represented: nulls, or a specific code? Are the representations consistent?

Investigate Null Values

ETL tools reveal, on a column-by-column basis, the percentage of null values. Using Power Query, **Illustration 5.27** shows this information for the MaritalStatus column in the Employee table. This information is useful in many ways:

- For each column, decide whether null values are allowed. Primary keys cannot contain null values. Also, the Rate column in the Employee table cannot contain any null values because

ILLUSTRATION 5.27
Incompleteness Profiling

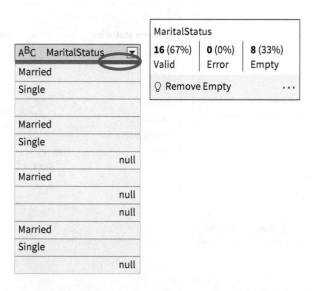

it is used to determine the fee to be paid by the client. The percentage shows whether this is the case.

- A high or higher than expected percentage might make the column unusable.

It is also important to analyze how incompleteness is represented and how this affects the data's reliability. What does a null value in the MaritalStatus column imply? Is this a different way to state that an employee is single, or do we not know the employee's marital status?

Remove the Column or Replace the Null Values

The correction scenario depends on the situation. If null values are not allowed but they exist, they should be replaced. If the number of null values is too high to be useful, then remove the column from the analytical database. If there is inconsistency in representing missing values, design a consistent schema and correct the values in terms of that schema. For the MaritalStatus column, values could be Married, Single, and blank. Blank values indicate that the values are unknown.

Pattern 9 Summary

Problem	Incompleteness might make data unusable and unreliable and result in poor decision-making.
Detect (Data Profiling)	Investigate null values.
Correct (ETL)	Remove the column or replace the null values.

Data Preparation Pattern 10: Invalid Values

Domain-specific rules that determine whether data are acceptable can be created for most columns. Data that do not meet these expectations are considered invalid.

Create and Apply Validation Rules

For some validation rules, we can rely on the profiling information automatically generated by the ETL tool. For a mandatory column, which cannot contain null values, the statistics about null values provided by ETL tools can be used for validation. However, in most cases the validation rule must be implemented with a scripting language. **Illustration 5.28** shows a few examples of validation rules that apply to the Beans case. The syntax used in the sample code column is general, as no specific scripting language is used.

ILLUSTRATION 5.28 Design and Implementation of Validation Rules

Description	Sample Code
The actual hours for a service must be positive and can't exceed 14.	ACTUALHOURSVALID = IF SERVICE.ACTUALTIME > 0 AND SERVICEACTUALTIME <= 14, THEN "YES", ELSE "NO"
The minimum employee rate is $150, and the maximum employee rate must be lower than $500.	RATEVALID = IF EMPLOYEE.RATE >= 150 AND EMPLOYEE.RATE < 500, THEN "YES", ELSE "NO"
Valid job titles are: {Manager, Partner, Senior, Sr. Manager, and Staff}.	JOBTITLEVALID = IF EMPLOYEE.JOBTITLE IN {"MANAGER", "PARTNER", "SENIOR", "SR. MANAGER", "STAFF"}, THEN "YES", ELSE "NO"

Modify Invalid Values

If a questionable value is identified, eliminate the root cause, change the value in the source, or change the value in the analytical database. In the Beans data set, no invalid data were detected.

Pattern 10 Summary

Problem	Invalid data might result in poor decision-making.
Detect (Data Profiling)	Create and apply validation rules.
Correct (ETL)	Modify invalid values.

APPLY IT 5.4

Use Column Transformation Patterns

Data One of Shanice's assistants at Stufan prepared four files called Customer, Item, Sale, and Salesperson and gave them to you. These files have several data issues. Identify them using the column transformation patterns in this section.

For each data issue, you identify:

1. Describe the issue.

2. Identify the data preparation pattern you applied to detect the issue.

3. Explain how you would correct it.

SOLUTION

Issue 1:

1. The data in the LoyaltyRating column in the Customer table are not useful for analytical purposes.

2. Data Preparation Pattern 3: Irrelevant and Unreliable Data.

3. Remove the LoyaltyRating column from the analytical database.

Issue 2:

1. The Sales table has a column with ambiguous heading-SP.

2. Data Preparation Pattern 4: Incorrect and Ambiguous Column Names.

3. Replace the ambiguous abbreviation SP with SalesPerson.

Issue 3:

1. The State column in the Customer table contains the value DN, which might be incorrect, inconsistent, and/or invalid.

2. Data Preparation Patterns 7, 8, and 10: Incorrect, Inconsistent, and Invalid Values.

3. Replace the DN value with DE.

5.5 Which Patterns Transform Tables?

LEARNING OBJECTIVE ❺
Apply patterns to transform tables.

Transformation patterns at the table level look for data issues in a single table, such as ambiguously named tables, missing primary keys, and overlapping columns.

Data Preparation Pattern 11: Nonintuitive and Ambiguous Table Names

Like column names, table names are part of both the data model and the data set's vocabulary, so they must be correct, intuitive, and clear.

Scan Tables for Incorrect or Ambiguous Names

Examining a table's content and its data dictionary definition can help determine whether the name accurately reflects its content. The rules for naming tables are the same as those for naming columns. They should be intuitive, avoid spaces, underscores, and special coding:

- For example, use CashReceipt instead of Cash Receipt.
- Avoid special coding like DCustomer (the D refers to a dimension table, but not everyone will understand that).

Rename Tables

To correct this issue, rename the table with an ETL tool, as name changes are automatically propagated to all formulas. For the Beans example, make two changes. First, replace ClData with Client and then replace E-Dem with EmployeeDemographics.

Pattern 11 Summary

Problem	Incorrect or ambiguous table names make it harder to understand and work with a data set.
Detect (Data Profiling)	Visually scan tables for incorrect or ambiguous names.
Correct (ETL)	Rename tables.

Data Preparation Pattern 12: Missing Primary Keys

This pattern focuses on primary keys. Tables are descriptions of entities, and each instance of an entity should be uniquely identified. To be a primary key, a column must have a unique value for each instance and no null values. Primary keys are normally already in place when data are extracted from a relational database. However, a primary key will not be in place when data are extracted from a spreadsheet, such as in the Beans case. To establish a primary key, the field must be selected and both rules must be validated.

Identify Tables with a Primary Key Missing

Every table needs at least one column—or combination of columns—that meet the two criteria discussed earlier. Columns that meet both criteria are candidate keys, and ETL tools can help identify them. The column profile provided by Power Query, first shown in Illustration 5.15 and repeated in **Illustration 5.29**, provides the information necessary to identify a candidate key:

- The value for Empty should be zero.
- The values for Count, Distinct, and Unique should be the same. A unique value is a value that occurs only once in the column.

Column Statistics	...
Count	4,632
Error	0
Empty	0
Distinct	4,632
Unique	4,632
NaN	0
Zero	0
Min	1
Max	4,632
Average	2,316.5
Standard deviation	1,337.28...
Even	2,316
Odd	2,316

ILLUSTRATION 5.29 Column Profile in Power Query

Create a Primary Key

The EmployeeDemographics table does not have a candidate key. We could combine the first and last names into the same field (Name), but names generally should not be used as primary keys because they are rarely unique. For scenarios like this, create an artificial key, such as a number. As **Illustration 5.30** shows, ETL tools can help with that:

- In Power Query, click **Add Column** in the Main Menu.
- Select **Index Column**.
- Click **From 1**.

ILLUSTRATION 5.30 Creating a Primary Key

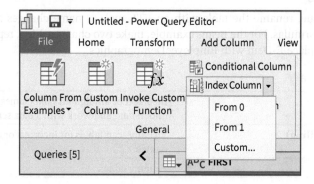

The situation for the Beans data set is more complicated, so there is an alternative solution, which is presented with Pattern 15.

Pattern 12 Summary

Problem	Some tables do not have a primary key.
Detect (Data Profiling)	Identify tables missing a primary key.
Correct (ETL)	Create a primary key.

Data Preparation Pattern 13: Redundant Content Across Columns

This pattern looks for redundancies that create inconsistencies. Data inconsistencies occur when the same data are recorded more than once and changed in one place but not the other, such as a customer's email address. Here are two scenarios where two or more columns in a table might have the same content:

- When there is overlap such as an address that contains state information and a separate state field.
- When there is dependency, which exists when one column's values are dependent on the values of another column in the same table. Assume both age and date of birth are recorded. However, the values of age change when time passes and the data will become inconsistent. Therefore, instead of transferring age from the data source, it should be calculated as part of the analytical database.

Perform Column-By-Column Comparisons

Performing column-by-column comparisons for overlaps or dependencies would detect this issue. Doing so within the Beans data set would show there is currently no redundant content.

Delete Redundant and Dependent Columns

Columns that contain redundant information can be deleted. When there is dependency, delete the column that contains the dependent value. Instead, use a formula to recreate the column in the analytical database.

Pattern 13 Summary

Problem	Redundant content among columns in a table might result in inconsistencies.
Detect (Data Profiling)	Perform column-by-column comparisons.
Correct (ETL)	Delete redundant and dependent data.

Data Preparation Pattern 14: Find Invalid Values with Intra-Table Rules

Pattern 14 is similar to Pattern 10 in that it also defines acceptable values for a column. However, Pattern 14 determines the validity of a column's values based on the values in one or more other columns in the same table.

Create and Apply Intra-Table Validation Rules

The goal of the validation rule is to identify invalid data. Creating validation rules requires in-depth knowledge of the business, and they are implemented using a scripting language. **Illustration 5.31** shows an intra-table validation rule for the Beans case. The values in the Rate column depend on the values in the JobPosition column. Applying this validation rule to the Beans data set shows that the rates are too low for five employees—Alex Messi, Thibaut Martens, Paulo Lukaku, Ed Diamond, and Molly McCarthy.

ILLUSTRATION 5.31 Design and Implementation of Intra-Table Validation Rules

---

DESCRIPTION

The rate of Beans' employees is determined by their job position. The table shows the minimum and maximum rates, in dollars, for each job position.

Position	>=	<
Staff	150	200
Senior	200	250
Manager	250	300
Sr. Manager	300	350
Partner	350	500

SAMPLE CODE

```
RATEVALIDBASEDONJOBTITLE =
IF EMPLOYEE.JOBTITLE = "Staff" AND (EMPLOYEE.RATE >= 150 AND EMPLOYEE.RATE < 200), THEN "YES", ELSE,
IF EMPLOYEE.JOBTITLE = "Senior" AND (EMPLOYEE.RATE >= 200 AND EMPLOYEE.RATE < 250), "YES", ELSE,
IF EMPLOYEE.JOBTITLE = "Manager" AND (EMPLOYEE.RATE >= 250 AND EMPLOYEE.RATE < 300), "YES", ELSE,
IF EMPLOYEE.JOBTITLE = "Sr. Manager" AND (EMPLOYEE.RATE >= EMPLOYEE.RATE < 350), "YES", ELSE,
IF EMPLOYEE.JOBTITLE = "Partner" AND (EMPLOYEE.RATE >= 350 AND EMPLOYEE.RATE < 500), "YES", ELSE,
"NO"
)
```

Modify Invalid Values

At Beans, modifying employee rates or the rate policy requires approval from the CEO, so there can be no rate changes until approval is granted.

Pattern 14 Summary

Problem	Invalid data might result in poor decision-making.
Detect (Data Profiling)	Create and apply intra-table validation rules.
Correct (ETL)	Modify the invalid values.

APPLY IT 5.5

Transform Tables
with Patterns

At Stufan, CEO Shanice wonders whether it would be possible to integrate sales and purchases information for analysis. Purchase information is currently recorded in an Excel worksheet titled PTS, a sample of which is shown.

	A	B	C	D	E
1	Invoice	Item	Price	Quantity	Vendor
2	1	DOCL	20	10	DITV
3	1	DOCS	15	10	DITV
4	2	TINL	10	10	BIC
5	2	SNOWL	7	10	BIC
6	3	DUCH	20	10	STWS
7	4	GRUML	20	10	DELT
8	4	SNOWL	25	10	DELT
9	5	TINL	9	10	STIMP

Use the table transformation patterns to identify two data issues in the PTS file.

1. First, describe the data issue.
2. Next, identify the data exploration pattern you could apply to detect it.
3. Finally, explain how you would correct the problem.

SOLUTION

Issue 1:

1. The current name of the worksheet/table is ambiguous. PTS stands for PurchaseTransactions, but that is not clear from the title.
2. Use Data Exploration Pattern 11: Nonintuitive and Ambiguous Table Names.
3. Rename the worksheet "Purchases."

Issue 2:

1. The table currently does not have a primary key, and none of the columns contain unique values. Each row in the table represents an invoice line. The first two rows in the table represent two line items for invoice 1, one for the item DOCL and another for the item DOCS.
2. Use Data Exploration Pattern 12: Missing Primary Keys.
3. Create an artificial key consisting of unique sequential numbers.

5.6 Which Patterns Transform Models?

LEARNING OBJECTIVE ❻

Apply patterns to transform models.

Transformation patterns at the model level search for data issues across tables, such as data that describe the same entity spread across multiple tables, data models with a structure that is difficult to understand, and data models that do not support efficient processing.

Data Preparation Pattern 15: Data Spread Across Tables

Analysis becomes more challenging when data that describe the same entity are spread across multiple tables. **Illustration 5.32** shows two possible scenarios.

1. In panel (A) both tables, JanuarySales and FebruarySales, have the same structure but different rows. It is the sales table shown in panel (C) split horizontally. Questions about total sales amounts are easier to answer if all data are in one table.

2. In panel (B) the two tables describe different characteristics of the same entity—Product. Some information for the product with ID 1 is in the ProductDescriptions table. Other information for the same product, ID = 1, is in the ProductAccounting table. In this case, it is the product table shown in panel (D) split vertically.

(A) Monthly Sales Data Across Tables

JanuarySales

Number	Date	Amount
189	1/10/2025	$ 17,450
190	1/15/2025	$ 23,890
191	1/24/2025	$ 19,001

FebruarySales

Number	Date	Amount
192	2/9/2025	$ 25,451
193	2/10/2025	$ 34,881
194	2/14/2025	$ 7,282
195	2/23/2025	$ 13,209

(B) Product Information Across Tables

ProductDescriptions

ID	Type	Category
1	Stuffed Animals	Toys
2	Radio	Electronics
3	Soccer Balls	Toys

ProductAccounting

ID	QOH
1	84
2	133
3	354

(C) Monthly Sales Data Union

Sales

Number	Date	Amount
189	1/10/2025	$ 17,450
190	1/15/2025	$ 23,890
191	1/24/2025	$ 19,001
192	2/9/2025	$ 25,451
193	2/10/2025	$ 34,881
194	2/14/2025	$ 7,282
195	2/23/2025	$ 13,209

(D) Product Information Merge

Product

ID	Type	Category	QOH
1	Stuffed Animals	Toys	84
2	Radio	Electronic	133
3	Soccer Balls	Toys	354

ILLUSTRATION 5.32
Combining Tables

Identify Similarly Structured Tables/Tables Describing Different Characteristics of the Same Entity

To identify similarly structured tables, look for two or more tables with the same structure. These tables would have the same columns and similar data. Another option is to search for tables that describe different characteristics of the same entity. In the Beans case, Employee and EmployeeDemographics are such tables. The goal is to create a single table with all the employee information.

Combine Tables

Recall from earlier in the chapter that combining two tables with a similar structure is called a union. In Illustration 5.32, the table in panel (C) combines the two tables in panel (A). Combining two tables with different characteristics for the same entity is a merge or a join. The table in panel (D) combines the two tables in panel (B). For the Beans case, both the Employee and Employee-Demographics tables contain employee information, so they should be merged into one table (Data See How To 5.2 to learn how to merge these tables with Power Query.).

How To

Illustration 5.33 shows the structure of the combined table, which is named Employee.

ILLUSTRATION 5.33
Combined Employee Table

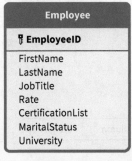

Employee

🔑 **EmployeeID**

FirstName
LastName
JobTitle
Rate
CertificationList
MaritalStatus
University

Pattern 15 Summary

Problem	An entity's data are spread across multiple tables, which complicates analysis.
Detect (Data Profiling)	Identify tables with a similar structure or tables that describe different characteristics of the same entity.
Correct (ETL)	Union or merge tables.

Data Preparation Pattern 16: Data Models Do Not Comply with Principles of Dimensional Modeling

Dimensional modeling is the technique of creating data models with fact tables surrounded by dimension tables. These data models, such as star schemas, are easy to understand and result in efficient data processing.

Analyze a Data Model's Compliance with Dimensional Modeling Principles

Use these dimensional modeling principles by determining the fact and dimension tables and ensuring all fields belong to the correct table. In an accounting context, fact tables correspond to business transactions. Dimension tables, on the other hand, describe *who* participates in the transactions, *when* the transactions occurred, and *what* was given up or acquired. (Chapter 6 discusses who, what, and when analysis of accounting transactions in more detail.)

Illustration 5.34 structures the current analytical database as a star schema. The Service table is the fact table, the Employee table is a *who* dimension, and the Client table is also a *who* dimension.

Note that the *when* and *what* dimensions seem to be missing. There is only the Date field in the Service table, and we opted not to specify a separate *when* dimension. However, TaskId,

ILLUSTRATION 5.34 Current Beans Star Schema

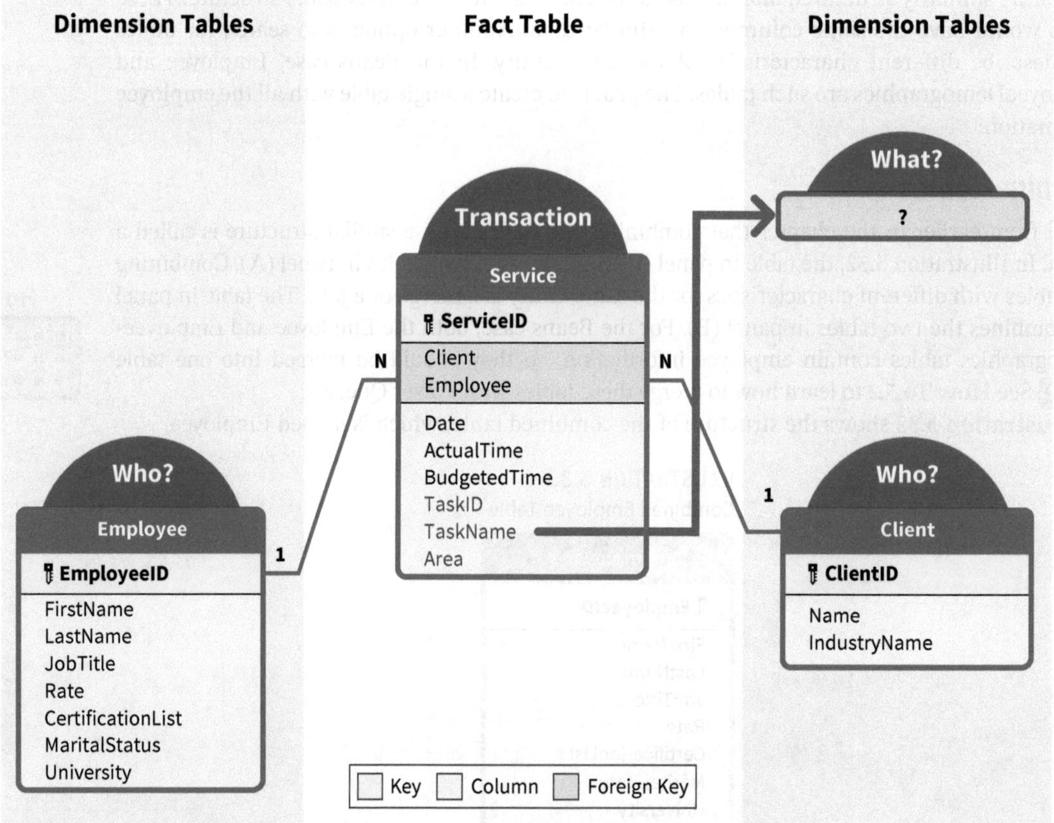

TaskName, and Area are all *what* descriptions—What does Beans sell to their clients? Therefore, a new dimension table named Task can be created. Further, recall from Pattern 6 that the CertificationList column in the Employee table is a multi-valued column. Creating a new table transforms it into a single-valued column. **Illustration 5.35** shows the data model we would like to create.

ILLUSTRATION 5.35 An Ideal Beans Star/Snowflake Schema

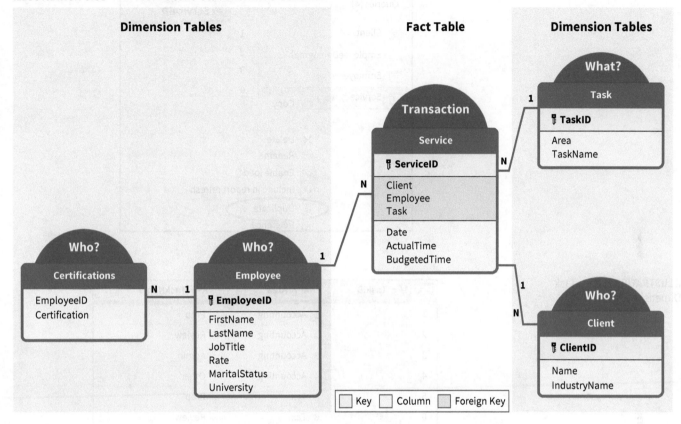

Creating a separate table for Certifications results in a snowflake schema. In a **snowflake schema**, the information for a dimension is spread across multiple tables. The schema in Illustration 5.35 can be created using Power Query as the ETL tool.

Reconfigure the Data Model as a Star/Snowflake Schema

First, create a Task Dimension table that captures the descriptions for services.

Step 1: Duplicate the Service table and rename the duplication "Task" (**Illustration 5.36**). For both the Service and Task tables, keep only the columns that are shown in Illustration 5.35.

Be sure to retain the TaskID field in the Service table and to rename it "Task." The Service table has now been split into two tables. Service is a fact table, and Task is a dimension table.

Step 2: Delete the duplicate rows in the Task table by selecting the **Home** tab in Power Query's main menu. Select **Remove Rows**, then select **Remove Duplicates**.

The Task table should now mirror the one shown in **Illustration 5.37**.

Second, address the problem of CertificationList, which is a multi-valued column in the Employee table:

Step 1: Use the same process as before to create the CertificationList table:

- Duplicate the Employee table and name the duplication "Certifications."
- Remove the CertificationList column from the Employee table.
- In the new Certifications table, keep only the EmployeeID and the CertificationsList columns.

ILLUSTRATION 5.36 Duplicate
Service Table

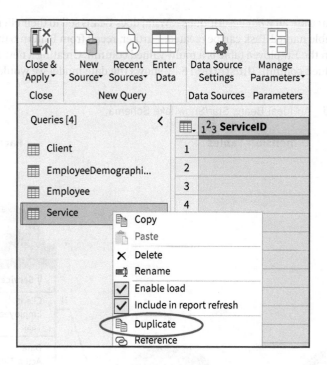

ILLUSTRATION 5.37 Task
Dimension Table

	1^2_3 TaskID	ABC Area	ABC TaskName
1	1	Accounting	Prep
2	2	Accounting	Review
3	3	Accounting	Admin
4	4	Accounting	Other
5	5	Tax	Prep
6	6	Tax	Review
7	7	Tax	Admin
8	8	Tax	Other

Step 2: Transform the CertificationList from a multi-valued column into a single-valued column:

- In Power Query, split the CertificationList column and select the **Each Occurrence of the delimiter** option.
- Click on the EmployeeID column and select **Transform** in the main menu.
- Finally, select **Unpivot Columns** in the ribbon, and choose **Unpivot other Columns** (Illustration 5.38).

Step 3: In the resulting table, delete the Attribute column and change the Value column's name to "Certificate." An employee's certifications are now recorded in a single-valued column.

This completes the transformation of the Beans data set into a star/snowflake schema.

Pattern 16 Summary

Problem	Data models that are not structured following the principles of dimensional modeling are typically more difficult to analyze.
Detect (Data Profiling)	Analyze a data model's compliance with dimensional modeling principles.
Correct (ETL)	Reconfigure the data model as a star/snowflake schema.

ILLUSTRATION 5.38   Unpivoting Columns

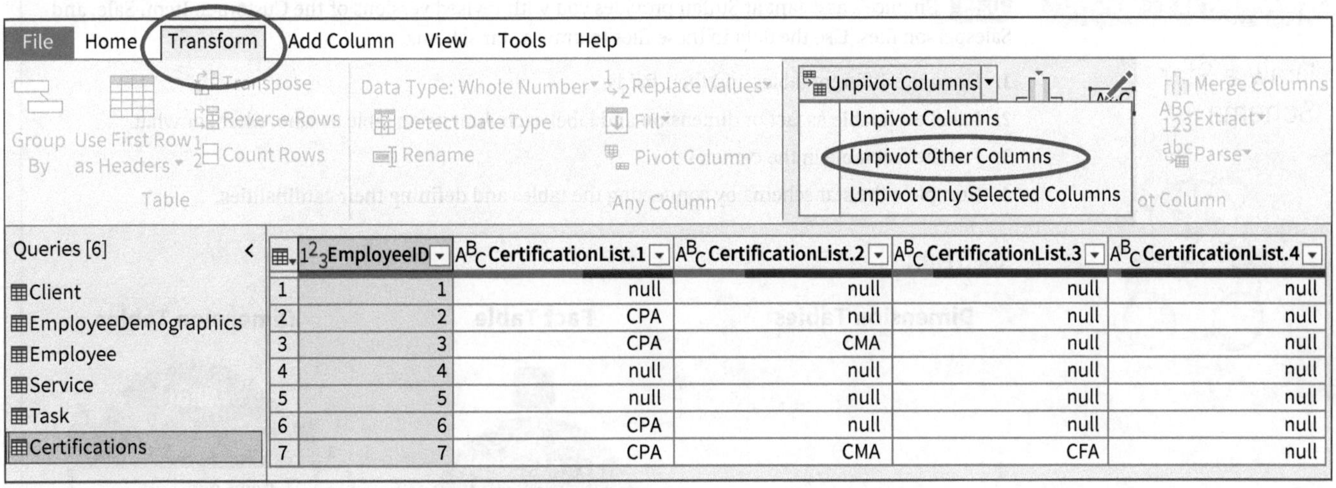

	EmployeeID	CertificationList.1	CertificationList.2	CertificationList.3	CertificationList.4
1	1	null	null	null	null
2	2	CPA	null	null	null
3	3	CPA	CMA	null	null
4	4	null	null	null	null
5	5	null	null	null	null
6	6	CPA	null	null	null
7	7	CPA	CMA	CFA	null

Queries [6]:
- Client
- EmployeeDemographics
- Employee
- Service
- Task
- Certifications

Ribbon: File | Home | **Transform** | Add Column | View | Tools | Help

Transform ribbon items: Transpose, Reverse Rows, Count Rows, Group By, Use First Row as Headers, Table, Data Type: Whole Number, Replace Values, Detect Date Type, Fill, Rename, **Unpivot Columns** (dropdown: Unpivot Columns, **Unpivot Other Columns**, Unpivot Only Selected Columns), Pivot Column, Merge Columns, Extract, Parse

Data Exploration Pattern 17: Find Invalid Values with Inter-Table Rules

Patterns 10, 14, and 17 are similar because they define the acceptable values for a column. However, Pattern 17 determines the validity of a column's values based on the values in one or more other tables. An example of a widely used inter-table validation rule is **referential integrity**, which refers to the fact that all values in a foreign key should also exist as values in the corresponding primary key. (**Data** How To 5.3 at the end of the chapter explains how to implement referential integrity with Microsoft Access.)

How To

Create and Apply Inter-Table Validation Rules

Inter-table validation rules identify invalid data. Their creation requires in-depth knowledge of the business. **Illustration 5.39** shows an example of an inter-table validation rule applied to the Beans case. It is part of the Service table, and it specifies that only managers, sr. managers, and partners can review an engagement. The rule has detected that service 3971 was reviewed by a senior, and a staff employee reviewed service 4193.

ILLUSTRATION 5.39   Design and Implementation of an Inter-Table Validation Rule

Description	Sample Code
Only managers, sr. managers, and partners can review an engagement.	NOAUTHORITY = IF TASK.TASKNAME = "REVIEW" AND EMPLOYEE[JOBTITLE] IN {"MANAGER", "SR. MANAGER", "PARTNER"}, THEN "OK", ELSE "ISSUE"

Modify Invalid Values

If you were working on the Beans case, you would consult with the CEO to find out if a policy violation, incorrect entry of the data, or another reason caused the error. Once identified, the issue can be corrected by putting a control in place to avoid further policy violations, correcting the values in the source data, or correcting the values in the analytical database.

Pattern 17 Summary

Problem	Invalid data might result in poor decision-making.
Detect (Data Profiling)	Create and apply inter-table validation rules.
Correct (ETL)	Modify the invalid rules.

APPLY IT 5.6

Draw a Star
Schema

Data Shanice's assistant at Stufan provides you with revised versions of the Customer, Item, Sale, and Salesperson files. Use the data in these files to draw a star schema.

1. Draw the different tables and their fields.
2. Label each table as fact or dimension and label each dimension table as who, when, or what.
3. Put the fact table in the center.
4. Complete the star schema by connecting the tables and defining their cardinalities.

SOLUTION

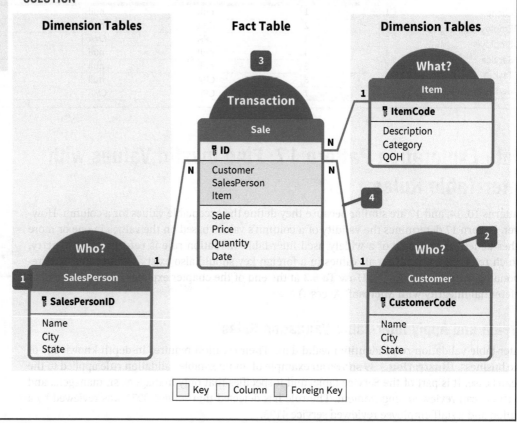

5.7 Which Patterns Apply to Data Loading?

LEARNING OBJECTIVE ❼
Apply patterns to data loading issues.

Once the data are cleaned and transformed, it is time to load them into the software for analysis. Data loading is the process of making the analytical database available for use. Since both extraction and loading are transfer processes, they have similar issues when it comes to the completeness and correctness of transferred data. It is also important that the data model of the analytical database is validated, that is, all relationships have been defined.

Data Preparation Pattern 18: Incomplete Data Loading

Loading moves the data from the ETL tool to the analytical database. **Illustration 5.40** shows how to transfer data from the ETL tool, in this case Power Query, to the analytical database.

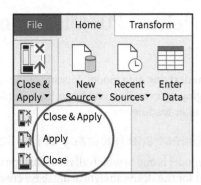

ILLUSTRATION 5.40 ETL-Analytical Database Transfer

There are three options:

- **Close and apply:** Close Power Query and apply all transformations to the analytical database.
- **Apply:** Apply all the transformations to the analytical database, but keep Power Query open.
- **Close:** Close Power Query without applying any transformations to the analytical database.

If we choose one of the first two options, then it is important to confirm that all data were transferred.

Compare Row Counts

Like Pattern 1, the row count for the analytical database can be compared with the row count of the data set in the ETL tool. The ETL tool will also issue an alert if any errors occurred when the transformations are applied to the analytical database.

Add Missing Rows

If the numbers do not match, determine which rows were not transferred and why. Once identified, add the missing rows to the analytical database.

Pattern 18 Summary

Problem	All the data did not transfer during loading.
Detect (Data Profiling)	Compare row counts.
Correct (ETL)	Add the missing data.

Data Preparation Pattern 19: Incorrect Data Loading

Even when all the rows have been transferred, the data might not have been transferred correctly. Pattern 19 addresses this potential issue.

Compare Control Amounts

Like Pattern 2, an effective way to validate the correct transfer of data is by comparing sums, averages, or any other control amounts.

Modify Incorrect Values

If the numbers do not match, determine which data were transferred incorrectly and what caused the problem. Once identified, modify the incorrectly transferred values in the analytical database.

Pattern 19 Summary

Problem	The correct data did not transfer during loading.
Detect (Data Profiling)	Compare control amounts.
Correct (ETL)	Modify incorrect values.

Data Preparation Pattern 20: Missing or Incorrect Data Relationships

Analytics rely heavily on the underlying data model. Missing or incorrectly defined data relationships make analytics challenging or even impossible, so the completeness and accuracy of the data model must be validated after loading.

Investigate the Completeness and Accuracy of the Data Model

A complete and accurate data model is one in which all relationships are correct. **Illustration 5.41** shows the finalized data model for the Beans analytical database created with Power Query. Compare this with your data model, and determine that no relationships are missing, there are no unnecessary relationships, and that all relationships are defined correctly.

ILLUSTRATION 5.41 Beans Data Model

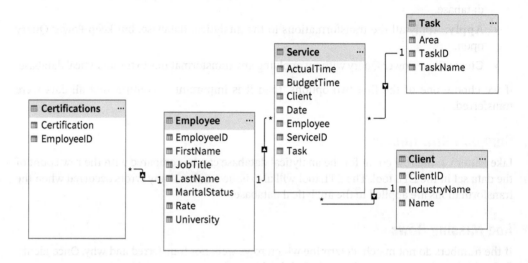

Modify the Data Model

To do this in Power BI, select the **Home** tab in the Main Menu and click **Manage Relationships** in the ribbon. The window shown in **Illustration 5.42** will appear. Select the buttons at the bottom of the window to create, edit, or delete a relationship.

ILLUSTRATION 5.42 Manage Relationships

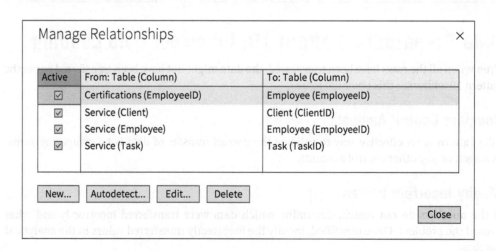

Illustration 5.43 shows some of the aspects of a relationship that can be defined:

- The data fields between which the relationship is specified.
- The cardinalities that apply to the relationship.
- The navigation direction used to aggregate data.

ILLUSTRATION 5.43 Define Relationships

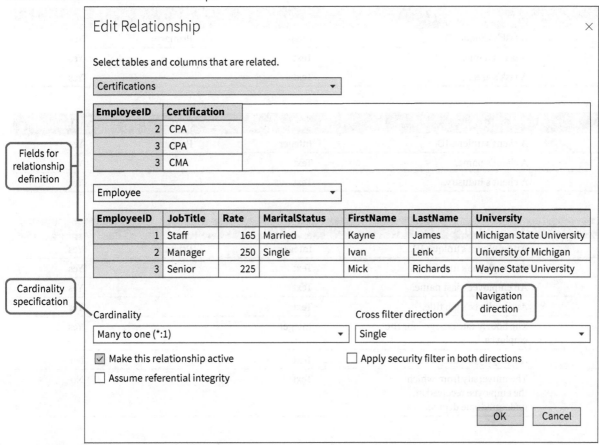

Fields for relationship definition

Cardinality specification

Pattern 20 Summary

Problem	Missing or incorrectly defined data relationships make analysis challenging or even impossible.
Detect (Data Profiling)	Investigate the completeness and accuracy of the data model.
Correct (ETL)	Modify the data model.

The transformation of the Beans data set and its preparation for analytics is now complete.

Illustration 5.44 shows the revised data dictionary for the analytical database in Illustration 5.41.

ILLUSTRATION 5.44 Beans Revised Data Dictionary

Service

Name	Description	Data Type	Key	Mandatory
Client	A client's unique ID.	Integer	Foreign	Yes
Employee	An employee's unique ID.	Integer	Foreign	Yes
Task	A task's unique ID.	Integer	Foreign	Yes
ServiceID	A service's unique ID.	Integer	Primary	Yes
Date	The date the service occurred.	Date		Yes
ActualTime	The actual time spent on the service provided.	Decimal		Yes
BudgetedTime	The budgeted time for the service provided.	Decimal		Yes

Task

Name	Description	Data Type	Key	Mandatory
TaskID	A task's unique ID.	Integer	Primary	Yes
TaskName	A task's name.	Text		Yes
Area	A task's area.	Text		Yes

Client

Name	Description	Data Type	Key	Mandatory
ClientID	A client's unique ID.	Integer	Primary	Yes
Name	A client's name.	Text		Yes
IndustryName	A client's industry.	Text		Yes

Employee

Name	Description	Data Type	Key	Mandatory
EmployeeID	An employee's unique ID.	Integer	Primary	Yes
FirstName	An employee's first name.	Text		Yes
LastName	An employee's last name.	Text		Yes
JobTitle	An employee's job title.	Text		Yes
Rate	The hourly rate charged for the employee.	Integer		Yes
MaritalStatus	An employee's marital status.	Text		No
University	The university from which the employee received an undergraduate degree.	Text		No

Certifications

Name	Description	Data Type	Key	Mandatory
EmployeeID	An employee's unique ID.	Integer	Foreign	Yes
Certification	A certification earned by the employee.	Text		Yes

---

APPLY IT 5.7

Evaluate Relationships Between Tables

The following two illustrations show the current relationship between the Sale and Customer tables for the Stufan data set. There are two issues that would dramatically distort any analytics related to this relationship. Identify them and describe why they are problems.

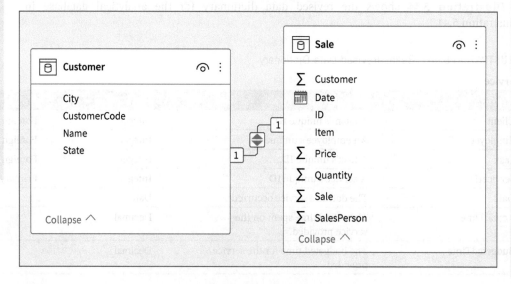

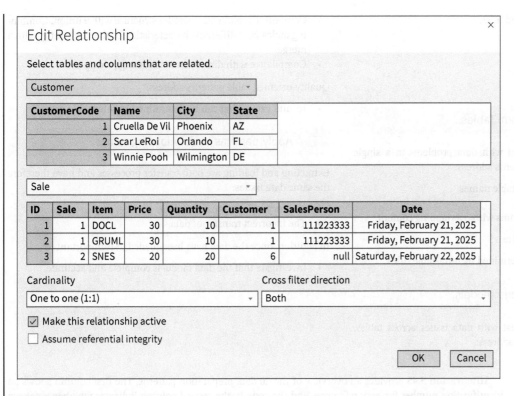

Edit Relationship

Select tables and columns that are related.

Customer

CustomerCode	Name	City	State
1	Cruella De Vil	Phoenix	AZ
2	Scar LeRoi	Orlando	FL
3	Winnie Pooh	Wilmington	DE

Sale

ID	Sale	Item	Price	Quantity	Customer	SalesPerson	Date
1	1	DOCL	30	10	1	111223333	Friday, February 21, 2025
2	1	GRUML	30	10	1	111223333	Friday, February 21, 2025
3	2	SNES	20	20	6	null	Saturday, February 22, 2025

Cardinality

One to one (1:1)

Cross filter direction

Both

☑ Make this relationship active

☐ Assume referential integrity

OK   Cancel

SOLUTION

1. The relationship is defined between the wrong fields: CustomerCode and ID. ID is a sequential number assigned to each row in the Sale table. As a result, the wrong customers are being assigned to the sales. The relationship should have been designated between the CustomerCode field in the Customer table and the Customer field in the Sale table.

2. A 1-N cardinality pattern is expected for a relationship between a dimension table (customer) and a fact table (sale). Customers can make more than one sale, but only one customer is specified for each sale.

Chapter Review and Practice

Learning Objectives Review

❶ Explain the process of data profiling.

Data profiling is the process of investigating data quality and structure. It has three parts:

- Investigating data quality: Identify if there are anomalies in the data. Stated differently, are the data dirty?
- Investigating data structure: Improve the organization of the data for the purpose of analysis.
- Deciding and informing: Decide whether to address the issues identified, the cost of doing so, and the consequences of not addressing the issues.

❷ Describe the extract-transform-load (ETL) process.

The extract-transform-load (ETL) is a process that corrects data issues:

- Extraction is moving the data to a staging area for transformation purposes.
- Transformation involves improving the data during three sub-processes: cleaning, restructuring, and integration.
- Loading occurs when the data are moved to the area where they will be used for analysis.

❸ Apply patterns to extract data.

Data preparation patterns are a robust tool for data preparation projects. They help identify data issues and provide guidance for detecting and correcting them. Data extraction patterns address:

- The incomplete transfer of data.
- The incorrect transfer of data.

❹ Apply patterns to transform columns.

Transformation cleans the data by correcting values (quality) and restructuring and integrating the data structures for analytics (structure). It can be gradually conducted at the column, table, and model level.

Column transformation patterns deal with data issues in a single column. Structure-oriented column patterns address:

- Columns that contain irrelevant and unreliable data.
- Incorrect and ambiguous column names.
- Incorrect data types.
- Combined or multi-valued columns.

Quality-oriented column patterns address:

- Columns with incorrect data.
- Inconsistent data in columns.
- Columns with incomplete data.
- Columns with invalid data.

⑤ Apply patterns to transform tables.

Table transformation patterns deal with data problems in a single table. Structure-oriented table patterns address:

- Nonintuitive and ambiguous table names.
- Tables without a primary key.
- Tables with two or more columns with overlapping content.

Quality-oriented table patterns address:

- Invalid values that can be determined by intra-table rules.

⑥ Apply patterns to transform models.

Model transformation patterns deal with data issues across tables. Structure-oriented model patterns address:

- Combining tables with a similar structure with a union. Combining tables with different characteristics for the same entity with a merge.
- Compliance with dimensional modeling principles.

Quality-oriented table patterns address:

- Invalid values that can be determined by inter-table rules.

⑦ Apply patterns to data loading issues.

Extracting and loading are both transfer processes and have therefore the same data issues:

- The incomplete transfer of data.
- The incorrect transfer of data.

In addition, once the data have been loaded, it is important to:

- Investigate that the data model is complete and accurate.

Illustration 5.45 provides an overview of the 20 data preparation patterns. The first column shows an identification number for easy reference, and the code in the second column indicates whether a pattern focuses on values (V) or restructuring the data (S). The chart also includes the data issue and how to detect and correct it.

ILLUSTRATION 5.45 Overview of Data Preparation Patterns

Data Preparation Patterns

Id	Code	Issue	Detect (Data Profiling)	Correct (ETL)
Extraction				
1	V	All the data did not transfer.	Compare row counts.	Add missing rows.
2	V	Data was not correctly transferred.	Compare control amounts.	Modify incorrect values.
Transformation				
Id	Code	Issue	Detect (Data Profiling)	Correct (ETL)
Column				
3	S	Irrelevant or unreliable data.	Visually scan columns for irrelevant and unreliable data.	Remove columns with irrelevant and unreliable data.
4	S	Incorrect or ambiguous data.	Scan column for incorrect or ambiguous names.	Rename column.
5	S	Incorrect data types.	Inspect the data type.	Change data type.
6	S	Columns are not single-valued.	Examine the values in the columns.	Split composite columns. Create a separate table for multi-valued columns.
7	V	Incorrect values.	Detect incorrect values with outliers.	Modify incorrect values.
8	V	Inconsistent values.	Identify inconsistent values.	Modify inconsistent values.
9	V	Incomplete values.	Investigate null values.	Remove the columns or replace the null values.
10	V	Invalid values.	Create and apply validation rules.	Modify invalid values.

(*Continued*)

Transformation				
Id	Code	Issue	Detect (Data Profiling)	Correct (ETL)
Table				
11	S	Incorrect or ambiguous table names.	Visually scan the table for incorrect or ambiguous names.	Rename tables.
12	S	Missing primary keys.	Identify tables missing a primary key.	Create a primary key.
13	S	Redundant column content.	Perform column-by-column comparisons.	Delete redundant and dependent data.
14	V	Invalid values detected with intra-table rules.	Create and apply intra-table validation rules.	Modify the invalid data.
Model				
15	S	Data spread across tables.	Identify tables with a similar structure or tables that describe different characteristics of the same entity.	Union or merge tables.
16	S	Compliance with dimensional modeling principles.	Analyze a data model's compliance with dimensional modeling principles.	Restructure model as a star/snowflake schema.
17	V	Invalid values detected with inter-table rules.	Create and apply inter-table validation rules.	Modify the invalid rules.
Loading				
Id	Code	Issue	Detect (Data Profiling)	Correct (ETL)
18	V	Incomplete data loading.	Compare row counts.	Add the missing data.
19	V	Incorrect data loading.	Compare control amounts.	Modify incorrect values.
20	S	Missing or incorrect data relationships.	Investigate the completeness and accuracy of the data model.	Create, modify, and delete relationships Modify the data model.

Key Terms Review

How To Walk-Throughs

HOW TO 5.1   Profile Data with Power Query

How To

Power Query integrates excellent data profiling tools. Let's examine how it can help with row counts, control amounts, and distribution information.

What You Need: `Data` The How To 5.1 data file.

STEP 1: Extract the data from the data file. There are different steps for extracting data from Excel versus Power BI. If you are using Excel:

- First, open a Blank workbook and click **Data > From File > From Excel Workbook** (**Illustration 5.46**).

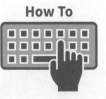

ILLUSTRATION 5.46 Extract Data from an Excel File

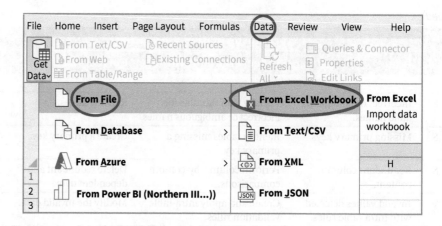

- Next, select the Beans Excel file and click **Import**. A Navigator dialog box will open. Select the **Service** table and click **Load** (**Illustration 5.47**).

ILLUSTRATION 5.47 Select and Load the Service Table

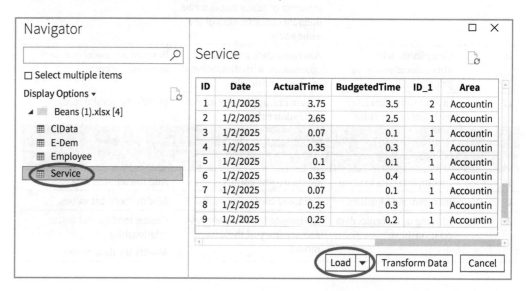

- Finally, click the **Data** tab and then the down arrow in **Get Data**. Next, you will see the option to **Launch Power Query Editor**. Click to open the Query Editor (**Illustration 5.48**).

ILLUSTRATION 5.48 Open Power Query

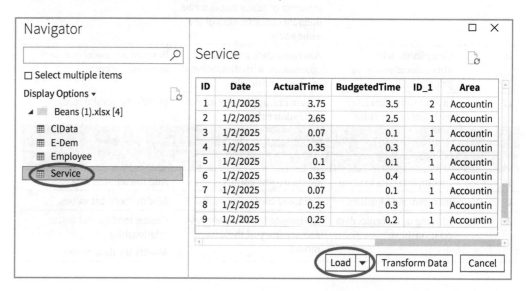

If you are using Power BI:

- Open a new Power BI file and select **Excel** in the **Data** group. **Illustration 5.49** shows Power BI's Home tab, which includes the Data group.

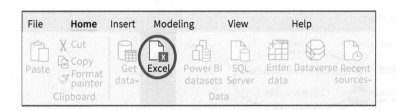

ILLUSTRATION 5.49   Extract Data from an Excel File

- Next, select the Beans Excel file and click **Open**. A Navigator dialog box will open. Select the **Service** table and click **Load** (**Illustration 5.50**).

ILLUSTRATION 5.50   Select and Load the Service Table

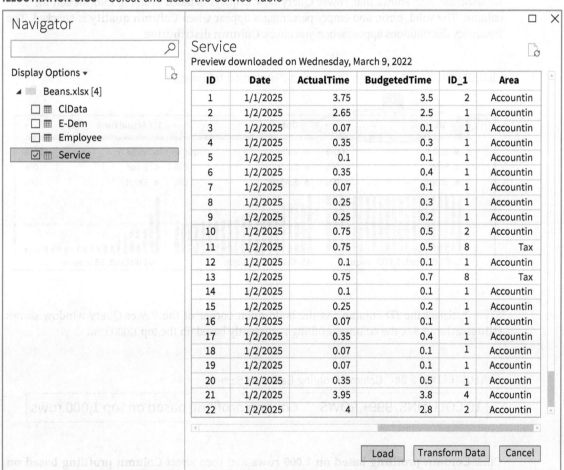

Navigator

Display Options ▾

▲ Beans.xlsx [4]
  ☐ ClData
  ☐ E-Dem
  ☐ Employee
  ☑ Service

Service
Preview downloaded on Wednesday, March 9, 2022

ID	Date	ActualTime	BudgetedTime	ID_1	Area
1	1/1/2025	3.75	3.5	2	Accountin
2	1/2/2025	2.65	2.5	1	Accountin
3	1/2/2025	0.07	0.1	1	Accountin
4	1/2/2025	0.35	0.3	1	Accountin
5	1/2/2025	0.1	0.1	1	Accountin
6	1/2/2025	0.35	0.4	1	Accountin
7	1/2/2025	0.07	0.1	1	Accountin
8	1/2/2025	0.25	0.3	1	Accountin
9	1/2/2025	0.25	0.2	1	Accountin
10	1/2/2025	0.75	0.5	2	Accountin
11	1/2/2025	0.75	0.5	8	Tax
12	1/2/2025	0.1	0.1	1	Accountin
13	1/2/2025	0.75	0.7	8	Tax
14	1/2/2025	0.1	0.1	1	Accountin
15	1/2/2025	0.25	0.2	1	Accountin
16	1/2/2025	0.07	0.1	1	Accountin
17	1/2/2025	0.35	0.4	1	Accountin
18	1/2/2025	0.07	0.1	1	Accountin
19	1/2/2025	0.07	0.1	1	Accountin
20	1/2/2025	0.35	0.5	1	Accountin
21	1/2/2025	3.95	3.8	4	Accountin
22	1/2/2025	4	2.8	2	Accountin

Load   Transform Data   Cancel

- Finally, click **Transform data** in the **Queries** group of the **Home** tab to launch Power Query (**Illustration 5.51**).

ILLUSTRATION 5.51   Open Power Query

Power BI

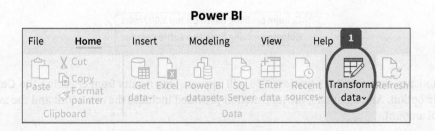

The remaining steps are identical for Excel and Power BI.

STEP 2: Click the **View** tab in the main menu (**Illustration 5.52**). Select **Column quality**, **Column distribution**, and **Column profile**.

ILLUSTRATION 5.52 Column Profiling Options

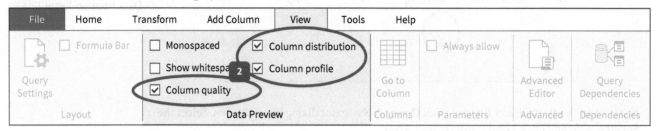

Illustration 5.53 shows that Power Query now displays detailed profiling information for each column. The valid, error, and empty percentages appear when **Column quality** is checked. The frequency distributions appear when you check **Column distribution**.

ILLUSTRATION 5.53 Column Quality and Distribution Information

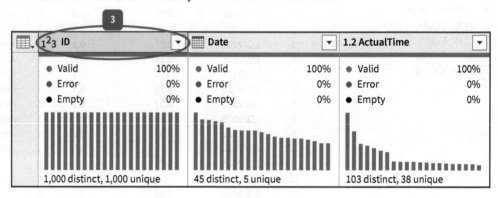

STEP 3: Select the **ID** column. As the bottom-left corner of the Power Query window shows (**Illustration 5.54**), the column profiling is currently based on the top 1,000 row.

ILLUSTRATION 5.54 Column Profiling Based on Sample

10 COLUMNS, 999+ ROWS   Column profiling based on top 1,000 rows

Click **Column profiling based on 1,000 rows** and then select **Column profiling based on entire data set** (**Illustration 5.55**).

ILLUSTRATION 5.55 Column Profiling
Based on Entire Data Set

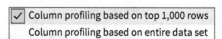

The statistics shown in **Illustration 5.56** will appear. This results from checking the **Column profile** option. Among others, the information provided includes the row count and the average control amount.

ILLUSTRATION 5.56   Column Profile

Column statistics	...
Count	4,632
Error	0
Empty	0
Distinct	4,632
Unique	4,632
NaN	0
Zero	0
Min	1
Max	4,632
Average	2,316.5
Standard deviation	1,337.28...
Even	2,316
Odd	2,316

HOW TO 5.2   Merge Tables with Power Query

How To

In the Beans case the goal is to join the Employee and EmployeeDemographics tables. If both tables share the same primary key, a join, or merge, is straightforward. But the Employee-Demographics table does not have a primary key and there are matching issues between the names. Let's explore how these different issues can be addressed with Power Query.

What You Need: [Data] The How To 5.2 data file.

STEP 1: If you are using Excel, open the file and click the **Data** tab in the main menu. Select **Get Data** in the ribbon, then **Launch Power Query Editor**. In Power BI, open the file and click on the **Home** tab in the main menu. Select **Transform data**.

In both cases, Power Query will open. Make sure you are connected to the BeansEmployeeData file. Create this connection by clicking the wheel next to **Source** in the **Applied Steps** pane. Under **File path**, specify where the data set is located on your device. If you don't define this connection correctly, you will receive an error message like the one shown in **Illustration 5.57**.

ILLUSTRATION 5.57   Incorrect Connection to Data Set

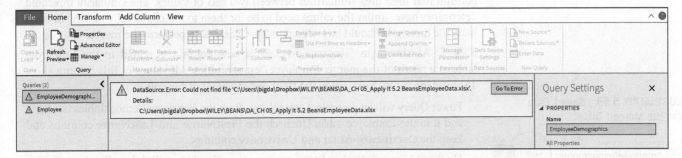

STEP 2: Select the Employee table in the Queries pane. Next, select the **Home** tab in Power Query's main menu and select **Merge Queries** in the **Combine** group.

STEP 3: Select the EmployeeDemographics table to join it with the Employee table.

STEP 4: Choose **FirstName** and **LastName** in both tables. Using Pattern 6 to split the name in the Employee table now pays off!

Illustration 5.58 visually shows how to perform steps 3, 4, and 5.

ILLUSTRATION 5.58 Merge Tables with Fuzzy Matching

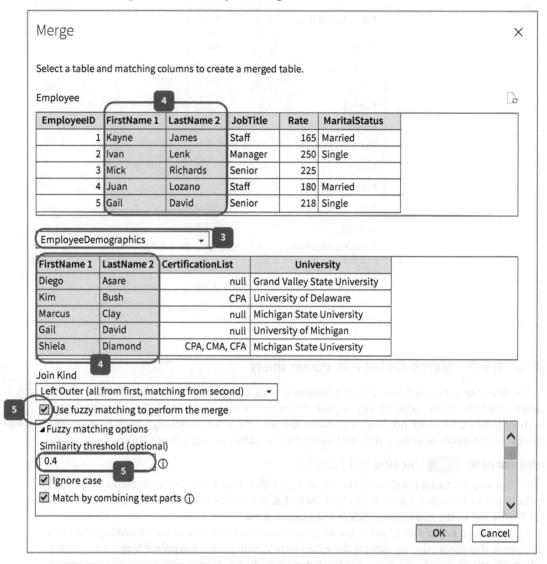

STEP 5: To address data issues resulting from nicknames, typos, and reversed names, click the checkbox **Use fuzzy matching to perform the merge**. Fuzzy matching is an algorithm that measures similarities between two sets of values. The similarity threshold determines how similar the values need to be for them to match. To fully match both sets here, the threshold should be lowered to 0.4. Click **OK** to perform the merge.

STEP 6: As shown in **Illustration 5.59**, a new column is added to the Employee table as a result of the merge: EmployeeDemographics. All values in this column show **Table** as the value. Next, Click the right upper corner of the column:

ILLUSTRATION 5.59 Select Data from the Merged Table

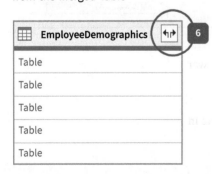

- Power Query will let you select any column from the EmployeeDemographics table and add it to the Employee table. Uncheck the **FirstName** and **LastName** columns and keep the **CertificationList** and **University** columns.

- Uncheck **Use original column name as prefix**. This will delete EmployeeDemographics from the CertificationList and University column names.

At this point, you have successfully merged the two tables into one.

STEP 7: Only the Employee table is needed for analytical purposes. **Illustration 5.60** shows how to instruct Power Query not to load a table. Right-click on **EmployeeDemographics** and unclick the checkbox before **Enable Load**. Tables that are not loaded into the analytical database are shown in italics. *Note*: This option is available in power BI only, not in Excel

ILLUSTRATION 5.60   Select Tables That Should Not Be Loaded

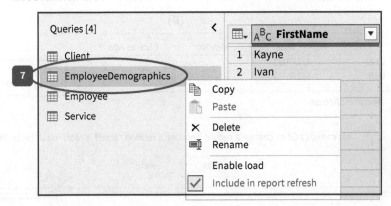

HOW TO 5.3   Implement Referential Integrity with Microsoft Access

To improve data quality, referential integrity is best implemented at the data entry level. Database software such as Microsoft Access makes this easy.

What You Need: `Data` The How To 5.3 file.

STEP 1: The Microsoft Access database contains the Vendor and Purchase tables:

- As shown in **Illustration 5.61**, the relationship between the two tables is defined between the ID field in the Vendor table and the Vendor field in the Purchase table.

- The bottom of Illustration 5.61 shows that when creating this relationship (by dragging the vendor field into the Purchase table, or the other way around), Microsoft Access provides an **Enforce Referential Integrity** option.

ILLUSTRATION 5.61   Enforcing Referential Integrity with Microsoft Access

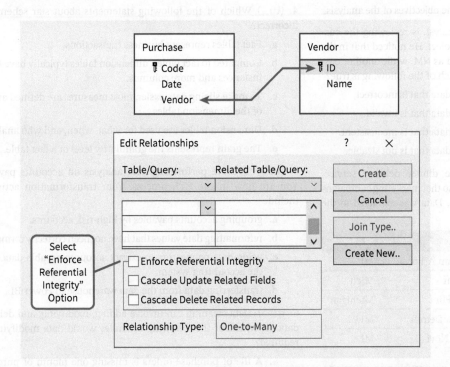

STEP 2: Illustration 5.62 demonstrates what happens if you select this option. Panel (A) shows all existing vendors. Panel (B) shows what happens if you try to add a nonexisting vendor—the vendor with ID 6—to the Purchase table. Access generates an error preventing you from entering the *invalid* vendor.

ILLUSTRATION 5.62 Entering an Invalid Vendor

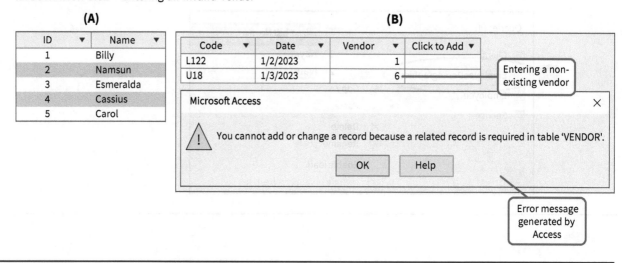

Data The Data tag appears when the data to answer a question or complete an exercise are available in the book's product page on www.wiley.com.

Multiple Choice Questions

1. (LO 1) Data preparation includes the process of

a. gathering and integrating data during the data analysis phases.

b. capturing data from transactional systems.

c. profiling, cleaning, and restructuring data prior to analysis.

d. assessing if the data will address the objectives of the analysis.

2. (LO 1) Hao, an accounts receivable analyst, is reviewing the customer master file for use in an analysis project. He noticed that in the Address field one customer's state is listed as NM, while another customer's state is listed as New Mexico. Which of the following is true?

a. Hao has identified an instance of data that is incorrect.

b. Hao has identified an instance of data that is invalid.

c. Hao has identified an instance of data that is inconsistent.

d. Hao has identified an instance of data that is not sizable.

3. (LO 1) Harvest Dinners is an online dinner delivery service. Analysis by customer location is required so that marketing campaigns can highlight locally-sourced ingredients. Data was extracted to the following table:

Customer ID	Address	State
203211	245 Fleet St., Ann Arbor	MI
203212	14 First St., Flint	Mich
203213	3403 Main St., Flint	Michigan
203214	3306 Second St., Detroit	MI
203215	341 Liberty St., Novi	MI
…	…	…

What data problem exists in the table?

a. The address field should have the city separated into its own column, and the State field has inconsistent values.

b. The address field should have the city separated into its own column, and the State field has incomplete values.

c. The address field has incomplete data, and the State field has incorrect values.

d. The address field has incomplete data, and the State field has incomplete values.

4. (LO 1) Which of the following statements about star schemas is incorrect?

a. Fact tables represent business transactions.

b. Compared to fact tables, dimension tables typically have fewer instances and more columns.

c. To make slicing data easier, most measures are defined as part of the dimension tables.

d. Dimension tables are used for what, when, and who analysis.

e. The grain represents the granularity level of a fact table.

5. (LO 2) You are performing data analysis on accounts payable. You are now in the ETL process. Your transformation activities include

a. grouping accounts payables by high-risk accounts.

b. reformatting date values that have not been correctly formatted.

c. using data connectors to extract accounts payable data from the accounting system.

d. transferring data from the data warehouse to Power BI.

6. (LO 2) Data cleaning can involve adding, modifying, and deleting data. In which of the following examples would data modifying be required?

a. A file of purchase orders is missing one month of purchase orders.

b. You are preparing an analysis of how many purchase orders are greater than $500. The file you are working with has a row at the beginning of each new month with the month name listed in the date column. There is no other data in the row with the month name.

c. While examining the purchase orders data, you note that the vendor's name, street address, city, and state are listed in separate columns. In some cases, the state column displays the state name, in other cases the state abbreviation is shown.

d. During your analysis of purchase orders, you note that some of the orders include the vendor phone number.

7. (LO 3) Validation of data transfers is done by comparing the source data with the data in the ETL tool. Which of the following statements about data transfer is incorrect?

a. The number of rows helps validate the completeness of data transfers.

b. Sequence gap analysis helps validate the completeness of data transfers.

c. Comparing the averages of a numeric field helps validate the accuracy of data transfers.

d. Comparing column headers helps validate both completeness and accuracy.

e. Comparing the sum of numeric fields helps validate the accuracy of data transfers.

8. (LO 3) What is the method to check for completeness when data is extracted or transferred?

a. Compare the Excel worksheet's row count with the row count in the ETL tool.

b. Compare the Excel worksheet's average of a value with the average in the ETL tool.

c. Create a time-series chart to see if there are missing periods in the data.

d. All of the answer choices are correct.

9. (LO 4) Lizelle is a financial analyst preparing an analytical database to analyze manufacturing data to determine the most efficient processes. She is currently identifying irrelevant and unreliable data in columns within a table. Which of the following is the most appropriate response when she identifies irrelevant or unreliable data?

a. Remove the column with irrelevant or unreliable data.

b. Abandon the project because the data are not valid and cannot be analyzed.

c. Unpivot the column so that the data are separated into distinct fields.

d. Put the relevant, irrelevant, reliable, and unreliable data in separate columns.

10. (LO 4) Hofflak is a large construction company in the Northwest United States. Their ERP system keeps track of all their assets. The data dictionary for the asset table looks as follows:

Asset

Name	Description
ID	An asset's unique ID.
Description	An asset's description.
AssetCategory	An asset's category.
Price	The price paid for the asset.
Salvam	The estimated book value of the asset at the end of its useful life.
EstimatedLifetime	An asset's estimated lifespan.
DprMethod	The depreciation method that applies to the asset.

What column names would you change for data analysis purposes?

a. ID, Salvam, DprMethod

b. ID, Price, EstimatedLifetime, DprMethod

c. Price, Salvam, EstimatedLifetime, DprMethod

d. AssetCategory, Price

e. Salvam, EstimatedLifetime, DprMethod

f. EstimatedLifetime, DprMethod

11. (LO 4) To restructure a composite column you should

a. remove the column data that is not needed.

b. split the column data into separate columns.

c. create a separate table.

d. move the column to another table.

12. (LO 4) You are performing ETL on the vendor master table. The table has several data issues. The transformed table will be used to analyze spend by commodity and state. You are reviewing the data preparation pattern for irrelevant and unreliable data. Describe the data issue and how you would correct it.

VendorID	Address	State	Commodity	Telephone
20211	245 Fleet St., Rockville	MA	Cleaning Supplies	240.243.2400
20212	14 First St., Rockville	Maryland	Office Equipment; Office Supplies	
20213	3403 Main St., Rochester	NY	Beverages; Kitchen Supplies	585-450-9910
20214	3306 Second St., Buffalo	New York	Toys; Clothing; Household Goods	2995229
20215	341 Liberty St., Springfield	N/A	Cleaning Equipment	241.233.4111
…	…	…	…	…

a. The Address column has an ambiguous name since it combines the street and address, and city. Split the column into Street and City.

b. The Telephone column has data that is unreliable and not relevant for the analysis. Correct the data that is unreliable and keep the column in the analytical database.

c. The State column has data that is unreliable for the analysis. Remove the State column from the analytical database.

d. The Telephone column has data that is unreliable and not relevant for the analysis. Remove the Telephone column from the analytical database.

13. (LO 5) The following table showing employee information doesn't have a primary key defined. What should be the primary key?

FirstName	LastName	Department	Birthday
James	Peter	Accounting	9/2/1986
Lee	Wong	Facilities	7/4/2000
Sandra	Ng	Accounting	6/20/1985
Sally	Singh	IT	12/6/2001
Kevin	Brock	IT	11/22/1988
Harold	Young	Facilities	8/20/1977
Pamela	McCain	Accounting	9/30/1980
...	...	...	...

  a. LastName should be the primary key since it has unique values.

  b. The combination of FirstName and LastName should be the primary key since it has unique values.

  c. An artificial primary key should be created to ensure that the key has unique fields.

  d. All of the answer choices are correct.

14. (LO 5) You are examining the columns in a data set that you are analyzing. The following columns are in the data set:

HotelPropertyID	Contains a unique identification number for each hotel.
HotelAge	How many years the hotel has been operating since opening?
OpeningDate	The date the hotel opened.
RoomsAvailable	The number of rooms in the hotel.
RoomsRented	The number of rooms rented during the year.
Revenue	The amount of money collected for rooms rented during the year.

After reviewing the column headings and description, which of the following would you note?

  a. There is no overlap between the columns.

  b. There is an overlap between HotelAge and OpeningDate.

  c. There is redundancy between RoomsAvailable and RoomsRented.

  d. There is dependency between HotelAge and OpeningDate.

15. (LO 5) Consider a scenario where the following validation rule was applied to the Employee table shown:

```
VALID =
IF EMPLOYEE.AGE < 24 AND EMPLOYEE.DEGREE = "COLLEGE",
THEN "YES",
ELSE "NO"
```

Employee

Code	Age	Degree
1	23	High School
2	23	College
3	25	College
4	21	

Which of the following statements is incorrect?

  a. The value for the Valid column for the employee with code "1" is "No."

  b. The value for the Valid column for the employee with code "2" is "No."

  c. The value for the Valid column for the employee with code "3" is "No."

  d. The value for the Valid column for the employee with code "4" is "No."

16. (LO 6) Mithali, a financial analyst, is preparing data to engage in a data analysis project to predict revenue for the next period based on environmental considerations. She is currently reviewing the tables to validate inter-table rules for referential integrity. Which of the following is true about referential integrity?

  a. The primary and foreign key fields must have the same name.

  b. The primary key must be single-valued, but the foreign key can be multi-valued.

  c. The primary and foreign key fields can have different data types.

  d. All values in a foreign key should also exist as values in the corresponding primary key.

17. (LO 6) Skyline is a national plumbing and heating company. Skyline's CFO is preparing the employee performance data for further analysis. Samples of four of the files are shown. How would you suggest combining these four files?

JanuaryPurchases

PurchaseID	Date	Amount	Employee
14399	1/1/2025	1,432.24	7
14400	1/1/2025	799.99	14
14401	1/1/2025	320	12
14402	1/1/2025	822.21	22

EmployeeDemographics

ID	Name	DateOfBirth
14399	Ben Jespers	3/3/1975
14400	Bei Shi	7/17/1985
14401	Michael Rodman	5/20/1984
14402	Benita Alvarez	11/11/1979

EmployeeWages

ID	HourlyWage
14399	25
14400	38
14401	36
14402	45

FebruaryPurchases

PurchaseID	Date	Amount	Employee
15021	2/1/2025	123.89	4
15022	2/1/2025	540.99	1
15023	2/1/2025	183.12	14
15024	2/1/2025	744.41	21

  a. Merge JanuaryPurchases and EmployeeDemographics and merge FebruaryPurchases and EmployeeWages.

  b. Union JanuaryPurchases and FebruaryPurchases and union EmployeeDemographics and EmployeeWages.

  c. Union JanuaryPurchases and FebruaryPurchases and merge EmployeeDemographics and EmployeeWages.

  d. Union JanuaryPurchases and EmployeeDemographics and merge FebruaryPurchases and EmployeeWages.

18. (LO 6) Which of the following would result in transforming this star schema into a snowflake schema?

a. EmployeeName is a combined field that contains both the employee's first name and last name.

b. For some employees, their position is not known.

c. It is possible to have multiple contacts for a vendor.

d. Weekday, Month, and Year are extensively used for analysis purposes.

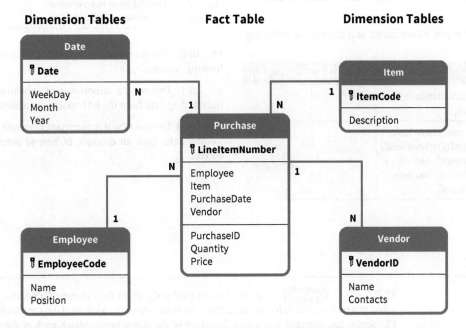

Dimension Tables   **Fact Table**   **Dimension Tables**

19. (LO 7) Hamza is transferring data into an analytical database for analysis. Which steps should he take to identify whether all the data transferred?

a. Review the columns for appropriate naming conventions.

b. Establish data validation rules and identify which data do not comply with the data validation rules.

c. Inspect distinct values and analyze frequencies.

d. Compare the row count for the analytical database with the row count of the data set in the ETL tool.

20. (LO 7) You are preparing an analysis for a food delivery company called Dine At Home. Dine At Home picks up food orders from restaurants and delivers them to the customer. Customers can order many times, but an order is for one customer only. Restaurants may have many orders, but an order is only for one restaurant. Which of the following cardinality specifications is incorrect?

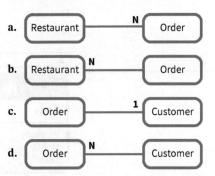

Review Questions

1. (LO 1) Describe data preparation. Why is data preparation necessary prior to analyzing data?

2. (LO 1) Assume you are preparing an analytical database. You have downloaded raw data from the information system and are now examining the data for consistency. Discuss two profiling techniques you might use to identify inconsistencies in the data.

3. (LO 2) Define and describe the three subprocesses of data transformation.

4. (LO 2) Compare and contrast the two forms of data integration: linking and combining.

5. (LO 2) What is data matching and why is it a challenge for data integration?

6. (LO 3) Describe what a data dictionary is and why it is an important part of data analysis.

7. (LO 3) Discuss why a pattern-based approach to data preparation is appropriate for data analysis projects.

8. (LO 3) Discuss the tools and features available in Microsoft Excel to ensure the transfer of all data when extracting data.

9. (LO 4) Compare and contrast the data types of whole number and text. Include how variables that are noted as whole numbers and variables that are coded as text are used in data analysis.

10. (LO 4) Discuss the difference between a composite column and a multi-valued column and give an example of each.

11. (LO 4) Describe the profiling techniques for detecting inconsistent values, and explain how to modify inconsistent values. Give an example of an inconsistent value.

12. (LO 5) Discuss the importance of minimizing redundant data among columns in an analytical database.

13. (LO 5) Discuss why it is important to verify the presence of primary keys. Explain how to identify a missing primary key and how to create one.

14. (LO 6) Describe dimensional modeling and discuss the importance of complying with dimensional modeling principles when building an analytical database.

15. (LO 6) What is the difference between a union and a merge? Give an example of when a union cannot be used.

16. (LO 6) Discuss the benefits of single-valued columns and flat tables for slicing data.

17. (LO 6) Explain how you would detect and correct the following issues:

Issues	Detection	Correction
A table in your analytical database does not have a primary key.		
A column in the fixed assets table has a column for date acquired (DateAcquired) and the asset age (AssetAge). Age represents how long the asset has been held since the date acquired.		
A table with vendor information is named VINFO.		
Invalid data might have been entered into one of the tables in the database.		

18. (LO 6) Discuss transforming models and how it differs from transforming columns.

19. (LO 7) Discuss the importance of validating relationships when transferring data from the ETL tool to the analytical database.

20. (LO 7) Discuss why it is important to ensure correct transfer when loading data. Give an example of how to determine if the data are correct.

Brief Exercises

BE 5.1 (LO 1) Auditing You are an audit staff assigned to the Coleman Cable, Inc. audit. You have been asked to develop a star schema to illustrate the structure of the analytical data model for your sales analysis. The senior has provided you with a first draft of the star schema. Match each of the following terms to its appropriate location in the star schema:

a. Dimension tables

b. Fact table

c. N

d. Measure

e. TotalAmountPurchased

f. PurchasingClerk

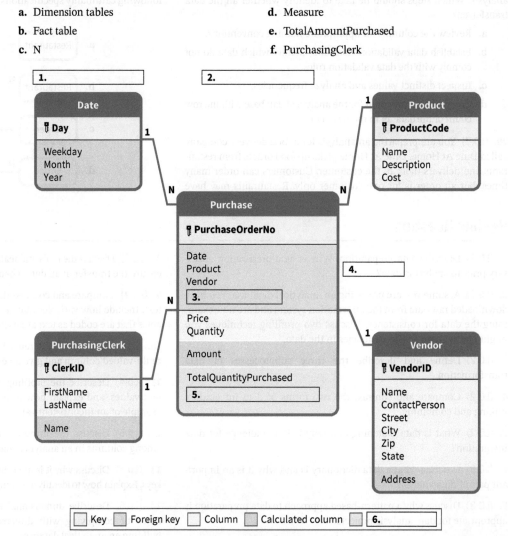

BE 5.2 (LO 1) You are a financial analyst and must use slicing measures to answer specific questions required by the senior management. Identify the most appropriate question that matches the dimension and measures.

Measures	Dimension
Total Sales Amount	Customer
Total Sales Quantity	Salesperson
	Product
	Month

1. What is the total sales amount (dollars) for a specific customer?
2. Who is the salesperson with the highest total sales amount (dollars) for a specific product?
3. What is the total quantity sold of a specific product?
4. Which month has the highest total sales amount (dollars)?

BE 5.3 (LO 1) You have been provided with a data table that contains customer data collected for a retail company's customer loyalty program. An excerpt of that data table follows. Identify at least three data quality issues.

CustomerInfo	Gender	Date	Email
Steve Millier, 121 South Beach St	M	10/21/1978	steve.miller
Sara Stevens, 435 Parker St	Female	9/21/2008	sara.stevens@mail.com
Libby Ralston, 812 Foster Ave	Female	6/28/2956	libby123@mail.com
Able Meyers, 902	Male	1/4/2009	smileyone@mail.com
Spring Stevens, 639 Bulldog Ct	Undisclosed	6/14/1982	sparkie.steven
Kevin Hogan, 3098 N. Tier St. Apt 392	M	7/22/1955	doglover@mail.com
Libby Ralston, 812 Foster Ave	Female		
Sara Stevens, 435 Parker St	Female	9/21/2008	sara.stevens@mail.com
Cooper Mazzu, 2342 Lincoln Way	Male	4/17/1955	coop8623
Molly White	F	10/21/1977	molly.white.123@mail.com
Janet Jones, 909 Hwy 78	F		

BE 5.4 (LO 2) The following two tables must be integrated into one combined table. The combined table must include the following fields for each record: Description, QOH, Location, Cost, Price, and Sale. Review each table and identify three data-matching challenges.

Table A		
Description	QOH	Location
Blue Dog Collar	5	A10
Red Doc Collar	3	A11
7 Inch Rope Sturdy Lead	10	B10
10 Inch Rope Sturdy Lead—Green	3	B10
10 Inch Rope Sturdy Lead—Black	5	B10

Table B			
ProductDescription	Cost	Price	Sale
Dog Collar—Blue	12.54	16.93	Y
7 Inch Rope Sturdy Lead	15.44	20.85	N
Red Dog Collar	15.54	20.98	N
10 Inch Rope Sturdy Lead—Bk	20.38	27.52	N
Green 10 Inch Rope Sturdy Lead	28.34	38.26	Y

BE 5.5 (LO 2) Panels (A) and (B) represent alternative data models for the same data set. Compare and contrast the two models.

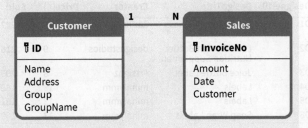

(A)

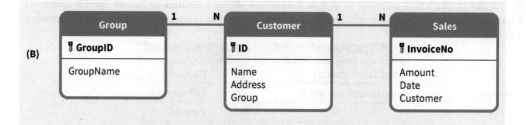

BE 5.6 (LO 3) [Tax Accounting] You have been asked to develop an analytical database to analyze the salary taxes of employees. An excerpt of your data is presented in the table. All amounts are in dollars.

ID	BasicSalary	Conveyance	MedicalExp	SpecialWork Allowance	TotalWorking Hours
1	30,000	1,600	1,250	6,150	53,850
2	15,000	1,600	1,250	6,150	28,350
3	10,000	1,000	1,250	750	19,250
4	12,500	1,600	1,250	900	24,100
5	11,000	1,100	1,250	950	21,050
6	7,000	700	1,250	150	13,850

You have started the process and are now ready to create the data dictionary. Identify the sentence with the unique identifier.

Sentence	Solution
The base salary is on which further calculations for salary and tax shall be made.	
The medical expenses that the employee will be reimbursed.	
Number of working hours put in by an employee.	
The unique identifier of an employee.	
The transportation expenses allowed for the employee.	
Additional payments paid in recognition of outstanding performance by the employee.	

BE 5.7 (LO 3) [Data] You receive a text file with December purchase order information. Before you start your analysis, use Power Query (Excel or Power BI) to determine whether the data have been completely and correctly transferred. A total of 34 purchases with an average total cost per product (orderline) of $610.98 were made during the month of December.

1. Name the preparation pattern you used to verify all transactions were transferred and explain how you verified this.

2. Name the preparation pattern you used to verify that all data were transferred correctly and explain how you verified this.

BE 5.8 (LO 4) Dimple Floral Artist, with a network of designers, provides floral design services for special events. The business uses designs from the community of designers. In return, the designers are paid for the designs that Dimple Floral Artist accepts. The business collects designer information and assigns a unique designer ID to track the designer's rewards, designs made, and appointments.

DesignerID	DesignTitle	Creator	Price(€)	Design Sold	Rewards	Reviews Favorable	NumberOf Appointment
D1	Box Set for Business Cards	Zarins	9	222	4	10	1
D2	Label Design Bottle: Nutrition Supplement	designstudios	9	216	4	0	2
D3	Juice Bottle Label	Artsignz	8	203	2	5	1
D4	Labels	mihalymm	13	188	2	3	1
D5	Labels	mihalymm	13	181	2	5	1
D6	Soap Wrap Labels	mihalymm	13	169	2	4	2

For each column, identify the most appropriate data type—Text, Decimal number, Whole number, Time, and Percentage.

BE 5.9 (LO 4) `Data` With the provided data, use an ETL tool to perform the following:

1. Modify the data type for the CustomerId column from text to whole number. How many records report an error after this change?

2. Determine the highest number of rewards a customer earned.

3. Identify any incorrect data in the AppointmentDuration column.

BE 5.10 (LO 5) `Data` Your boss gives you a text file that contains sales information including amounts, discounts, and coupons. An excerpt is shown here:

InvoiceNo	SaleDate	Amount	Discount	Coupon	Customer
1203	1/6/2025	$ 621	0	25	23
1204	1/6/2025	$ 682	2	0	144
Cash	1/7/2025	$ 477	0	5	
1206	1/7/2025	$ 779	5	25	233
1207	1/8/2025	$ 742	5	0	17
Cash	1/8/2025	$ 452	2	0	
1208	1/8/2025	$ 233	0	10	101
1209	1/9/2025	$ 539	0	5	224
Cash	1/10/2025	$ 985	0	2	
Cash	1/10/2025	$ 320	0	0	
1210	1/10/2025	$ 398	5	0	301
1211	1/10/2025	$ 354	10	0	24
Cash	1/11/2025	$ 863	0	5	
1212	1/11/2025	$ 944	2	15	144

Based on a discussion with your boss, you put together the following data dictionary:

Name	Description
InvoiceNo	A unique code given to Credit sales for which an invoice is prepared. The label Cash is used for cash sales.
SaleDate	The date the sale occurred.
Amount	The dollar amount the customer owes before discounts and coupons.
Discount	The discount percentage given to the customer.
Coupon	A coupon with a dollar provided by the customer. It should be noted that a coupon can only be considered when no discount applies.
Customer	A customer's ID. For cash sales, this field is left blank.

List the table transformation patterns (patterns 11–14) that are relevant for this data set and explain how you would apply each.

BE 5.11 (LO 5) Your supervisor has asked you to understand sales and the discounts and coupons applied to them. They provided you with a spreadsheet for your analysis. Here is an excerpt of that spreadsheet:

SaleDate	Amount	Discount	Coupon	Approved
10/21/2025	$ 197	0	0	1
10/22/2025	$ 113	2	32	2
10/23/2025	$ 155	0	1	1
10/24/2025	$ 423	12	0	
10/25/2025	$ 88	10	0	2
10/26/2026	$ 250	3	45	
10/27/2025	$ 4,680	2	0	3
10/28/2025	$ 584	0	0	
10/29/2025	$ 997	1	1	1
10/30/2025	$ 258	2	10	1

1. Apply data preparation Pattern 11. The table is titled Amounts & Discounts. Propose a table name that is less ambiguous.

2. Apply data preparation pattern 12. Does the table have a primary key? If not, describe how you would create a primary key for this table.

BE 5.12 (LO 6) `Data` You are given two files. One file contains employee information and the other contains employee performance information. These are the data dictionaries for both tables.

Employee (Generic Employee Information)	
Name	**Description**
LastName	An employee's last name.
FirstName	An employee's first name.
Location	The city where the employee is located.
Gender	An employee's gender.

EmployeePerformance (Information About Employee Performance)	
Name	**Description**
LastName	An employee's last name.
FirstName	An employee's first name.
Level	An employee's level with 1 being the lowest and 7 being the highest.
2024Hours	The number of hours an employee worked in 2024.
RatePerHour	An employee's hourly rate.

Using data preparation pattern 15, combine both files to achieve the result shown here:

	ABC LastName	ABC FirstName	ABC Location	ABC Gender	123 Level	123 2024Hours	123 RateperHour
1	James	Kayne	Houston	Male	1	3,521	27
2	Lenk	Ivan	Texarcane	Male	3	3,811	35
3	Richards	Mick	Chicago	Male	5	2,901	39
4	Lozano	Juan	Boston	Male	4	3,477	37
5	David	Gail	Chicago	Female	7	3,420	40
6	Petroni	Ann	Houston	Female	1	1,709	27
7	Diamond	Shiela	Boston	Female	3	2,331	35
8	Sutherland	Yvonne	Chicago	Female	4	3,871	37
9	Clay	Marcus	Boston	Male	5	1,942	39
10	McCarthy	Molly	Chicago	Female	1	3,665	27

BE 5.13 (LO 6) `Data` HoneyBees is a high-end restaurant in Northern California. They just installed table-side point-of-sale (POS) systems on each of their 20 tables. They provide you the data for the first two days of using the new system. The data dictionary describes the data captured by the POS systems on both days.

HoneyBees Day 1 Data Dictionary	
Name	**Description**
Date	The day the sales transaction occurred.
Time	The time the sales transaction occurred.
Amount	The dollar amount of the sales transaction.
Tip	The tip received as a percentage.
Customer	Name of the customer—name on the credit card used.
Server	The name of the server (employee).
POS	The POS number—between 1 and 20—that was used to record the sales transaction.

| HoneyBees Day 2 Data Dictionary ||
Name	Description
Date	The day sales transaction occurred.
Time	The time the sales transaction occurred.
Amount	The dollar amount of the sales transaction.
Tip	The tip received as a percentage.
Server	The name of the server (employee).
Customer	Name of the customer—name on the credit card used.
POS	The POS number—between 1 and 20—that was used to record the sales transaction.

Combine the data in the two files for analysis purposes. The new file should have 46 transactions.

BE 5.14 (LO 6) **Managerial Accounting** You are evaluating a data set to determine if the data are valid. The data model for the data set is shown.

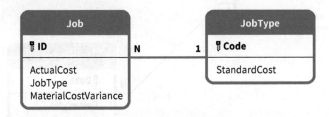

MaterialCostVariance = StandardCost − ActualCost

If negative, it's unfavorable variance.

Your team designs a number of validation rules, including the following inter-table validation rule:

```
IF MATERIALCOSTVARIANCE < 0
THEN RED
OTHERWISE GREEN
```

1. Specify the validation rule in terms that are easy for a business person to understand.

2. Discuss what might cause the formula to generate the value red.

BE 5.15 (LO 7) Tin Fos, a midsize information service company, received a data set from one of its clients. They are trying to design analytics reports, but the results are either empty or wrong. Evaluate the following data dictionary and data model to identify the two issues that are causing the problems:

Data Dictionary

| PurchaseOrder (Information About Orders Placed) ||
Name	Description
Amount	The dollar amount to be paid to the vendor.
Date	The date on which the order was placed.
ID	The purchase order's unique ID.
Vendor	The ID of the vendor from whom the goods were purchased.

| Delivery (Information About Goods Delivered) ||
Name	Description
Date	The date on which the goods were delivered.
DeliveryNo	The delivery's unique ID.
PurchaseOrder	The purchase order number associated with the delivery.

Vendor (Information About Vendors)	
Name	**Description**
Address	The vendor's address.
ID	The vendor's unique ID.
Name	The vendor's name.

Data Model:

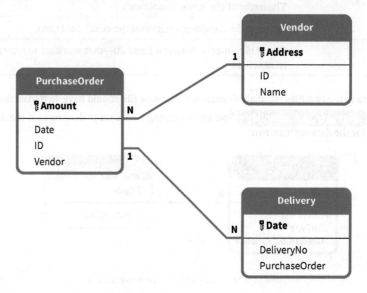

Relationships:

Manage Relationships

Active	From: Table (Column)	To: Table (Column)
☑	Delivery (DeliveryNo)	PurchaseOrder (ID)
☑	PurchaseOrder (Vendor)	Vendor (Name)

Exercises

EX 5.1 (LO 1, 2, 4, 5) Data **Basic Data Transformations** You are running your own accounting practice. Your clients are small to midsize companies that need assistance with transaction processing, bookkeeping, and financial reporting. Your newest client, Healthy Pets, is a pet supply retailer with 10 locations across the region. The company owner has provided you with customer loyalty data. Each customer can join the customer loyalty program to earn points for discounted purchases.

1. Remove duplicate customer entries (*Hint*: There are 11 records in the original table; the clean table should only include 9 records).

2. Replace values in the gender column so that records labeled "M" are replaced with Male, and records with "F" are replaced with Female.

3. Rename the Date column as DOB (date of birth of the customer).

4. Transform the CustInfo column into two single-valued columns. Label one column Name and the second column Street.

EX 5.2 (LO 1, 2, 4, 6) Data **Column and Model Transformations** You are an accountant for Bargain, which is a franchise that buys items all over North America, fixes and cleans them, and then sells them with a substantial markup. You have been asked to create an analytical database to understand purchases in anticipation of a business cycle review and efficiency project. Your supervisor provided you with three CSV files and a PDF file with the data dictionaries for each. Apply the appropriate data preparation patterns to the three files to create an analytical database that is consistent with the one shown here:

BargainVendors

	A^B_C ID	A^B_C Name	A^B_C Email
1	US1	Cohen, Sandra	scohen@vstores.com
2	US2	Gray, Sev	sev-gray@lbox.com
3	US3	Leroy, Shanice	sleroy@google.com
4	US4	Morales, Benita	bmor@hf.com
5	US5	Wang, CeCe	cece@cch.com
6	CAN1	Zhu, Jim	jzhu@outlook.com
7	CAN2	Coyle, Irene	Irene@coyle.com
8	CAN3	Dabrowski, Elizbieta	ElzDab@gmail.com
9	CAN4	King, Laura	LauraKing@fmh.com
10	CAN5	Jackson, Kiara	kiaraj@ncn.com

BargainPurchases

	$^{12}_3$ LineItemID	$^{12}_3$ OrderNo	Date	A^B_C Type	A^B_C Category	$^{12}_3$ Price	$^{12}_3$ Quantity	A^B_C Vendor
1	1	8992	1/2/2025	Rice Cooker	Kitchen	$ 69	2	US1
2	2	8993	1/2/2025	Phone	Electronics	$ 113	1	CAN3
3	3	8994	1/2/2025	Fryer	Kitchen	$ 181	1	CAN5
4	4	8894	1/2/2025	Stuffed Animal	Toys	$ 14	5	US2
5	5	8896	1/2/2025	TV	Electro	$ 79	1	CAN2
6	6	8897	1/3/2025	Stuffed Animal	Toys	$ 67	1	CAN1
7	7	8897	1/3/2025	Microwave	Kitchen	$ 205	1	US1
8	8	8898	1/3/2025	Headphone	Electronics	$ 45	1	US4
9	9	8898	1/3/2025	Jewelry	Toys	$ 13	2	CAN1
10	10	8899	1/3/2025	Printer	Electro	$ 199	2	CAN3

EX 5.3 (LO 1, 2, 3, 4, 5, 7) `Data` `Financial Accounting` **Extraction, Column and Table Transformations** As the accountant for El Azteco, a restaurant in Knoxville, TN, you are asked to prepare data for analysis of the restaurant's sales. The data dictionary details the data recorded for each sales transaction:

Name	Description
ID	A number that uniquely identifies the sale.
SaleDate	The date the sale occurred.
Amount	The dollar amount the customer owes before discounts and coupons.
Discount	A discount percentage given to the customer.
LoyaltyDiscount	A loyalty discount percentage given to the customer.
LolyaltyNumber	A unique number given to loyalty customers. Only customers enrolled in El Azteco's loyalty program can receive a loyalty discount.

All data recorded thus far is given to you in a CSV file. The data are also shown here. Notice that currently, all data are stored in one column. Further, Fernando, El Azteco's owner, informs you that the average sales amount thus far is $212.1.

A
SalesInformation
1,1/6/2025,97,0,0
2,1/6/2025,113,2,3,49
3,1/6/2025,55,0,1,23
4,1/7/2025,423,2,0
5,1/7/2025,88,0,0
6,1/7/2025,250,3,5,53
7,1/8/2025,680,2,0
8,1/8/2025,58,0,0
9,1/8/2025,99,1,1
10,1/8/2025,258,2,0

Examples of questions you need to answer using this data include:

- What is the actual amount paid for each sale?
- What is the average discount per sale?
- What is the total discount given to loyal customers?

Apply the necessary data preparation patterns to prepare an analytical database that makes it easy to answer these questions. Make sure to consider the patterns that help with detecting and correcting inconsistent and invalid data.

EX 5.4 (LO 4, 5, 7) **Managerial Accounting** **Apply Principles of Dimensional Modeling** MEQ is a medical equipment manufacturer that sells their products in the United States, Canada, and several European countries. All sales are conducted by salespeople. As MEQ's accountant, you are asked to perform an analysis of your entity's sales by salesperson. You will calculate key performance indicators (KPIs) for each salesperson as part of their annual performance review. Currently, all information is stored in a single table (named Sales) in a relational database. The data dictionary is given here:

Name	Description
Address	A customer's address.
Category	An item's category.
CCode	A code that uniquely identifies a customer.
CName	A customer's name.
Date	The day a sale occurred.
Description	An item's name.
DOH	The day a salesperson was hired.
InvoiceId	An ID that uniquely identifies a sale.
ItemCode	A code that uniquely identifies an item or product.
LiId	A unique ID given to each line item. A sale can have multiple line items. A line item specifies an item's ID and description, the quantity sold, and the price asked per unit.
PaymentTerms	The payment terms that apply to a customer.
Price	The price paid for a line item as part of a sale.
Quantity	The quantity sold of a line item as part of a sale.
QOH	Current quantity on hand for a product.
Region	The different regions in which a salesperson operates. Each region is assigned to exactly one salesperson.
SpCode	A code that uniquely identifies a salesperson.
SpName	A salesperson's name.

1. Apply the principles of dimensional modeling to the Sales table by creating a star or snowflake schema.

2. List the patterns you would use to detect and correct data issues, and explain why you would use each pattern.

EX 5.5 (LO 6) **Data** **Auditing** **Combine Tables and Identify Invalid Data** Assume you are a financial analyst working in the controller's group at a public company. You are asked to prepare an analytical database that shows the consolidated fixed assets for your entity. This analytical database will be used by the auditor to verify depreciation expenses and by your controller when they are preparing the financial statement footnotes. Your company has locations in the United States and Mexico. Each location's technology group provided you with a data file that contains data about fixed assets and depreciation. Apply the appropriate data preparation patterns to the data files to create an analytical database that helps verify the 2025 depreciation expenses and the accumulated depreciation expenses. You can assume that all data were transferred correctly.

EX 5.6 (LO 4) [Data] **Use Patterns to Detect and Correct Data Issues** Dunn Motors is a Honda dealership in Tallahassee, FL. They keep a list of all vehicles available for the salespeople in their used car department. A sample of the list and the table's data dictionary follows:

ID	ProductCode	Price
3044	Accord-Black-2017-*13,14,15*	12,350
3045	CRV-White-2019-*11,22,27*	16,990
3046	Accord-Green-2012-*4,7*	9,766
3047	Civic-White-2015-*4,5,6*	10,889
3048	Pilot-Red-2018-*1,7,11,18*	22,998
3049	Civic-Gray-2017-*2,6,9,20*	11,150
3050	Odyssey-White-2020-*4,7,11,12,17,*	24,551
3051	Ridgeline-Black-2012-*1,13*	12,990
3052	Pilot-White-2016-*7*	17,000
3053	Accord-Black-2018-*12,14,17*	13,500

Name	Description
ID	A car's unique ID.
ProductCode	A car's code that captures the following information: model, color, year, and list of extra features (between **). Each feature has an internal code between 1 and 30.
Price	A car's price (before negotiation).

1. Describe the table's data problems.
2. Address these issues by transforming the table.

EX 5.7 (LO 2, 5, 6) [Data] [Financial Accounting] **Prepare Data for Financial Analysis** Hikko is a technology firm headquartered in California with sales in three regions: United States, Europe, and Asia. It publishes the following report regarding its quarterly revenues:

Region	2022:Q1	2022:Q2	2022:Q3	2022:Q4	2023:Q1	2023:Q2	2023:Q3	2023:Q4	2024:Q1	2024:Q2	2024:Q3	2024:Q4
UNITED STATES	77,265,889	57,176,758	57,748,525	78,811,207	97,265,889	71,976,758	80,613,969	94,347,912	107,467,822	78,451,510	89,434,721	102,094,431
EUROPE	53,761,998	47,848,178	51,197,551	53,224,378	65,534,311	58,325,537	67,074,367	67,500,340	73,666,129	54,512,935	54,512,935	72,929,468
ASIA	32,188,799	27,038,591	31,094,380	32,832,575	31,777,112	23,197,292	23,661,238	32,094,883	29,778,112	22,035,803	24,239,383	28,289,206

You would like to compare Hikko's revenues across regions, quarters, and years. How would you reorganize the data to make such analysis easy?

EX 5.8 (LO 1, 4, 5, 6) [Data] [Managerial Accounting] **Prepare Data for Cost Analysis** Wilkinson, a luxury custom home builder in southern Nevada, uses job time cards to track labor costs for its different properties. They create weekly reports. Samples of the 2025 week 1 and week 2 reports are shown here:

WilkinsonWeek1

ID	Employee	JobNo	WeekNo	Thursday: 1/2/2025	Friday: 1/3/2025	Saturday: 1/4/2025
3405	1	ERF007	1	4	8	4
3406	1	ERF008	1	4		4
3407	13	ERF007	1	8	8	8
3408	25	IR68	1	4	8	0

WilkinsonWeek2

ID	Employee	JobNo	WeekNo	Monday: 1/6/2025	Tuesday: 1/7/2025	Wednesday: 1/8/2025	Thursday: 1/9/2025	Friday: 1/10/2025	Saturday: 1/11/2025
4608	25	ERF008	2	8	8	8	8	8	4
4609	13	ERF008	2	8	8	4			4
4610	13	IR68	2			4	8	8	
4611	1	IR101	2	6	8	10	8	8	4

How would you prepare Wilkinson's data for labor cost analysis purposes?

EX 5.9 (LO 4) Data **Detect Data Issues** HomePrinter is a distributor of laser and inkjet printers for the home office. You receive a data set that describes the different models they buy (and sell) and their January purchases. Profile the data set and identify any data issues.

EX 5.10 (LO 5) Data **Detect Data Issues** Know It All Group is a small accounting firm with 20 employees. They keep track of their employees' salaries, bonuses, and other information in a data file. Profile this data set and identify any data issues.

EX 5.11 (LO 6) Data **Create and Test Validation Rules** Vroomba manufactures and sells state-of-the art robot vacuums. All units sell for $279. Salespeople receive a large bonus if they sell more than 1,000 units in a single week. Salespeople can sell to a pre-approved list of customers, which are distributors, only. Every customer (distributor) has a unique name. They provide you with a sample of sales transactions for the week of January 6, 2025. What validation rule would you test? Are there any transactions that require further investigation?

EX 5.12 (LO 5) Data **Identify Inconsistent, Incomplete, or Invalid Data** TryIt is a new ride-sharing company. They believe their employees are the keys to their success. They keep track of a wide range of employee information in a custom cloud application. On January 1, 2025, they provide you with a sample of employee information. The data dictionary for the Driver table follows:

Name	Description
DriverNumber	A TryIt driver's unique number.
DateOfBirth	A driver's birthday.
State	The state in which the driver lives.
DateDriverLicense	The day a driver license was obtained by the driver.
AverageRating	The driver's average rating, with 1 being the worst possible rating and 5 being the best possible.
Customer	A six-digit unique code used to text a driver pickup information.

Profile this data set and identify any inconsistent, incomplete, or invalid data problems.

EX 5.13 (LO 1, 4) Data **Prepare Data for Analysis** Baking Sweetness is an industrial bakery in Singapore. They produce baked goods in large batches. For each batch they record a range of information. A sample of this information is provided in a data file. The data dictionary for the Batch table follows:

BATCH

Name	Description
ID	Uniquely identifies a batch.
Product	The product, a baked good, produced by the batch.
EstThrough	The estimated throughput time for the batch. How many minutes it should take to complete the batch.
ActThrough	The actual throughput time for the batch. How many minutes actually it takes to complete the batch.
EstQuantity	The estimated number of baked goods units that will be produced by the batch.
ActQuantity	The actual number of baked goods units produced by the batch.
Facility	Records which of the two facilities, A or B, produced the batch.
Supervisor	The employee who supervised the batch.

What changes would you make to the file before it is used for analysis?

Professional Application Case ToysRFun

ToysRFun is a fast-growing company in North Dakota that creates and ships customized stuffed animals to all 50 U.S. states. There are several options for customization, from customers submitting their own designs to sending the company a rough design idea that ToysRFun then develops and creates. While business is going well, the company's information system is a disaster and they are not able to do any analytics. The priority is to integrate their data into an analytical database. They hire your firm to help them.

PAC 5.1 Auditing: Identify Data Issues

Auditing You are given access to ToysRFun's vendors, purchases, and employees files. Samples of the three files appear here:

Vendors

Code	Name	Address
1	Discount store	4326 Lochmere Lane, Groton, CT, 06340
2	Lebron Jordan	1177 Gore Street, Houston, TX, 77027
3	Duffy Warehouse	4457 Lonely Oak Drive, Mobile, AL, 36603
4	Bob Dylan	3764 Courtright Street, Fargo, ND, 58102
5	Segher's Fabrics	2170 Metz Lane, Camden, NJ, 08102

Purchases

Number	Date	Amount	Employee
1	1/6/2025	$ 4,176	1
2	1/7/2025	$ 660	3
3	1/9/2025	$ 1,680	5
4	1/14/2025	$ 4,703	4
6	1/20/2025	$ 3,108	2
7	1/21/2025	$ 2,263	4
8	1/23/2025	$ 1,597	6
8	1/23/2025	$ 1,597	6
9	1/30/2025	$ 3,433	2
10	1/31/2025	$ 1,833	4

Employees

Code	Name	Address
1	Joan Waddington	Phillps Circle 12, Fargo, ND, 58102
2	Matt Anthony	1012 Catherine Drive, St. Thomas, ND, 58276
3	Elizabeth Petroni	2490 Findley Avenue, Hope, ND, 58046
4	Andrea Dylan	3764 Courtright Street, Fargo, ND, 58102
5	Jimmy John	4000 Findley Avenue, Minot, ND, 58701

Using the data preparation patterns, review the sample data and identify at least three issues. Where applicable, specify which pattern you applied to detect and correct an issue.

PAC 5.2 Financial Accounting: Determine and Analyze Accounts Receivable

Data **Financial Accounting** ToysRFun allows their customers to pay in installments. In the current system, sales orders and payments are recorded in two separate files. The SalesOrders file records the amount the customer owes ToysRFun and the payments that have been received. The CashReceipts file records all payments received. Samples of both files are shown here:

SalesOrders

OrderNo	Date	Amount	Payments
1	1/6/2025	$ 838.46	1
2	1/7/2025	$ 100.03	2
3	1/9/2025	$ 245.67	3,10
4	1/13/2025	$ 3,632.16	
5	1/15/2025	$ 386.90	5
6	1/20/2025	$ 753.15	4
7	1/20/2025	$ 611.00	7,9,11
8	1/23/2025	$ 63.00	
9	1/25/2025	$ 1,496.72	
10	1/28/2025	$ 194.80	11

CashReceipts

CashReceiptNo	Date	Amount	Type
1	1/6/2025	$ 838.46	Cash
2	1/7/2025	$ 100.3	Credit Card
3	1/9/2025	$ 150	Check
4	1/20/2025	$ 350	Credit Card
5	1/24/2025	$ 386.9	Cash
6	1/27/2025	$ 200	Check
7	1/27/2025	$ 500	Check
8	1/30/2025	$ 403.15	Check
9	1/30/2025	$ 200	Check
10	1/31/2025	$ 95.67	Check
11	1/31/2025	$ 194.8	Check

1. Identify and explain the primary issue in the data set.
2. Describe how you would reorganize the data to enable the calculation of accounts receivable.

PAC 5.3 Managerial Accounting: Analyze Costs

Data **Managerial Accounting** Cost analysis is extremely important for ToysRFun. In addition to producing the stuffed animals and providing standard shipping, they also offer a range of other services, such as express shipping, packing, and design. In fact, any service requested by a customer will be considered by ToysRFun. When the company outsources a service, such as express shipping, the customer simply pays the amount charged to ToysRFun. ToysRFun has a standard markup for everything produced in-house, the stuffed animals, designs, and packing.

No	Price:100	StandardShipping:0	ExpressShipping:0	Packing:25	Design:50
1010	700	38	0	50	0
1011	280	0	154	125	225
1012	1,590	50	0	0	0
1013	906	57	0	25	0
1014	142	49	0	250	150
1015	1,728	44	0	125	0
1016	664	0	252	35	0
1017	208	66	0	35	0
1018	778	60	0	0	0
1019	296	62	0	10	0
1020	800	75	0	0	0

The sample data file shows how they currently record their cost and markup information. For example, for Order # 1010:

- The cost to make the products sold is $350. The price they charge is $700. As indicated by the column header, the markup on stuffed animals is 100%.
- There is no markup for shipping or express shipping.
- The markup for packing is 25%. The packing cost for Order # 1010 is $40. There is a 25% markup ($10), and the customer pays $50 ($40 + $10).
- The overall cost for Order 1010 is $350 (stuffed animals) + $38 (standard shipping) + $40 (packing) = $428. The markup for the same order is $350 (stuffed animals) + $10 (packing) = $360. The total price to be paid by the customer is $788.

ToysRFun would like to use their data to answer questions such as:

- What is the total revenue generated?
- What is the overall cost structure of orders based on the services offered?
- How do additional services affect the overall profit margin?

How would you restructure the data to make it easier to answer these questions through analysis?

PAC 5.4 Tax Accounting: Validate Sales Tax Amounts

Tax Accounting Currently, ToysRFun's salespeople are responsible for creating and sending orders to customers. All salespeople have access to the Excel file that contains the sales tax rates for each state. They use that information to manually determine the sales tax of an order and enter it in the accounting system.

SalesTaxRate

State	SalesTaxRate
Connecticut	6.35
Delaware	N/A
Hawaii	4.17
Kentucky	6
Maryland	6
Michigan	6
Rhode Island	7

At the end of each week, ToysRFun's accounting system generates a list of all orders called Sales Orders. As ToysRFun's accountant, you must collect sales taxes and remit them to applicable states. You must check whether the sales tax amounts are accurate. A sample with 10 orders from the sales orders file is shown next.

SalesOrder

OrderNo	Amount	SalesTax	State
1	$ 791	$ 47.46	KY
2	$ 88	$ 12.03	RI
3	$ 231	$ 14.67	CT
4	$ 3,488	$ 144.16	RI
5	$ 365	$ 21.90	MD
6	$ 723	$ 30.15	HI
7	$ 611	$ 0.00	DE
8	$ 55	$ 8.00	MD
9	$ 1,412	$ 84.72	MI
10	$ 187	$ 7.80	HI

It would help if you could combine the information in both tables to automatically calculate the sales tax per order and compare the tax information by state. Are there any data issues that would prevent this? List the patterns you used to identify the issues.

Analysis: Information Modeling

After planning the project and completing the data preparation, you are probably excited to finally explore the data and generate insights. While the data may be ready for analysis, there is still a missing piece—the information necessary to perform the analysis. For example, the data selected and prepared for analysis might include a set of transactions, but without knowing the total revenue or profit generated, they cannot be analyzed to determine which products are profitable.

There are two important information modeling tasks to complete before data exploration. First, you must understand what information is required for analysis and what data are needed to produce that information. You did this in the planning stage when you developed a strategy to select the best data and analysis to answer accounting questions. The second task is identifying the specific measures you want to use for analysis based on the prepared data set, and then writing the code that generates this information.

Information modeling is a process. This chapter will help you develop the skills to do it successfully by offering a menu of patterns for common coding structures and for identifying information used in accounting analytics.

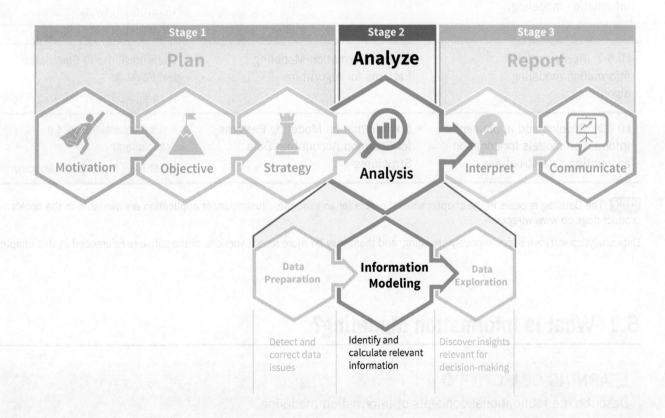

After earning his accounting degree, Dan started working as a tax consultant for one of the Big Four public accounting firms, which is where he fell in love with data and data analytics. More recently, he moved to a multinational telecommunications corporation where he works as a data analyst.

As a data analyst, I must be versatile. I process raw data sets from multiple sources and am heavily involved in ETL (Extract-Transform-Load). I also explore data to generate insights for stakeholders across multiple departments and develop dashboards. **Continuously facing new challenges is what I really like about my job.** Two days ago, I worked on processing unstructured data (text), yesterday I coded a new algorithm, and today I am working on a dashboard that presents an interrelated set of KPIs.

While I spend most of my time on ETL, I think **information modeling is the heart of data analytics.** It involves coding the calculations, testing whether they are correct, and making sure the information necessary for the different business cases is available. **This is where my accounting degree pays off, as I can understand the business context.**

Chapter Roadmap

LEARNING OBJECTIVES	TOPICS	APPLY IT
LO 6.1 Describe the foundational concepts of information modeling.	• The Information Modeling Process • A Structured Approach	**Complete a Star Schema** (Example: Accounting Information Systems and Financial Accounting)
LO 6.2 Apply common information modeling algorithms.	• Seven Information Modeling Patterns for Algorithms	**Use Algorithms to Calculate Net Revenue** (Example: Financial Accounting)
LO 6.3 Develop and implement information models for common accounting data structures.	• Six Information Modeling Patterns for Common Accounting Data Structures	**Answer Questions with a Star Schema** (Example: Managerial Accounting)

Data The Data tag appears in the chapter when the data for an example, illustration, or application are available in the book's product page on www.wiley.com.

Data analytics software is continuously changing, and there may be more recent versions of the software referenced in this chapter.

6.1 What Is Information Modeling?

LEARNING OBJECTIVE ❶
Describe the foundational concepts of information modeling.

Information modeling is the process of generating additional knowledge from data that is relevant for analysis purposes. Next, we examine how this is performed in an accounting context.

The Information Modeling Process

In information modeling, data are the input. They are the raw figures and facts. **Algorithms** are sets of instructions that transform the data into **information**, which is the output of additional knowledge gained from the data (**Illustration 6.1**).

ILLUSTRATION 6.1 The Information Modeling Process

Information Modeling

Data	→	Algorithm	→	Information
Input		Transforms		Output

Algorithms are the link between the input of facts and the output of useful information. Keep in mind that data (input) for one application can also be information (output) for another application. One example is how financial statements are information (output) for financial statement preparers, but they are data (input) for financial analysts.

Algorithms are intrinsic to the work of accountants. These instructions calculate depreciation, cost, financial ratios, and more. They range from simple to complex and can be coded with a host of languages, including Excel functions, Power BI's Data Analysis Expressions (DAX) language, and the Python programming language. In this chapter, we will rely on general descriptions of the algorithms.

The first seven columns in **Illustration 6.2** are data fields. They are factual descriptions about sales transactions, such as a transaction's identification number and the date it occurred. In accounting, these descriptions can range from the social security numbers of employees to the names of customers who have made payments. The last two columns in Illustration 6.2 contain information that was calculated with an algorithm.

ILLUSTRATION 6.2 Data, Information, and Algorithms for Sales Transactions

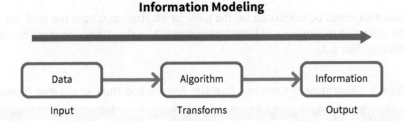

IF the NetAmount of a transaction is smaller than $1,000,
THEN the TransactionSize is S (small),
ELSE
   IF the NetAmount of a transaction is at least $1,000 but smaller than $2,500,
   THEN the TransactionSize is M (medium),
   ELSE the transaction size is L (large).

Algorithm for TransactionSize

Amount—Discount

Algorithm for NetAmount

ID	Date	Product	Amount	Discount	Customer	SalesPerson	NetAmount	TransactionSize
1	1/3/2025	Dishwasher	$ 825	0	Jeremy	Ed	$ 825	S
2	1/3/2025	Refrigerator	$ 2,500	100	Jane	Juana	$ 2,400	M
3	1/3/2025	Refrigerator	$ 2,500	250	Molly	Hakeem	$ 2,250	M
4	1/4/2025	Cooktop	$ 1,250	75	Whitney	Ed	$ 1,175	M
5	1/4/2025	Dishwasher	$ 900	125	Zuzu	Juana	$ 775	S
6	1/4/2025	Cooktop	$ 1,500	250	Carmen	Cindy	$ 1,250	M
7	1/4/2025	Oven	$ 1,500	150	Ben	Hakeem	$ 1,350	M
8	1/4/2025	Cooktop	$ 1,000	50	Lebron	Juana	$ 950	S
9	1/4/2025	Cooktop	$ 900	0	Trisha	Hakeem	$ 900	S
10	1/5/2025	Dishwasher	$ 500	50	Xuomin	Cindy	$ 450	S

Data   Information

There are two types of information fields:

- In Illustration 6.2, both NetAmount and TransactionSize are a **calculated column** in the SalesTransactions table because a value is calculated for each cell in the columns. They are integral parts of the table.

- The second type of information field is a **measure**, which is an aggregate, or total, that can be used in reports, and thus for analytical purposes. Measures are created by algorithms, but they are not integral parts of a table.

Two measures that could be calculated for the table in Illustration 6.2 are the total net amount generated by sales and the number of large transactions. The algorithms for these measures are shown in **Illustration 6.3**.

ILLUSTRATION 6.3 Algorithms to Calculate Total Net Amount and Number of Large Transactions

Measure	Algorithm
TotalNetAmount	Sum of all the values in the NetAmount column
NumberOfLargeTransactions	Count the number of cells in the TransactionSize column that have the value "L"

Measures are at the center of data analytics. They can be calculated and then sliced in many ways during data exploration. Data analytics software, such as Power BI and Tableau, make it easy to create and slice them.

A Structured Approach

Performing data analysis requires determining the numbers to analyze (these are the measures) and how to analyze them (these are the **dimensions**, or the fields that can slice them). This chapter describes a structured approach to developing accounting information models by defining dimensions of *who*, *what*, and *when* in transactions to help make accounting sense of data. A measure such as total revenue can be broken down by the following dimensions:

- Customer (*who?*).
- Product category (*what?*).
- Year (*when?*).

Dimensions like these, and the measures they can slice, are typically configured in a star schema. (As you learned earlier in this course, star schemas are the preferred data structures for data analysis.) Let's use an example to help illustrate this. **Data** KLUB is a retail store located in Interlochen, MI:

KLUB

- KLUB's owner uses business connections in different retail spaces to negotiate bulk purchases at heavily discounted prices and signs no-return policies with all vendors to further lower the prices.

- The company sells the items at prices lower than its competitors, but still with a substantial profit margin.

- The owner handles all negotiations, contracts, and deliveries with vendors.

- Salespeople are contractors who are paid a commission on sold goods.

KLUB's website shows currently available items, but sales are exclusively made over the phone. The company regularly sends marketing emails to a list of 100,000 potential customers. When customers want to buy something, they email the company and a salesperson contacts them.

After six months in business, the owner is curious where the company stands from a sales-and-profit perspective and hires you to provide some insights. You are given the company's available data. The data set is clean and structured as star schemas.

From Data Model to Information Model

Illustration 6.4 shows the two star schemas for the KLUB data set. The information model has not been created yet.

ILLUSTRATION 6.4 KLUB's Sales and Purchases Star Schemas

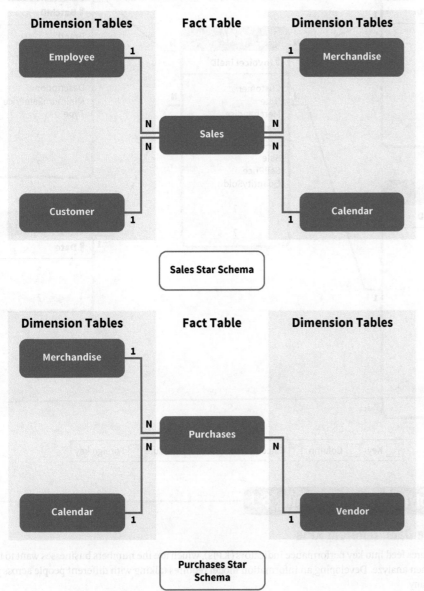

A star schema is a data model. A **data model** shows the structure of a data set. It shows the concepts being described, the tables, and the fields used to describe the concepts. An **information model** extends the data model because it also includes calculated columns and measures. It has additional information that is calculated from the data set, which can be used for analysis purposes.

Illustration 6.5 shows the extended Sales star schema with field names such as Brand, Country, and Gender. In this illustration, the fact table describes sales transactions. The fields with question marks indicate the information model's calculated columns and measures that will be developed in this chapter.

Create Measures and Dimensions

There are two goals for building an information model for a star schema. The first is to create a rich set of measures for the fact table. Recall that in a star schema, fact tables typically hold

ILLUSTRATION 6.5 Extended Sales Star Schema

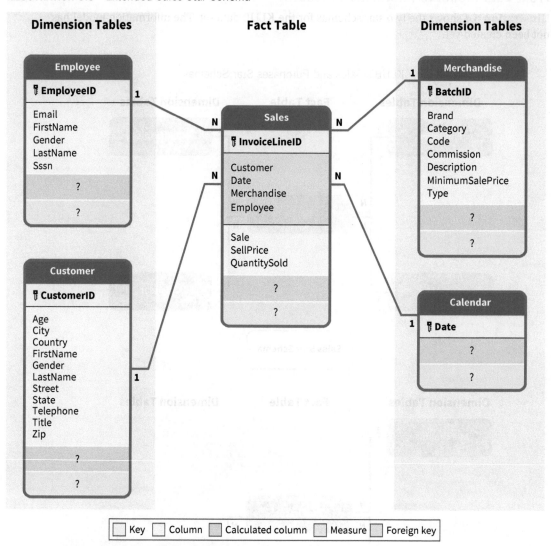

| Key | Column | Calculated column | Measure | Foreign key |

Applying Critical Thinking 6.1

Same Data, Different KPIs

Measures feed into key performance indicators (KPIs), which are the numbers businesses want to track and then analyze. Developing an information model requires talking with different people across your company:

- People who are impacted by the analysis all likely want their own KPIs included. Consider sales data—the marketing manager might be interested in analyzing churn rates, while the accountant might be interested in analyzing accounts receivable and bad debt expenses. The same data is being analyzed, but different KPIs must be applied (**Stakeholders**).

- One KPI might mean different things to different people. What if you are asked to analyze profit margin? Is it the gross profit margin or the net profit margin? Make sure you understand the algorithm (**Knowledge**)!

business transactions. For example, in Illustration 6.2 the NetAmount column was created and then used to create the TotalNetAmount measure, which is an aggregate. The calculated fields in the fact table are often used as building blocks for the measures.

The second goal for building an information model is a rich set of dimensions that can break down, or slice, measures in many ways. Helpful dimensions in Illustration 6.5 include Gender, State, Country, Brand, Type, and Category. In the KLUB example, it may be useful to compare profit across product brands, types, categories, and countries. More dimensions can be created through calculated columns. An example of a dimension we will develop with calculated columns for KLUB's Sales star is AgeCategory, which differentiates between junior and senior customers.

Dimension tables can describe specific characteristics of transactions: who participated, what was involved, and when they occurred[1]:

- A dimension table that describes the agents involved in the transactions is a **who table**. Internal agents are the employees who participate in the transaction. External agents, such as customers and vendors, are parties external to the organization involved in the accounting transactions. A **participates relationship** links agents to specific transactions.

- A dimension table that describes the resources that were given up or acquired as part of a transaction is a **what table**. In the KLUB example, purchases increase merchandise, while sales decrease merchandise. A **flows relationship** links resources to specific transactions.

- A dimension table that describes when a transaction occurs is a **when table**. Such tables often take the form of a Calendar table. An **occurs relationship** links the calendar to specific transactions.

Illustration 6.6 is KLUB's Sales star schema labeled with who, what, and when dimension tables and their relationships.

ILLUSTRATION 6.6 Sales Star with Who, What, and When Dimension Tables

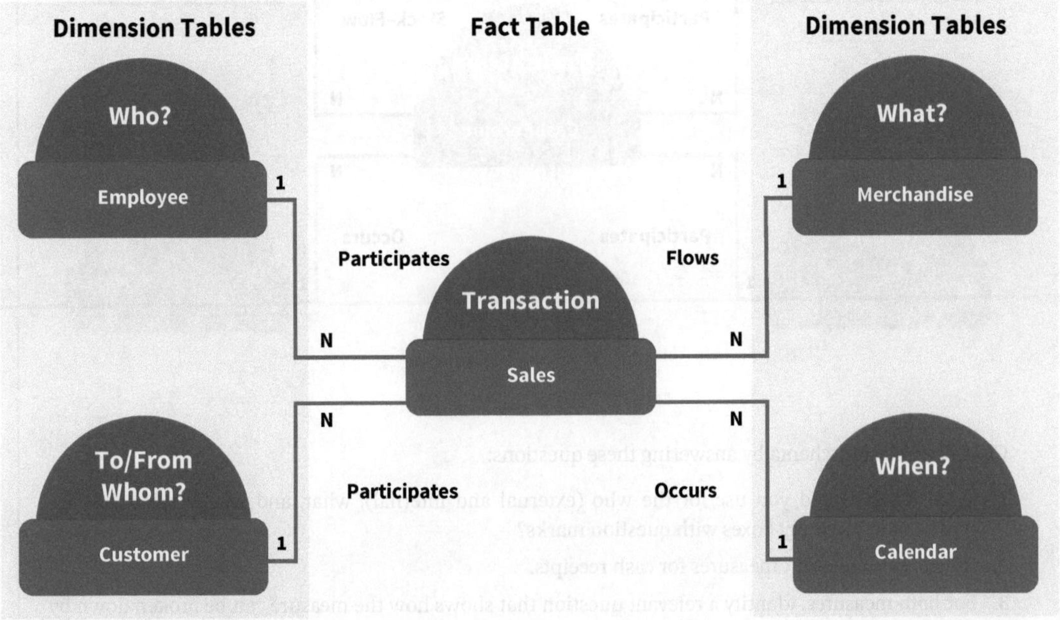

Stars like the one shown in Illustration 6.6 are designed for accounting analytics. They make it easy to answer transaction questions that include who, what, and when characteristics. For example, an accountant at KLUB could ask: How much revenue (the measure) was generated by selling garden items (what) to customers living in Texas (who) during the 2025 spring season (when)?

When developing stars like this, it is critical to determine:

- The accounting measures to break down.
- The who, what, and when dimensions for analysis purposes.

This chapter explains how to do both. Information modeling is the heart of data analytics. Rich, robust information models lead to rich and robust analyses. Creating measures and dimensions

---

[1]Who-what-when dimensions of accounting transactions were first recognized in McCarthy, William E. (1982). The REA accounting model: A generalized framework for accounting systems in a shared data environment. *Accounting Review*: 554–578.

that are relevant for analysis requires coding skills. But once these measures and dimensions are in place, software, such as Power BI or Tableau, makes it easy to do the analysis. Whatever software and language you use, invest some time into learning how to code. It will pay off!

APPLY IT 6.1

Complete a Star Schema

Accounting Information Systems **Financial Accounting** Abroad is a store in the King of Prussia mall near Philadelphia, PA, that sells stylish suitcases and bags. Sales are spectacular, but management believes data analytics are the key for more growth. The company is in the process of building their application and the owner asks you for help.

The illustration shows an empty star schema for cash receipts transactions, or payments made by a customer.

Draft Cash Receipt Star Schema

Dimension Tables	Fact Table	Dimension Tables
Who? · ? · 1	Participates ··· Stock-Flow	What? · ? · 1
	N — Transaction — N	
	CashReceipt	
	N N	
To/From Whom? · ? · 1	Participates ··· Occurs	When? · ? · 1

Complete the star schema by answering these questions:

1. What labels would you use for the who (external and internal), what, and when tables that are represented by empty boxes with question marks?

2. Indicate two relevant measures for cash receipts.

3. For both measures, identify a relevant question that shows how the measure can be broken down by the information in the who, what, and when tables.

SOLUTION
(*Note*: Solutions will vary. What follows are examples.)

1. Who Table External: Customer (Who makes the payments?)
   Who Table Internal: Employee/Cashier (Who is handling the payments by the customers?)
   What Table: Account (A payment from a customer increases an account's balance. An account can be cash, a bank, etc.)
   When Table: Calendar (The calendar contains information regarding the date the payment was made.)

2. Measure 1: Total number of cash receipt transactions.
   Measure 2: Total amount of dollars received.

3. Measure 1: How does the number of cash receipt transactions (measure) in the first quarter of 2025 (when) compare across employees (who)?
   Measure 2: What are the monthly trends (when) for the amounts (measure) received for the different accounts (what), and are there any fluctuations?

6.2 Which Patterns Implement Information Modeling Algorithms?

LEARNING OBJECTIVE ❷

Apply common information modeling algorithms.

This section presents seven implementation patterns that each represent a different type of algorithm. The first four create calculated columns, while the final three patterns create measures. (**Data** How To 6.1 at the end of the chapter walks through how to create calculated columns and measures with Power BI.) The details of each pattern are illustrated with the KLUB example and data set. **Data** Download the available data set to create the information model as you work through the chapter.

How To

Information Modeling Pattern 1: Within-Table Numeric Calculation

The within-table numeric calculation pattern creates a new field (a calculated column) from one or more numeric columns, or fields in the same table. Basic arithmetic operations of addition, subtraction, multiplication, and division can do this. A typical example is determining the dollar total for an order line or invoice line by multiplying price and quantity. **Illustration 6.7**(A) shows how to create a Revenue field in KLUB's sales table with such a calculation. Illustration 6.7(B) shows the result: the Revenue field that is part of the Sales table. Later, we will use the Revenue field as a building block for the TotalRevenue measure.

ILLUSTRATION 6.7 Within-Table Numeric Calculation to Determine Revenue

(A)

Table: Sales	
Calculated Column	**Algorithm**
Revenue	SellPrice × QuantitySold

Result of Algorithm

SellPrice × QuantitySold

(B)

InvoiceLineID	Sale	Date	Merchandise	Customer	Employee	SellPrice	QuantitySold	Revenue
1	1	1/5/25	8	223	7	60	12	720
2	1	1/5/25	9	223	7	20	4	80
3	1	1/5/25	16	223	7	320	1	320
4	2	1/6/25	19	80,968	635	9	40	360
5	2	1/6/25	20	80,968	635	20	40	800

Information Modeling Pattern 2: Within-Table Text Calculation

The second implementation pattern also involves creating a new calculated column from one or more fields in the same table. However, the information in the new column is created from text fields. For example, different pieces of location information could be linked, or concatenated, into an address so it can be read by a map service such as Bing Maps or Google Maps.

Illustration 6.8(A) shows an algorithm that creates an address field in KLUB's Customer table. (The ampersand symbol represents concatenation.) The new field in the Customer table in Illustration 6.8(B) is the result of applying this calculation.

ILLUSTRATION 6.8 Within-Table Text Calculation to Determine Customer Address

(A)

Table: Customer	
Calculated Column	**Algorithm**
Address	Street & "," & City & "," & State & "," & Zip & "," & Country

Street + City + State + Zip + Country

Result of Algorithm

(B)

CustomerID	Street	City	State	Zip	Country	Address
1	3462 MacLaren Street	Ottawa	ON	K1P 5M7	CA	3462 MacLaren Street,Ottawa,ON,K1P 5M7,CA
2	2608 Laurel Lane	Terminal	TX	79703	US	2608 Laurel Lane,Terminal,TX,79703,US
3	4679 Byrd Lane	Albuquerque	NM	87102	US	4679 Byrd Lane,Albuquerque,NM,87102,US
4	975 Armbrester Drive	Malibu	CA	90265	US	975 Armbrester Drive,Malibu,CA,90265,US
5	3251 St. John Street	Bruno	SK	S4P 3Y2	CA	3251 St. John Street,Bruno,SK,S4P 3Y2,CA

Once implemented, the Address field can be used to create maps.

Using similar formulas, KLUB's information model can be extended with Name fields for both the Customer and Vendor tables (**Illustration 6.9**). If you are following along building KLUB's information model, make sure to create both columns.

ILLUSTRATION 6.9 Within-Table Text Calculations to Determine Customer and Vendor Names

Table: Customer	
Calculated Column	**Algorithm**
Name	LastName & " , " & FirstName

Table: Vendor	
Calculated Column	**Algorithm**
Name	LastName & " , " & FirstName

Information Modeling Pattern 3: Within-Table Classification

The number of classification algorithms that can be applied to a data set is, in essence, unlimited. You may be familiar with airlines' tiered loyalty programs classifications (such as silver, gold, and platinum) where an algorithm determines your status based on miles flown or money spent. The statistical technique of data binning is another example, where numbers are grouped into smaller numbers of "bins," such as age groups. In fact, classifications are omnipresent in accounting, such as classifying accounts receivable by age to determine bad debt expense.

The third implementation pattern is used when classifications are determined based on data that are part of the same table. Most classification algorithms rely on Boolean logic, so it is necessary to understand Boolean operators like AND, OR, NOT, and IF functions and how to create them.

With both code (A) and a flowchart (B), **Illustration 6.10** shows how an IF function can split customers into two categories: junior (up to 40 years old), and senior (older than 40). Illustration 6.10(C) is the result of applying this algorithm. The new AgeCategory field is now part of the Customer table.

Once implemented, we can use the AgeCategory field for analysis. **Illustration 6.11** shows the proportional number of KLUB's junior and senior customers, respectively.

ILLUSTRATION 6.10 Within-Table Classification Using an IF Function to Determine Customer Age Category

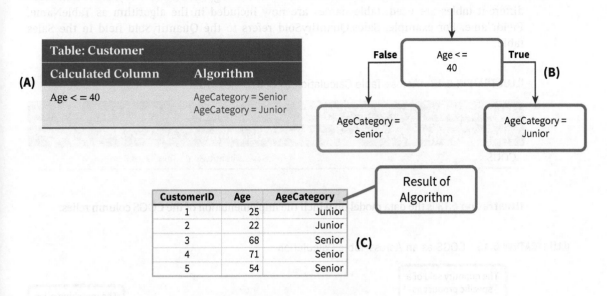

ILLUSTRATION 6.11 Pie Chart Created with AgeCategory Field

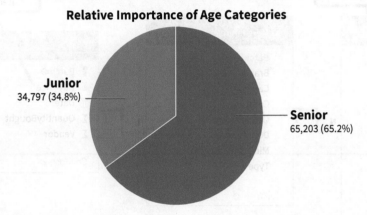

Information Modeling Pattern 4: Across-Table Calculation

The calculations for this pattern are like the first three—a new column is created from existing data using arithmetic, text calculation, or classification. But this pattern is different from the earlier patterns because data from different tables are used to create a new column. This means the tables must be linked. How this is accomplished depends on the software being used. Excel uses a VLOOKUP, in a relational database this is done with a join, and in DAX it is accomplished with the RELATED function. Regardless of the software, there are multiple questions to consider when linking tables:

- Are there properly defined relationships between the tables?
- What is the nature of the relationship, and what type of join should be considered?
- What cardinalities apply to the relationship: 1-1, 1-N, N-1, or N-N? For example, calculations become more complex when navigating a 1-N relationship.

Let's use an example of an across-table calculation that illustrates some of these issues. Recall that KLUB buys products in batches:

- The buy price, or cost per unit, in a batch is recorded in the Purchase table.
- The revenue of sold items is determined by multiplying the SellPrice and QuantitySold fields in the Sales table, which results in the Revenue field (which is a calculated column) discussed earlier.
- The matching cost is determined by multiplying the BuyPrice in the Purchase table with QuantitySold in the Sales table.

Illustration 6.12 is an algorithm that calculates cost of goods sold (COGS). Since data from different tables are used, table names are now included in the algorithm as TableName. FieldName. For example, Sales.QuantitySold refers to the QuantitySold field in the Sales table.

ILLUSTRATION 6.12   Across-Table Calculation to Determine COGS

Table: Sales	
Calculated Column	**Algorithm**
COGS	Sales.QuantitySold × Purchases.BuyPrice

Illustration 6.13 is the data model on which the implementation of the COGS column relies.

ILLUSTRATION 6.13   COGS as an Across-Table Calculation

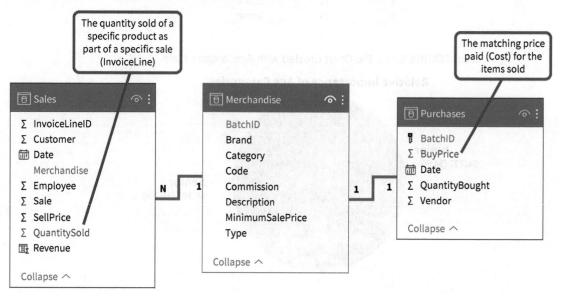

The values in the COGS column in the Sales table are calculated by multiplying the QuantitySold field in the Sales table by the corresponding BuyPrice field in the Purchase table. Corresponding values are determined by following the relationships, which is known as the navigation path. Here are some characteristics of the navigation process for the execution of this formula:

- A green line indicates the navigation path in Illustration 6.13. The Merchandise field in the Sales table is linked to the BatchID field in the Merchandise table based on matching values. A similar relationship is created between the BatchID field in the Merchandise table and the BatchID field in the Purchases table. If KLUB sells a hairdryer to a customer, the navigation path will reveal which batch it belongs to and thus from whom they bought it, when, and for what price (cost).

- The navigation path has 1-1 cardinalities. There is one merchandise item (Merchandise) per invoice line (Sales), and one purchase (Purchase) for a merchandise item (Merchandise).

- There are no join issues. There is exactly one merchandise for each invoice line, and there is exactly one purchase for each merchandise.

Once implemented, the COGS field can be used for analysis. The clustered column chart created with the COGS field in **Illustration 6.14** can be used by KLUB management to compare revenue and COGS across three product categories: electronics, garden, and office.

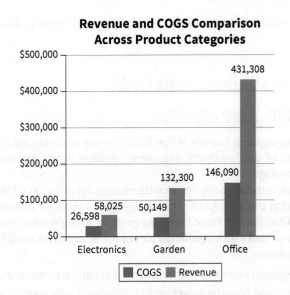

Revenue and COGS Comparison Across Product Categories

ILLUSTRATION 6.14 Column Chart Created with COGS and Revenue Fields

Applying the first four implementation patterns has extended KLUB's Sales star schema (**Illustration 6.15**) with the following calculated columns:

- Address (Customer)
- AgeCategory (Customer)
- COGS (Sales)

- Name (Customer)
- Revenue (Sales)

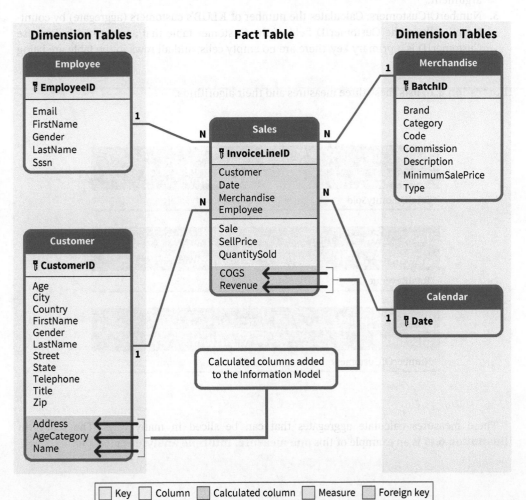

ILLUSTRATION 6.15 KLUB's Information Model Extended with Calculated Columns

In addition, a Name calculated field was added to the Vendor table in KLUB's Purchases star schema.

Information Modeling Pattern 5: Single-Column Aggregation

The single-column aggregation pattern is the first to focus on measures, which, as you have learned, are the heart of data analytics. Measures calculate aggregates that can be sliced, or broken down, in many ways.

In its simplest form, a measure applies a mathematical operation to *all* the values of a single column. Operations that can be applied include aggregate functions such as SUM, AVERAGE, COUNT, MIN, and MAX. Each of these functions generate a single value. For most applications, single-column measures make up a significant part of the information model. A few more things about aggregation functions:

- Except for aggregation functions that count, most require a numeric data type.
- Be sure to understand how the aggregate functions deal with specific values, such as null, as this can differ depending on the implementation platform.

Three measures can be created using single-column aggregations for KLUB's data set:

1. TotalQuantitySold: Calculates the total number of units (aggregate) sold by KLUB by using the SUM function to add all values in the QuantitySold field in the Sales table.
2. TotalRevenue: Calculates the total revenue (aggregate) generated by KLUB thus far. Notice that the SUM aggregation function uses the calculated field Revenue as an argument.
3. NumberOfCustomers: Calculates the number of KLUB's customers (aggregate) by counting all cells in the CustomerID field of the Customer table that are not blank. Because CustomerID is a primary key, there are no empty cells, and all rows in the table are being counted.

Illustration 6.16 lists these three measures and their algorithms.

ILLUSTRATION 6.16 Single-Measure Aggregation to Create TotalQuantitySold, TotalRevenue, and NumberOfCustomers Measures

Table: Sales	
Measure	**Algorithm**
TotalQuantitySold	SUM(QuantitySold)

Table: Sales	
Measure	**Algorithm**
TotalRevenue	SUM(Revenue)

Table: Customer	
Measure	**Algorithm**
NumberOfCustomers	COUNT(CustomerID)

These measures calculate aggregates that can be sliced in many ways. The report in **Illustration 6.17** is an example of this **one measure, multiple analyses principle**.

ILLUSTRATION 6.17 The One Measure, Multiple Analyses Principle

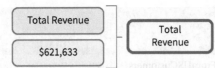

Name	Revenue ▾
Frazier, Theodore	$ 27,500
Morris, Bonnie	$ 11,573
Moncrief, Richard	$ 11,400
Fisher, Rebecca	$ 11,145
Fennell, Mary	$ 10,975
Beaver, Daniel	$ 10,200
Vaughn, Anthony	$ 9,960
Zebrowski, Connie	$ 9,565
Uren, Harold	$ 9,385
Newby, Annie	$ 8,750
Deaton, Andrew	$ 8,515
Henderson, Teresa	$ 7,785
Engel, Dexter	$ 6,825
Nevius, Scott	$ 6,090
Black, Candice	$ 5,884
Flynn, Casey	$ 5,700

State	Country	Revenue ▾
ON	CA	$ 132,867
BC	CA	$ 58,258
AB	CA	$ 57,254
CA	US	$ 41,466
FL	US	$ 39,572
QC	CA	$ 33,404
NY	US	$ 18,049
TX	US	$ 17,959
PA	US	$ 16,999
GA	US	$ 13,647
NJ	US	$ 12,218
WI	US	$ 11,941
MA	US	$ 11,358
MS	US	$ 11,305
MI	US	$ 9,891
SK	CA	$ 8,665

Category	Revenue ▾
Office	$ 431,308
Garden	$ 132,300
Electronics	$ 58,025

Total Revenue
Sliced by: Customer, State, and (Product) Category

It breaks revenue down by customer, state, and product category. There are many more types of analysis that could be performed with TotalRevenue, including a breakdown by the AgeCategory field we calculated (which is a classification).

Applying Critical Thinking 6.2

Evaluate Algorithms

Implementing an algorithm (or writing a program) is not an exact science. There are often multiple appropriate solutions, but also some bad ones. The most important criterion for a good program is that the output is correct. But it should also be fast, and this is especially true for large data sets. An algorithm should use the least amount of memory possible and be readable (**Alternatives**).

Information Modeling Pattern 6: Filtered Aggregation

It is often necessary to analyze aggregates based on filtered data sets. One example is analyzing the total revenue generated by sales to U.S. customers. There are different ways to implement filtered aggregations. The method often depends on the software being used.

- In Excel, use the SUMIF, COUNTIF, AVERAGEIF, etc., functions.
- In SQL, use the WHERE clause. (**Data** How To **6.2** demonstrates how to implement a filtered aggregation with SQL.)
- In Power BI, create filters in the Filters pane, or use the CALCULATE function.

Illustration 6.18(A) is an example of a filtered aggregation that determines the total revenue generated by KLUB from sales to its U.S. customers. Illustration 6.18(B) recreates the report from Illustration 6.17 using the total revenue from U.S. customers measure.

How To

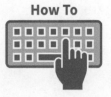

ILLUSTRATION 6.18 Filtered Aggregation to Calculate Total Revenue from U.S. Customers

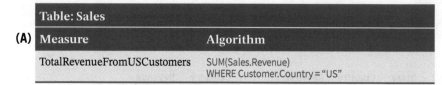

Table: Sales

(A)

Measure	Algorithm
TotalRevenueFromUSCustomers	SUM(Sales.Revenue) WHERE Customer.Country = "US"

Total Revenue
from U.S. Customers

$325,125

Total Revenue
from U.S. Customers

(B)

Name	Total Revenue from U.S. Customers ▼
Adams, Ramon	$ 1,160
Alfonso, Henry	$ 4,965
Archer, Greg	$ 2,150
Armstrong, Rita	$ 300
Arnold, Charles	$ 710
Baker, Nancy	$ 1,030
Ball, Martha	$ 320
Banks, Ingrid	$ 1,465
Barnhart, Richard	$ 885
Batts, Andrea	$ 1,680
Beaver, Daniel	$ 10,200
Bentley, Earnest	$ 1,750
Bernard, Caleb	$ 1,418
Blocher, Harold	$ 990
Bloss, John	$ 828

State	Country	Total Revenue from U.S. Customers ▼
AK	US	$ 5,148
AL	US	$ 750
AR	US	$ 6,310
AZ	US	$ 4,050
CA	US	$ 41,466
CO	US	$ 2,160
CT	US	$ 980
DC	US	$ 6,023
DE	US	$ 4,550
FL	US	$ 39,572
GA	US	$ 13,647
HI	US	$ 113
ID	US	$ 1,520
IL	US	$ 4,715
IN	US	$ 5,217

Category	Total Revenue from U.S. Customers ▼
Electronics	$ 34,553
Garden	$ 80,012
Office	$ 210,560

Total Revenue
from U.S. Customers
Sliced by: Customer,
State, and (Product)
Category

Information Modeling Pattern 7: Measure Hierarchies

A **measure hierarchy** is used when a new, more complex measure is created using existing measures. In fact, complex problems can sometimes be solved by dividing the problem into smaller problems, then combining the different solutions. Measure hierarchies are especially useful when calculating ratios and benchmarks.

Illustration 6.19(A) visualizes a measure hierarchy. The first measure, TotalRevenueFrom CanadianCustomers, determines the total revenue generated by KLUB's customers in Canada. The second measure, TotalRevenueFromUSCustomers, determines the total revenue generated by KLUB's U.S. customers. The third measure reuses the first two measures to calculate a ratio that compares Canadian revenue with U.S. revenue, using the latter as the benchmark.

Illustration 6.19(B) shows a possible implementation for the view hierarchy. The slash symbol represents division. Finally, Illustration 6.19(C) shows one way to use the Canadian/ USRevenueRatio measure. The red line, a ratio with value 1, indicates the equal contribution to revenue by both countries. With this analysis, management at KLUB can see that while Canada generates slightly more revenue for office products, most of the revenue for Electronics and Garden products are generated in the United States.

ILLUSTRATION 6.19 Measure Hierarchy for Canadian/U.S. Revenue Ratio: Visualization and Implementation[2]

Measure Hierarchy

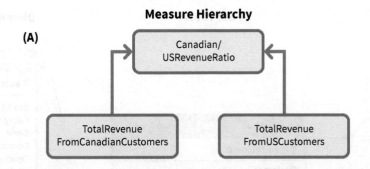

Measure Hierarchy to Calculate the Canadian/USRevenueRatio Measure

(B)

Table: Sales	
Measures	**Algorithm**
TotalRevenueFromCanadianCustomers	SUM(Revenue) WHERE Customer.Country = "CA"
TotalRevenueFromUSCustomers	SUM(Revenue) WHERE Customer.Country = "US"
Canadian/USRevenueRatio	TotalRevenueFromCanadianCustomers/TotalRevenueFromUSCustomers

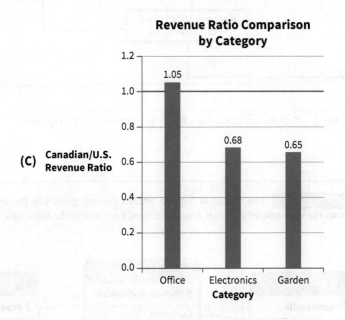

After creating the NumberOfCustomers, TotalQuantitySold, TotalRevenue, TotalRevenue-FromUSCustomers, TotalRevenueFromCanadianCustomers, and Canadian/USRevenueRatio measures, KLUB's information model is growing (**Illustration 6.20**). Remember, the richer your information model is, the richer your analysis will be!

---

[2]The TotalRevenueFromUSCustomers measure is the same as the measure in Illustration 6.18.

ILLUSTRATION 6.20   KLUB's Information Model Extended with Measures

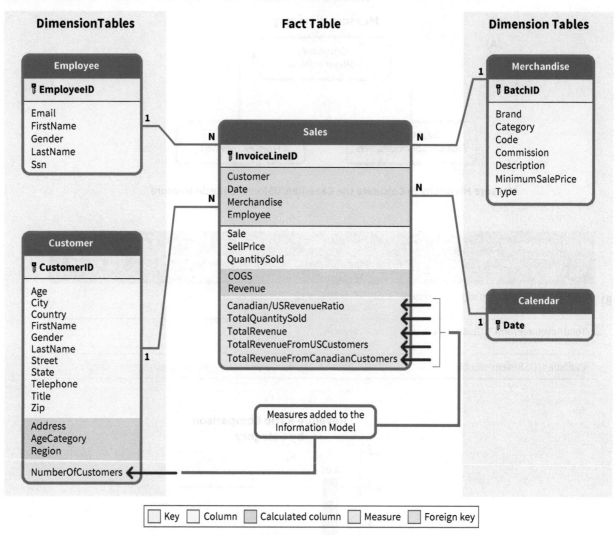

APPLY IT 6.2

Use Algorithms
to Calculate
Net Revenue

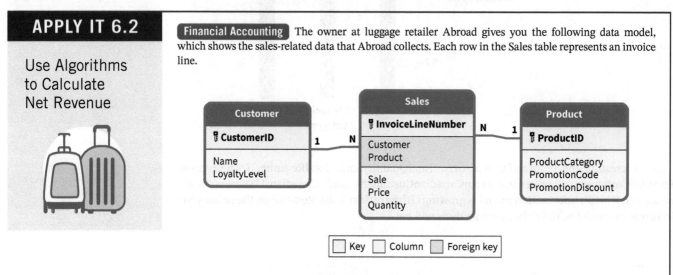

Financial Accounting   The owner at luggage retailer Abroad gives you the following data model, which shows the sales-related data that Abroad collects. Each row in the Sales table represents an invoice line.

Some products have a promotion code and a promotion discount. For products with no promotion code, the discount is 0. Abroad has three loyalty levels: Fish, Eagle, and Lion. The discounts given to each of the loyalty levels is shown in the table.

Level	Discount
Fish	0
Eagle	3
Lion	5

Abroad's owner asks you to calculate the total net revenue generated thus far. When calculating the total net revenue, be sure to consider both the loyalty and promotion discounts. Assume that both discounts are recorded as percentages, e.g., 5%. For each of the following, indicate which pattern(s) you applied, then show your algorithms:

1. Loyalty discount
2. Net revenue
3. Total net revenue

SOLUTION

1. Pattern 2
Algorithm (calculated column): LoyaltyDiscount =
IF Level = "Fish" THEN 0, ELSE
IF Level = "Eagle" THEN 3, ELSE 5

2. Pattern 3 and Pattern 4
Algorithm (calculated column): NetRevenue =
IF Customer.LoyaltyDiscount > 0 and Product.PromotionDiscount > 0
THEN
Sales.Price × Sales.Quantity × (1 − ((Customer.LoyaltyDiscount/100) +
(Product.PromotionDiscount/100)))
ELSE
IF Customer.LoyaltyDiscount = 0 and Product.PromotionDiscount > 0
THEN Sales.Price × Sales.Quantity × (1 − Product.PromotionDiscount/100)
ELSE
IF Customer.LoyaltyDiscount > 0 and Product.PromotionDiscount = 0
THEN Sales.Price × Sales.Quantity × (1 − Customer.LoyaltyDiscount/100)
ELSE Sales.Price × Sales.Quantity

3. Pattern 5
Algorithm (measure): Total Net Revenue = SUM(Amount)

6.3 Which Patterns Help Develop and Implement Accounting Information Models?

LEARNING OBJECTIVE ❸
Develop and implement information models for common accounting data structures.

Earlier in the course, you learned the importance of applying dimensional modeling to accounting data. Organizing data properly in specific ways makes analysis easier. Information modeling, or identifying and implementing measures and dimensions, also benefits from having similiar structures in place. The previous section covered seven common patterns for implementing calculated columns and measures. Here, we present six more patterns that help identify measures to analyze who, what, and when characteristics of accounting transactions.

Information Modeling Pattern 8: How Many

Tables usually describe concepts like customers, vendors, sales, and products. The next pattern creates a measure that counts the number of rows, or instances, of a concept within a table.

This pattern can count resources, transactions, and agents, which means it can be used for both fact (transactions) and dimension (resources and agents) tables.

The example in **Illustration 6.21** determines the number of rows in the Merchandise table, which reveals how many batches KLUB has purchased.

ILLUSTRATION 6.21 The How Many Pattern

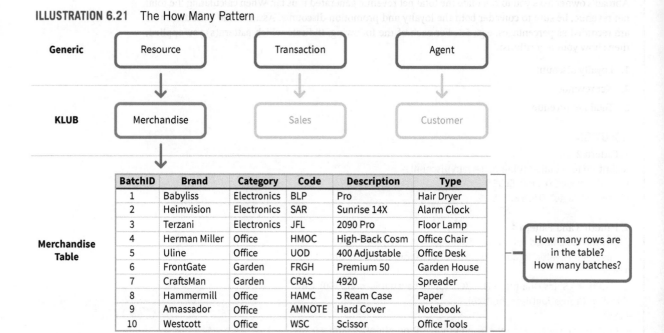

In the KLUB example, we can create "how many" measures for:

- Resources: Merchandise.
- Transactions: Sales and purchases.
- Agents: Customer, vendor, and employee.

Information Model

These measures can be broken down further. Using the KLUB data set, we could explore questions like the following by applying these measures to transactions, who, and what tables:

- Transactions: How many sales have occurred, and how many purchases?
- Agents (Who): How many customers does KLUB have, how many employees, and how many vendors do they work with? It is also possible to drill down further to reveal how many customers or vendors KLUB has per country, per state, or per province.
- Resources (What): How many products does KLUB have? It is then possible to find the number of products per brand, per product type, and per product category.

When answering questions about agents and resources, we can analyze relationships between dimensions in the same table, such as the number of customers for a state or province, or the number of product types per category. **Illustration 6.22** shows how some dimensions in the Merchandise table are related. Remember the N-1 cardinalities for the relationship between Batch ID and Brand:

- 1: One brand is specified for a batch.
- N: There can be many batches of the same brand.

The algorithms in **Illustration 6.23** show that implementing measures to answer questions about the number of transactions, agents (who), and resources (what) is straightforward. Implementation is performed with a single-column aggregation—Count. A similar formula was used for the NumberOfCustomers measure earlier in this chapter.

ILLUSTRATION 6.22 Relationships Between the Merchandise Dimensions

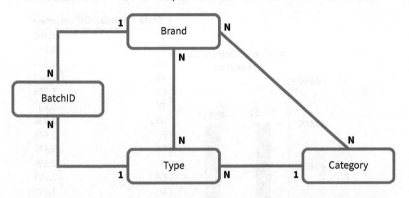

ILLUSTRATION 6.23 How Many Measures for KLUB's Information Model

Table: Vendor	
Measure	**Algorithm**
NumberOfVendors	COUNT(VendorID)

Table: Sales	
Measure	**Algorithm**
NumberOfSales	COUNT(InvoiceLineID)

Table: Purchase	
Measure	**Algorithm**
NumberOfPurchases	COUNT(BatchID)

Table: Employee	
Measure	**Algorithm**
NumberOfEmployees	COUNT(EmployeeID)

Table: Merchandise	
Measure	**Algorithm**
NumberOfBatches	COUNT(BatchID)

Once in place, filters can be applied to the measures. For example, tables that describe agents (who) often contain location information, so it is also possible to determine the number of KLUB customers living in California, or any other location. On the other hand, tables that describe resources (what) often contain information about categories that can be used as filters. For example, it is possible to determine how many electronic batches KLUB bought.

Analysis

The NumberOfCustomers measure can determine how potential customers are spread out across countries by provinces in Canada and states in the United States (**Illustration 6.24**). Clicking a bar in the column chart filters the state/provinces in the table, so management at KLUB could select the Canadian provinces only.

ILLUSTRATION 6.24 Analysis with the Number of Customers Measure

Number of Customers by Location

State	NumberOfCustomers
ON	21,290
BC	8,641
QC	7,664
AB	7,445
CA	5,286
TX	3,837
NY	2,938
FL	2,606
SK	2,440
IL	2,389
PA	2,127
MI	1,979
OH	1,880
NJ	1,474
MA	1,472
GA	1,380
NC	1,375
VA	1,172
MO	1,098
WA	1,068
WI	1,064
IN	1,034
MN	1,031
MD	1,013

Chart: Number of Customers by Location — United States: 50,151; CA: 49,849 (Country)

Information Modeling Pattern 9: Participates | Transaction—Who

The participates relationship describes *who* is involved in a transaction (**Illustration 6.25**).

ILLUSTRATION 6.25 The Participates Relationship

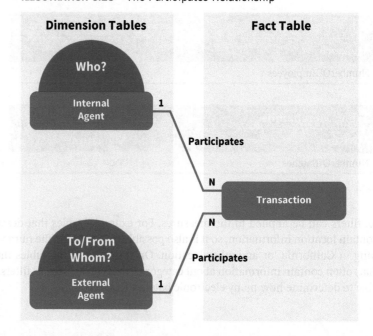

In KLUB's data model, there are three participates relationships:

- From Sales to Customer (the customer is an external agent).
- From Sales to Employee (the employee is an internal agent).
- From Purchases to Vendor (the vendor is an external agent).

There are also other types of participates relationships that do not appear in the KLUB data set:

- CashReceipts to Customer.
- CashReceipts to Employee.
- CashDisbursements to Vendor.
- CashDisbursements to Employee.

Because the information captured by these relationships is similar, the same types of analyses apply to all of them.

Information Model

Following the principles of dimensional modeling, measures must be developed for the sales transactions and broken down by agent dimensions, such as customer tables:

- What are relevant measures for transactions that can be broken down by agents? **Illustration 6.26**(A) shows that the number of transactions is a key measure for the participates relationship information model. For example, how many flights (transaction) has an airline customer taken (agent)?
- What dimensions can be defined for agents? Analysis can be performed for individual customers, but typically customers are grouped in a variety of ways for analysis purposes, including by location, membership group, or performance category.

ILLUSTRATION 6.26   Information Model Pattern for the Participates Relationship

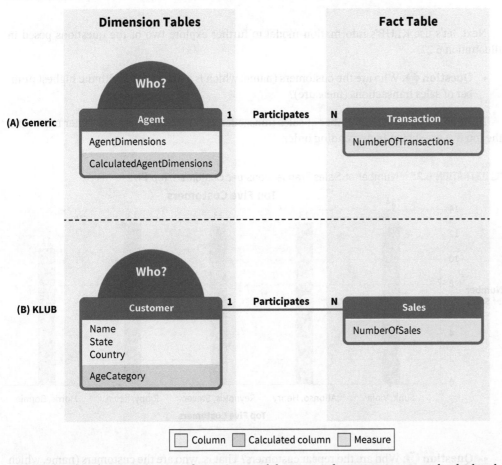

To implement the participates information model, create relevant measures and calculated columns in the Transaction (fact) and Agent (dimension) tables. The actual measures and calculated fields will depend on a business's specific needs. Illustration 6.26(B) applies the participates model to KLUB's Customer–Sales relationship. The additional calculated columns and measures create a richer information model and, therefore, a richer analysis. The algorithms to implement the NumberOfSales measure and the AgeCategory calculated field in Illustration 6.26 were discussed earlier in this chapter.

Analysis

KLUB could use the participates relationship to answer several questions using data analysis (**Illustration 6.27**).

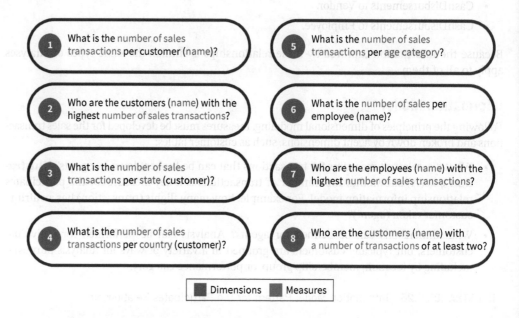

Next, let's use KLUB's information model to further explore two of the questions posed in Illustration 6.27.

- **Question ❷:** Who are the customers (name, which is a dimension) with the highest number of sales transactions (measure)?

In **Illustration 6.28** the number of sales transactions is broken down by customer name, and the top five are shown in descending order.

ILLUSTRATION 6.28 Number of Sales Transactions per Customer: Top Five

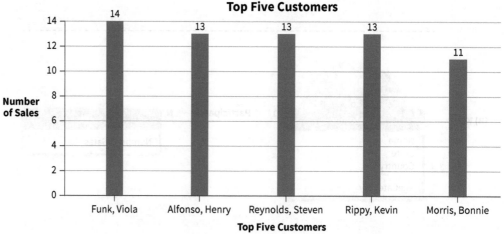

- **Question ❽:** Who are the repeat customers? That is, who are the customers (name, which is a dimension) with a number of transactions (measure) of at least two?

Illustration 6.29 is a partial list of customers who have bought at least twice from KLUB.

Name	NumberOfSales
Funk, Viola	14
Alfonso, Henry	13
Reynolds, Steven	13
Rippy, Kevin	13
Morris, Bonnie	11
Moore, Steven	9
Williams, Mary	9
Zebrowski, Connie	9
Garza, Jeffrey	8
Uren, Harold	8
Barnhart, Richard	7
Edens, Blaine	7
Jenkins, Toni	7
Ward, Jenny	7
Younce, Stacey	7

ILLUSTRATION 6.29 List of Repeat Customers

Information Modeling Pattern 10: Flows | Transaction—What

The flows relationship describes *what* is involved in a transaction, such as goods and services (**Illustration 6.30**). A transaction results in either an increase or a decrease of the resources.

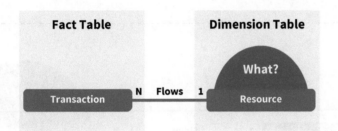

ILLUSTRATION 6.30 The Flows Relationship

In KLUB's data model, there are two flows relationships:

- From Sales to Merchandise.
- From Purchases to Merchandise.

There are also other types of flows relationships that do not appear in the KLUB data set:

- Cash Receipts to Cash.
- Cash Disbursements to Cash.

Because the information captured by these relationships is similar, the same types of analysis apply to all of them.

Information Model

The first step is to develop measures for the transactions, such as sales, that can be broken down by dimensions that are part of the Resource tables, such as merchandise. For flows relationships, consider measures that summarize the physical and monetary flows:

- The physical flows describe *how many*. How many units were bought? How many units were sold?
- The monetary flows describe *how much*. What is the value of the units sold, and for how much have they been sold?

In addition, we can use the number of transactions and number of resources measures discussed earlier.

Illustration 6.31(A) shows the generic information model for flows relationships. Panel (B) in the same illustration applies this pattern to KLUB's Sale–Merchandise flows relationship, which results in four measures: NumberOfSales, TotalCOGS, TotalQuantitySold, and TotalRevenue.

ILLUSTRATION 6.31 Information Model Pattern for the Flows Relationship

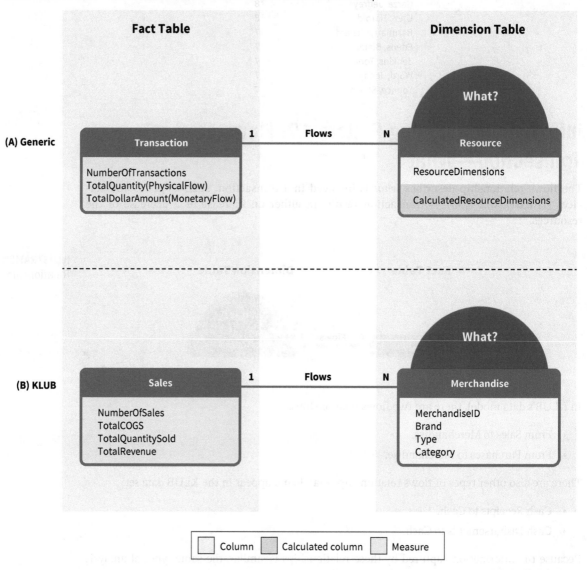

Implementing the flows information model involves creating measures in the Transaction table and creating Resource dimensions through algorithms. All dimensions in Illustration 6.31 are given; that is, additional calculations are unnecessary. How to implement the NumberOfSales, TotalQuantitySold, and TotalRevenue measures was discussed earlier. TotalCOGS, a measure in the Sales table, is a single-column aggregation that sums all the values in the COGS column—SUM(COGS).

There are two additional flows-related measures that should be added to the information model (**Illustration 6.32**). The TotalQuantityBought measure uses the single-column aggregation pattern to determine the total units bought by KLUB, and it is added to the Purchases table. The TotalQuantityOfPrintersSold measure uses the filtered aggregation pattern to determine the total quantity of printers sold.

Table: Purchases	
Measure	**Algorithm**
TotalQuantityBought	SUM(QuantityBought)

Table: Sales	
Measure	**Algorithm**
TotalQuantityOfPrintersSold	SUM(QuantitySold) WHERE Type = "Printer"

ILLUSTRATION 6.32 Additional Measures for KLUB's Flows Information Model

Analysis

In the KLUB flows information model, the TotalQuantityBought measure in the Purchases table and the TotalQuantitySold measure in the Sales table summarize the physical flows, while the TotalCost measure in the Purchases table and the TotalRevenue and TotalCOGS measures in the Sales table summarize the monetary flows. Brand, Type, and Category are resource dimensions.

What questions can the data described by a flows relationship answer? **Illustration 6.33** presents some that can be analyzed using KLUB's flows information model.

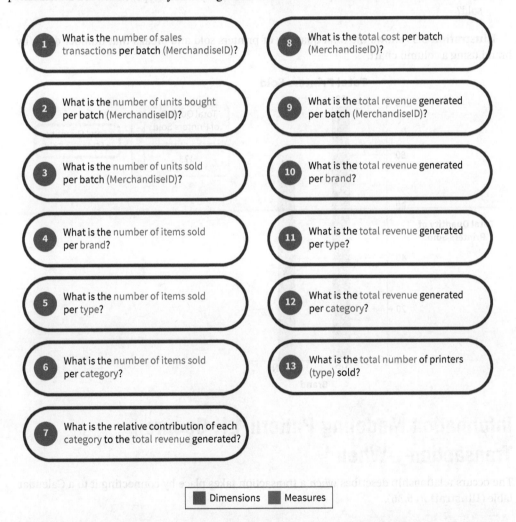

1. What is the number of sales transactions per batch (MerchandiseID)?

2. What is the number of units bought per batch (MerchandiseID)?

3. What is the number of units sold per batch (MerchandiseID)?

4. What is the number of items sold per brand?

5. What is the number of items sold per type?

6. What is the number of items sold per category?

7. What is the relative contribution of each category to the total revenue generated?

8. What is the total cost per batch (MerchandiseID)?

9. What is the total revenue generated per batch (MerchandiseID)?

10. What is the total revenue generated per brand?

11. What is the total revenue generated per type?

12. What is the total revenue generated per category?

13. What is the total number of printers (type) sold?

■ Dimensions ■ Measures

ILLUSTRATION 6.33 Answering Questions with the Flows Relationship

Next, use KLUB's information model to explore two of the questions posed in this illustration.

- **Question ⑦**: What is the relative contribution of each category (dimension) to the TotalRevenue (measure)?

In **Illustration 6.34**, the TotalRevenue measure in the Sales table is broken down by the category dimension in the Merchandise table. Pie chart slices represent the relative importance of each category. The pie chart shows that KLUB generates most of its revenue from its office products.

ILLUSTRATION 6.34 Relative
Contribution of Categories to
Total Revenue

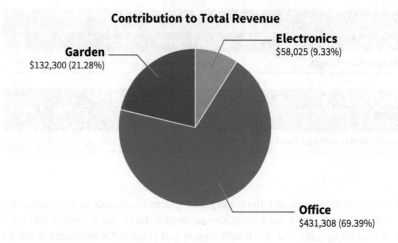

Now, explore another question.

- **Question 13:** What is the total number (measure) of printers (type, which is a dimension) sold?

Illustration 6.35 shows the total quantity of printers sold and breaks that number down by brand using a column chart.

ILLUSTRATION 6.35 Total
Number of Printers Sold

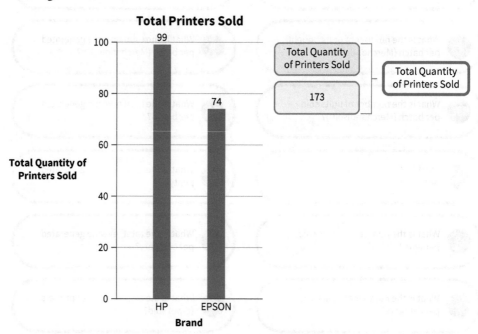

Information Modeling Pattern 11: Occurs | Transaction—When

The occurs relationship describes *when* a transaction takes place by connecting it to a Calendar table (**Illustration 6.36**).

ILLUSTRATION 6.36 The
Occurs Relationship

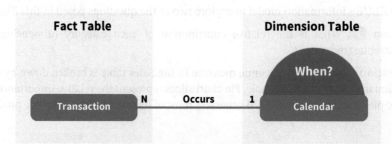

There are two occurs relationships in KLUB's data model:

- Sales to Calendar.
- Purchases to Calendar.

There are other occurs relationships that do not appear in the KLUB data set:

- CashReceipts to Calendar.
- CashDisbursements to Calendar.

Because the information captured by these relationships is similar, the same types of analyses apply to all of them.

Information Model

Following the principles of dimensional modeling, measures must be developed for the transactions (such as Sales) and broken down by dimensions that are part of the Calendar table:

- The measures developed earlier for the Transaction tables, such as NumberOfSales, can also be used here.
- In addition to dates, a Calendar table contains a series of time units as dimensions for analysis, including weekday, week number, month, quarter, and year. Because there are only six months of data for KLUB, year dimensions are not relevant.

Illustration 6.37(A) shows the generic information model for occurs relationships. Panel (B) of the same illustration applies this pattern to KLUB's Sales–Calendar occurs relationship. NumberOfSales can be analyzed by weekday, month, and quarter.

A calendar table contains all dates between a start date and an end date. Software such as Power BI makes it easy to create a Calendar table. Once that is done, time unit dimensions such as month, quarter, and year can be added and used for analysis. Creating these dimensions is usually easy. An example of this is Excel's year function, which returns the year component of a date.

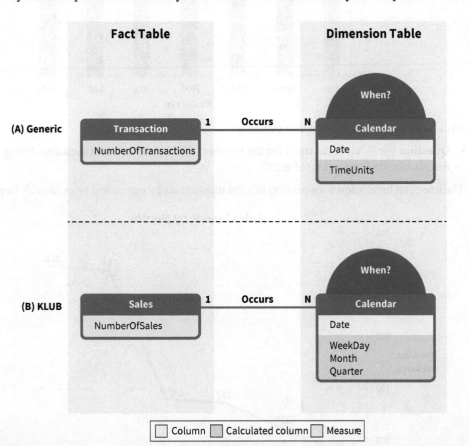

ILLUSTRATION 6.37
Information Model Pattern for the Occurs Relationship

Analysis

Illustration 6.38 presents some example questions that can be analyzed using KLUB's occurs relationships.

ILLUSTRATION 6.38 Answering Questions with the Occurs Relationship

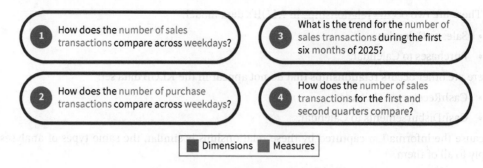

Once again, we can use the information model to explore two of these questions. **Illustration 6.39** explores the first question with KLUB's occurs information model.

- **Question ❶:** How does the number of sales transactions (measure) compare across weekdays (dimension)?

The column chart breaks down the number of sales transactions by weekday.

ILLUSTRATION 6.39 Comparing Number of Sales Transactions Across Weekdays

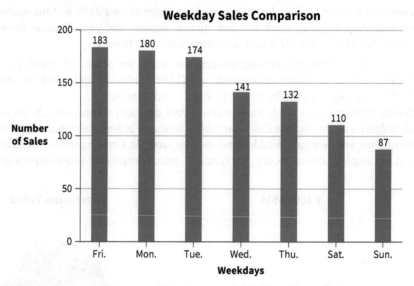

Illustration 6.40 explores another question:

- **Question ❸:** What is the trend for the number of sales transactions (measure) during the first six months (dimension) of 2025?

The line chart breaks down the number of sales transactions by month and helps identify trends.

ILLUSTRATION 6.40 Identifying Trends for the Number of Sales Transactions Across Months

Information Modeling Pattern 12: Who-What-When Star Schema

While patterns 9, 10, and 11 analyze the who, what, and when dimensions of accounting transactions, this pattern integrates these three relationships (**Illustration 6.41**).

ILLUSTRATION 6.41 The Who-What-When Star Schema Pattern

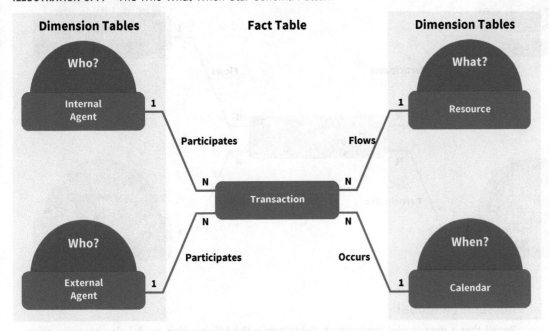

KLUB's data model integrates two instances of the who-what-when pattern. The first is for the acquisition of items, which are purchases (**Illustration 6.42**). There is no employee information to record for purchases because the owner of the company oversees the acquisition process.

ILLUSTRATION 6.42 The Purchases Who-What-When Star Schema Pattern

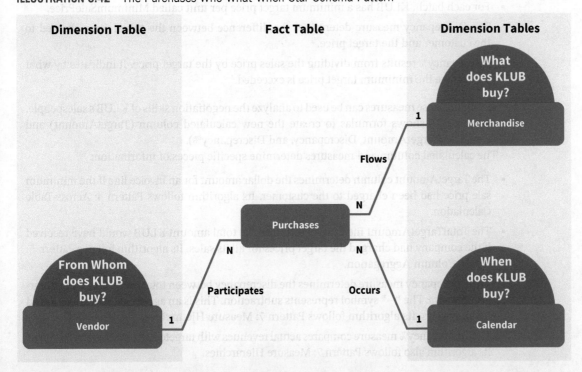

The second is for selling the items, or sales (**Illustration 6.43**).

ILLUSTRATION 6.43 The Sales Who-What-When Star Schema Pattern

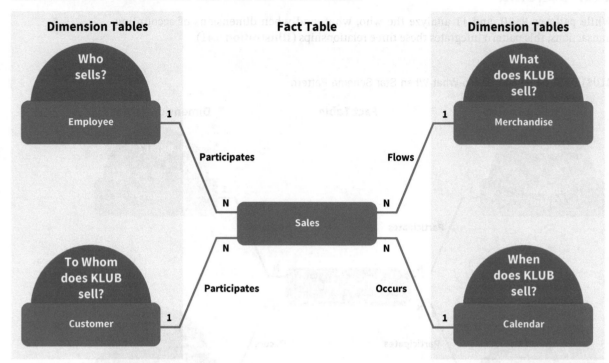

Information Model

Recall that a data model contains all fields, while the information model also contains calculated columns and measures created for analysis purposes. Information models can be extended depending on the business' specific needs. **Illustration 6.44** is the data model and information model for KLUB's Sales star schema.

To create a richer information model for KLUB, we added an extra calculated column called TargetAmount, as well as the three extra measures of TotalTargetAmount, Discrepancy, and Discrepancy% to the Sales star schema:

- For each batch, KLUB has a minimum target price per unit called MinimumSalePrice.
- The Discrepancy measure determines the difference between the actual price charged to the customer and the target price.
- Discrepancy% results from dividing the sales price by the target price. It indicates by what percentage the minimum target price is exceeded.

Among others, these measures can be used to analyze the negotiation skills of KLUB's salespeople. **Illustration 6.45** shows formulas to create the new calculated column (TargetAmount) and measures (TotalTargetAmount, Discrepancy, and Discrepancy%).

The calculated column and measures determine specific pieces of information:

- The TargetAmount column determines the dollar amount for an invoice line if the minimum sale price had been charged to the customer. Its algorithm follows Pattern 4: Across-Table Calculation.
- The TotalTargetAmount measure determines the total amount KLUB would have received if the company had charged the target prices for all its sales. Its algorithm follows Pattern 5: Single-Column Aggregation.
- The Discrepancy measure determines the discrepancy between total revenues and total target amounts. The "−" symbol represents subtraction. This is an aggregate that can be sliced in many ways. Its algorithm follows Pattern 7: Measure Hierarchies.
- The Discrepancy% measure compares actual revenues with targeted revenues as a percentage. Its algorithm also follows Pattern 7: Measure Hierarchies.

ILLUSTRATION 6.44 Data and Information Models for the Who-What-When Sales Star Schema

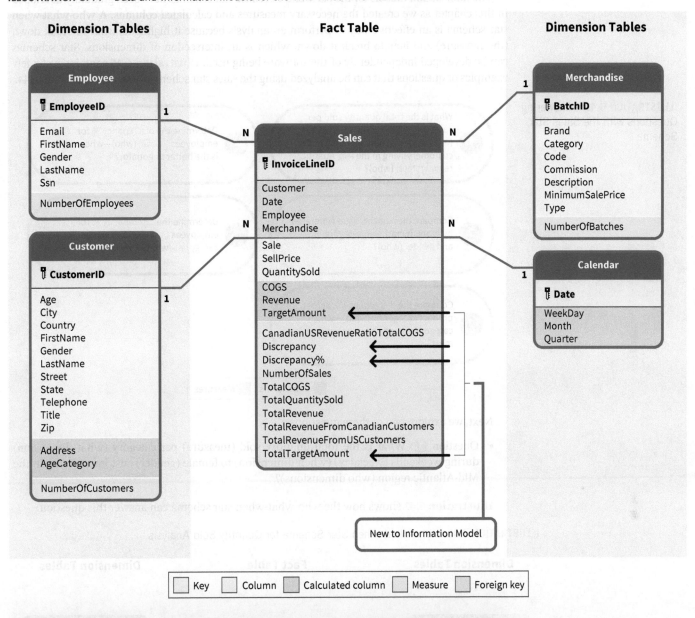

ILLUSTRATION 6.45 Additional Calculated Columns and Measures for the Who-What-When Sales Star Schema

Table: Sales	
Calculated Column	**Algorithm**
TargetAmount	Sales.QuantitySold × Merchandise.MinimumSalePrice

Table: Sales	
Measures	**Algorithm**
TotalTargetAmount	SUM(TargetAmount)
Discrepancy	[TotalRevenue] − [TotalTargetAmount]
Discrepancy%	[TotalRevenue] / [TotalTargetAmount]

Analysis

A who-what-when star schema is a powerful structure for the analysis of accounting data. Any transaction measures in the fact table can be broken down by any combination of dimensions (who, what, and/or when), and these breakdowns can be shaped through a variety of visualizations.

The information models for the Sales and Purchase star schemas have been gradually developed in this chapter as we created the necessary measures and calculated columns. A who-what-when star schema is an effective way to perform an analysis because it highlights *what* to break down (the measure) and *how* to break it down, which is an intersection of dimensions. Star schemas can be developed independently of the software being used. **Illustration 6.46** contains just a few examples of questions that can be analyzed using the sales star schema shown in Illustration 6.44.

ILLUSTRATION 6.46 Answering Questions with the Sales Star Schema

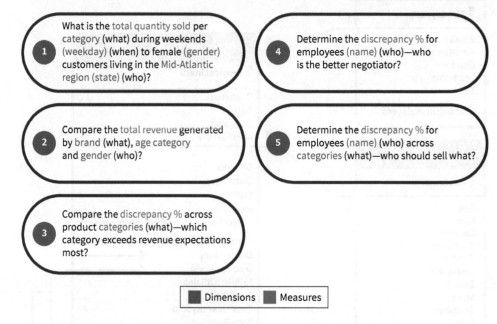

1. What is the total quantity sold per category (what) during weekends (weekday) (when) to female (gender) customers living in the Mid-Atlantic region (state) (who)?

2. Compare the total revenue generated by brand (what), age category and gender (who)?

3. Compare the discrepancy % across product categories (what)—which category exceeds revenue expectations most?

4. Determine the discrepancy % for employees (name) (who)—who is the better negotiator?

5. Determine the discrepancy % for employees (name) (who) across categories (what)—who should sell what?

■ Dimensions ■ Measures

Next, we explore two of these questions.

- Question **1**: What is the total quantity sold (measure) per category (what dimension) during weekends (weekday) (when dimension) to female (gender) customers living in the Mid-Atlantic region (who dimensions)?

Illustration 6.47 shows how the who-what-when star schema can answer this question.

ILLUSTRATION 6.47 Who-What-When Star Schema for Quantity Sold Analysis

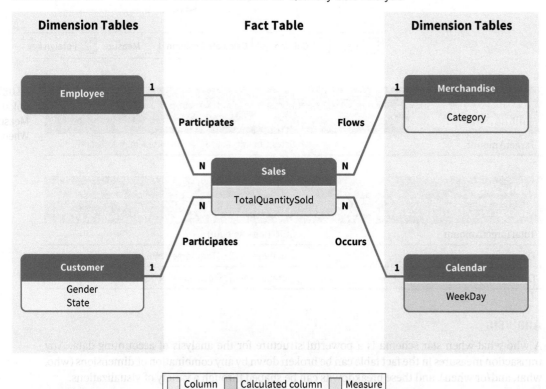

□ Column ■ Calculated column □ Measure

This is a query-type question that uses filters, so the next step is to create the algorithm that integrates these filters (**Illustration 6.48**).

ILLUSTRATION 6.48 Implementation of the QuantitySoldOnWeekdaysToFemaleMidAtlanticCustomers Measure

Table: Sales	
Measure	**Algorithm**
QuantitySoldOnWeekdaysToFemaleMidAtlantic Customers	SUM(QuantitySold) WHERE Calendar.Weekday = 1 or 7, AND Customer.Gender = "Female", AND Customer.State = "PA" OR "MD" OR "DC" OR "VA" OR "WV" OR "DE" OR "NJ" OR "NY"

Finally, the number generated by QuantitySoldOnWeekdaysToFemaleMidAtlanticCustomers must be sliced by product category. The column chart in **Illustration 6.49** shows this slicing.

ILLUSTRATION 6.49 Product Category Comparison: Quantity Sold to Mid-Atlantic Female Customers on Weekdays

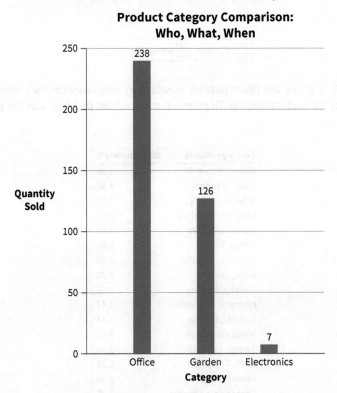

Next, use the information model to explore another question.

- **Question ❹:** Determine the discrepancy % (measure) for employees (name, which is a who dimension).

The answer to this question can reveal which employees are the better negotiators. This is an exploration-type of question. **Illustration 6.50** shows how the who-what-when star schema answers this question.

ILLUSTRATION 6.50 Who-What-When Star Schema for Discrepancy% Analysis

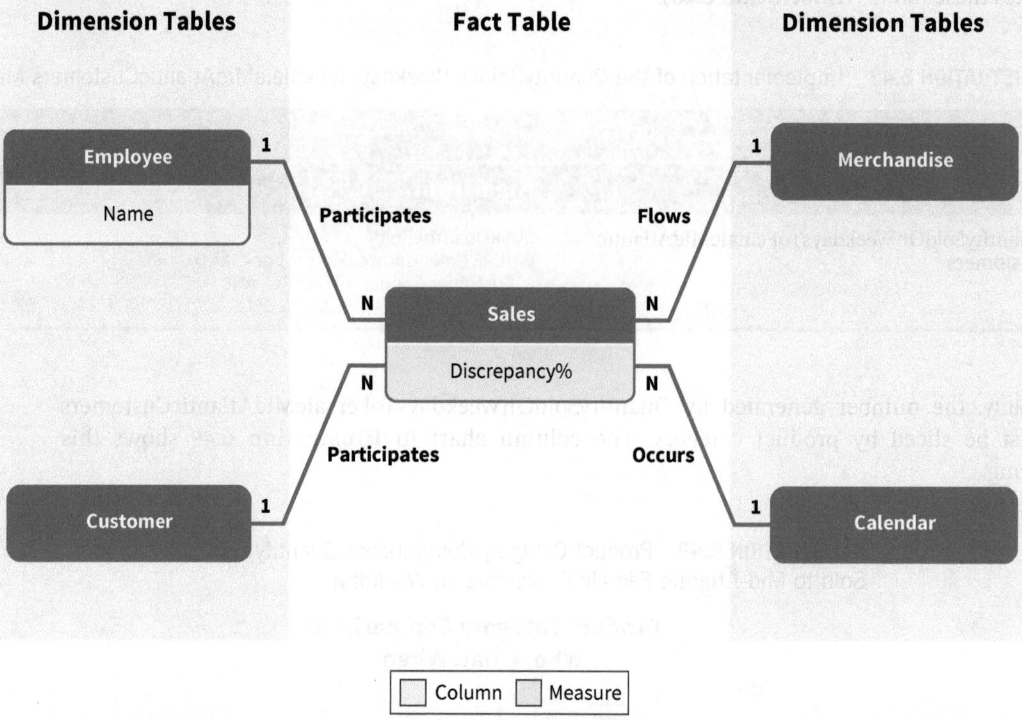

Illustration **6.51** slices the Discrepancy% measure by employee (name), which reveals the negotiation power for each employee. To generate more robust insights, sort the percentages in descending order.

ILLUSTRATION 6.51 Comparing Employees Based on Discrepancy%

EmployeeName	Discrepancy%
Gianni, Kobierski	12.06
Jade, Steeden	4.80
Arlyn, McCreery	3.43
Rosabel, Gabbitus	2.94
Dalenna, Patillo	2.86
Valery, Bayles	2.86
Catherin, Tolliday	2.66
Haze, Coomer	2.59
Florella, McAllan	2.56
Hermina, Jeandillou	2.47
Padriac, Parlour	2.44
Alyda, Greenhall	2.40
Tamra, Lambdin	2.38
Berti, Pridding	2.36
Loreen, Polye	2.36
Catharine, Laimable	2.35
Audie, Braniff	2.33
Charlie, Libri	2.27
Clim, Orhtmann	2.25
Chancey, Donke	2.25
Aarika, Bircher	2.20
Edik, Knowles	2.19
Silvain, MacTague	2.07
Sally, Blizard	1.94
Timmie, Brookzie	1.93

Information Modeling Pattern 13: Integrated Star Schemas

Illustration **6.52**(A) shows how who-what-when stars are connected through resources. Resources are being acquired for a purpose—to sell or to use them for manufacturing, for example.

Illustration 6.52(B) applies the pattern to KLUB. Because KLUB buys items in batches and sells them to make a profit, the Sales and Purchases star schemas are connected through the Merchandise table.

ILLUSTRATION 6.52   Integrated Star Schemas Pattern

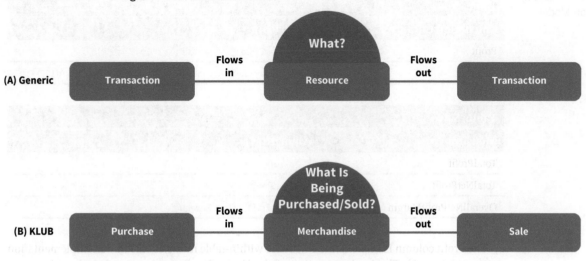

Additional examples of integrated stars that are not part of the KLUB data set are:

- Cash Receipts to Cash to Cash Disbursements.
- Fixed Asset Acquisitions to Fixed Asset to Depreciation.

Information Model

This pattern describes the flow of resources in terms of quantity and value. It helps answer questions about how many resources have been acquired, which is the inflow, how many are in stock, and how many have been used and how (such as sales). **Illustration 6.53** provides an overview of accounting concepts, the information model, that can be derived from integrating KLUB's Sale and Purchase star schemas as shown in Illustration 6.52.

ILLUSTRATION 6.53   Information Model for KLUB's Integrated Star Schemas

Concept/Field	Field Type	Description
Revenue	Calculated Column	The dollar amount paid by the customers for items sold.
COGS	Calculated Column	The dollar amount paid by KLUB for the items they sold.
Profit	Calculated Column	The profit KLUB made on the items they sold.
NetProfit	Calculated Column	The net profit KLUB made on the items sold after paying a commission (additional cost) to their employees (salespeople).
TotalRevenue	Measure	Total revenue generated from sales.
TotalCOGS	Measure	Total dollar amount paid by KLUB for items they sold.
TotalProfit	Measure	Total profit generated from sales.
TotalNetProfit	Measure	Total net profit generated from sales. Commissions for employees are considered.
OverallNetProfit Margin	Measure	The overall net profit margin for KLUB's sales. Total net profit / total revenue.

Again, there are many ways to implement the enhanced information model associated with the integrated star schemas. The formulas for the additional columns and measures are shown in **Illustration 6.54**.

ILLUSTRATION 6.54 Extending KLUB's Information Model

Table: Sales	
Calculated Columns	**Algorithm**
Profit	Revenue – COGS
NetProfit	Sales.Profit – (Sales.Revenue × (Merchandise.Commission)/100)

Table: Sales	
Measure	**Algorithm**
TotalProfit	SUM(Profit)
TotalNetProfit	SUM(NetProfit)
OverallNetProfitMargin	[TotalNetProfit] / [TotalRevenue]

The Profit column is implemented with the within-table numeric calculation implementation pattern (Pattern 1). The implementation of the NetProfit column is more complex, given that information from both the Sales table and the Merchandise table is needed. This is an application of the across-table calculation implementation pattern (Pattern 4).

The implementation of the TotalProfit and TotalNetProfit measures are both applications of the single-column aggregation implementation pattern (Pattern 5), summing the values of a calculated column. Finally, the OverallNetProfitMargin measure is an application of the measure hierarchy implementation pattern (Pattern 7).

The information model can be further expanded with more specific measures. For example, we could calculate the total profits resulting from electronics sales in the United States. A possible implementation for this measure is shown in **Illustration 6.55**, which is an application of the filtered aggregation implementation pattern (Pattern 6).

ILLUSTRATION 6.55 Implementation of the ProfitsForUSElectronicSales Measure

Table: Sales	
Measure	**Algorithm**
ProfitsForUSElectronicsSales	TotalProfit Where Customer.Country = "US" AND Merchandise.Category = "Electronics"

Analysis

This extended information model can answer a variety of questions regarding KLUB's financial situation (**Illustration 6.56**).

ILLUSTRATION 6.56 Answering Questions with KLUB's Integrated Star Schemas

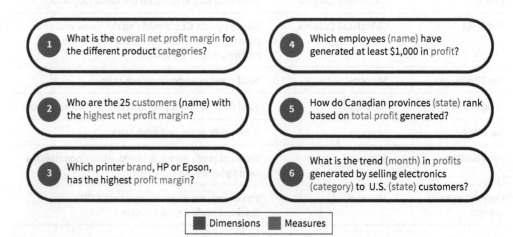

1. What is the overall net profit margin for the different product categories?

2. Who are the 25 customers (name) with the highest net profit margin?

3. Which printer brand, HP or Epson, has the highest profit margin?

4. Which employees (name) have generated at least $1,000 in profit?

5. How do Canadian provinces (state) rank based on total profit generated?

6. What is the trend (month) in profits generated by selling electronics (category) to U.S. (state) customers?

Dimensions Measures

Next, we use KLUB's integrated star schemas to further explore two of these questions.

- **Question ❶:** What is the overall net profit margin (measure) for the different product categories (dimension)?

Illustration 6.57 shows how the star schema can be used to answer this question.

ILLUSTRATION 6.57 Star Schema for Net Profit Margin Analysis

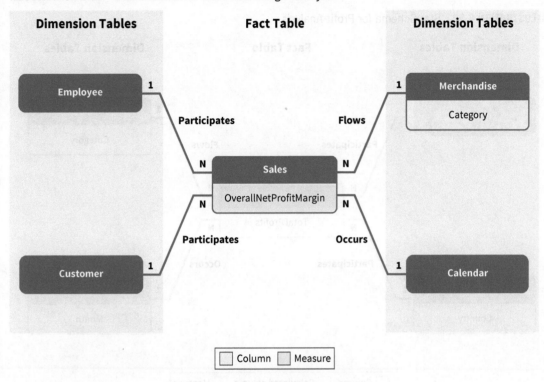

The corresponding report is shown in **Illustration 6.58**.

ILLUSTRATION 6.58 Comparing Product Categories by Net Profit Margin

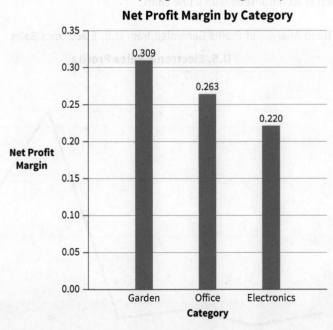

Category is used as a dimension, and net profit margin is calculated for each category (garden, office, and electronics) and represented as a bar. KLUB's negotiation power seems to be strongest for garden items.

- **Question 6**: What if we wanted to know the trend (month, which is a dimension) in profits (measure) generated by selling electronics (category, which is a dimension) to U.S. (country, which is a dimension) customers?

Illustration 6.59 shows the star schema for this question. It should be noted that an alternative star schema could be created where the ProfitsForUSElectronicSales measure is sliced by month.

ILLUSTRATION 6.59   Star Schema for Profit Analysis

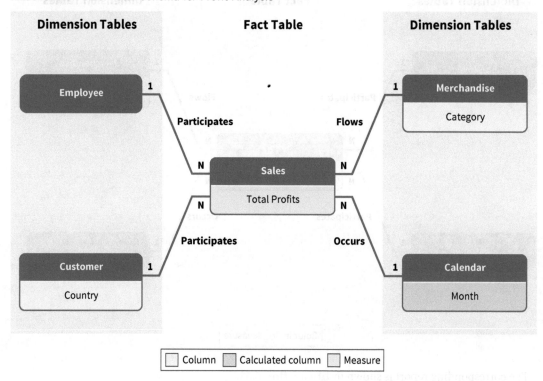

The corresponding report is shown in **Illustration 6.60**. Profits for U.S. electronics sales are sliced by month, which is accomplished with a line chart.

ILLUSTRATION 6.60   Trend Analysis of Profits Generated from U.S. Electronics Sales

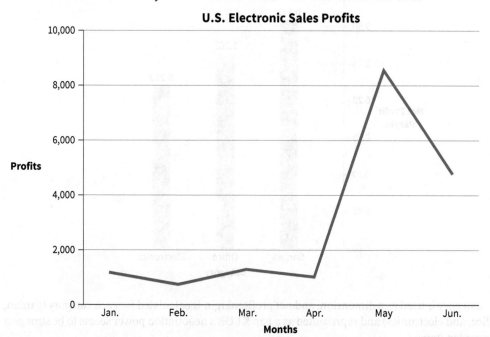

Thirteen different patterns were applied to complete KLUB's information model. Keep in mind that patterns are best practices. They are a guide for determining what information, or content, is relevant and how to implement it. These 13 patterns will help you identify a range of relevant accounting information and code the algorithms that can generate such information.

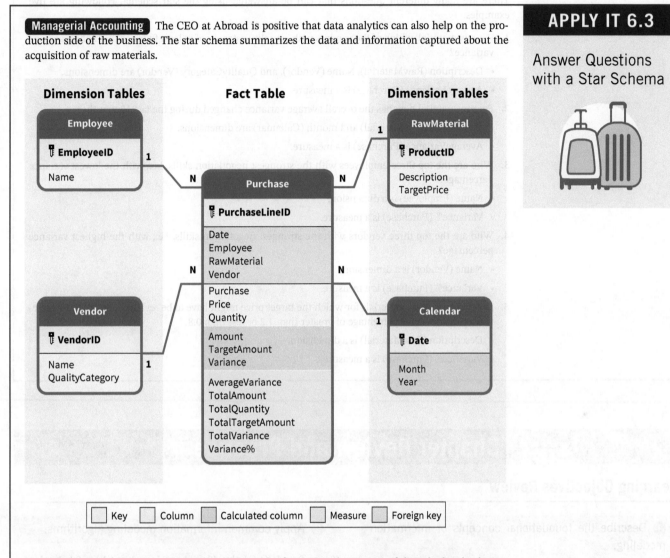

Managerial Accounting The CEO at Abroad is positive that data analytics can also help on the production side of the business. The star schema summarizes the data and information captured about the acquisition of raw materials.

APPLY IT 6.3

Answer Questions with a Star Schema

You are given the following table that has additional information about some of the calculated columns and measures:

Table	Field	Description/Algorithm
RawMaterial	TargetPrice	What Abroad is expected to pay for one unit of the raw material.
Purchase	Amount	Price × Quantity
	TargetAmount	TargetPrice × Quantity
	AverageVariance	TotalVariance/TotalQuantity
	Variance	TargetAmount − Amount
	Variance%	TotalAmount/TotalTargetAmount
Vendor	QualityCategory	Assessment of the vendor's quality on a 1 to 5 scale, with 1 being the worst and 5 being the best.

You are asked to develop three questions that can be explored with this information model. Abroad's owner is especially interested in questions related to variances. Identify three potential questions and the dimensions and measures you would use to answer them.

SOLUTION

There are many different questions that can be answered using the star schema. Following are five examples:

1. Per raw material, which of the vendors with a quality category of at least four has the highest average variance?

   - Description (RawMaterial), Name (Vendor), and QualityCategory (Vendor) are dimensions.
   - AverageVariance (Purchase) is a measure.

2. Per raw material how has the overall average variance changed during the last 12 months?

   - Description (RawMaterial) and month (Calendar) are dimensions.
   - AverageVariance (Purchase) is a measure.

3. Who are the top three employees with the strongest negotiation skills, i.e., with the lowest variance percentage?

   - Name (Employee) is a dimension.
   - Variance% (Purchase) is a measure.

4. Who are the top three vendors with the strongest negotiation skills, i.e., with the highest variance percentage?

   - Name (Vendor) is a dimension.
   - Variance% (Purchase) is a measure.

5. Determine the raw materials for which the target price might have to be reviewed, i.e., the raw materials with a variance percentage of greater than 1.2 or less than 0.8.

   - Description (RawMaterial) is a dimension.
   - Variance% (Purchase) is a measure.

Chapter Review and Practice

Learning Objectives Review

❶ Describe the foundational concepts of information modeling.

Successful information modeling requires an in-depth understanding of its foundational concepts:

- Information modeling is a process. Algorithms transform data into information.
- Information models are built using calculated columns and measures. Calculated columns are new columns with values that are calculated, row-by-row, from existing data. Measures are aggregates resulting from vertical calculations that can be broken down in many different ways.
- Star schemas are the preferable data structure for data analytics. Measures are created for the fact table and are sliced, or broken down, with the fields in the dimension tables. A robust set of measures and dimensions results in a rich information model that enables analytics.
- Who-what-when stars structure accounting data and make accounting analytics easier.

❷ Apply common information modeling algorithms.

Seven foundational algorithms provide a strong base for developing information models:

- Pattern 1 is within-table numeric calculation. It adds a new column to a table by applying arithmetic operators such as addition, subtraction, multiplication, and division to columns in the same table.
- Pattern 2 is within-table text calculation. It adds a new column to a table by applying text manipulation operators such as concatenation, extraction, and replacement to columns in the same table.
- Pattern 3 is within-table classification. It adds a new column to a table by applying a classification algorithm to data in other columns in the same table.
- Pattern 4 is across-table calculation. It creates a new column by using data from different tables. Tables are linked through relationships, and algorithms are required to navigate these relationships.

- Pattern 5 is single-column aggregation. It aggregates all the values in a single column using mathematical operators such as SUM, AVERAGE, and COUNT.
- Pattern 6 is filtered aggregation. It filters the data in a single column based on one or more criteria and then aggregates the remaining values.
- Pattern 7 creates a measure hierarchy. It creates a new, more complex measure using existing measures.

❸ Develop and implement information models for common accounting data structures.

Six common accounting data structures can help identify an information model's measures and dimensions:

- Pattern 8 is the how many pattern. It counts existing agents, transactions, and resources.

Illustration 6.61 is an overview of the 13 patterns.

- Pattern 9 is the participates | transaction-who pattern. It captures information about who is involved in the transactions. Agents participating in an accounting transaction can be external to an organization, e.g., customer, or internal, e.g., salesperson.
- Pattern 10 is the flows | transaction-what pattern. It captures information about what resources are involved in the transaction. A transaction can result in an inflow or outflow of resources.
- Pattern 11 is the occurs | transaction-when pattern. It captures information about when a transaction occurs.
- Pattern 12 is the who-what-when star schema pattern. It integrates the who, what, and when dimensions of transactions and supports a wide range of accounting analyses.
- Pattern 13 is the integrated star schemas pattern. It combines multiple star schemas and enables integrated analyses of resource inflows and outflows.

ILLUSTRATION 6.61 Overview of Information Modeling Patterns

Id	Algorithm	Description	Implementation
Implementation Patterns			
1	Within-Table Numeric Calculation	Creates a new calculated column by applying arithmetic operators to columns in the same table.	Basic arithmetic operators: addition, subtraction, multiplication, division, or exponentiation.
2	Within-Table Text Calculation	Creates a new calculated column by applying text manipulation operators to columns in the same table.	Text manipulation operators such as concatenate, extract, or replace.
3	Within-Table Classification	Creates a new calculated column that contains new knowledge by applying conditional logic.	Boolean expressions and Boolean operators such as AND, OR, and NOT.
4	Across-Table Calculation	Data from different, linked tables are used to create a new calculated column.	Navigation operators such as joins.
5	Single-Column Aggregation	Creates a new measure that aggregates all the values of a single column.	Aggregate functions such as SUM, COUNT, AVERAGE, MIN, and MAX.
6	Filtered Aggregation	Creates a new measure that aggregates a subset of the values of a single column.	Apply filters. Examples are SUMIF, COUNTIF, and AVERAGEIF functions in Excel or the WHERE clause in SQL.
7	Measure Hierarchies	Creates a new, more complex measure using existing measures.	Apply arithmetic operators to measures such as addition, subtraction, multiplication, or division.
Content Patterns			
8	How Many	Analyzes how many of a concept exists.	Create measures that counts rows in tables.
9	Participates | Transaction-Who	Analyzes who is involved in a transaction.	Create measures for transactions and calculated columns for agents.
10	Flows | Transaction-What	Analyzes what is involved in a transaction.	Create measures for transactions and calculated columns for resources.
11	Occurs | Transaction-When	Analyzes when a transaction occurred.	Create measures for transactions and calculated columns for calendars.
12	Who-What-When Star Schemas	Integrates analysis of the who, what, and when transactions.	Create measures for transactions and calculated columns for agents, resources, and calendars.
13	Integrated Star Schemas	Analyze how inflows and outflows affect resources.	Create measures for transactions and calculated columns for resources.

Key Terms Review

How To Walk-Throughs

How To

HOW TO 6.1   Create Calculated Columns and Measures with Power BI

Calculated columns and measures are the building blocks of information models. Here, we illustrate how they can be specified with Power BI.

What You Need: **Data** The How To 6.1 data file.

STEP 1: In the **Fields** pane, select the table to which you want to add a column or a measure. In **Illustration 6.62**, the Customer table is selected.

STEP 2: Next to the table name, click **More Options** and select either **New Measure** or **New Column**.

ILLUSTRATION 6.62   Creating Columns and Measures

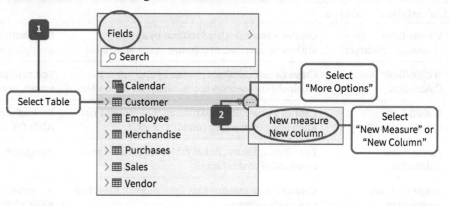

STEP 3: An area in which to enter the formula that creates the new column, or measure, will appear (**Illustration 6.63**).

ILLUSTRATION 6.63   Entering a Formula

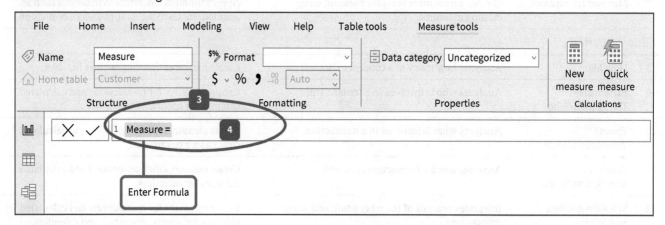

STEP 4: Enter a formula. For example, enter the following formula to create a measure which determines the number of customers:

NUMBER OF CUSTOMERS = COUNT(Customer[CustomerID]).

Then, press the **Enter** key.

HOW TO 6.2   Implement a Filtered Aggregation with SQL

How To

The patterns discussed in this chapter are not specific to a software or language. Here, you can practice implementing filtered aggregation with relational database software (e.g., Microsoft Access) using the Structured Query Language (SQL).

What You Need: **Data** The How To 6.2 data file.

STEP 1: Open the file using Microsoft Access and select the **Create** tab in the Main Menu. Click **Query Design** in the **Queries** group of the ribbon.

STEP 2: When a new ribbon appears in the **Results** group, select **SQL View**.

STEP 3: Enter the SQL command shown in **Illustration 6.64**.

ILLUSTRATION 6.64   SQL Query for Determining the Total Revenue Generated from Sales to U.S. Customers by Product Category

Query: Total Revenue from U.S. Customers by Product Category

```
SELECT Category, SUM([SellPrice] * [QuantitySold]) AS [TotalrevenueFromUSCustomers]
FROM Merchandise INNER JOIN (Customer INNER JOIN Sales ON Customer.CustomerID = Sales.Customer)
ON Merchandise.BatchID = Sales.Merchandise
WHERE Country="US"
GROUP BY Category
```

Detailed Descriptions Code

Code	Description
SUM([SellPrice] * [QuantitySold])	Calculates the total revenue generated from sales.
WHERE Country="US"	A filter defined through a Boolean expression. Only sales from U.S. customers are considered.
GROUP BY Category	The total revenue is broken down by category. There are three values for CATEGORY: Electronics, Garden, and Office.
FROM Merchandise INNER JOIN (Customer INNER JOIN Sales ON Customer.CustomerID = Sales.Customer) ON Merchandise.BatchID = Sales.Merchandise	Defines the joins between the tables and thus the navigation path.

STEP 4: Select the Exclamation Mark (!) in the **Results** group of the ribbon. The table shown in **Illustration 6.65**, which summarizes revenues generated from sales to U.S. customers by (product) category, will appear.

ILLUSTRATION 6.65   Query Results

Category	Total Revenue from U.S. Customers
Electronics	34,553
Garden	80,012
Office	210,560

> **Data** The Data tag appears when the data required to answer a question or complete an exercise are available in the book's product page on www.wiley.com.

Multiple Choice Questions

1. (LO 1) A calculated column

   a. should always result in a measure.

   b. is the result of the arithmetic function of other columns.

   c. should always result in a numeric data type.

   d. is the result of an algorithm that was applied using other columns.

2. (LO 1) Information modeling is the process of

   a. defining relationships between tables and the constraints that apply to them.

   b. generating additional knowledge from data that is relevant for analysis purposes.

   c. creating star and/or snowflake schemas.

   d. creating data structures that make analytics easy.

3. (LO 1) An algorithm is a

   a. set of instructions that transform the data into information.

   b. set of instructions used to clean the data prior to loading the data into analytical databases.

   c. set of instructions used to validate the completeness and the correctness of the data prior to loading the data into analytical databases.

   d. set of instructions used to integrate data from various data sources.

4. (LO 1) Assume a grocery store recorded the following information for each transaction:

TransactionID	Date	Amount	Loyalty	LoyaltyDiscount
1	2/1/2025	$ 144.17	Y	1.44
2	2/1/2025	$ 35.80	N	0
3	2/2/2025	$ 289.09	N	2.89
4	2/2/2025	$ 134.88	Y	1.35
5	2/3/2025	$ 99.50	N	1

The information model consists of three measures and a calculated column. Which of the following is the calculated column?

   a. Calculation of the loyalty discount. Members of the loyalty program get a 1% discount on all transactions.

   b. Calculation of the % of transactions from members of the loyalty program.

   c. Calculation of the total dollar amount generated on a specific day.

   d. Calculation of the total loyalty discount amount paid on a specific day.

5. (LO 1) Star schemas represent data structures that help determine which numbers to break down (facts) and how (what, who, and when) to break them down (dimensions). Which of the following scenarios is *not* compliant with such a structure?

Scenario	Facts	Dimensions		
		What	Who	When
a.	Total revenue	Product category	Customer	Month
b.	Total revenue		Region	
c.	Total profit	Product type	Region	Weekday
d.	Total number of customers		Region	
e.	Total number of sales	Product category	Customer	
f.	Total number of sales			Month
g.	Total cost	Product type		

6. (LO 2) Which of the following statements regarding algorithms would you disagree with?

   a. Boolean expressions are an integral part of classification algorithms.

   b. Analytics based on data from multiple tables heavily rely on properly defined relationships among the tables.

   c. A measure hierarchy defines a relationship between measures from two different tables.

   d. SUM, AVERAGE, and COUNT are mathematical operations often used to define measures.

7. (LO 2) When applying the following classification algorithm to the data set, which of the four customers (CustomerID) is assigned the value B?

Algorithm

IF ((Age < 30 AND LoyaltyProgram = "Yes") OR (Sales > 10,000 AND Number-OfIssues = 0))
THEN "A"
ELSE "B"

Data set

CustomerID	Name	Age	LoyaltyProgram	Sales	NumberOfIssues
1	Kinsun	32	Yes	$ 13,833	0
2	Barbara	29	No	$ 15,000	2
3	Jon	29	Yes	$ 15,000	2
4	Gabriella	25	Yes	$ 20,000	0

   a. 1   c. 3

   b. 2   d. 4

8. (LO 2) Creating a new field from one or more numeric columns in the same table is called

   a. a within-table numeric calculation.

   b. an in-table calculation.

   c. an in-table classification.

   d. a single-column aggregation.

9. (LO 2) When applying the following algorithm to the data set, which of the following implementation patterns are used?

Algorithm

PRICE TYPE =
IF Price < 25,000 THEN "LOW-END" ELSE
IF Price >= 25,000 AND PRICE < 50,000 THEN "MID-RANGE" ELSE
"HIGH-END"

Data set

ProductID	Description	Year	Price
1	VW Beetle	2019	$ 14,322
2	Honda Pilot	2018	$ 25,119
3	BMW X7	2019	$ 50,432
4	Chevrolet Cru..	2019	$ 11,654
5	Mercedes ML	2017	$ 29,750
6	Ford Explorer	2019	$ 32,881
7	Honda Civic	2017	$ 9,811
8	Chevrolet Tah..	2016	$ 42,889
9	Jeep Wrangler	2007	$ 9,999
10	Maserati Leva..	2020	$ 69,922

a. Within-table numeric calculation

b. Within-table text calculation

c. Within-table classification

d. Filtered aggregation

10. (LO 2) You are a financial accountant, and you are asked to analyze financial ratios for the company. You are provided with a table showing accounts and their values. Define the algorithm for creating the current ratio using the measure hierarchies' pattern.

Category	Description	Amount
Current Assets	Cash and Cash Equivalents	$33,203
Current Assets	Short-Term Investments	$22,034
Noncurrent Assets	Long-Term Investments	$131,334
Current Liabilities	Accounts Payables	$45,536
Current Assets	Accounts Receivables	$62,344
...	...	...

11. (LO 3) The information modeling pattern of how many can be used to

a. count the number of instances in fact tables but not in dimension tables.

b. determine average values in dimension tables but not in fact tables.

c. determine average values in fact tables and in dimension tables.

d. count the number of instances in fact tables and dimension tables.

12. (LO 3) Which of the following statements regarding dimensional modeling is incorrect?

a. Dimensional modeling aims to create data structures that make data analytics easier.

b. Dimensions can be used for filtering purposes.

c. Calculated columns can function as dimensions.

d. How many measures can be specified for dimension tables only.

13. (LO 3) The following diagram is a part of a star schema that describes a manufacturing process.

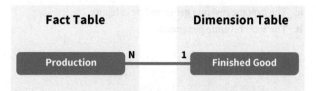

How would you describe the nature of the relationship between production and finished goods?

a. A participates relationship

b. An occurs relationship

c. A flows relationship resulting in a decrease or outflow of finished goods

d. A flow relationship resulting in an increase or inflow of finished goods

14. (LO 3) Which of the following questions does *not* rely on a participates relationship?

a. Which vendor offers the lowest price for a specific product?

b. What is the total units sold for each product category?

c. For each product category, who is the customer that bought the highest quantity last year?

d. Which employee has the worst return ratio?

15. (LO 3) What question represents a physical flow relationship?

a. What is the value of material waste due to machine failures?

b. What are product costs and period costs for this month's production?

c. How many units of each product category were produced in the last fiscal quarter?

d. All of the answer choices are correct.

16. (LO 3) Who-what-when stars are connected through

a. transactions (e.g., sales).

b. resources (e.g., finished goods).

c. internal agents (e.g., employees).

d. external agents (e.g., customers).

17. (LO 3) This column chart was generated by a car manufacturer.

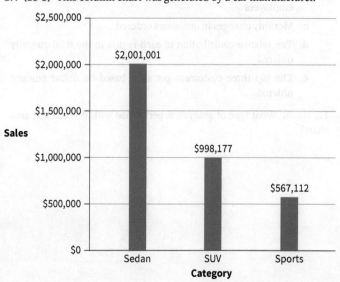

Which is the most accurate description of the accounting information captured by this chart?

a. The average revenue generated by category.

b. The total revenue generated.

c. How much revenue each category has generated (inflow).

d. How much revenue each category has generated (outflow).

18. **(LO 3)** Which of the following analyses *cannot* be explored with this information model?

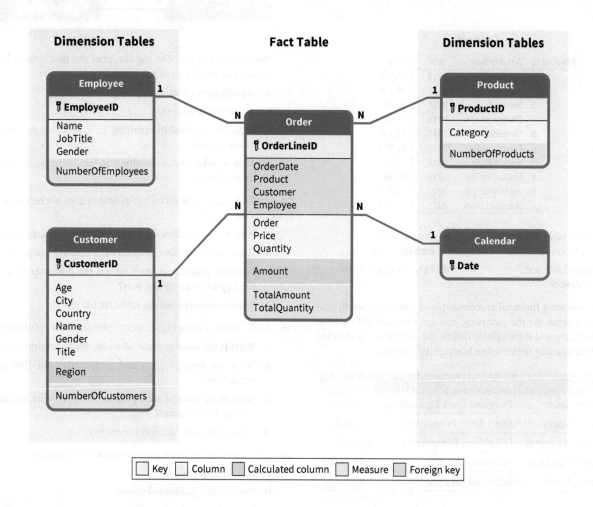

a. The number of different products ordered by region

b. The total quantity ordered by female customers from female employees

c. Monthly changes in quantities ordered

d. The relative contribution of each region to the total quantity ordered

e. The top three customers per state based on dollar amount ordered

19. **(LO 3)** What type of analysis is performed with this stacked area chart?

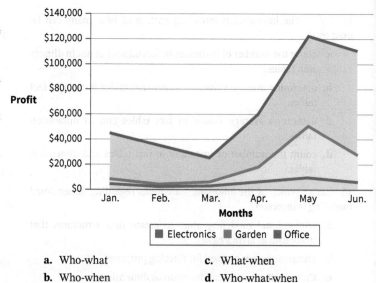

a. Who-what

b. Who-when

c. What-when

d. Who-what-when

Review Questions

1. **(LO 1)** Describe the goal of information modeling.

2. **(LO 1)** What are the two main tasks involved in information modeling?

3. **(LO 1)** What is the difference between a data model and an information model?

4. **(LO 1)** What are the two different types of information fields and how do they differ?

5. **(LO 1)** What are the two goals of star schema information models?

6. **(LO 1)** What is an algorithm? Provide an example of an accounting algorithm.

7. **(LO 2)** Provide two examples of text calculations.

8. **(LO 2)** What is Boolean logic and how can it be used for classification purposes?

9. **(LO 2)** Calculations might require information from multiple tables. Describe the mechanism that is used to connect tables.

10. **(LO 2)** Describe the one measure, multiple analyses principle.

11. **(LO 2)** For each operator, describe whether you most likely would use it to create a calculated column or a measure.

Mathematical Operator	Type of Information Field
Sum	
Multiplication	
Count	
Concatenation	
Average	
Division	
Exponentiation	
Standard Deviation	

12. **(LO 2)** What are filtered measures?

13. **(LO 2)** For what purpose is a measure hierarchy used?

14. **(LO 3)** What are the who, what, and when dimensions of accounting transactions?

15. **(LO 3)** What accounting information is captured by a flows relationship?

16. **(LO 3)** What is the difference between physical and monetary flow information?

17. **(LO 3)** Examine this model.

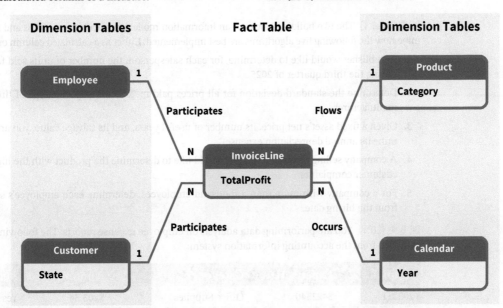

| **Dimension Tables** | **Fact Table** | **Dimension Tables** |

1. What are you comparing?
2. What field do you use for comparison purposes?
3. What fields are you using for filtering purposes?

18. **(LO 3)** What kind of information do calendar tables contain?

19. **(LO 3)** Describe the difference between internal and external agents. For purchase transactions, who are the internal and external agents?

20. **(LO 3)** What information is captured by the occurs relationship, and why is such information crucial in an accounting context?

21. **(LO 3)** For the Customer table, what relationships between the dimensions can you identify? Describe how such relationships can be used for analysis purposes by identifying a few questions that can be answered using these relationships.

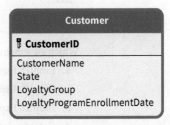

Brief Exercises

BE 6.1 (LO 1) Use the following terms to complete the sentence:

a. algorithm

c. information model

b. data

d. star schema

1. A(n) _____ is a data model extended with calculated columns and measures.

2. The formula that determines the break-even point is an example of a(n) _____.

3. A(n) _____ is the preferred data structure for data analysis.

4. _____ is the input of an information model.

BE 6.2 (LO 1) Match the appropriate term to each definition.

a. Algorithm

d. Information model

b. Calculated column

e. Measure

c. Data model

f. Star schema

Definition	Term
1. An aggregate that is calculated from a set of data that can be used for analytical purposes.	
2. A specification of the structure of a data set showing what concepts are described as tables and what characteristics are used to describe the concepts.	
3. An extension to the data model that consists of calculated columns and measures.	
4. A set of instructions that transform data into information.	

BE 6.3 (LO 1) The two building blocks of an information model are calculated columns and measures. Determine how the following five algorithms are best implemented: Either as a calculated column or measure.

1. A publisher would like to determine, for each salesperson, the number of units sold for a specific title during the third quarter of 2025.

2. Determine the standard deviation for all prices paid in 2025 for a specific type of tire used by a bike manufacturer.

3. Given a fixed asset's net price, its number of useful years, and its salvage value, you are asked to determine its annual depreciation expense.

4. A company selling electronic gadgets would like to determine the product with the highest number of customer complaints.

5. For a company with more than a thousand employees, determine each employee's seniority starting from the hiring date.

BE 6.4 (LO 1) You are performing data analysis on employee expense reports. The following table has been extracted from the accounting information system:

EmpID	ExpenseID	Category	Amount	ReceiptExists
203211	3422340	Office Supplies	$203.34	Yes
203212	3422341	Furniture	$22.52	Yes
203213	3422342	Computer Equipment	$13.34	Yes
203214	3422343	Computer Equipment	$205.36	Yes
203215	3422344	Furniture	$123.44	No
...	...		...	...

Which statement is correct?

a. EmpID, ExpenseID, and Amount are measures, and Category and ReceiptExists are dimensions.

b. EmpID, ExpenseID, Category, and ReceiptExists are measures, and Amount is a dimension.

c. EmpID, ExpenseID, Category, and ReceiptExists are dimensions, and Amount is a measure.

d. Category is the only dimension, and Amount is the only measure.

BE 6.5 (LO 2) `Data` `Financial Accounting` Tesla is an Austin, Texas, based electric vehicle and clean energy company. You just downloaded its inside trading report for the first quarter of 2022.

1. Build an information model for this data set that lets you compare the fluctuations in the total value of shares sold during the first three months of 2022.

2. Use your information model to create the following line chart:

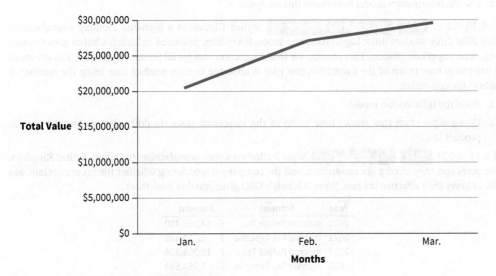

BE 6.6 (LO 2) `Data` `Managerial Accounting` OCE is a large chemical company with headquarters in Birmingham (United Kingdom). One of the responsibilities of their controller is to manage projects. In January 2025, 200 projects were completed. The controller would like to know how many of them did not exceed their budgeted expenses.

1. Create the information model by writing the algorithms.

2. Create a pie chart that shows the number of projects that did and did not exceed their budgeted expenses.

BE 6.7 (LO 2) `Data` `Financial Accounting` Nerdy Us is a small university with a sizeable endowment. Part of their endowment is invested in stocks. At the end of their fiscal year, they provide you the following information regarding their stocks:

- Ticker symbol
- Market Sector
- Price
- Number of stocks

They ask you to determine the total value of their stock portfolio and the relative importance of each market sector in it, presented as a pie chart.

1. Build the information model needed to generate such chart.

2. Create the pie chart.

BE 6.8 (LO 2) `Managerial Accounting` GoToOffice is a supplier of office furniture and office supplies. Their catalog is available to their customers' electronic procurement systems. Data analysis of their catalog pricing is required to ensure that they adhere to their minimum contracted discount percentage. The following table has been extracted from their pricing file:

ProductID	Product	ListPrice	NetPrice	Discount
213611	Copy Paper	$15.80	$12.64	20%
213612	Staples	$8.69	$6.95	20%
213613	Office Chair	$249.99	$187.49	25%
213614	Dry Erase Marker	$14.49	$11.59	20%
...	...	...	...	...

An information modeling algorithm was created to calculate the Discount column. What information modeling technique was used to create the Discount column?

BE 6.9 (LO 2) `Data` `Financial Accounting` KOE is a small dairy company in southeast Canada. They track a variety of financial information on a monthly basis. They provide you with some financial information for the year 2025 and ask you to determine their 2025 net profit margin and compare the 2025 monthly net profit margins.

1. Build the information model.

2. Use the information model to perform this analysis.

BE 6.10 (LO 2) `Data` `Managerial Accounting` Stylish Clothes is a high-end clothing manufacturer. They offer three product lines: bags, coats, and shoes. Every item produced at Stylish Clothes goes through a rigorous inspection process. Last month, the total inspection cost for all items was $45,750. You are asked to determine how much of the inspection cost pool is allocated to each product line, using the number of units as the cost driver.

1. Build the information model.

2. Create a pie chart that shows how much of the inspection costs (in dollars) was allocated to each product line.

BE 6.11 (LO 2) `Data` `Tax Accounting` Wear It Nicely is a shoe manufacturer in Oxford, United Kingdom. Five years ago, they hired a tax accountant, and the company is wondering whether the tax accountant was able to lower their effective tax rate. Wear It Nicely's CEO gives you this worksheet.

Year	Account	Amount
2021	Income Before Tax	£ 14,365,450
2021	Income Tax Expense	£ 1,120,505
2022	Income Before Tax	£ 15,299,804
2022	Income Tax Expense	£ 1,254,584
2023	Income Before Tax	£ 165,998,110
2023	Income Tax Expense	£ 12,947,853
2024	Income Before Tax	£ 13,489,990
2024	Income Tax Expense	£ 1,025,239
2025	Income Before Tax	£ 175,009,898
2025	Income Tax Expense	£ 12,950,732

1. Develop the information model that calculates the effective tax rate.

2. Use it to create the following report:

Year	EffectiveTaxRate
2021	7.80%
2022	8.20%
2023	7.80%
2024	7.60%
2025	7.40%

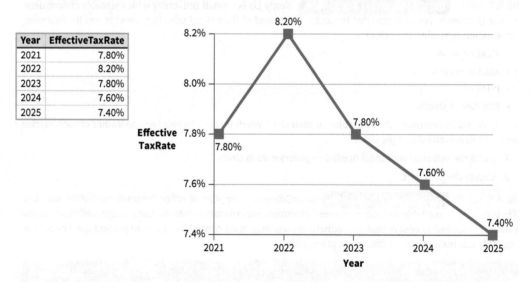

BE 6.12 (LO 3) TrustUs Bank is an investment bank. With interest rates increasing during inflationary times, clients are investing in more fixed-income investments compared to equity investments. The star schema summarizes the investment transactions.

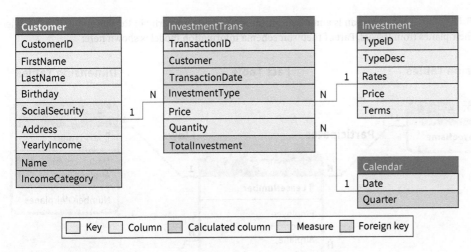

1. What type of schema is used?
2. What is a characteristic of the schema used?
3. Which month had the greatest number of investment transactions? Explain.

BE 6.13 (LO 3) The following are star schema diagrams of Freshly Made Coffee that sells coffee to customers across the country. You are required to describe the relationship between the following:

Schema				Explain Relationship Between
TaxRemittance	N	1	**State**	TaxRemittance and State
Attacks	N	1	**Calendar**	Attacks and Calendar
Purchases	N	1	**Approver**	Purchases and Approver
Sales	N	1	**Product**	Sales and Product

Identify the relation from the following: participated relationship, flow relationship, and occurs relationship.

BE 6.14 (LO 3) Assume you would like to explore how the total revenue generated by sales from senior salespeople to U.S. customers in 2025 differs across product categories. Salespeople are considered senior when they are with the company for at least 10 years after their hiring date. Complete the star schema.

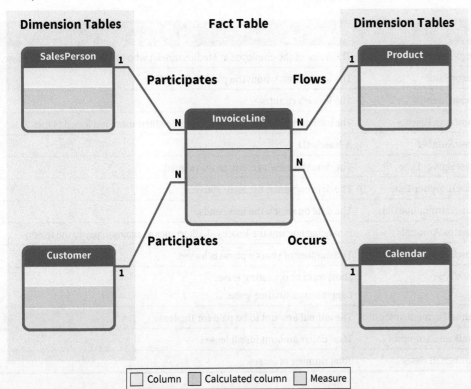

BE 6.15 (LO 3) Mediterranean is a mid-size airline with flights primarily in Europe and Africa. They lease all their planes from lessors. Part of their star schema information model is shown here:

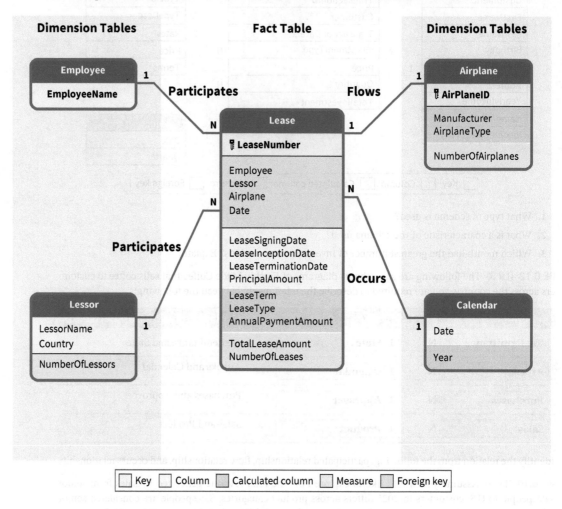

The table is the data dictionary for this information model.

Name	Description
EmployeeName	The name of the employee at Mediterranean who is accountable for the lease.
LessorName	The lessor from whom the plane is leased.
LessorCountry	The lessor's country.
NumberOfLessors	The total number of lessors from whom Mediterranean has leased planes.
LeaseNumber	A lease's ID.
LeaseSigningDate	The date the lease agreement was signed.
LeaseInceptionDate	The date on which the lease starts.
LeaseTerminationDate	The date on which the lease ends.
PrincipalAmount	Financing amount the lessee (Mediterranean) agrees to pay to the lessor.
LeaseTerm	The number of years a plane is leased.
LeaseType	Short-term or operating lease. Long-term or finance lease.
AnnualPaymentAmount	The annual amount to be paid for the lease.
TotalLeaseAmount	Total dollar amount for all leases.
NumberOfLeases	Total number of leases.

(*Continued*)

Name	Description
AirPlaneID	An airplane's unique ID.
Manufacturer	The airplane's builder—Boeing, Airbus, or Embraer.
AirplaneType	The airplane's type. For example, a (Boeing) 787 model.
NumberOfAirplanes	The total number of airplanes leased.

Determine at least five questions that can be analyzed starting from this information model.

Exercises

EX 6.1 (LO 1) Identify Data Relationships For each of the scenarios described, identify which relationship or relationships they describe: participates, flows, or occurs.

1. Generating cash receipts.
2. Raising loans.
3. Generating quarterly sales reports.
4. Receiving of goods returned by a customer.
5. Manufacturing a custom-made electric car.

EX 6.2 (LO 2) Build an Information Model for Reporting Net Revenues and Taxes PaintedByUs is a custom-design paint store. They provide you with a spreadsheet that contains the following information regarding their Q1 2025 purchase of paints:

- InvoiceNumber: Used to uniquely identify purchase transactions.
- Amount: A cost of purchase gross dollar amount.
- Discount: The discount amount to be deducted from the (purchase) amount to arrive at the actual purchase cost.

1. Create an information model that enables you to determine the total purchase cost and discount received from the purchases.
2. Once the information model is in place, create this report.

| Total Purchase Cost | $3,326,283.38 |
| Total Discount Amount | $142,547.62 |

EX 6.3 (LO 2) `Data` `Managerial Accounting` **Build an Information Model for Reporting Standard Costs** FonzieBikes is a niche Canadian manufacturer of bikes and buggies. Their engineers and accountants have worked together to specify a Bill of Materials (BoM) which determines what raw materials are needed to make a finished good (product), how many (quantity), and what the expected (standard) cost is for each of them. You are given a data set that contains a sample of the BoM data.

FinishedGood	RawMaterial	STDQuantity	STDCost
Tricycle	Trike tire, large front	1	$ 96
Tricycle	Tricycle frame	1	$ 150
Tricycle	4" tire	1	$ 64
Tricycle	Tricycle pedals	2	$ 28
Mountain bike	18" Frame	1	$ 213
Mountain bike	26" wheels and tires	2	$ 34
Mountain bike	Mountain Bike handle	2	$ 44
Mountain bike	Gear system	1	$ 81
Buggy	Nuts	2,500	$ 0.01
Buggy	Bolts	2,750	$ 0.01
Buggy	Radio	1	$ 111
Buggy	Truck body	1	$ 430
Buggy	Engine	1	$ 1,015
Buggy	Automotive tires	4	$ 69
Buggy	Black Paint	40	$ 2

1. Create an information model.
2. Use the information model to generate a report that shows the total estimated standard cost for each of the three products: tricycle, mountain bike, and buggy.

FinishedGood	TotalStandardCost
Buggy	$ 1,964.50
Mountain bike	$ 450.00
Tricycle	$ 366.00

EX 6.4 (LO 2) `Data` `Managerial Accounting` **Create a Report for Hotel Spending** Emory & Grant is a regional accounting firm in the southeastern United States. When traveling to clients, their employees can stay at any Hilton or Marriott hotel. You receive a spreadsheet with all February 2025 hotel transactions and the amount paid for each stay. You are asked to build an information model that can determine two things:

- The amount spent on Hilton hotels, the amount spent on Marriott hotels, and the amount spent on other hotels.
- The relative proportion of Hilton, Marriott, and other hotels in lodging expenses.

1. Develop the information model.
2. Then, create the following two reports:

Report 1: Amount spent per hotel chain

Hotel	TotalAmountSpent
Hilton	$ 170,154.52
Marriott	$ 73,376.80
Other	$ 2,225.38
Total	**$ 245,756.70**

Report 2: Relative proportion of lodging expenses per hotel chain

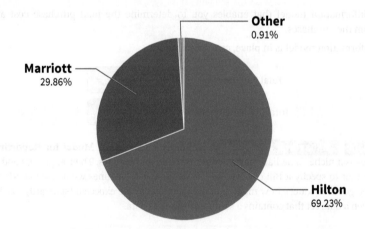

EX 6.5 (LO 2) `Data` **Create an Information Model to Support a Hiring Decision** CreativeX is hiring a CFO. To be considered qualified, a candidate must meet the following three criteria:

- Between 30 and 50 years old ($\geq$30 and $\leq$50).
- Expertise in either auditing or tax, or both.
- Currently employed as level 3 (manager) or higher.

The company provides you with the spreadsheet containing the information they received from the candidates.

Candidate	Age	Audit	Tax	Level
Liz Smith	33	Y	N	4
Jada Vaughn	29	Y	Y	3
Jenny Wang	52	N	N	1
Eric Kim	47	Y	Y	3
Misty Harrison	41	N	Y	4
George Star	39	Y	N	5
Elton Seger	25	N	N	3
Isabella Fernande	38	Y	N	2
Elise Jackson	41	Y	Y	2
Brenda Swift	25	N	N	5
Lindsay Lauper	56	N	Y	4
Nicole Sardo	35	N	N	2
Cindy Rafferty	40	N	N	2
Greg Cuddy	45	Y	N	3
Mateo Rodriguez	31	N	Y	4
Caleb Cooke	28	Y	N	2
Jane Harris	41	N	Y	5
Debra Pollack	29	Y	N	1
Sheldon Andrews	49	Y	Y	2

1. Create the information model.

2. Use the information model to generate a list with the names of the candidates that are qualified.

EX 6.6 (LO 2) `Data` `Financial Accounting` **Build an Information Model for Reporting Net Revenues** Old Marine (OM) is a Michigan clothing manufacturer. You are given a spreadsheet that contains information regarding all January 2025 orders. It has two worksheets:

- Orders: For each order, a unique ID, date, dollar amount, and shipment ID are provided.
- Shipments: For each shipment, a unique ID, the shipment type, the shipping cost (Amount), and the shipping company are provided.

There are two types of shipping:

- FOB Origin (**O**): The customer pays for the shipping costs.
- FOB Destination (**D**): Old Marine pays for the shipping costs.

The net revenue for an order is the order's amount minus the shipping cost paid by OM.

1. Create an information model that enables you to generate the total net revenue for January 2025 orders.

2. Use the information model to create a report that shows this number.

EX 6.7 (LO 2) `Data` `Financial Accounting` **Build an Information Model for Profit Margin Analysis** Berok is a small investment company that wants to invest in one of the following three companies: ABC Groceries, Neighborhood Groceries, or Worldwide Groceries. They assembled a spreadsheet with revenue and profit data for each firm for the last five years. A key ratio for their financial analysis is profit margin.

1. Develop an information model that calculates the profit margin ratio.

2. Use the information model to create the following two visuals:

   a. The profit ratios for each of the five previous years (2021–2025) for each of the three companies:

Name	2021	2022	2023	2024	2025
ABC Groceries	7.55%	7.94%	7.55%	7.14%	8.05%
Neighborhood Groceries	6.83%	6.76%	7.02%	6.67%	6.78%
Worldwide Groceries	7.62%	8.57%	7.52%	8.27%	8.59%

   b. The profit ratio based on the total revenues and profits for the 2021–2025 period for each of the three companies:

Name	Profit Margin 2021–2025
ABC Groceries	7.65%
Neighborhood Groceries	6.82%
Worldwide Groceries	8.08%

EX 6.8 (LO 2) `Data` `Managerial Accounting` **Create an Information Model to Determine Employee Bonuses** Ruppetware is a small manufacturer of innovative kitchen products. In addition to their fixed salaries, salespeople at Ruppetware can earn a substantial bonus at the end of the year. This is the algorithm to determine bonuses for 2025:

- The 2025 target sales amount for each salesperson is determined by adding 5% to the average 2024 sales amount for all salespeople.
- Only salespeople that meet that target are considered for a bonus. The magnitude of the bonus is determined as follows:
  - If the target is exceeded by less than 5%, the bonus is $5,000.
  - If the target is exceeded by at least 5% but less than 10%, the bonus is $10,000.
  - If the target is exceeded by at least 10%, then the bonus is $15,000.

1. Create the information model needed for such an analysis.
2. Generate a list that shows the 2025 bonus amounts for all salespeople.

EX 6.9 (LO 2) `Data` `Managerial Accounting` **Build an Information Model for Truckload Management** Leno Transportation Services (LTS) is a transportation company that compiles a daily schedule linking available trucks to pallets that need to be transported that day. All transportations are local. They keep their data in three worksheets:

- The Truck worksheet contains a list of all available trucks. For each truck, LTS records a unique ID and the maximum weight it can carry (truckload).
- The Pallet worksheet contains a list of all pallets that must be transported on a given day. For each pallet, LTS records a unique ID and the total weight of the goods currently on a it. Pallet weights are in kilograms (note, 1 kilogram = 2.20462 pounds).
- The Schedule table contains the daily schedule and therefore determines which pallets must be loaded on which trucks.

Using the three worksheets, LTS asks you to create an information model that enables them to explore the following two questions:

- Is the maximum weight for any truck exceeded?
- What trucks have a truckload of less than 75%?

1. Create the information model.
2. Once your information model is in place, use it to create a table that provides a list of all trucks scheduled to go out today. For each truck, the table shows its ID, its maximum weight, its scheduled weight, and its scheduled load. Use a red background for trucks that exceed their maximum weight and a yellow background for trucks that have a truckload less than 75%. The report should look as follows:

TruckID	MaximumWeight	TotalWeight	Load
1	10,000	7,826.40	0.78
2	25,000	25,974.83	1.04
3	15,000	11,794.72	0.79
4	20,000	16,997.62	0.85
5	20,000	8,267.33	0.41
6	25,000	19,246.33	0.77
7	15,000	4,078.55	0.27

EX 6.10 (LO 2) `Data` `Financial Accounting` **Create an Information Model to Show Employees' Pension Account Contributions** Maurer and Cook is a small accounting firm in downtown Reno, Nevada. They offer to match $0.75 of each dollar of their employees' pension account contributions following the graded vesting schedule shown here:

Years Employed	Vesting Schedule
0	0%
1	0%
2	20%
3	40%

(Continued)

4	60%
5	80%
6	100%

The managing partner gives you an Excel worksheet with the names of all employees, their years of service, and their total employee contributions.

1. Develop the information model.
2. Generate a report that shows each employee's total vested pension account contribution.

Employee	Total Vested Contribution
David Maurer	705,047.00
Mike Cook	638,946.00
Bernard Espinosa	438,663.75
Susan Hoover	437,302.25
Jamal Coleman	321,413.75
Elzbieta Jacek	234,108.00
Gail Wolcott	78,167.25
Billy Houston	50,912.40
Carlos Martinez	37,590.80
Amy Winter	30,483.70

EX 6.11 (LO 2, 3) `Data` `Financial Accounting` **Create an Information Model for Cash Flow Analysis** Valentina Turner owns The Blue Ballroom, which is a dance studio in Nevada. She has a spreadsheet that records incoming and outgoing payments since the beginning of the year (2025). The structure of the data set is shown here:

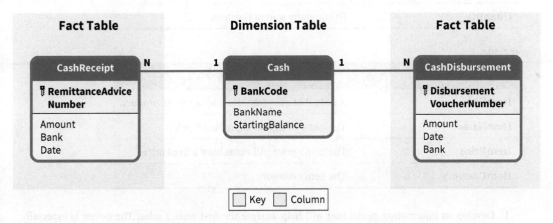

She would like to use the summary table shown here to show the overall cash flows and the cash flows for each of her three bank accounts.

BankName	StartingBalance	Inflow	Outflow	CustomerBalance
Fulton	$ 23,009	$ 953.34	$ 1,148.36	$ 22,813.98
MTB	$ 89,012	$ 2,116.00	$ 900.23	$ 90,227.77
PNC	$ 44,099	$ 2,408.04	$ 2,987.36	$ 43,519.68
Total	$ 156,120	$ 5,477.38	$ 5,035.95	$ 156,561.43

1. Create the information model.
2. Generate the report.

EX 6.12 (LO 2, 3) `Data` `Financial Accounting` **Create an Information Model for Revenue Analysis** Jane Jones (JJ) just opened a small food truck, Gourmet@5, on Fifth Avenue in New York City. The menu is simple, offering hamburgers, hot dogs, water bottles, and a variety of soda and candy bars. She gives you a spreadsheet that contains all the transactions for the first week from Monday through Sunday. The diagram shows what data was collected:

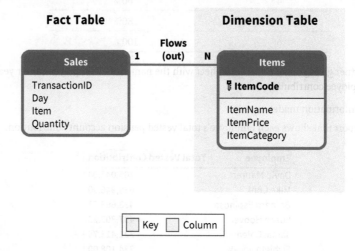

The data dictionary provides a brief description for each of the fields.

SALES

Name	Description
TransactionID	An ID used to identify the transaction.
Day	The day of the week the transaction occurred.
Item	The item sold to the customer (code).
Quantity	The quantity sold of the item.

ITEMS

Name	Description
ItemCode	A code that uniquely identifies a type of product.
ItemName	The name of the item (product type).
ItemPrice	The item's price. All items have a fixed price.
ItemCategory	The item's category.

1. Develop an information model that will help analyze the first week's sales. The owner is especially interested in knowing which products generate the most revenue.

2. Generate at least two reports using the information model you created.

EX 6.13 (LO 2, 3) Data **Create an Information Model for Employee Performance Analysis** Giuseppina's is a popular, family-owned, pizza store in Bourbon, Missouri. The store's owner has collected the following information regarding all deliveries on February 14, 2025: order number, driver, order amount, and tip amount received by the driver. The owner would like to rank the drivers based on two criteria:

- Total tip amount received.
- Average tip percentage received.

1. Develop an information model for such an analysis.

2. Use the information model to create a table for each ranking that shows the names of the drivers.

Professional Application Case **359**

Professional Application Case   VibeToUs

VibeToUs is a ballroom studio in Pocatello, Idaho. The studio's owner has collected data regarding the studio's sales for lessons in January 2025. You are interning with them as an accountant. The owner has a series of questions that can be answered using data that has already been given to you. You have already developed the data dictionary and the data model for the data set.

VibeToUs Data Dictionary

INSTRUCTORS

Column Name	Field Description
InstructorID	An ID that uniquely identifies an instructor.
InstructorName	An instructor's name.
NumberOfHoursTaught	The number of hours an instructor has taught for VibeToUs.
NumberOfAwards	The number of local and regional awards an instructor has received during the last three years.
NumberOfNationalAwards	The number of national recognitions an instructor has received.
Salary	For full-time employees, the salary the instructor earns.
JobTitle	An instructor's job title.

CLASSES

Column Name	Field Description
ClassCode	A code that uniquely identifies a class.
ClassDescription	A brief description of the class.

STUDENTS

Column Name	Field Description
StudentID	An ID that uniquely identifies a student.
StudentName	A student's name.
Level	Student's Skill Level: B = Beginner I = Intermediate A = Advanced
Gender	A student's gender.

LESSONS

Column Name	Field Description
LessonID	An ID that uniquely identifies a lesson.
Date	The date on which the lesson occurred.
Class	The type of class taught during this lesson.
Instructor	The ID of the instructor teaching this class.

PARTICIPATES

Column Name	Field Description
Lesson	The ID of the lesson taken by the student.
Student	The ID of the student taking the lesson.

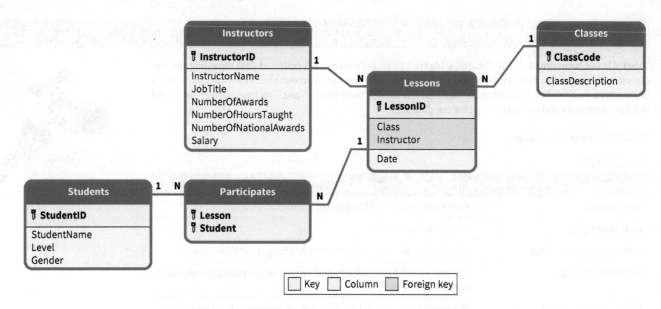

PAC 6.1 Financial Accounting: Analyze VibeToUs' Profitability

Data **Financial Accounting** VibeToUs has four categories of instructors:

- Apprentice.
- Intermediate.
- Advanced.
- Champion.

The following rules are used to assign instructors to their category:

- Instructors who have taught less than 250 hours are apprentices.
- Instructors who have taught more than 250 hours are considered intermediate.
- Intermediate instructors who have won at least three awards, from a list of approved local and regional tournaments during the last three years, are considered advanced.
- Instructors who have earned national recognition, from a list of highly prestigious awards, are classified as champions.

Instructors' pay is determined by their category:

Category	Hourly Rate
Apprentice	$ 45
Intermediate	$ 65
Advanced	$ 85
Champion	$ 110

This hourly rate applies to any class an instructor teaches: initiation, private, or group. The only exception is the Friday evening parties, for which an instructor is paid $250. The price paid by students is the instructor's hourly rate plus $30. So, for a one-hour lesson with an apprentice, the student pays $75. For a one-hour lesson with a champion, the students pays $140. The standard rate for any group lesson (swing, cha-cha, etc.) is $40 per person. Admission to the weekly Friday party is $25. Every student receives a free initiation lesson.

1. Develop an information model that enables you to determine the gross profit for last month. When calculating gross profit, the only cost to consider is what the owner pays the instructors. Do not include the salaries paid to full-time employees.

2. Create a report that shows the total gross profit generated, gross profit generated per class, and gross profit generated per instructor.

PAC 6.2 Auditing: Analyze Potential Fraud

Data **Auditing** VibeToUs' policy is that potential customers can have a free initiation lesson. However, instructors are still paid for these lessons. The owner does not want to change this policy, but understands that it creates an opportunity for fraud. You are asked to analyze the following four questions. Build an information model to explore each question. Then, create a report for each of them.

1. What is the cost of the initiation lessons. What investment has been made thus far?

2. Are there students that took more than one initiation lesson?

3. Are there instructors with an unusually high number of initiation lessons?

4. What is the conversion rate? That is, how many students who signed up for an initiation lesson also eventually paid for a lesson or a Friday night party?

PAC 6.3 Managerial Accounting: Create a Break-even Analysis of Group Classes

Data **Managerial Accounting** VibeToUs policy is to keep group classes only when there is a net revenue of at least $150 after paying the instructor. Currently, the price paid by students for a group class is $40. Explore the following two questions:

1. Create an information model to determine how many students are required per lesson to break-even, and which lessons have not yet reached that goal.

2. Generate a report that shows which classes are not meeting the break-even point. What classes would you suggest canceling?

PAC 6.4 Tax Accounting: Determine Withholdings for Salaried Employees

Data **Tax Accounting** For the two salaried employees, VibeToUs must withhold the employer portion of FICA taxes every month from their wages. FICA tax is a combination of Social Security tax and Medicare tax. The 2025 FICA tax rate is 7.65%, which includes Social Security tax of 6.2% and Medicare tax of 1.45%. The owner does not need to withhold Social Security tax for any earnings above $168,900. Therefore, the studio must only withhold Medicare tax on wages above this amount. Create an information model that will allow you to design a worksheet similar to the one shown that will help the studio determine the FICA tax payments for each month.

		Month	Deduction
Salary	200,000	January	1,275.00
FICA%	0.0765	February	1,275.00
SocialSecurity%	0.062	March	1,275.00
Medicare%	0.0145	April	1,275.00
SocialSecurityMaximum	168,900	May	1,275.00
		June	1,275.00
		July	1,275.00
		August	1,275.00
		September	1,275.00
		October	1,275.00
		November	380.13
		December	241.67

Analysis: Data Exploration

So far in the analyze stage of the data analysis process, you have prepared the data, completed information modeling, and created an analytical database. Now, it is time to explore the data and collect insights. This step investigates data to uncover anomalies, new patterns, and anything that might improve decision-making. This chapter will help you develop the skills needed for successful data exploration, which is a process that includes asking the right questions and identifying and exploring data relationships to find insights. The patterns presented in this chapter will help you effectively and efficiently explore the data sets you will work with during your career.

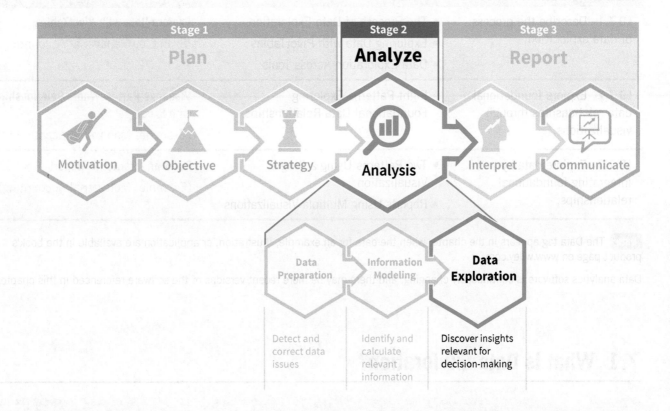

Stage 1			Stage 2	Stage 3	
Plan			**Analyze**	**Report**	
Motivation	Objective	Strategy	Analysis	Interpret	Communicate

Data Preparation	Information Modeling	**Data Exploration**
Detect and correct data issues	Identify and calculate relevant information	Discover insights relevant for decision-making

After earning her master's in accounting, Yuqi joined the data analytics department of a large financial institution.

My transition into the workplace was not without challenges. **In school I was given complex problems for which I had to find elegant solutions, and I really excelled at that. However, when I started my job, there were no neatly defined questions.** For example, the financial data team continuously asked us for new insights. What can you tell us that we don't know yet? **So, I needed to learn more skills—specifically data exploration. I started looking at data sets from as many different angles as possible.** I looked at trends, distributions, grouped data in ways that no one had done before, correlated all kinds of variables, looked for outliers, and so much more. I developed a unique data exploration skill set and became good at it. **Honestly, I feel like I have become a data researcher.** What is next for me? After doing this for almost 10 years, I plan to get my PhD in data science.

Chapter Roadmap

LEARNING OBJECTIVES	TOPICS	APPLY IT
LO 7.1 Describe the process of data exploration.	• The Process of Data Exploration • Exploring Data with PivotTables • Data Exploration Across Tools	**Explore Data with PivotTables** (Example: Managerial Accounting)
LO 7.2 Explore foundational data relationships through visualizations.	• Eight Patterns Exploring Foundational Data Relationships	**Visualize Part-to-Whole Relationships with Excel** (Example: Managerial Accounting)
LO 7.3 Explore data by integrating foundational relationships.	• Two Patterns Using a Single Visualization • Reports Using Multiple Visualizations	**Build an Interactive Report** (Example: Managerial Accounting)

Data The Data tag appears in the chapter when the data for an example, illustration, or application are available in the book's product page on www.wiley.com.

Data analytics software is continuously changing, and there may be more recent versions of the software referenced in this chapter.

7.1 What Is Data Exploration?

LEARNING OBJECTIVE ❶
Describe the process of data exploration.

In Chapter 6, you learned how to add information useful for analysis to an analytical database. Now you are ready to start exploring the data. **Data exploration,** or exploratory data analysis, is the discovery process of looking for something new and previously unknown. This is accomplished by looking for patterns, outliers, or, more generally, for insights. An **insight** is an observation that might significantly affect a business' decision-making. Remember, decisions are not based on data. Rather, decisions are informed by the insights generated from data.

This process of generating insights is what distinguishes data analysis from the simple act of reporting numbers. Calculating and presenting the total dollar amount of donations per year for a non-for-profit organization is reporting, but recognizing there is a downward trend of donations over the years and that donors in different age groups behave differently is a result of data exploration. While they might share some tools, it is essential to differentiate between data exploration, interpretation, and reporting:

- **Exploration:** Discovering insights.
- **Interpretation:** Contextualizing and understanding insights.
- **Reporting:** Communicating insights.

Interpretation and reporting are covered in their own chapters. For now, let's summarize the process of data exploration.

The Process of Data Exploration

Data exploration is an integral part of what accountants do every day. They look for insights, from identifying if there are seasonal fluctuations in sales and whether those fluctuations affect the bottom line, to how changes in credit policy affect sales and uncollectible accounts receivable. It is a four-step process of identifying questions, identifying data relationships, exploring data relationships, and, finally, generating insights (**Illustration 7.1**).

ILLUSTRATION 7.1   Data Exploration as a Process

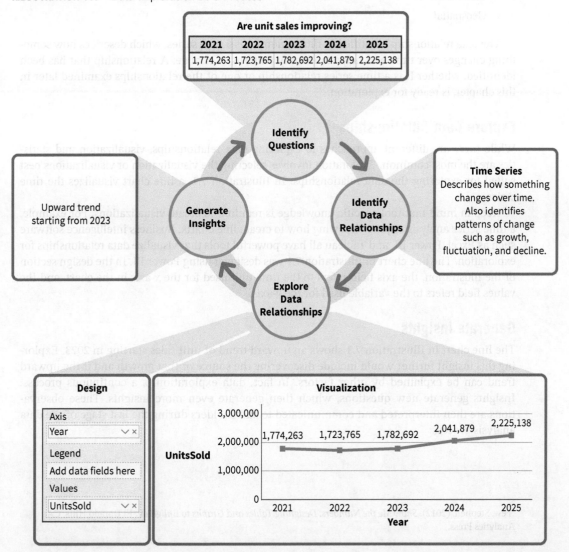

Identify Questions

Data exploration helps answer accounting questions such as whether sales and profits are improving, which products deserve investment, if bad debts are appropriately managed, and more. An analytical database should provide answers to both anticipated and unanticipated (unplanned) questions. Once the question is determined, such as the question about whether unit sales are improving in Illustration 7.1, then the underlying data relationships can be identified.

Identify Data Relationships

If we want to know if sales are improving and the available data indicated a change in both the marketing budget and in unit sales, then the relationship between those two elements could generate valuable insights. A **data relationship** describes how data elements (or values) relate to each other. But before aspects of data relationships can be analyzed, they have to be identified. Stephen Few,[1] an expert in data visualizations, differentiates eight foundational data relationships:

- Nominal comparison
- Distribution
- Deviation
- Ranking
- Part-to-whole
- Correlation
- Time series
- Geospatial

The data relationship identified in Illustration 7.1 is a time series, which describes how something changes over time and helps to identify patterns of change. A relationship that has been identified, whether it is a time series relationship or one of the relationships examined later in this chapter, is ready for exploration.

Explore Data Relationships

While there are different approaches to exploring data relationships, visualization and statistics are the most common. Exploration involves selecting the visualization or visualizations best suited for exploring the data relationships. In Illustration 7.1, a line chart visualizes the time series.

Keep in mind that tool-specific knowledge is required to create visualizations. For example, a time series analysis requires knowing how to create line charts. Business intelligence software such as Excel, Power BI, and Tableau all have powerful tools that visualize data relationships for exploration. The line chart in Illustration 7.1 was designed using Power BI. In the design section of the illustration, the axis field refers to the time unit used for the x-axis in the chart, and the values field refers to the variable used for the y-axis.

Generate Insights

The line chart in Illustration 7.1 shows an upward trend of unit sales starting in 2023. Exploring this insight further would include discovering the source of that growth and if the upward trend can be explained by other factors. In fact, data exploration is a continuous process. Insights generate new questions, which then generate even more insights. These observations are then interpreted and communicated to stakeholders during the last stage of the data analysis process.

---

[1]Few, Stephen. (2012). *Show Me the Numbers: Designing Tables and Graphs to Enlighten.* El Dorado Hills, CA: Analytics Press.

Think Critically During Data Exploration

Critical thinking is an integral part of data exploration:

- Exploring requires in-depth understanding of data relationships, how they are presented, and the insights they can generate. For example, many visualizations can present and explore time series, including area charts, column charts, line charts, sparkline charts, and waterfall charts. You must know which chart to use and when. When exploring time series, you are looking for trends, cycles, and irregularities (**Knowledge**).

- Data exploration is often pattern-based. You will look for patterns and structures you have encountered before and develop more that you can leverage in future analyses. One example is breaking trends down to better understand the reason for changes. If there is an upward trend in units sold, is this also true for all products and regions (**Self-Reflection**)?

Exploring Data with PivotTables

Data exploration investigates data from different angles to collect insights. A widely-used tool for this is the Excel PivotTable. You learned in Chapter 2 that a PivotTable can quickly rearrange data to help answer important business questions. Here, we illustrate the key elements of data exploration using a PivotTable.

Data The data set in **Illustration 7.2**(A) summarizes unit sales for Honda Motors North America (HNA) for the period 2021–2025 in a cross tabulation table.[2] Illustration 7.2(B) shows the same data as a flat table.[3] Recall that for data analytics, flat tables are preferred over cross-tabulation tables because the column headers in flat tables do not contain data values useful for analysis purposes. The flat table in Illustration 7.2(B) will be used to build PivotTables.

ILLUSTRATION 7.2 HNA Data Set

Country	Model	Type	2021	2022	2023	2024	2025
USA	Civic	Sedan	320,981	301,882	292,331	291,002	255,423
USA	Accord	Sedan	243,192	245,998	231,441	309,885	344,771
USA	CR-V	SUV	175,883	160,886	190,001	220,877	252,019
USA	Pilot	SUV	140,444	142,980	139,441	142,917	125,090
USA	Odyssey	Minivan	188,664	167,123	150,872	150,881	139,009
USA	Ridgeline	Truck	58,322	55,897	56,889	55,899	54,891
Canada	Civic	Sedan	230,887	242,998	275,667	381,998	480,871
Canada	Accord	Sedan	195,232	200,872	210,665	253,988	319,755
Canada	CR-V	SUV	135,423	129,809	126,592	114,119	98,077
Canada	Pilot	SUV	40,998	35,672	39,811	43,125	47,329
Canada	Odyssey	Minivan	25,229	7,761	26,981	22,099	19,822
Canada	Ridgeline	Truck	19,008	31,887	42,001	55,089	88,081

Country	Model	Type	Year	UnitsSold
Canada	Accord	Sedan	2021	195,232
Canada	Accord	Sedan	2022	200,872
Canada	Accord	Sedan	2023	210,665
Canada	Accord	Sedan	2024	253,988
Canada	Accord	Sedan	2025	319,755
Canada	Civic	Sedan	2021	230,887
Canada	Civic	Sedan	2022	242,998
Canada	Civic	Sedan	2023	275,667
Canada	Civic	Sedan	2024	381,998
Canada	Civic	Sedan	2025	480,871

(A) Cross Tabulation Structure of HNA Data Set

(B) Flat Structure of HNA Data Set

Illustration 7.3(A) is a PivotTable made with Excel using the HNA data set. It lists HNA's models in descending order of total units sold. Illustration 7.3(B) shows how the PivotTable in panel A is created using the PivotTable Fields dialog box, which is Excel's tool for defining a PivotTable's content.

The five components used for data exploration with PivotTables are fields, values, rows, columns, and filters [Illustration 7.3(B)].

---

[2]The data set is fictitious.
[3]Illustration 7.2(A) shows the full data set. Illustration 7.2(B) shows a partial data set; the first 10 rows of the flat table.

ILLUSTRATION 7.3 Excel PivotTable and PivotTable Dialog Box

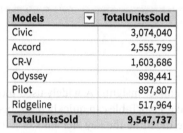

Models ▼	TotalUnitsSold
Civic	3,074,040
Accord	2,555,799
CR-V	1,603,686
Odyssey	898,441
Pilot	897,807
Ridgeline	517,964
TotalUnitsSold	**9,547,737**

(A) PivotTable: Total Units Sold per Model[4]

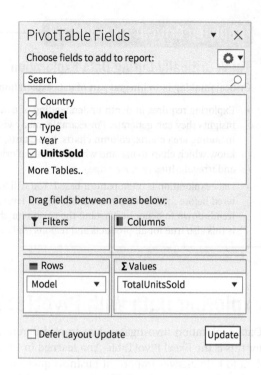

(B) PivotTable Creation

Fields

The Fields area lists all the data elements available for exploration purposes. They can be dragged and dropped to other areas to build data relationships and filter the data. In Illustration 7.3, the Model and UnitsSold fields are used for exploration.

Values

The Values area in Illustration 7.3(B) represents the number or numbers to be analyzed. It can be used to explore data in different ways:

- Drag and drop any field into the Values area and apply mathematical operations such as average, count, or sum to it.
- Create calculated fields.

Examples of accounting-related values that could be analyzed include gross revenue, net revenue, taxes, cost, profit, and more. For HNA, the values in the UnitsSold field are summed, generating the total number of units sold during the 2021–2025 period.

Rows and Columns

In Illustration 7.3(B), the Model field has been dragged to the Rows area so the table will calculate and show the total units sold per model. The TotalUnitsSold column in Illustration 7.3(A) can then be sorted and formatted.

When the Country field is added to the Columns area in Illustration 7.3(B), the resulting cross tabulation table (**Illustration 7.4**) shows the total units sold per model, represented by the rows, and per country, which is represented by the columns.

Any fields can be dragged to the Rows and Columns areas and dropped. For example, we can analyze the number of units sold per Type (Rows) per Country (Columns). It is also possible to drag and drop more than one field into the Rows and Columns sections to drill further down into the data.

---

[4]Some minor formatting was applied.

Total UnitsSold Models	Countries ▾ Canada	USA	TotalUnitsSold
Accord	1,180,512	1,375,287	2,555,799
Civic	1,612,421	1,461,619	3,074,040
CR-V	604,020	999,666	1,603,686
Odyssey	101,892	796,549	898,441
Pilot	206,935	690,872	897,807
Ridgeline	236,066	281,898	517,964
TotalUnitsSold	**3,941,846**	**5,605,891**	**9,547,737**

ILLUSTRATION 7.4 Excel PivotTable Total Units Sold per Model per Country

Filters

Using filters further enhances data exploration with Excel PivotTables. Filters let us determine what data should be considered for analysis, and they can be created for any field. The PivotTable in **Illustration 7.5**(A) creates a filter for the Country field, while Illustration 7.5(B) shows how to use this filter by selecting a value for the Country field. In this case, the selected value is United States.

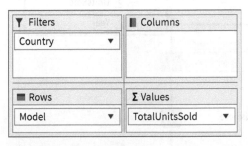

ILLUSTRATION 7.5 Excel PivotTable Filters

Country	USA ▾
Models ▾	**TotalUnitsSold**
Accord	1,375,287
Civic	1,461,619
CR-V	999,666
Odyssey	796,549
Pilot	690,872
Ridgeline	281,898
TotalUnitsSold	**5,605,891**

(A) Creating a PivotTable Filter

(B) PivotTable with Filter Applied

Creating Relationships, Filtering, and Dragging and Dropping

The PivotTable definition in Illustration 7.3(B) brings together some key techniques for data exploration—creating data relationships, filtering, and dragging and dropping.

First, data relationships can be created between the variables in the Values, Rows, and Columns areas and explored. Here are two examples of such data relationships:

- How can the Values variable number be broken down by the values of the Rows and Columns variables? For HNA, what is the share of each model (rows) in the total number of units sold (values)?

- How can the different models (rows) be ranked based on total units sold (values)? What are HNA's best-selling models?

There are some similarities between this discussion and the concept of information modeling, which was covered earlier in this course. The numbers in the Values area can be compared to measures, while the fields in the Rows and Columns areas can be compared to dimensions.

Next, filtering helps identify what data should be considered for analysis. An example of this is applying a filter that would exclude outliers in an analysis. Finally, the ability to drag and drop fields makes exploring different scenarios effortless. Here are some questions that can be answered by dragging and dropping fields using the HNA data set in a PivotTable:

- What is the total number of units sold (values) per country (rows) per model (columns) and how do the numbers compare?

- What is each country's share (rows) in the total number of units sold (values)?

- How do U.S. (filter) sales, in terms of total units sold (values), compare across the different models (rows)?

Data Exploration Across Tools

Excel is not the only business intelligence software that uses data relationships, filtering, and drag and drop for data exploration. **Illustration 7.6**(A) is a Power BI PivotTable that summarizes HNA's total units sold per model during the last five years. In Power BI, a PivotTable is called a matrix. The second part of the illustration(B) shows how it was created.[5]

ILLUSTRATION 7.6 Creating a Power BI Matrix

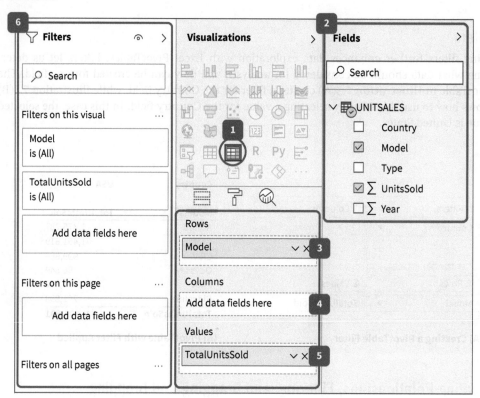

Model	TotalUnitsSold
Accord	2,555,799
Civic	3,074,040
CR-V	1,603,686
Odyssey	898,441
Pilot	897,807
Ridgeline	517,964
Total	**9,547,737**

(A) Power BI Matrix

(B) Power BI Matrix Creation

Notice the similarity between creating an Excel PivotTable in Illustration 7.3(B) and a Power BI matrix in Illustration 7.6(B):

1. In Power BI, we can choose between many drag and drop visualizations. In this example, matrix was selected.

2. The Fields pane corresponds to the fields list in the PivotTable Fields dialog box.

3. The Rows slot in the Fields tab of the matrix visualization corresponds with the Rows area in an Excel PivotTable definition.

4. The Columns slot in the Fields tab of the matrix visualization corresponds with the Columns area in an Excel PivotTable definition.

5. The Values slot in the Fields tab of the matrix visualization corresponds with the Values area in an Excel PivotTable definition.

6. The Filters pane is an enhanced version of the Filters area in an Excel PivotTable definition.

Charts are often more effective than tables for analysis. Power BI charts, which are visualizations, represent one or more data relationships and have a drop and drag structure. In Excel

---

[5]We used Power BI's matrix visualization. However, since no columns are defined, we could have used the table visualization.

it is easy to convert PivotTables into charts with the PivotChart tool. PivotCharts graphically represent the data relationships in PivotTables. **Illustration 7.7** is a pie chart for the PivotTable in Illustration 7.3(A). It highlights each model's share in the total units sold, a part-to-whole relationship, which is discussed later.

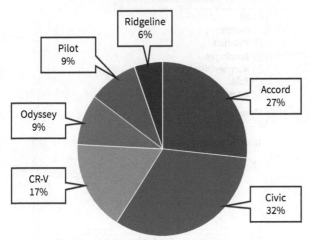

Breakdown of Total Units Sold by Model: 2021–2025

- Ridgeline 6%
- Pilot 9%
- Accord 27%
- Odyssey 9%
- CR-V 17%
- Civic 32%

ILLUSTRATION 7.7   Excel PivotChart

Next, let's examine how charts can represent and explore data relationships.

APPLY IT 7.1

Explore Data with PivotTables

Data **Managerial Accounting** Happy Colors is a small paint company that prepares paint cans that are sold to retailers. CEO Angela Lee supervises three employees, and there are three types of products—low, high, and premium paint. Regardless of the type of paint, it should take about three minutes to prepare a can. The cost of a can depends on the type of product:

- Low: $5
- High: $10
- Premium: $14

Since defective paint cans cannot be sold, Angela inspects each can herself. Losses resulting from defective cans are an important issue for Happy Colors, so Angela hires your firm to help understand this issue. Here is the data dictionary for this data set:

Data Dictionary for Happy Colors

Name	Description
ID	A unique ID for each recording of an employee's output per month per product type.
Month	The name of the month.
Product	The name of the product type: low, high, or premium.
Employee	The name of the employee.
NumberOfDefectiveItems	The number of defective cans by an employee for a product type in a specific month.
Total	The total number of cans by an employee for a product type in a specific month.
Cost	The total loss (in dollars) resulting from the detective items by an employee for a product in a specific month.

1. Create a PivotTable that helps you understand the losses per employee per product type.
2. What insights does the PivotTable generate?

SOLUTION

1. Using Excel, the PivotTable can be created by selecting the product, employee, and cost fields. Drag the Cost field to Values, the Employee field to Rows, and the Product field to Columns.

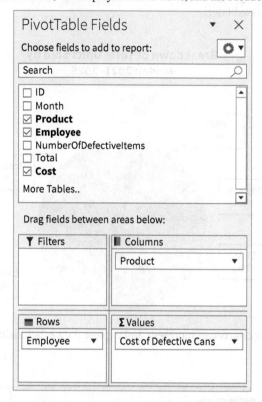

After applying some formatting, the resulting PivotTable looks like this:

Cost of Defective Cans	Product Type 🔽			
Employee 🔽	**High**	**Low**	**Premium**	**Total**
Andre	$ 30,500	$ 20,750	$ 1,530	$ 52,780
Bianca	$ 24,750	$ 24,250	$ 1,147	$ 50,147
Camille	$ 35,500	$ 14,750	$ 825	$ 51,075
Total	**$ 90,750**	**$ 59,750**	**$ 3,502**	**$ 154,002**

2. The table shows that the losses resulting from defective items are somewhat similar for the three employees. However, Andre has the highest losses for premium paint cans, Bianca has the highest losses for low paint cans, and Camille has the highest losses for high paint cans.

7.2 How Are Data Relationships Visualized for Exploration?

LEARNING OBJECTIVE ❷
Explore foundational data relationships through visualizations.

You have learned that a data relationship describes how data elements, or values, relate to each other. Each data analytics project will have a unique set of data relationships. While there is no single, best approach for investigating data relationships, a structured set of data exploration patterns can help answer questions about which data relationships can be explored, how they can be illustrated in visualizations, how to create those visualizations, and what they can tell us.

There are two types of data exploration patterns. Some patterns explore a foundational data relationship with a single visualization, while others explore data by integrating data relationships. This section presents eight foundational data exploration patterns. Each pattern identifies and describes the data relationship and visualizations that could represent it. The pattern also shows how to explore the relationship and the insights that can be collected from doing so.

Applying Critical Thinking 7.2

Use Patterns to Explore Data

Data exploration patterns are *real-world* best practices for using data relationships for exploration. They describe which data relationships exist and how to effectively visualize and explore them (**Knowledge**):

- **Data relationship:** Time series data relationships compare observations over time.
- **Visualization:** Line charts are considered the most effective visualization for exploring time series. Best visualization practices include starting the line chart's *y*-axis at zero.
- **Exploration:** Line charts generate insights by identifying trends, cycles, and irregularities.

Data Exploration Pattern 1: Nominal Comparison

A **nominal comparison data relationship** compares the values of a nominal variable based on the values of a second, numeric variable. **Illustration 7.8** shows its **exploration structure**, which is a visual that describes the different elements used in the exploration and how they are related. For nominal comparisons, the exploration structure is a nominal variable, which is what is being compared, and a numeric variable, which is how the values of the nominal variable are compared.

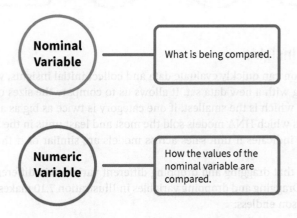

ILLUSTRATION 7.8 Exploration Structure for a Nominal Comparison Data Relationship

Visualizations

Visualizations for nominal comparisons include bar charts, column charts, dot plots, and lollipop charts. Let's go back to the Honda North America example from earlier in the chapter. **Illustration 7.9** is a column chart that compares HNA's models, which is the nominal variable, using the number of units sold, which is the numeric variable. Each model is presented by a column (*x*-axis), and the length of the column is determined by the number of units sold for that model (*y*-axis).

ILLUSTRATION 7.9   Visualizing a Nominal Comparison Data Relationship with a Column Chart

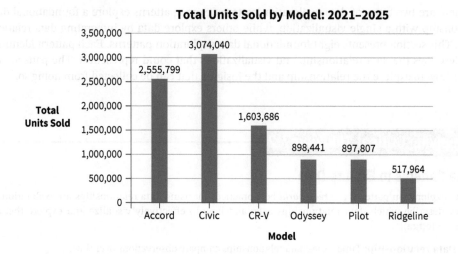

The Excel PivotTable used to create this column chart is shown in **Illustration 7.10**.

ILLUSTRATION 7.10   Excel PivotTable Definition

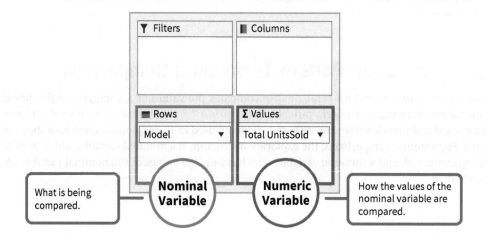

Exploration and Insights

A nominal comparison can quickly evaluate data and collect initial insights, which is especially useful when working with a new data set. It allows us to compare the sizes of each category—which is the biggest, which is the smallest, if one category is twice as big as another, and more. Illustration 7.9 shows which HNA models sold the most and least units in the 2021–2025 period. The same chart also indicates if unit sales across models are similar or if there are significant differences.

You have learned that dragging and dropping different variables in different areas is the key to data exploration. Dragging and dropping variables in Illustration 7.10 makes the opportunities for nominal comparison endless:

- Any nominal variable, or *what* is being analyzed, can be compared using any numeric variable, or *how* the nominal variable is being analyzed.

- Filters can also be applied to both the nominal variable and the numeric variable.

What if an accounting firm regularly analyzes the performance of its staff members? How would they do this? First, the staff members (*what*) are being compared, and they would be selected with a filter. We could use many measures (*how*) to compare them, including total hours worked, total revenue generated, number of clients, average revenue per client, and average client response time. All these variables can be dragged to the numeric variable slot labeled Values. This is why the information modeling step is important for data exploration—it allows creating additional measures that you can later use in analysis.

Data Exploration Pattern 2: Distribution

A **distribution data relationship** (Illustration 7.11) shows how the values of a numeric variable are distributed, or spread out, by providing the lowest value, the highest value, the median, the interquartile range, and so on.

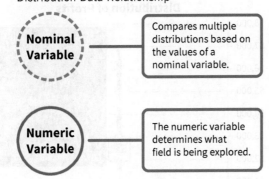

ILLUSTRATION 7.11 Exploration Structure for a Distribution Data Relationship

A common scenario, shown in Illustration 7.11, is to create and compare multiple distributions of the same numeric variable based on the different values of a nominal variable. The dotted line indicates that such a variable is valuable for exploration, but optional when defining a distribution data relationship.

Visualizations

Several visualizations portray distributions, including histograms, violin plots, and box-and-whisker charts (or boxplot charts). Box-and-whisker charts are both powerful and detailed, so they are used here to illustrate a visualization for this pattern.

Let's go back to the HNA example. **Data** The company has a spreadsheet from one of its New York dealerships. They want to know how the profits generated by selling cars vary. **Illustration 7.12** summarizes the spreadsheet data about the cars sold by the dealership last December.

ILLUSTRATION 7.12 Data Structure of the Dealership Profit Data

Field Name	Description
ID	The internal ID that identifies the car.
Model	The car's model.
Profit	The profit made when selling the car is selling price minus dealer invoice. This is also known as front-end gross profit.

Illustration 7.13 shows the first 10 rows of the data set.

ID	Model	Profit
1	Civic	$ 2,125
2	CR-V	$ 2,798
3	Odyssey	$ 2,144
4	Accord	$ 2,749
5	Accord	$ 1,810
6	Accord	$ 1,844
7	Odyssey	$ 4,446
8	Civic	$ 1,912
9	Pilot	$ 3,107
10	Civic	$ 2,101

ILLUSTRATION 7.13 First 10 Rows of the Dealership Profits Data Set

Illustration 7.14 shows a box-and-whisker chart for the Profit field. The red circle represents the average. The bottom of the green box is the first quartile, and the top of the orange box is the third quartile. The median is the intersection between the green and orange boxes, and the length of the green and orange boxes combined is the interquartile range. Finally, the lower fence portrays the minimum value, while the upper fence portrays the maximum value.

ILLUSTRATION 7.14
Visualizing a Distribution Data Relationship with a Box-and-Whisker Chart

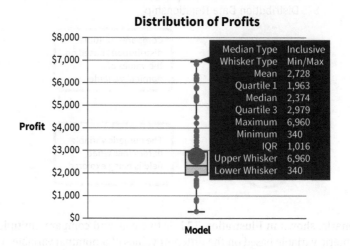

Distribution of Profits

Median Type	Inclusive
Whisker Type	Min/Max
Mean	2,728
Quartile 1	1,963
Median	2,374
Quartile 3	2,979
Maximum	6,960
Minimum	340
IQR	1,016
Upper Whisker	6,960
Lower Whisker	340

How To

Illustration 7.15 shows how this chart would be created in Power BI. Power BI requires dragging a field into the Axis slot. The values for this field represent the data points. Dragging a primary key into this slot is good practice because all data points and their unique values are then represented. A similar box-and-whisker chart can also be created in Excel. (**Data** See **How To 7.1** at the end of the chapter to learn how to do this.)

ILLUSTRATION 7.15 Creating a Box-and-Whisker Chart in Power BI

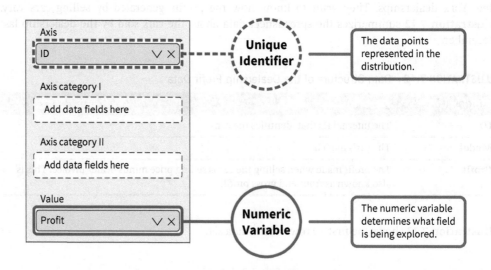

As mentioned earlier, creating and comparing multiple distributions of the same numeric variable based on the different values of a nominal variable is common in this kind of analysis. **Illustration 7.16** shows how to make a chart with this comparison using Power BI:

- Drag Model to the Axis category I slot.
- A separate distribution is then created for each model.

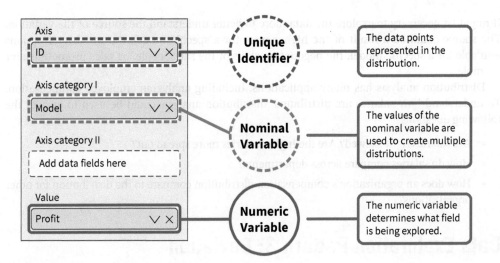

ILLUSTRATION 7.16 Creating a Box-and-Whisker Chart with Multiple Distributions

Illustration 7.17 is the resulting chart.

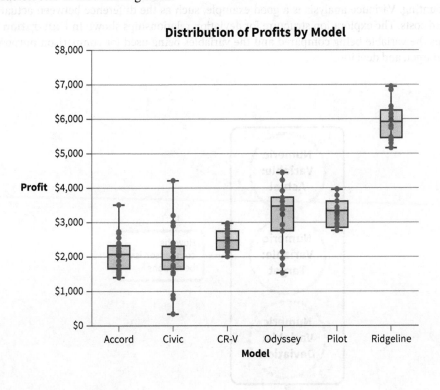

ILLUSTRATION 7.17 Parallel Profit Distributions for HNA Car Models

Exploration and Insights

Dragging and dropping variables also supports data exploration using this pattern. Using the exploration structure for a distribution data relationship, we can quickly examine the distribution of any numeric field in a data set and use any nominal field in the data set to compare data distributions.

Illustration 7.14 showed the distribution information provided by Power BI, including the median, the mean, the interquartile range (IQR), the lowest value, and the highest value. This makes it possible to investigate outliers, skewness, and more. The chart in Illustration 7.17 allows even more comparison across distributions:

- The profits for the Ridgeline model are higher than for the other models.
- The profits for the CR-V and Pilot models are consistent, which means there is little variation.
- The profits for the Odyssey and especially the Civic models are more spread out.

It might be necessary to explore the data more to better understand the source of the variation. The source could be a result of the higher price for a specific model, the number of options available for a specific model, the negotiation skills of the salespeople, or sales promotions, for example.

Distribution analysis has many applications, including analyzing employee compensation. To understand how salaries are distributed, distribution analysis could be used to answer the following questions:

- Are salaries right-skewed? Are the higher salaries more spread out?
- How do salaries compare across departments?
- How does an organization's compensation distribution compare to the distribution for other organizations?

Data Exploration Pattern 3: Deviation

A **deviation data relationship** shows how a set of actual values deviate from their reference values, which are budgeted or forecasted values. Deviation relationships are everywhere in accounting. Variance analysis is a good example, such as the difference between actual and standard costs. The exploration structure for deviation relationships shown in **Illustration 7.18** contains the variable being compared and the variables being used for comparison purposes—actual, target, and deviation.

ILLUSTRATION 7.18
Exploration Structure for a Deviation Data Relationship

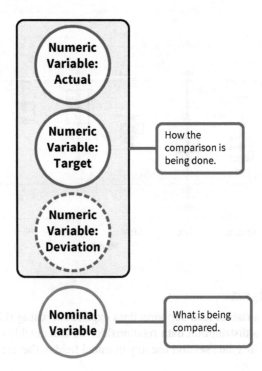

Visualizations

Clustered bar and column charts (used in the following example), gauges, bullet charts, and more can be used for deviation analysis. Imagine that HNA would like to explore whether each vehicle model met its sales expectations. **Data** The company has another data set that includes both the actual and the budgeted unit sales for the 2025 period (**Illustration 7.19**).

ILLUSTRATION 7.19   HNA Budgeted Unit Sales—2025

Country	Model	Type	ActualUnits	BudgetedUnits
USA	Civic	Sedan	255,423	300,000
USA	Accord	Sedan	344,771	350,000
USA	CR-V	SUV	252,019	25,000
USA	Pilot	SUV	125,090	160,000
USA	Odyssey	Minivan	139,009	145,000
USA	Ridgeline	Truck	54,891	55,000
Canada	Civic	Sedan	480,871	425,000
Canada	Accord	Sedan	319,755	275,000
Canada	CR-V	SUV	98,077	110,000
Canada	Pilot	SUV	47,329	45,000
Canada	Odyssey	Minivan	19,822	30,000
Canada	Ridgeline	Truck	88,081	65,000

This data set was used to create the clustered column chart in **Illustration 7.20** with Power BI.

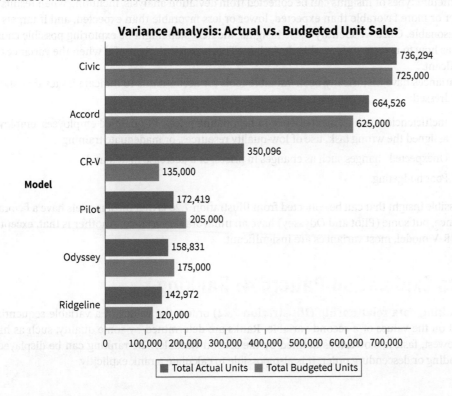

ILLUSTRATION 7.20
Visualizing a Deviation Data Relationship with a Clustered Column Chart

Illustration 7.21 shows how the chart was created.

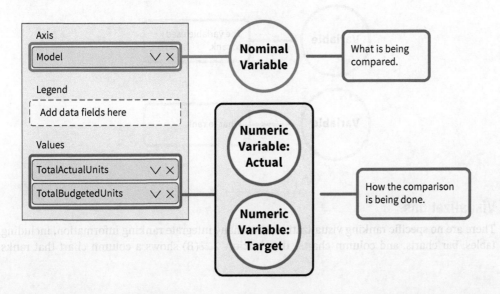

ILLUSTRATION 7.21   Creating a Clustered Column Chart in Power BI

Unlike a column chart, a clustered column chart uses multiple variables for comparison purposes. While the clustered column chart can make comparisons across models, it also provides a comparison within a model. For example, the comparison in Illustration 7.20 is between the actual number of units sold and the budgeted number of units sold, which are the two variables in the Values area:

- TotalActualUnits represents the sum of all values in the ActualUnits field.
- TotalBudgetedUnits represents the sum of all values in the BudgetedUnits field.

Exploration and Insights

Additional variables can be dragged into the Values slot in Illustration 7.21. For example, variance, a variable that is calculated as the difference between the actual and the budgeted units, could be added. There are also three nominal variables in this data set to choose from: country, type, or model.

Different types of insights can be collected from deviation analysis, including when results are higher or more favorable than expected, lower or less favorable than expected, and if targets are unreasonable. Once we identify these insights, the next step might be exploring possible causes, such as how to reverse unfavorable deviations. This is particularly useful when the variances are significant.

Variances have historically been valuable tools for accountants to indicate issues that should be addressed:

- Inefficiencies such as inexperience in negotiating prices, ill-qualified employees, employees assigned the wrong task, use of low-quality resources, or inadequate training.
- Unexpected changes such as changes in prices, or a decrease in demand.
- Poor budgeting.

A possible insight that can be collected from Illustration 7.20 is that most models have a favorable variance, but some (Pilot and Odyssey) have an unfavorable variance. Another is that, except for the CR-V model, most variances are insignificant.

Data Exploration Pattern 4: Ranking

A **ranking data relationship** (**Illustration 7.22**) orders the values of a variable sequentially based on the values of a second variable. Ranks are determined by some quality, such as highest, lowest, fastest, slowest, as defined by the second variable. The ranking can be displayed in ascending or descending order. It is also possible to calculate a rank explicitly.

ILLUSTRATION 7.22
Exploration Structure for a
Ranking Data Relationship

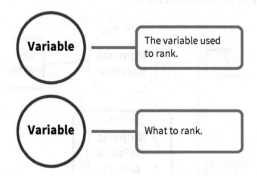

Visualizations

There are no specific ranking visualizations, but many integrate ranking information, including tables, bar charts, and column charts. **Illustration 7.23**(B) shows a column chart that ranks

HNA's models (*what to rank*) based on the units sold in the 2021–2025 period (*how to rank*). Illustration 7.23(A) shows this ranking relationship created for a PivotTable in Excel.

ILLUSTRATION 7.23 Integrating a Ranking Data Relationship into a Column Chart

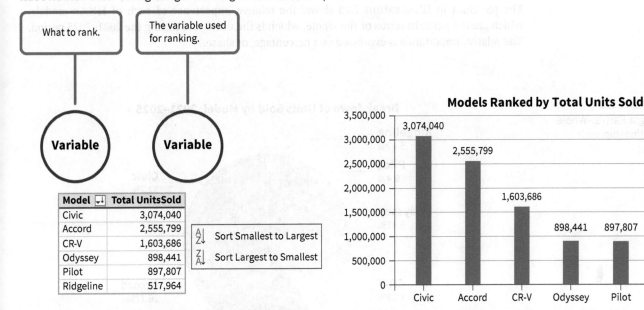

(A) Creating a Ranking Relationship for a PivotTable

(B) Integrating a Ranking Relationship with a Column Chart

Exploration and Insights

Different ranking relationships can be explored by dragging and dropping. Customers can be ranked based on their sales amount or their age; employees can be ranked based on their salaries or their seniority. Measures, such as total outstanding debt of at least 60 days, can also be used to rank customers. Ranking can determine, for example, the top 25 or bottom 25 customers based on revenue. The column chart in Illustration 7.23 indicates a model's rank based on units sold during the 2021–2025 period. The Civic is the best-selling model, followed by the Accord.

Data Exploration Pattern 5: Part-to-Whole

A **part-to-whole data relationship** (Illustration 7.24) compares parts to wholes and looks at how the different parts compare to each other. For example, an organization might generate $100,000 in sales, which is the whole. The home, office, and garden product categories generate $30,000 (30%), $50,000 (50%), and $20,000 (20%), respectively. These three product categories represent the parts.

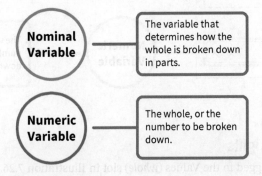

ILLUSTRATION 7.24
Exploration Structure for a Part-to-Whole Data Relationship

A part-to-whole visualization should define the number that is the whole and how the whole should be broken down into parts.

Visualizations

Multiple visualizations can model part-to-whole relationships, including pie charts, donut charts, stacked bar charts, stacked column charts, and tree maps. While tree maps are considered superior for portraying part-to-whole relationships, here the more commonly used pie chart is shown. The pie chart in **Illustration 7.25** shows the relative importance of each of HNA's models, which are the parts, in terms of the whole, which is the units sold during the 2021–2025 period. The relative importance is expressed as a percentage, or share.

ILLUSTRATION 7.25
Visualizing a Part-to-Whole
Data Relationship with
a Pie Chart

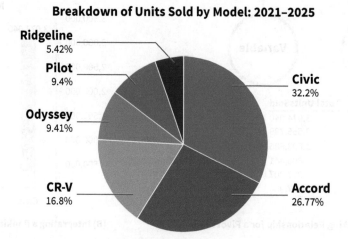

Breakdown of Units Sold by Model: 2021–2025

Ridgeline 5.42%
Pilot 9.4%
Odyssey 9.41%
CR-V 16.8%
Civic 32.2%
Accord 26.77%

Illustration 7.26 shows how this pie chart is created using Power BI:

- The Values slot defines the *what*: This refers to the number that is broken down. Here, it is the TotalUnitsSold measure.
- The Legend slot defines the *how*: This refers to how to break down the whole. Here, this is done by model. For each value of model the number of units sold is calculated, determining the size of its share of the pie. This visual shows the size of its share as a percentage.

ILLUSTRATION 7.26 Creating
a Pie Chart in Power BI

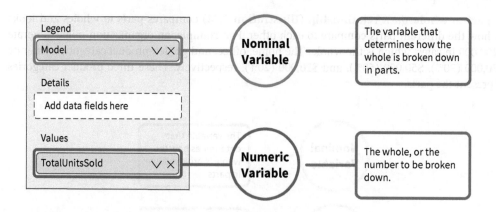

Legend
Model

Details
Add data fields here

Values
TotalUnitsSold

Nominal Variable — The variable that determines how the whole is broken down in parts.

Numeric Variable — The whole, or the number to be broken down.

Exploration and Insights

Any measure can be dragged to the Values (*whole*) slot in Illustration 7.26. Measures tailored to specific needs can also be created, such as July sales to non-U.S. customers. Any nominal variable can be dragged to the Legend slot (*parts*).

Part-to-whole relationships are often used in accounting. Examples include the breakdown of expenses in multiple categories such as administrative expenses, depreciation, marketing expenses, and the breakdown of costs in terms of materials, labor, and overhead.

The pie chart in Illustration 7.25 shows how each model contributes, in relative terms, to the total units sold in the 2021–2025 period. It further shows that the Accord and Civic models combined count for more than 50% of the unit sales. The share of other models, such as the Ridgeline, is relatively small.

Data Exploration Pattern 6: Correlation

A **correlation data relationship** indicates the degree to which two variables move in the same or the opposite direction. For example, if the marketing expenses for a product increase, then it is likely that the sales for the same product also increase. There are two key features to consider with these relationships. The first is direction:

- The direction is positive if both variables move in the same direction.
- The direction is negative if both variables move in opposite directions.

The second feature is the strength of the correlation. Strength indicates the degree of correlation between the two variables, ranging from no correlation to perfect correlation. **Illustration 7.27** shows the exploration structure of a correlation data relationship between numeric variables.

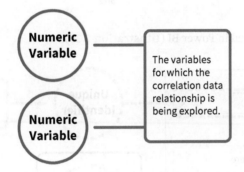

ILLUSTRATION 7.27
Exploration Structure for a Correlation Data Relationship

Visualizations

The most common visualization for exploring correlation is the scatterplot, which is also referred to as a scatter chart. It plots the coordinates for two variables for each data point.

Let's illustrate a scatterplot with an example from a new company. Buzz Cut is a landscaping business with two owners. These small business owners continuously face tough strategic, financial, and operational decisions, such as price estimates for properties. **Data** They have a spreadsheet that contains data about the size and average cutting time, in minutes, for all their properties (**Illustration 7.28**).

Price estimation is a critical decision for all landscape businesses. Buzz Cut uses the following decision model to make price estimates:

- It takes one minute to mow 1,000 square feet, and Buzz Cut charges a dollar per minute ($60 per hour). They would charge $50 for mowing a 50,000 square foot property.
- The minimum price per cut is $25.
- Reduced rates are offered for large lots.

All prices are rounded up: $25, $30, $35, and so on. In some cases, Buzz Cut's owners negotiate with the customers. Price estimation decisions rely on two assumptions:

1. The size of a lawn determines the time needed to cut it.
2. Time determines the cost and thus price.

ILLUSTRATION 7.28 First 10 Rows of the Property Data Size Time Spreadsheet

Property	Size	Time
1	4,500	9
2	3,000	6
3	50,000	50
4	25,000	45
5	4,000	8
6	18,000	18
7	21,000	17
8	100,000	120
9	22,000	55
10	23,000	25

The first assumption can be rephrased: "There is a strong positive correlation between lawn size and time: the bigger the lawn, the more time it will take to mow it."

Correlation is a data relationship. Strong correlation and positive direction are assumptions regarding the data relationship made by Buzz Cut. The scatterplot in **Illustration 7.29** explores the validity of these assumptions.

ILLUSTRATION 7.29
Scatterplot Showing
Correlation Between Size
and Time

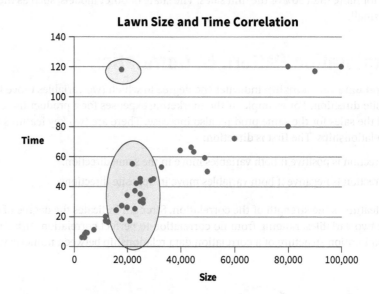

This scatterplot was created in Power BI (**Illustration 7.30**).

ILLUSTRATION 7.30 Creating a Scatterplot in Power BI

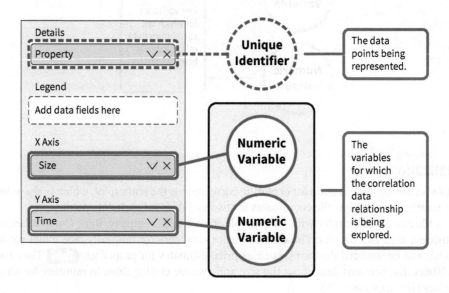

Exploration and Insights

Scatterplots are created by dragging and dropping numeric variables from a data set into the two areas shown in Illustration 7.30. Several insights could be collected once the scatterplot is created. For instance, there is a strong, positive correlation between lawn size and time. There are also two additional insights:

1. The data point with a yellow background shows an outlier. Talking to the owners of Buzz Cut reveals this is the result of a data entry issue. It takes 18 minutes to cut the property, but "118 minutes" was recorded.

2. The chart indicates that there might be other factors than just size influencing time. The data points with a green background in Illustration 7.29 indicate properties that are approximately the same size but require different amounts of time, with times ranging between 17 and 55 minutes (ignore the outlier here).

While the data do not indicate what the other factor or factors might be, the owners mention that properties with many trees, plants, and corners take more time to mow. This means that difficulty, or complexity, is another factor that influences time and cost, and the decision model should be adjusted to reflect this.

Applying Critical Thinking 7.3

Evaluate Your Assumptions

The Buzz Cut scatterplot example shows that critical thinking is an integral part of data exploration:

- Unrealistic assumptions might result in insights that pose a significant risk. Underpricing might result in losses (**Risks**).
- These insights could negatively affect all stakeholders. If there are other factors that drive time, employees could be evaluated unfairly, and underpricing might mean that Buzz Cut cannot pay creditors (**Stakeholders**).

Data Exploration Pattern 7: Time Series

A **time series data relationship** defines the values of a variable at sequential points in time (Illustration 7.31).

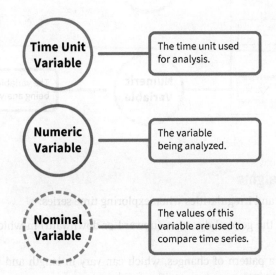

ILLUSTRATION 7.31
Exploration Structure for a
Time Series Data Relationship

To display a time series, a visualization requires a time unit such as a minute, hour, day, or week, and a variable that changes over time.

Visualizations

A line chart is the most common visualization for time series, but bar charts, column charts, area charts, waterfall charts, and sparkline charts can also be used. Let's go back to the Honda Motors North America (HNA) example. **Illustration 7.32** is a Power BI line chart that explores how HNA's unit sales changed during the 2021–2025 period.

ILLUSTRATION 7.32 Line Chart Showing Changes in HNA's Unit Sales During the 2021–2025 Period

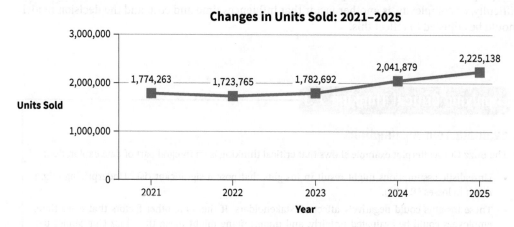

It was created in Power BI by using year as the time unit and total unit sales as the numeric variable (**Illustration 7.33**).

ILLUSTRATION 7.33 Creating a Line Chart in Power BI

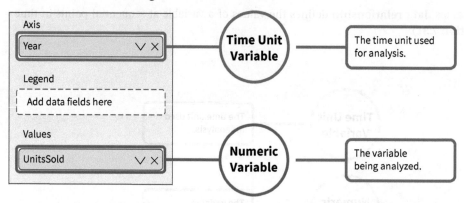

Exploration and Insights

Look for trends, cycles, and irregularities when exploring time series:

- A trend indicates the general direction (upward or downward) in which a variable moves over time.
- A cycle indicates a pattern of changes, which can vary in length and intensity over time. Seasonality refers to intra-year cycles with a fixed nature.
- Irregularities are unsystematic, typically short-term, fluctuations.

The time series in Illustration 7.32 shows a strong upward trend for HNA's unit sales starting from 2023. Dragging and dropping can explore this trend in more detail by comparing the trends for Canada and the United States. This new line chart (A) and how it was made (B) are shown in **Illustration 7.34**. This chart shows a very different picture: U.S. sales are flat, and growth is a result of increasing sales in Canada. Additional insights might be generated by also comparing trends for units sold by model or type.

ILLUSTRATION 7.34 Trend Analysis Units Sold by Country

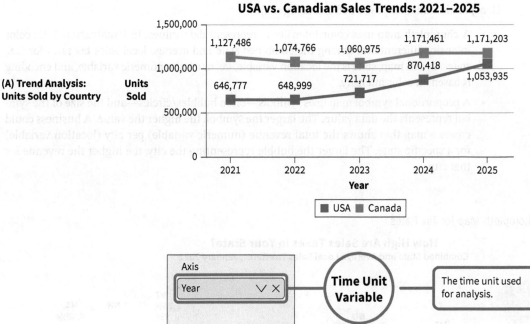

(A) Trend Analysis: Units Sold by Country

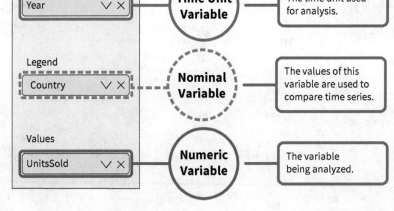

(B) Creating a Line Chart with Multiple Time Series

Data Exploration Pattern 8: Geospatial

In a **geospatial data relationship**, numeric values are assigned to locations and encoded through coloring or shading and the size of the bubbles within the visualization (**Illustration 7.35**).

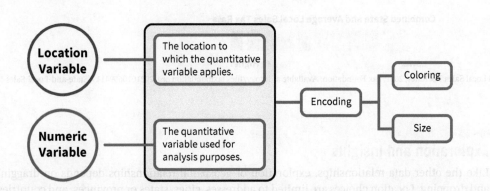

ILLUSTRATION 7.35
Exploration Structure for Geospatial Data Relationships

Visualizations

Geospatial relationships are defined using maps:

- A choropleth map uses color intensity to represent data values. In **Illustration 7.36**, color intensity differentiates among the combined state and average local sales tax rates for U.S. states. In this map, state is the location variable, tax rate is the numeric variable, and encoding is based on color intensity.

- A proportional symbol map uses symbols—often bubbles/circles—and the size of the symbol represents the data value. The larger the symbol, the higher the value. A business could create a map that shows the total revenue (numeric variable) per city (location variable) for a specific state. The larger the bubble representing the city, the higher the revenue for that city.

ILLUSTRATION 7.36 Choropleth Map for Tax Rates

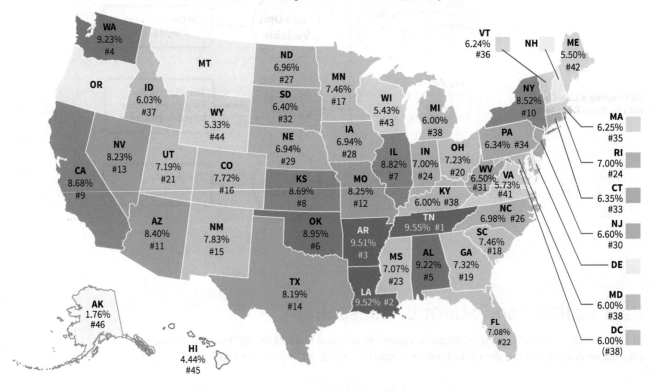

How High Are Sales Taxes in Your State?
Combined State and Average Local Sales Tax Rates, January 2021

Source: Janelle Cammenga, State and Local Sales Tax Rates, 2021, Tax Foundation. Available at https://files.taxfoundation.org/20210106094117/State-and-Local-Sales-Tax-Rates-2021.pdf

Exploration and Insights

Like the other data relationships, exploration of geospatial relationships depends on dragging and dropping. Location choices are limited to addresses, cities, states or provinces, and countries, and the location information must be formatted so that a map service, Google Maps or Bing Maps, for example, can recognize it.

On the other hand, a variety of numeric variables can be used for exploration. A map created for the HNA example could show the total revenue generated per dealership and use color intensity for encoding. That same map could display the new-to-used car sales ratio, which is an important key performance indicator (KPI) for car dealerships, and use size for encoding purposes.

APPLY IT 7.2

Visualize Part-to-Whole Relationships with Excel

Data **Managerial Accounting**   The CEO at Happy Colors needs to understand the relative importance of the company's different product types, Low, High, and Premium quality paint, in terms of the total units, or cans, being produced. Complete these three steps to perform this analysis:

1. Determine what data relationship underlies this question.
2. Identify and create a visual that could explore the data relationship.
3. Describe the insights generated by the visual.

SOLUTION

1. A part-to-whole relationship is being explored.
2. Several visualizations can be used to explore part-to-whole relationships, including pie charts, donut charts, stacked bar charts, stacked column charts, and tree map charts. The Illustration shows a pie chart (A) and the dialog box of the Excel PivotTable used for its creation (B).

Part-to-Whole Relationship with Pie Chart

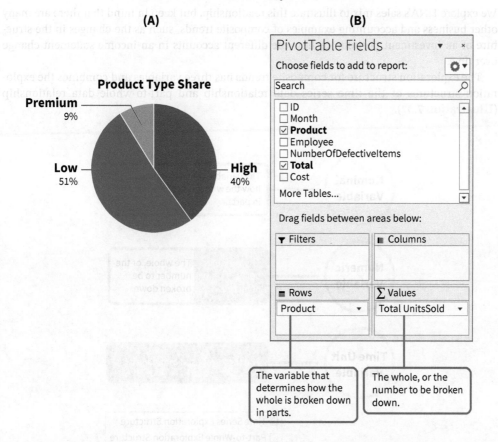

3. The pie chart shows that more than half of the production is for cans of Low product type, while Premium cans have a relatively small share—lower than 10%.

7.3 How Are Data Explored by Integrating Data Relationships?

While patterns 1–8 explore a single, foundational data relationship with one visualization, data exploration often requires integrating two or more data relationships. Integrated data relationships can be represented with a single visualization or by using different visualizations as part of a report. Composite trends and Pareto analysis are two examples of combined data relationships that can be represented in one chart, both of which are discussed next.

Data Exploration Pattern 9: Composite Trends

A **composite trend data relationship,** or the change in a part-to-whole relationship over time, is an integrated data relationship that is often analyzed. One example is an analysis of how a business' sales mix changes over time:

- Sales mix is the relative proportion of each product in a business' total sales, which means that it is a part-to-whole relationship.
- Change over time is a time series.

We explore HNA's sales mix to illustrate this relationship, but keep in mind that there are many other business and accounting examples of composite trends, such as the changes in the structure of an investment portfolio or how the different accounts in an income statement change over time.

The exploration structure for composite trends has three variables and combines the exploration structures of the time series data relationship and part-to-whole data relationship (**Illustration 7.37**).

ILLUSTRATION 7.37
Exploration Structure for
Composite Trend Data
Relationships

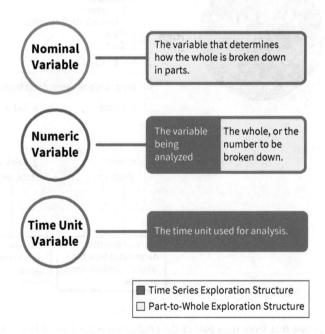

- ■ Time Series Exploration Structure
- □ Part-to-Whole Exploration Structure

Visualizations

Several visualizations, all of which rely on the exploration structure shown in Illustration 7.37, can explore composite trends. In **Illustration 7.38**, the stacked area chart is used to explore changes in HNA's unit sales mix.

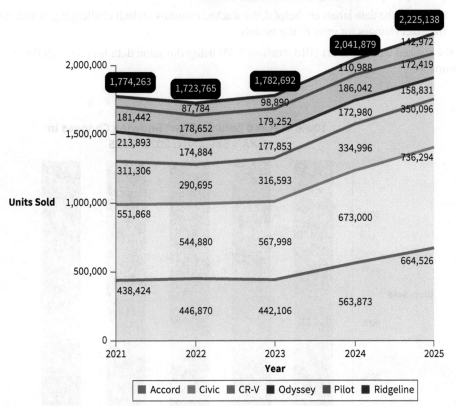

Stacked Area Chart Showing Changes in HNA's Sales Mix: 2021–2025

ILLUSTRATION 7.38 Exploring Changes in HNA's Sales Mix with a Stacked Area Chart

Illustration 7.39 shows how to build this chart with Power BI.

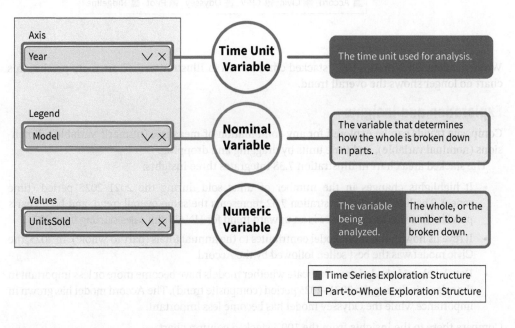

ILLUSTRATION 7.39 Power BI Definition of Stacked Area Chart

There are a few things to note about Illustration 7.38:

- The top shows how the total units sold (the numeric variable) has changed during the 2021–2025 period (the time unit variable).

- For each year, the total units sold (numeric variable) is broken down by model (the nominal variable).

- The horizontal bands reveal how the share of each model changed during the 2021–2025 period (composite trend).
- Although the data labels are helpful, the stacked columns make it challenging to understand the exact changes for most of the models.

A 100% stacked column chart (**Illustration 7.40**) using the same data is created in Power BI in the same way.

ILLUSTRATION 7.40 Exploring HNA's Sales Mix with a 100% Stacked Column Chart

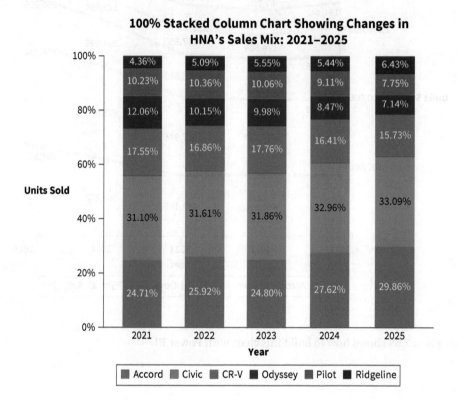

While the data labels in the 100% stacked chart shown in Illustration 7.40 are more precise, this chart no longer shows the overall trend.

Exploration and Insights

Composite trends can be explored for any combination of measures (numeric variable), dimensions (nominal variable), and time units by dragging and dropping.

The stacked area chart in Illustration 7.38 integrates three insights:

- It highlights changes in the number of units sold during the 2021–2025 period (time series). The line chart in Illustration 7.32 represents the same overall trend, and both charts provide the same insight: there is an upward trend for HNA's unit sales starting from 2023.
- It reveals how much each model contributes to the annual totals (part-to-whole). In 2025, the Civic model was the best seller, followed by the Accord.
- Data labels and shaded areas indicate whether models have become more or less important in the sales mix during the 2021–2025 period (composite trend). The Accord model has grown in importance while the Odyssey model has become less important.

Compare these to the insights from the 100% stacked column chart:

- It does not show an overall trend.
- It shows the exact share each model contributes to the annual totals (part-to-whole). Of the total cars sold in 2025, 33.09% were Civics and 29.86% were Accords.

- Expressed as percentages, it reveals how a model's share in the sales mix has changed during the 2021–2025 period. The share of the Accord model grew from 31.1% in 2021 to 33.09% in 2025.

Applying the composite trend pattern can also provide insights for a business exploring how the contribution of its different regions (nominal variable) to its revenue (numeric variable) has changed during the last five years (time unit variable). A composite trend pattern can also show how the relative importance of the different accounts in an income statement changed in a specific period. This is a combination of vertical (part-to-whole) and horizontal (time series) financial statement analysis.

Data Exploration Pattern 10: Pareto Analysis

Pareto analysis (Illustration 7.41) determines the importance of different categories, which is nominal comparison, ranks them, and shows how each, based on that ranking, contributes to the cumulative percentage (part-to-whole).

ILLUSTRATION 7.41 Exploration Structure for Pareto Analysis

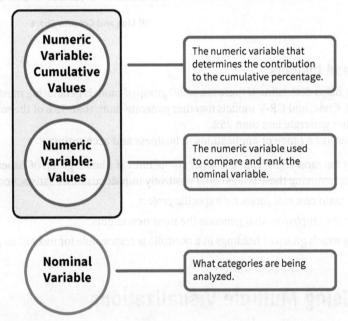

Numeric Variable: Cumulative Values — The numeric variable that determines the contribution to the cumulative percentage.

Numeric Variable: Values — The numeric variable used to compare and rank the nominal variable.

Nominal Variable — What categories are being analyzed.

Visualizations

A Pareto chart visualizes the combination of the relationships shown in the exploration structure. Some tools, like Excel, offer Pareto charts. They can also be created as line and column charts, which are supported by most tools. (**Data** **How To 7.2** shows how to create a Pareto chart using both Power BI and Excel.)

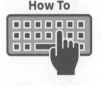

How To

Here, a line and column chart was created using Excel. **Illustration 7.42**(A) shows a PivotTable created from the HNA Unit Sales data set. It contains the different models, units sold per model, and cumulative units sold per model. Models are ranked in descending order (ranking) based on units sold. In terms of the exploration model:

- Model represents the nominal variable.
- Total units sold represents the numeric variable (values).
- Cumulative percentage represents the numeric value (cumulative values).

Illustration 7.42(B) is the line and column chart created from the PivotTable. Along the *x*-axis are the different models ranked based on total units sold. They are the items being analyzed. The line indicates the cumulative number of units sold. A second *y*-axis was added to emphasize that the line is expressed as a percentage. A point on the line shows how the models to the left of it cumulatively contribute to the total unit sales, as a percentage.

ILLUSTRATION 7.42 Exploring HNA's Unit Sales with Pareto Analysis

Model	TotalUnitsSold	CumulativePercentage
Civic	3,074,040	32.20%
Accord	2,555,799	58.97%
CR-V	1,603,686	75.76%
Odyssey	898,441	85.17%
Pilot	897,807	94.58%
Ridgeline	517,964	100.00%
Total	**9,547,737**	

(A) PivotTable

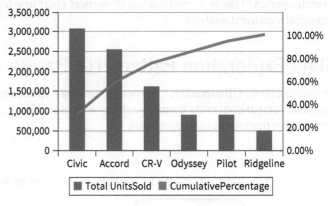

(B) Line and Column Chart

Exploration and Insights

The Pareto chart helps determine if there is a small group of models generating most sales. In this case, the Accord, Civic, and CR-V models together generate more than 75% of the sales, while the other three models generate less than 25%.

Pareto analysis has a range of applications in business and accounting:

- Identifying the most significant customer complaints. If a small group of issues causes most complaints, removing these issues could positively impact customer satisfaction.

- Indicating main cost categories for a specific project.

- Identifying the employees that generate the most new clients.

- Illustrating which group of holdings in a portfolio is responsible for most of its growth.

Reports Using Multiple Visualizations

Data relationships are often integrated using multiple visualizations as part of a report. Mostly interactive, these visualizations provide endless exploration opportunities. A report that combines part-to-whole and time series relationships explores trends for not only the whole, but also for each of the individual parts. A more advanced example, with multiple interactive visualizations representing different relationships, can illustrate this.

Visualizations

Illustration 7.43 is an HNA Interactive Report, which integrates data relationships with multiple visualizations.

The report in Illustration 7.43 integrates five elements:

1. A slicer to select one or more years, which operates as a filter.[6]

2. A card showing the total number of units sold.

---

[6]We wanted to show the use of slicers as part of a report. However, this slicer is redundant since the years in the line chart and the 100% stacked column charts can be used for the same purpose.

ILLUSTRATION 7.43 Interactive Report Integrating Multiple Data Relationships

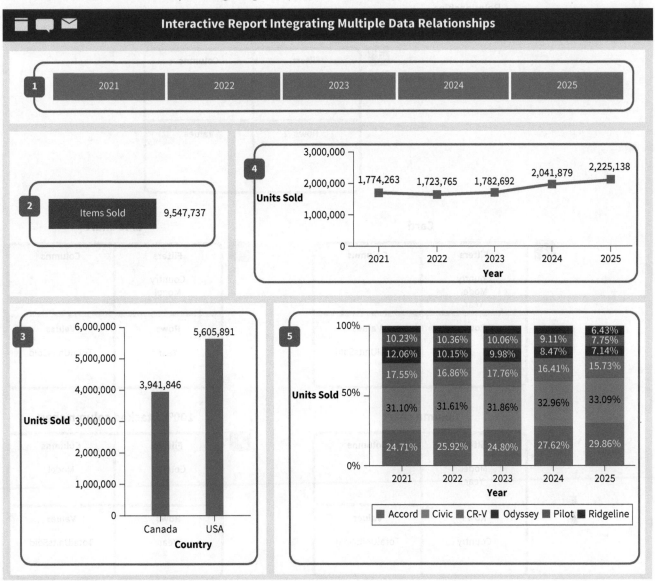

3. A column chart showing a nominal comparison—countries are compared by the total number of units sold.

4. A line chart representing a time series that reveals how the total number of units sold changed during the 2021–2025 period.

5. A 100% stacked column chart that shows composite trends.

Additionally, the report shows three different part-to-whole relationships. First, the column chart (3) breaks down the total number of units (2) by country. Second, the line chart (4) breaks down the total number of units (2) by year. Finally, the 100% stacked column chart reveals how models break down each total (per year) as percentages.

Since the report is interactive, different variables can be used for filtering purposes. The total units sold (2) can be filtered by year (1), country (3), and model (5). Also, the trendline (4) can be filtered by country (3) and model (5).

Illustration 7.44 is the exploration structure of the report in Illustration 7.43. Note that fields in one visualization, such as countries represented as bars in the column chart (3), can be used as filters for the other visualizations. How this structure is supported might differ across different software tools.

ILLUSTRATION 7.44 Exploration Structure for an Interactive Report That Integrates Multiple Relationships

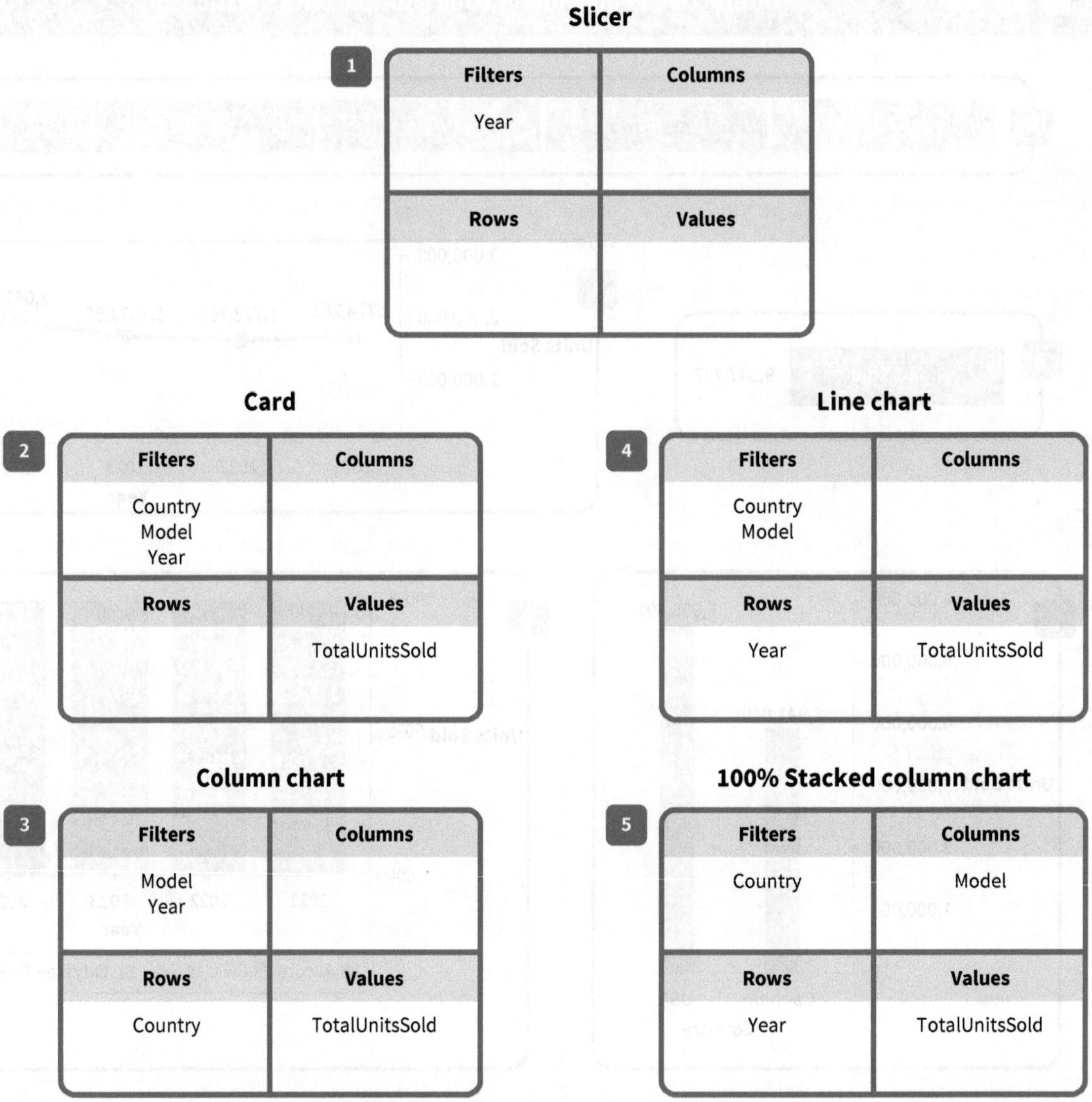

Slicer

1	Filters	Columns
	Year	
	Rows	**Values**

Card

2	Filters	Columns
	Country Model Year	
	Rows	**Values**
		TotalUnitsSold

Line chart

4	Filters	Columns
	Country Model	
	Rows	**Values**
	Year	TotalUnitsSold

Column chart

3	Filters	Columns
	Model Year	
	Rows	**Values**
	Country	TotalUnitsSold

100% Stacked column chart

5	Filters	Columns
	Country	Model
	Rows	**Values**
	Year	TotalUnitsSold

Exploration and Insights

What follows is an overview of the data relationships that can be explored, the insights that can be generated, and questions that can be answered with the exploration structure shown in Illustration 7.44:

- As shown in the upper-left corner of Illustration 7.44, the value shown by the card (2)—Total-UnitsSold—can be filtered by any combination of Country, Model, and Year. One example of this is how many units were sold in the United States (country) of the Pilot model (model) in 2022 (year).
- The column chart (3) compares the units sold (TotalUnitsSold) across countries. Using Model and Year as filters (from the other visualizations), makes it possible to compare Canadian and U.S. sales of the Accord and Civic models in 2025.
- The line chart (4) analyzes the overall sales trend. However, trends could also be shown for specific combinations of country and model, such as exploring trends for Ridgeline sales in Canada.
- The 100% stacked column chart (5) determines the units sold per model per year and presents them as a percentage.

Once again, using filters allows exploring more specific scenarios, such as selecting United States in the column chart (3) and 2025 in the line chart (4).

Illustration 7.45 shows how the report would look after using these filters.

ILLUSTRATION 7.45   U.S. 2025 Sales Mix

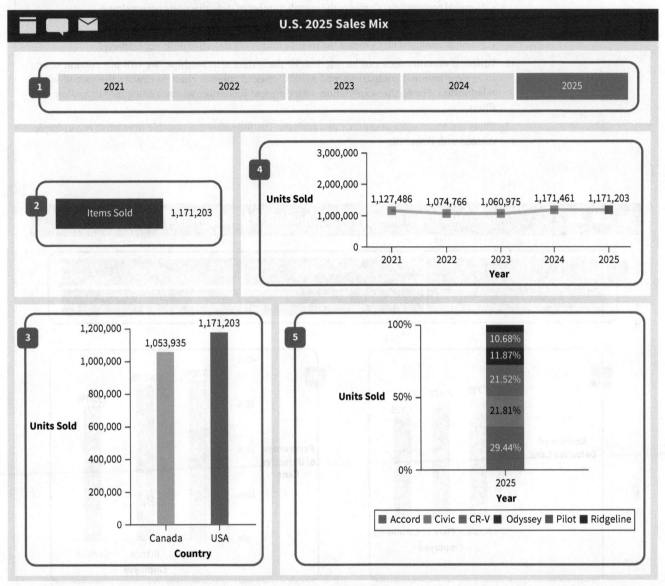

Data exploration patterns are best practices for performing analysis. They make us more aware of data relationships, how they can be represented and explored, the insights that can be generated, and how they can be integrated.

Data Managerial Accounting   Defective paint cans are an issue for Angela at Happy Colors, so she would like to explore the following:

- Compare the overall number of defective units (paint cans) per employee.
- Determine how the relative proportion of defective units across products differs among employees.
- Compare the relative number of defective units per employee.

Implement the following four steps to help perform the analysis:

1. Determine what data relationships underlie this analysis.
2. Identify the visualizations that could be used to explore these data relationships.
3. Build an interactive report with these visualizations and draw the report's exploration structure.
4. Identify the insights generated by your analysis.

APPLY IT 7.3

Build an Interactive Report

SOLUTION

1. The data relationships underlying this analysis:
   - Nominal comparison: Compare the overall number of defective units per employee.
   - Part-to-whole: Per employee, relative proportion of defective units across products.
   - Nominal comparison: Compare the relative number of defective units per employee.

2. Different visualizations can be selected for these data relationships. We will use column charts to explore nominal comparison and a 100% stacked column chart to explore the part-to-whole relationship. For further exploration with different scenarios, we are adding month and product filters.

3. There are many ways to conduct this analysis. The following is a possible interactive report implemented with Power BI:

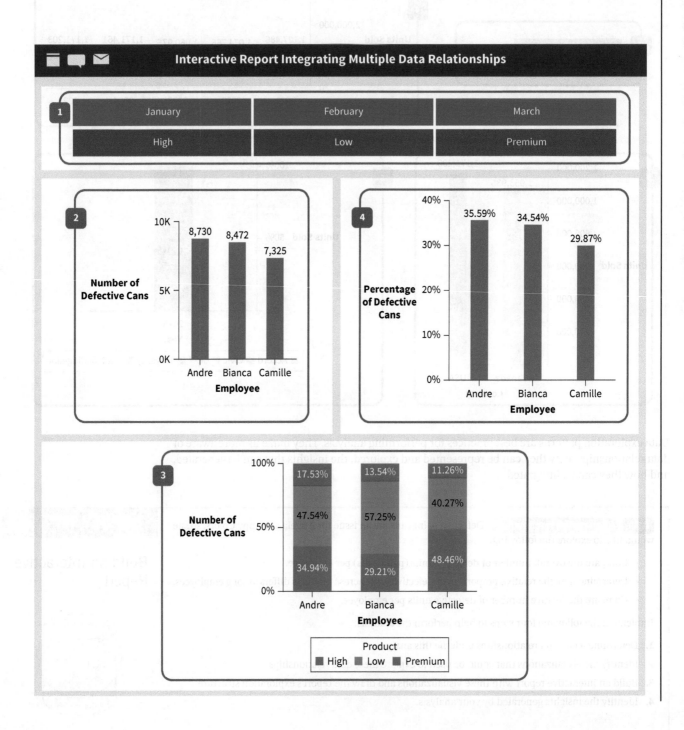

The exploration structure for this report looks as follows:

Exploration Space: Happy Colors Defective Cans Analysis

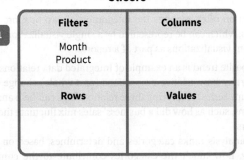

1 **Slicers**

Filters	Columns
Month Product	

Rows	Values

3 **100% Stacked column chart**

Filters	Columns
Month	Product

Rows	Values
Employee	Total Number of Defective Cans

2 **Column chart**

Filters	Columns
Month Product	

Rows	Values
Employee	Total Number of Defective Cans

4 **Column chart**

Filters	Columns
Month Product	

Rows	Values
Employee	Relative Number of Defective Cans

4. These insights can be collected from the report:

   - The column chart (2) can compare the number of defective cans per employee. This is nominal comparison. Andre has the highest number and Camille the lowest.
   - The 100% stacked column chart (3) breaks down the number of defective cans by employee and product. This is a part-to-whole relationship. Most of Bianca's defective cans are for Low products. For Camille, most of the defective cans are for High products.
   - The second column (4) chart mirrors the first column chart (2) and is also a nominal comparison. However, here, an employee's number of defective cans is shown as a percentage of the total number of defective cans (part-to-whole relationship).
   - Using filters (1), select any combination of month and product, which generates additional insights. For example, in January, Andre had more defective cans than Rebecca. However, in February it was the other way around.

Chapter Review and Practice

Learning Objectives Review

❶ Describe the process of data exploration.

Data exploration is the discovery process of looking for something new and previously unknown:

- Data exploration has four steps: identifying questions, identifying data relationships, exploring those relationships, and generating insights.
- A widely used tool for data exploration is the Excel PivotTable. It enables exploration by selecting, from a list of fields, the numbers to be analyzed, how the numbers will be broken down in terms of rows and columns, and the filters that apply to the data.
- PivotTables integrate the key techniques of data exploration: identifying data relationships, filtering, and dragging and dropping.

❷ Explore foundational data relationships through visualizations.

Investigating data relationships is at the heart of data exploration. Eight foundational patterns can help answer questions about which data relationships can be explored, how they can be illustrated in visualizations, how to create those visualizations, and what insights can be generated from them:

- A nominal comparison data relationship compares the values of a nominal variable based on the value of a second, numeric variable. For example, we can compare product categories (nominal variable) based on the total profit they have generated (numeric variable).
- A distribution data relationship shows how the values of a quantitative variable are spread out. This relationship can show

the highest price paid for a product, the lowest price, the price range, etc.

- A deviation data relationship shows how a set of actual values deviate from their reference values. Exploring a deviation relationship can show how the actual profit for 2025 compares with the budgeted profit.
- A ranking data relationship orders the values of a variable sequentially based on the values of a second variable. An example of what it can show is how different products rank based on profit.
- A part-to-whole data relationship displays how each part compares to the whole and how the parts compare to each other. It helps to understand issues such as the relative contribution of each product category to a business' total revenue.
- A correlation data relationship indicates the degree to which two variables move in the same or opposite direction. For example, how ice cream sales are correlated with temperature.
- A time series data relationship defines the values of a variable at sequential points in time. For example, it can be used to explore how a business' profit changed during the last decade.
- A geospatial data relationship encodes locations through coloring, shades, and size, based on the values of a numeric variable.

States (location) can be colored based on the total profit (numeric variable) they have generated.

❸ Explore data by integrating foundational relationships.

Data exploration often requires the integration of two or more data relationships, which can be represented by a single visualization or by using different visualizations as part of a report:

- A composite trend is an example of integrated data relationships that portray how relative proportions (part-whole) change over time (time series). Exploring these relationships can help answer questions, such as how did a business' sales mix fluctuate the last ten years.
- Pareto analysis ranks categories and determines, based on that ranking, how much the categories contribute to the cumulative percentage. Pareto charts can explore data to determine, for example, the most frequent surgical errors in a hospital.
- Interactive reports with multiple visualizations that represent different data relationships provide endless exploration opportunities. A business' profit total (visual 1) can be broken down by product category (visual 2) while product categories can be further broken down by region (visual 3) or the other way around.

Illustration 7.46 is an overview of the 10 data exploration patterns presented in this chapter.

ILLUSTRATION 7.46 Overview of Data Exploration Patterns

Id	Data Relationship	Description	Visualization Examples (Bold Indicates Chapter Example)
Foundational Data Relationships			
1	Nominal Comparison	Compares the values of a nominal variable based on the values of a second, numeric variable.	Bar chart, **column chart**, dot plot, and lollipop chart
2	Distribution	Shows how the values of a numeric variable are distributed, or spread.	Histogram, **box-and-whisker (boxplot) chart**, and violin plot
3	Deviation	Shows how a set of actual values deviate from their reference values such as budgeted or forecasted values.	**Clustered bar** and column **charts**, gauge, and bullet chart
4	Ranking	Orders the values of a variable sequentially based on the values of a second variable.	Defined as part of a table, bar chart, or **column chart**
5	Part-to-Whole	Shows how each part compares to the whole and how the parts compare to one another.	**Pie chart**, donut chart, stacked bar chart, stacked column chart, and tree map chart
6	Correlation	Indicates the degree to which two variables move in the same or the opposite direction.	**Scatterplot**
7	Time Series	Shows the values of a variable at sequential points in time.	Area chart, bar chart, column chart, **line chart**, sparkline chart, and waterfall chart
8	Geospatial	Assigns numeric values to locations and encodes them through coloring (shade) and size (bubble size).	**Maps**
Integrated Data Relationships			
9	Composite Trends	Shows how a composite structure (part-to-whole) changes over time (time series).	Stacked column chart, **100% stacked column chart, and stacked area chart**
10	Pareto Analysis	Illustrates the importance of different categories (nominal comparison), ranks them (ranking), and shows their cumulative percentage (part-to-whole).	Pareto chart, **line and column chart**

Key Terms Review

How To Walk-Throughs

HOW TO 7.1   Create a Box-and-Whisker Chart with Excel

Box-and-whisker charts are excellent tools for exploring distribution relationships. Illustration 7.14 showed an example of a box-and-whisker chart created with Power BI, but you can also create one with Excel.

What You Need: **Data** The How To 7.1 data file.

STEP 1: Select the data in the **Profit** column as shown in **Illustration 7.47**, then click the **Insert** tab (1). Go to the **Charts** group and select **Insert Statistic Chart** (2) and **Box-and-Whisker** (3).

ILLUSTRATION 7.47   Creating a Box-and-Whisker Chart with Excel

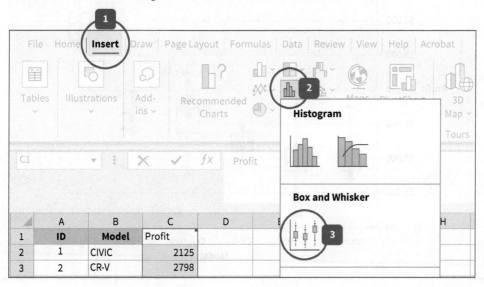

This creates the box-and-whisker chart shown next (**Illustration 7.48**).

ILLUSTRATION 7.48   Excel Box-and-Whisker Chart for Profit Distribution

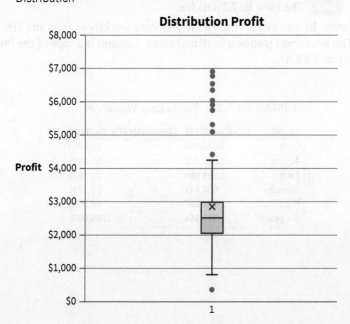

The ✕ symbol represents the average. Outliers, defined as being 1.5 times of the interquartile range (IQR) below the first quartile or above the third quartile, are also shown as part of the chart. To see all the data points, click one of the boxes and select **Format Data Series**. Then, select **Show Inner Points**. We applied some additional formatting to the chart.

STEP 2: To create parallel profit distributions for the different models, select both the **Model** and **Profit** columns. To recreate the chart in **Illustration 7.49**, sort the **Model** column in ascending order.

ILLUSTRATION 7.49 Parallel Profit Distributions for HNA Car Models

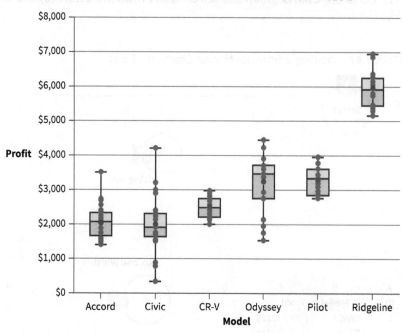

HOW TO 7.2 Create a Pareto Chart with Excel and Power BI

When conducting a Pareto analysis, you must calculate the data, create the chart, and perform the analysis. This can be done in Excel or in Power BI. Here, we illustrate how to combine both tools.

What You Need: Data The How To 7.2 data file.

STEP 1: Open Power BI and extract the Pareto raw data worksheet from the HNA Pareto raw data Excel file. The worksheet is shown in **Illustration 7.50** and is a copy of the PivotTable data shown in Illustration 7.42(A).

ILLUSTRATION 7.50 Pareto Data Worksheet

Model	TotalUnitsSold	CumulativePercentage
Civic	3,074,040	32.20%
Accord	2,555,799	58.97%
CR-V	1,603,686	75.76%
Odyssey	898,441	85.17%
Pilot	897,807	94.58%
Ridgeline	517,964	100.00%

STEP 2: Select the Line and Stacked Column chart in the **Visualizations** pane. The definition for the Pareto chart is shown in **Illustration 7.51**.

ILLUSTRATION 7.51   Creating a Line and Column Chart for Pareto Analysis in Power BI

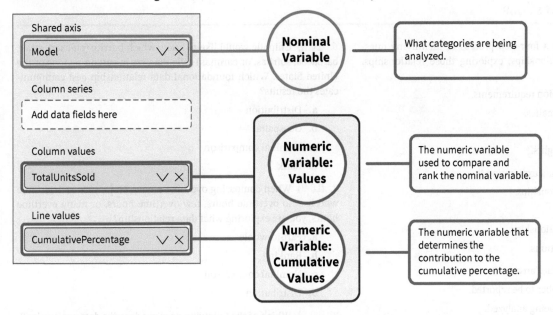

The corresponding chart is shown in **Illustration 7.52** and is similar to the chart in Illustration 7.42(B). Some additional formatting was applied.

ILLUSTRATION 7.52   Pareto Analysis of HNA's Unit Sales

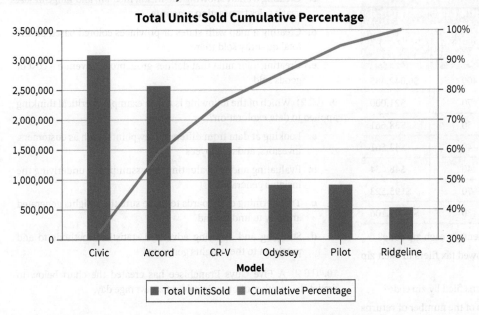

Combining multiple tools for a data analytics task and integrating their strengths is common practice.

> **Data** The Data tag appears when the data required to answer a question or complete an exercise are available in the book's product page on www.wiley.com.

Multiple Choice Questions

1. (LO 1) Exploring data is a four-step process of identifying questions, identifying data relationships, exploring those relationships, and

  a. identifying information requirements.

  b. correcting data anomalies.

  c. identifying insights.

  d. communicating insights.

2. (LO 1) The first step in data exploration is

  a. exploring data relationships.

  b. generating insights.

  c. identifying data relationships.

  d. identifying the questions.

3. (LO 1) A PivotTable's values area

  a. determines the number to be reported.

  b. determines what is being analyzed.

  c. represents the variables used for slicing and dicing.

  d. represents data points.

4. (LO 1) Using the IRS data set below, what questions can be asked using a PivotTable?

Zip Code	Number of Single Returns	Number of Joint Returns	Number of Heads of Household Returns	Adjusted Gross Income (AGI)
90210	5,020	3,590	400	$6,042,485
60653	1,700	160	70	$21,000
27114	810	160	50	$38,661
46410	570	140	40	$47,561
39111	350	140	40	$48,634
20053	690	560	70	$195,523
10003	900	2,430	130	$5,691,106

  a. How many households have dependents in each zip code?

  b. What is the average number of widowed tax filers in each zip code?

  c. What is the total number of tax returns filed by zip code?

  d. Which zip code is an outlier in terms of the number of returns filed?

5. (LO 1) Which of the following tools explores data?

  a. Microsoft Excel

  b. Microsoft Power BI

  c. Tableau

  d. All of these tools can explore data.

6. (LO 2) Chipotle would like to know which burrito (chicken, steak, barbacoa, sofritas, or carnitas) sells the best in certain regions of the United States. Which foundational data relationship best communicates the results?

  a. Distribution

  b. Geospatial

  c. Nominal comparison

  d. Rank

7. (LO 2) When comparing overtime among employees to determine who has no overtime hours, few overtime hours, or many overtime hours, you are exploring what data relationship?

  a. Part-to-whole

  b. Ranking

  c. Nominal comparison

  d. Distribution

8. (LO 2) Which of the following does *not* describe data exploration?

  a. Creating a list of products, ordered by Facebook "likes," in descending order

  b. Creating a visualization showing, per product, the 2025 actual and targeted number of units sold

  c. Creating a chart showing the mean, median, and range of last year's sales transaction amounts

  d. Creating a map with states or provinces colored based on the total quantity sold there

  e. Creating a formula that defines gross profit: revenue – cost of goods sold

9. (LO 2) Which of the following is *not* an example of critical thinking applied to data exploration?

  a. Looking at data from different viewpoints, such as customers, investors, and employees

  b. Evaluating and re-evaluating the assumptions underlying the insights generated

  c. Transforming dashboards to make sure the insights generated are easy to understand

  d. Studying and applying advanced statistical methods to add precision to the insights generated

10. (LO 2) A Five Guys Franchisee has created the chart below to depict the number of burgers sold on an average day.

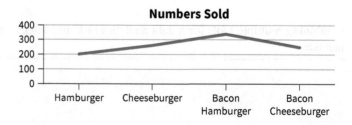

Determine what data exploration pattern/visualization would more aptly display the data to generate insights on the burger sales mix.

   a. Nominal comparison/Bar chart

   b. Part-to-whole/Pie chart

   c. Ranking/Bar chart

   d. Time series/Time series line chart

11. (LO 2) Flame, a U.S. company that sells electronic products worldwide, gives you this data set:

Region	2025 Profits
North-America	19,922,189
South-America	89,900,011
Western-Europe	3,008,223
Eastern-Europe	2,347,781
Africa	890,002
Asia	122,343

What data relationship is *not* relevant for this data set?

   a. Nominal comparison

   b. Ranking

   c. Geospatial

   d. Part-to-whole

   e. Deviation

   f. All of these are relevant.

12. (LO 2) Which of the following aspects is *not* relevant for a time series data relationship?

   a. Trend

   b. Seasonal pattern

   c. Magnitude of discrepancies

   d. Irregularities

   e. Forecasts

13. (LO 2) Which of the following aspects is *not* relevant for a correlation data relationship?

   a. Clusters

   b. Strength (correlation coefficient)

   c. Direction (positive or negative)

   d. Outliers

   e. Forecasts

14. (LO 3) Hyatt HeavyLoads company bought a machine with an estimated useful life of 10 years for $80,000 (cost). The residual (salvage) value of the machine is $8,000.

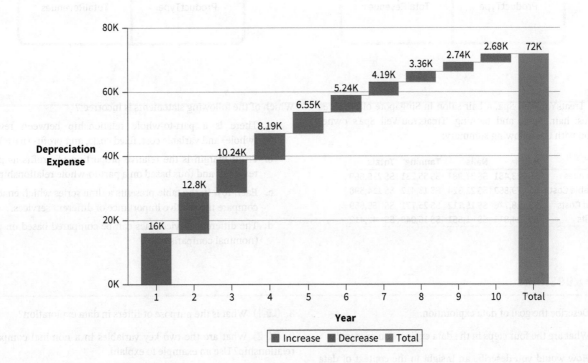

The waterfall chart visualizes the machine's depreciation using what data relationships?

   a. Part-to-whole, time series

   b. Deviation, time series

   c. Time series, nominal comparison

   d. Ranking, time series

   e. Deviation, part-to-whole

15. (LO 3) Chipotle would like to know how the sales mix for burritos (steak, chicken, veggie, barbacoa, and carnitas) has changed from 2015 to 2020. What data exploration pattern will best explore the data and provide insights?

   a. Composite trend

   b. Part-to-whole

   c. Ranking

   d. Time series

16. (LO 3) Cone Canoes (CoCaN) is a high-quality canoe manufacturer that sells their products worldwide. They make four different types of canoes: recreational, whitewater, racing, and fishing. They would like to further explore the total revenues generated by U.S. sales of whitewater and racing canoes for all four quarters in 2025. Through their ERP, they have access to their sales data for the last 10 years. Which of the following represents the exploration structure for such an analysis?

A

Filters	Columns
Country ProductType	Year

Rows	Values
ProductType	TotalRevenues

C

Filters	Columns
ProductType Year	

Rows	Values
Country Year	TotalRevenues

B

Filters	Columns
Country Year ProductType	Quarters

Rows	Values
ProductType	TotalRevenues

D

Filters	Columns
Country Year	Quarters

Rows	Values
ProductType	TotalRevenues

17. (LO 3) TreatsYouWell Spa, a hair salon in Singapore offers three service lines: hair, nails, and tanning. TreatsYouWell Spa's owner provides you with the following summary:

	Hair	Nails	Tanning	Totals
Revenues	S$ 123,451	S$ 37,987	S$ 55,231	S$ 216,669
Variable Costs	S$ 79,862	S$ 21,324	S$ 13,412	S$ 114,598
Fixed Costs	S$ 18,776	S$ 15,112	S$ 25,771	S$ 59,659
Profits	S$ 24,813	S$ 1,551	S$ 16,048	S$ 42,412

Which of the following statements is incorrect?

a. There is a part-to-whole relationship between revenues (whole) and variable cost, fixed costs, and profits (parts).

b. Profit margin is the relative proportion of profits as part of revenues and thus based on a part-to-whole relationship.

c. Each row in the table presents a time series which enables to compare the relative importance of different services.

d. The different service lines can be compared based on profits (nominal comparison).

Review Questions

1. (LO 1) Describe the goal of data exploration.

2. (LO 1) What are the four steps in the data exploration process?

3. (LO 1) How would you describe an insight in the context of data exploration?

4. (LO 1) Briefly describe the role of charts in data exploration.

5. (LO 1) What is a PivotTable's key strength?

6. (LO 1) What three key data exploration techniques are supported by PivotTables?

7. (LO 1) Discuss the purpose of the Values area in a PivotTable.

8. (LO 1) What is the purpose of filters in data exploration?

9. (LO 2) What are the two key variables in a nominal comparison relationship? Use an example to explain.

10. (LO 2) Discuss two insights that can be generated from exploring a distribution relationship. Use a corporation's earnings during the last 20 years as the example for your discussion.

11. (LO 2) List at least five different pieces of information that a box-and-whisker chart provides about a distribution.

12. (LO 2) What role does a nominal variable play when creating a box-and-whisker chart?

13. (LO 2) A university compares its faculty salaries with peer institutions (peer salary comparison). What kind of relationship are they exploring? What kind of insights might they generate and what decisions can be affected by such insights?

14. (LO 2) The pie chart summarizes the expenses of a household, as shown below:

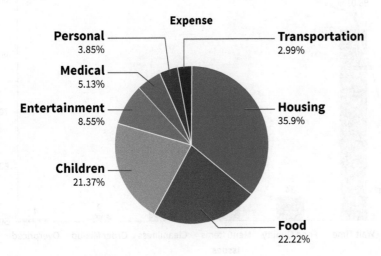

Expense

Personal — 3.85%
Medical — 5.13%
Entertainment — 8.55%
Children — 21.37%
Transportation — 2.99%
Housing — 35.9%
Food — 22.22%

1. What data relationship is being explored?
2. What are two insights that can be generated from the pie chart?

15. (LO 2) DeMorris is a hospital in southern Delaware that employees 50 surgeons. For insurance purposes they must provide detailed data regarding surgical errors. One of the reports they prepare is shown here:

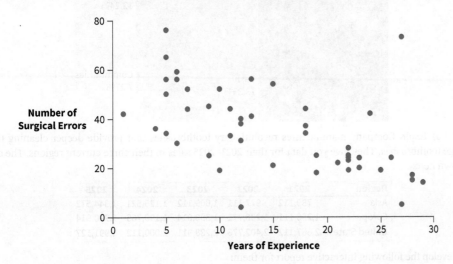

1. What chart is being used?
2. What data relationship is being presented?
3. What two insights regarding the data relationship can you identify?

16. (LO 2) What are the two mechanisms that can be used to encode locations?

17. (LO 3) Analysis of composite trends is based on three variables: a nominal variable, a numeric variable, and a time unit variable. Discuss the role of each of these variables in the analysis. Use the medal count per country during the last five summer Olympics as an example for your discussion.

18. (LO 3) Aurora is a pizza restaurant in Johannesburg, South Africa. Recently, business has been significantly slower than normal for them. To better understand why this is happening, they created a Pareto chart using data from the complaints they received on Dineplan. A Pareto chart combines several data relationships. Name these relationships and discuss them in the context of the chart shown:

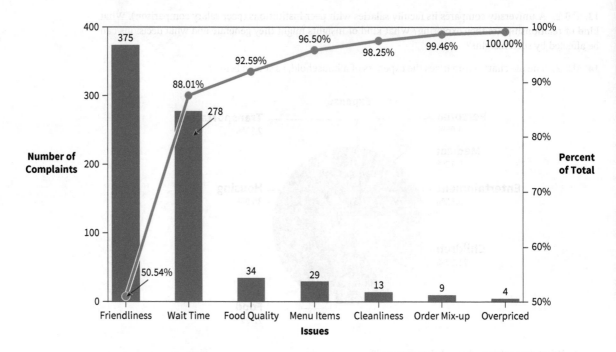

19. (LO 3) What are the two relationships integrated by a tree map? Explain how the following tree map shows these relationships:

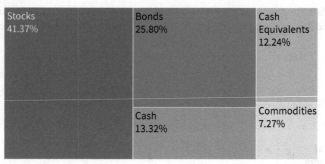

20. (LO 3) ESpin Company manufactures revolutionary toothbrushes that provide deeper cleaning than average toothbrushes. They give you data for their 2021–2025 sales in their three current regions. The data is shown here:

Region	2021	2022	2023	2024	2025
Asia	789,112	977,111	1,009,112	1,125,521	1,344,572
Europe	1,256,111	1,238,771	1,398,814	1,199,765	1,290,914
United States	2,667,112	2,402,776	2,288,911	2,000,112	1,991,127

You develop the following interactive report for them:

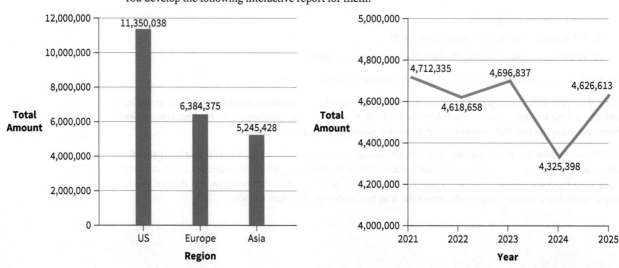

The corresponding exploration structure follows:

Bar Chart

Filters	Columns
Year	

Rows	Values
Region	Total Amount

Line Chart

Filters	Columns
Region	

Rows	Values
Year	Total Amount

Determine at least three questions that can be answered with this report.

Brief Exercises

BE 7.1 (LO 1) Match the appropriate term to each definition. Terms can be used once, more than once, or not at all.

a. Outlier
b. Correlation
c. Insight
d. Analytical database
e. Drag and drop
f. Data interpretation
g. Data exploration

Statement	Term
1. An observation that might significantly affect a business' decision-making.	
2. Input of data exploration.	
3. Output of data exploration.	
4. The discovery process of learning something new and previously unknown from data.	

BE 7.2 (LO 1) Data exploration is based on three elements: (1) the number being analyzed, (2) variables that break down the number, and (3) _____.

BE 7.3 (LO 1) **Data** **Financial Accounting** Nazmi runs a Food Truck, the Treat Buggy, in Sydney, Australia. Use the data file provided by Nazmi to determine the percentage of his revenues during summer months (June, July, August) generated from ice cream sales compared to sales from other items.

BE 7.4 (LO 1) **Data** **Managerial Accounting** Mauretius is a boutique car builder. They manufacture 5,000 cars each year. There are two different car models: Perfic and Fortis. A critical component for all their cars is a high-performance battery. The company outsources the manufacturing of the batteries for both models to three vendors: Optima, Champion, and Diehard. Specifications and prices are the same for all three vendors. Because of this, vendors are rated based on reliability. They are evaluated as to the extent they comply with Mauretius' specifications. Batteries that are not compliant are returned. Using the data set provided by Mauretius, compare vendors' reliability as a percentage for both models. Based on reliability, who should be the preferred vendor for each battery type?

BE 7.5 (LO 2) Which type of visualization is appropriate for the statements given below?

Statement	Solution	Explanation
Chart that is best for visualizing time series		
Chart type best suited for visualizing a part-to-whole relationship		
Chart type that is best used to depict a distribution data exploration pattern		
Chart type that is best used to depict a ranking data exploration pattern		
Chart type that is best used to depict a nominal comparison data exploration pattern		

BE 7.6 (LO 2) `Managerial Accounting` Monar is a trendy shoe store on Oxford Street in London that employs 10 in-store salespeople. Monar's CEO uses the following chart when analyzing the performance of the company's salespeople. The chart shows salespeople in descending order of seniority. Maurice Ayoade is the most recent hire.

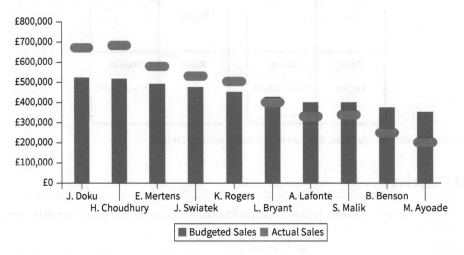

1. What data relationship is being explored?
2. What insights can be generated from this chart?

BE 7.7 (LO 2) `Data` `Managerial Accounting` Raisin is an electronics manufacturer with headquarters in Dijon, France. Its CEO wants a dashboard that shows the progress made for each product line compared to last year's unit sales. The goal is a 10% increase in unit sales for each of the four product lines. The CEO provides you the data.

ProductLine	LastYear	ThisYear
Computers	122,322	132,889
Phones	789,112	998,325
Printers	67,891	32,445
TVs	322,112	401,223

1. What data relationship are you exploring?
2. What visuals would you use to explore this relationship?
3. What insights can you collect from your exploration?

BE 7.8 (LO 2, 3)

1. What insights can be generated from the Pareto chart below that depicts the composition of a high school by class?

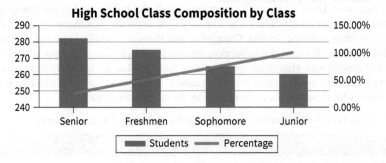

2. The Pareto chart below depicts customer complaints for the four locations of McDowell's Burgers for the month of July 2025. The labor market has been tight for the past 12 months as McDowell's has had difficulty hiring.

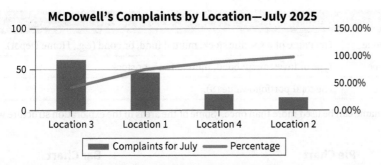

Based on the insight ranking complaints by location, what might be the remedy for Location 3?

BE 7.9 (LO 2, 3) The Hilton hotel chain is attempting to understand the profitability of frequent guests (i.e., those guests that log over 75 nights per year). Since there is a large variability in revenue per night due to hotel location, the percentage of net profit per guest per year is used to compensate for the variability in location. Some guests tend to ask for additional customer service more than others. Customer service may include everything from extra towels to comped nights due to noise complaints, etc. Excessive customer service lowers the average profitability of the customer, even though they spend a large number of nights at Hilton hotels. The data will be used to revoke those customers' frequent stay status so the focus can be on more profitable customers. What data exploration pattern can best identify the least profitable frequent guests?

BE 7.10 (LO 3) `Data` `Financial Accounting` Poisson is a manufacturer of swimwear. They provide you the following financial summary for the period 2021–2025:

Account	2021	2022	2023	2024	2025
Revenues	$ 3,476,811	$ 3,337,714	$ 3,197,633	$ 3,159,912	$ 3,087,761
Gross Profit	$ 1,890,556	$ 1,735,551	$ 1,640,941	$ 1,554,891	$ 1,438,664
Net Profit	$ 753,891	$ 827,714	$ 970,022	$ 1,000,033	$ 1,110,989

Explore the data. Create two visualizations. Briefly describe what data relationships they represent and the insights you derived from each.

BE 7.11 (LO 2, 3) Napigem is a Florida-based biotech company. They invest some of their assets in stocks, bonds, and mutual funds. The following dashboard helps them manage their investment portfolio:

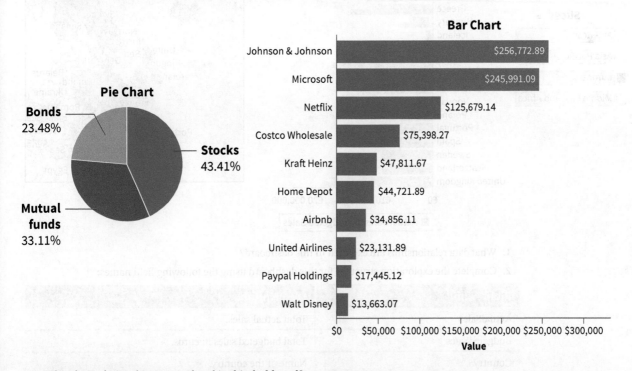

1. What data relationships are explored in this dashboard?
2. Complete the exploration structure for this dashboard using the following field names:

Field Name	Description
InvestmentName	The name of a specific stock, mutual fund, or bond (e.g., Home Depot).
InvestmentType	Type of investment: bond, mutual fund, or stock.
TotalValue	The total portfolio value ($).

The same field name can be used more than once. (Some of the areas in the exploration structure will remain empty.)

Pie Chart

Filters	Columns
Rows	**Values**

Bar Chart

Filters	Columns
Rows	**Values**

BE 7.12 (LO 3) DotSoft is company with headquarters in Brussels, Belgium, that sells babycare products worldwide. They created the following dashboard to make it easy for the C-Suite to monitor sales:

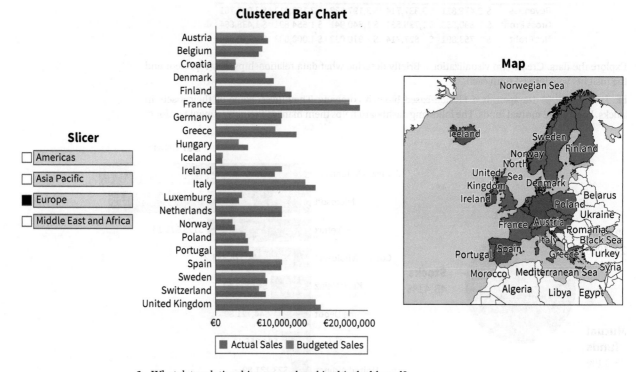

Clustered Bar Chart

Slicer
- ☐ Americas
- ☐ Asia Pacific
- ☑ Europe
- ☐ Middle East and Africa

Map

■ Actual Sales ■ Budgeted Sales

1. What data relationships are explored in this dashboard?
2. Complete the exploration structure for this dashboard using the following field names:

Field Name	Description
ActualSales	Total actual sales.
BudgetedSales	Total budgeted sales in euros.
Country	Name of the country.
Region	Name of the region.
Variance	Total sales – total budgeted sales.

Each field name can be used more than once. There will be some blank areas in the completed exploration structure.

Slicer		**Clustered Bar Chart**		**Map**	
Filters	**Columns**	**Filters**	**Columns**	**Filters**	**Columns**
Rows	**Values**	**Rows**	**Values**	**Rows**	**Values**

Exercises

EX 7.1 (LO 1) `Data` `Tax Accounting` **Explore Tax Expenses** Instant Pest Control (IPC) is a medium-sized company with offices in Delaware, Maryland, New Jersey, and Pennsylvania. IPC's controller wants two tax-related questions answered.

1. For tax purposes, IPC is required to file Form 1099s for contractors and Form W-2s for employees. How many of both forms do they need to prepare for each state? Because IPC pays their tax accountants per prepared form, this information can help the controller estimate the fee to be paid.

2. IPC has established an internal policy to hire only in-state employees to simplify its tax filings. The state the office is located in and the employee's state of residency should be the same. Per state, to what extent are the offices compliant with this policy (as a percentage)?

EX 7.2 (LO 2) `Data` `Managerial Accounting` **Explore Salary Distribution** The Benford Group is a U.S. top-50 public accounting firm with more than 1,400 employees. Their managing partner, Tuhina, provides you with a list of the salaries of all employees. What can you tell Tuhina about the salary distribution at the Benford Group?

EX 7.3 (LO 2) `Data` `Financial Accounting` **Growth Analysis** Shrek, a mid-size bike manufacturer in Oxford, PA, targets a 5% growth in 2025 for all its product lines. As Shrek's controller, you have received the data set generated by the company's ERP system.

ProductLine	2024 UnitsSold	2025 UnitsSold
Adventure	2,771	5,741
City	8,001	6,799
Cyclocross	13,998	14,881
Family	23,488	22,476
Fitness	8,112	11,665
Mountain	7,500	7,430
Tandem	1,089	722
Touring	3,801	4,022

1. Starting from the data you received, what are two key questions you would like to answer?

2. What data relationship is being explored?

3. What visualizations can be used for exploration purposes?

4. What insights are generated by your analysis?

EX 7.4 (LO 2, 3) `Data` `Managerial Accounting` **Daily Sales Comparison** Meier is a chain of grocery stores. Their store in Big Rapids, MI gives you their 2025 February sales data for four products: deli, meat, chicken, and fish. A sample is shown below:

Day	Deli	Meat	Chicken	Fish
2/1/2025	$ 27,234	$ 87,665	$ 17,074	$ 5,992
2/2/2025	$ 34,889	$ 43,141	$ 38,827	$ 10,436
2/3/2025	$ 19,067	$ 61,675	$ 15,447	$ 12,024
2/4/2025	$ 17,812	$ 46,855	$ 32,029	$ 5,285
2/5/2025	$ 22,357	$ 42,584	$ 31,342	$ 9,361
2/6/2025	$ 11,525	$ 55,635	$ 42,466	$ 9,019
2/7/2025	$ 12,052	$ 38,495	$ 41,091	$ 24,889
2/8/2025	$ 28,554	$ 82,009	$ 24,739	$ 7,563
2/9/2025	$ 41,776	$ 45,106	$ 15,990	$ 12,569
2/10/2025	$ 16,200	$ 44,461	$ 25,780	$ 11,666

Create a visualization for each of the two questions they ask you to explore:

1. How do weekdays rank based on total February sales?
2. How does the sales share of each product compare across weekdays?

EX 7.5 (LO 2) `Data` **Identify and Explore Data Relationships** Ice Cow is a popular ice cream store in New York City's theater district. They created the following report for their July 2025 sales:

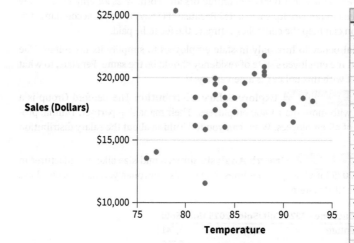

Date	Temperature	Sales
7/1/25	82	$ 16,820
7/2/25	81	$ 16,128
7/3/25	81	$ 18,412
7/4/25	79	$ 25,373
7/5/25	83	$ 17,396
7/6/25	85	$ 17,236
7/7/25	83	$ 18,628
7/8/25	84	$ 18,393
7/9/25	86	$ 17,773
7/10/25	88	$ 21,761
7/11/25	88	$ 20,411
7/12/25	91	$ 17,558
7/13/25	93	$ 18,104
7/14/25	82	$ 11,498
7/15/25	76	$ 13,497
7/16/25	77	$ 13,985
7/17/25	82	$ 15,825
7/18/25	84	$ 16,031
7/19/25	88	$ 20,248
7/20/25	92	$ 18,333
7/21/25	91	$ 16,442
7/22/25	90	$ 17,872
7/23/25	88	$ 20,923
7/24/25	82	$ 19,752
7/25/25	83	$ 19,919
7/26/25	84	$ 19,153
7/27/25	83	$ 19,494
7/28/25	85	$ 18,361
7/29/25	87	$ 20,311
7/30/25	86	$ 19,544
7/31/25	84	$ 17,790

1. What question is being explored?
2. What data relationship is being explored?
3. What insights does the data relationship generate?

EX 7.6 (LO 2, 3) `Data` `Managerial Accounting` **Identify and Explore Data Relationships** Gummy is a chain with candy trucks selling in five cities: Chicago, Los Angeles, New York, Philadelphia, and San Francisco. They provide you the following report:

Number of Candy Trucks

Year	Chicago	Los Angeles	New York	Philadelphia	San Francisco
2021	1,240	1,712	1,350	750	920
2022	1,267	1,650	1,245	730	920
2023	1,270	1,590	1,240	690	975
2024	1,300	1,575	1,243	720	1,044
2025	1,320	1,420	1,225	730	1,055

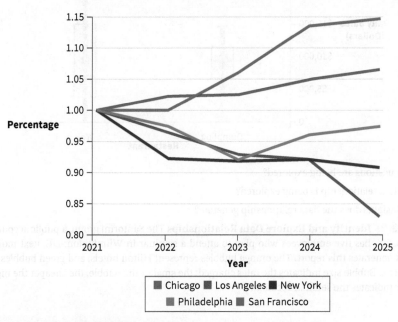

1. What question is being explored?
2. What data relationships are being explored?
3. What insights do the data relationships generate?

EX 7.7 (LO 2, 3) `Data` `Managerial Accounting` **Identify and Explore Data Relationships** Cook Cars is a small car dealership that employs three salespeople: Carlos, Arun, and Shanice. The dealership's owner asked you to prepare the following report:

1. What questions are being explored?
2. What data relationships are being explored?
3. What insights do the data relationships generate?

EX 7.8 (LO 2) `Data` **Identify and Explore Data Relationships** Benji owns two take-out restaurants called Wok and Dumpling. Wok is located in downtown Denton, Texas. Dumpling is in the business district of the same city. Both restaurants serve a similar menu. At the end of the first quarter, Benji receives a report he requested from his accountant.

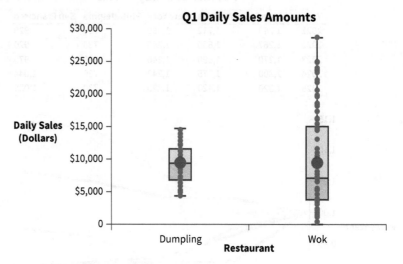

1. What questions are being explored?
2. What data relationship is being explored?
3. What insights does the data relationship generate?

EX 7.9 (LO 2, 3) Identify and Explore Data Relationships The Santorini group, a public accounting firm in Amarillo, TX, has five employees who plan to attend a seminar in Wilmington, DE, next month. Their data analyst generates this report. The orange bubbles represent Hilton hotels, and green bubbles represent Marriott hotels. Bubble size indicates the rates charged: the smaller the bubble, the cheaper the nightly rate. The red star indicates the seminar location.

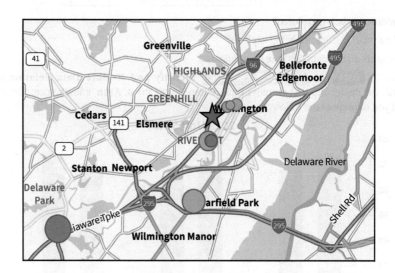

Chain	Hotel	Location	Rate/Night
Marriott	Courtyard Wilmington Downtown	1102 N West Street, Wilmington, Delaware, 19801	127
Hilton	DoubleTree by Hilton Hotel Wilmington	4727 Concord Pike, Wilmington, DE 19803	118
Marriott	Fairfield Inn & Suites Wilmington New Castle	2117 N Dupont Hwy, New Castle, DE 19720-6308	202
Hilton	Homewood Suites by Hilton Wilmington Downtown	820 Justison St, Wilmington, DE 19801	145
Hilton	Hotel Wilmington/Christiana	100 Continental Drive Newark, Delaware 19713-4301, USA	224
Marriott	Residence Inn Wilmington Downtown	1300 North Market Street, Wilmington, Delaware 19801	142
Marriott	Sheraton Suites Wilmington Downtown	422 Delaware Avenue, Wilmington, Delaware, 19801	136
Marriott	The Westin Wilmington	818 Shipyard Drive, Wilmington, Delaware 19801	175

1. What questions are being explored?
2. What data relationships are being explored?
3. What insights do the data relationships generate?

EX 7.10 (LO 2, 3) `Data` **Identify and Explore Data Relationships** Perez & Sons (PS) are the exclusive northeast distributors for South Track treadmills. There are four types of treadmills: M1750, M2450, M2950, and M3750. PS has four warehouses, one each in Boston, New York, Philadelphia, and Baltimore. To meet demand, they want 1,300 units of each type of treadmill in stock at any time, for a total of 5,200. They provide you with the data set.

Warehouse	Product	QOH
Boston	M1750	412
New York	M1750	288
Philadelphia	M1750	298
Baltimore	M1750	396
Boston	M2450	49
New York	M2450	658
Philadelphia	M2450	321
Baltimore	M2450	199
Boston	M2950	420
New York	M2950	519
Philadelphia	M2950	344
Baltimore	M2950	618
Boston	M3750	400
New York	M3750	400
Philadelphia	M3750	150
Baltimore	M3750	55

The three diagrams show possible exploration structures for this data set: A, B, and C.

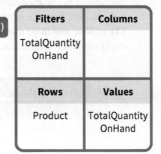

(A)

Filters	Columns
	Product

Rows	Values
Warehouse	TotalQuantity OnHand

(B)

Filters	Columns
	Product

Rows	Values
Warehouse	TotalQuantity OnHand

(C)

Filters	Columns
TotalQuantity OnHand	

Rows	Values
Product	TotalQuantity OnHand

Do the following for each exploration structure:

1. Identity a data relationship that could be explored.
2. Determine questions that could be answered.
3. Create a visualization to support your analysis.
4. Explain insights that could be generated.

EX 7.11 (LO 2, 3) `Data` `Financial Accounting` **Identify and Explore Data Relationships** Bethany Beach, a small beach community, has three ice cream stores: Laureen's, Softer-Ice, and YuMeeS. The following data summarizes their revenue for the 2021–2025 period:

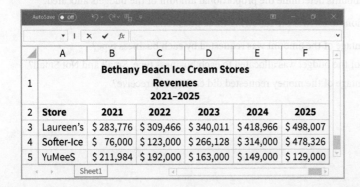

Store	2021	2022	2023	2024	2025
Laureen's	$ 283,776	$ 309,466	$ 340,011	$ 418,966	$ 498,007
Softer-Ice	$ 76,000	$ 123,000	$ 266,128	$ 314,000	$ 478,326
YuMeeS	$ 211,984	$ 192,000	$ 163,000	$ 149,000	$ 129,000

Bethany Beach Ice Cream Stores Revenues 2021–2025

Generate at least three insights from the perspective of Laureen's. For each insight, discuss what data relationship you explored and what visual you used to generate it.

EX 7.12 `Data` `Tax Accounting` **Identify and Explore Data Relationships** The following table was taken from the IRS 2018 Statistics of Income report. It summarizes the Income Subject to Tax and Total Income Tax After Credits amounts on the federal returns filed by active corporations.

Size Total Assets	Income Subject To Tax	Total Income Tax After Credits
Zero Assets	$ 55,884,102	$ 11,594,836
$1 under $500,000	$ 7,829,008	$ 1,569,228
$500,000 under $1,000,000	$ 4,829,204	$ 956,103
$1,000,000 under $5,000,000	$ 17,223,201	$ 3,496,487
$5,000,000 under $10,000,000	$ 10,086,326	$ 2,015,713
$10,000,000 under $25,000,000	$ 19,143,340	$ 3,805,232
$25,000,000 under $50,000,000	$ 14,384,822	$ 2,811,835
$50,000,000 under $100,000,000	$ 16,854,446	$ 3,293,822
$100,000,000 under $250,000,000	$ 25,807,956	$ 4,772,611
$250,000,000 under $500,000,000	$ 26,192,384	$ 4,679,319
$500,000,000 under $2,500,000,000	$ 126,273,758	$ 20,835,589
$2,500,000,000 or more	$ 1,632,169,980	$ 184,855,832

Explore whether large companies with more assets have a higher tax rate.

1. What data relationships are you exploring?
2. Design a report with a visualization that enables you to explore this data relationship.
3. What insights can you collect from your exploration?

EX 7.13 (LO 2, 3) `Data` `Tax Accounting` **Exploring R&D Tax Credit Allocations** In 1997, the state of Pennsylvania enacted a research and development (R&D) tax credit to increase R&D activities within the commonwealth to enhance economic growth. The state's budget for the tax year 2020 was $55 million. The legislation required the state to set aside $11 million to support startups and small businesses (Small). The remaining $44 million was to be awarded to other businesses (Not-Small). The 2021 report summarizes the 2020 R&D credit amount requested and awarded.

PENNSYLVANIA RESEARCH & DEVELOPMENT TAX CREDIT – 2021 REPORT

2020 RECIPIENTS

			R&D CREDITS - DECEMBER 2020 ($M)		
BUSINESS TYPE	APPLICANTS	% OF APPLICANTS	TENTATIVE	ACTUAL	% OF ACTUAL
SMALL	470	42.2%	$18.1	$11.0	20.0%
NOT SMALL	643	57.8%	$189.7	$44.0	80.0%
TOTAL	**1,113**	**100.0%**	**$207.7**	**$55.0**	**100.0%**

Source: Adapted from the Research & Development Tax Credit Report to the Pennsylvania General Assembly.

- The Tentative column represents the taxpayers' total requested credit amount on their R&D credit applications.
- The Actual column represents the total amount awarded to those submitting applications.
- The actual amounts determine the proportional amount of the budgets allocated.

Create visualizations to answer the following three questions:

1. What percentage of the amount was requested by each business type?
2. How much of the budget was allocated to each business type, Small and Not Small?
3. What percentage of the money requested did each group receive?

EX 7.14 (LO 3) Data **Perform Pareto Analysis** Nicole, manager of the Rainbow hotel, provides you this summary table regarding customer complaints received in January 2025.

Type	Source	Number
Dirty Rooms	Hotel Website	4
Dirty Rooms	Calls	22
Elevator	Calls	2
Poor Wifi	Hotel Website	4
Poor Wifi	ratemyhotel.com	2
Poor Wifi	Calls	7
Rodents	Calls	2
Room Temperature	Calls	2
Unexpected Fees	Letter	14
Unexpected Fees	Hotel Website	60
Unexpected Fees	ratemyhotel.com	16
Unexpected Fees	Calls	90
Unfriendly Staff	Letter	2
Unfriendly Staff	Hotel Website	105
Unfriendly Staff	ratemyhotel.com	44
Unfriendly Staff	Calls	45

1. Use the data file to create a Pareto chart.
2. Discuss the insights it generates.

EX 7.15 Data **Explore with an Interactive Report** Jumpers is a grocery store in Indianapolis with locations in NIndy (North Indy) and SIndy (South Indy). They compiled a five-year report with revenues generated for each of their seven product categories (meat, drinks, vegetables and fruits, snacks, freezer, diary, other).

1. Create an interactive report based on the following exploration structure:

Filters	Columns
Store	

Rows	Values

Filters	Columns
Store ProductName	Store

Rows	Values
Year	TotalAmount

Filters	Columns
ProductName	

Rows	Values

Filters	Columns
	ProductName

Rows	Values
Year	TotalAmount

2. Describe the relationships that are part of your dashboard.
3. Identify questions that can be explored with your dashboard.

ComfyFurn is a furniture store in Halfway, Oregon, that manufactures custom-designed wooden tables of exceptional quality. Most of their customers are collectors, including several movie stars. Their business model is simple: a customer contacts them, they work with the customer on a design, build the table, and deliver it to the customer's residence. ComfyFurn just hired you as an intern for their accounting department. They hope your data analytics skills can help them with some of the decisions they face. They provide you with an Excel file that contains several worksheets with data generated from their ERP system. The underlying data model is shown here, followed by a data dictionary.

Data Model

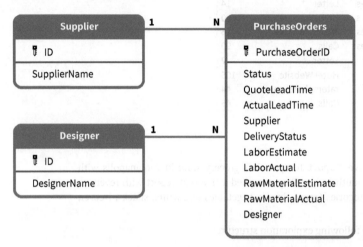

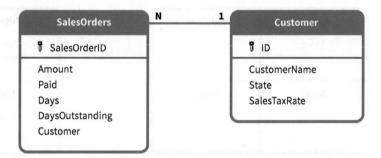

Data Dictionary
PURCHASEORDERS

Name	Description
PurchaseOrderId	Uniquely identifies a purchase order.
Status	A purchase order's status: Canceled, Delivered, Open, or Returned.
QuotedLeadTime	The number of days the vendor committed to deliver the goods.
ActualLeadTime	The number of days it took the vendor to deliver the goods.
Supplier	ID of the vendor from whom the goods are purchased.
DeliveryStatus	An order is canceled, delivered, open, or returned. For orders that have been delivered, it is specified whether they were early, ontime, late, or disruptive. Disruptive implies that the production process was disrupted.
LaborEstimate	The estimated dollar amount for labor for the production order.
LaborActual	The actual dollar amount used for labor for the production order.
RawMaterialEstimate	The estimated dollar amount for raw materials for the production order.
RawMaterialActual	The actual dollar amount for raw materials for the production order.
Designer	ID of the designer who designed the production order (table).

Supplier

Name	Description
ID	Uniquely identifies a vendor.
Name	A vendor's name.

SalesOrders

Name	Description
SalesOrderId	Uniquely identifies a sales order.
Amount	The amount the customer owes ComfyFurn.
Paid	Has the order been paid in full: Yes or No.
Days	For orders that are fully paid, the number of days it took to pay them.
DaysOutstanding	For orders that are not fully paid yet, the number of days the receivable has been outstanding.
Customer	ID of the customer to whom the table was sold.

Customer

Name	Description
ID	Uniquely identifies a customer.
Name	A customer's name.
State	The state in which a customer lives.
SalesTaxRate	The sales tax rate for the state in which the customer lives.

Designer

Name	Description
ID	Uniquely identifies a designer.
Name	A designer's name.

PAC 7.1 Auditing: Explore Vendor Reliability

Data **Auditing** Part of ComfyFurn's success rests on its use of premium wood such as Bubinga and Dalbergia. One of its main challenges is to find suppliers for such wood. They currently work with 11 different suppliers, and selection is exclusively based on price: the order goes to the supplier with the lowest price. You point out that supplier performance, particularly on-time delivery, should be considered as well. Risks related to late deliveries include lost sales, downtime, or not meeting the delivery schedule. Late deliveries can dramatically impact the bottom line. You decide to use the data to support your statement. You start by developing an algorithm to create a field called DeliveryStatus that contains one of the following values: Early, Ontime, Late, Disruptive, Canceled, Returned. You already added that column to the ComfyFurn file.

1. Using the values in the DeliveryStatus field, explore the delivery risks ComfyFurn is facing.

2. Assess the risk of each supplier, and assign them one of the following labels: Safe, Risky, High-Risk.

3. To mitigate supplier risk, how would you suggest tiering ComfyFurn's suppliers?

PAC 7.2 Managerial Accounting: Manage Variances

Data **Managerial Accounting** Another key part of ComfyFurn's success is its designers, highly-paid artists who design the tables with and for customers. They currently have five designers, and one is assigned to each purchase order. They meet extensively with each of the customers and develop comprehensive specifications. Production steps and required raw materials are specified with the highest level of detail. Accuracy of cost estimates are of utmost importance for ComfyFurn given that they determine a table's price.

You receive data generated by ComfyFurn's ERP system that show the estimated and actual labor and material cost in dollars for each production order (table). You can find these data in the PurchaseOrders worksheet. You are asked to analyze how accurate the design specifications are both overall and among designers.

1. Determine and analyze the overall variances.

2. Compare variances among designers.

PAC 7.3 Financial Accounting: Manage Accounts Receivable

Data Financial Accounting ComfyFurn's management would like to include additional information about credit risk in their financial report. They ask you to explore accounts receivable and provide some insights. They provide you with sales orders and payment data generated by their ERP system. You can find these data in the SalesOrders and Customer worksheets. The following is some additional information regarding ComfyFurn's credit policy:

- All payments are due within 30 days.
- Early payments: There is a 3% discount for all orders paid in full within two weeks (15 days).
- On time payments: There is no discount or no penalty for sales orders paid on time.
- Late payments: There is a 3% penalty for all sales orders with a late payment.

1. Explore whether ComfyFurn's credit policy works. For orders that already have been paid, compare early, on time, and late payments.
2. For the orders that have not been fully paid yet, explore the aging of the outstanding balances. What insights can you collect?
3. Analyze accounts receivable by customer. Explore whether there is an issue with accounts receivable concentration.

PAC 7.4 Tax Accounting: Analyze Sales Tax

Data Tax Accounting ComfyFurn delivers items to customer residencies. You notice that no sales tax was collected for any of the sales.

1. Determine the total sales tax amount that ComfyFurn should have collected.
2. Determine how much sales tax should have been collected and remitted to the different states.

CHAPTER

8

Interpreting Data Analysis Results

CHAPTER PREVIEW

Your data analysis skill-building journey continues in this chapter with a focus on interpreting data analysis results. You have been developing your data analytics mindset, identifying and analyzing the motivation for data analytics projects, learning how to identify relevant questions, data, and concepts, and designing data analysis strategies. You also learned the skills necessary to prepare data for analysis, build information models, and explore data. Now, it is time to interpret the analyses' results so they can be communicated to stakeholders.

It might initially seem that data exploration and data interpretation are the same thing. While some aspects are similar, there are also key differences. The data exploration step focuses on analyzing rather than interpreting. Interpreting data analysis results is a critical step in the data analysis process.

There will be times during your career when you must interpret a data analysis that was prepared by someone else in your organization, clients, creditors, or supply chain partners. This chapter focuses on interpreting the meaning of both your own final analyses and results prepared by others.

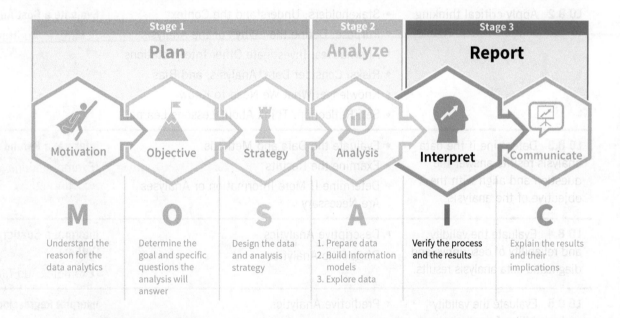

Stage 1			Stage 2	Stage 3	
Plan			**Analyze**	**Report**	
Motivation	Objective	Strategy	Analysis	Interpret	Communicate
M	**O**	**S**	**A**	**I**	**C**
Understand the reason for the data analytics	Determine the goal and specific questions the analysis will answer	Design the data and analysis strategy	1. Prepare data 2. Build information models 3. Explore data	Verify the process and the results	Explain the results and their implications

PROFESSIONAL INSIGHT — **Do the Analysis Results Make Sense?**

Megan, a senior tax accountant, works at one of the 10 largest U.S. accounting firms.

When I first graduated, the firm I worked in outsourced all tax return and analysis preparation. Right away I was expected to review analyses prepared by other people and explain those results to the partner. It was really difficult to suddenly be in a review role rather than a preparer role. I knew how to check the numbers to see if they were correct, but interpreting what the results meant was much more challenging.

As I have transitioned into a senior role, I have seen the importance of critical thinking even more. My favorite staff to work with are those who review their results and ask questions. They don't just assume that, because the numbers were input correctly, the results are correct. **You can check all the numbers to see if they are correct, but when you do the analysis, you need to be able to determine if the results make sense.**

A staff member once input all the data correctly into the tax software and prepared a tax liability analysis that showed the client's tax liability went up. However, this didn't make sense because that client had a $100 thousand loss from one of their businesses. So, the tax liability should have gone down. When I pointed this out, the staff member responded, "I was so caught up in the details that I rationalized the results instead of asking more questions." Stepping back to evaluate if something makes sense is difficult. As a student I didn't practice doing that. I was just focused on getting the right answers and getting a high grade.

Chapter Roadmap

LEARNING OBJECTIVES	TOPICS	APPLY IT
LO 8.1 Compare data analysis interpretation and data exploration.	• Data Analysis Interpretation Versus Data Exploration • Data Analysis Interpretation	**Interpret Revenue Visualization** (Example: Financial Accounting)
LO 8.2 Apply critical thinking to data analysis interpretation.	• Stakeholders: Understand the Context • Purpose: Define the "Why" of the Analysis • Alternatives: Investigate Other Interpretations • Risks: Consider Data, Analysis, and Bias • Knowledge: What We Need to Know • Self-Reflection: Think About Lessons Learned	**Evaluate a Cost Analysis** (Example: Auditing)
LO 8.3 Determine if the data analysis results answer the question and align with the objective of the analysis.	• Evaluate the Data and Methods • Examine the Results • Determine If More Information or Analyses Are Necessary	**Interpret a Refund Analysis** (Example: Managerial Accounting)
LO 8.4 Evaluate the validity and reliability of descriptive and diagnostic data analysis results.	• Descriptive Analytics • Diagnostic Analytics	**Interpret a Scatterplot for Outliers** (Example: Auditing)
LO 8.5 Evaluate the validity and reliability of predictive and prescriptive data analysis results.	• Predictive Analytics • Prescriptive Analytics	**Interpret Regression Results** (Example: Managerial Accounting)

Data The Data tag appears in the chapter when the data for an example, illustration, or application are available in the book's product page on www.wiley.com.

Data analytics software is continuously changing, and there may be more recent versions of the software referenced in this chapter.

8.1 How Do We Draw Conclusions from Data Analysis?

LEARNING OBJECTIVE ❶
Compare data analysis interpretation and data exploration.

Data analysis interpretation is the process of evaluating an analysis to understand and explain its meaning. Similar to interpreting a weather forecast when planning an outdoor party, the insights gained from data analysis interpretation help us make good business decisions. Data analysis interpretation and data exploration probably seem very similar. In fact, you are interpreting even as you are exploring the data.

Data Analysis Interpretation Versus Data Exploration

The goal of data exploration is understanding the data, whereas data interpretation involves understanding the analysis. The focus, however, is what differentiates exploration and interpretation.

An example can illustrate the difference. Imagine conducting an audit of accounts receivable. The client has given the audit team access to the available accounts receivable data. An excerpt from the data is shown in **Illustration 8.1**. The first step is exploring the data to understand it. Recall that data exploration is a process with four steps:

1. Identify questions about the data.
2. Identify data relationships.
3. Explore data relationships.
4. Generate insights.

ILLUSTRATION 8.1 Accounts Receivable Database

	A	B	C	D	E	F	G	H	I
1				Client Accounts Receivable Database Excerpt					
2	CustomerID	PaperlessDate	InvoiceNumber	InvoiceDate	DueDate	InvoiceAmount	Disputed	SettledDate	PaperlessBill
3	0379-NEVHP	4/5/2025	611365	1/1/2025	1/31/2025	$ 55.94	No	1/14/2025	Paper
4	8976-AMJEO	3/2/2024	7900770	1/25/2025	2/24/2025	$ 61.74	Yes	3/2/2025	Electronic
5	2820-XGXSB	1/24/2024	9231909	7/2/2025	8/1/2025	$ 65.88	No	7/7/2025	Electronic
6	9322-YCTQO	4/5/2024	9888306	2/9/2025	3/11/2025	$ 105.92	No	3/16/2025	Electronic
7	6627-ELFBK	11/25/2024	15752855	10/24/2024	11/23/2024	$ 72.27	Yes	11/27/2024	Paper
8	5148-SYKLB	8/27/2025	18104516	1/25/2024	2/24/2024	$ 94.00	Yes	2/20/2024	Paper
2466	7050-KQLDO	9/28/2024	9989225541	4/26/2024	5/26/2024	$ 53.16	No	5/17/2024	Paper
2467	9758-AIEIK	4/22/2024	9990243864	7/3/2025	8/2/2025	$ 68.66	No	7/17/2025	Electronic
2468									

The data could be explored to calculate the total accounts receivable by aging category, and the data and payment information could be used to identify relationships in the data:

- Column G represents accounts where the customer disagrees with the invoice amount.
- Exploration: Is there a relationship between accounts receivable being disputed and how overdue the payment is?

An alternative relationship could also be explored:

- Column I data show whether a customer receives an electronic or paper bill.
- Exploration: Does paper or electronic billing have a relationship with how long it takes a customer to pay?

The insight gained from analyzing the relationships can be used to estimate uncollectible accounts. Performing many exploratory analyses will eventually lead to the analysis that accurately explains the accounts receivable and uncollectible accounts.

Now, it is time to move into interpretation mode. At this point, we understand the data, but we must understand what the analyses mean in terms of supporting the audit tests of completeness and reasonableness of the allowance for doubtful accounts. Data analysis interpretation happens at the end of the data exploration process. We move from exploring for insights to interpreting so we can make informed decisions.

Data Analysis Interpretation

Data analysis interpretation is the process of reviewing an analysis. There are two steps, each with specific questions that should be answered.

Step 1: Determine if the analysis makes sense.

- Question 1: Does the analysis answer the intended question and align with the original objective?
- Question 2: Were the correct data and methods used to perform the analysis?
- Question 3: Are the results reasonable, or are more analyses necessary?

Step 2: Verify that the results are valid and reliable.

- Question 4: Does the analysis measure what it was intended to measure?
- Question 5: Are the results accurate?

These steps probably seem familiar because they mirror the data analysis process in previous chapters. When interpreting our own analysis, the first two questions in Step 1 are answered during the planning and analyzing stages of the MOSAIC process:

- Does the analysis answer the original question or objective of the analysis? (**Motivation** and **Objective**)
- Were the correct data and appropriate method used to perform the analysis? (**Strategy** and **Analysis**)

The remaining questions from both steps would then be answered during the reporting stage of the data analysis process (**Interpretation**). However, if someone else prepared the analysis, then it is necessary to address each question for both steps. This chapter works through the five questions assuming the analysis was prepared by someone else.

Let's continue with the accounts receivable example. During an audit, the audit team will review the accounts receivable balance to confirm two things:

1. The receivables exist and are legitimate.
2. The amount reflected in the balance sheet contains all the accounts receivable and is complete.

Understanding accounts receivable involves reviewing an analysis prepared by a client, which must be interpreted. **Illustration 8.2**, a column chart, is an example of an accounts receivable analysis called an accounts receivable aging report. The chart breaks total accounts receivable into categories based on when the receivables are due. Each bar in the chart represents the total of accounts receivable due for each category of due dates.

ILLUSTRATION 8.2 Accounts Receivable Aging Analysis

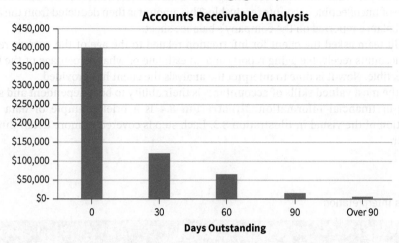

This analysis could be one of many that the audit team must interpret. It helps auditors understand the relationship between the accounts receivable total and the breakdown of how much of that total is past due and for how long.

Imagine the audit team is testing whether the valuation of the allowance for doubtful accounts is appropriate. The client has provided the visualization in **Illustration 8.3**.

ILLUSTRATION 8.3 Accounts Receivable Aging and Percent of Uncollectible Accounts

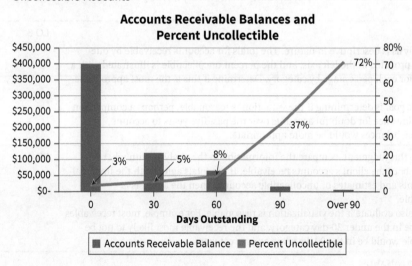

Some important points about this visualization:

- This is a dual axis chart, which helps illustrate the relationship between variables with different measurement scales.
- This example examines the total amount of accounts receivable in each of the five aging categories and the percentage of those receivables that are uncollectible.
- The left axis shows the amount of accounts receivables in U.S. dollars. The right axis is the percentage of receivables that are uncollectible.
- Including both variables in the visualization shows the total accounts receivable by aging category and what percent of those receivables are considered uncollectible.

Recall from your first financial accounting course that the allowance for doubtful accounts is an estimate of uncollectible accounts receivable. This amount is then deducted from the accounts receivable balance reported on the company's balance sheet.

The audit team asked the client for information related to the age of the current receivable balances (accounts receivable aging report) and an estimate of what percentage of the balances are uncollectible. Now it is time to interpret the analysis the client has provided.

One of the most valued skills of accountants is their ability to be independent and skeptical evaluators of financial information. **Illustration 8.4** is a brief example of data analysis interpretation of the visual in Illustration 8.3. Each step is covered in more detail throughout the chapter.

ILLUSTRATION 8.4 Overview of Data Analysis Interpretation

Interpretation Process	Example: Interpretation of Illustration 8.3	Learning Objective
Step 1: Determine if the analysis makes sense.		
1. Does the analysis answer the intended question and align with the original objective?	• The question is whether the allowance for doubtful accounts seems reasonable. The analysis does reveal some insight, but more information is needed. • For example, we do not know the balance in the allowance for doubtful accounts.	LO 3
2. Were the correct data and methods used to perform the analysis?	Data: • To make this judgment, check the data to confirm the correct accounts receivable data were used in the analysis. • Confirm that the data used to calculate the uncollectible percentage amounts are correct.	LO 3
	Methods: • The analysis is descriptive in nature. The totals for accounts receivable by due date are provided in the left axis, and the percent uncollectible is illustrated with a call out for each percentage by category. Determine if this is the most appropriate method. • Since the goal is determining if the valuation is reasonable, perhaps a comparison of the allowance for doubtful accounts over the past five years to account receivable balances would be more appropriate.	LO 3
3. Are the results reasonable, or is more analysis necessary?	• To make this judgment, compare the information in the analysis with what is known about the client's accounts receivable. If the totals agree with the financial statements and estimates of uncollectible accounts, then the analysis is reasonable. • We can also evaluate if the visualization is reasonable. For example, most receivables should be in the under 30-day category, and the receivable most likely to not be collectible would be in the 90 days late or over category.	LO 3
Step 2: Verify the results are valid and reliable.		
4. Does the analysis measure what was intended?	Validity refers to how well the analysis represents reality: • In this example, determine if the visualization represents an analysis of the allowance for doubtful accounts valuation.	LO 4 and LO 5
5. Are the results accurate?	Accuracy means that the measures used in the analysis are correct and without mistakes: • The measures used in the visualization are account balances, days outstanding, and a calculation of the percent of uncollectible accounts. These are all correct measures. • Confirm the amounts are correct by comparing the accounts receivable to the amounts in the financial statements.	LO 4 and LO 5

Data Financial Accounting Denton Hospitality, Inc. (DHI) is a hotel chain in the southwestern United States. Dante Garcia started the hotel chain in Denton, Texas, in 1968 with one hotel. Since then, the chain has grown to 48 hotels in four states. Dante retired in 2002 and was succeeded as CEO by his daughter, Luciana.

DHI's hotels are in the economy lodging segment. Properties are in Colorado, Oklahoma, New Mexico, and Texas. A typical economy lodging hotel has an average of 84 rooms, although DHI's hotels average 117 rooms. Properties are staffed by a general manager, front desk staff of six persons, a head housekeeper, seven housekeepers, and a maintenance worker. Except for the general manager, employees are paid hourly and their assigned hours vary based on demand. A summary of DHI's financial performance is provided.

APPLY IT 8.1

Interpret Revenue Visualization

Summary of DHI Financial Performance

State	Number of Hotels	Revenue 2024	Revenue 2025	Profit 2024	Profit 2025
CO	5	$ 6,972,316	$ 6,942,074	$ 3,701,428	$ 3,582,689
NM	7	$ 8,491,172	$ 8,414,229	$ 4,025,218	$ 3,862,043
OK	5	$ 6,223,433	$ 6,156,051	$ 3,178,742	$ 2,928,290
TX	31	$ 41,220,622	$ 40,071,922	$ 18,320,989	$ 16,548,176
Grand Total	**48**	**$ 62,907,543**	**$ 61,584,276**	**$ 29,226,377**	**$ 26,921,198**

DHI would like to know how revenue compares by state and if revenues are rising or falling. Luciana has asked you to interpret this analysis.

Denton Hospitality, Inc.—Revenue by State

Revenue (y-axis, $0 to $45):

- CO: $7.0 (2024), $6.9 (2025)
- NM: $8.5 (2024), $8.4 (2025)
- OK: $6.2 (2024), $6.2 (2025)
- TX: $41.2 (2024), $40.1 (2025)

State (x-axis)

Legend: 2024, 2025

1. List the questions you would ask to interpret this analysis, and provide the answers.
2. Is this exploratory data analysis or data analysis interpretation?

SOLUTION

1. Does the analysis answer the question and align with the objective? Yes:

   - The question is how the states' revenues compare and if revenues are increasing.
   - The chart shows revenue by state and a comparison to the prior year.

   Were the correct data and methods used to perform the analysis? Yes:

   - DHI is interested in revenue performance. This chart includes revenue.
   - DHI also wants to know performance by state and if revenue is increasing. This bar chart shows that information by grouping revenue by state and showing current year compared to prior year.

Are the results reasonable? Maybe:

- It is necessary to confirm an understanding of DHI and their revenue to make a final decision about reasonableness.
- The bar chart shows how many hotels are in each state. It seems reasonable that Texas has the highest amount of revenue because about 65% of all the hotels are in Texas.

Is the analysis valid? That is, did it measure what it was intended to measure? Maybe:

- The results seem to be valid because the analysis measured what was intended—revenue by state and comparisons to prior year.

Is the analysis accurate (reliable)? Maybe:

- More research is necessary to compare the results to the financial statements to ensure all the revenue is represented and that the analysis is accurate.

2. Since DHI asked for an interpretation of the analysis, it would seem logical that this is an interpretation. If the task was interpreting this analysis to determine additional analyses that could be performed based on the outcome, it could be considered exploratory.

8.2 What Is the Relationship Between Critical Thinking and Data Analysis Interpretation?

LEARNING OBJECTIVE ❷
Apply critical thinking to data analysis interpretation.

In the chapter opener, Megan discussed the importance of critical thinking in data analysis. Thinking deeply about the analysis helps interpret the results and avoids being ". . . *so caught up in the details that I rationalized the results instead of asking more questions.*" Applying a critical thinking framework to the analysis being interpreted ensures that we are consistently thinking critically about every analysis.

Let's use critical thinking to interpret a data analysis prepared by someone else. The manufacturing firm Super Scooters makes four models of scooters:

- The Captain and Lazer models are electric scooters.
- The Kicks model is not powered.
- The Celeritas is a gas-powered scooter.

Super Scooters has benefited from the increase in scooter-sharing systems in large cities. Like bike-sharing, a scooter-sharing system is a service that provides scooters for short-term rentals. The global market for electric scooters is estimated to reach $34.7 billion by 2028.[1] Companies such as Lime and Bird are purchasing large quantities of electric scooters as the market for scooter-sharing expands. Super Scooters believes the time may be right to move to manufacturing only electric scooters to potentially increase sales to companies like Lime and Bird. Imagine you are a staff accountant who is part of a team evaluating whether to continue producing the Celeritas model gas scooter. Let's apply the elements of critical thinking (**Illustration 8.5**) to this example.

Stakeholders: Understand the Context

Before interpreting the analysis provided by the Celeritas marketing team, consider who the stakeholders are in this decision. Identifying stakeholders (**Illustration 8.6**) provides insight

---

[1]https://www.grandviewresearch.com/industry-analysis/electric-scooters-market

ILLUSTRATION 8.5 The SPARKS Critical Thinking Framework

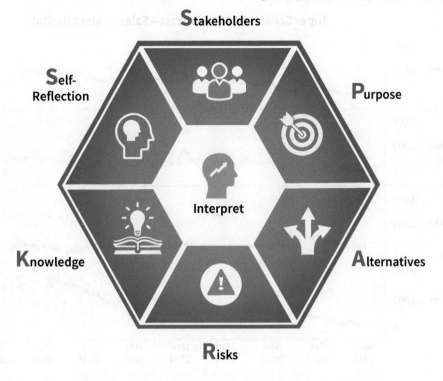

ILLUSTRATION 8.6 Super Scooters' Internal and External Stakeholders

Internal Stakeholders	External Stakeholders
• Super Scooters Managers	• Investors
• Super Scooters Employees	• Creditors

into the situation within which the data analysis was created. This knowledge can help explain the results.

Failing to identify the stakeholders means potentially interpreting the results from the wrong perspective. In this example, if you were not thinking about Super Scooters' creditors, you may not consider the impact of dropping the Celeritas scooter on the company's ability to pay their existing loans.

Purpose: Define the "Why" of the Analysis

In addition to recognizing relevant stakeholders, identify the purpose of the analysis. It is easy to forget this and immediately start interpreting. Be careful not to fall into this trap! We cannot fully interpret an analysis until we know its purpose.

In this example, Super Scooters is considering eliminating the Celeritas scooter. The Celeritas marketing team has prepared an analysis of sales for the last four years and a forecast for 2026. The shaded part of the line represents the 2026 forecast. The purpose of the analysis is to understand the sales trends for the four models of powered scooters that Super Scooters currently manufactures and sells.

Overlooking the purpose could mean interpreting the analysis incorrectly. If you did not know the purpose of the analysis in **Illustration 8.7** was to evaluate the Celeritas model, you might waste time evaluating a different model.

ILLUSTRATION 8.7 Super Scooters Forecast

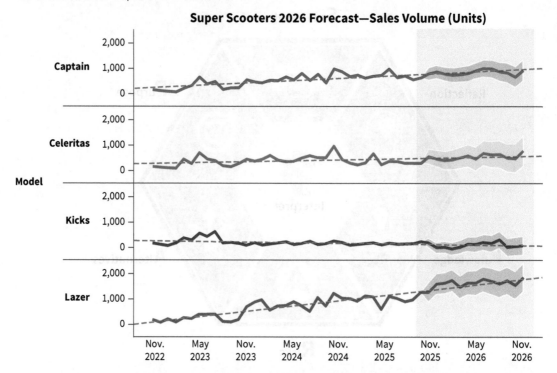

Alternatives: Investigate Other Interpretations

Always consider if there are alternative ways to view the results of an analysis. Additionally, consider if there are alternative methods to conduct the analysis that were not addressed. Finally, decide if more analysis is needed. Thinking about these different alternatives helps determine whether the most appropriate analysis was used, which can increase confidence when interpreting the results.

In the Super Scooters example, alternative interpretations may include:

- The trend analysis assumptions do not include potential impact to sales of the other models should the Celeritas be eliminated.
- The trend analysis assumptions may be too aggressive.
- The trend analysis alone is not enough information on which to base a decision to keep or drop the Celeritas scooter.
- The Kicks model has the poorest performance. Perhaps that model should be evaluated for elimination instead of the Celeritas.

Risks: Consider Data, Analysis, and Bias

Examine all aspects of the analysis to identify potential risks. This begins with the data and extends to potential biases—both our own and those of stakeholders. Asking certain questions can help evaluate these potential risks. **Illustration 8.8** lists the risks and questions that could be asked to evaluate them, and applies a Super Scooters example. Keep in mind that if you are the preparer of the analysis, then you will have already addressed some of these issues.

Knowledge: What We Need to Know

To interpret any analysis, determine the knowledge necessary to understand it. We may not have the correct background or experience, so identifying the required understanding will reveal if we need to do additional research. It helps to ask these questions:

- Is specific accounting knowledge necessary?
- Would industry knowledge be helpful?

Potential Risks	Questions	Super Scooters Examples
Data	• Completeness: Is the analysis missing relevant data? • Accuracy: Are the data used in the analysis correct? • Timeliness: Are the data used in the analysis the most recent available? • Internal controls: Were appropriate internal controls in place to ensure the data used were correct?	• Some of the sales data were not included or may be incorrect. • The data starts in 2022 and continues through 2026, so they appear timely.
Analysis	• Method: Was the correct method used to perform the analysis? • Data: Did the analysis use the right data? • Purpose: Did the analysis answer the question?	• The purpose of the analysis was to understand sales trends for the Super Scooter models. • The analysis uses sales amounts from 2022 to 2025, so it does show how sales are trending. • The risk of using the wrong estimates to forecast the 2026 figures should be considered.
Bias	• Data biases: Were all the necessary and appropriate data included in the analysis? • Preparer biases: Did the preparer have any potential biases that could have influenced the preparation of the analysis? • Evaluator biases: Does the evaluator (you) have any biases that could influence the interpretation of the results?	• The data could be biased if the analysis did not include all the available sales data. • The preparer could be biased to provide a positive analysis if they do not want to eliminate the Celeritas model. • The evaluator could be biased in favor of eliminating the Celeritas or in favor of keeping the Celeritas model.

ILLUSTRATION 8.8 Questions That Help Identify Risks

- Is technology knowledge important to interpret the analysis?
- Is additional research necessary, or should we seek the help of an expert?

What types of knowledge are required for interpreting the Celeritas marketing team's analysis?

- **Accounting knowledge:** Understanding the sales forecast requires knowing the sales revenue and how the forecast was calculated. To determine whether to discontinue the Celeritas model, an understanding of costs, cost volume profit analyses, and how to perform a keep or drop analysis are necessary.

- **Industry knowledge:** Super Scooters operates in the automotive and transportation industry, so you would need information about the manufacturing industry of gas-powered scooters and electric-powered scooters. Learning about the supply chain for the manufacture of gas and electric scooters, as well as the competitors in scooter manufacturing, would also be important.

- **Technology knowledge:** In this example, the visualization shows the sales and sales forecast for the Celeritas model (Illustration 8.7). Understanding how this visualization was created would be helpful since that software knowledge will help you better evaluate the visualization.

- **Other knowledge:** If there is accounting, industry, or technical knowledge you need, do additional research and/or solicit the help of someone with that knowledge.

Self-Reflection: Think About Lessons Learned

Each data analysis project should include reflecting on lessons learned from previous analyses performed or interpreted. We can also learn from the current data analysis being performed or interpreted and apply that to future data analysis projects. Reflecting on previous experiences helps us perform interpretations quickly, thoroughly, and accurately.

In the Super Scooters example, reflect on other analyses you have performed that may be similar. Did you do any keep or drop analyses in your college courses? Have you analyzed sales trend analyses prior to this? If so, how can you apply those experiences to this interpretation?

APPLY IT 8.2

Evaluate a Cost Analysis

Auditing Denton Hospitality, Inc. (DHI) CEO Luciana Garcia is concerned about growing costs in some of the hotels and has asked the internal audit department to evaluate which hotels have increasing costs over the past two years. As an internal auditor for DHI, your manager asked you to prepare and interpret an analysis of costs by hotel for the past two years and identify the locations with the highest increases.

List each critical thinking element and identify how you would apply it to this example.

SOLUTION

Critical Thinking Element		Example
	Stakeholders	Internal: Purchasing department, hotel management External: Creditors, vendors
	Purpose	Evaluate expenses by hotel site and determine which locations have experienced increases.
	Alternatives	There may be alternative analyses that could or should be prepared. There could also be different explanations for why expenses have increased. For example, increases in hotel occupancy could drive increases in hotel expenses.
	Risks	Data may be missing or incorrect. An analysis could be incorrectly interpreted.
	Knowledge	Knowledge about the company and the industry, hotel expenses, and the preparation and interpretation of data analyses is necessary.
	Self-Reflection	There could be expense analyses from prior projects that could be applied to this one. Consider whether you could apply what was learned during this project to future projects.

8.3 How Do We Know the Analysis Makes Sense?

LEARNING OBJECTIVE ❸

Determine if the data analysis results answer the question and align with the objective of the analysis.

Recall that the first step in data interpretation is determining if the analysis makes sense. This may seem like an obvious question, but it is one that is often overlooked. It is even more important when trying to understand an analysis of something unfamiliar. In terms of data analysis, asking if the analysis "makes sense" means confirming the analysis has a clear meaning.

Using critical thinking skills, determine if the analysis answers the intended question and aligns with objective, if the correct data and methods were used, and if the results are both reasonable and sufficient for the project's purpose.

Evaluate the Data and Methods

Questions we can ask to determine if the analysis makes sense include thinking about *how* we got the results:

- Are the data used in the analysis reasonable given the question/objective of the analysis?
- Is the analysis method reasonable given the question/objective of the analysis?

Illustration 8.9 is an analysis designed to show if Super Scooters' labor expenses in the Charlotte, NC, location increased as sales volume increased.

ILLUSTRATION 8.9 Dual Axis Chart of Sales Volume and Labor Expenses

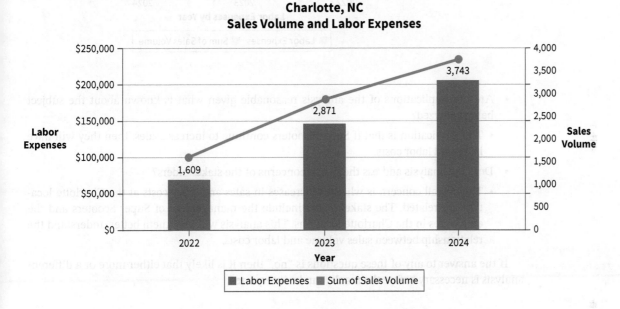

Are the data used in the analysis reasonable given the question/objective of the analysis?

- The data used in this chart are labor expenses and sales volume. It is reasonable to use these two measures since we want to know if they are related. In other words, do both measures move in the same direction?

Is the analysis method reasonable given the question/objective of the analysis?

- A dual axis chart compares two different measures in one graph. Labor expense numbers ($50,000–$250,000) are much larger than sales volume numbers (1,000–4,000). If a clustered column chart (**Illustration 8.10**) was used instead, the sales volume bar would be too small to distinguish a relationship.

Examine the Results

There are also questions that evaluate the reasonableness of the results themselves:

- Are the results of the analysis reasonable given what is known about the subject being analyzed?
  - Super Scooters manufactures the scooters they sell. It makes sense that as the number of scooters sold increases, they would need to produce more scooters. Increased production would lead to increased labor.

ILLUSTRATION 8.10 Clustered Column Chart of Sales Volume and Labor Expenses

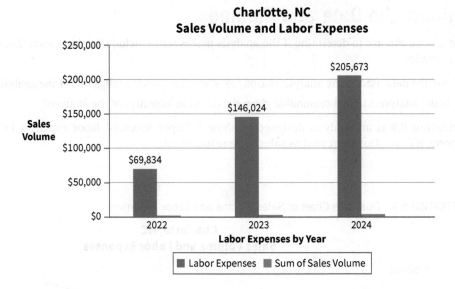

- Are the implications of the analysis reasonable given what is known about the subject being analyzed?
  - The implication is that if Super Scooters continue to increase sales, then they will have increased labor costs.
- Does the analysis address the needs/concerns of the stakeholders?
  - The overall concern is whether increases in sales and labor costs at the Charlotte location are related. The stakeholders include the management of Super Scooters and the employees in the Charlotte locations. This analysis will help them better understand the relationship between sales volume and labor costs.

If the answer to any of these questions is "no," then it is likely that either more or a different analysis is necessary before the results can be interpreted.

Applying Critical Thinking 8.1

Ask If the Analysis Makes Sense

Notice the relationship between these questions and the previous discussion about applying critical thinking. To answer these questions, you need to know:

- Who is impacted by the analysis (**Stakeholders**).
- The reason for performing the analysis (**Purpose**).
- Whether the results are reasonable given what you know (**Knowledge**).
- If you can apply past experience or knowledge to the current context and whether what you learn now can be leveraged in future analyses (**Self-Reflection**).

Determine If More Information or Analyses Are Necessary

Even if the interpretation makes sense, sometimes more information or additional analyses are still necessary to thoroughly answer the question. It is easy to believe we have the information necessary to decide on a course of action. This is a common human bias that Nobel Prize winning psychologist Daniel Kahneman refers to as the "what you see is all there is" bias.

This bias can be particularly strong if the data analysis supports preconceived ideas or conclusions about the question. Accountants must be skeptical evaluators of information, so we must diligently review data analyses to be sure they provide enough information and support to make a well-informed decision.

There are more biases to be aware of when interpreting data analyses:

- **Confirmation bias:** The person performing the analysis wants to prove a predetermined assumption, so they look for data that support their existing belief. The person interpreting the analysis can also have this bias. Being aware of the preparer's potential biases, as well as our own, can help to mitigate confirmation bias.

- **Selection bias:** This bias occurs when the data used in the analysis are selected subjectively. Selection bias is a concern if the analysis being interpreted is based on a sample of data rather than the entire population. An example is when an analysis of sales transactions is based on a sample of transactions rather than on all the transactions. If the sample is not a good representation of the full population, then the results will be biased.

Continuing the Super Scooters example, additional analyses are necessary before making a keep or drop decision. Imagine that you asked for additional information about costs and were given the analysis in **Illustration 8.11**. (Assume you have already determined that the analysis makes sense.)

ILLUSTRATION 8.11 Variable Costs by Super Scooters Model

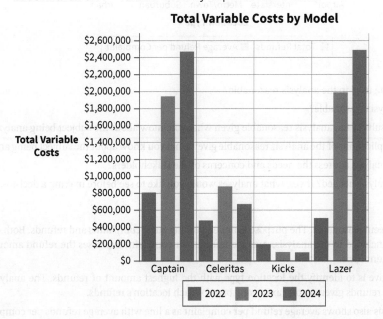

This analysis provides some key cost information, but do you need more? Variable costs will be eliminated if the Celeritas model is dropped, but what about fixed costs? Ask for that information as well. Do not assume that the sales and variable costs analyses are all that is needed to decide whether the Celeritas model should be dropped. There is also the potential for selection bias and confirmation bias. Consider a few questions to look for selection bias:

- Did the preparer of the sales and variable cost analyses use all the information available, or did they select just a sample of that information?
- If it was a sample, is the sample representative of all sales and all variable costs?

To mitigate the potential of confirmation bias, examine your perspective about the analyses. Was the interpretation approached with an open mind, or were you already leaning in favor of or against dropping the Celeritas model?

APPLY IT 8.3

Interpret a Refund
Analysis

Data **Managerial Accounting** Luciana at DHI is concerned about the amount of refunds given to customers. She has asked you to speak to the hotel area managers to gain more insight, and then interpret an analysis prepared by another employee to identify the type of location with the highest amount of refunds. After speaking with the hotel area managers, you learn:

- Front desk employees can give refunds to hotel guests without approval from the general manager.
- Area managers think the number of guest complaints is strongly related to the total amount of refunds. If there are many guest complaints, there will likely be a higher amount of total refunds.

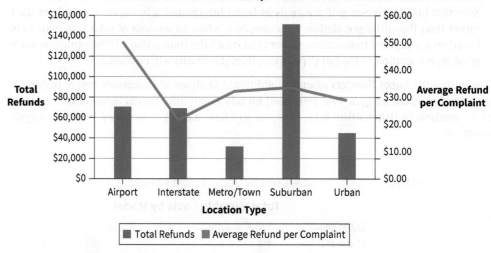

DHI Refunds and Guest Complaints Dual Axis Chart

1. Are the data used in the analysis reasonable?
2. Is the analysis reasonable?
3. Are the results of the analysis reasonable given what you know about the subject being analyzed?
4. Are the implications of the analysis reasonable given what you know about the subject being analyzed?
5. Does the analysis address the needs and concerns of the stakeholders?
6. Is more analysis needed? If yes, what analyses would you like to see before making a decision?

SOLUTION

1. The data seem reasonable. The purpose is understanding guest complaints and refunds. Both of those items are included in the analysis. Average refunds per complaint expresses the refund amount on a per complaint basis.

2. The objective is to identify the location type with the highest amount of refunds. The analysis does show total refunds given on one axis using bars for each location's refunds.

   The analysis also shows average refund per complaint as a line with average refunds per complaint on the right axis. This is a reasonable way to evaluate the relationship between complaints and refunds because using the average refund per complaints helps look at each location based on its performance rather than size.

3. The area managers were convinced that the number of complaints is related to the total amount of refunds. The analysis shows the average amount of refunds is highest for airport locations even though the suburban locations have a higher total.

4. There are much higher total refunds in the suburban locations, so it might seem they would have the highest number of complaints. However, if there are more hotels in that category, that may also be driving the total number of complaints. By using average refund per complaint, we can see that airport locations are giving very high refunds to guests even though the total refund amount is not as high as suburban locations.

5. The analysis addresses the needs of the stakeholders to an extent. The analysis is one piece of this puzzle.

6. Yes, more analysis is necessary. To be sure that we have addressed the stakeholders, further analysis is required to address the concern about hotels offering too many refunds.

8.4 How Are Validity and Reliability Determined in Descriptive and Diagnostic Analyses?

LEARNING OBJECTIVE ❹

Evaluate the validity and reliability of descriptive and diagnostic data analysis results.

Once it is clear that the analysis makes sense, the results can be assessed for validity and reliability. If the results are not valid, then it does not matter how "good" the analysis is. Sometimes it is easy to be fooled by data analyses because we take them at face value. Recall the example at the start of the chapter. Megan's staff tax accountant checked the numbers and assumed the analysis was correct. However, the analysis result was an increase in tax liability when it should have been a decrease. The staff accountant should have been more skeptical of the analysis and considered that a large loss should have caused a decrease in the tax liability.

First, what does valid and reliable mean in the context of data analysis?

- Evaluating the **validity** of a data analysis involves confirming that it measures what it is supposed to measure and represents reality.

- **Reliability** means that the data used are dependable and trustworthy, and the measures used in the analysis are consistent and accurate. In this context, **accurate** means the measures used in the analysis are correct and without mistakes.

During your career, you will interpret the validity and reliability of different types of analyses. **Illustration 8.12** summarizes the types of analyses most common in the four areas of analytics.

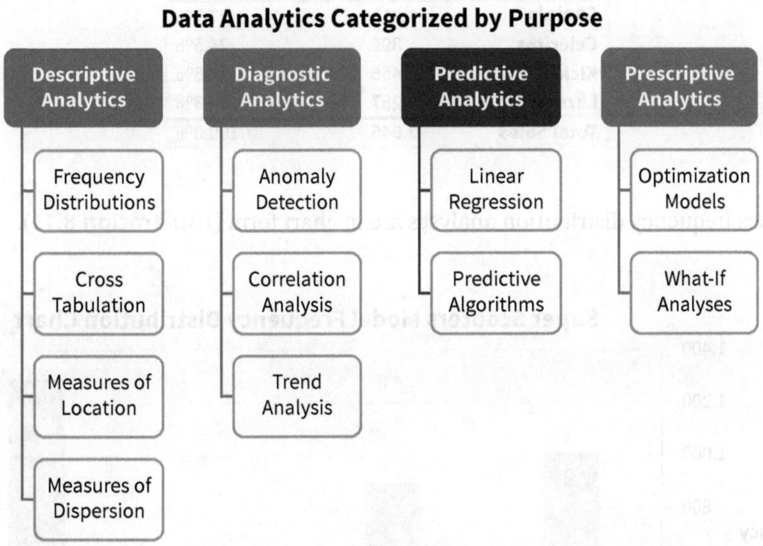

Data Analytics Categorized by Purpose

ILLUSTRATION 8.12 Summary of Analyses by Analytics Area

This section reviews the most common types of analyses used in descriptive and diagnostic analytics, how to identify appropriate measures for each type, and how to determine if the results are valid.

Descriptive Analytics

Descriptive analytics help to better understand the data underlying the analysis being interpreted. To assess validity and reliability of the analyses, ensure the correct method is used and that the data are accurate. **Illustration 8.13** is a summary of valid descriptive analyses based on the objective of the analysis. For an analysis to be valid, the method must match the objective. In a reliable analysis, the measures used are accurate and consistent.

ILLUSTRATION 8.13
Descriptive Objectives,
Questions, and Valid Analyses

Objective	Example Questions	Valid Analyses
Understand categories of data.	What product category is selling the most? Which business unit has the highest revenue?	Frequency distribution Histogram
Summarize by categories and subcategories.	Which products are selling the most in each region? How much were total expenses each year by business unit?	Cross tabulation analysis
Identify an average observation in the data.	What is the average tax liability for each business unit?	Mean (if no outliers) Median
Evaluate the distribution of data.	How different are the expenses in each business unit from the company average?	Standard deviation

Understand Categories of Data

Grouping data into categories is sometimes part of an analysis. An example is when the goal is to understand sales by product. If the analysis is based on groups or categories of data, a valid analysis would be a frequency distribution or a cross tabulation analysis.

A **frequency distribution** reveals how many times something has occurred within a group or interval. The example in **Illustration 8.14** was prepared using the Super Scooters data set. (**Data** How To 8.1 at the end of the chapter shows how to create this visual in Power BI.) The frequency column reports sales orders for each model for the years 2023–2025. The relative frequency column indicates the percentage of total sales orders for each model.

How To

ILLUSTRATION 8.14 Super
Scooters Model Frequency
Distribution

Model	Frequency	Relative Frequency
Captain	1,010	27.7%
Celeritas	892	24.5%
Kicks	456	12.5%
Lazer	1,287	35.3%
Total Sales	3,645	100.0%

Sometimes frequency distribution analyses are in chart form (**Illustration 8.15**).

ILLUSTRATION 8.15 Super
Scooters Model Frequency
Distribution Chart

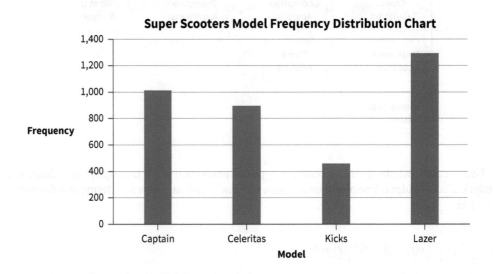

Summarize by Categories of Data

Suppose the objective is knowing the number of orders each year, from 2023 to 2025, by scooter model. A **cross tabulation analysis** would answer that question. A cross tabulation analysis shows the number of observations in a data set for different subcategories (**Illustration 8.16**).

Number of Orders	Year			
Model	2023	2024	2025	Grand Total
Captain	244	397	369	1,010
Celeritas	248	327	317	892
Kicks	261	107	88	456
Lazer	207	517	563	1,287
Grand Total	960	1,348	1,337	3,645

ILLUSTRATION 8.16 Super Scooters Cross Tabulation Analysis of Sales Orders by Model

Note that a cross tabulation analysis does not have to be in table format. **Illustration 8.17** is a column chart visualization of the table in Illustration 8.16.

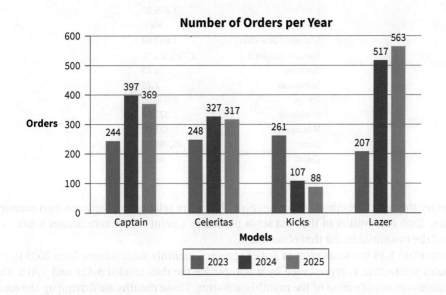

ILLUSTRATION 8.17 Super Scooters Cross Tabulation Analysis Column Chart

What can we interpret from these analyses? First, the Lazer is the best-selling model, accounting for 35.3% of total sales volume (Illustration 8.14). Second, the Lazer is the only model that shows an increase in sales volume each year from 2023 to 2025 (Illustration 8.17). Are these analyses valid and reliable? Since the objective is analyzing sales volume by model, then the frequency distribution and the cross tabulation analyses are valid methods to use. Reliability will be determined by confirming the totals agree to the actual sales volume in the financial records.

Identify an Average Observation in the Data

Sometimes the analysis question is not about groups or categories of data, but instead asks about the averages in the data. In addition to frequency and cross tabulation, measures of location are used in descriptive analytics. When evaluating the validity and reliability of an analysis that includes measures of location, ensure that the correct measure is being used.

Measures of location include the mean, median, and mode measures that reveal the average or typical observation in the data set:

- **Mean:** The sum of all observations in a data set divided by the total number of observations.
- **Median:** The middle value when the data is arranged from smallest to largest.
- **Mode:** The observation that occurs most frequently.

All three measures are valid measures of location, but under different conditions some measures of central tendency will be more appropriate than others.

For example, a mean can be affected by extreme values in the data, whereas the median is not affected by these kinds of values, which are **outliers**. There are two methods to determine if there are outliers in a data set:

- Search for a large difference between the mean and median.
- Plot the data to visually determine if there is an outlier.

How To

Let's start by examining the mean and the median. **Illustration 8.18** shows descriptive statistics for Super Scooters' monthly sales volume amounts. (**Data** How To 8.2 illustrates how to create these statistics in Microsoft Excel.) The mean monthly sales volume is 2,132 and the median monthly sales volume is 1,879. The mean is much larger than the median. But we know that if we are searching for the central location of the data set, the median is right in the middle. This large difference is a good indication that there are extreme values in the data set.

ILLUSTRATION 8.18
Descriptive Statistics for
Super Scooters' Sales Volume

Super Scooters, Inc.	
Monthly Sales Volume	
Mean	2,132.39
Standard Error	275.34
Median	1,879.00
Mode	#N/A
Standard Deviation	1,652.02
Sample Variance	2,729,183.96
Kurtosis	8.82
Skewness	2.73
Range	8,050.00
Minimum	371.00
Maximum	8,421.00
Sum	76,766.00
Count	36.00

Now try the second method. A **scatterplot** shows the relationship between two numerical variables. Each observation in the data set is plotted as a point whose coordinates relate to the values of the two variables for that observation.

Illustration 8.19 is a scatterplot of Super Scooters' monthly sales volume from 2023 to 2025. Each sales transaction is represented by a dot. Notice the dots labeled 8,421 and 7,810. These observations are outside most of the monthly amounts. Those months are driving up the mean.

ILLUSTRATION 8.19
Scatterplot of Super Scooters'
Sales Volume

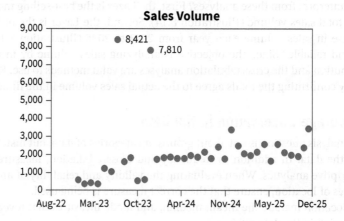

When evaluating measures of location, keep in mind the potential impact of outliers on the results. If you were responsible for creating the sales budget for Super Scooters, then you might choose between using the mean or the median sales volume from prior year to budget for the next year's production budget. (Refer to Illustration 8.18 for the calculation of mean and median for Super Scooters' descriptive statistics.)

Illustration 8.20 summarizes the two options. Using the mean as a measure of the average amount of monthly sales production needs overstates production needs.[2] There is a difference of

---

[2]Keep in mind that this is a very simplified example of preparing a budget. Sales budgets include more than just estimating a single sale transaction amount, particularly if there are multiple products and locations. However, the danger of using the wrong measure is still a valid concern.

3,036 (13%) between the two options. It would be difficult to explain to your boss next year why you were off by 13% on projected production!

Estimated Sales Based on Mean Sales Volume	Estimated Sales Based on Median Sales Volume
2,132 × 12 months = 25,584	1,879 × 12 months = 22,548
Difference Between Estimated Sales Volume = 3,036	

ILLUSTRATION 8.20
Estimated Sales Using Mean vs. Median Sales Volume

In summary, when evaluating the validity and reliability of an analysis that includes measures of location, confirm the correct measure is being used. If the correct measure is used, then the results are valid. In Illustration 8.20, using the mean instead of the median to estimate sales volume would not be valid because of the difference between mean and median monthly sales volume. Using the mean sales volume inflates the estimate due to the outliers of higher sales volume in the data. That is not a reliable budget estimate.

Evaluate the Distribution of Data

The final type of descriptive analyses discussed here are measures of dispersion. Dispersion refers to the amount of variation in the data. Are the data spread out or are they compact? In other words, how far apart are all the observations (data points) from the mean? The two most widely used measures of dispersion are variance and standard deviation.

The **standard deviation** shows how spread out the data are from the mean. It is in the same units as the mean. Standard deviation can help determine the validity and reliability of an analysis. **Illustration 8.21** shows a list of descriptive statistics for Super Scooters' sales volume. Standard deviation is highlighted.

Super Scooters, Inc.	
Monthly Sales Volume	
Mean	2,132.39
Standard Error	275.34
Median	1,879.00
Mode	#N/A
Standard Deviation	1,652.02
Sample Variance	2,729,183.96
Kurtosis	8.82
Skewness	2.73
Range	8,050.00
Minimum	371.00
Maximum	8,421.00
Sum	76,766.00
Count	36.00

ILLUSTRATION 8.21
Descriptive Statistics for Super Scooters' Sales Volume

In this example, the mean amount of monthly sales volume is 2,132.39. The standard deviation is 1,652.02. So, the average distance between an observation (in this case a sale volume amount) and the mean is 1,652.02. Standard deviation can indicate the data points' relationship to the mean:

- A low standard deviation indicates the data points tend to be close to the mean.
- A high standard deviation indicates the data points are spread out over a large range of values.

Does the amount of 1,652.02 seem like a high or a low standard deviation for sales volume? Considering that the standard deviation is about 77% of the mean, it does seem to be a high deviation. Review the scatterplot in Illustration 8.19 to visually determine if there are many observations (data points) far from the mean of 2,132.39. The scatterplot does show data points that are much higher than the mean.

Taken together, descriptive analytics help us better understand the data underlying the analysis being interpreted. Assessing validity and reliability of the analyses involves ensuring the correct method is used and that the data are accurate. Frequency distributions and cross tabulations can help group data into meaningful categories. Measures of location can show what the average observation looks like or if there are outliers, while measures of dispersion reveal the distribution of the data underlying the analysis.

Applying Critical Thinking 8.2

Evaluate Reliability and Validity

It may not seem like you are applying critical thinking skills when evaluating the reliability and validity of descriptive analytics, but you are thinking critically before you even begin:

- You must identify the reason behind the analysis to decide if it is a question that should be answered with descriptive analytics (**Purpose**).
- Then, you identify the information necessary to interpret the analysis. Do you need to know how to interpret frequency distributions? Cross tabulations? Measures of location? Measures of dispersion? Do you have that knowledge (**Knowledge**)?
- You could apply experiences with past interpretations of analyses to the current context (**Self-Reflection**).

Diagnostic Analytics

If the objective of the analysis is to understand *why* something has occurred, then you will be interpreting diagnostic analytics. **Illustration 8.22** provides some common diagnostic objectives and the analyses that could be used.

ILLUSTRATION 8.22 Diagnostic Objectives, Questions, and Valid Analyses

Objective	Example Questions	Valid Analyses
Find anomalies in the data set.	Are there revenue transactions that are different or suspiciously high?	Scatterplot Boxplot
Examine relationships in the data.	Is there a relationship between maintenance expense and equipment hours?	Scatterplot Correlation coefficient
Identify patterns in the data set.	Is there a seasonal sales pattern?	Bar chart Column chart Line graph Trendline

Find Anomalies

Assessing validity and reliability includes identifying any potential anomalies in the data. An **anomaly** is an observation in the data set that deviates from what is normal or expected. Identifying anomalies is a common diagnostic analytics procedure. An anomaly may seem the same as an outlier, as discussed in the section on descriptive analytics. However, there are some key differences:

- **Outlier:** This is a legitimate observation that lies an abnormal distance from other values in the data. For example, in retail stores sales are much higher during the holidays than during the summer. A high sale amount in December may be an outlier, in that it is much higher than the other months, but it is legitimate because sales are expected to be higher in December.
- **Anomaly:** This is an illegitimate observation. Illegitimate observations could be mistakes or unusual occurrences that we do not expect to see again. These observations may be outliers that are determined to be illegitimate, hence an anomaly. An example of this is if supplies expense is significantly higher in one month due to an erroneous journal entry.

Detecting anomalies could be the purpose of the analysis, such as when searching for unusually large transactions in an audit where fraud is suspected. However, detecting an anomaly could also be unintentional.

Recall that Illustration 8.19 identified two potential outliers—the sales volume amounts of 8,421 and 7,810. These amounts are much larger than the other monthly volume amounts that occurred over the 2022–2025 period. Why are those sale volume amounts so high? This is an example of anomaly detection. These two points might be legitimate observations (outliers) or illegitimate (anomalies).

The next step in the interpretation is to determine the reason for the high monthly volume amount and investigate other potential anomalies in the data. First, examine all the amounts that are over 1,500 and determine if they are accurate. If they are accurate, then investigate potential reasons for the high volume.

Examine Data Relationships

Part of understanding data is knowing how the data are related. **Correlation analysis** shows relationships in the data by measuring the linear relationship between two variables. If the goal of the analysis is to determine the strength of a relationship between objects of interest (variables), then a correlation analysis would be appropriate. Assessing the validity and reliability of a correlation analysis requires knowing how to interpret the correlation coefficient.

Linear correlation is measured by the **correlation coefficient**, also known as the Pearson product-moment correlation coefficient. This measure is a numerical value between –1 and +1. The higher the absolute number, the greater the strength of the relationship. A positive correlation coefficient indicates that as one variable increases, so does the other variable. There is a positive relationship between ice cream sales and outdoor temperature, for example. As the temperature rises, ice cream sales tend to rise as well.

A negative correlation is an inverse relationship. As one variable increases, the other decreases and vice versa. Consider sales of soup. There is a negative relationship between soup sales and temperature. As temperatures decrease, the sales of soup increase. **Illustration 8.23** is a guide to interpreting the value of the correlation coefficient.

Correlation *r*	Interpretation
Exactly −1	A perfect negative linear relationship
−0.70	A strong negative linear relationship
−0.50	A moderate negative linear relationship
−0.30	A weak negative linear relationship
0	No linear relationship
+0.30	A weak positive linear relationship
+0.50	A moderate positive linear relationship
+0.70	A strong positive linear relationship
Exactly +1	A perfect positive linear relationship

ILLUSTRATION 8.23
Interpreting Correlation Coefficients

Correlation is a valid measure for examining linear relationships between variables in data, and the interpretation of the correlation should be based on the correlation coefficient. Correlation analysis is reliable if the correlation coefficients are consistent and accurate relative to the data being analyzed. In the ice cream and soup examples, the correlation is valid because we are examining a logical correlation using the correlation coefficient. It is reliable if we believe the correlation coefficients are consistent and accurate.

A correlation analysis can be performed using the Super Scooters data:

- Super Scooters management is reviewing variable marketing costs and would like to know if there is a relationship between the amount spent on variable marketing (discounts given as incentives for dealers to buy Super Scooters products) and sales volume.

- Management is concerned that they spent $1.1 million on variable marketing in 2024, and they are not sure if that spending resulted in increases in sales.

Illustration 8.24 is a summary of the correlation coefficients for gross sales, sales volume, and variable marketing expenses.

ILLUSTRATION 8.24
Correlation Coefficients Summary for Super Scooters

	Correlation Coefficient
Gross Sales	0.9650
Sales Volume	0.7749

The correlation coefficient for variable marketing and gross sales is 0.9650. The interpretation of that number is that there is a strong positive correlation between gross sales and variable marketing costs. As variable marketing costs increase, so do gross sales. There is also a strong correlation between sales volume and variable marketing with a correlation coefficient of 0.77410. While we cannot prove causation, we can say that there appears to be a strong positive correlation between the amount spent on variable marketing and both sales volume and gross sales.

Identify Patterns

A **trend analysis** is a statistical tool that uses historical data to identify patterns. It can explain why something is happening. A **trendline** indicates the general course or tendency of the data and is created using the historical data points to estimate a line.[3] Examining trends helps detect patterns and relationships, which can identify opportunities or potential threats to a business.

The best way to identify trends is to graph the data over time. **Illustration 8.25** is a trend analysis of material costs and sales volume for Super Scooters for the years 2023–2025. The trend analysis was prepared with data visualization software. A trend analysis can also be prepared in Microsoft Excel using the trendline tool that is available when the data is charted.

ILLUSTRATION 8.25   Super Scooters' Material Costs and Sales Volume Trend Analysis

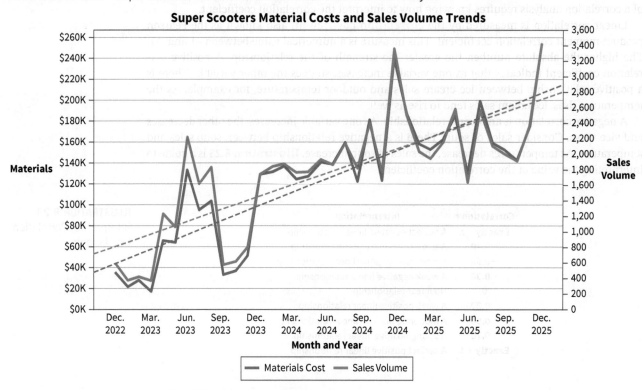

Super Scooters is examining why material costs have been increasing. The analysis in Illustration 8.25 shows that sales volume and material costs move in the same pattern over the years and that both are increasing:

- It is logical that sales volume increases will result in rising material costs. There are similar peaks and valleys in the lines. This is an indication that there could be a seasonal pattern to sales.

- The trendlines in the analysis (the dashed straight lines) reveal that while both trend lines are increasing, material costs are increasing at a higher rate.

After reviewing this analysis, we can conclude that material costs are increasing due to increases in sales volume.

---

[3]Trend analysis can also be used as a predictive analytic method.

This analysis of sales volume and material costs is valid because it uses the appropriate method for understanding the relationship between trends of sales and expenses. The measures used in the analysis are accurate and consistent and the data is dependable and trustworthy, so the analysis is also reliable. However, understanding why material costs are rising at a faster rate than sales will require more investigation.

Applying Critical Thinking 8.3

Interpret Diagnostic Analytics

When explaining why something happened, use diagnostic analytics:

- The results of diagnostic analyses can be used to develop other explanations. For example, sales trends seem to alternate with increases and then decreases the following quarter. Perhaps sales promotions are driving this pattern (**Alternatives**).

- Look for potential threats to the analyses, such as anomalies. Are there any observations in the trend analysis that are unusual or unexpected (**Risks**)?

- Consider what is required to understand analyses, such as correlation analysis and trend analysis (**Knowledge**).

Data **Auditing** Roberto Jimenez is the operations manager for DHI. He has asked the internal audit department to help him perform an analysis of housekeeping hours. Roberto would like to know how efficiently different locations are performing. You have been given a scatterplot that displays the housekeeping hours worked and the number of rooms rented by hotel location. The line through the graph is a trendline indicating the linear relationship between hours worked and rooms rented. Note that the numbers listed below the dots are the hotel location numbers. All data in the scatterplot are legitimate observations.

1. Review the scatterplot, identify potential outliers, and explain why you identified them as outliers.

2. Recommend how to address the outliers.

APPLY IT 8.4

Interpret a Scatterplot for Outliers

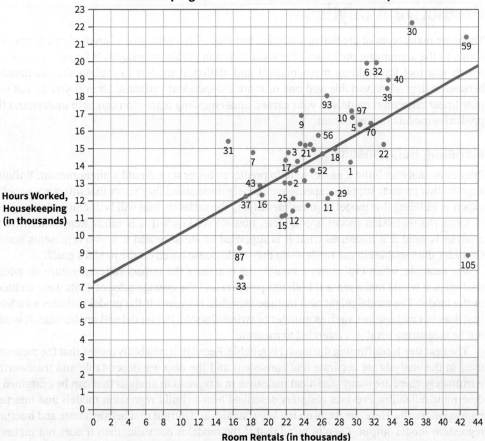

Housekeeping Hours Worked and Rooms Rented per Location

Hours Worked, Housekeeping (in thousands)

Room Rentals (in thousands)

SOLUTION

1. There is a positive relationship between housekeeping hours and room rentals. As the number of rooms rented increases, so does the number of housekeeping hours. This makes sense because rooms that have been rented must be cleaned.

   There are several hotel location observations that are further from the trendline than other observations:

   - Location 30 has the highest hours of housekeeping, but not the highest number of room rentals.
   - Location 105 has low housekeeping hours but a high number of room rentals.

2. Recommendations:

   - Further investigation into Location 30 to identify the cause of inefficient housekeeping hours.
   - Further investigation into Location 105 to identify efficiencies that could be applied to less efficient locations.

8.5 How Are Validity and Reliability Assessed in Predictive and Prescriptive Analyses?

LEARNING OBJECTIVE ❺
Evaluate the validity and reliability of predictive and prescriptive data analysis results.

As you have learned, the other two types of analytics are predictive and prescriptive analytics. The next section covers the types of analyses in these areas that you are likely to encounter in your career and how to determine if the analyses are reliable and valid.

Predictive Analytics

There are many types of predictive analytics, but they all have the goal of predicting a future outcome. In the accounting profession, the most common predictive analysis is **linear regression**, which is a tool for building mathematical and statistical models to explain the relationship between a dependent variable and one or more independent variables. Even if you do not prepare linear regression models in your career, understanding regression can help understand the predictive models you encounter.

Modeling Relationships

Predictive analytics build a model to help predict or better understand a phenomenon. Building a model that predicts supplies expense would help understand the factors that influence supplies expense. Building this model requires identifying the variables that will be included in it.

Once the regression model is complete, how do we know if it is valid? Remember that an analysis is valid if it measures what it is supposed to measure and if it also represents reality. Consider the variables in the model—do they make sense based on the model's goal?

For example, when evaluating a model that examines the impact of temperature on winter coat sales, it would make sense if both temperature and the average price of coats were included in the model. The model might also include snowfall. However, if the model includes a variable that does not make sense, such as number of swimsuits sold, the model will not be valid. It would not be measuring what it is intended to measure.

The next step is confirming the model is reliable. Recall that reliability means that the measures used in the analysis are accurate and consistent and the data are dependable and trustworthy. Fortunately, there are many statistical measures in a regression analysis that can be examined to determine reliability. Previous chapters described how to build regression models and interpret regression results. Here, we focus on the key statistics and output that help evaluate and interpret regression model output. Keep in mind that if the model is not valid, then it does not matter if it is reliable. An accurate and consistent measure of the model does not mean the model represents reality. So, this first step of determining if the model variables are logical is important.

Reliability of the Regression Model

Assess the reliability of the regression analysis by reviewing the model's statistics. **Illustration 8.26** depicts the output of a multiple regression model used to predict purchasing department expenses for Super Scooters. Note that purchasing department expenses are those expenses incurred by the purchasing department to process purchase orders (payroll, administrative, and overhead). These are not the same as the cost of the purchase. The model is based on historical data, collected from each production location, for variables believed to influence total purchasing department expenses.

ILLUSTRATION 8.26   Super Scooters Purchasing Department Expense Regression Model

Super Scooters Purchasing Department Expense Regression

SUMMARY OUTPUT					
Regression Statistics					
Multiple R	0.892897453				
R Square	0.797265861				
Adjusted R Square	0.777957848				
Standard Error	1,337.156824				
Observations	24				
ANOVA					
	df	*SS*	*MS*	*F*	*Significance F*
Regression	2	147,659,116.6	73,829,558.29	41.29196782	5.2812E-08
Residual	21	37,547,755.8	1,787,988.371		
Total	23	185,206,872.4			
	Coefficients	*Standard Error*	*t Stat*	*P-value*	
Intercept	−994.5719771	877.1183137	−1.133908575	0.269611889	
# of Purchase Orders	180.0127037	31.32217805	5.747132382	1.05165E-05	
Sales Volume	1.191401172	0.351035522	3.393961854	0.002736568	

In this model, total purchasing department expense is the dependent variable, and sales volume and the number of purchase orders processed are the independent variables.

The regression in Illustration 8.26 was performed using Microsoft Excel. The Summary Output is split into three sections. First are the **regression statistics**, which are the statistical measures used to evaluate the model. **Illustration 8.27** shows the regression statistics from Illustration 8.26.

Regression Statistics	
Multiple R	0.892897453
R Square	0.797265861
Adjusted R Square	0.777957848
Standard Error	1,337.156824
Observations	24

ILLUSTRATION 8.27
Regression Statistics for Purchasing Department Expenses

All the regression statistics provide insight into a regression model. Each of these statistics was covered in Chapter 2. Here are some of the most important statistics to evaluate for model reliability:

- **Adjusted R square (R^2):** Explains how well the regression line fits the data. The adjusted R^2 is a statistic that modifies the value of R^2 by incorporating the sample size and the number of independent variables. In general, use adjusted R^2 to evaluate a multiple regression model. The closer the R^2 is to 1, the better the fit of the regression line to the data.

- **Standard error:** In Excel regression output, standard error represents the variability of the observed dependent variable values from the values that are predicted by the model.

In other words, it compares the actual dependent variable to the predicted value that the model provides. If the data are clustered close to the regression line, then the standard error will be small. If the data are more scattered, then the standard error will be larger. A small standard error is optimal.

Illustration 8.27 shows the regression statistics for Illustration 8.26:

- The adjusted R square in Illustration 8.27 is 0.778. We would interpret that 77.8% of total expenses can be explained by how many purchase orders are processed and by sales volume.

- The standard error in this model is $1,337.16. To determine if this is a large or a small standard error, compare it to the standard deviation of the dependent variable. In this example, compare the standard error to the standard deviation of total expenses. **Illustration 8.28** provides the mean and standard deviation for total expenses.

ILLUSTRATION 8.28 Super Scooters Purchasing Department Expenses

Super Scooters Purchasing Department Costs 2022–2024	
Mean	$ 3,725.30
Standard Deviation	$ 2,837.69

- The standard deviation of $2,837.69 is higher than the standard error of $1,337.16 in the regression model. The standard error in this model would be considered somewhat small.

The next section of regression summary output is the analysis of variance (ANOVA) output. **Illustration 8.29** is the ANOVA section from the regression model. The ANOVA is a test for the significance of the entire model:

- In a multiple linear regression such as this, significance is a test of whether the regression model is better than a model with no independent variables. In other words, is the model better than no model at all?

- Generally, a model is considered significant if the F statistic (Significance F in Illustration 8.29) is less than 0.05.

ILLUSTRATION 8.29 ANOVA Regression Statistics for Purchasing Department Expenses

Purchasing Dept. Expenses ANOVA Results

ANOVA	df	SS	MS	F	Significance F
Regression	2	147,659,116.6	73,829,558.29	41.29197	5.2812E-08
Residual	21	37,547,755.8	1,787,988.371		
Total	23	185,206,872.4			

So, is the model significant? The ANOVA in Illustration 8.29 has a Significance F of 5.2812E-08. The notation "E-08" after 5.2812 represents scientific notation, also known as exponential notation. 5.28.12E-08 is the same as 0.000000052812. This is a number well below 0.05, so the model is significant. In other words, the independent variables can explain some variation of total expenses, so it is better than no model at all.

The last section of the regression summary output provides information to create the equation that predicts the dependent variable. If the adjusted R square and standard error are acceptable and the model is significant, then we can interpret the equation of the model.

The intercept and coefficients of the model represent the equation of the line that best fits the data. The key statistic to analyze in this section is the p-value for each of the independent variables. Like the F statistic, the p-value provides a test of significance. It is a test as to whether the independent variable improves the ability of the model to predict the dependent variable. A p-value of 0.05 or less is considered significant.

Let's use the output in **Illustration 8.30** to identify the prediction model for Super Scooters' purchasing department total costs, and then interpret the coefficients. Notice that the p-values for all the independent variables meet the test of being less than 0.05 and are therefore significant.

Purchasing Dept. Regression Model

	Coefficients	Standard Error	t Stat	P-value
Intercept	−994.572	877.1183137	−1.133908575	0.269612
# of Purchase Orders	180.0127	31.32217805	5.747132382	1.05E-05
Sales Volume	1.1914012	0.351035522	3.393961854	0.002737

ILLUSTRATION 8.30
Regression Model Example

The prediction model will be equal to the intercept, plus the coefficients of the independent variables, multiplied by the predicted values for those variables. Based on the regression model in Illustration 8.30, the equation to predict total purchasing department costs is:

($994.57) + $180.01 (number of purchase orders) + $1.19 (sales volume)

Illustration 8.31 is the calculation of predicted total expenses if 12 purchase orders are processed and 2,200 scooters are sold.

Purchasing Dept. Predicted Expenses

	Model Coefficient	Variable Values	Prediction
Intercept	$ (994.57)	1	$ (994.57)
# of Purchase Orders	$ 180.01	12	$ 2,160.15
Sales Volume	$ 1.19	2,200	$ 2,621.08
			$ 3,786.66

ILLUSTRATION 8.31
Prediction Model Example

Add the product of each independent variable coefficient and each variable's predicted value to the intercept for a total prediction of $3,786.66 purchasing department costs for the year.
The model could be interpreted like this:

- Intercept: The intercept does not have a practical interpretation. It is a result of the model that represents the mean for the response when all the independent variables are zero. It is where the equation function crosses the y-axis.

- # of Purchase Orders: Each purchase order adds $180.01 to total costs.

- Sales Volume: For each additional scooter sold, purchasing department costs increase by $1.19.

Using a model like the one in Illustration 8.31 helps businesses predict future outcomes. The combination of evaluating the variables included in the model to see if they make sense and then assessing the regression model statistics will help determine if the model is both valid and reliable.

Applying Critical Thinking 8.4

Interpret Predictive Analytics

If the analysis being interpreted predicts a future outcome, then you will be interpreting predictive analytics:

- In the Super Scooters' purchasing department costs example, the purpose of the model is to better understand and predict the department's costs **(Purpose)**.
- Making this prediction requires understanding how to interpret a regression analysis **(Knowledge)**.

Prescriptive Analytics

Prescriptive analytics prescribe what should happen to achieve desired results. The most common prescriptive analytics in accounting are what-if analyses and optimization models. The same rules that apply to the other analytics methods also apply here. The analysis must be valid and reliable. Since a prescriptive model prescribes action, it is crucial to verify that the inputs and outputs of the model are valid and reliable to avoid making poor business decisions.

A spreadsheet model that evaluates how changes to values and assumptions affect an outcome is called a **what-if analysis**. A what-if analysis is an easy way to change values in a spreadsheet and recalculate the outputs.

Excel tools that are commonly used for what-if analysis include Scenario Manager and Goal Seek. (Optimization models are discussed in Chapter 3.) Regardless of which tool is used, assessing the validity and reliability of the model output is the same:

- Understand what the model is addressing.
- Determine if the model measures what it is supposed to measure and if it does, in fact, represent the objective (validity).
- Review the model measures to confirm they are accurate and consistent (reliability).

What-If Analysis: Scenario Manager

Let's look at a scenario analysis and assess validity and reliability. An international dance company, DanceTillYouDrop, is performing in Atlanta, Georgia. They have three performances scheduled and are determining if they should add a fourth. **Illustration 8.32** provides a summary model.

ILLUSTRATION 8.32 Ballet Performance Financial Model

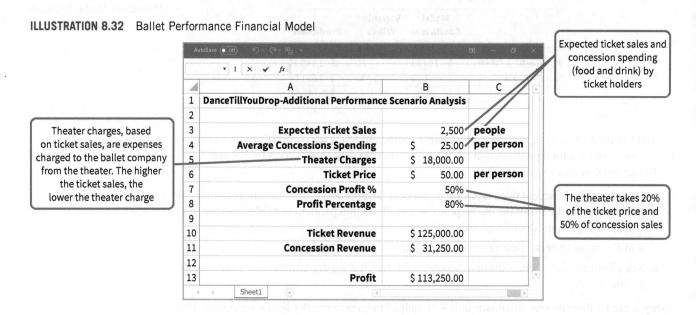

DanceTillYouDrop believes there are three possible scenarios, which are shown in **Illustration 8.33**.

ILLUSTRATION 8.33
DanceTillYouDrop
Performance Scenarios

DanceTillYouDrop Scenario Analysis Model

	Likely	Optimistic	Pessimistic
Expected Ticket Sales	2,500	4,500	1,500
Concessions Spending	$ 25.00	$ 40.00	$ 10.00
Theater Charges	$ 18,000.00	$ 10,000.00	$ 25,000.00

A scenario analysis was performed using Scenario Manager in Microsoft Excel. The scenario summary shows the results when cells B3, B4, and B5 (Illustration 8.32) are changed to the values shown in Illustration 8.33.

The result of the analysis is shown in **Illustration 8.34.**

ILLUSTRATION 8.34
DanceTillYouDrop Scenario
Analysis

DanceTillYouDrop Scenario Analysis Results

Scenario Summary	Current Values	Optimistic	Pessimistic	Likely
Changing Cells				
$B$3	2,500	4,500	1,500	2,500
$B$4	$ 25.00	$ 40.00	$ 10.00	$ 25.00
$B$5	$ 18,000.00	$ 10,000.00	$ 25,000.00	$ 18,000.00
Result Cells				
$B$13	$ 113,250.00	$ 260,000.00	$ 42,500.00	$ 113,250.00

The interpretation of this analysis is that even in the pessimistic scenario DanceTillYouDrop will make a profit on an additional performance.

How do we know this analysis is valid and reliable? DanceTillYouDrop would like to evaluate different ticket and concession sales scenarios to determine if they should add an additional performance. A scenario analysis is a valid method to use for this type of analysis, and the model represents three realistic possibilities. As to reliability of the model, that can be confirmed by verifying the profit calculation is correct and the assumptions are realistic (ticket prices, concession purchases, and theater costs). If the model inputs are accurate and consistent, then the model is reliable.

What-If Analysis: Goal Seek

Another tool for performing what-if analysis is Goal Seek:

- Goal Seek is used if the desired result is already known but the input value to achieve that result is not.
- Goal Seek is limited because it can only use one input variable. If the analysis being performed requires more than one variable to change, then an optimization model using Excel Solver would be needed.

In the previous example, DanceTillYouDrop wanted an analysis comparing different ticket and concession sales scenarios to determine if they should add a performance. What if an additional performance is not possible due to theater availability, and DanceTillYouDrop instead must consider how to set ticket prices to meet a specific target profit?

- DanceTillYouDrop has determined they need a profit of $150,000 from their performance.
- Currently the ticket prices are $50, and they anticipate 2,500 ticket sales based on last year's performances.

Illustration 8.35 shows the financial information for DanceTillYouDrop and the Goal Seek box that appears after clicking the **Data** tab in Excel and selecting **What-If Analysis** and **Goal Seek**.

ILLUSTRATION 8.35 Ticket Price and Target Profit—Goal Seek

	A	B	C	Goal Seek	
1	**DanceTillYouDrop—Profit Target Goal Seek**				
2					
3	**Expected Ticket Sales**	2,500	People	Set cell:	$B$13
4	**Average Concessions Spending**	$ 25.00	Per person		
5	**Theater Charges**	$ 18,000.00		To value:	150,000
6	**Ticket Price**	$ 50.00	Per person	By changing cell:	$B$6
7	**Concession Profit %**	50%			
8	**Profit percentage**	80%		OK	Cancel
9					
10	**Ticket Revenue**	$ 125,000.00			
11	**Concession Revenue**	$ 31,250.00			
12					
13	**Profit**	$ 113,250.00			

Sheet1

- The **Set cell** represents the profit calculation in cell B13 in the Excel spreadsheet.
- Note the current profit amount of $113,250. The desired profit is $150,000, so that value was entered in the **To value** box.
- The variable being manipulated is ticket price, so the cell reference for the ticket price (B6) was entered in the **By changing** cell box.

After the user clicks **OK**, Excel will calculate the ticket price necessary to meet the profit goal of $150,000. **Illustration 8.36** is the solution generated by Excel. To meet a profit target of $150,000, DanceTillYouDrop must charge $68.38 per ticket.

ILLUSTRATION 8.36 Ticket Price and Target Profit—Goal Seek Solution

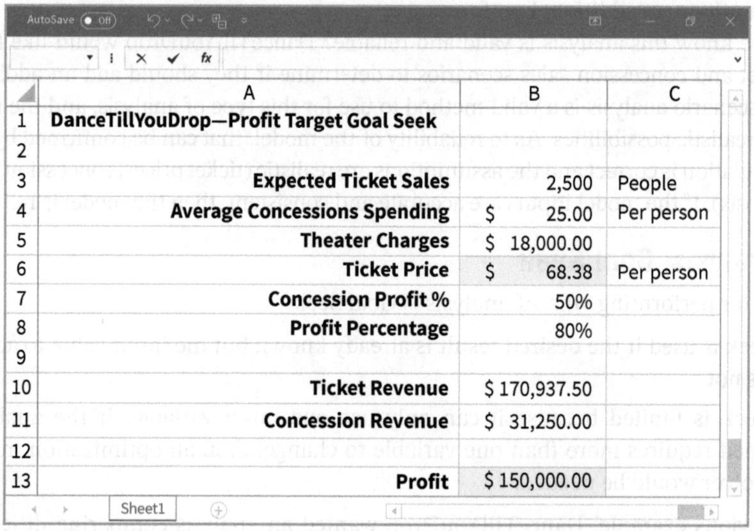

	A	B	C
1	**DanceTillYouDrop—Profit Target Goal Seek**		
2			
3	**Expected Ticket Sales**	2,500	People
4	**Average Concessions Spending**	$ 25.00	Per person
5	**Theater Charges**	$ 18,000.00	
6	**Ticket Price**	$ 68.38	Per person
7	**Concession Profit %**	50%	
8	**Profit Percentage**	80%	
9			
10	**Ticket Revenue**	$ 170,937.50	
11	**Concession Revenue**	$ 31,250.00	
12			
13	**Profit**	$ 150,000.00	

To assess the reliability and validity of a goal seek model, determine if the model measures what it is supposed to measure (reliability) and if it represents the reality of the question/objective (validity):

- In this model, confirm the profit calculation is accurate.
- Additionally, determine if the model answers the question of how much DanceTillYouDrop should charge per ticket to achieve a profit of $150,000, and if the model's suggested ticket price is realistic. If $68.38 is unrealistic for a ticket to a performance, then DanceTillYouDrop must consider other ways to reach profit goals.

Applying Critical Thinking 8.5

Interpret Prescriptive Analytics

Use the elements of critical thinking when interpreting a prescriptive model:

- Knowing who will use predictions helps determine if the model addresses their concerns and confirm that it represents reality (**Stakeholders**).
- An understanding of why the analysis is being performed is required to evaluate if the variables make sense (**Purpose**).
- Knowing how to interpret regression analyses and evaluate optimization models is necessary to interpret them (**Knowledge**).

Data **Managerial Accounting** DHI would like to understand what is driving total expenses for the hotel chain. Luciana feels strongly that the following variables have the most influence on expenses:

- Age of the hotel
- The number of maintenance employees
- Total housekeeping hours
- Total rooms rented

She has asked you to prepare a regression model using those variables to predict expenses. The following illustration is the result of that model:

Housekeeping Hours and Rooms Rented by Location Regression Model

Regression Statistics	
Multiple R	0.7215151
R Square	0.520584
Adjusted R Square	0.4714132
Standard Error	93,901.466
Observations	44

ANOVA					
	df	SS	MS	F	Significance F
Regression	4	3.73412E+11	9.3353E+10	10.58724498	6.62556E-06
Residual	39	3.43882E+11	8,817,485,253		
Total	43	7.17293E+11			

	Coefficients	Standard Error	t Stat	P-value
Intercept	413,314.47	107,148.5543	3.85739665	0.000418405
Room Rentals	11.015461	2.918679199	3.77412543	0.000534577
Hours Worked, Housekeeping	6.0934507	5.531393108	1.1016123	0.277382666
Age	−3,565.695	1,674.938087	−2.12885155	0.039637083
Employees, Maintenance	16,762.392	6,906.902129	2.42690446	0.019949355

1. What does the adjusted R square reveal about the model?
2. Is the model better than not having a model?
3. Are there any variables you would recommend Luciana remove from the model? Why?

SOLUTION

1. The adjusted R square is 0.471, meaning that room rentals, housekeeping hours worked, the age of the hotel, and the number of maintenance employees can explain 47.1% of total expenses.
2. The model is significant—Significance F is less than 0.05—so, it is better than no model at all.
3. The p-value for Hours Worked, Housekeeping is greater than 0.05, so it should be removed from the model.

Chapter Review and Practice

Learning Objectives Review

❶ Compare data analysis interpretation and data exploration.

While data exploration and interpretation seem similar, there are important differences:

- Data exploration is the process of analyzing data to determine whether we need to perform additional analyses. The objective in data exploration is getting to a point where we are sufficiently confident we understand what is happening in the data.

- Data analysis interpretation is the process of evaluating an analysis to understand it and explain its meaning. The insights gained from interpretation lead to good business decisions.

❷ Apply critical thinking to data analysis interpretation.

- Understanding the stakeholders enables understanding the context of the analysis and the implications of the results.
- Identifying the purpose of the analysis maintains focus on its goal and avoids misdirection in the interpretation.

- When interpreting an analysis, consider if there are alternative explanations or alternative analyses that should be conducted.
- Identify potential risks such as data risks, analysis risks, and risks of bias.
- All analysis interpretation requires specific knowledge. Identifying the necessary accounting, industry, and technology knowledge gives us the tools to interpret the analysis.
- Similar analysis interpretation performed in the past could be applied in the current context.

❸ Determine if the data analysis results answer the question and align with the objective of the analysis.

The answers to some specific questions can be helpful when interpreting a data analysis:

- Is the method and the result reasonable given current knowledge about the subject being analyzed? Does the analysis and its interpretation make sense? Consider whether the analysis has clear meaning. Does it address the objective or question posed? Consider also whether the interpretation is reasonable.
- Sometimes more information or analysis is needed before a final interpretation can be completed. Avoid risks like the "what you see is all there is" bias or confirmation bias.

❹ Evaluate the validity and reliability of descriptive and diagnostic data analysis results.

Descriptive analytics determine what has happened in the past, while diagnostic analytics investigate why it happened.

- Common descriptive analytics techniques include frequency distributions, cross tabulation, measures of location, and measures of dispersion.
- Common diagnostic analytics techniques include anomaly detection, correlation analysis, and trend analysis.
- A data analysis is valid if it measures what it is supposed to measure and represents reality.
- A data analysis is reliable if the measures used in the analysis are accurate and consistent and the data used are dependable and trust worthy.

❺ Evaluate the validity and reliability of predictive and prescriptive data analysis results.

Predictive analytics are used when the objective of the analysis is to predict a future outcome. Prescriptive analytics aim to prescribe actions that would result in best outcomes in the future.

- Linear regression is the foundation for most predictive modeling techniques. The validity of a regression model is assessed by how well the model represents the phenomenon of interest. Reliability of the model is assessed by evaluating the regression statistics, model statistics, and the p-value of the coefficients.
- Optimization models and what-if analysis are commonly used for prescriptive analytics. In the accounting profession, what-if analysis can help evaluate several choices (Scenario Analysis) or determine a specific input (Goal Seek).
- Regardless of the tool used to create the what-if analysis, assess validity by determining if the model is measuring what it is supposed to measure (validity) and that the measures are accurate and consistent (reliability).

Key Terms Review

How To Walk-Throughs

How To

HOW TO 8.1   Create a Frequency Distribution with Power BI

Illustration 8.14 is a frequency distribution for Super Scooters' different models. It was created in Excel, but other tools, such as Power BI, can also create frequency distributions.

What You Need: **Data** The How To 8.1 data file.

STEP 1: Extract the data. Open Power BI and select the **Home** tab on the top horizontal menu (**Illustration 8.37**).

- Select the Excel icon below.
- When the file dialog box opens, navigate to the Super Scooters Excel file and select **Open** in the bottom-right corner.

ILLUSTRATION 8.37   Extract and Load Super Scooters Data

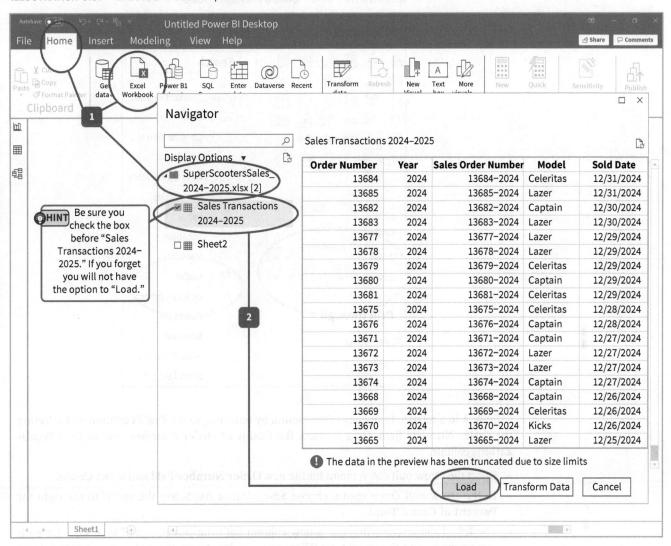

STEP 2: Load the data (Illustration 8.37). From Power BI's **Navigator** window, which automatically opens once the data source is selected, select the data for this exercise: Sales Transactions 2023–2025. Next, click **Load** on the bottom right to upload this data.

STEP 3: Transform the data to create a frequency table (**Illustration 8.38**). The screen will return to the main Power BI screen. The **Fields** column will be on the far right of the screen.

- Click the drop-down arrow next to Sales Transactions 2023–2025 to view all column names from the spreadsheet.

- Drag the data fields **Model** and **Σ Order Number** to the spaces provided directly under **Values**.

- Each field has a down arrow indicating a menu of options. Select this arrow for the **Σ Order Number** field and the pull-down menu appears.

- Select **Count**. The field name will change to **Count of Order Number**.

- On the left is a table with the results containing the four Super Scooter models, the count of order number, and a grand total. You may enlarge that new table to see all the columns.

ILLUSTRATION 8.38 Build a Frequency Table

Visualizations 〉 | **Fields** 〉

Search

∨ 🔲 Sales Transactions 20...
- ☐ Color
- ☐ ∑ Contribution M...
- ☐ Country
- ☐ ∑ Days in Inventory
- ☐ ∑ Gross Sales
- ☐ ∑ Labor
- ☐ Location
- ☐ ∑ Materials
- ☑ Model
- ☑ ∑ Order Number
- ☐ ∑ Overhead
- ☐ ∑ Revenue
- ☐ Sales Order Nu...
- ☐ ∑ Sales Tax

Values

Model ∨ ✕

Order Number ∨ ✕

Drill through

Cross-report

Off ○—

STEP 4: Add a relative frequency table column by returning to the **Fields** column and selecting the **Order Number** field. Drag it below the **Count of Order Number** field in the **Visualizations** column.

- Select the arrow pull down menu for the new **Order Number** field and select **Count**.
- In the arrow pull down menu, choose **Show Value As**. Select the arrow to the right for **Percent of Grand Total**.
- The left of the screen will show a new column with the percentage of total sales for each scooter model and the grand total (**Illustration 8.39**). Again, it may be necessary to enlarge the table to see the new column.

ILLUSTRATION 8.39 Final Super Scooters Frequency Table

Model	Frequency	Relative Frequency
Captain	1,010	27.71%
Celeritas	892	24.47%
Kicks	456	12.51%
Lazer	1,287	35.31%
Total Sales	3,645	100.00%

- Finally, it is possible to change the names of the columns to "Frequency" and "Relative Frequency" by clicking the same down arrow used to select **Count** and instead choosing **Rename for this Visual**.

It is also possible to do a frequency distribution using PivotTables or by using data visualization software.

How To

HOW TO 8.2 Calculate Descriptive Statistics in Microsoft Excel

To create the Illustration of Super Scooters' sales volume in Illustration 8.18, use the Descriptive Statistics option in the Data Analysis Tool in Microsoft Excel.

What You Need: `Data` The How To 8.2 data file.

STEP 1: Open the worksheet by clicking **Data** in the toolbar (**Illustration 8.40**).

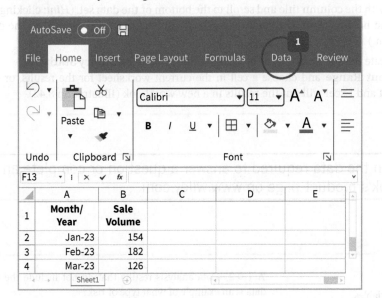

ILLUSTRATION 8.40   Super Scooters Data

STEP 2: Select **Descriptive Statistics** (**Illustration 8.41**).

ILLUSTRATION 8.41   Analysis Tools Dialog Box

STEP 3: In the **Descriptive Statistics** box, designate the input range (**Illustration 8.42**).

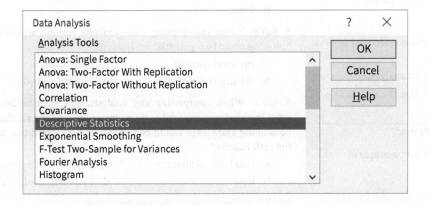

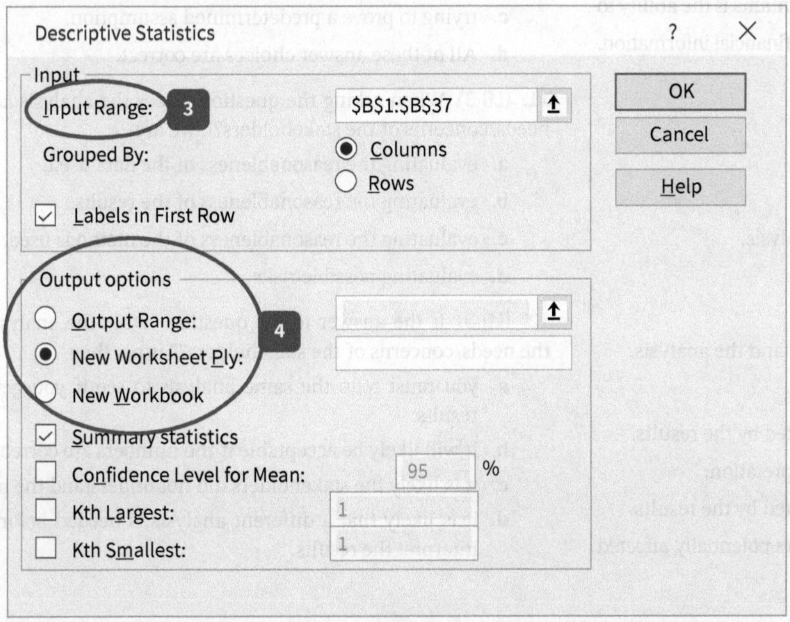

ILLUSTRATION 8.42
Descriptive Statistics Box

- The input range is the data used to calculate descriptive statistics. In this example, it is column B.
- Start with the column title and scroll to the bottom of the data set. (*Hint*: clicking in the title cell and holding Shift, Ctrl, and the keyboard down arrow will capture all the data in that column.)

STEP 4: Create the statistics output by clicking **Labels** and **Summary Statistics**.

Select **Output Range** and choose a cell in the current worksheet for the results, or click **New Worksheet** and Excel will put the results in a new workbook (Illustration 8.42).

Data   The Data tag appears when the data required to answer a question or complete an exercise are available in the book's product page on www.wiley.com.

Multiple Choice Questions

1. (LO 1) Data exploration may involve

a. identifying data relationships between variables.

b. understanding the analysis results.

c. interpreting results for making informed decisions.

d. assessing the validity of the analysis.

2. (LO 1) Which of the following is *not* a question addressed in data analysis results interpretation?

a. Were the correct data used to perform the analysis?

b. Was the correct technology used to perform the analysis?

c. Is the analysis biased?

d. Were the appropriate analysis methods used?

3. (LO 1) Missing relevant data in an analysis is an example of

a. potential bias risk.

b. potential analysis risk.

c. potential data risk.

d. potential selection risk.

4. (LO 1) One of the most valued aspects of accountants is the ability to

a. be independent and skeptical evaluators of financial information.

b. perform difficult calculations.

c. identify employees committing fraud.

d. remember financial information.

5. (LO 2) To fully interpret data analysis results,

a. identify the person who prepared the analysis.

b. identify the purpose of the analysis.

c. prepare the analysis yourself.

d. have all the knowledge needed to understand the analysis.

6. (LO 2) When interpreting data analysis results,

a. consider only internal stakeholders affected by the results.

b. stakeholders are not relevant to the interpretation.

c. consider only external stakeholders affected by the results.

d. consider internal and external stakeholders potentially affected by the results.

7. (LO 2) Data analysis results that do not include the most recent data is an example of what type of risk?

a. Incorrect method of analysis

b. Preparer bias

c. Timeliness

d. Completeness

8. (LO 2) When interpreting data analysis results, which of the following could be a potential analysis risk?

a. Incorrect method

b. Missing relevant data

c. Data biases

d. Internal controls

9. (LO 2) When interpreting any analysis, you need to determine what knowledge is required to help you understand the results. What accounting knowledge would be required to help interpret a decreasing cash balance?

a. Goodwill calculations

b. Revenue trends

c. Depreciation expense

d. Fair market value of land

10. (LO 3) Confirmation bias can exist while

a. interpreting the analysis.

b. selecting data to support existing beliefs.

c. trying to prove a predetermined assumption.

d. All of these answer choices are correct.

11. (LO 3) When asking the question "Does the analysis address the needs/concerns of the stakeholders?", we are

a. evaluating the reasonableness of the data used.

b. evaluating the reasonableness of the results.

c. evaluating the reasonableness of the methods used.

d. evaluating possible risks.

12. (LO 3) If the answer to the question "Does the analysis address the needs/concerns of the stakeholders?" is no, then

a. you must redo the same analysis to see if you get different results.

b. it will likely be acceptable if the numbers are correct.

c. it is likely the stakeholders did not understand the problem.

d. it is likely that a different analysis is needed before you can interpret the results.

13. **(LO 3)** When comparing two variables with different measurement scales
   a. a clustered column chart is best to visually compare the variables.
   b. a clustered bar chart is best to visually compare the variables.
   c. a dual axis chart is best to visually compare the variables.
   d. a line graph is best to visually compare the variables.

14. **(LO 4)** When determining sales trends by year for each product category, what valid analyses can be used?
   a. Crosstab bar chart
   b. Frequency distribution chart
   c. Dual axis chart
   d. Scatterplot chart

15. **(LO 4)** An appropriate analysis to determine how many times an event has occurred would be
   a. a measure of location.
   b. a measure of dispersion.
   c. a frequency distribution.
   d. linear optimization.

16. **(LO 4)** An anomaly is
   a. always an outlier.
   b. an observation that deviates from what is normal or expected.
   c. always eliminated.
   d. an indication of fraud.

17. **(LO 4)** If gross margin is increasing as sales revenue is increasing, the data relationship is
   a. perfectly correlated.
   b. uncorrelated.
   c. a positive correlation.
   d. a negative correlation.

18. **(LO 4)** If the objective is to use historical data to identify patterns, which is the best analysis to use?
   a. Linear optimization
   b. Frequency distribution
   c. Trend analysis
   d. Linear regression

19. **(LO 5)** Which of the following analyses can predict a future outcome?
   a. Standard deviation
   b. Linear optimization

   c. Cross tabulation analysis
   d. Linear regression

20. **(LO 5)** The goal of predictive analytics is to build a model that
   a. can help predict or better understand a phenomenon in which you are interested.
   b. can be performed using statistical software.
   c. can identify how frequently a phenomenon has happened in the past.
   d. is not too complicated.

21. **(LO 5)** An example of an outlier is
   a. a high sales total of student textbooks in September.
   b. a high sales transaction that was recorded as an error.
   c. a system error in October causing erroneous sales transactions.
   d. inventory balances in May being understated due to some recent shipments not being included in the inventory counts.

22. **(LO 5)** In a regression model prepared to predict revenue, which of the following is the correct interpretation of an adjusted R-square of 0.85?
   a. Revenue will increase by 85% next year.
   b. The independent variables in the model can explain 85% of the change in revenue.
   c. The dependent variable in the model can explain 85% of the change in independent variables.
   d. The adjusted R-square is too small of a number for us to rely on the model.

23. **(LO 5)** A spreadsheet model that allows evaluating how changes to values and assumptions affect an outcome is called a
   a. regression equation.
   b. linear optimization model.
   c. best guess model.
   d. what-if analysis.

24. **(LO 5)** Which is the best tool when the desired result is known, but not the input value for a single variable will achieve that result?
   a. Goal Seek
   b. Scenario Manager
   c. Linear regression
   d. Data analysis

Review Questions

1. **(LO 1)** Compare and contrast data exploration with data analysis interpretation.

2. **(LO 1)** Discuss the two overall steps in the process of interpreting a data analysis.

3. **(LO 2)** When applying the SPARKS critical thinking model to interpreting data analyses, how does identifying the stakeholders help interpret that analysis?

4. (LO 2) The following visualization was published on the Target Investors Relations website:

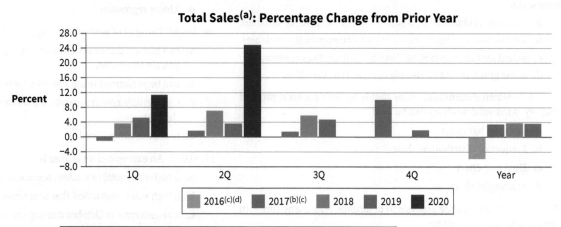

Total Sales(a): Percentage Change from Prior Year

Legend: 2016(c)(d) ■ 2017(b)(c) ■ 2018 ■ 2019 ■ 2020

Fiscal Year	1Q	2Q	3Q	4Q	Year
2020	11.3 %	24.8 %			
2019	5.1 %	3.6 %	4.7 %	1.8 %	3.6 %
2018	3.5 %	7.0 %	5.7 %	– %	3.7 %
2017 (b) (c)	(1.1)%	1.6 %	1.4 %	10.0 %	3.4 %
2016 (c) (d)					(5.8)%

(a) *Total sales include merchandise sales, net of expected returns, from our store and digital channels, as well as gift card breakage.*

(b) *The fourth quarter and full year 2017 consisted of 14 weeks and 53 weeks, respectively, compared with 13 weeks and 52 weeks in the comparable periods presented.*

(c) *Beginning with the first quarter 2018, we adopted the new accounting standards for revenue recognition, leases, and pensions. We are presenting certain prior period results on a basis consistent with the new standards and conformed to the current period presentation. We provided additional information about the impact of the new accounting standards on previously reported financial information in a Form 8-K filed on May 11, 2018.*

(d) *2015 sales include $3,815 million related to our former pharmacy and clinic businesses, which Target sold to CVS in December of 2015.*

Source: Target's Consolidated Financial Statements as filed with the U.S. Securities and Exchange Commission Public Domain.

Assume the role of the preparer of this visualization.

1. Who are the stakeholders?

2. What is the purpose of the analysis?

3. What applicable knowledge do you need in order to prepare this visualization?

Then, assume the role of the reviewer of this visualization and answer the following:

4. What are the risks when interpreting this visualization?

5. What conclusions can be identified from the visualization?

5. (LO 2) Explain why it is important to identify and evaluate alternative explanations of results.

6. (LO 3) Discuss what it means to ask "does the analysis make sense?"

7. (LO 3) What questions should be asked when evaluating the data and methods of an analysis?

8. (LO 3) What questions should be asked when evaluating the results of an analysis?

9. (LO 4) Explain what reliability and validity mean in the context of data analysis interpretation.

10. (LO 4) Explain the difference between an anomaly and an outlier.

11. (LO 5) Discuss how to evaluate a regression model for validity.

12. (LO 5) Explain how adjusted R-square can be used to evaluate the reliability of a regression model.

13. (LO 5) Explain how to interpret whether an independent variable in a regression model is a reliable measure of the dependent variable.

Brief Exercises

BE 8.1 (LO 1) Which of the following statements regarding data exploration and data interpretation are true? Select all that apply.

1. Data exploration and data interpretation are very similar, but there are differences.

2. Generally, data exploration is done before data interpretation.

3. Data exploration and data interpretation are two distinct activities and do not overlap.

4. Informed decisions are made after data exploration and before data interpretation.

BE 8.2 (LO 1) `Managerial Accounting` `Financial Accounting` Blue Steel Motors is an automaker of gasoline-based engines. It recently introduced electric vehicles into their product offerings. As a result, determining the inventory value for raw materials, work-in-process, and finished goods is a complex valuation process since some of its inventory is obsolete or has lost market value. U.S. GAAP requires that inventory is reported as the lesser of cost or net realizable value. Analyses were conducted to valuate the inventory. Identify the right question that should be asked when interpreting the results of the inventory valuation analyses and why.

a. Were inventory counts conducted accurately?

b. Was the classification of the work-in-process and finished goods assessed correctly?

c. Does it make sense that the market value of raw materials is lower than the historic cost?

d. Can the market value be used as a substitute for the net realizable value of raw materials?

BE 8.3 (LO 1) [Financial Accounting] You are a financial analyst working for the city of Boulder, Colorado. Your manager has asked you to review the accounts payable analysis prepared by the accounts payable department. The analysis preparer told you the analysis is intended to determine which Boulder, Colorado, city department has the highest level of spending in U.S. dollars during the year 2025. The analysis was prepared using all the transaction data for the year 2025 for every department. The preparer also verified that the total agreed to the appropriate line item for expenditures in the general ledger, and that there were no intercompany transactions to eliminate.

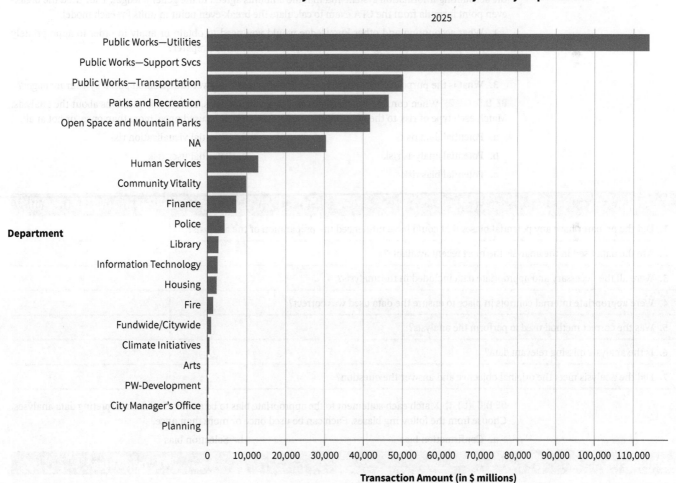

City of Boulder 2025 Accounts Payable by Department

1. The original question for the analysis was "Which department has the highest spending amount during year 2025?" Does the analysis answer this question? Why or why not?

2. Based on the information from the analysis preparer, was the correct data used in the analysis? Why or why not?

3. What information in the analysis preparer's statement allows you to conclude that the results of the analysis are accurate?

BE 8.4 (LO 2) Financial Accounting Managerial Accounting As a senior financial analyst at Super Scooters, you received the following graph from a financial analyst in your department. Your manager would like to know the quantity of units that must be sold for each model before it will have a profit.

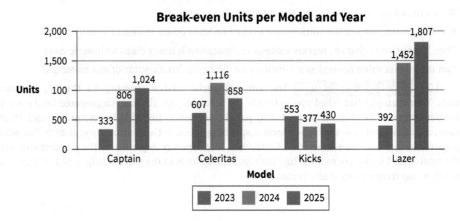

The preparer of the graph told you that total sales price, variable costs, and total fixed costs were pulled from the accounting information system and that the amounts agreed to the general ledger. They used the break-even point formula from the CPA exam to calculate the break-even point in units for each model.

1. What accounting and other knowledge would you need to obtain or apply in order to appropriately interpret the prepared graph or the statement made by the preparer?

2. Who are the stakeholders for this analysis?

3. What is the purpose of the analysis, and does the graph answer the question posed by your manager?

BE 8.5 (LO 2) When considering possible risks of a data analysis, always ask questions about the analysis. Match each type of risk to the question that addresses it. Each be used once, more than once, or not at all.

a. Potential data risk

b. Potential analysis risk

c. Potential bias risk

d. Potential visualization risk

e. Potential user risk

Question	Type of Risk Addressed
1. Did the preparer have any potential biases that could have influenced the preparation of the analysis?	
2. Are the data used in the analysis the most recent available?	
3. Were all the necessary and appropriate data included in the analysis?	
4. Were appropriate internal controls in place to ensure the data used was correct?	
5. Was the correct method used to perform the analysis?	
6. Is the analysis missing relevant data?	
7. Did the analysis meet the original objective and answer the question?	

BE 8.6 (LO 3) Match each statement to the appropriate bias to be aware of when interpreting data analyses. Choose from the following biases. Each can be used once or more than once.

a. Confirmation bias

b. Selection bias

Statement	Type of Bias
1. The person performing the analysis wants to prove a predetermined assumption.	
2. The person performing the analysis selected the data subjectively.	
3. The person interpreting the analysis wants to prove a predetermined assumption.	
4. The person interpreting the analysis focuses on results that support the existing assumption.	
5. The person interpreting the analysis considers only a sample of the data rather than the entire population.	
6. The person interpreting the analysis ignores aspects of the analysis that contradicts the existing assumption.	

BE 8.7 (LO 3) `Auditing` Roberto is the operations manager for Denton Hospitality Co. He has asked you to interpret the analysis of guest complaints. Internal audit provided the following analysis and information:

"We prepared a dual axis graph to show the relationship between guest complaints and customer satisfaction. The x-axis shows the hotel properties. The left y-axis is the number of complaints, and the right y-axis is the customer satisfaction score. The line across the graph is the customer satisfaction score for each hotel property. There is a strong correlation between customer satisfaction score and guest complaints."

1. Roberto would like to know if guest complaints are related to maintenance expenses. Does the visualization and information provided by the internal audit department make sense given Roberto's question? Why or why not?

2. Roberto would like to know if there is a statistical correlation between customer satisfaction scores and guest complaints. Is the analysis sufficient to answer this question? Why or why not?

3. Roberto wants to present a visual depiction of the relationship between customer satisfaction score and guest complaints as part of a presentation to the board. Is the analysis method reasonable? Why or why not?

BE 8.8 (LO 4) `Auditing` In 2020, the National Retail Association reported that 5.9% of returns are fraudulent. This report has prompted you, a risk analyst, to analyze the returns data for fraud for your retail company. The data will be used to implement a real-time fraud detection system to prevent potential fraud as returns are being processed. What data relationship can be used for this analysis?

BE 8.9 (LO 4) `Financial Accounting` CleanItUp is a commercial cleaning and lawn care service company. Your manager wants to understand whether there is a relationship between the results of a customer satisfaction survey and key performance measures of each cleaning crew.

	Correlation: Customer Satisfaction Score
Customer Satisfaction Score	1
Annual Customer Complaints	−0.826124807
Minutes Spent at Property	0.938922087
Number of Employees	0.681057818

The preparer of the correlation analysis provided the data definitions:
- Customer Satisfaction Score: Score from the customer survey.
- Annual Customer Complaints: Number of customer complaints filed each year.
- Minutes Spent at Property: Number of minutes each cleaning crew spent cleaning a property.
- Number of Employees: Number of employees assigned to work at the property for a cleaning.

Use this information to match the appropriate answer to each question. Responses can be used once, more than once, or not at all.

a. A positive correlation coefficient.

b. A negative correlation coefficient.

c. There is a strong positive correlation between the variables.

d. There is a strong negative correlation between the variables.

e. There is a moderate positive correlation between the variables.

f. There is a moderate negative correlation between the variables.

g. There is no relationship between the variables.

Question	Answer
1. What does an inverse relationship mean between two variables?	
2. How would you interpret the correlation coefficient for annual customer complaints and customer satisfaction score?	
3. How would you interpret the correlation coefficient for minutes spent at the property and customer satisfaction score?	
4. How would you interpret the correlation coefficient for number of employees and customer satisfaction score?	

BE 8.10 (LO 5) **Managerial Accounting** Your client, We Care For You Hospital, needs to understand the cost drivers of their total hospital expenses. Your team ran regression analysis based on input from the hospital CFO. The regression equation follows:

$$\text{Hospital expenses} = (\$39{,}702) + \$564\,(\text{Beds}) + \$0.65\,(\text{Outpatient Visits}) + \$26.76\,(\text{Births})$$

Summary Output	
Regression Statistics	
Multiple R	0.87254918
R Square	0.76134208
Adjusted R Square	0.76098337
Standard Error	158,773.661
Observations	2,000

1. Identify the independent variables in the regression model.
2. Identify the dependent variable in the regression model.
3. Identify the regression statistic that indicates how well the model's independent variables explain the dependent variable.
4. What percentage of the variance in hospital expenses do beds, births, and outpatient visits explain?

BE 8.11 (LO 5) **Tax Accounting** One consideration of tax planning is understanding and projecting the amount of net revenue that a company expects for the upcoming year. Your team has created a what-if analysis to predict Super Scooters' net revenue for next year. Based on current year data, the team has performed three sensitivity analyses:

- Best-case scenario: They expect sales to increase by 10%.
- Likely-case scenario: They expect sales to increase by 5%.
- Worst-case scenario: They expect sales to decrease by 7%.

The current calculation of net revenue follows. Variable costs are 47% of sales, and Super Scooters expects variable costs to remain stable over the next year.

Net Revenue

	2025
Gross Sales	£ 12,165,162
Total Variable Costs	£ 5,722,777
Contribution Margin	£ 6,442,385
Total Fixed Costs	£ 1,696,822
Net Revenue	£ 4,745,563

What-If Analysis

	Best-Case	Likely-Case	Worst-Case
Gross Sales	£ 12,165,162	£ 12,165,162	£ 12,165,162
Total Variable Costs	£ 6,008,916	£ 5,837,232	£ 6,123,371
Contribution Margin	£ 6,156,246	£ 6,327,930	£ 6,041,791
Total Fixed Costs	£ 1,696,822	£ 1,696,822	£ 1,696,822
Net Revenue	£ 4,459,424	£ 4,631,108	£ 4,344,969

1. What knowledge would you need to understand how the best-case, likely-case, and worst-case scenarios should be interpreted?
2. Assume the objective of the analysis is to estimate sales tax for the upcoming year. Would the available what-if analysis provide the appropriate information to begin your estimation?

Exercises

EX 8.1 (LO 1) **Auditing** **Accounting Information Systems** **Interpret and Evaluate a Data Visualization** The following analysis was prepared to evaluate business expenses for the city of Dublin, Ireland. You work for the internal audit department for the city. Your manager asked you to review an analysis to evaluate business expense reimbursement for the city departments.

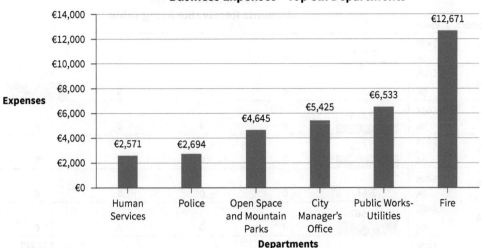

Business Expenses—Top Six Departments

Answer the five data interpretation questions to determine if the analysis and visualization make sense and whether they are valid and reliable.

EX 8.2 (LO 1) `Auditing` `Accounting Information Systems` **Interpret and Evaluate a Data Visualization** An anonymous tip was called into the city's fraud hotline alleging that contracts are being awarded without the appropriate bidding process. An analysis was prepared to identify the top 10 vendors so the bidding process for those vendors could be reviewed. The data used was all accounts payable for the current year. The vendors with the highest number of transactions were identified as top vendors.

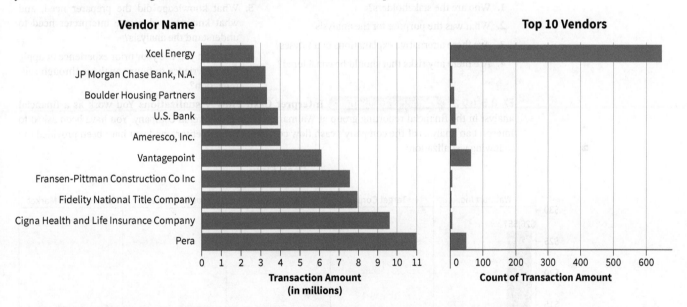

Answer the five data interpretation questions to determine if the analysis makes sense and is valid and reliable.

EX 8.3 (LO 2) `Accounting Information Systems` **Evaluate a Data Visualization** Go to the Tableau Gallery website and search for an accounting topic. Choose a visualization and analyze it using the critical thinking framework:

1. Who are the stakeholders ?
2. What was the purpose for analysis?
3. Are there alternative explanations or analyses?
4. Are there any risks that should be considered?
5. What knowledge did the preparer need and what knowledge does the interpreter need to understand the analysis?
6. How can you use your prior experience or apply this experience to future analyses?

EX 8.4 (LO 2) `Financial Accounting` **Interpret Accounts Receivable Analyses** Assume you are a financial analyst working in the controller's group at Super Scooters. You have been asked to analyze accounts receivable and have prepared the following aging table. The bars represent total accounts receivable balances.

Super Scooters, Inc.
Accounts Receivable Aging Table

Customer	Value	Less than 30	31 to 60	61 to 90	91 to 180	More than 180...
C1036	$40K–0K	$7,184	0	0	0	0
C1282	$40K–0K	0	0	0	0	$32,478
C1423	$40K–0K	$17,635	0	0	0	0
C1671	$40K–0K	$23,038	0	0	0	0
C2036	$40K–0K	$763	0	0	0	0
C2274	$40K–0K	$23,562	0	0	0	0
C3168	$40K–0K	0	0	0	0	$32,229
C9591	$40K–0K	$10,840	0	0	0	0
C9917	$40K–0K	0	0	0	0	$31,046

Days

1. Who are the stakeholders?
2. What was the purpose for the analysis?
3. Are there alternative explanations or analyses?
4. Are there any risks that should be considered?
5. What knowledge did the preparer need, and what knowledge does the interpreter need to understand the analysis?
6. How can you use your prior experience or apply this experience to future analyses through self-reflection?

EX 8.5 (LO 2) Financial Accounting **Interpret Cash Flow Visualizations** You work as a financial analyst in the financial reporting group at Walmart, a large public retail company. You have been asked to interpret an analysis of the company's cash flow compared to competitors, and you have been provided the following visualization:

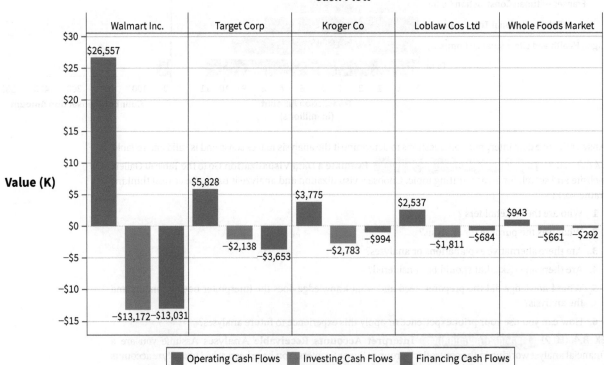

Cash Flow

1. Who are the stakeholders ?
2. What was the purpose for analysis?
3. Are there alternative explanations or analyses?
4. Are there any risks that should be considered?

5. What knowledge did the preparer need, and what knowledge does the interpreter need to understand the analysis?
6. How can you use your prior experience or apply this experience to future analyses through self-reflection?

EX 8.6 (LO 3) `Data` `Financial Accounting` **Interpret Reasonableness of a Data Analysis** As a financial analyst at Best Bakes Bakery, you are often tasked with conducting and evaluating data for decision-making. The Best Bakes owners have asked you to identify their top five customers. You performed an analysis of profit margin by customer and prepared the following visualization using the Best Bakes data file:

Profit Margin by Customer

Cust Name	2021	2022	2023	2024
Bluebird Cafe	45.83%	45.15%	47.28%	53.04%
Butters AM Eatery	44.85%	21.98%	45.51%	50.90%
Home Cookin Café	42.77%	39.14%	48.17%	55.14%
Krispy Kreme	48.84%	49.21%	31.18%	47.92%
Lucile's Creole Café	46.52%	48.44%	49.44%	40.91%
Red Rooster Restau..	44.31%	41.04%	50.38%	50.02%
Rocky Mountain Bag..	50.02%	45.32%	47.82%	40.53%
Snooze AM Eatery	47.11%	47.41%	47.37%	33.27%
Syrup Downtown	42.23%	56.82%	43.61%	43.47%
Ziggi's Coffee	41.69%	42.60%	56.57%	38.71%

Avg. Profit Margin

21.98%   56.82%

1. Are the data used in the analysis reasonable given the question/objective of the analysis?
2. Is the analysis method reasonable given the question/objective of the analysis?
3. Are the results of the analysis reasonable given what you know about the subject being analyzed?
4. Are the implications of the analysis reasonable given what you know about the subject being analyzed?
5. Does the analysis address the needs/concerns of the stakeholders?

EX 8.7 (LO 3) `Auditing` `Accounting Information Systems` **Interpreting Reasonableness of Journal Entries Data Analysis** You are an audit associate responsible for the audit of journal entries for a public company client. Part of the audit procedures are analyzing journal entry activity to identify any unusual activity. You have prepared the following analysis of journal entry activity. It shows the total dollar amount, the average dollar amount, and the total number of journal entries made automatically by the accounting system and made by three key employees at your client.

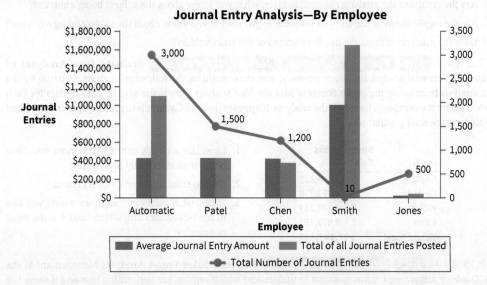

1. Are the data used in the analysis reasonable given the question/objective of the analysis?
2. Is the analysis method reasonable given the question/objective of the analysis?

3. Are the results of the analysis reasonable given what you know about the subject being analyzed?

4. Are the implications of the analysis reasonable given what you know about the subject being analyzed?

5. Does the analysis address the question/objective of the analysis?

EX 8.8 (LO 3) **Managerial Accounting** **Interpreting Reasonableness of Sales Forecast Analyses** Super Scooters is considering dropping the Celeritas scooter model and expanding their electric-powered scooter offerings to take advantage of changing market demand. You acquired the following information:

- The market for electric scooters is growing rapidly due to the increase in scooter-sharing programs.

- Celeritas is the only gas-powered scooter that Super Scooters manufactures.

- The Lazer and Captain models are electric-powered scooters, whereas the Kicks model is a manually propelled scooter.

Your analytics team prepared this visualization to contribute to the decision-making process.

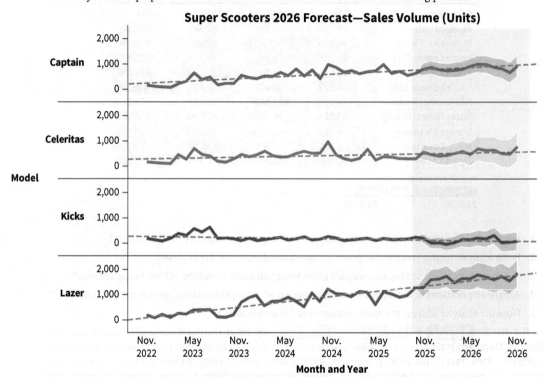

1. Are the data used in the analysis reasonable given the question/objective of the analysis?

2. Is the analysis method reasonable given the question/objective of the analysis?

3. Are the results of the analysis reasonable given what you know about the subject being analyzed?

4. Are the implications of the analysis reasonable given what you know about the subject being analyzed?

5. Does the analysis address the needs/concerns of the stakeholders?

EX 8.9 (LO 3) **Data** **Financial Accounting** **Managerial Accounting** **Evaluate Data Analyses of Sales** As a financial analyst for Super Scooters, you must evaluate the following analysis prepared by the data analysis team using the Super Scooters data set. The analysis reports the sum of sales dollars for each model sold by the company. Based on the analysis, it appears that the Captain is the most popular model and the Kicks is the least popular model.

Model	Sum of Gross Sales
Captain	$ 12,324,133
Celeritas	$ 4,792,338
Kicks	$ 1,108,183
Lazer	$ 8,922,753
Grand Total	**$ 27,147,407**

1. Does the analysis confirm the most and least popular models? Why or why not?

2. Do you think more analysis is needed?

3. If yes, what additional analyses would you like to see before deciding which model is the most popular?

EX 8.10 (LO 3) **Data** **Managerial Accounting** **Evaluate Sales Trend Analysis** Management at the U.S. Outdoor Adventure Company wants to understand which regions are performing best and if there is a trend in sales over the years within the regions. Your team has analyzed sales and prepared a visualization using the U.S. Outdoor Adventure Company Tableau file.

Yearly Region Sales

Region	2022	2023	2024	2025
Central	$103,838	$102,874	$147,429	$147,098
East	$128,680	$156,332	$180,529	$213,239
South	$103,846	$ 71,301	$ 93,539	$122,977
West	$147,883	$139,766	$186,976	$250,633

$0 $300,000

1. Does the analysis address the objective? Why or why not?

2. Do you think more analysis is needed?

3. If yes, what additional analyses would you like to see before deciding which region is performing the best?

EX 8.11 (LO 4) `Managerial Accounting` **Interpret Correlation Analysis** All Care Hospital would like to better understand cost drivers of total expenses. As a first step, they have prepared a correlation analysis to determine factors that are correlated with total expenses.

Cost Drivers	Beds	Outpatient Visits	Births	Gen Med/ Surg or Not	Total Expense
Beds	1				
Outpatient Visits	0.61584604	1			
Births	0.66665244	0.496333644	1		
Gen Med/Surg or Not	0.25764602	0.322183655	0.359453	1	
Total Expense	0.77739236	0.782692108	0.62695	0.249571064	1

Interpret the correlations:

1. Outpatient visits and total expense

2. Number of beds and total expense

3. Number of beds and births

EX 8.12 (LO 4) `Financial Accounting` **Interpret Descriptive Statistics** You are a financial analyst at the hotel chain Denton Hospitality. You have been asked to provide a better understanding of their profit from the past year. Your data analysis team has prepared two analyses. The first is a scatterplot that shows the total annual profit for each hotel. The second is a descriptive statistics analysis of profit from the past year.

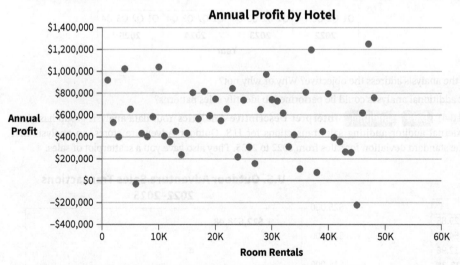

Profit	
Mean	547,691.05
Standard Error	44,607.48
Median	553,868.00
Mode	#N/A
Standard Deviation	309,049.66
Sample Variance	95,511,689,341.06
Kurtosis	0.07
Skewness	0.00
Range	1,472,109.00
Minimum	(224,305.00)
Maximum	1,247,804.00
Sum	26,289,170.25
Count	48.00

1. Interpret the following descriptive statistics:

    a. Mean   b. Median   c. Standard Deviation

2. Does the scatterplot support your explanation of the descriptive statistics? Why or why not?

EX 8.13 (LO 4) `Data` `Financial Accounting` `Managerial Accounting` **Interpret Descriptive Analytics** You are a financial analyst for One Stop Shop, which is a wholesale distributor of consumer products to convenience stores. The company operates in Canada, Mexico, and the United States. One Stop Shop has two sales channels:

- Online sales made through the One Stop Shop website.
- Offline sales made directly with One Stop Shop sales representatives.

One Stop Shop would like to evaluate whether they should move to only online sales. They believe this will save a significant amount of money since they will not need as many sales representatives and will not have to pay sales commissions. Following is an analysis prepared by One Stop Shop using the One Stop Shop data set:

Row Labels	Sum of Total Sales
Canada	**$ 788,914,146**
Offline	$ 392,731,724
Online	$ 396,182,421
Mexico	**$ 710,979,369**
Offline	$ 400,360,732
Online	$ 310,618,637
United States	**$ 1,452,693,443**
Offline	$ 720,489,036
Online	$ 732,204,407
Grand Total	**$ 2,952,586,958**

1. What information does the PivotTable provide to One Stop Shop?
2. What additional analyses should One Stop Shop consider?

EX 8.14 (LO 4) `Financial Accounting` `Managerial Accounting` **Interpret Diagnostic Analytics** The management team at One Stop Shop wants to know if there is a seasonal pattern to sales. The data analysis team prepared the following visualization:

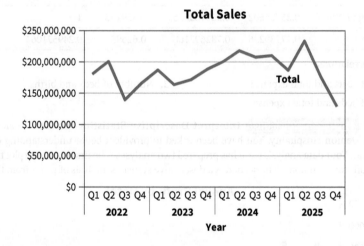

Total Sales

1. Does the analysis address the objective? Why or why not?
2. What additional analyses could be performed to identify sales patterns?

EX 8.15 (LO 4) `Data` `Auditing` **Interpret Descriptive Analytics** Your data analysis group has given you, an external auditor auditing sale transactions for U.S. Outdoor Adventure stores, an analysis that includes the standard deviation for sales from 2022 to 2025. They also gave you a scatterplot of sales.

Descriptive Statistics	
Sales 2022–2025	
Mean	229.86
Median	54.49
Mode	12.96
Standard Deviation	**623.25**
Sample Variance	**388,434.46**
Minimum	0.44
Maximum	22,638.48
Count	9,994.00

U.S. Outdoor Adventure Sales Transactions 2022–2025

The preparer of the analysis used all the sales transaction data and agreed total sales in their file to the sales line item in the general ledger.

1. Interpret the variance and standard deviation for U.S. Outdoor Adventure Stores sales.

2. Does the scatterplot support your explanation of standard deviation? Why or why not?

3. Use the provided data file to recreate the analyses.

EX 8.16 (LO 5) `Financial Accounting` `Managerial Accounting` **Interpret Regression Analysis** Denton Hospitality Inc. has hired your consulting firm to evaluate and manage cashflows. Specifically, you have been asked to build a valid and reliable model to predict total expenses so management can better manage cashflows. You and your team prepared the following regression:

Denton Hospitality Inc.—Total Expenses Prediction Model					
SUMMARY OUTPUT					
Regression Statistics					
Multiple R	0.810435721				
R Square	0.656806059				
Adjusted R Square	0.62160668				
Standard Error	79,448.54158				
Observations	44				
ANOVA					
	df	*SS*	*MS*	*F*	*Significance F*
Regression	4	4.71E+11	1.18E+11	18.65959	1.211E–08
Residual	39	2.46E+11	6.31E+09		
Total	43	7.17E+11			
	Coefficients	*Standard Error*	*t Stat*	*P-value*	
Intercept	(131,136.43)	121071.9	−1.08313	0.285403	
Number of Rooms	2,670.21	587.7595	4.543032	5.23E–05	
Hours Worked, Front Desk	29.30	9.270823	3.160299	0.003044	
Hours Worked, GM	52.01	18.93043	2.747581	0.009043	
Hours Worked, Housekeeping	13.41	4.683324	2.862522	0.006728	

1. Interpret the regression statistics.

2. Explain whether the model is significant.

3. What are the coefficients of the model?

4. Do the variables used in the model make sense? Why or why not?

5. Identify other variables that may improve the model.

6. Use the model to predict expenses for a hotel with the following characteristics:
   - Opened in 1975
   - 150 rooms
   - 9,200 hours worked—Front Desk
   - 1,500 hours worked—GM
   - 12,100 hours worked—Housekeeping
   - Location—Airport

EX 8.17 (LO 5) `Data` `Managerial Accounting` **Interpret Sensitivity Analysis** Super Scooters is preparing revenue forecasts for the next year. Based on current year data, you performed three sensitivity analyses:

- Best-case scenario: Variable costs will decrease by 5%.
- Likely-case scenario: Variable costs will increase by 2%.
- Worst-case scenario: Variable will increase by 7%.

The current calculation of net revenue is provided.

	2025
Gross Sales	$ 12,165,162
Total Variable Costs	$ 5,722,777
Contribution Margin	$ 6,442,385
Total Fixed Costs	$ 1,696,822
Net Revenue	$ 4,745,563

The best-case, likely-case, and worst-case scenario analysis is provided. Super Scooters expects sales to remain stable over the next year.

	Best-Case	Likely-Case	Worst-Case
Gross Sales	$ 12,165,162	$ 12,165,162	$ 12,165,162
Total Variable Costs	$ 6,008,916	$ 5,837,232	$ 6,123,371
Contribution Margin	$ 6,156,246	$ 6,327,930	$ 6,041,791
Total Fixed Costs	$ 1,696,822	$ 1,696,822	$ 1,696,822
Net Revenue	$ 4,459,424	$ 4,631,108	$ 4,344,969

Recreate the what-if analysis and answer the questions:

1. What is the question/objective of the analysis?
2. Does the model measure what it is supposed to measure?
3. Are the model measures accurate and consistent?

EX 8.18 (LO 5) `Data` `Managerial Accounting` **Interpret Goal Seek Analysis** U.S. Outdoor Adventure Sales has asked your accounting team to determine the break-even sales for their tent product. The team discussed potential methods to estimate break-even sales, and determined that Goal Seek is the most effective method. The sales team provided you with price and costs information:

- Sales price = $70
- Variable cost per unit = $25
- Fixed costs = $10,000

With the spreadsheet model used to calculate profit using this data, use Goal Seek to answer the following questions:

1. What are the number of break-even units needed?
2. How many tents must U.S. Outdoor Adventures sell to make a profit of $100,000?
3. How would you verify the validity and reliability of the model and model results?

EX 8.19 (LO 5) `Data` `Financial Accounting` **Interpret Predictive Analytics** You are a financial analyst at Best Bakes Bakery. Your manager has asked you to build a model to predict sales for 2026 using sales data from 2022 to 2025. The following is the trendline equation using the variables gross sales in dollars and month of sale:

$$\text{Gross Sales} = \$74,739.90 - (\$1.56 \times \text{Month of Sale}).$$

Model statistics include:

$$R\text{-square} = 0.0487$$

$$p\text{-value is } 0.1406$$

The trendline equation was used to develop the following visualization. The month and year of sale is on the x-axis and gross sales are on the y-axis.

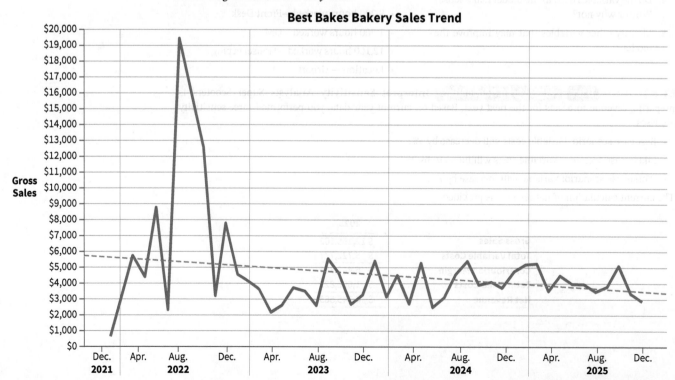

Best Bakes Bakery Sales Trend

Examine the analysis in the provided data file and interpret the sales trend analysis.

1. What is the question/objective of the analysis?
2. Does the model and visualization provide adequate information to address it?
3. Are the model variables valid?

EX 8.20 (LO 5) `Financial Accounting` `Managerial Accounting` **Interpret Regression Analysis** You are asked to build a model to predict sales at U.S. Outdoor Adventures. Management believes that the region, discount percentage, and discount dollar amount are good predictors of sales. You used the data in the regression file to prepare the following regression analysis:

SUMMARY OUTPUT					
Regression Statistics					
Multiple R	0.6260322				
R Square	0.3919164				
Adjusted R Square	0.391612				
Standard Error	486.1264				
Observations	9994				
ANOVA					
	df	*SS*	*MS*	*F*	*Significance F*
Regression	5	1,521,272,575	304,254,515	1,287.47445	0.00
Residual	9,988	2,360,352,937	236,318.876		
Total	9,993	3,881,625,512			
	Coefficients	*Standard Error*	*t Stat*	*P-value*	
Intercept	221.75141	12.60104565	17.5978578	2.7291E-68	
Discount	–438.73427	24.64841598	–17.799694	8.4529E-70	
Discount $	2.4154052	0.030141825	80.1346697	0.00	
Region West	0.1232541	15.12802917	0.0081474	0.99349955	
Region East	–17.727807	14.84929891	–1.1938481	0.23256576	
Region Central	18.590415	15.9032368	1.16897054	0.2424434	

1. Interpret the regression statistics.
2. Is the model significant? Why or why not?
3. What are the coefficients of the model?
4. Do the variables used in the model make sense? Why or why not?
5. Identify other variables that may improve the model.
6. Based on this model, what is the predicted sale when the discount percentage is 20%, the sale is in the west region, and the discount dollar amount is 100?

Problems

PR 8.1 (LO 1) `Data` `Financial Accounting` **Interpret Descriptive Analytics** Management at U.S. Outdoor Adventures is evaluating their shipping policy to customers. Currently, the company offers free shipping, but they are considering charging customers for shipping. Management would like to better understand how shipping costs are changing and if there is a relationship between the type of shipping method and order priority.

Products are shipped either first class, same day, second class, or standard class. The method of shipping is decided by the customer but is usually related to the order priority. The priority categories are critical, low, medium, or high.

The data analysis team provided the following descriptive analyses, which indicate that total shipping costs increased from 2022 to 2025. They also prepared a frequency distribution of the number of shipments by priority and shipping mode for 2022, 2023, 2024, and 2025 combined.

Shipping Cost per Year

Year ▾	Total Shipping Cost
⊞ 2022	$ 49,769.30
⊞ 2023	$ 50,198.57
⊞ 2024	$ 60,925.19
⊞ 2025	$ 77,280.73
Grand Total	**$ 238,173.79**

Number of Shipments by Shipping Mode

Priority and Shipping Mode ▾	Number of Shipments
⊟ **Critical**	**783**
First Class	340
Same Day	154
Second Class	289
⊟ **High**	**3,069**
First Class	703
Same Day	273
Second Class	744
Standard Class	1,349
⊟ **Low**	**432**
Standard Class	432
⊟ **Medium**	**5,710**
First Class	495
Same Day	116
Second Class	912
Standard Class	4,187
Grand Total	**9,994**

1. Identify the following:
   a. Who are the stakeholders ?
   b. What was the purpose for analysis?
   c. Are there alternative explanations or analyses?
   d. Are there any risks that should be considered?
   e. What knowledge did the preparer need and what knowledge does the interpreter need to understand the analysis?
   f. How can you use your prior experience or apply this experience to future analyses through self-reflection?

2. Are the data used in the analysis reasonable given the question/objective of the analysis?
3. Is the analysis method reasonable given the question/objective of the analysis?
4. Are the results of the analysis reasonable given what is known about the subject being analyzed?
5. Are the implications of the analysis reasonable given what you know about the subject being analyzed?
6. Does the analysis address the needs/concerns of the stakeholders?
7. Prepare an additional descriptive analysis that will help U.S. Outdoor Adventures understand the costs associated with each mode of shipping. Interpret your analysis.

PR 8.2 (LO 1, 2, 3, 5) `Data` `Financial Accounting` `Managerial Accounting` **Interpret Predictive Analyses** All Care Hospital, which operates 2,000 hospitals in the United States, is preparing their operating budgets for 2026. Executive management would like to understand the factors driving total expenses. As a member of the data analytics team in the accounting department, you are asked to prepare and interpret data analyses to provide management with information about total hospital expenses.

The data analytics team provided descriptive analyses summarizing the number of hospitals in each region and total hospital expenses by region. In 2025, total expenses for All Care Hospitals were $386.8 million. They also gave you the raw data file.

Region ▾	Number of Hospitals
East North Central	262
East South Central	136
Mid Atlantic	168
Mountain	160
New England	100
Pacific	259
South Atlantic	252
West North Central	214
West South Central	449
Grand Total	**2,000**

Total Expenses by Region—2025

Region	
East North Central	$52,941,169
East South Central	$19,037,967
Mid Atlantic	$60,506,505
Mountain	$26,438,517
New England	$25,634,270
Pacific	$71,210,066
South Atlantic	$57,893,598
West North Central	$26,015,206
West South Central	$47,082,098

Total Expense

19M   71M

According to management, the following variables are predictors of total hospital expenses: admissions, census, outpatient visits, births, payroll expenses, personnel, and whether there was a birth or not. The analytics team prepared a regression model using those variables with the following output:

SUMMARY OUTPUT

Regression Statistics	
Multiple R	0.982051941
R Square	0.964426014
Adjusted R Square	0.964301005
Standard Error	61,360.99522
Observations	2,000

ANOVA

	df	SS	MS	F	Significance F
Regression	7	2.03E+14	2.9E+13	7,714.85352	0
Residual	1,992	7.5E+12	3.77E+09		
Total	1,999	2.11E+14			

	Coefficients	Standard Error	t Stat	P-value	Lower 95%	Upper 95%	Lower 95%	Upper 95%
Intercept	-4,191.07786	2,275.171	-1.84209	0.06561006	-8,653.042868	270.8871	-8653.04	270.8871
Admissions	6.013726131	0.387068	15.5366	1.8108E-51	5.254624717	6.772828	5.254625	6.772828
Census	-57.72122789	19.55346	-2.95197	0.00319445	-96.06861315	-19.3738	-96.0686	-19.3738
Outpatient Visits	-0.019727175	0.009985	-1.97573	0.04832264	-0.039308781	-0.00015	-0.03931	-0.00015
Births	-9.977260409	1.656594	-6.02276	2.0367E-09	-13.22609855	-6.72842	-13.2261	-6.72842
Payroll Expense	1.804388653	0.036122	49.95226	0.00000000	1.733547274	1.87523	1.733547	1.87523
Personnel	30.9359429	2.697418	11.46872	1.5657E-29	25.64588566	36.226	25.64589	36.226
Births or Not	-5,932.874462	3329.682	-1.78181	0.07493183	-12,462.8985	597.1496	-12,462.9	597.1496

1. Identify the following:

   a. Who are the stakeholders?

   b. What was the purpose of analysis?

   c. Are there alternative explanations or analyses?

   d. Are there any risks that should be considered?

   e. What knowledge did the preparer need and what knowledge does the interpreter need to understand the analysis?

   f. How can you use your prior experience or apply this experience to future analyses?

2. Use the Summary Output for the following:

   a. Interpret the regression statistics.

   b. Is the model significant? Why or why not?

   c. Identify the coefficients of the model.

   d. Do the variables used in the model make sense? Why or why not?

   e. Identify other variables that may improve the model.

3. Prepare a regression model that predicts total expenses using the variables: admissions, outpatient visits, births, and personnel.

   a. Is this model better than the previous model?

   b. Interpret the regression statistics and the coefficients of the model.

Professional Application Case   KneeCap Inc.

Data KneeCap Inc. is a medical device manufacturer based in San Diego, California. The company produces and sells custom-made knee replacement implants:

- It is a privately held company and files U.S. GAAP-based financial statements with its bank as part of its debt covenants.

- The board of directors is very involved and continues to emphasize the importance of well-designed and effective internal controls.

- KneeCap is a decentralized organization, with five manufacturing and sales sites across the United States employing a total of 28 product managers and 29 sales managers. Each site operates independently and is responsible for procurement of raw materials, production, and sales of finished products in its own

geographic region. Sales managers maintain their own customer relationships, while product managers monitor inventory levels and order raw materials as needed.

- Silicone and plaster are used to create the molds for all the company's knee replacements. The materials poured into molds vary by product—some are metal, some are plastic, and some are ceramic.

The company has invested significantly in the development and maintenance of its information system to collect and report complete and accurate data. Company management uses the data captured in the information system to create reports and support decision-making. The data dictionary includes the most relevant data used by management, accountants, auditors, and other professionals.

Data Dictionary

Material Master Table

Name	Primary Key	Definition
MaterialCategory	☐	Constant stating raw material
Material	☑	Material item identifier
MaterialDescription	☐	Description of material

Note: The Material Master table contains information about different raw materials purchased by KneeCap.

Product Master Table

Name	Primary Key	Definition
ProductCategory	☐	Constant stating knee implant
Product	☑	Product item identifier
ProductDescription	☐	Description of product

Note: The Product Master table contains information about different products sold by KneeCap.

Transactions Table

Name	Primary Key	Definition
TransType	☑	Indicates the type of transaction (O for orders and S for sales)
TransNumber	☑	Identifier for orders and sales
SiteCode	☐	Transaction site (one of five locations)
Manager	☐	Employee associated with the transaction
EntityID	☐	Supplier/Customer associated with the transaction
Quantity	☐	Transaction quantity
Unit	☐	Unit of transaction (lb or kg for orders, ea for sales)
UnitPrice	☐	Price per unit
TransDate	☐	Sales/purchase order date
CompleteDate	☐	Shipping/receiving date (sales/orders)
Item	☐	The material purchased or product sold
CreatedBy	☐	The source of the data (e.g., daily batch)
Subtotal	☐	Transaction total before tax (UnitPrice * Quantity)
Tax	☐	Tax amount

Note: The Transactions table contains a combination of purchase order, sales order, and sales return transactions.

Sites Table

Name	Primary Key	Definition
SiteCode	☑	Identified for company sites (five state abbreviations)
SiteName	☐	Name of site (states)

Note: The Sites table contains the name of each site, which is the name of the state where the site is located.

Employee Master Table

Name	Primary Key	Description
EmployeeID	☑	Employee identifier
FirstName	☐	Employee first name
LastName	☐	Employee last name

(Continued)

Name	Primary Key	Description
SiteCode	☐	Company site identified (state)
Position	☐	Employee position
OrderApproval	☐	Employee order approval authority

Note: The Employee Master table contains information about employees associated with the sales order and purchase order transactions, e.g., sales and product managers.

Entity Master Table

Name	Primary Key	Description
EntityID	☑	Entity (supplier/customer/KneeCap Inc.) identifier
SiteCode	☐	Indicates which KneeCap site the entity is associated with
EntityName	☐	Entity company name
ContactFirstName	☐	Entity contact first name
ContactLastName	☐	Entity contact last name
Phone	☐	Entity phone
Email	☐	Entity email
StreetAddress	☐	Entity street address
City	☐	Entity city
State	☐	Entity state
Zip	☐	Entity zip code
EntityType	☐	Entity type ("S" for customer and "O" for supplier)

The entity-relationship diagram (ERD) shows the relationships among the tables in the information system.

Entity-Relationship Diagram (ERD)

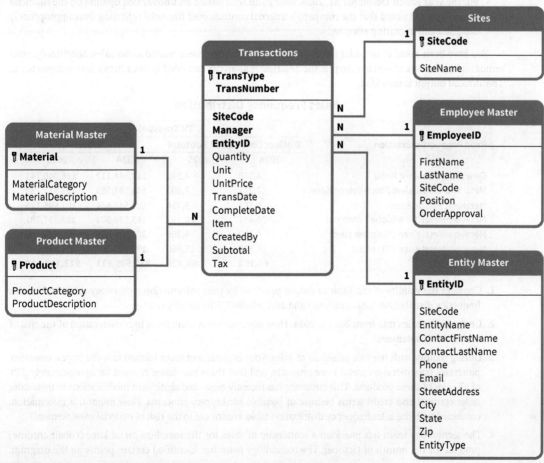

(*Note:* The ERD indicates which tables to join and which columns to use in the joins.)

The comparative income statement shows income for 2024 and 2025.

KneeCap Inc. Comparative Income Statement

Comparative Income Statement
(in millions)

	2024 (audited)	2025 (unaudited)
Net sales	$913	$854
Cost of sales	579	542
Gross profit	334	312
Research and development	57	59
Selling, general and administrative	191	196
Recall charges, net of insurance proceeds	5	5
Intangible asset amortization	3	2
Total operating expenses	256	262
Operating income	78	50
Other income (expenses), net	1	2
Earnings before income taxes	79	52
Income taxes	11	8
Net earnings	$ 68	$ 44

PAC 8.1 Auditing: Interpret Descriptive and Diagnostic Analytics

Data **Auditing** You are on the external audit team auditing KneeCap's financial statements as of and for the year ended December 31, 2025:

- Note that the amounts presented in the comparative income statement for 2024 are audited, whereas the amounts presented for 2025 are unaudited.
- For the year ended December 31, 2024, your audit firm issued an unqualified opinion on the financial statements and noted that the company's internal controls over financial reporting were appropriately designed and operating effectively.

You have been asked to consider the risks of material misstatement related to net sales. Specifically, your senior auditor has asked you to interpret the descriptive analytics provided by your firm's data analysis team. The Tableau output is provided.

Sales Frequency Distribution

Prod ProductDescription	TR TransDate			
	Distinct Count of TR Subtotal		TR Subtotal	
	2024	2025	2024	2025
Ceramic-on-Ceramic Knee	4,378	4,196	113,844,112	116,040,741
Metal and Crosslinked Polyethylene Knee	7,217	7,208	145,197,885	153,572,138
Metal and Plastic Knee	9,567	9,714	103,546,449	107,545,175
Metal-on-Metal Knee (Cobalt chrome)	20,457	20,331	185,198,302	198,397,781
Metal-on-Metal Knee (Stainless steel)	4,153	4,306	106,320,616	116,722,920
Metal-on-Metal Knee (Titanium)	16,526	16,760	199,398,247	220,828,360
Grand Total	**60,102**	**60,424**	**853,505,611**	**913,107,114**

1. Consider the validity of the Tableau output provided by your information technology team. Is the sales frequency distribution table analysis valid and reliable? Why or why not?

2. Compare the sales mix from 2025 to 2024. How does sales mix contribute to consideration of the risk of material misstatement?

3. During inquiry with the vice president of sales, your engagement team learned that the largest customer purchases only metal-on-metal knee products, and that these purchases account for approximately 35% of all sales of these products. This customer has recently requested significant modifications to their sales order contract and credit terms because of possible bankruptcy concerns. How might this information, combined with the sales frequency distribution table, contribute to the risk of material misstatement?

4. The technology team has provided a scatterplot of sales for the metal-on-metal knee (cobalt chrome) product for the month of October. The technology team has identified certain points on the diagram.

Explain whether each of the identified points on the diagram would need further investigation, or if they should be included in normal substantive testing for sales.

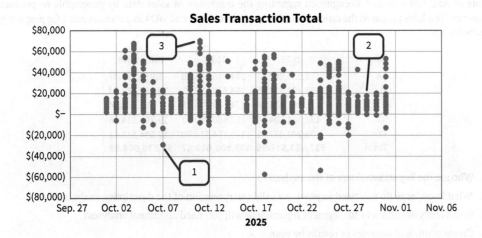

Sales Transaction Total

5. Use the KneeCap data sets to create additional descriptive analytics. Consider creating a cross tabulation analysis of sales by product description and/or sales by site code. These descriptive statistics provide insight into the company's net sales for the year under audit. Describe your analysis, and interpret your results.

PAC 8.2 Managerial Accounting: Interpret Diagnostic Analytics

Data **Managerial Accounting** You have been tasked with understanding the relationship between sales orders and purchase orders to acquire raw materials. Currently, production sites are individually responsible for all purchases. The benefit of this decentralized organization is that the sites can quickly respond to changes in production demand. The downside is that sourcing for purchases is not coordinated between the sites. There is a concern that some sites' purchasing departments have been buying more raw materials than needed.

Your manager has asked you to analyze purchases compared to sales. You prepared the following analyses:

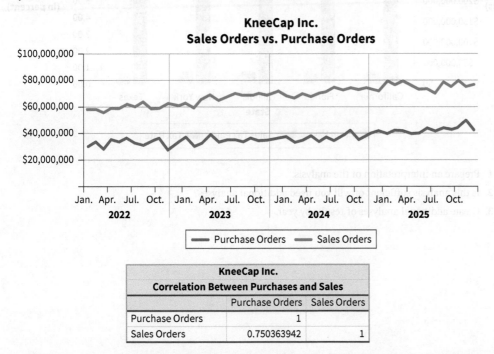

KneeCap Inc.
Sales Orders vs. Purchase Orders

KneeCap Inc.		
Correlation Between Purchases and Sales		
	Purchase Orders	Sales Orders
Purchase Orders	1	
Sales Orders	0.750363942	1

1. How do these analyses help evaluate if the sites are purchasing more raw materials than they need?
2. List some additional analyses that would be useful.
3. Create additional analyses and interpret your results.

PAC 8.3 Financial Accounting: Interpret Descriptive Analytics

Data **Financial Accounting** The Controller at KneeCap Inc. has asked you to understand the requirements of ASC 606 Revenue Recognition regarding the disclosure of sales data by geographic or product categories. You have prepared the cross tabulation analysis for 2025 and 2024 as a starting point for preparing the disclosure.

Site	2025	2024	Difference
CA	172,934,662.11	174,888,045.18	–1,953,383.07
FL	183,493,309.15	164,530,136.81	18,963,172.34
IL	175,041,416.59	174,872,628.25	168,788.34
NY	193,364,104.19	163,660,289.73	29,703,814.46
TX	188,249,027.51	175,554,510.70	12,694,516.81
Total	**913,082,519.55**	**853,505,610.67**	**59,576,908.88**

1. Who are the key stakeholders of the analysis?
2. What knowledge do you need to provide a valid interpretation of the descriptive analysis?
3. Is this analysis sufficient for segment reporting or will you need additional analyses?
4. Create additional analyses of results by year.

PAC 8.4 Tax Accounting: Interpret Descriptive and Diagnostic Analytics

Data **Tax Accounting** KneeCap's management would like to identify potential opportunities for cost savings. One aspect of purchasing costs that management has not yet considered is sales tax paid on purchases. Management has requested an analysis of sales tax paid by site. As a staff tax accountant for KneeCap, you have prepared the following trend analysis of sales tax paid by location:

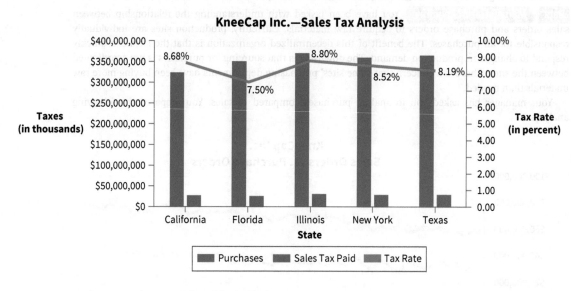

1. Prepare an interpretation of the analysis.
2. Is this analysis sufficient or will you need additional analyses?
3. Create additional analyses of results by year.

Communicating Data Analysis Results

CHAPTER PREVIEW The last step in the data analysis process is to explain the results of our analyses and their implications. Whether the goal is to inform or persuade, effectively communicating results is critical. If the intended audience does not understand the information, then it does not matter how well the analysis was performed.

Data analysis results can be communicated through memos, reports, or oral presentations, to name a few methods. Regardless of the form of communication, analyses must be supported using data visualizations, data stories, or interactive data visualizations. This chapter focuses on best practices for the common forms of data analysis communication you will encounter in your accounting career, including preparing effective data visualizations (both static and interactive) and creating data stories.

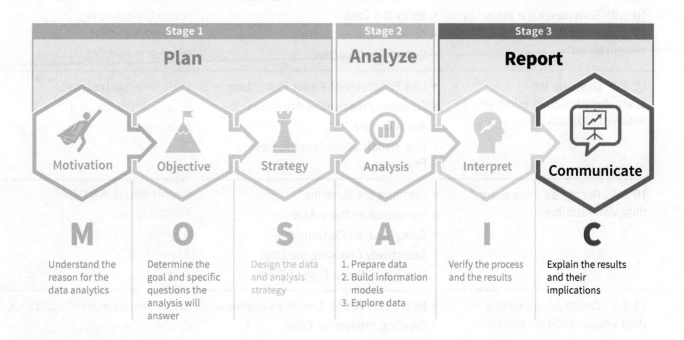

Stage 1			Stage 2	Stage 3	
Plan			**Analyze**	**Report**	
Motivation	Objective	Strategy	Analysis	Interpret	Communicate
M	**O**	**S**	**A**	**I**	**C**
Understand the reason for the data analytics	Determine the goal and specific questions the analysis will answer	Design the data and analysis strategy	1. Prepare data 2. Build information models 3. Explore data	Verify the process and the results	Explain the results and their implications

Can Data Visualization Knowledge Distinguish You from the Crowd?

Jenna is a senior accounting student who recently finished an audit internship with a large international accounting firm.

One of my biggest takeaways was how much high-quality communication was valued by my internship firm. This was especially true when it came to communicating the results of data analyses.

I was the only intern on the audit client that had experience using data visualization software. I was able to create data visualizations for a presentation that the team prepared for the client. As a result, I was invited to attend the presentation. Being involved in the client meeting allowed me to interact with the partner on the audit. **I believe it really helped me stand out from the other interns and is one of the reasons I was offered a full-time position.**

Chapter Roadmap

LEARNING OBJECTIVES	TOPICS	APPLY IT
LO 9.1 Explain how a data story communicates data analysis results.	• Develop Data Literacy • Communicate Effectively • Tell a Data Story	**Communicate Accounting Information** (Example: Financial Accounting)
LO 9.2 Summarize the steps for creating effective data visualizations.	• Verify the Data • Consider the Audience • Define the Objective	**Match Objectives to Visualization Types** (Example: Auditing)
LO 9.3 Describe the characteristics of an effective data visualization.	• Use Principles of Visual Perception • Consider Preattentive Attributes • Avoid Clutter • Use Visualization-Specific Best Practices	**Evaluate Visualizations** (Example: Managerial Accounting)
LO 9.4 Recognize misleading data visualizations.	• Omitting the Baseline • Manipulating the y-Axis • Going Against Conventions • Selectively Choosing the Data • Using the Wrong Type of Graph	**Identify Misleading Data Visualizations** (Example: Managerial Accounting)
LO 9.5 Create an interactive data visualization presentation.	• Best Practices for Live Presentations • Creating Interactive Data Visualizations	**Create an Interactive Visualization** (Example: Financial Accounting)

Data The Data tag appears in the chapter when the data for an example, illustration, or application are available in the book's product page on www.wiley.com.

Data analytics software is continuously changing, and there may be more recent versions of the software referenced in this chapter.

9.1 How Do We Tell a Data Story?

LEARNING OBJECTIVE ❶

Explain how a data story communicates data analysis results.

Finding valuable insights in data and then communicating them effectively is, in the words of Google's Chief Economist Hal Varian, a "hugely important skill."[1] This is particularly important for accountants who frequently communicate data analysis findings to a variety of stakeholders.

Develop Data Literacy

Effectively communicating these findings requires **data literacy**, which is the ability to understand and communicate data. Why is data literacy so important? A study by the data visualization software company Qlik and the consulting firm Accenture found that 63% of employees use data to make a decision at least once a week.[2] Further, another study by the consulting firm McKinsey & Company found that companies where employees consistently use data in decision-making were more likely to report revenue growth of more than 10% in the past three years.[3]

Data Let's use an example to illustrate data literacy. Imagine you are an accountant for Huskie Motor Corporation (HMC).[4] HMC is an international automobile manufacturer that produces and sells cars in 15 countries. The countries are grouped into three regions—Europe, North America, and South America (**Illustration 9.1**).

Europe	North America	South America
France	Canada	Argentina
Germany	Mexico	Bolivia
Poland	USA	Brazil
Spain		Chile
Sweden		Colombia
United Kingdom		Venezuela

ILLUSTRATION 9.1 Huskie Motor Corporation (HMC) International Operations

HMC has three brands of vehicles, and each brand has five unique models (**Illustration 9.2**).

	Brands		
	Apechete	**Jackson**	**Tatra**
	Chare	Brutus	Advantage
	Island	Crux	Bloom
Models	Pebble	Fiddle	Jespie
	Robin	Rebel	Mortimer
	Summet	Wood	Rambler

ILLUSTRATION 9.2 HMC Brands and Models

[1]McKinsey & Company. (2009). Hal Varian on How the Web Challenges Managers. https://www.mckinsey.com/industries/technology-media-and-telecommunications/our-insights/hal-varian-on-how-the-web-challenges-managers (accessed July 2022).

[2]Qlik and Accenture. (2020). The Human Impact of Data Literacy. Data Literacy Project. https://thedataliteracyproject.org/humanimpact (accessed July 2022).

[3]McKinsey. (2019). Catch Them If You Can: How Leaders in Data and Analytics have Pulled Ahead. https://www.mckinsey.com/business-functions/quantumblack/our-insights/catch-them-if-you-can-how-leaders-in-data-and-analytics-have-pulled-ahead (accessed July 2022).

[4]Ann C. Dzuranin, Johan Perols, and Dana L. Hart. (2018). "Huskie Motor Corporation: Visualizing the Present and Predicting the Future," *IMA Educational Case Journal*, Volume 11, Issue 2. ©2022, Institute of Management Accountants, www.imanet.org. Used with permission.

You have been asked to prepare an analysis of sales trends by month for each brand. **Illustration 9.3** provides sales information by brand for each month, but does it show what you need to understand about sales trends?

ILLUSTRATION 9.3 HMC Gross Sales by Brand

Gross Sales Trends by Brand: 2024–2025 (in $ millions)

	Apechete	Jackson	Tatra
January	$2.4M	$1.2M	$2.5M
February	$4.3M	$2.2M	$2.8M
March	$6.5M	$3.4M	$3.7M
April	$0.2M	$0.2M	$1.3M
May	$2.5M	$1.2M	$2.0M
June	$4.6M	$2.3M	$2.9M
July	$2.3M	$1.2M	$3.2M
August	$2.4M	$1.2M	$3.7M
September	$2.4M	$1.2M	$3.5M
October	$2.6M	$1.7M	$3.2M
November	$2.7M	$1.6M	$2.9M
December	$2.2M	$1.4M	$1.9M

Analyzing this table determines which months had the highest sales and which had the lowest. Preparing a line chart would accomplish the same thing (**Illustration 9.4**).

ILLUSTRATION 9.4 HMC Gross Sales Trends Line Chart

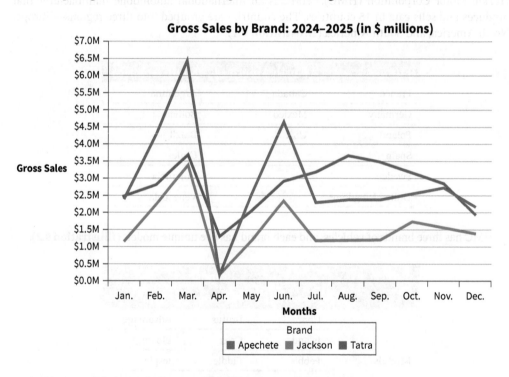

The chart in Illustration 9.4 more clearly shows the sales trends:

- March is the highest selling month, and April is the lowest selling month.
- Sales peak again in June for the Apechete and Jackson brands, then level off for the remainder of the year.
- The Tatra brand has increasing sales from April to August.

While the figures in Illustration 9.3 can be used to determine the sales trends, it is easier to do so with Illustration 9.4. Because data literacy skills are necessary for a successful accounting career, this chapter examines the data literacy skill of communicating data analysis results.

Communicate Effectively

The final step in the data analysis process is summarizing the project's findings and communicating them to the intended audience. This requires explaining the meaning of the data by writing memos or reports or preparing presentations that explain the data analysis results clearly and concisely. This is not easy, and it takes practice. Effectively reporting the results of data analysis requires being aware of the audience, focusing on the message, putting that message in context, and making sure it is clearly presented as an engaging story.

Understand the Audience

Have you ever attended a presentation where the presenter didn't provide enough background information for you to understand the topic? It is like walking into an advanced physics class when you have never taken a physics course. Understanding to whom we are communicating is critical. The audience (or reader) must be provided with enough background and explanation to follow the presentation.

Applying Critical Thinking 9.1

Identify the Audience

When communicating data analysis results, identifying the stakeholders of the analysis is an important first step. They are the audience to whom you are communicating (**Stakeholders**):

- Internal stakeholders will likely have some knowledge of what you are communicating.
- When communicating to external stakeholders, consider what information they will find most relevant and focus on that.

Knowing if the audience is comprised of internal or external stakeholders makes it possible to develop communication that is both relevant and understandable. In the HMC example, if the communication is for internal stakeholders such as company management, it is safe to assume they will have knowledge of the company's background. Whereas if the presentation was for external stakeholders such as investors, it should include more background information about the company.

Focus on the Message

Accountants are comfortable reading and interpreting numbers, so it is easy to focus solely on the numbers when communicating data analyses. However, an audience is likely more interested in the relationship between the numbers and the message. For example, if the objective of the analysis is to identify expense trends, ensure the communication explains the trends and does not only focus on the amounts.

Put It in Context

The third suggestion for communicating effectively is to put the data in **context**, or perspective. There are two aspects to context when communicating data analyses results:

1. The context of the overall purpose of the analysis. Is the purpose to inform or persuade the audience?
2. The context of the individual analyses. Are the analyses based on all the company data or just one department? Are the figures in whole dollars or in millions?

When communicating data analysis results, give the audience the information they need to understand the context of the analysis. We will discuss other aspects of context throughout this chapter.

Strive for Clarity

The fourth suggestion for effective data analysis communication is to make sure the communication is easy to understand. Do this by clearly explaining the data and the results in the narrative of the communication and including effective visualizations. The last suggestion for effective communication is to engage the audience with a memorable story.

Tell a Data Story

People have communicated knowledge and information using stories for thousands of years—they are an integral part of human communication. In fact, the human mind is wired to absorb stories. Research has shown that when we hear or read a story our brains are activated. The emotional part of the brain releases chemicals to stimulate feelings of connection, reward, and recognition.[5] In other words, a story creates both a physical and emotional response. Research has also shown that facts are up to 22% more memorable when they are part of a story.[6] So, how can storytelling help communicate the results of data analysis?

Data Story Elements

There are three elements to a data story—data, narrative, and visuals (**Illustration 9.5**).

ILLUSTRATION 9.5 Elements of Effective Storytelling

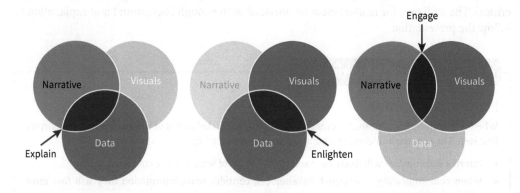

The author of *Effective Data Storytelling*, Brent Dykes, describes how these elements combine to explain, enlighten, and engage the audience:[7]

- The intersection of data and narrative explains the data story. The story's narrative provides the context and commentary needed to understand the results of the analysis. It provides structure to the data and guides the reader through the meaning of the analysis.
- Data also intersects with visuals to enlighten the reader with insights. Visualizing the data reveals patterns or trends that may have gone unnoticed without the help of visualizations. In fact, humans process visual images 60,000 times faster than text.[8]
- Finally, combining narrative with visuals engages the audience in the story. A good story can hold the attention of the reader and increases the likelihood of action.

In addition to including these three elements, a good data story must be structured effectively.

Data Story Structure

Most stories have a similar structure. They introduce the characters and set the scene, then a series of events build to the most climatic or important point of the story. Following the climax of the story, the rest of the events unravel until conflicts are resolved and the story concludes.

This structure is called Freytag's pyramid, also sometimes referred to as a storytelling arc (**Illustration 9.6**). The pyramid was developed by the German playwright and novelist Gustav Freytag to understand the structure of Greek and Shakespearian drama. It is one of the most taught dramatic structures in the world.

[5]Rutledge, P. (2011). The Psychological Power of Storytelling. *Psychology Today*. https://www.psychologytoday.com/us/blog/positively-media/201101/the-psychological-power-storytelling (accessed July 2022).

[6]Harrison, K. (2015). A Good Presentation Is About Data and Story. *Forbes*. https://www.forbes.com/sites/kateharrison/2015/01/20/a-good-presentation-is-about-data-and-story/#1f9a2f54450f (accessed July 2022).

[7]Dykes, B. (2020). *Effective Storytelling: How to Drive Change with Data, Narrative, and Visuals*. Hoboken, NJ: Wiley.

[8]Thermopylae Sciences and Technology. (2014). Humans Process Visual Data Better. https://www.t-sciences.com/news/humans-process-visual-data-better (accessed July 2022).

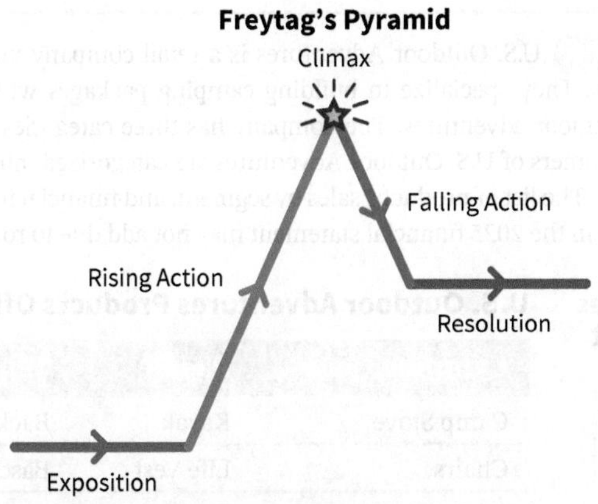

Freytag's Pyramid

ILLUSTRATION 9.6 Freytag's Pyramid[9]

Freytag's pyramid can be applied to data storytelling using the HMC example:

- The audit team received an anonymous tip that one of the purchasing managers was receiving kickbacks from vendors.
- The team prepared an analysis investigating potential kickback fraud in the purchasing department. They identified the location of the possible kickback activity and the employee and vendors potentially involved.

If you were on the audit team, you would now be ready to create a story using the data analyses prepared in the audit of the purchasing department. **Illustration 9.7** provides an example of how to adapt the Freytag pyramid to a data story.

ILLUSTRATION 9.7 Anatomy of a Data Story

Freytag's Pyramid	Data Story Application	Kickback Analysis Example
Exposition	Introduce the problem or issue.	Briefly discuss the background information relevant to the analysis. Include interesting details to engage the reader's attention. Example: "Is kickback fraud occurring in the Purchasing Department? Based on an anonymous tip, we took a closer look at the purchasing department."
Rising Action	The subject of the analysis is explored at a deeper level.	In this part of the story, methodically peel back layers of the kickback analyses.
Climax	The main finding or insight is shared. This is the "aha moment" of the story.	After building the case in the previous section, announce the suspected employee(s) and vendor(s).
Falling Action	Share the solution.	Identifying a suspected employee and vendor does not prove kickback fraud has occurred. Next, provide more details and recommendations as to specific transactions that should be investigated further.
Resolution	Conclude the story and provide next steps.	Make suggestions for additional internal controls to avoid future kickback fraud.

Following the storytelling arc described in Illustration 9.7 is a simple and effective way to structure a data story. Once the structure is set, the elements of a story (data, narrative, and visuals) can be applied to bring the data story to life.

[9]Glatch, S. (2020). The 5 Elements of Dramatic Structure: Understanding Freytag's Pyramid. Writers.com. https://writers.com/freytags-pyramid (accessed July 2022).

APPLY IT 9.1

Communicate Accounting Information

Data **Financial Accounting** U.S. Outdoor Adventures is a retail company that sells camping travel supplies in the United States. They specialize in building camping packages with all the supplies customers will need for their outdoor adventures. The company has three categories of products: Camping Gear, Paddle, and Tents. Customers of U.S. Outdoor Adventures are categorized into segments: Consumer, Corporate, and Travel Agency. The list of products, sales by segment, and financial information for 2025 are provided. (*Note*: the numbers in the 2025 financial statement may not add due to rounding.)

U.S. Outdoor Adventures 2025 Sales by Segment

Segment	Total Sales
Consumer	$ 512,711
Corporate	$ 359,264
Travel Agency	$ 232,095
Grand Total	**$ 1,104,070**

U.S. Outdoor Adventures Products Offered

Camping Gear	Paddle	Tents
Camp Stove	Kayak	Backpacking Tent
Chairs	Life Vest	Base Camp Model
Cook Set	Paddle Board	Mountain Tent—4 Person
Fasteners	Paddles	Northface Subzero
Firestarter Kit		
First Aid Kit		
Micro Cooking Unit		
Propane Portable Grill		
Sleeping Bag		

U.S. Outdoor Adventures 2025 Financial Information

	Camping Gear	Paddle	Tents	Total
Sales	$ 321,964	$ 243,580	$ 538,526	$1,104,070
Discount	$ 34,170	$ 40,030	$ 96,864	$ 171,063
Net Sales	$ 287,794	$ 203,550	$ 441,663	$ 933,006
Cost of Goods Sold	$ 114,903	$ 87,682	$ 193,681	$ 396,265
Shipping Cost	$ 36,900	$ 31,066	$ 64,646	$ 132,611
Profit	$ 135,992	$ 84,802	$ 183,336	$ 404,130

The company would like to expand their business internationally, but they must raise additional capital to do so. If you were tasked with presenting this information to a group of potential investors, describe why each of the following are important to consider and give an example of each related to U.S. Outdoor Adventures:

1. Identify the audience.
2. Focus on the message, not the numbers.
3. Put the data in context.
4. Make it easy to understand.
5. Create a memorable story.

SOLUTION

1. Provide enough background and explanation so the audience can follow the presentation. In this case, potential investors are the audience. They will likely understand the numbers but may need additional background about the business.

2. This audience probably wants to know how the numbers relate to the message being communicated, which is how likely the business is to be successful internationally.

3. First, there is the context of the overall objective of the analysis, which is to attract investment into the company. There is also the context of the individual analyses. These include the company's customers, the products they sell, and their current profits. Finally, there is the context of how the company compares to its competitors.

4. Clearly explain the data and the results. Make communication easy to understand by using effective visualizations. In this example, it may make sense to create visuals other than the tables.

5. Engaging the audience with a data story makes it easier for the reader to remember the results. The story in this example could focus on U.S. Outdoor Adventures' prior success and how investing in an international expansion will build on that success.

9.2 What Are the Steps for Creating Effective Data Visualizations?

LEARNING OBJECTIVE ❷
Summarize the steps for creating effective data visualizations.

Data visualization is the process of displaying data to provide meaning and insights for the audience. A well-designed visualization conveys the results of an analysis clearly and concisely. **Illustration 9.8** is a visualization Ford Motor Company used in their presentation of third quarter 2021 results to investors.

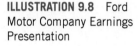

ILLUSTRATION 9.8   Ford Motor Company Earnings Presentation

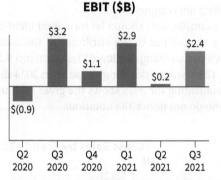

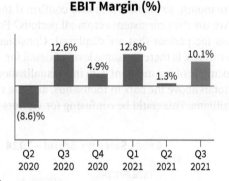

Source: Ford, Q3 2021 Earnings Review, October 27, 2021.

As an overview of Ford's North America performance, this illustration is an example of a well-designed visualization. It combines information about the number of vehicles sold (wholesale units), revenue generated from those sales (revenue), earnings before interest and taxes on those sales (EBIT), and the percent profit margin of earnings before interest and taxes (EBIT Margin %). Note the color differentiation of the third quarter data. By using a different color for Q3 2021, the objective of the visualization (to convey third quarter 2021 results) is immediately clear. Creating well-designed visualizations like this starts with verifying the data, considering the audience, and defining the objective of the analysis.

Verify the Data

The saying "garbage in, garbage out" is as relevant to data analysis communication as it is to performing data analyses. Incorrect data leads to incorrect visualizations. To avoid this, data should have the attributes of accuracy, completeness, consistency, freshness, and timeliness.

Accurate Data

Accurate data are free from errors. They are reliable and representative of the problem or issue being visualized. Imagine preparing information for the shareholders of the fictitious HMC company. The goal is to provide information about monthly sales in 2025 for each brand. The data provided in **Illustration 9.9** are representative of 2025 sales performance of the Apechete brand. If the data are confirmed to be free of error, then they are also reliable.

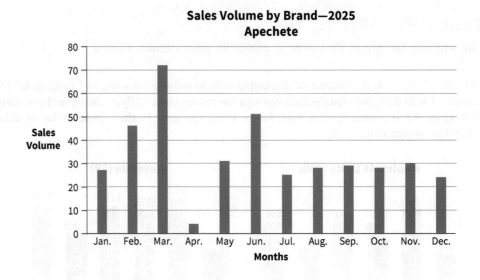

Complete and Consistent Data

Data are complete when there are no missing data. Illustration 9.9 shows monthly sales volume, but it is missing data for the month of April. It would be unusual to have only four sales for the entire month, so the next step is to confirm if the data are complete.

Are the data consistent across all periods? For example, data should be formatted identically across the periods that are displayed. Consistency also relates to the attributes of the data. In other words, is there the same level of detail for each period being displayed? **Illustration 9.10** is an example of inconsistent data in a visualization. The visualization for gross sales in 2024 shows the totals above the bars in thousands, and the visualization for 2025 shows the gross sales totals in millions. This could be confusing for viewers who do not notice the notations.

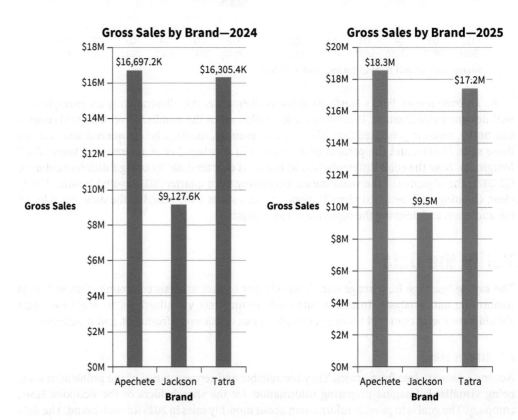

Fresh and Timely Data

Data is considered fresh if they are the most recent data available. Avoid using outdated data in visualizations. Consider the earnings presentation in Illustration 9.8. If Ford had used data from the second quarter in their third quarter presentation, investors would not have useful information about third quarter results.

Data are considered timely when they are available in time to be used for a visualization. When designing a visualization, ensure that the targeted data are available so that the visualization is fresh.

Consider the Audience

After verifying the data, consider who will be viewing the visualization. Audiences can be separated into four categories (**Illustration 9.11**).[10]

Category	Description	What They Want
Novice	Has never encountered the information.	Enough detail to gain understanding.
Managerial	Has some knowledge of the topic.	Actionable results.
Expert	Has deep knowledge of the topic.	Investigation and discovery.
Executive	Has a broad, high-level knowledge of the topic.	Only the most important insights.

ILLUSTRATION 9.11 Types of Audiences

Novice Audiences

A novice audience, which can be internal or external to the organization, needs enough background information to understand the results. An analysis for an external client or one presented to an internal department unfamiliar with the topic would both have novice audiences. **Illustration 9.12** is an example of the type of visualization that might be used to explain sales trends to a novice audience.

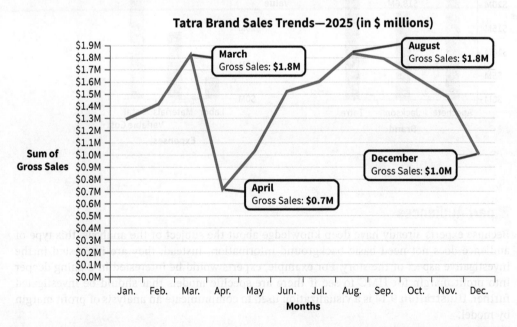

Tatra Brand Sales Trends—2025 (in $ millions)

ILLUSTRATION 9.12
Visualization Sample for a Novice Audience

The visualization is clearly labeled to show the viewer the highest and lowest months of sales.

---

[10]Stikeleather, J. (2013). How to Tell a Story with Data. *Harvard Business Review*. https://hbr.org/2013/04/how-to-tell-a-story-with-data (accessed July 2022).

Managerial Audiences

How To

A managerial audience generally has some knowledge of the topic, so detailed background information may be unnecessary. However, this audience is looking for actionable results, so the visualization should include recommendations for actions based on the results.

The dashboard in **Illustration 9.13** communicates to the managers profit margin as well as gross sales and cost analysis. (**Data** **How To 9.1** at the end of the chapter explains how to create this dashboard in Tableau.) The filters for year sold and brand let the managers customize the visual by year and brand. It provides quick, actionable information.

ILLUSTRATION 9.13 Performance Dashboard Sample for a Managerial Audience

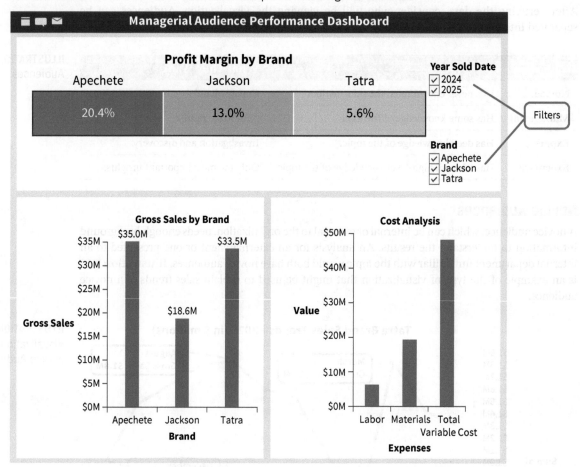

Expert Audiences

Because experts already have deep knowledge about the subject of the analysis, this type of audience does not need basic background information. Instead, they are interested in the investigative aspect of the story. For example, experts would be interested in digging deeper into profit margin for HMC to see if there are specific models that should be investigated further. **Illustration 9.14** is a visualization used to communicate an analysis of profit margin by model.

ILLUSTRATION 9.14 Sample Visualization for an Expert Audience

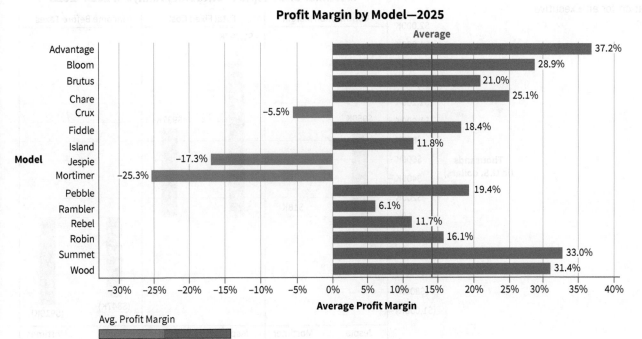

This illustration provides detailed information about each model's profit margin as compared to the average profit margin for all HMC models. The models with negative profit margin are clearly identified by the orange bars. From here the expert can determine which model to investigate further.

Applying Critical Thinking 9.2

Give the Audience the Information They Need

It is easy to lose the audience's attention if they lack background knowledge or information necessary to interpret and understand data analysis results (**Knowledge**):

- Consider what information is necessary to understand the message being communicated.
- Include background necessary for the audience to understand the analysis.

For the HMC analysis prepared in Illustration 9.15, the audience are executives, so they understand how to use contribution margin, total fixed costs, and income before taxes to decide whether to discontinue a product. Therefore, they do not need detailed information about how to interpret those figures.

Executive Audiences

An audience composed of executives will be interested in only the most important insights. Discuss the important insights first, then discuss the support for those insights. **Illustration 9.15** is a visualization that might be used when communicating to an audience of executives who want details about the two least profitable models, which are Mortimer and Jespie.

Illustration 9.15 shows the contribution margin, total fixed costs, and income before taxes for each model. If the decision being made is whether to discontinue the models, this visual communicates information relevant to that decision. Specifically, it shows how much contribution margin would be lost and the impact of fixed costs on the decision. Executives would need to determine if the fixed costs are avoidable when the models are discontinued.

ILLUSTRATION 9.15 Sample Visualization for an Executive Audience

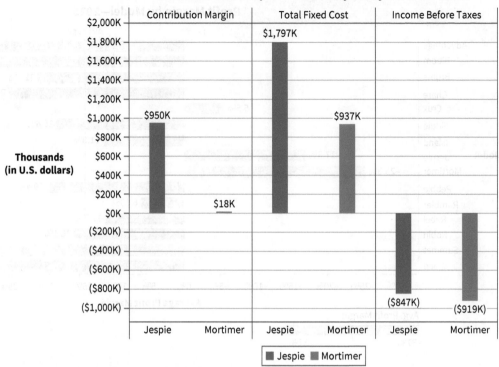

Mortimer and Jespie Profitability Analysis: 2024–2025

Applying Critical Thinking 9.3

Address the Objective

It is common to prepare many visualizations in the process of performing your analysis. When you decide which visuals to use in presentations, stay focused on the purpose of the analysis (**Purpose**). This helps exclude visuals that are not related to the original objective of the analysis.

The purpose of the HMC analysis is to evaluate how the various brands are performing. Remain focused on that objective while preparing the presentation. For example, if the purpose is to compare the performance of five categories, choose a column chart rather than an area chart.

Define the Objective

Once data are verified and the audience has been considered, the next step is to understand the objective of the analysis, or the question/issue to be addressed in the visualization. The objective of the analysis helps determine the types of visualizations that are appropriate. It might be to show composition, relationships, distributions, trends, or comparisons of the data (**Illustration 9.16**).

ILLUSTRATION 9.16 Visualization Objectives

Objective	Explanation	Example
Composition	Show how part of the data compares to the whole.	How much revenue has each region contributed to total revenue?
Relationships	Show how the data are related.	Is there a relationship between machine hours and maintenance expense?
Distributions	Reveal how data are spread out or grouped.	Are there transactions that might be considered outliers?
Trends	Display patterns in the data.	Is there a seasonal pattern in revenue?
Comparisons	Compare values between groups of data.	How does the revenue for 2024 compare to 2025 by product?

Once the objective of the data analysis communication is identified, choose the visualization that will best convey the message. **Illustration 9.17** is a decision tree for selecting a visualization if the objective is to show composition, relationships, or distributions.

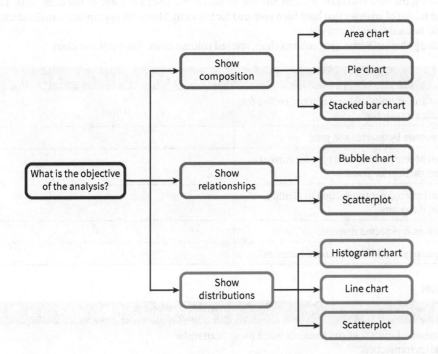

ILLUSTRATION 9.17
Visualization Decision Tree for Showing Composition, Relationships, and Distributions

Illustration 9.18 provides guidance when the objective is to show trends or comparisons.

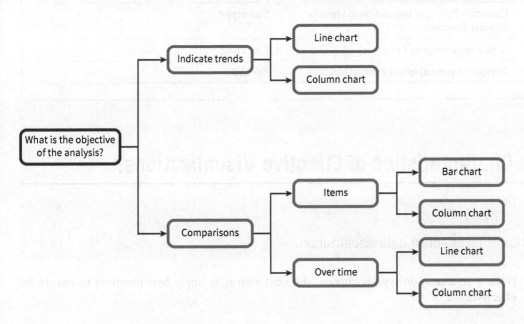

ILLUSTRATION 9.18
Visualization Decision Tree for Showing Trends or Comparisons

Next, we discuss best practices for creating visualizations.

APPLY IT 9.2

Match Objectives to Visualization Types

Auditing You have been assigned to the audit team for U.S. Outdoor Adventures. You are responsible for preparing the data visualizations that will communicate the results of some of the audit tests. The following is a list of analyses that have been prepared for the audit. Match the appropriate visualization(s) that could be used for each analysis.

Matching choices: Scatterplot, column chart, stacked column chart, line chart, bar chart

Audit Test	Possible Visualization
Comparison of units sold and amounts billed for every sales transaction.	
Sales revenue by quarter and year.	
Number of tents sold by tent type for current year and three prior years.	
Discount offered per transaction to identify unusual discounts.	
Actual versus expected revenue.	
Changes in general ledger account balances.	

SOLUTION

Audit Test	Possible Visualization
Comparison of units sold and amounts billed for every sales transaction.	Scatterplot
Sales revenue by quarter and year.	Column chart or stacked column chart
Number of tents sold by tent type for current year and three prior years.	Stacked column chart or separate line charts for each product
Discount offered per transaction to identify unusual discounts.	Scatterplot
Actual versus expected revenue.	Line chart
Changes in general ledger account balances.	Bar chart

9.3 What Are the Characteristics of Effective Visualizations?

LEARNING OBJECTIVE ❸
Describe the characteristics of an effective data visualization.

Once a visualization type is chosen, the next step is to apply best practices to ensure its effectiveness.

Use Principles of Visual Perception

The human brain prefers simplicity and order in visual images because it prevents us from becoming overwhelmed with information. We can process simple patterns faster than complex patterns. Gestalt is an area of psychology that was the foundation for the modern study of perception.

Gestalt principles of visual perception describe how humans gain meaning from the stimuli around them. These principles address the natural need for humans to find order. We can create effective visualizations by considering relevant principles such as continuity, similarity, proximity, and focal point.

Continuity

The **law of continuity** refers to how people tend to perceive any line as continuing in its established direction and how objects aligned with each other are perceived as a single path or shape. We follow lines, curves, or a sequence of shapes to determine if there is a relationship between the elements. Effective data visualizations will arrange visual objects in a line to simplify grouping and comparison. **Illustration 9.19** shows gross sales by model for HMC sales in the United Kingdom.

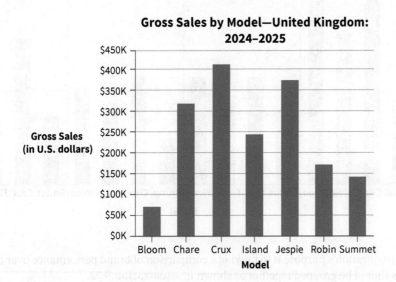

ILLUSTRATION 9.19   Gross Sales by Model—United Kingdom

The bars in this chart are in alphabetical order, an organization that makes it difficult for the viewer to compare the models. In contrast, **Illustration 9.20** shows the bars in descending order by gross sales. Illustration 9.20 is a more readable chart because the viewers' eyes follow a continuous path. The viewer can easily see which are the highest selling and lowest selling models.

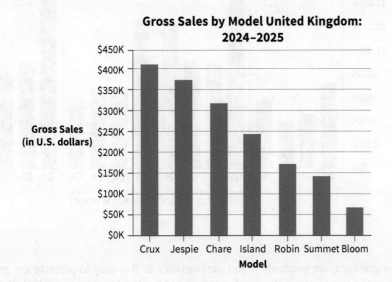

ILLUSTRATION 9.20   Gross Sales by Model Sorted in Descending Order

Now we can compare quarterly performance as it is easy to perceive the grouping by brand. Using the law of similarity can help viewers identify the groups to which the displayed data belong.

Similarity

The **law of similarity** states that similar elements tend to be perceived as a unified group. Items similar in color, shape, size, or location evoke the perception that they belong to the same group. **Illustration 9.21** is a bar chart showing sales by quarter for four HMC car models. This chart makes it easy to compare the brands within each quarter, but it is difficult to compare the sales of the individual brands over time.

ILLUSTRATION 9.21 Quarterly Sales by Model

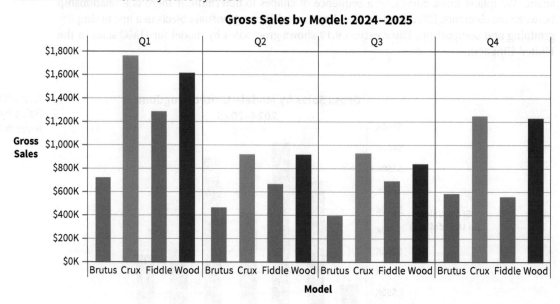

If the visualization's purpose is to provide a comparison of brand performance over time, then the brands should be grouped together as shown in **Illustration 9.22**.

ILLUSTRATION 9.22 Quarterly Sales by Model (Revised)

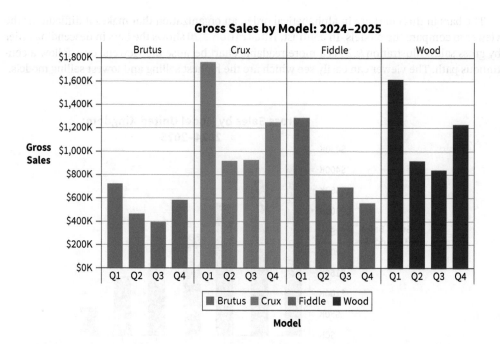

Now we can compare quarterly brand performance as it is easy to perceive the grouping by brand. Using the law of similarity can help viewers identify the groups to which the displayed data belong.

Proximity

The **law of proximity** states that people will perceive visual elements based on how closely they are positioned to one another. Each point in the scatterplot in **Illustration 9.23** is an individual sale. It is obvious that there are two groupings of sales:

1. Sales between $70,000 and $85,000.
2. Sales between $11,000 and $55,000.

ILLUSTRATION 9.23   Gross Sale Amount by Transaction

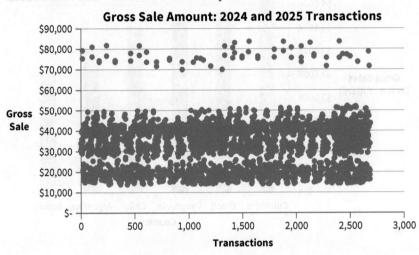

The law of proximity helps a viewer make sense of a large set of data very quickly.

Focal Point

The **law of focal point** refers to how we are more attentive to whatever stands out visually. The focal point tends to be the starting point for the viewer. Illustrations 9.21 and 9.22 are examples of the focal point principle. Imagine you have prepared an analysis of HMC sales in Venezuela. You begin your presentation with an overview of sales for all the South America countries shown in **Illustration 9.24**.

ILLUSTRATION 9.24   Sales Performance in Venezuela

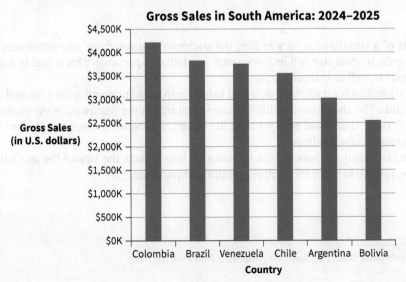

You have followed the law of continuity by sorting the bars from highest to lowest. However, you can improve this visual by highlighting the country you want your viewers to focus on (**Illustration 9.25**).

ILLUSTRATION 9.25 Sales Performance Graph with Focal Point

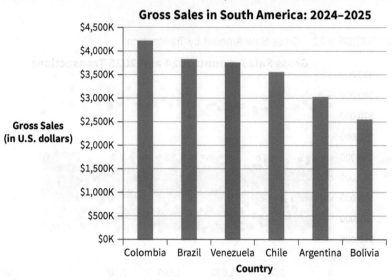

Illustration 9.25 still provides the information about the other South American countries, but using a different color for Venezuela focuses the viewers' attention on that country.

Consider Preattentive Attributes

Gestalt principles help create visualizations that are easily consumed by viewers. But how do we capture their attention? Studies have shown that someone will decide within three to eight seconds whether to continue looking at a visualization or turning their attention to something else.[11] **Preattentive attributes** are visual properties we notice without realizing it. Size, color, and position are preattentive attributes in visualizations that can direct the audience's attention.

Size

If elements of a visualization vary in size, the audience assumes those size differences matter. In other words, relative size will be interpreted as relative importance. This is true in individual visualizations as well as in dashboards.

Illustration 9.26 is a dashboard designed to help management monitor the sales and revenue of their brands. The visualization with the largest font size in the dashboard is the profit margin by brand. Because this visual is larger than the others, the viewer focuses on it before viewing gross sales and the cost analysis.

While a visualization's relative size indicates its importance, the size of the text within the illustration, relative to other text, will also indicate importance.

---

[11]Knaflic Nussbaumer, C. (2015). *Storytelling with Data*. Hoboken, NJ: Wiley.

ILLUSTRATION 9.26 Profit Margin by Brand Dashboard

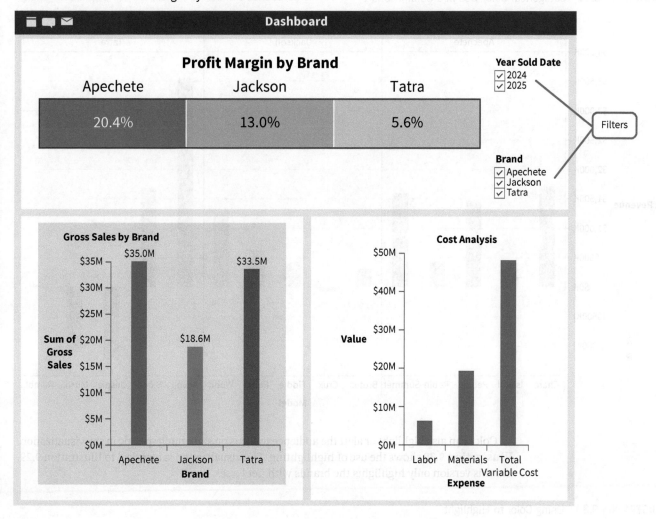

Color

As you learned in the discussion of Gestalt principles, color can make visualizations more effective. There are three ways to use color in visualizations:

1. **Sequential:** Color is ordered from low to high (**Illustration 9.27**).

ILLUSTRATION 9.27
Sequential Color Scale

2. **Diverging:** There are two sequential colors with a neutral midpoint (**Illustration 9.28**). This type of scale is useful for showing gains and losses.

ILLUSTRATION 9.28   Diverging
Color Scale

3. **Categorical:** There are contrasting colors for individual comparison. This is a common use for color when comparing categories. **Illustration 9.29** shows how contrasting colors can be used in a column chart.

ILLUSTRATION 9.29   Categorical Color Use in a Column Chart

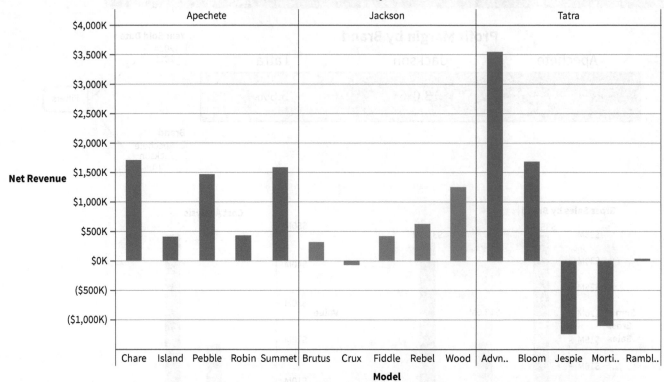

Color can also highlight or alert the audience to focus on something specific in the visualization. **Illustration 9.30** shows the use of highlighting. The visualization is identical to Illustration 9.29, but this version only highlights the brands with net losses.

ILLUSTRATION 9.30   Using Color to Highlight

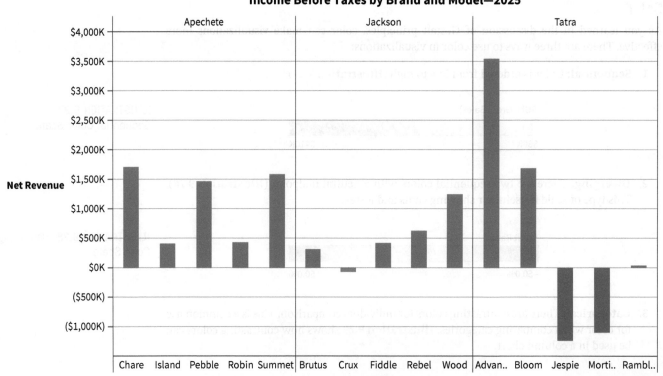

Highlighting the brands with net losses and making all the other bars fade out encourages the audience to immediately focus on the darker bars. Using color this way is also another example of applying Focal Point Law.

What if the intention is to grab the audience's attention and alert them to an issue or problem? **Illustration 9.31** changes the color of the losses in Illustration 9.30 to convey a sense of urgency.

ILLUSTRATION 9.31   Using Color to Alert the Viewer

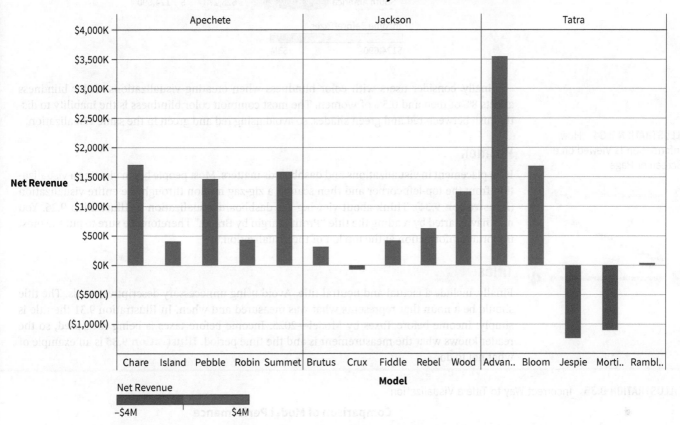

Income Before Taxes by Brand and Model—2025

Color evokes emotion, so be thoughtful of the tone conveyed by the color. For example, red evokes a sense of urgency. In visuals with financial information, red is also an indication of poor performance. By highlighting the models with negative net revenue (Illustration 9.31), the viewer can quickly see that Crux, Jespie, and Mortimer are losing money. Regardless of its tone, color should be used both consistently and sparingly:

- If the visualization includes color, variables should be indicated by the same color to avoid confusion.
- Interpreting too many colors can overwhelm the audience, so only add color that makes it easier to interpret the visualization.

Illustrations 9.32 visualizes net revenue by region using multiple colors in a diverging color scale.

Income Before Taxes by Region			
Region	**Apechete**	**Jackson**	**Tatra**
Europe	$ 1,246,353	$ 1,010,446	$ 136,006
North America	$ 2,013,345	$ 963,145	$ 2,719,779
South America	$ 2,372,282	$ 625,278	$ 124,690

Net Revenue

$124,690 $3M

ILLUSTRATION 9.32
Visualization with Too Much Color

Due to the additional cognitive load created by the colors, interpreting the table is more difficult. The viewer must interpret the numbers, regions, brands, and seven different colors to understand the table.

On the other hand, the single-color gradient scale in **Illustration 9.33** makes it easier for the audience to quickly see that the Tatra in North America has the highest net revenue.

ILLUSTRATION 9.33 Revised Visualization Using a Single-Color Gradient Scale

Income Before Taxes by Region

Region	Apechete	Jackson	Tatra
Europe	$ 1,246,353	$ 1,010,446	$ 136,006
North America	$ 2,013,345	$ 963,145	$ 2,719,779
South America	$ 2,372,282	$ 625,278	$ 124,690

Income Before Taxes

$124,690 $3M

Finally, consider users with color blindness when creating visualizations. Color blindness affects 8% of men and 0.5% of women. The most common color blindness is the inability to distinguish between red and green shades, so avoid using red and green in the same visualization.

ILLUSTRATION 9.34 How Information Is Viewed on a Screen or Page

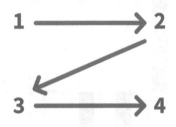

Position

Item placement in visualizations and dashboards matters. Most people begin viewing a visualization from the top-left corner and then scan in a zig-zag motion through the entire visualization (**Illustration 9.34**). Think about viewing the dashboard visualization in Illustration 9.26. You may have started by reading the title "Profit Margin by Brand." Therefore, be sure to put the most important information at the top left of the visualization.

Titles

Finally, include a factual and neutral title. Avoid using unnecessary descriptive words. The title should be a noun that represents what was measured and when. In Illustration 9.31 the title is simply: Income before Taxes by Model—2025. Income before taxes is being measured, so the reader knows what the measurement is and the time period. **Illustration 9.35** is an example of what not to do.

ILLUSTRATION 9.35 Incorrect Way to Title a Visualization

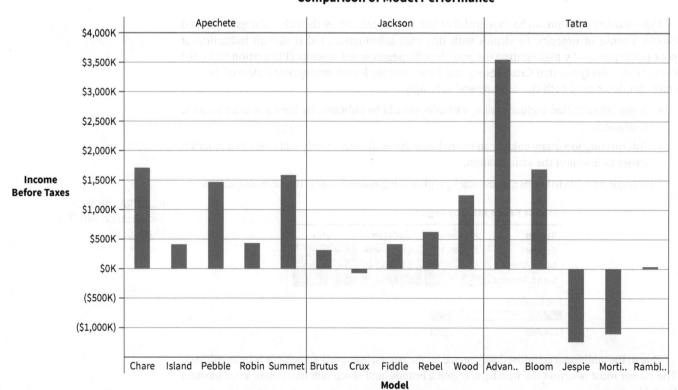

The title of the visual does not give the reader a clear description of what is being measured (income before taxes by model) or the time period represented (2025). A better title would be: "Income Before Taxes by Model—2025."

Avoid Clutter

After considering principles of perception and preattentive attributes, consider visual clutter in visualizations. Clutter is the enemy of a good visualization. The more cluttered the visualization, the harder it is for the viewer to understand the results. Remove any nondata-related details from the visualization and check for redundant information. The purpose of **Illustration 9.36** is to show gross sales for each model produced under the Jackson Brand and identify the bestselling model.

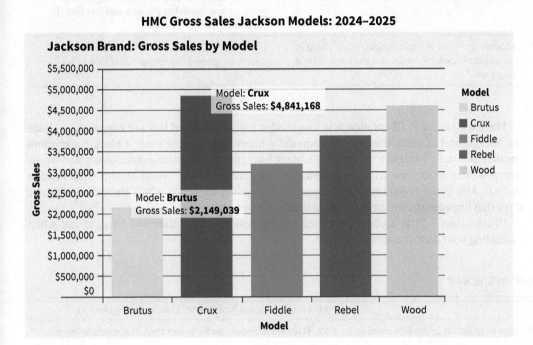

ILLUSTRATION 9.36
Visualization Containing
Clutter

The visual does show sales for the Jackson brand models. However, there are so many elements that the viewer could become overwhelmed. **Illustration 9.37** uses the same data but removes the unnecessary aspects of the visualization.

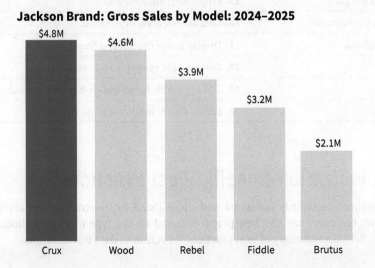

ILLUSTRATION 9.37 Revised
Visualization with Clutter
Removed

Recall that the purpose of the visualization was to show how the various models are performing for the Jackson brand. The changes are summarized in **Illustration 9.38**.

ILLUSTRATION 9.38 Summary: Before and After Reducing Visualization Clutter

Cluttered Visualization	Revised Visualization
Too many colors are not adding to the meaning of the graph because the models are also directly labeled.	The visual is a single color.
Axis labels are provided, but the audience must guess the exact amount.	Label each bar directly with the sales volume amount and remove the axis. Sales volume is in the title of the graph, so remove the axis header.
Annotation text boxes identify the bestselling model.	Sort the data from highest to lowest.
Background color of the graph is unnecessary.	Remove background color. Remove gridlines since we are removing the axis and labeling the columns directly.
Models are listed in alphabetical order. There is no indication which model the audience should focus on.	The bestselling model is highlighted and the others are grayed out to draw attention to it.

The background in Illustration 9.36 was shaded a gray color, but it is not necessary to shade the background of visualizations. It is especially important to avoid using a black background because although it might look striking, a black background can make lighter colors and words appear blurry to anyone with an astigmatism. According to the World Health Organization (WHO), 43% of the population have astigmatism, a visual condition where there is a refractive error that impedes the eye from focusing light evenly on the retina.

Illustration 9.39 is a checklist, based on the best practices discussed here, to use when evaluating your data visualizations.

ILLUSTRATION 9.39 Data Visualization Checklist

1. Data have been verified.	**11.** Graph does not have border line (reducing clutter).
2. Visualization addresses the objective or question being addressed in the analysis.	**12.** Data are labeled directly rather than in a separate legend.
3. It is appropriate for the intended audience.	**13.** Redundant labels are removed.
4. The type of visual is appropriate for the data and the level of precision needed.	**14.** y-axis scales start at zero.
5. A descriptive title is left-justified in the upper left corner.	**15.** Proportions are accurate.
6. Subtitle and/or annotations provide additional information.	**16.** Data are intentionally ordered.
7. Significant findings or conclusions are highlighted.	**17.** Display is free from distractions.
8. Text size is hierarchical and readable.	**18.** Color is used sparingly and consistently.
9. Text is horizontal when possible.	**19.** Color is legible for people with color blindness.
10. Gridlines, if used, are muted.	**20.** Spatial flow is intuitive for the viewer.

Use Visualization-Specific Best Practices

The best practices previously discussed and those listed in Illustration 9.39 are an essential starting point, but there are also best practices based on the type of visualization to consider. **Illustration 9.40** is a summary of best practices for common data visualizations.

Visualization	Best Practices
Area Chart 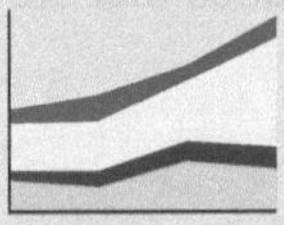	• Do not use with more than four categories to avoid confusion and clutter. • Start the y-axis at zero. • Put highly variable data on the top and data with low variability on the bottom.
Bar Chart 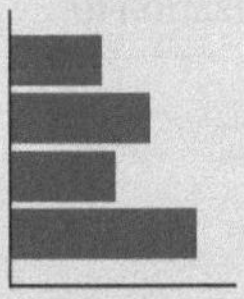 Column Chart 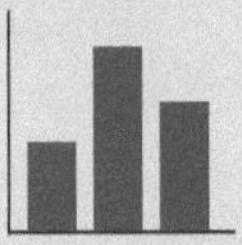	• Use horizontal bars if there are more than seven categories or long category labels. • Use horizontal labels for better readability. • Space bars appropriately and consistently. • Use color sparingly, or as an accent. • Always have a zero baseline (the y-axis begins at zero). • Compare 2–7 categories with vertical columns.
Bubble Chart 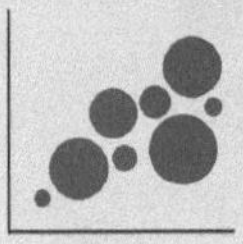	• Label bubbles and make sure they are visible. • Scale bubble size by area and not diameter. • Do not use bubbles if they are all similar in size.

Histogram Chart 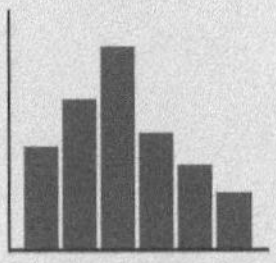	• Use a zero baseline.
	• Choose an appropriate number of bins:
	  • Bins are numbers that represent the intervals into which the data will be grouped.
	  • Bins define the groups used for the frequency distribution.
	  • Generally, include between 5–15 bins.

Line Graph 	• Time runs from left to right. • Be consistent when plotting time points. • Use solid lines, not dotted. • Use a zero baseline. • Do not plot more than four lines. Use multiple charts, instead.
Pie Chart 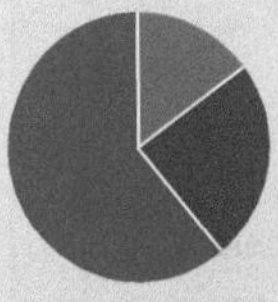	• Most impactful with small data sets. • Best to use when showing differences within groups based on one variable. • Ensure the data adds to 100%. • Limit the chart to a maximum of five segments. • Start the first segment at 12 o'clock position.
Stacked Bar Chart 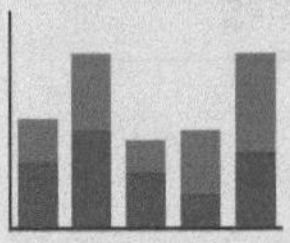	• Can be vertical or horizontal. • Follow same best practices as bar charts. • Used to show comparisons of subcomponents between categories. • Best used when there are not too many subcomponents. • Consider using a 100% stacked bar to make comparisons between the bars and subcomponents easier.
Scatter Chart 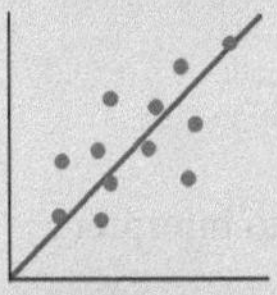	• Data set should be in pairs with an independent variable (x-axis) and a dependent variable (y-axis). • Use if order is not relevant—otherwise use a line graph. • Do not use if there are only a few pieces of data or if there is no correlation.
Tree Map 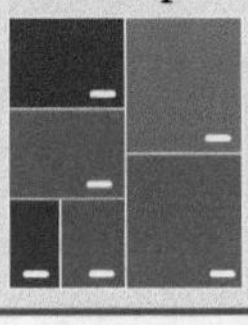	• Appropriate when precise comparisons are not important. • Use bright, contrasting colors so that each box is easily defined. • Label boxes with text or numbers.

ILLUSTRATION 9.40 Best Practices by Visualization Type

Applying best practices for each specific visualization, the principles of visual perception, and appropriately using preattentive attributes will help ensure you are creating a good visualization and communicating results effectively. Failing to do so can lead to visualizations that are misleading, which is the topic of the next section.

APPLY IT 9.3

Evaluate Visualizations

Data **Managerial Accounting** U.S. Outdoor Adventures has prepared the following visualization to help better understand which products are their bestselling products:

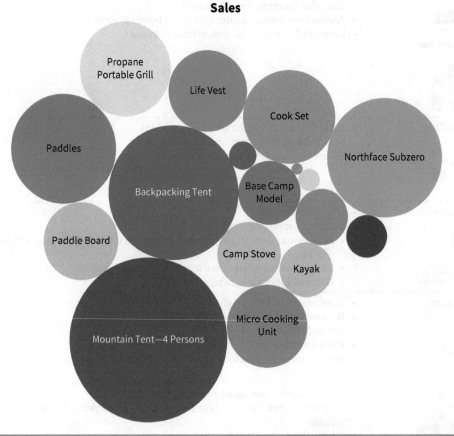

Sales

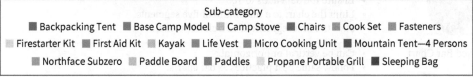

Sub-category
■ Backpacking Tent ■ Base Camp Model ■ Camp Stove ■ Chairs ■ Cook Set ■ Fasteners
■ Firestarter Kit ■ First Aid Kit ■ Kayak ■ Life Vest ■ Micro Cooking Unit ■ Mountain Tent—4 Persons
■ Northface Subzero ■ Paddle Board ■ Paddles ■ Propane Portable Grill ■ Sleeping Bag

1. Discuss the effectiveness of this visualization using the best practices for data visualizations.
2. Use the U.S. Outdoor Adventures data set to create an improved visualization.

SOLUTION

1. Some issues with the visualization include:
   - The title is not clear. It should be more specific and include dates from the data.
   - A bubble chart is not the correct choice. There are too many bubbles, and it is difficult to interpret the extent of the difference between the sub-categories.
   - The visualization uses too many colors.
   - There are no numbers or scale, so the sales in each sub-category are unclear.
   - It is unclear if the visualization is showing sales dollars or number of sales.

2. The suggested visualization has a clear title and sorts the products from highest selling to lowest. The scale is clearly indicated as net sales in thousands of dollars.

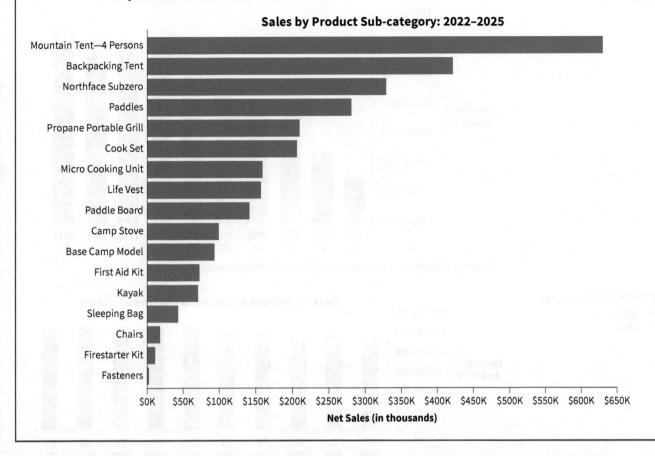

9.4 What Makes Data Visualizations Misleading?

LEARNING OBJECTIVE ❹
Recognize misleading data visualizations.

Ethics and data visualization are not best practices; the best practices of data visualization and ethics are intertwined. Because visualizations can significantly influence how data are used to make decisions, there is an ethical obligation to not mislead the viewer. Using best practices is the first step for mitigating the risk of creating a misleading data visualization. The second is developing an awareness of how visualizations can mislead to avoid making those mistakes. Visualizations may mislead by omitting the baseline, manipulating the *y*-axis, selectively picking the data, using the wrong type of graph, and going against conventions.

Omitting the Baseline

Illustration 9.41 is a visualization that was posted in a USA Today blog.

The data shows that there was an alarming increase in federal welfare spending. However, notice the starting point is 94 million, not zero. The same data is presented in **Illustration 9.42** with a zero baseline.

Notice the difference between the two visualizations? The increase in welfare spending does not seem nearly as dramatic. Always graph data with a zero baseline to avoid misleading the audience.

ILLUSTRATION 9.41   Federal
Welfare Spending:
Omitted Baseline

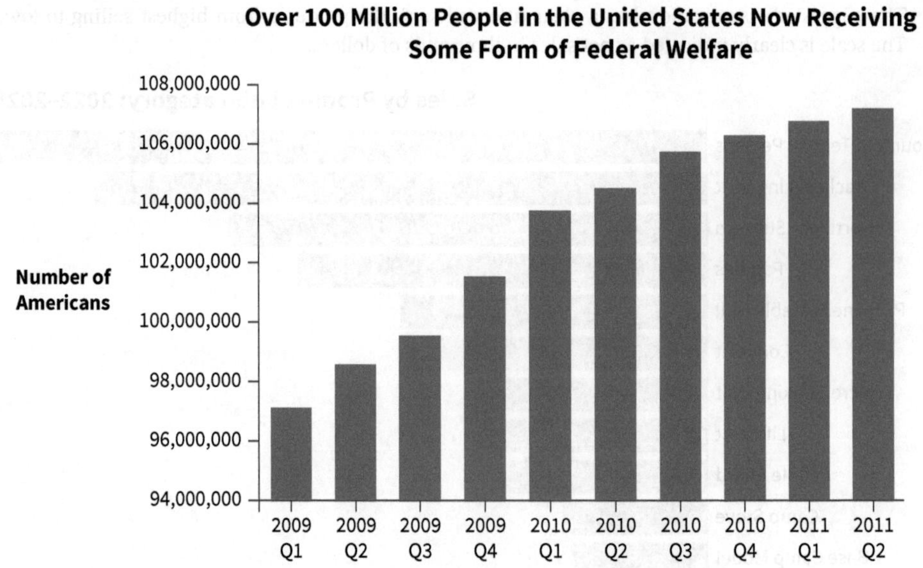

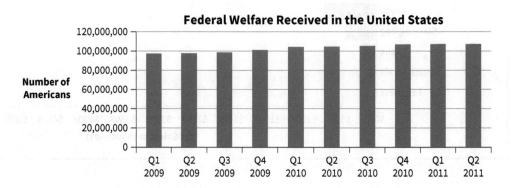

Over 100 Million People in the United States Now Receiving Some Form of Federal Welfare

Source: U.S. Census survey/U.S Department of Commerce/Public Domain.

ILLUSTRATION 9.42   Federal
Welfare Spending:
Zero Baseline

Federal Welfare Received in the United States

Manipulating the *y*-Axis

Like omitting the baseline, manipulating the scale on the *y*-axis can affect how the data are interpreted. Expanding or compressing the scale on the *y*-axis can make changes in the data seem more or less significant. **Illustration 9.43** is a comparison of two visualizations using the same data.

ILLUSTRATION 9.43
Manipulating the *y*-Axis
Examples

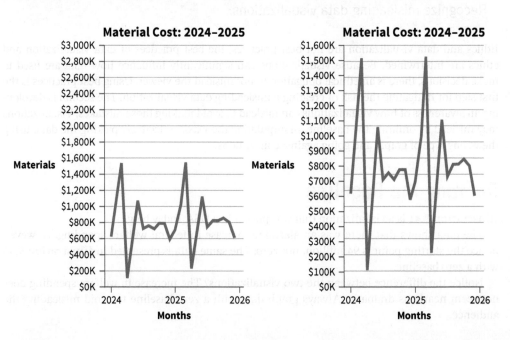

Material costs look much more volatile in the graph on the right. If the preparer wanted to make costs look less volatile, the *y*-axis can be manipulated like the graph on the left by increasing the scale maximum.

Going Against Conventions

A general standard in data visualization is that darker colors indicate higher numbers in a color scale. **Illustration 9.44** provides an example of what happens when that standard is violated.

ILLUSTRATION 9.44 Going Against Conventions Example

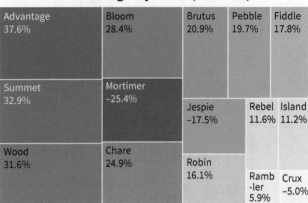

If the viewers did not concentrate on the numbers in the visualization, they would assume the Mortimer has the highest profit margin according to the tree map on the left. The tree map on the right follows general color conventions, and it is immediately clear that the Mortimer has the lowest profit margin.

Applying Critical Thinking 9.4

Consider Visualization Risks

When creating data visualizations, think about the risks involved (**Risk**):

- The viewer may not understand the visual.
- The visual is unclear.
- The visual is misleading.

For the HMC visualization in Illustration 9.44, if you did not consider the risk of creating a misleading visualization, you may not realize that the color convention is misleading.

Selectively Choosing the Data

Including only some data points in a visualization may also create a false impression of the data. **Illustration 9.45** is an example of what happens when data are selectively used.

The graph on the left plots the sum of sales for the year 2024 and the year 2025, whereas the graph on the right plots sales for each month. Notice that the graph on the left creates the impression that sales have gradually increased. However, as the graph on the right shows, there is a great deal of variability in monthly sales.

ILLUSTRATION 9.45 Selectively Choosing the Data Example

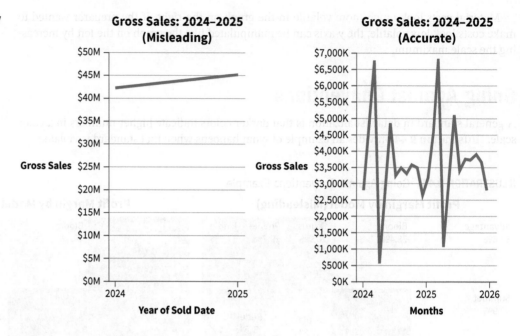

Using the Wrong Type of Graph

Sometimes choosing the wrong type of graph can make it difficult to interpret the data and results in misleading the viewer. A visualization that is not appropriate for the type of data or analysis results being reported makes it difficult for the audience to interpret the message.

Consider the two visualizations in **Illustration 9.46**.

ILLUSTRATION 9.46 Using the Wrong Type of Graph Example

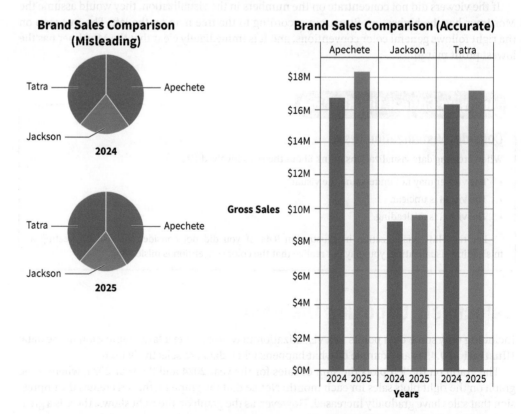

If the objective is to show a comparison of how each brand performed by year, a bar chart is a better choice. Unlike a pie chart, bar charts make it easy to determine if amounts have increased or decreased. This is because it is difficult for the human eye to interpret proportions and changes in proportions in a pie chart.

Data | Managerial Accounting You are a managerial accountant for U.S. Outdoor Adventures reviewing data analyses prepared by someone in your department. For each visualization, identify if it is or is not misleading, and correct those that are misleading.

1.

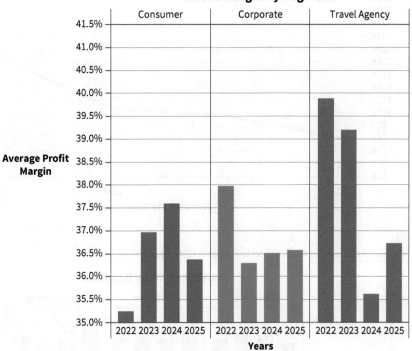

Profit Margin by Segment

2.

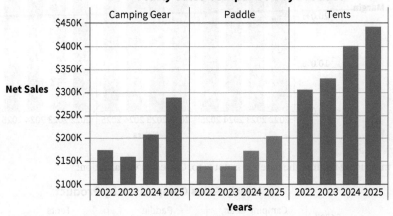

Yearly Sales Comparison by Product

3.

Shipping Costs by Order Priority and Shipping Mode				
Order Priority	**First Class**	**Same Day**	**Second Class**	**Standard Class**
Critical	$ 5,505	$ 2,664	$ 1,654	
High	$ 16,132	$ 13,516	$ 7,687	$ 13,881
Medium	$ 13,215	$ 2,611	$ 8,898	$ 41,628
Low				$ 5,220

Shipping Cost

$1,654 $41,628

4.

Same Day Shipping Costs

SOLUTION

1. This is misleading because the baseline is not zero. Corrected visualization:

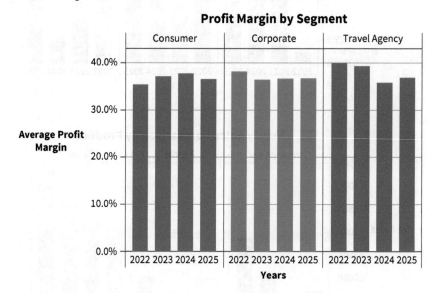

Profit Margin by Segment

2. This is misleading because the baseline is not zero. Corrected visualization:

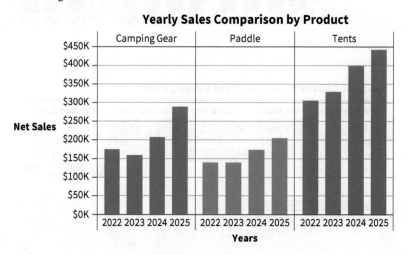

Yearly Sales Comparison by Product

3. This visual is misleading because it goes against conventions by reversing the color scale. Corrected visualization:

Shipping Cost by Mode and Order Priority: 2024–2025

Order Priority	First Class	Same Day	Second Class	Standard Class
Critical	$ 5,505	$ 2,664	$ 1,654	
High	$ 16,132	$ 13,516	$ 7,687	$ 13,881
Medium	$ 13,215	$ 2,611	$ 8,898	$ 41,628
Low				$ 5,220

Shipping Cost

$1,654 $41,628

4. This is misleading because the *y*-axis was manipulated. Corrected visualization:

Same Day Shipping Costs

Shipping Cost

$20K
$18K
$16K
$14K
$12K
$10K
$8K
$6K
$4K
$2K
$0K

2022   2023   2024   2025

Year of Order Date

9.5 How Are Data Used in Live Presentations?

LEARNING OBJECTIVE ❺

Create an interactive data visualization presentation.

Because accountants are often asked to present data stories, oral communication skills are essential for a successful career. Results of data analyses are commonly communicated via a live presentation to the intended audience, either in-person or in a virtual meeting. These presentations often include interactive data visualizations.

Best Practices for Live Presentations

Whether presenting to a live audience or virtually, a presentation should be clear and engaging. There is nothing worse than preparing a great data analysis and then presenting it to an uninterested audience. Business writer Joel Schwartzberg provides seven best practices to follow when presenting data analyses:[12]

1. **Ensure the audience can see the data.** A visualization that looks fine on a screen may be too small for someone in the back of the room to see.

---

[12]Schwartzberg, J. (2020). Present Your Data Like a Pro. *Harvard Business Review*. https://hbr.org/2020/02/present-your-data-like-a-pro (accessed July 2022).

2. Focus on the points the data illustrates by explaining the meaning of the data analysis. Stating facts without showing how they tell a story will leave the audience confused.

3. Share one major point on each chart to avoid overwhelming with details. Rather than showing several visualizations, only share those that support the data story.

4. Label chart components clearly. Review them and ask: "If I was seeing this for the first time, would I understand it?"

5. Visually highlight the "a-ha" point, or the insight or discovery, in the story. Smart presenters explain the relevance of the "a-ha" moment both orally and with a visual highlight in the chart or graph.

6. Slide titles should reinforce the data's point. Avoid generic titles and choose those the audience will notice and remember.

7. Present to the audience by looking at them and not reading from a slide presentation. Engaging the audience requires connecting with them, and the best way to do that is by focusing on them rather than the slides.

Following these seven best practices will help create a powerful presentation. However, the work does not stop there, as an effective oral presentation requires planning and practice.

Creating Interactive Data Visualizations

A powerful way to communicate data analysis results in a live presentation is by inviting the audience to explore the representation of the data. An **interactive data visualization** is a visualization that allows users to explore, manipulate, and interact with graphical representations of data. They help connect the presenter with the audience by drilling down into the data based on the audience's needs. This allows the presenter to quickly answer any questions from the audience.

Besides following best practices for creating data visualizations and telling a story with data, interactive data visualizations should provide an easy and intuitive way for the user to interact with the data. Consider the visualization in **Illustration 9.47**, which is a dashboard that reflects gross sales and profit margin by brand of vehicle sold by Huskie Motor Corporation (HMC).

This static visualization does not have the functionality to dive deeper into the data. What if, during the presentation for this analysis, the CEO of HMC asked how the model Advantage

ILLUSTRATION 9.47 Static Dashboard of Gross Sales and Profit Margin

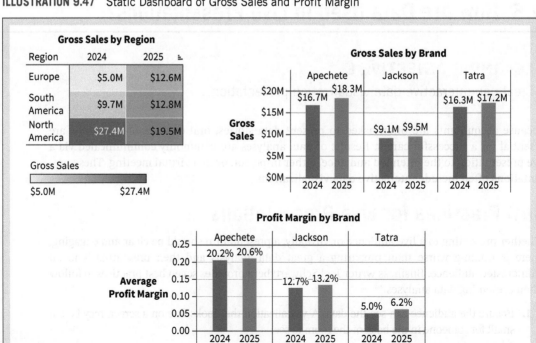

performed? An interactive visualization would make it possible to answer the CEO's question quickly. How do we make visualizations interactive? The most common method is to add a filter that allows filtering for the specific information. The best interactive visualizations allow the user to view detailed information.

Adding filters to the dashboard in Illustration 9.47 makes it interactive, letting the user see the same information at a more detailed level—by region and model (**Illustration 9.48**).

ILLUSTRATION 9.48 Interactive Dashboard of Gross Sales and Profit Margin

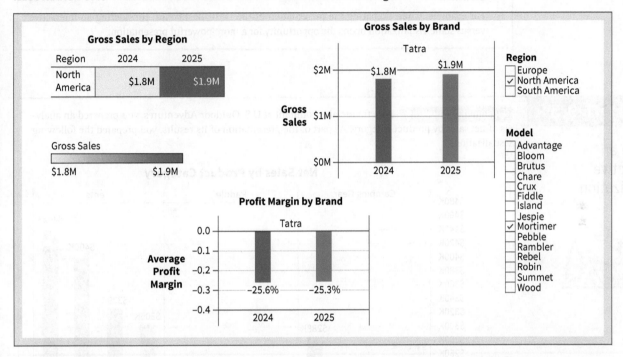

Users of Illustration 9.48 can choose the region and the car model and see either all the data or any combination of the data. In this illustration, the user has chosen the North American region and the Mortimer model. They can quickly see how that model performed in 2024 and 2025. (**Data** **How To 9.2** illustrates how to create an interactive dashboard in Tableau.)

The benefit of interactive data visualization is that it allows engagement with the data. An interactive visualization helps users:

- Quickly identify trends.
- Efficiently identify relationships.
- Provide useful data storytelling.
- Simplify complex data.

Keep in mind that interactive data visualization is not limited to live presentations. In general, the more interactive the visual, the more engaged the user will be regardless of the communication medium.

> ### Applying Critical Thinking 9.5
>
> #### Plan the Best Presentation
>
> Creating data visualizations for a presentation takes planning. Part of that planning should include considering different ways to present your findings as well as possible alternative visualizations (**Alternatives**):
>
> - Be open-minded about visualizations so that you consider all possible options and create the best presentation.
> - For example, when preparing the presentation of the HMC dashboard, considering an interactive versus static visualization opens the opportunity for a more powerful presentation.

APPLY IT 9.5

Create an Interactive Visualization

Financial Accounting As a financial accountant at U.S. Outdoor Adventures, you prepared an analysis of net sales by product category. As part of the presentation of its results, you prepared the following visualization:

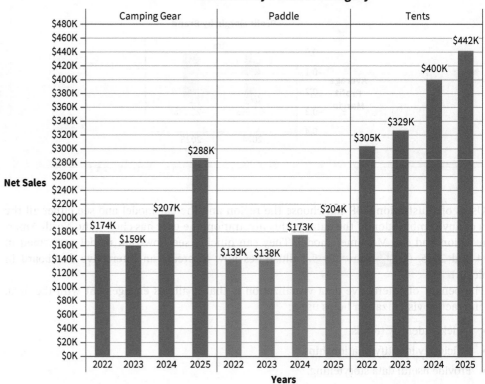

During the presentation of the analysis to the accounting team, you were asked about the sales for a specific product (Micro Cooking Set) in the Camping Gear product category for the year 2024 in California. List what should be included in this visual to make it interactive so you can answer the question posed during the presentation.

SOLUTION

To create an interactive visualization, identify which aspects of the visual a user would be interested in changing. In this example, a filter is necessary to see how a specific sub-category of the product is performing. To quickly answer questions about sales in a specific state, a filter for state is also necessary. It is also a good idea to have a filter for product category to answer questions about the entire category, as well as specific sub-categories.

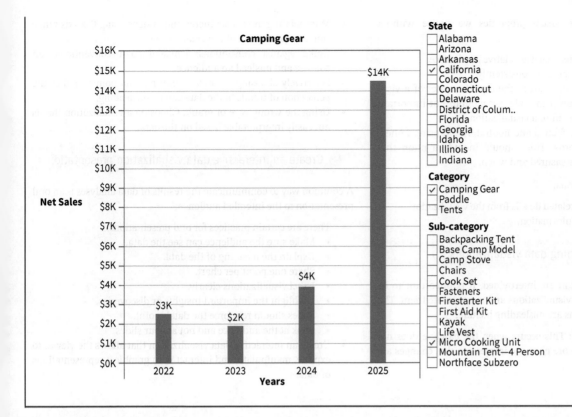

Chapter Review and Practice

Learning Objectives Review

❶ Explain how a data story communicates data analysis results.

The final step in data analysis is to summarize the findings and communicate them to the intended audience:

- Data literacy is the ability to understand data and communicate their meaning clearly and concisely.
- Communicate data analysis results effectively by understanding the audience, focusing on the message rather than the numbers, providing context for the data, making it easy to understand the results, and telling a data story.
- A data story includes three elements: data, narrative, and visuals. Effective data stories have a specific structure. First, the problem or issue is introduced and explored. Next, the main insight is identified and a solution is shared. The final part of the story is a conclusion that includes next steps.

❷ Summarize the steps for creating effective data visualizations.

There are three steps to follow before creating effective data visualizations:

- Verify the data: Make sure they are accurate, complete, consistent, fresh, and timely.
- Consider the audience: Who will be viewing the visualizations? Consider what the audience needs so that they are engaged and understand the visualization.
- Define the objective: Is the objective to show composition, relationships, distributions, trends, or comparisons? Choose the visual that matches the project's goal.

❸ Describe the characteristics of an effective data visualization.

Once the visualization is chosen, follow best practices to be sure it effectively communicates the results.

Consider the principles of visual perception:

- Continuity: Effective visualizations arrange visual objects in a line to simplify grouping and comparison.
- Similarity: Items similar in color, shape, size, or location evoke the perception that they belong to the same group.
- Proximity: People perceive visual elements are related by how closely they are positioned to one another.
- Focal point: The viewer of a visualization will pay more attention to whatever stands out visually.

Preattentive attributes are visual properties we notice without realizing it:

- Size: Relative size is interpreted as relative importance.
- Color: Use color sparingly and consistently.
- Position: People typically start at the top-left corner of a visualization and then scan it in a zig-zag motion. Put important information at the top left of a visualization.
- Titles: They should be factual and neutral. Avoid using unnecessary descriptive words. Titles should include a noun that represents what was measured and when.

Avoid cluttering visualizations:

- Remove any nondata-related details from the visualization.
- Eliminate redundant information.

④ Recognize misleading data visualizations.

Ethics and data visualization are intertwined. It is important to be able to identify misleading visualizations and to not create them. The common ways visualizations are misleading include:

- Omitting the baseline: This occurs when the baseline does not start at zero and therefore gives the impression that changes are more dramatic.

- Manipulating the y-axis: Increasing or decreasing the axis range can alter perception of the data.
- Going against conventions: Unusual color conventions can confuse and mislead an audience.
- Selectively choosing the data: Omitting data points to alter the perception of trends in the data can be misleading.
- Using the wrong type of graph: Choosing a visualization that is not easily interpretable based on the data.

⑤ Create an interactive data visualization presentation.

A common way to communicate the results of data analyses is an oral presentation to the intended audience:

- There are certain practices for oral presentations:
  - Make sure the audience can see the data.
  - Explain the meaning of the data.
  - Share one point per chart.
  - Label visualizations clearly.
  - Highlight the important insights or discoveries.
  - Slides should reinforce the data's point.
  - Look at the audience and not at your slides.
- Create an interactive data visualization that allows the viewer to explore, manipulate, and interact with graphical representations of data.

Key Terms Review

How To Walk-Throughs

How To

HOW TO 9.1   Create a Dashboard in Tableau

The dashboard in Illustration 9.13 was created using the visualization software Tableau. Follow these steps to create it yourself:

What You Need: **Data** The How To 9.1 data file.

STEP 1: Open the workbook to find the three visualizations that have already been created: profit margin by brand, gross sales by brand, and cost analysis.

STEP 2: Open a dashboard worksheet by selecting **Dashboard** in the main toolbar or by clicking the dashboard icon next to the worksheets (**Illustration 9.49**).

ILLUSTRATION 9.49 Tableau Dashboard Option in the Toolbar

STEP 3: In the dashboard worksheet, click and drag any of the visualizations listed under **Sheets** to the box **Drop Sheets Here**.

STEP 4: In the **Objects** section on the left, choose **Floating** (see **Illustration 9.50**). Manually locate and size the visualizations.

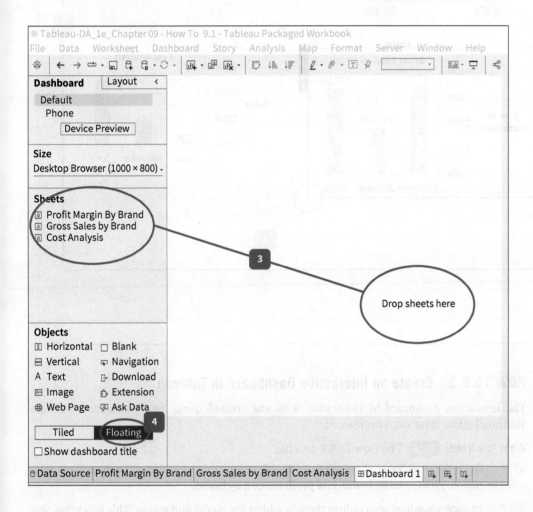

ILLUSTRATION 9.50 Tableau Dashboard Canvas

STEP 5: Recreate the dashboard shown in Illustration 9.13 by dropping the visualizations into the dashboard (**Illustration 9.51**).

STEP 6: Move the visualizations around the dashboard by clicking on the visual and dragging it. It can be re-sized by clicking on the visual and then hovering at the corner (Illustration 9.51).

ILLUSTRATION 9.51   Moving Visualizations and Sizing Dashboard Visualizations

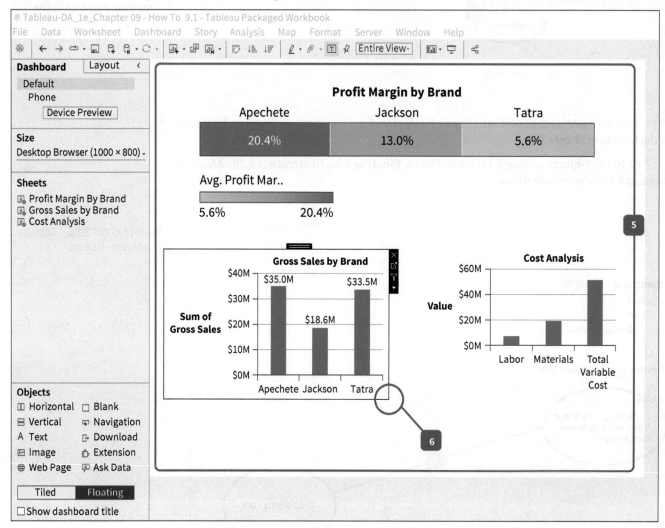

How To

HOW TO 9.2   Create an Interactive Dashboard in Tableau

The interactive dashboard in Illustration 9.48 was created using the visualization software Tableau. Follow these steps to create it:

What You Need: `Data` The How To 9.2 data file.

STEP 1: Open the workbook. There are three visualizations that have already been created: gross sales by region, gross sales by brand, and profit margin by brand.

STEP 2: In each visualization, confirm there is a filter for model and region. This will allow you to filter to the lowest level of detail within the dashboard (**Illustration 9.52**).

STEP 3: Follow the instructions in How To 9.1 to drag all three visualizations onto the dashboard canvas and format to mirror the dashboard in Illustration 9.48.

STEP 4: To link the worksheets in the dashboard so the filters will apply to each, click on the **Filter List**. Choose the option **Apply to Worksheets** and then **Selected Worksheets** (**Illustration 9.53**).

ILLUSTRATION 9.52 Confirm Filters for Region and Model

Pages	
	iii Columns ⊞ YEAR(Sold Date)
	☰ Rows Region

Filters ②

🔳 Region: Europe
🔳 Model: Advantage

Gross Sales by Region

Region	2024	2025
Europe	$0.2M	$0.5M

Marks

□ Square ▼

Color	Size	Label
Detail	Tooltip	

:: SUM(Gross Sal..
T SUM(Gross Sal..

ILLUSTRATION 9.53 View of Dashboard After the Filter List Down Arrow Is Selected

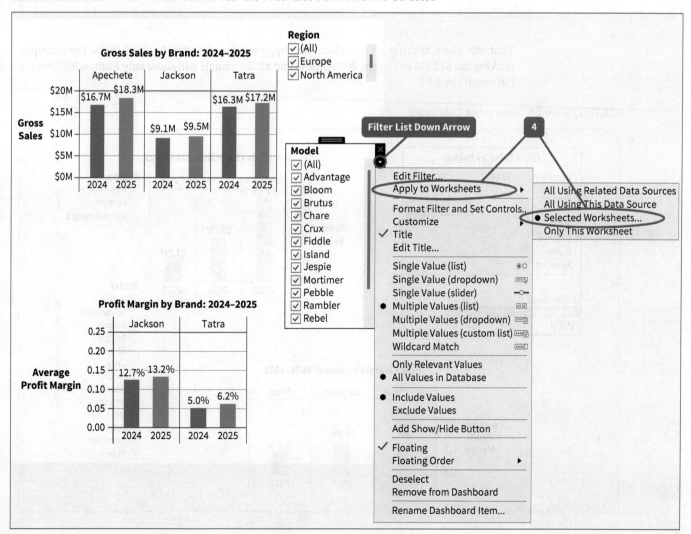

STEP 5: Click each visual in the dashboard and create a filter by selecting the filter icon.

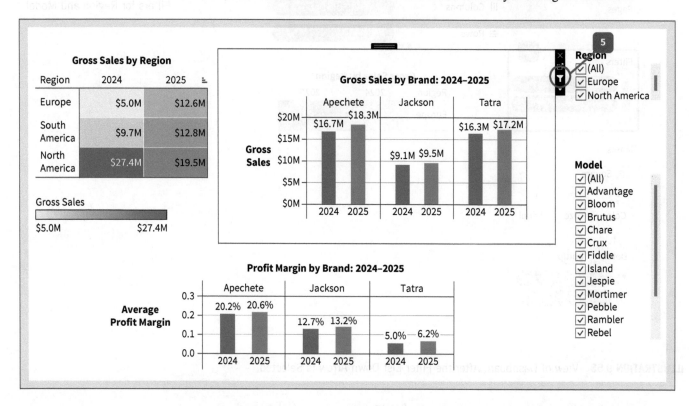

That will allow clicking on one visual and applying the selection to all of them. For example, clicking the $12.6M in Europe 2025 means that all the visuals will show only Europe 2025 results (**Illustration 9.54**).

ILLUSTRATION 9.54 Interactive Dashboard

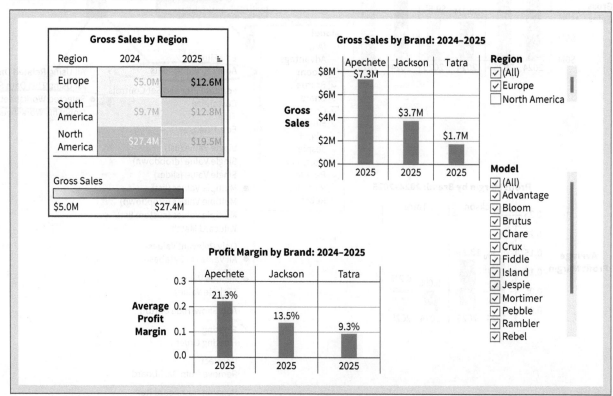

> **Data** The Data tag appears when the data required to answer a question or complete an exercise are available in the book's product page on www.wiley.com.

Multiple Choice Questions

1. (LO 1) Data literacy is

   a. one of the characteristics of an effective visualization.

   b. the knowledge of a project's data perspective.

   c. the communication of the objective of data analysis.

   d. the ability to understand and communicate data.

2. (LO 1) Dara prepared a data analysis of profitability by product for the current year for her company. She felt it was also important to show how this year's profitability compared to prior years. This is an example of

   a. putting the analysis in context.

   b. understanding the audience.

   c. creating a memorable story.

   d. a composition analysis.

3. (LO 1) Gwei is a financial accountant for a retail company who was asked to do an analysis of sales over the past five years to prepare a sales forecast. The company is seeking additional investors so they can expand their operations. Gwei's supervisor has asked her to prepare a report that will be given to the potential investors. The investors would be considered the _____ of the report.

   a. stakeholders

   b. preparers

   c. purchasers

   d. regulators

4. (LO 1) Filip is a financial accountant for a computer software company. He was asked to do an analysis of cashflows over the past five years and to prepare a revenue forecast. The company is seeking additional investors so that they can expand their operations. Filip's supervisor has asked him to prepare a report that will be given to the potential investors. If the investors have a bias against the type of software the company sells, Filip should consider this bias as a(n)

   a. key alternative.

   b. uncontrollable event.

   c. risk.

   d. negative outcome.

5. (LO 1) You are explaining company results to a group of managers. You provide a narrative that gives context, you comment on the results of the analysis, and you structure the data to guide the viewer or reader through the analysis. This interaction of two elements of the data story

   a. educates.

   b. engages.

   c. enlightens.

   d. explains.

6. (LO 1) Methodically peeling back layers of the analysis in a data story is the _____ section of the story.

   a. exposition

   b. rising action

   c. climax

   d. falling action

7. (LO 2) The process of displaying data to provide meaning and insights for the audience is

   a. data communication.

   b. data description.

   c. data explanation.

   d. data visualization.

8. (LO 2) Which visualization audience is most likely looking for actionable results?

   a. Department managers

   b. Industry experts

   c. New employees

   d. The CEO, CFO, and COO

9. (LO 2) An area chart is best used for which of the following objectives?

   a. Showing composition

   b. Showing relationships

   c. Showing distributions

   d. Showing comparisons

10. (LO 2) A scatterplot is best used for which of the following objectives?

   a. Showing composition

   b. Showing relationships

   c. Indicating trends

   d. Showing comparisons

11. (LO 2) Jamie was preparing a visualization to show the results of an analysis of sales trends. Jamie has data for each month's sales from all the company's regions. All the sales data is reported in whole dollars except for the east region. The east region reports sales in thousands. This is an example of what type of data verification attribute?

   a. Accuracy

   b. Completeness

   c. Consistency

   d. Freshness

12. (LO 3) You are preparing a visualization about company division performance. Each bar is labeled with division revenues in thousands of dollars. The visual is a single color. The divisions are presented in alphabetical order. The title is at the top. There is no background color. Which preattentive attribute still needs the most attention?

   a. Clutter

   b. Color

   c. Size

   d. Title

13. (LO 3) You want to illustrate the relationships between three data fields for each product line: total sales, sales growth, and market share. You have prepared a scatter chart to illustrate these relationships. What is a better visualization for this purpose?

   a. Area chart

   b. Bar chart

   c. Bubble chart

   d. Pie chart

14. (LO 3) When showing correlation between two variables, which is the most appropriate chart to use?

   a. Tree map

   b. Stacked bar chart

   c. Bubble chart

   d. Scatterplot

15. (LO 4) A bar graph visualization that misleads by making the data look like it has more differences across categories than it really does is an example of misleading by

   a. manipulating the *y*-axis.

   b. omitting the baseline.

   c. selectively picking data.

   d. using the wrong graph.

16. (LO 4) The following visualization was prepared to allow the viewer to compare sales quantity by type of product for Pizza My Heart Food truck:

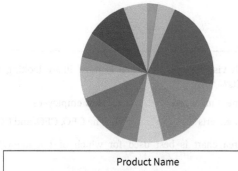

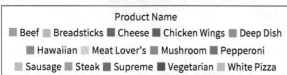

Product Name

■ Beef ■ Breadsticks ■ Cheese ■ Chicken Wings ■ Deep Dish
■ Hawaiian ■ Meat Lover's ■ Mushroom ■ Pepperoni
■ Sausage ■ Steak ■ Supreme ■ Vegetarian ■ White Pizza

How might this visualization be misleading?

a. There is no baseline.

b. The data has been selectively chosen.

c. The wrong type of visualization was used.

d. The color scale goes against conventions.

17. (LO 4) The following visualization was prepared for a management dashboard to monitor profit margin:

Profit Margin by Brand—2025

Apechete	Jackson	Tatra
20.4%	13.0%	5.6%

How might this visualization be misleading?

a. There is no baseline.

b. The data has been selectively chosen.

c. The wrong type of visualization was used.

d. The color scale goes against conventions.

18. (LO 5) Which of the following is a characteristic of an interactive data visualization? Select all that apply.

a. It helps connect the presenter with the audience.

b. It allows the user to drill down into the data.

c. It allows for quick answers to audience questions.

d. It provides the presenter's view of the data.

19. (LO 5) A static visualization

a. allows the user to dig deeper into the analysis.

b. is best suited for live presentations.

c. does not allow the user to dig deeper into the analysis.

d. cannot be used in a data story.

20. (LO 5) The law of continuity

a. states that a viewer pays attention to whatever stands out visually.

b. states that lines are perceived as going further along the same path.

c. states that the closeness of visual objects impacts people's perceptions.

d. states that matching objects tend to be perceived as a whole group.

Review Questions

1. (LO 1) List and discuss each suggestion for effectively communicating to your audience.

2. (LO 1) What is meant by "putting the data in context"?

3. (LO 1) Imagine you are presenting a data analysis that shows expense trends for the last three years. You have found that one region had a significant jump in labor expenses in the second year of the analysis. Upon further analysis, you identified a specific location that is paying much higher wage rates than other locations in the same region. Discuss how you would build a data story for these analyses. Include the elements of an effective data story.

4. (LO 1) Discuss why data stories are an effective way to communicate data analysis results.

5. (LO 2) Discuss why it is important to verify your data prior to preparing your data analysis communication.

6. (LO 2) Compare and contrast communicating to a novice audience versus an executive audience.

7. (LO 2) Compare and contrast communication to a managerial audience versus an expert audience.

8. (LO 2) Discuss how a dashboard can help communicate data analysis results to managers.

9. (LO 2) Discuss how the objective of an analysis can help determine the type of visualization that should be used.

10. (LO 3) Discuss how the law of continuity applies to data visualization.

11. (LO 3) Discuss how the law of similarity applies to data visualization.

12. (LO 3) Discuss how the law of proximity applies to data visualization.

13. (LO 3) Discuss how the law of focal point applies to data visualization.

14. (LO 3) What are preattentive attributes, and why do they matter when preparing a visualization?

15. (LO 4) Give an example of how manipulating the y-axis could cause a visualization to be misleading.

16. (LO 4) In terms of creating a visualization, discuss what going against conventions means and give an example.

17. (LO 4) Discuss why omitting the baseline in a visualization may be misleading.

18. (LO 5) Compare and contrast static visualizations with interactive visualizations.

19. (LO 5) Discuss the benefits of using interactive data visualizations and give an example of how an interactive data visualization could be used in a live presentation.

20. (LO 5) Discuss best practices for presenting data analysis results to a live audience.

Brief Exercises

BE 9.1 (LO 1) `Financial Accounting` You are explaining company results to a group of managers.

1. You provide a narrative that gives context, you comment on the results of the analysis, and you structure the data to guide the viewer or reader through the analysis. What element of the data story is involved here?

2. You provide a narrative that gives context, you comment on the results of the analysis, and you use visuals in the story. This interaction of two elements of the data story _____ the audience.

3. You show both the data and visuals that reveal patterns and trends. What element is this in the data story?

BE 9.2 (LO 1) `Tax Accounting` U.S. Outdoor Adventures is concerned about sales tax compliance. The tax department director has asked you to analyze company sales this year and the sales tax that should have been collected. You have performed the analysis and are preparing to communicate your results to the director. Describe how each of the following applies to the presentation of your results to the tax director:

1. Understand the audience.
2. Focus on the message.
3. Put the data in context.
4. Make it easy to understand.
5. Create a memorable story.

BE 9.3 (LO 1) `Auditing` You are an auditor who has performed an analysis of your client's purchase card (P-card) transactions. The objective of the analysis was to test the controls the client has over the use of employee purchase cards. You used all the P-card transactions data for the year under audit to evaluate the following controls:

- Employees have not exceeded their spending limit per transaction.
- Employees have not exceeded their monthly spending limit.
- All purchases are recorded with descriptions.
- All purchases have supervisor approval.

During your analysis you discovered there were several violations of policy, but they were generally small and involved various employees/supervisors. However, one employee and supervisor had very suspicious violations. Upon deeper analysis, you were able to identify a pattern of suspicious spending. Use Freytag's pyramid to draft how you will tell this story.

BE 9.4 (LO 2) `Financial Accounting` Identify the appropriate audience that is classified as executive audience, expert audience, managerial audience, and novice audience based on the statements given:

Statement	Solution Audience
You are presenting a visualization about product line performance to employees of a major retailer. You explain that the company was started five years ago with a focus on kitchenware but has expanded in the past year to include product lines such as small kitchen appliances, kitchen tools, kitchen and dining linens, bed and bath linens, and small home (nonkitchen) appliances.	
Sam is presenting a visualization about product line performance to employees of a retailing company. She recommends the company drop two product lines that have resulted in losses for the past four quarters, and the company should expand two product lines that have produced the highest profit margins.	
Johanna is presenting a visualization about department performance to employees of a retailing company. Her presentation includes variances in expenses, revenues, and profit margins for each department and identifies anomalies that warrant additional research.	
Dale is presenting a visualization about company performance to employees of a manufacturing company. In their presentation, Dale highlights the product lines that are performing the best and those that are performing the worst, as well as the company segments that are controlling costs well and those that are having major cost overruns. Dale also provides data backing up these highlights.	

BE 9.5 (LO 2) **Auditing** **Financial Accounting** **Managerial Accounting** Match each of the following to the best visualization. Visualization choices can be used once, more than once, or not at all.

- **a.** Bar chart
- **b.** Line chart
- **c.** Stacked bar chart
- **d.** Scatterplot
- **e.** Bubble chart

Purpose	Visualization
1. Show the distribution of prices for a specific product.	
2. Show the composition of total expenses.	
3. Show the relationship between temperatures and soup sales at a restaurant.	
4. Show sales trends over time.	
5. Show the distribution of sales by country.	
6. Show sales comparisons by year.	

BE 9.6 (LO 3) **Data** **Financial Accounting** **Managerial Accounting** Using the available data, create a line chart that shows the trend in overtime pay over the year. Be sure to follow best practices for creating line charts.

BE 9.7 (LO 3) **Data** **Financial Accounting** Create a column chart comparing product sales in 2024 and 2025 for the following cities: Denver, Loveland, Lafayette, and Brookfield. Be sure to follow best practices for creating charts.

BE 9.8 (LO 2, 3) **Data** **Financial Accounting** **Tax Accounting** The following visualization was prepared to communicate the analysis of employee reimbursement to city employees. The audience for the visualization is the internal audit team. The objective is to identify the departments with the highest amount of employee reimbursement over the years 2022 to 2025.

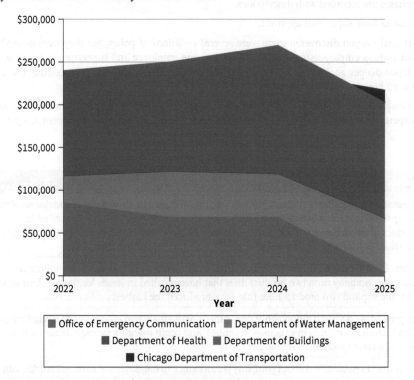

1. Identify possible corrections/improvements for this visualization.
2. Prepare a corrected visualization.

BE 9.9 (LO 3) `Auditing` `Financial Accounting` `Managerial Accounting` The following visualization was prepared to show seasonal profitability of a bakery for the prior year:

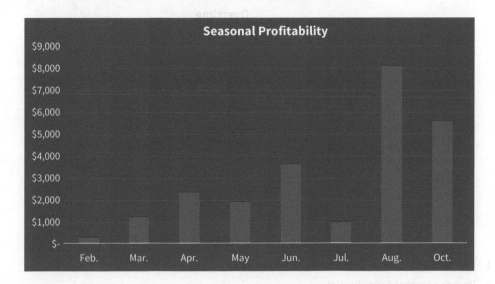

1. Identify possible corrections/improvements that should be considered to improve the visualization.
2. Discuss why your suggested improvements are necessary.

BE 9.10 (LO 3, 4) `Data` You are an AIS accountant for WaveStream, an online television streaming service. WaveStream has operations across the United Kingdom and its staff log into the accounting information system daily. The CIO has concerns about system security since there have been an increased number of data breaches and ransomware in recent years. A visualization was created to show the number of unauthorized login attempts in the last two years. The CIO's objective is to understand if the problem is more serious and if immediate action is required.

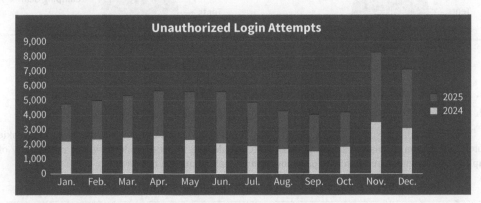

1. Discuss if the data visualization is appropriate for this analysis.
2. Prepare another visualization that is more appropriate for meeting the objectives of the analysis.
3. Use Freytag's pyramid to tell the story. Ensure the story includes recommendations to the CIO.

BE 9.11 (LO 4) Data Financial Accounting You are a city accountant analyzing overtime pay for the fire department. Review the visualization prepared by someone else in your department.

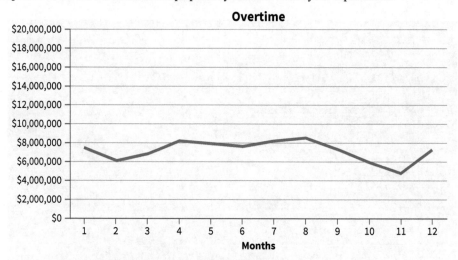

1. Discuss whether the visualization is misleading, and if so, how?

2. Prepare a corrected visualization.

BE 9.12 (LO 4) Data Financial Accounting Managerial Accounting U.S. Outdoor Adventures has asked for an analysis of sales for 2024 and 2025. The objective of the analysis is to compare sales from 2024 to 2025 and determine if any product categories are increasing or decreasing. The following analysis was prepared for the management team:

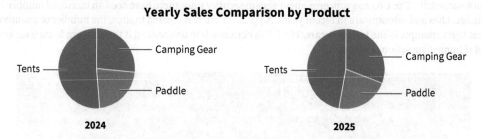

1. Is this data visualization appropriate for this analysis? Discuss why it is or is not appropriate.

2. Prepare another visualization. Explain why your visualization is more appropriate.

BE 9.13 (LO 5) Data Managerial Accounting The following visualization was prepared for Huskie Motor Corporation to analyze sales channels. HMC would like to better understand the profitability of employee, government, and purchase payment options (cash, financing, or leasing).

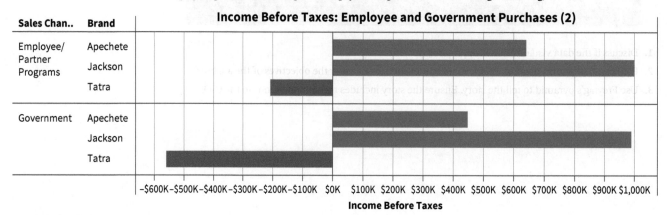

1. Recommend how this visualization could be made interactive.

2. Create the interactive visualization you recommended.

BE 9.14 (LO 2, 5) `Data` `Auditing` `Financial Accounting` `Managerial Accounting` The following visualization was prepared to help Denton Hospitality analyze profit by hotel location. Each dot on the scatter-plot represents an individual hotel location. The audience for the presentation will be experts.

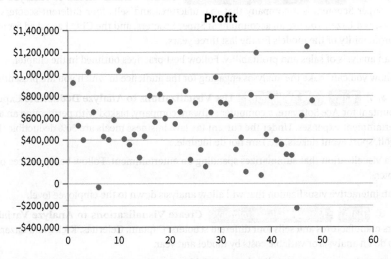

1. Based on the audience being experts, what would you change or enhance for a live presentation?
2. Prepare a corrected scatterplot based on your recommendations.

BE 9.15 (LO 5) `Data` `Financial Accounting` `Managerial Accounting` The following visualization was prepared for U.S. Outdoor Adventures to help them analyze sales:

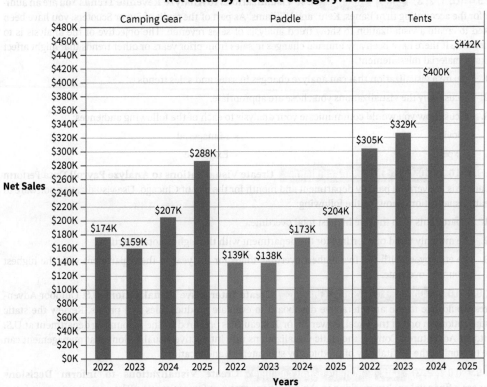

Identify ways to make this visualization interactive so the user can drill down and see how the various products are performing. Then, create the visualization.

Exercises

EX 9.1 (LO 1, 2, 3, 5) `Data` `Managerial Accounting` **Create Visualizations to Analyze Sales and Profitability** Super Scooters is a company that manufactures and sells four different scooters: Captain, Celeritas, Kicks, and Lazer. You are an accountant at Super Scooters, and the CEO has asked for an analysis of sales and profitability of the models for the last three years.

1. Prepare an analysis of sales and profitability. Follow best practices outlined in the chapter.
2. Discuss how you can make the analyses engaging for the audience to which you are presenting.

EX 9.2 (LO 2, 3, 5) `Data` `Tax Accounting` **Use Visualizations to Analyze Deductible Expenses** You are a tax accountant for Ace Software, a computer software company, tasked with performing an analysis of business entertainment expenses. Under the current tax law, business meals are 50% deductible. Entertainment costs (golf, sport event tickets, etc.) are not deductible.

1. Prepare a visualization that summarizes spending on entertainment. Follow best practices outlined in the chapter.
2. Design an interactive visualization that will allow analysis down to the employee level.

EX 9.3 (LO 2, 3) `Data` `Managerial Accounting` **Create Visualizations to Analyze Variable Costs** Super Scooters manufactures and sells four different scooters: Captain, Celeritas, Kicks, and Lazer. You have been asked to do an analysis of variable costs by model and year.

1. Prepare an explanatory data visualization of variable costs. You may use Excel, Power BI, or Tableau to prepare the visualizations. Be sure to follow all best practices.
2. Discuss how you would communicate your analysis to each of the following audiences:

   - Novice
   - Expert
   - Managerial
   - Executive

EX 9.4 (LO 1, 2, 3) `Data` `Auditing` **Use Visualizations to Analyze Revenue Trends** You are an auditor for the accounting firm Banes, Kent, and Williams. As part of the audit of Super Scooters, you have been asked to create a visualization to show trend analysis of sales revenue. The objective of the analysis is to determine if there have been any unusual changes in sales from prior years or other trends that might affect risks of material misstatement.

1. Prepare a visualization that can analyze changes in sales and sales trends.
2. Discuss why the visualizations you chose are appropriate.
3. Discuss how you would communicate your analysis to each of the following audiences:

   - Novice
   - Expert
   - Managerial
   - Executive

EX 9.5 (LO 3) `Data` `Financial Accounting` **Create Visualizations to Analyze Payroll Data** Perform an analysis of overtime paid by department and month for the city of Chicago. Use visualization software to create visualizations showing the following:

1. Departments with the five highest total overtime.
2. The monthly trend of overtime for the department with the highest total overtime.
3. The employees with the five highest overtime totals for the year in the department with the highest amount of overtime.

EX 9.6 (LO 5) `Data` `Financial Accounting` **Create Interactive Visualizations** U.S. Outdoor Adventures would like to use an interactive dashboard to evaluate product sales and profits. Review the static visualizations in one of the Excel, Power BI, or Tableau files prepared by the accounting department at U.S. Outdoor Adventures. Convert the static visualizations into interactive visualizations that management can use to monitor the profitability of products by sub-category and location.

EX 9.7 (LO 1, 2, 3) `Data` `Managerial Accounting` **Create Visualizations to Inform Decisions** You are a financial analyst working in the operations group at Super Scooters. The executive team is interested in the sales trends by scooter models. Specifically, they want to understand gross sales by model and sales volume by model to identify those models that are increasing in these measures. Those high-performing models should receive more marketing dollar allocation.

1. Analyze sales dollars, sales volume, and sales volume mix by model for the last three years. Present visualizations to communicate the results to the executive team. You will need more than one visualization to create an adequate story for the executive team.
2. Use Freytag's pyramid to tell the story. Provide recommendations to the executive team regarding the allocation of marketing dollars to high-performing models.

EX 9.8 (LO 2, 3) `Data` `Financial Accounting` **Create Visualizations to Describe Warranty Expenses**
High-End Hubs (HEH) is a private entity that manufactures and sells bicycle wheel parts. Their primary customers are high-end mountain bike manufactures. The controller has asked you to understand warranty returns this year compared to last year. Your objective is to identify models and part numbers that have warranty issues in the current year and to identify assumptions to use in the warranty accrual calculation for year-end. Prepare descriptive visualizations of warranty returns compared to sales by model for this year and last year.

EX 9.9 (LO 1, 2, 3) `Data` `Audit` **Communicate Risk of Material Misstatement Using Visualizations**
You are an auditor for the accounting firm Banes, Kent, and Williams. As part of the audit of Super Scooters, you must create a visualization to communicate the trend of sales revenue by model. The objective of the analysis is to communicate changes in sales trends from prior year that inform your consideration of the risk of material misstatement related to revenue recognition for the current year audit.

1. Create a visualization to show yearly gross sales by location.
2. Create a visualization to show yearly gross sales by model and location.
3. Use Freytag's pyramid to tell the story of each visualization and how it might inform the audit of Super Scooters. Remember that your audience for these visualizations and story are the audit team and the audit files.

EX 9.10 (LO 1, 2) `Financial Accounting` `Managerial Accounting` **Create a Story Based on Audience**
You are a financial analyst for SWI, Inc. SWI is a Germany-based manufacturer and distributor of microchips and microprocessors. The company sells its products to customers in several countries and regions including Australia, Europe, North America, and South America. You have prepared the following table and visualization that show sales in each of the various regions in 2024 compared to 2025:

Sales by Location

Location	Sold Date 2024	Sold Date 2025
Australia	€ 1,417,584	€ 1,134,785
Europe	€ 1,252,712	€ 1,376,503
North America	€ 1,239,689	€ 1,624,719
South America	€ 1,515,744	€ 1,742,311
Grand Total	**€ 5,425,729**	**€ 5,878,318**

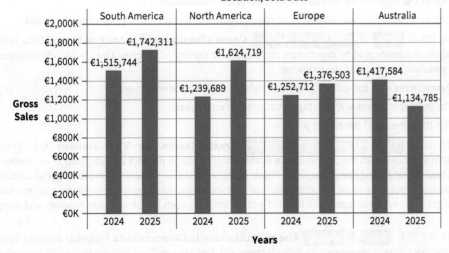

With the visualization and the table, use Freytag's pyramid to tell the story of your company's sales by country from the perspective of an executive discussing performance on an investor call. Then, tell the story from the perspective of an executive making managerial decisions about sales performance.

EX 9.11 (LO 2, 3, 4) `Data` `Auditing` **Review Data Analytics Workpapers** Assume you are a senior auditor staffed to the SWI, Inc. engagement. SWI is a public company that manufactures and distributes microchips and microprocessors internationally. Your engagement team staff has prepared a series of visualizations to identify the extent of testing that should be performed in each region by model. Specifically, the engagement team needs to understand the regions and models with the largest changes over the prior year.

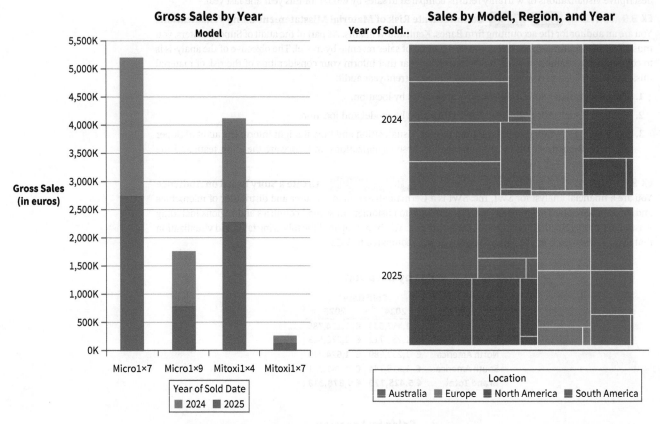

1. Provide review comments to improve the dashboard. Identify misleading visualizations and provide feedback to improve the overall effectiveness of the visualization.

2. Prepare a dashboard visualization that communicates differences in sales by region by model.

EX 9.12 (LO 3) `Data` `Financial Accounting` **Create Visualizations to Analyze Payroll Data** Perform an analysis of salaries paid by department and month for the city of Chicago. Use visualization software to create visualizations showing the following:

1. Departments with the three highest total salaries for full-time employees.

2. The five departments with the highest number of employees.

3. The 10 highest total salaries by job title.

EX 9.13 (LO 5) `Data` `Managerial Accounting` **Create Interactive Visualizations** U.S. Outdoor Adventures would like to use an interactive dashboard to evaluate product and shipping costs. Review the static visualizations using one of the Excel, Power BI, or Tableau files prepared by the managerial accounting department. Convert the static visualizations into interactive visualizations so management can monitor the costs of products by sub-category and location and the shipping costs by sub-category, location, and shipping mode.

EX 9.14 (LO 2, 3) `Data` `Auditing` **Use Visualizations to Communicate Unusual Journal Entries** HEH, Inc. is a private company with a calendar year-end. You are a staff auditor assigned to the engagement, and your senior auditor has asked you to analyze the general ledger transactions in the current year and identify any unusual items that may have been recorded. Create visualizations that illustrate unusual journal entries. For example, consider the following:

1. Journal entries that were recorded on a Saturday.

2. Journal entries where the memo item has the word "adjustment."

3. Journal entries where the memo item has the word "plug."

EX 9.15 (LO 2, 3) `Data` `Accounting Information Systems` **Use Visualizations to Communicate Log Analyses Results** You are an information systems accountant at your company, TBARk, which is a small retail company that sells both online and in brick-and-mortar stores. Quarterly, your team examines the log analysis of employees to ensure compliance with company policies. Key policies at the company include:

1. Employees should only login to one POS system at a time.

2. Employees should logout when they are not using the POS system to conduct a sale to a customer.

3. Corporate and back office employees should not login to the POS system.

You will communicate your results to the manager of your group, who is an expert in accounting information systems, controls, and log analyses. Prepare visualizations to test each of the policies using best practices to communicate the results of your analyses of each policy.

EX 9.16 (LO 3, 4) `Data` `Financial Accounting` **Identify Misleading Data Visualizations** You are a financial analyst for Adventure Sports and Outdoors, which is a retail company that sells boats, boating accessories, and safety gear. Your purchasing group is reviewing key vendor contracts. The purchasing group has performed analyses related to the dollar amount of spending with each vendor and has formed conclusions regarding purchasing behavior. The following purchasing group's analysis and conclusions were presented to you:

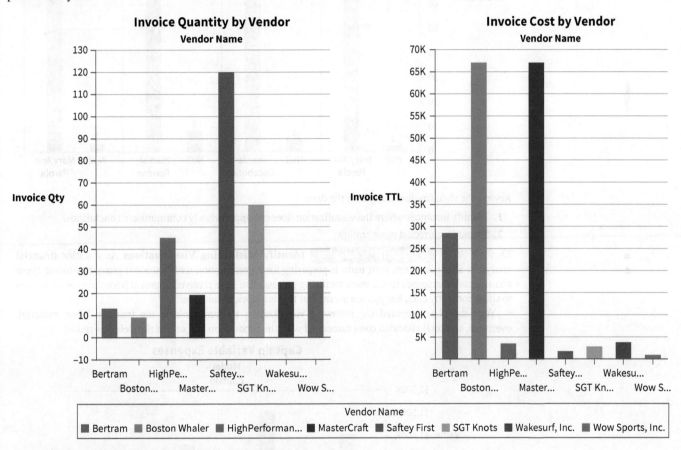

1. Identify misleading or ineffective elements of these visualizations.

2. Prepare visualizations that more accurately represent the purchasing activity for each vendor.

EX 9.17 (LO 4) `Data` `Accounting Information Systems` **Identify Misleading Visualizations in Control Testing** You are an accounting information systems accountant at SWI Inc. Your team is evaluating information technology controls associated with the sales approval process for the year 2025. SWI's sales approval process control is designed as follows:

- All sales above €10,000 and sales that have modifications to the general sales terms must be approved by the specified sales manager.

- There are three sales managers at SWI: Mary Ann Parola manages the Australia and South American regions, Hamish Rundan manages the North American regions, and Shonie Oscenbono manages the European region.

Your AIS accounting staff prepared the following visualizations to communicate the operating effectiveness of controls:

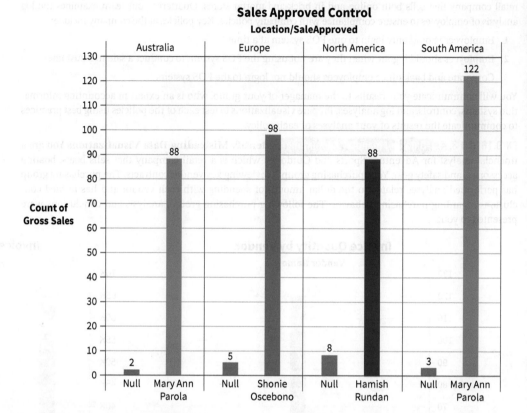

Review the visualization along with the data:

1. Identify instances where the visualization does not appropriately communicate conclusions.

2. Prepare a corrected visualization

EX 9.18 (LO 4) Managerial Accounting **Identify Misleading Visualizations** As a senior financial analyst at Super Scooters, your team is preparing for a presentation with a student group to educate them about variable expenses in the manufacturing process. You have received approval from the executive team to share company data, but you are aware that this is a novice audience.

Your staff has prepared the following visualization to communicate the trend in labor, material, overhead, and total allocated costs associated with the production and sale of the Celeritas model:

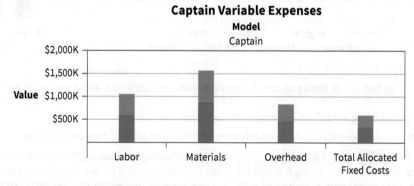

Review the visualization prepared by your staff and explain how it could be improved for presentation to a novice audience.

EX 9.19 (LO 5) Data Financial Accounting **Build an Interactive Data Visualization Presentation for Sales** HEH, Inc. sells bicycle parts B2B, which means that they sell primarily to companies that manufacture and assemble bicycles. Create two sales visualizations and an interactive dashboard that would allow you to present your analysis to the sales manager of the company. Remember to use best practices in creating your visualizations and creating the interactive dashboard.

EX 9.20 (LO 2, 3, 4) `Data` `Auditing` **Evaluate a Client-Prepared Analysis of Sales Trends** This is the first year your firm is auditing One Stop Shop. The team is performing analyses to gain an understanding of the client and the industry. One Stop Shop provided your team with an analysis of their sales trends and product mix from 2022 to 2025.

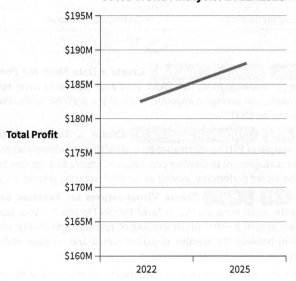

Sales Trend Analysis: 2022–2025

Product Sales Mix: 2022–2025

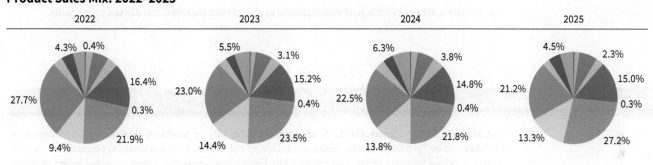

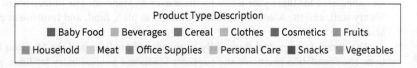

Product Type Description

■ Baby Food ■ Beverages ■ Cereal ■ Clothes ■ Cosmetics ■ Fruits
■ Household ■ Meat ■ Office Supplies ■ Personal Care ■ Snacks ■ Vegetables

1. Evaluate the visualizations provided by the client and identify potential issues or problems with the visualizations.
2. Create more effective visualizations.

Problems

Pueblo Hospitality, Inc. (PHI) operates a chain of 48 hotels located in several states. Stephanie Putnam is the president and CEO of PHI. PHI's hotels are in the economy lodging segment. A typical economy lodging hotel has an average of 84 rooms, although PHI's hotels average 117 rooms. Properties are staffed by a general manager, front desk staff of six persons, a head housekeeper, seven housekeepers, and a maintenance worker. Except for the general manager, employees are paid hourly and their assigned hours vary based on demand.

PHI uses the following performance benchmarks:

Measure	Target
Revenue per available room (RevPAR)	2% increase from prior year
Customer satisfaction	7.5
Housekeeping productivity	30 minutes per room
Audit score	7.0

PR 9.1 (LO 1, 3, 5) `Data` `Financial Accounting` **Create a Data Story for Profit Analysis** Prepare an analysis of revenue per available room (RevPAR). Your analysis should cover revenue, profit, average revenue per available room, and average competitor revenue per available room. Prepare interactive data visualizations to present to the CEO.

PR 9.2 (LO 1, 2, 3, 5) `Data` `Managerial Accounting` **Create a Dashboard for a Management Audience** Prepare an analysis of PHI's performance for each of the performance targets. Create a dashboard that would be useful for management to monitor performance. Ensure that the dashboard allows managers to see how individual hotels are performing, as well as the total company performance.

PR 9.3 (LO 1, 2, 3, 5) `Data` `Auditing` **Create Visualizations for Revenue Risk Assessment** You have been assigned to the audit team for the audit of Pueblo Hospitality. Your manager has asked you to use data visualization to gain a better understanding of revenue. Specifically, you have been asked to evaluate the relationship between the number of rooms rented and revenue, and identify any unusual patterns or observations.

1. Prepare an analysis that evaluates revenue in the current year compared to the prior year.
2. Prepare an analysis that shows potential outliers by property ID.
3. Prepare a data story with your visualizations to give to your manager, and discuss your results.

Professional Application Case — Madison Public Library

The Madison Public Library (MPL) is an agency of the City of Madison, Wisconsin. The mission of the library is to "provide free and equitable access to cultural and educational experiences." Its vision is to be a "place to learn, share, and create." The library is governed by a nine-member board of directors appointed for three-year terms by the mayor of Madison. The library board works with the mayor, library staff, and the Madison Common Council to plan, fund, and implement public library service in Madison.

The library is supported financially by the city of Madison and the Madison Public Library Foundation. The foundation promotes and supports Madison's public library facilities, services, and programs. Its board is comprised of 30 members. Board initiatives include growing restricted gifts, improving fundraising, building strategic collaboration to fund innovation and urgent needs, and supporting racial equity and inclusion in the library and foundation activities through funding, staff, and board makeup.

The library is comprised of eight locations.

Library Locations

Library Name	Street Address	City	State	Zip Code
Alicia Ashman	733 N High Point Rd	Madison	WI	53717
Central	201 W Mifflin St	Madison	WI	53703
Hawthorne	2707 E Washington Ave	Madison	WI	53704
Lakeview	2845 N. Sherman Ave	Madison	WI	53704
Meadowridge	5726 Raymond Rd	Madison	WI	53711
Pinney	516 Cottage Grove Rd	Madison	WI	53716
Sequoya	4340 Tokay Blvd	Madison	WI	53711
South Madison	222 S Park St	Madison	WI	53713

MPL operates as a not-for-profit entity. The financial information for the previous four years follows:

Library Financial Information

	Year Ended December 31			
Library Revenues	**2025**	**2024**	**2023**	**2022**
City of Madison Library Appropriation	$ 17,703,566	$ 17,779,030	$ 16,915,564	$ 16,288,835
South Central Library System Contractual Services	$ 395,478	$ 337,246	$ 337,361	$ 356,336
Dane County Library System Contractual Services	$ 1,144,935	–	–	–
LINK Contractual Services	$ 404,255	$ 454,290	$ 454,255	$ 454,255
Fines and Fees	$ 335,984	$ 383,403	$ 395,421	$ 404,399
Grants	$ 602,994	$ 149,459	$ 1,010,390	$ 370,254
Other	$ 74,538	$ 121,886	$ 104,631	$ 124,395
Endowment	$ 20,000	$ 20,000	$ 20,000	$ 20,000
	$ 20,681,750	$ 19,245,314	$ 19,237,622	$ 18,018,474
Library Expenses				
Salaries and Benefits	$ 13,026,440	$ 12,659,647	$ 12,352,852	$ 11,474,221
Library Books, Media, and Databases:	$ 1,040,746	$ 1,039,586	$ 1,000,816	$ 1,046,644
Dane County Library System Contractual Services	$ 1,537,180			
Facilities	$ 1,227,112	$ 1,515,114	$ 1,456,628	$ 1,357,358
LINKcat Online Computer Operations	$ 623,845	$ 609,444	$ 611,337	$ 592,158
Debt Retirement	$ 2,826,376	$ 2,648,112	$ 2,745,463	$ 2,720,545
Supplies and Capital Assets	$ 482,606	$ 497,976	$ 390,440	$ 330,283
Purchased Services, Miscellaneous	$ 541,895	$ 745,755	$ 578,811	$ 604,312
	$ 21,306,200	$ 19,715,634	$ 19,136,347	$ 18,125,521
Net Inflow/(Outflow)	$ (624,450)	$ (470,320)	$ 101,275	$ (107,047)

This financial information shows that the library has incurred an increase in net outflows in the last two years. The MPL Board is concerned that if the net outflows continue, the libraries will have to reduce their community services. The following is a list of metrics that can be used to evaluate MPL performance:

Metric	2025	2024	2023	2022
Checkouts	3,454,156	3,575,215	3,698,903	3,800,000
Digital Checkouts	462,416	382,068		289,309
Internet Uses	227,370	247,129	564,787	635,363
Library Card Registrations	15,544	12,154	11,775	13,245
Library Employees	137	135	131	128
Meeting Room Uses	22,714	22,278	23,010	20,782
Program Attendance (all ages)	107,447	136,303	134,666	110,744
Visits	1,779,552	1,911,287	1,965,014	2,170,000

PAC 9.1 Accounting Information Systems: Visualize Computer Systems Usage

Data **Accounting Information Systems** MPL has seen an increase in computer usage over the last two years. They want to ensure they are providing computers in the branches with the most usage and reducing the number of computers in the branches with lower usage. Use the MPL computer usage data to prepare an interactive visualization to help the accounting information systems department evaluate computer and technology usage by branch.

PAC 9.2 Auditing: Present Payroll Expense Analyses with a Data Story

Data **Auditing** As a member of the audit team examining MPL's payroll expense, you have gathered a list of current employees names and salary amounts. Prepare a descriptive analysis of payroll expense using data visualization. Summarize your findings in a data story.

PAC 9.3 Financial Accounting: Visualize Revenue and Expense Analysis

Data **Financial Accounting** You have been asked to prepare an analysis of revenue and expenses from 2016 to 2025. Use the MPL financial data to prepare visualizations that can be shown to your manager.

PAC 9.4 Managerial Accounting: Build an Interactive Performance Dashboard

Data **Managerial Accounting** You have been asked to prepare a dashboard that would allow management to view both financial and nonfinancial metrics for the library system. Use the managerial data to prepare a dashboard.

Recent Data and Analyses Developments in Accounting

This chapter reviews a variety of new data and analysis technologies that can add value and create opportunities for your professional work. These opportunities are limited only by your interest, creativity, and initiative. In fact, new data sources and analysis technologies are improving every step of the data analysis process.

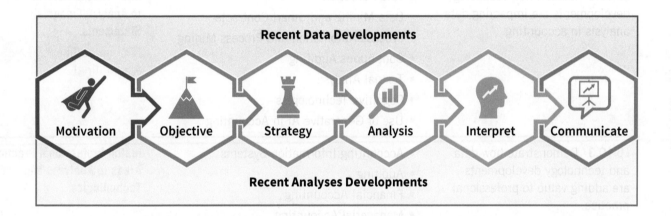

Recent Data Developments

Motivation ▸ Objective ▸ Strategy ▸ Analysis ▸ Interpret ▸ Communicate

Recent Analyses Developments

PROFESSIONAL INSIGHT — **What Opportunities Do Data and Analyses Developments Offer?**

Neo recently finished his internship in a financial institution and summarized his introduction to the endless possibilities and opportunities available by pursuing a career in accounting.

I discovered a passion for combining accounting and finance data during my internship. By analyzing accounting information trends, I could help define my client's capital needs and find the lowest cost capital sources. **I used diverse data sources and complex analyses to describe and predict my clients' financial value, cash flows, and capital needs to help me prescribe the best capital source alternatives.**

I loved developing models to predict my client's cash needs and prescribe the sources and costs associated with their capital sourcing options. For example, I helped one client decide whether to extend ownership or borrow funds with prediction models. Analyzing their cash flows revealed they could afford to leverage more debt. **I created my models from data from the accounting system, financial statements, electronic contracts, such as leases and loans, and company-related social media posts, using both structured and unstructured data.**

These experiences fostered the creative skills necessary to build models that measure future performance and economic valuation, whether the client is a public, private, nonprofit, or government organization. **I feel that my work had purpose because I was helping clients find opportunities to increase their sustainable competitive advantages. That sense of purpose has reinforced my choice to study accounting.**

Chapter Roadmap

LEARNING OBJECTIVES	TOPICS	APPLY IT
LO 10.1 Describe data trends impacting the accounting profession.	• Data Volume • Data Variety • Data Velocity • Data Veracity • Data Value • Data Ethics	**Identify Data Characteristics** (Example: Managerial Accounting)
LO 10.2 Explain how technology developments are impacting data analysis in accounting.	• Value Creation • Data Mining and Smart Contracts • Process Automation and Process Mining • Continuous Auditing • Textual Analysis • Cognitive Technologies • Use of Generative AI in Accounting	**Use Process Automation to Analyze Financial Statements** (Example: Financial Accounting)
LO 10.3 Demonstrate how data and technology developments are adding value to professional practice.	• Accounting Information Systems • Auditing • Financial Accounting • Managerial Accounting • Tax Accounting	**Match Professional Practice Areas to Analyses and Technologies**

Data The Data tag appears in the chapter when the data for an example, illustration, or application are available in the book's product page on www.wiley.com.

Data analytics software is continuously changing, and there may be more recent versions of the software referenced in this chapter.

10.1 Which Data Trends Are Impacting Accounting Practice?

LEARNING OBJECTIVE ❶
Describe data trends impacting the accounting profession.

More data from new and diverse sources are available every day. Consider the online course management platforms used by college students around the world. These learning management systems can track each selection a student makes during online learning. If your objective is to do well in a course, then this data can be analyzed to provide valuable feedback about which concepts you still need to master so you can focus on learning them.

Accountants are also encountering new data options and characteristics from sources both internal and external to their organizations. Whether that data is valuable depends on their objectives. If the objective is improving tax planning, then internet chatter data about upcoming tax policy changes could be valuable. Of course, this same chatter may not be valuable if the objective is to evaluate shipping costs for the year.

As accountants perform analyses using more data and increasingly powerful computers and analysis tools, they must consider how increases in data volume, variety, velocity, and veracity add value to their analyses. **Illustration 10.1** defines these five data characteristics and provides examples in each professional practice area.

ILLUSTRATION 10.1   The Five Data "V's"

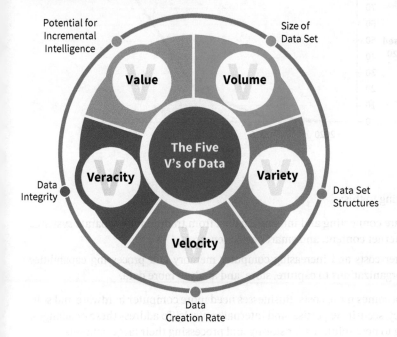

Characteristic	Examples
Volume	In AIS: • Process flow logs • Security alerts • System error logs • Transactions • Firewall traffic • System and application access logs
Variety	In auditing: • Codes, approval stamps, text, pictures, dates, and recorded values • Fair market values at year-end
Velocity	In financial accounting: • Cash transactions • Stock price changes • Social media content
Veracity	In managerial accounting: • Transactions • Prices and costs • Vendor and customer data • Sensor data from smart machines
Value	In tax accounting: • Local, national, and international tax changes • Sales tax jurisdictions and rates

This section covers the impact of each data characteristic on accounting data analytics, then explains the ethical implications accountants consider throughout the data analysis process stages.

Data Volume

Imagine if the number of clothes in your closet grew exponentially each year. Depending on your closet's size, you might run out of storage space and struggle to locate the items you need when you need them. Adding storage space and proper organization could cost you both time and resources.

Accountants are experiencing similar increases in data, which is leading to more data storage and organization costs and more data strategy options. **Data volume** refers to the amount of data selected for an analysis project. Data volume is typically limited by the computer and analysis tool capacities required for the data analyses.

Increases in Data Volume

Business operating cycles in large organizations are currently capturing and storing millions of sales, purchases, receipts, and payments each day, in addition to email, social media, and internet traffic content. Organizations are also storing more data than ever before. In fact, experts believe the volume of data produced by organizations will continue to increase exponentially in the next decade (**Illustration 10.2**).

ILLUSTRATION 10.2 Organizations Are Producing More Data

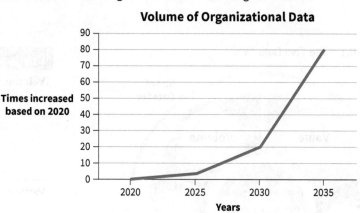

Two factors are contributing to this:

1. Technologies that are connecting and integrating data from traditionally separate systems, such as the AIS, internet content, and smart device sensors.

2. Decreasing computer costs and increasing computer memory and processing capabilities make it easier for organizations to capture, store, and analyze more data.

Of course, with more data comes more costs. Businesses need more computer hardware and software capacity, data privacy, security expertise, and internal controls. To address these challenges, organizations are turning to new solutions for storing and processing their large data sets.

Developments in Data Storage

A popular solution for storing high data volume are cloud data services. **Cloud data services** provide secure data storage on large servers, using the organization's own resources or resources provided by third parties. You might be familiar with some of the data clouds used by college students, such as Google Drive, Microsoft's OneDrive, pCloud, sync.com, mega.io, and box.com. What are the benefits of cloud data services? Benefits include:

- Easily expandable data storage capacities.
- Expert data management.
- Secure data, hardware, and software.
- IT expertise and advice.

There are three types of cloud data services. The key difference between them is if and how the cloud service provider's servers are shared:

- **Private clouds** are restricted access data storage centers created for the data of one organization or shared between an agreed upon set of companies. Private shared clouds often include a single large company, a group of supply chain partners, or noncompeting independent companies from different industries. Private clouds, provided by third parties such as HP Enterprise, VMWare, Microsoft, Cisco, and Amazon, are the fastest growing cloud sector.

- **Public clouds** securely store data from multiple companies on shared servers using virtual server data separators. Leading public cloud service vendors include Google Cloud Platform, Amazon Web Services (AWS), and Microsoft Azure.

- **Hybrid clouds** offer both private and public cloud data storage, serving the needs of the security and use characteristics of the data involved. Amazon and Microsoft are two leading vendors providing hybrid cloud solutions.

Applying Critical Thinking 10.1

Evaluate Cloud Data Services

Use critical thinking when deciding which data cloud type best serves your data needs by researching prices and services offered by viable data cloud vendors (**Knowledge**).

The best data cloud can also be selected by considering the following factors (**Alternatives**):

- The volume of data you need to store.
- How often and how much of the data needs to be added, modified, and retrieved.
- Data privacy and data security requirements.
- Your budget for cloud data services.
- The reputation of the vendor.

While organizations might prefer to store their data in private clouds, both private and public shared cloud services can provide significant cost savings. Think of it as living in a building with several separate apartments. Some people might prefer to live in a house by themselves, but a shared structure often means saving money on housing costs. **Illustration 10.3** summarizes the typical benefits and costs of each type of data cloud.

ILLUSTRATION 10.3 Comparing Cloud Data Services

Data Cloud	Benefits	Costs
Private Clouds		
Data storage for a single organization.	• Offers high data privacy and data security. • Offers high data interactivity. • More customization and adaptability are possible.	• Can be the most expensive option. • May be difficult to manage if developed in-house without hiring staff with cloud expertise.
Data storage that is shared by a set group of noncompeting organizations.	• All the benefits of single organization storage, especially for data interactivity between supply chain partners. • Sharing data storage makes it a less expensive option for each company.	• Can have some restrictions on customization and adaptability. • May involve shared contracts and joint revisions.
Public Clouds		
Public clouds are shared by many organizations who can easily come and go from the public cloud.	• Lowest individual company cost. • Fastest implementation. • Most appropriate for small businesses.	Least adaptable or customizable cloud data service.
Hybrid Clouds		
Include both private and public cloud virtual server sections.	The benefits and costs associated with both private and public clouds also apply to hybrid clouds. Hybrid clouds allow organizations to choose which data subset is best stored in a private cloud, while storing the rest in a public cloud for the cost efficiencies.	

Some vendors of cloud data services also offer cloud computing services, providing the software computing power that is often needed when organizations process and analyze large volumes of data. A recent market strategy pivot is the movement of high tech and internet service companies toward also providing private and public cloud data and computing services, leveraging their existing data storage, processing, and security service reputations.

Data Variety

Data variety refers to the diversity of data structures and measurement scales in the data we want to analyze. Let's return to the wardrobe example. We can describe our clothes with a variety of structured data fields: categorical scale fields such as color and type (shirts, shoes, etc.), ordinal scale fields such as size, interval scale fields such as how long we have owned the garment, or ratio scale fields such as how much it originally cost.

Accountants have traditionally selected and analyzed structured data that are easily represented in rows and columns, such as categorical account codes, interval transaction dates, and ratio values for the transaction amounts and account balances. Recently, accountants are combining structured data with unstructured data, including text, smart device sensor readings, and pictures and graphics, to increase the value created from their analyses.

Illustration 10.4 provides examples of unstructured data that can be combined with traditional transaction data from customer orders, inventory, shipments, invoices, and collections.

ILLUSTRATION 10.4 Analyzing the Sales Function: The Impact of Data Variety

Traditional Data Used in Sales Analysis	Enhanced with New Data Options
Sales Orders	Online Customer Reviews and Comments
Shipments	Weather Patterns
Invoices	GPS Locations
Collections by Inventory Product	Population Demographics
Customers	Targeted Promotions
Salespersons	Purchases Quality
Stores or Regions	
Budgeted Versus Actual Sales	

Valuable business intelligence can be created by combining unstructured data with traditional structured data for analysis:

- Shipping truck GPS data can be integrated with AIS data to find the most efficient delivery routes, reducing truck wear and tear by reducing mileage driven, reducing fuel costs, and improving delivery time.
- Integrating weather data with sales transaction data to anticipate customer traffic patterns and allow for better service.
- Combining customer reviews with inventory turnover to assess vendor and product effectiveness.
- Integrating GPA mapping data with cell phone location data can evaluate or develop targeted advertising campaigns or for marketing intelligence about future products.

Applying Critical Thinking 10.2

Consider the Impact of Data Variety on Data Strategy

As the variety of available data and how they are combined increase, the success of your data and analysis strategies can be improved by selecting an analysis that is appropriate for your data's measurement scales. One option is transforming unstructured data into structured data scales to increase your analysis options. For example, categorizing text comments as "positive" or "negative" transforms unstructured text fields into structured categorical data which better addresses the needs of marketing and sales managers. These two categories can be tested for correlation with other data, such as delays in shipments, to better understand how to best serve the stakeholder providing the comment (**Stakeholders, Purpose**).

Data Velocity

Most of us have experienced how rapidly information moves through social media platforms such as Instagram and Twitter. **Data velocity** refers to the speed with which new data points are generated. The higher the data velocity, the faster data volume grows (**Illustration 10.5**).

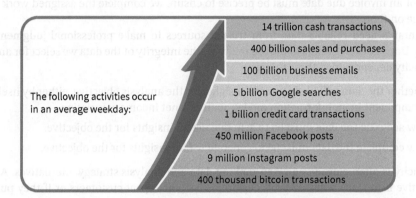

The following activities occur in an average weekday:

- 14 trillion cash transactions
- 400 billion sales and purchases
- 100 billion business emails
- 5 billion Google searches
- 1 billion credit card transactions
- 450 million Facebook posts
- 9 million Instagram posts
- 400 thousand bitcoin transactions

ILLUSTRATION 10.5 Data Velocity Continues to Increase

Accountants now regularly use high-velocity data. Internal high-velocity data can come from various sources:

- Equipment like HVAC (heating, ventilation, and air conditioning) and smart sensing and controlling devices for cost and quality control purposes.
- Business process tags indicating throughput progress for operational control.
- Tags on confidential data and sensitive word use for communications originating inside the organization to manage legal and market risk.

High-velocity data can also come from external sources:

- Mobile device location alerts indicating when customers are nearby for targeted advertising.
- Location, traffic, weather, and construction alerts for employees operating delivery or service trucks to optimize routes and service.
- Tags on sensitive words in tweets, posts, texts, emails, and blogs that originate outside the organization to identify legal risks and market intelligence.
- Weather and geographic map data for sales forecasting and transport safety.

Data velocity is also related to the terms *big data* and *internet of things*. Coined in 1987 to help market new computing systems, big data refers to how high data velocity can quickly increase data volume. When traditional AIS data is integrated with high-velocity data from smart devices, the resulting high variety data set is sometimes called the internet of things. Many technological advances, including the cloud data services discussed earlier, have been developed to provide solutions for the challenges experienced in storing and processing high-volume, high-variety, and high-velocity data.

Applying Critical Thinking 10.3

Tips for Using High-Velocity Data

While there are many tweets on X (formerly Twitter) every day, frequently only some are relevant to the purpose of an analysis:

- A common tool for evaluating high-velocity data as they are generated is using an "if, then" condition and only storing the data that pass the specific condition. For example, if a tweet mentions your company's name, then that tweet will be stored **(Purpose)**.
- The value of high-velocity data can be short-lived. The same "if, then" filters that identify which data have value can also be used for data purging when that value expires. Being alerted that there may be hail in the next hour can protect assets from hail damage, but hail alerts from yesterday will not protect assets today. (However, this data could still be valuable to insurance companies who are estimating future monthly hail damage claims.) **(Risks)**

Data Veracity

We often rely on data to help improve our decisions. Sometimes the data needs to be accurate for our objective, and other times data just needs to provide general direction. A weather forecast does not have to be exactly accurate to help us dress appropriately. Alternatively, an assignment due date or an invoice due date must be precise to ensure we complete the assigned work or pay the invoice on time.

Accountants need reliable data from trusted sources to make professional judgments and decisions. **Data veracity** refers to the reliability, or the integrity of the data we select for analysis. Data veracity depends upon three things:

1. Whether the data will likely provide insights for the analysis objective, either by itself or as a component in an information model, such as a net income calculation.

2. How accurate the data must be to generate useful insights for the objective.

3. How complete the data must be to generate useful insights for the objective.

Data veracity is often considered when ranking data and analysis strategy alternatives. Assume the objective is to learn whether prior customers become repeat customers or if they purchase from competitors instead. One data alternative might be analyzing the content of customers' related social media postings. Another choice is analyzing the last two years of sales data:

- Social media postings, when authentic, describe current or past customer experience satisfaction (or lack thereof), and may reveal if they are purchasing from competitors. The postings do not directly measure whether they would choose to be repeat customers in the future.

- Past sales data probably have higher data integrity and better identify prior repeat customers. We do not know if prior choices predict future choices or if customers are purchasing from competitors.

Applying Critical Thinking 10.4

Evaluate Data Veracity

Accurately evaluating data veracity helps you select the best data and analysis strategies and better interpret the results. Your biases, assumptions, and self-interests, or those of others who selected or analyzed the data, may impact how you judge the data's veracity (**Risks**):

- Data veracity can be overrated by the person selecting, preparing, and analyzing the data, as most people defend their own choices.

- Data veracity can also be under-rated when the data or results conflict with what is believed or expected about the phenomena, and when you do not know what, if any, controls were used when the data was selected, prepared, or analyzed. For example, if you expected sales revenues to increase, you may discount data which challenges your expectation.

Data Value

Data value refers to the benefits the data provides given the analysis' objective. Our clothes have a different value depending on the day's agenda. Professional attire is worth more when we have an interview, go into the office, or visit clients. Lounge wear, on the other hand, is more valuable when working remotely from home or enjoying personal time. Accountants' judgments regarding data value depend on the project's objective:

- If the objective is to describe profits or evaluate profit trends, then revenue and expense data are valuable data.

- When diagnosing the causes of decreasing operating cash flows, then data from the current asset and current liability accounts are valuable.

- If the objective is to predict bankruptcy risk, then liquidity and solvency data, such as a company's cash flows and all liabilities, would have data value.
- When prescribing asset utilization strategies, market data informing about future revenues and expenses have data value.

Let's illustrate data value with a managerial accounting example. Assume you work for a company that manufactures and sells a variety of computer keyboard product lines. You are considering dropping a product line because it is operating at a negative net income. Data that allows separating traceable fixed expenses from common allocated fixed expenses would make it possible to calculate segment contribution margin in addition to the product line net income (**Illustration 10.6**). (⬛Data See **How To 10.1** at the end of the chapter to learn how to create a comparative income statement in Excel, and then learn how to use an automated process to create it in **How To 10.2**.)

How To

ILLUSTRATION 10.6   Comparing Data Value of Net Income and Segment Margin

	Income Statement			
	Product A	Product B	Both Product Lines	Only Product A
Sales Revenues	$720,000	$1,200,000	$1,920,000	720,000
Less Variable Costs	432,000	960,000	1,392,000	432,000
= Contribution Margin	288,000	240,000	528,000	288,000
− Avoidable Fixed Expenses	210,000	225,000	435,000	210,000
= Segment Margin	78,000	15,000	93,000	78,000
− Unavoidable Common Fixed Expenses	42,000	42,000	84,000	84,000
= Net Income	**$ 36,000**	**$ (27,000)**	**$ 9,000**	**$ (6,000)**

Segment margin provides incremental intelligence value over the net income measure. This is because if the segment margin result is positive, then that product line of computer keyboards is generating wealth to cover the common fixed expenses. The final column in Illustration 10.6 shows that if Product B is dropped, the company would lose the $15,000 of segment margin generated by Product B and would make a loss ($6,000). This example shows that the separation of traceable and common fixed expense data has high data veracity.

Economists often measure the value of data by whether it is likely to confirm or change expectations about an objective's phenomena (e.g., the net income or the segment margin) or by how it reduces uncertainty about the phenomena (e.g., the dispersion of the data points). In fact, data value is often not fully understood until analysis hypotheses are tested and the results of the analysis are available.

Data Ethics

Using personally identifiable data can raise ethical issues for individuals and organizations. On a daily basis, accountants interact with the personal and confidential data of clients, employees, customers, investors, and creditors. These stakeholders rely on accountants' professional ethics to make judgments and communicate information while protecting their privacy and maintaining the confidentiality of their data. Unintentional and intentional personal data violations can occur in various ways:

- Collecting and sharing more than the minimally needed private data without explicit consent.
- Failing to provide easy and clear opt-in and opt-out consent for data collection, sharing, and deletion (pre-checked boxes on websites do not provide explicit consent).
- Limiting access or opportunities for those who opt-out of sharing their personal data.
- Inadequate data access controls, such as encryption, which lead to access violations.

Many specific types of data, such as personally identifiable information, client financial records, employee pay and health records, and a company's future strategic plans, are protected by laws and regulations.

Privacy Laws

Illustration 10.7 summarizes the leading data privacy laws in the United States.

ILLUSTRATION 10.7   U.S. Data Privacy Laws

Law	Description
The Privacy Act of 1974	Restricts use of data held by government agencies.
Health Information Privacy Protection Act of 2013 and the Health Insurance Portability and Accountability Act of 1996 (HIPAA)	Restricts the sharing of individual's healthcare data, with fines up to $10,000 per violation.
The Fair Credit Reporting Act (FCRA)	Limits and protects the credit-related personal data collected and shared.
The Family Educational Rights and Privacy Act (FERPA)	Protects the privacy of educational records.
The Gramm-Leach Bliley Act (GLBA)	Requires loan and investment service providers to disclose personal data sharing.
The Electronic Communications Privacy Act (ECPA) and Patriot Acts	Restricts when and how individuals' private data communications can be legally surveilled.
Children's Online Privacy Protection Act (COPPA)	Restricts personal data collected from minors and extends to third parties' data use.

U.S. states are also passing their own data privacy laws at varying speeds:

- California, Illinois, and Colorado were the first states to pass comprehensive consumer data privacy laws.
- Other states, such as Massachusetts, New York, Hawaii, Maryland, and North Dakota, are moving forward with both partial and comprehensive data privacy law proposals that are currently in committee at their state legislatures.

The progress of these laws can be tracked on websites such as the International Association of Privacy Professionals. To help accountants navigate this data privacy landscape, there are ethical standards, privacy policies, and codes of conduct.

Ethical Standards and Privacy Policies

Ethical standards for using personal data assume that accountants will stay current with the relevant data privacy laws and regulations. Inappropriately sharing a client's confidential contact information, financial status, or tax liability can result in losing client trust and a damaged professional reputation. Some data privacy infractions may have much more serious consequences, such as losing professional licenses or other sanctions:

- The Institute of Management Accountants' (IMA) ethical standards require managerial accountants to act with competence, confidentiality, integrity, and credibility when interacting with their organization's data, particularly the personally identifiable data of employees and customers.
- The Association of International Certified Professional Accountants (AICPA) has similar due care ethical standards for CPAs using private and confidential data. CPAs also have ethics requirements about their objectivity and avoiding conflicts of interest.
- Tax accountants, whether certified or not, must abide by the strict data confidentiality requirements of the Gramm-Leach-Bliley Act. The IRS code sections 6013 and 7213 require

tax accountants and IRS employees to maintain an individual's tax return data privacy and security. Violations risk misdemeanor charges, fines up to $5,000, and imprisonment up to five years per infraction.

Applying Critical Thinking 10.5

Learn About Data Laws and Regulations

Accountants must know the cultural, legal, regulatory, and transparency expectations for the collection, storage, and uses of personal data, both in the United States and globally. For example, if your company is expanding to the European Union, then per the GDP you must offer those customers the ability to opt out of having their private information stored after a sales transaction is fulfilled. You can find some of the current laws and regulation at the following sources (**Knowledge**):

- The European Union's General Data Protection Regulation (GDPR)
- Center for Internet Security's Critical Security Controls
- NIST Critical Infrastructure Security Framework
- National Conference of State Legislatures' Security Breach Notification Laws

---

Ethics and the Effects of Data Velocity and Volume

Whenever you activate your navigation app's location feature, either in your vehicle or cell phone, any data partner of that navigation app can access your location and movements throughout the day. This example of high data velocity and volume highlights new complexities when developing and maintaining compliant data privacy and security systems.

Data privacy is especially an issue for accountants when using internet browsers to access clients' or organizations' private data. A single website visit can place tracking cookies, as well as many third-party cookies, on our computers. If not immediately removed, these cookies can capture data retrieved from future website pages, username and password keystrokes, and cursor movements.

In the United States, it is legal for apps or cookies running in a browser's background to collect, use, and share data without explicit permission if the information collected does not include individual user identifiers and is not used for identity theft. However, the risk of personal data being gathered exists. An easy and cost-free preventative control for this is to go into the browser settings and clear stored cookies (also known as clearing the browsing history) at the beginning and end of every browser session. Of course, the most secure solution is accessing private data from within the security of a virtual private network.

Considering data volume, variety, veracity, velocity, value, and ethics within the context of your analyses' objectives can help you make the best choices when designing data and analysis strategies. Next, let's learn about the power we can harness from recent technological developments in analysis tools.

Managerial Accounting   You are an accountant for Limitless Outdoor, a leading outdoor gear company. The objective of your data analysis project is to learn more about your company's sales and product quality from last year. For each data field, indicate which data characteristics best describe it. (More than one data characteristic can be used to describe a data field.)

Data Field	Data Characteristic
Sleeping bag fabric durability rating from quality testing.	
Sales revenues from repeat customers and new customers during the last 12 months.	
Cell phone data captured from bicycle rides using a navigation app.	
Variability of manufacturing equipment performance every five minutes during use.	

APPLY IT 10.1

Identify Data Characteristics

(Continued)

(*Continued*)

Data Field	Data Characteristic
Naturally occurring bundles of camping equipment and outdoor clothing sales each month.	
Hourly outside temperatures during weekend days when most customers are using the equipment.	
Customer comments about their outdoor product satisfaction on social media platforms.	

SOLUTION

Data Field	Data Characteristic
Sleeping bag fabric durability rating from quality testing.	Value
Sales revenues from repeat customers compared to new customers during the last 12 months.	Veracity and value
Cell phone data captured from bicycle rides using a navigation app.	Volume and variety
Variability of manufacturing equipment performance every five minutes during use.	Volume
Naturally occurring bundles of camping equipment and outdoor clothing sales each month.	Value
Hourly outside temperatures during weekend days when most customers are using the equipment.	Volume
Customer comments about their outdoor product satisfaction on social media platforms.	Variety and volume

(This is a suggested solution; other relevant insights might also be correct.)

10.2 Which Recent Analyses Developments Are Accountants Adopting?

LEARNING OBJECTIVE ❷

Explain how technology developments are impacting data analysis in accounting.

Accountants can efficiently analyze more data than ever before by using established analysis tools such as Excel, as well as recently developed tools powerful enough to process a variety of data and at higher volume. In addition to tremendous analysis power, these tools have advanced visualization features that are improving how accountants analyze, interpret, and communicate analysis results.

Accountants often perform data analysis to prepare and verify appropriate recording of transactions and reporting of business operations and financial position. They are now also performing more data analysis to generate valuable business advice and professional judgments for their internal and external stakeholders. Several leading technologies are making this possible.

Value Creation

Accountants have a unique competitive advantage for creating value for their stakeholders since their perspectives integrate knowledge across disciplines. Thoughtful data analyses can help improve resources and processes to increase operational competitiveness and achieve financial objectives (**Illustration 10.8**).

ILLUSTRATION 10.8   The Data Analysis Value Creation Chain

These opportunities have led to changes in how professional accounting organizations and businesses present themselves:

- The Association of International CPAs (AICPA) and the Institute of Management Accountants (IMA) have recently rebranded how their members serve their organizations and society. They have declared that their primary purpose is to create value for stakeholders, which include investors, creditors, customers, suppliers, regulators, and management and employees.

- Similarly, the large international accounting firm PwC recently moved away from the traditional compliance-facing labels of tax accountant and auditor. PwC's operations in the United States have been reorganized to combine the traditional audit and tax regulatory expertise services into "Trust Solutions." PwC has further rebranded their professionals as transparent, trusted business advisors focused on creating value through recommending sustainable growth outcomes for their clients and the world.

Accounting firms, both large and small, are quickly changing their business models to present themselves as expert advisors who create value by performing data analyses to improve governance, operations, and compliance strategies for their clients. By following recommendations for better resource allocations and process improvements, organizations can improve access to capital, trading partners, and performance. For example, data analytics that reveal which product or service revenues are most associated with net income increases can grow both the client's and the public's trust in accountants' expertise and opinions.

Let's use a university example to illustrate how recent developments in data analysis have impacted value creation. Historically, faculty at institutions of higher education have evaluated internal student performance data to gain insights into how to improve their instruction. Access to new data options and analysis tools now allows colleges to analyze data from external stakeholders such as alumni, recruiters, advisory boards, and professional associations to learn which skills and knowledge are demanded by the profession (**Illustration 10.9**).

ILLUSTRATION 10.9   Accounting Knowledge and Skills Demanded by Recruiters and Professional Association Standards

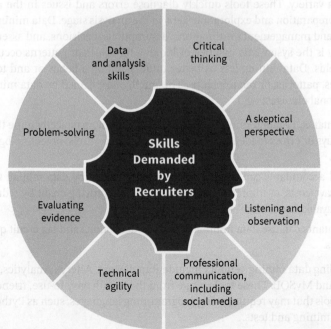

Accounting programs can now analyze a variety of valuable data from alumni and recruiter surveys, interviews, and high volume and velocity data from social media platforms, such as LinkedIn and Facebook, to create courses that produce successful graduates. They can also evaluate an accounting program's effectiveness by external metrics, such as how many internships turned into full time post-graduation job offers and by measuring how long it takes alumni to be promoted after graduation.

Similarly, accounting professionals are using more types of data and newer analysis tools to create value:

- Data mining tools and electronic contracts for revenue recognition and lease accounting.
- Routine process automation and process mining tools for improvements in process efficiency and control.
- Continuous auditing processes to reduce audit risk and improve audit quality.
- Textual analysis for insights from language used to describe accounting and business outcomes and predictions.
- Cognitive technologies using artificial intelligence modeling to predict and classify phenomena.

These tools improve the efficiency and productivity of accountants. Regained worktime can be repurposed for more activities that add value, such as finding service opportunities and interpreting and communicating analysis results to stakeholders.

Data Mining and Smart Contracts

Some may know from personal experience that food sensitivity symptoms are easily diagnosed. However, the process of identifying which food(s) are associated with which symptoms can require disciplined testing over time. Health professionals often advise eliminating the most likely food sensitivity culprits, and systematically, over weeks and months, adding each back into the diet to identify specific food allergies.

Similar to the trial and error method of food allergy identification, data mining helps accountants systematically understand and test hypotheses while reducing some of the labor involved with data analysis. Additionally, smart contract software solutions allow business contracts to be securely negotiated, settled, and signed online in a fraction of the traditional time.

Data Mining

Increasingly sophisticated data mining tools are better able to handle the recent increases in data volume and data variety. These tools quickly diagnose errors and issues in the accounting data during the data preparation and exploration steps in the analysis stage. Data mining is also used to improve and defend management's estimations, assumptions, decisions, and assertions.

Data mining is the systematic practice of looking for issues or patterns occurring within or between data fields. Data mining lets us better understand data behavior and test expectations about data values, patterns, or relationships. The intelligence gained by data mining can lead to valuable operational changes:

- AIS accountants, IT auditors, and application programmers typically mine their data to find system delays or errors to identify where new policies, controls, or technologies can improve operations.
- Managerial accountants can use the information provided by data mining to increase sales revenues, save costs, or improve operations, such as improving credit by reducing how often accounts payable invoices are paid late.
- Tax accountants can use data mining to find tax deductions and tax credit qualifications for their clients.

Some of the leading data mining vendors include RapidMiner, Alteryx Analytics, SAS Enterprise Miner, Sisense, and MySQL. These tools range from those with easy-to-use, friendly interfaces to more complex tools that may require using programming languages, such as Python or R, to write the desired data mining and tests.

Applying Critical Thinking 10.6

Reflect on Data Mining Results

You can improve data mining skills in a couple of ways (**Self-Reflection**):

- Think about how the data value and veracity contribute to creating reliable intelligence and insights for the objective of the analysis. This awareness includes watching for results that might be random correlations with little or no business value.

- Estimate the potential data value that could be created by mining the data, and compare that value to the costs and risks associated with continuing current strategies. For example, looking for sales revenues to customers from states far from each specific store's location may help to focus efforts on fraudulent invoices.

Retail grocery stores, such as Wegmans, Publix, and Kroger, are credited as the first industry to create value from sales data mining. Empowered by point-of-sale cash register machines that integrated sales and AIS inventory data, supermarkets performed data mining to understand what store, aisle, and shelf locations were associated with increases in product sales:

- The first step was to create a categorical data field in their inventory tables which indicated store location (aisle number, front cap, back cap, store front table, and register aisle) and shelf position (shelf number, and left or right side).

- The sales data with this location field was mined to learn which product locations were associated with high sales volume and which locations with low sales volume.

- Systematically and over time, each product's position in the store was moved to determine which positions resulted in higher sales for which products, as well as which products' sales were more resistant to location changes.

The next time you go to a grocery store you might notice some intentional product placement that is the result of mining store location data along with sales data. For example, temporary product promotions (e.g., strawberries during the spring) are best placed on the aisle end caps and store front display tables to capture customer attention (**Illustration 10.10**).

ILLUSTRATION 10.10   Product Placement Findings from Supermarket Data Mining

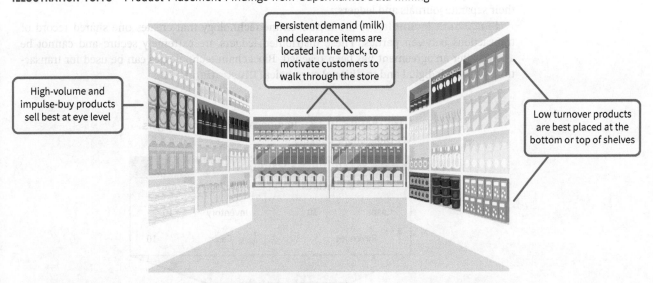

Let's consider an accounting data mining example. Assume you are hired as a consultant to help a law firm identify how to best use their limited professional staff resources. Your objective questions may include:

- Which legal service is the most profitable?
- Which service is performed most often?

- Which lawyer and paralegal team is currently earning the most client fee revenues for the law firm?
- Are any legal services being performed without being billed to clients?

Data mining tools can help gain insights to answer these questions. For example, you could use data mining to verify whether all services performed have corresponding invoices.

Data mining is perhaps the most common form of data analytics in accounting practice. It is useful for data preparation and data exploration. We can easily check for empty, incorrect, invalid, and duplicate data, and perform pattern identification tests, such as learning whether unusual logins indicate suspicious or unauthorized activity. Most data mining software displays the mining steps that have been performed on the data from left to right, which provides documentation for data verification procedures. **Illustration 10.11** illustrates a simple data mining process.

ILLUSTRATION 10.11 A Simple Data Mining Process for Identifying Suspicious Bank Deposits

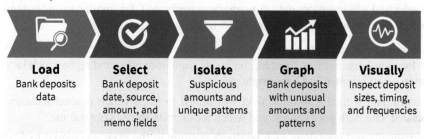

Load	**Select**	**Isolate**	**Graph**	**Visually**
Bank deposits data	Bank deposit date, source, amount, and memo fields	Suspicious amounts and unique patterns	Bank deposits with unusual amounts and patterns	Inspect deposit sizes, timing, and frequencies

Smart Contracts

A business contract is created whenever two parties, such as buyers and sellers, agree on the consideration (usually money) that one party will provide to the other party in exchange for goods or services. Business contracts can range from simple exchanges to complex agreements with many stipulations. Contract review is important for proper U.S. GAAP classifications, such as revenue recognition or lease treatment. Historically, contract content was not standardized, which meant that both parties had to conduct a detailed review of the contract to ensure proper accounting in their separate journals and ledgers.

Blockchain technologies are a new online technology that creates one shared record of transactions between parties. These distributed ledgers are extremely secure and cannot be altered after an agreement has been reached. Blockchain technologies can be used for transactions with both digital and traditional currencies (**Illustration 10.12**).

ILLUSTRATION 10.12 Traditional Accounting Ledgers vs. Blockchain Ledgers

Traditional Accounting Ledgers			
Seller S's Records		**Buyer B's Records**	
↑ Cash	10	↑ Inventory	10
↑ Revenues	10	↓ Cash	10

Blockchain Shared Ledger			
Seller	Buyer	Date	Amount
S	B	9.14.22	10
—	—	—	—
—	—	—	—
—	—	—	—

A specific and popular application of blockchain technology is a **smart contract**, which is a secure online shared digital contract. Smart contracts are now commonly used in healthcare, trading, lending, real estate, insurance, legal services, warranties, employment, and gaming contexts. **Illustration 10.13** shows some typical smart lease contract data fields.

ILLUSTRATION 10.13 Typical Smart Lease Contract Data Fields

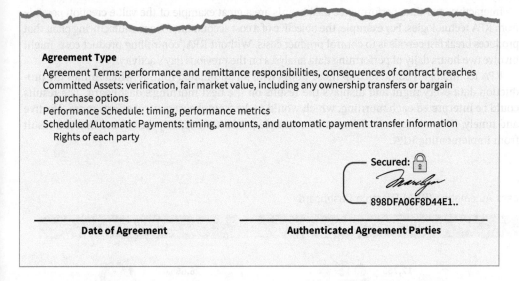

Agreement Type
Agreement Terms: performance and remittance responsibilities, consequences of contract breaches
Committed Assets: verification, fair market value, including any ownership transfers or bargain
    purchase options
Performance Schedule: timing, performance metrics
Scheduled Automatic Payments: timing, amounts, and automatic payment transfer information
    Rights of each party

Secured: 🔒

898DFA06F8D44E1..

| Date of Agreement | Authenticated Agreement Parties |

Smart contracts have important advantages over traditional contracts:

- Contract templates provide organized, approved, and clearly labeled data field options, many of which are required by contract law or by GAAP rules for revenue recognition or lease categorization.
- Contract parties collaboratively develop contract specifics using secured online shared documents, reducing the time needed for contract negotiation, verification, and signing, while providing stronger internal controls. Contract options can be activated or deactivated as needed.
- All signed contracts cannot easily be changed by either party and all changes made are documented with red flags to all parties, which can eliminate many misunderstandings and disagreements.
- Smart contracts can automatically identify contract performance milestones, determine performance outcomes, and automatically trigger agreed payments between parties.

The standardized data fields make it easy for financial accountants to review and evaluate contracts and determine which GAAP rules are applicable. Auditors can easily verify the contract accounting. In both cases, time traditionally spent data mining contracts can be spent on other services that create value.

Process Automation and Process Mining

From doorbell cameras to robotic vacuums, smart sensors and programmable controllers are making some homes operate more efficiently and effectively. In the same way, business process automation tools are now performing routine tasks, freeing accountants to create value with critical thinking, problem-solving, and their resulting professional judgments.

While automated processes within software programs and equipment controllers have been available for decades, the recent development of across-program and across-equipment integrative tools have transformed many accounting tasks. In addition to greater performance accuracy and consistency, these new capabilities are producing activity logs that can be used to analyze and improve business processes.

Robotic Process Automation

Robotic process automation (RPA) is the set of software technologies that record a specific order of human keystrokes and mouse activity steps within or across digital applications. Once saved or recorded, these routines can be repeated by simply re-running the tool. RPA tools are used for stable processes where the steps of the process do not change over time, such as when financial analysts download the closing stock prices of the same set of companies every day.

Interactive, real-time performance dashboards are a great example of the value creation possible from RPA technologies. For example, the objective of a cost accountant for a manufacturing plant that produces breakfast cereals is to control product costs. Without RPA, controlling product costs might involve two hours daily of performing data analyses on the previous day's activity.

RPA technologies could recoup those hours with an automated routine which mines the production data every night and displays the results on the next morning's dashboard. The results could be interpreted each morning, which would make factory cost control efforts more effective and timely. **Illustration 10.14** illustrates a sample production activity dashboard that can result from implementing RPA.

ILLUSTRATION 10.14   Robotic Process Automation (RPA) Example Dashboard

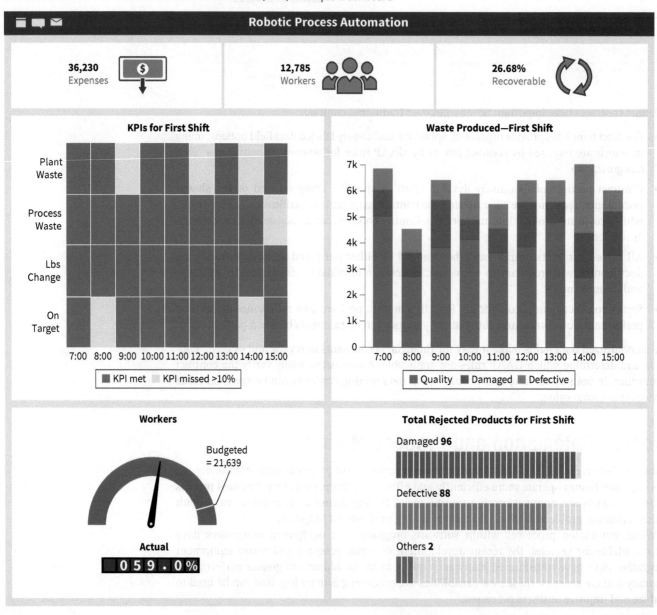

Illustration 10.15 summarizes more of the common accounting uses for RPA.

ILLUSTRATION 10.15
Accounting Tasks That Benefit
from RPA

PROFESSIONAL INSIGHT   How Can RPA Be Used in Financial Accounting?

The summer before the final year of her accounting program, Brigitte completed an internship where she gained valuable experience working for a financial analyst.

The first half of the summer I was gathering financial statement balances and totals for over 400 companies each day so I could calculate and compare 15 financial ratios. Evaluating these ratio trends over time and comparing them to a competitor's ratios or to the industry average can provide insights about profitability, asset utilization, liquidity, and solvency.

About halfway through my internship, my boss suggested I learn how to use a routine process automation tool, UiPath, to write a routine to automatically gather the financial data. My RPA routine opened the SEC data website and sequentially entered each company's code so the financial statement information would be displayed. My RPA script would then copy the data and paste it into an Excel worksheet, naming the sheet with that company's code.

I then learned how to write the RPA script for the calculation and comparison of all the financial ratios. What had previously taken me over six hours a day to perform was now running overnight so that I would have the information first thing the following morning. Then, I could critically evaluate the ratios' meaning. I feel like my internship was much more valuable after automating the routine part of my day and spending my time learning the value of the information models I had created.

Process Mining

Process mining tools measure the timing and flow of data captured as business events occur. They help financial, managerial, and tax accountants better evaluate business process efficiency and effectiveness. Systems accountants also use process mining tools to evaluate AIS risks and control effectiveness. By describing where processes have more exceptions and delays, process mining also helps auditors adjust their audit plans to spend more time on the accounts and processes that have the greatest risk of financial statement errors and omissions.

Process mining can improve, innovate, or control existing processes:

- Available data fields are typically extracted, joined, and transformed to create a process log.
- The process log records what happened where, who was involved, when it happened, and can capture which controls were implemented or skipped over.

Let's illustrate process mining with an example from a manufacturer of superhero figurines. **Illustration 10.16** depicts the three major events in their sales cycle:

- The sales department captures the sale and records it in the sales journal.
- The shipping department ships all sales notifications received from the sales department and reduces inventory.
- Accounts receivable matches sales orders and shipping notifications to create accurate invoices, which are sent to the customers.

ILLUSTRATION 10.16 Sales Cycle Example of Process Mining Tests

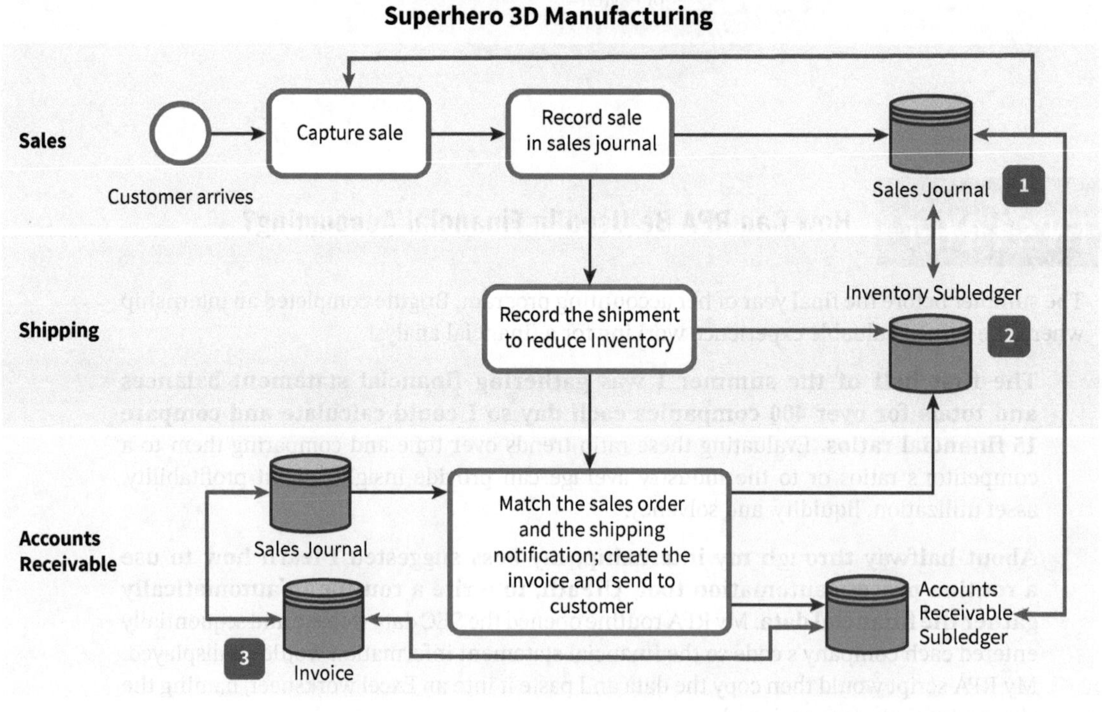

Superhero 3D Manufacturing

The red lines in Illustration 10.16 depict the specific tests to be conducted from the process mining, which can be expressed as these questions:

1. Are all sales captured reflected in the sales journal? What is the time delay between the capture and the recording of these sales?
2. Are all sales captured in the sales journal shipped? What is the time delay between the sales capture and the shipment to the customer? Are all shipments recorded as reductions in the inventory subledger? Are there any sales journal entries that are made and not shipped in the same accounting period? (GAAP rules state that revenue cannot be recognized until the sales transaction has been fulfilled.)

3. Do all invoices get posted to the accounts receivable subledger? How often and by how much are the sales journal entries different than the invoices? What is the time delay between the shipment and the invoice mailing to the customer?

The results may show that some captured sales are never shipped or do not ship in a timely fashion. Alternatively, there may be shipments that never turn into invoices, resulting in lost inventory. Finally, there may be differences between what is recorded in the sales journal and what invoice data is posted to the accounts receivable subsidiary ledger. To quickly show where and when the data variance happens for each of these questions, we could present process mining results as dashboard dials, as data tables, or as data visualizations.

Process mining results may also reveal violation of authorization or segregation of duties controls, such as the sales department both authorizing the sales capture and recording the sales journal entries. This insight would lead to changing the process so that accounts receivable is recording all sales transactions and sales events would not be recorded until after shipping and invoicing.

Two other examples help illustrate the value provided by process mining. In the AIS practice area, analyzing system access logs with process mining can ensure that system access for terminated employees is revoked in a timely manner. In managerial accounting, process mining can identify bottlenecks in business processes and establish relevant activity bases for activity-based costing systems. These examples document how process mining helps improve the internal controls over the accounting systems, reducing audit risk for both internal and external auditors.

Continuous Auditing

Have you ever wondered why auditors wait until after the year-end to perform their journal and ledger data tests under tremendous time pressure? Or why they use data sampling techniques to infer whether ledger balances are reasonable rather than evaluating the population of data?

Continuous auditing technologies are programmed modules embedded in an organization's AIS that evaluate transactions as they occur throughout the year:

- Routine transactions are typically captured and tested in automated routines for consistent processing.
- If transactions do not pass the tests to be categorized as a routine transaction, they are usually copied to an exception file to be evaluated by the external auditors at year-end. Examples of these exceptions are invoice totals that are too high or too low for what has been sold or payroll cash disbursements which do not match up to an authorized employee.

This testing of the entire population of transactions helps auditors develop a more accurate assessment of the risks inherent to amounts reported on the financial statements. Continuous auditing tools reduce the workload at year-end and provide faster audits with higher quality. **Illustration 10.17** illustrates continuous auditing modules employed at end of quarter throughout the year.

ILLUSTRATION 10.17   Quarterly Continuous Auditing Throughout the Year

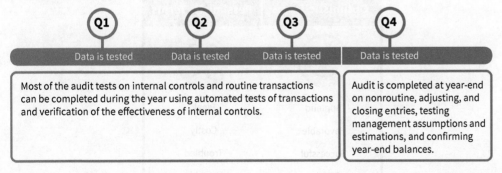

Q1	Q2	Q3	Q4
Data is tested	Data is tested	Data is tested	Data is tested

Most of the audit tests on internal controls and routine transactions can be completed during the year using automated tests of transactions and verification of the effectiveness of internal controls.	Audit is completed at year-end on nonroutine, adjusting, and closing entries, testing management assumptions and estimations, and confirming year-end balances.

The first users of continuous auditing were large banks and credit card companies. Both industries have millions of transactions occurring every day, which create a high data volume that is difficult to confidently sample by year-end. More recently, companies in extractive and manufacturing industries have joined auditors in embracing continuous auditing technologies to support their internal applications.

Continuous auditing technologies also make audits more proactive rather than reactive. Accounting record issues and errors can be evaluated and corrected when they occur, increasing the integrity and reliability of internal data gathered after those corrections are made:

- Evaluating emerging data patterns earlier in the year can identify new tax strategies or areas where more internal controls are needed.
- Logging unusual internet use data points can identify cybersecurity risks earlier, which means that controls can be implemented.
- Automated evaluation of routine transaction data frees auditors to focus time and energy on audit process steps that contain more financial statement risk.

Tests of revenue recognition, inventory valuation, and cash flows are a few examples of areas where both internal and external auditors are using continuous auditing.

Textual Analysis

Textual analysis tools analyze word choices in footnotes, investor communications, blogs, social media postings, and other documentation, such as contract language for revenue recognition treatment. **Textual mining** tools evaluate word choice and usage to reveal insights about honesty, transparency, intent, and sentiments in communications by management, elected officials, and customers. Text counts and text patterns can be coded into categories of meaning, which are then analyzed along with numerical data for insights.

These tools make harvesting data efficient from sources such as financial footnotes and management emails to online customer feedback. Textual analysis can generate business intelligence, audit intelligence, and tax planning value. There are a few examples of text mining sources in the accounting profession:

- Lease contract language
- Annual reports, financial statement footnotes, and 10K or 10Q filings
- xBRL text data fields
- Auditor letters and reports
- Investor relation press releases
- Correspondence from regulators
- Tax planning and response letters

We can also use textual analysis on formal and informal social media communications by analysts, auditors, and regulators to categorize the favorability or pessimism in those communications (**Illustration 10.18**).

ILLUSTRATION 10.18
Optimistic and Pessimistic Word Categories: Annual Report Examples

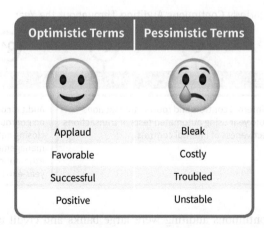

Optimistic Terms	Pessimistic Terms
Applaud	Bleak
Favorable	Costly
Successful	Troubled
Positive	Unstable

Diligent Institute is the leading technology solution designed to improve board of directors' fiduciary responsibilities to oversee management decisions. They create financial and textual analysis dashboard visualizations to focus board members' attention on the areas of the organization with the greatest risks. For example, they have used textual analysis to show corporate board members' sentiment rating over time. These results show how optimistic corporate board members are about the upcoming opportunities and performance possibilities in their organizations (**Illustration 10.19**).

ILLUSTRATION 10.19 Diligent Institute's Board Member Sentiment Tracker

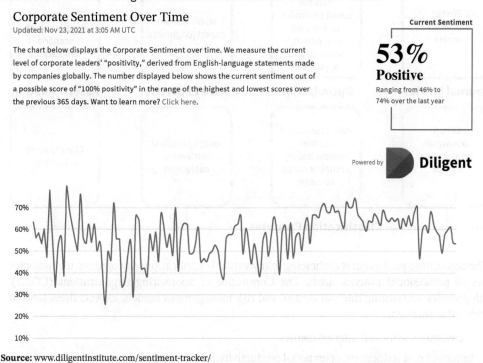

Corporate Sentiment Over Time
Updated: Nov 23, 2021 at 3:05 AM UTC

The chart below displays the Corporate Sentiment over time. We measure the current level of corporate leaders' "positivity," derived from English-language statements made by companies globally. The number displayed below shows the current sentiment out of a possible score of "100% positivity" in the range of the highest and lowest scores over the previous 365 days. Want to learn more? Click here.

Current Sentiment

53%
Positive

Ranging from 46% to 74% over the last year

Powered by **Diligent**

Source: www.diligentinstitute.com/sentiment-tracker/

Textual analysis that evaluates the use of passive versus active verbs and the ratio of positive words to negative words, often called the polarity of the communication, helps to categorize communications. These categories can then be analyzed in combination with financial statement totals or ratios to better predict future earnings, bankruptcy risk, or stock prices.

Cognitive Technologies

If you have interacted with Apple devices, then you have witnessed the power of Siri, the virtual assistant feature of Apple's operating system. Siri is a user-friendly artificial intelligence tool programmed to answer most questions and research requests. **Cognitive technologies** are artificial intelligence technologies that use a human expert judgment mimicking internal algorithm. Accountants typically use AIS data to train their models for accuracy for diagnosing and predicting objectives, and then adjust their model as new data is added. Cognitive technologies are used in many fields, including training, production, farming, banking, retail, healthcare, tourism, and utilities, and in a variety of business functions within organizations. They can range from simplistic decision models to dynamic, complex models.

Complex cognitive tools are also called artificial neural networks, machine learning, and expert systems. These models are programmed to accurately perform data classification tasks for diagnostic or prediction objectives. For the model to be accurate, the underlying phenomena variables should behave in stable or consistent patterns.

Cognitive technology tools perform best in stable environments because they use old data to define a complex mathematical algorithm which will, over time, produce an expert decision. The most advanced models, called adaptive cognitive technologies, can adjust their underlying models with every new data point, but these changes are typically very small, as the models were trained on very large data sets.

Illustration 10.20 lists a few common uses of cognitive technologies in accounting.

ILLUSTRATION 10.20 Cognitive Technologies in Accounting

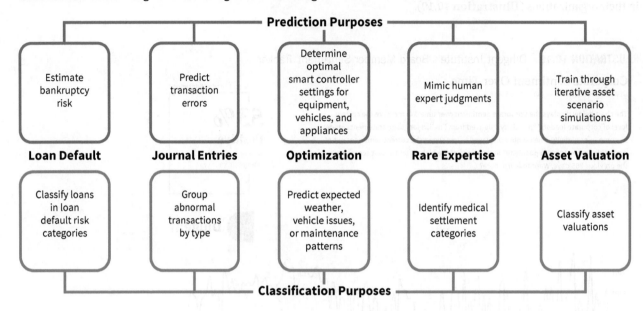

The accounting profession is embracing many valuable applications of cognitive technologies across all professional practice areas. The Committee of Sponsoring Organizations (COSO), which provides accounting internal control and risk management models, expects these tools to provide value through:

- Increased security and internal control.
- Improved cost reductions, operational productivity, and process quality.
- Predictive analytics.
- Innovation through iterative testing.

Applying Critical Thinking 10.7

Recognize Risks with Cognitive Technologies

Using cognitive technologies is not risk-free. For example, if a classification model incorrectly rejects a loan application due to a data error, then the lending institution could lose business. COSO suggests considering the following (**Risks**):

- Potential biases by the expert who developed the cognitive technology.
- High potential for errors from data and interpretation.
- Changing laws and regulations that may have been overlooked in the model.
- Changing underlying conditions or ranges of values that may make your model less predictive.
- Vulnerabilities to security attacks.
- Negative reactions from employees, customers, and other impacted stakeholders.

COSO also recommends cognitive technology policies to increase internal controls:

- Establish governance structure for all cognitive technology tool applications.
- Develop a risk management strategy.
- Regularly assess the risks of the organization's cognitive technology applications.
- Evaluate the cognitive technology applications as a portfolio rather than individual assets.
- Document and internally share the risk appetite and risk response commitments associated with cognitive technology use to increase transparency.

Use of Generative AI in Accounting

What Is Generative AI?

Combining computer science with robust data sets, AI facilitates problem-solving at a high level. Generative AI, a sub-domain of artificial intelligence technology, is capable of generating text, images, and audio forms of content. Numerous sectors are utilizing generative AI to execute various tasks, including generating code for application development and composing marketing copy, emails, and blogs, in addition to integrating chatbots for customer service.

The Transformative Impact of AI in Accounting

The implementation of generative AI in the accounting industry has the capacity to fundamentally alter established workflow procedures. An area where AI has made a substantial impact is in the automation of routine workflow tasks such as reconciliation, invoice processing, and data input. These responsibilities can now be executed with efficiency and precision by AI systems. Additionally, AI improves financial reporting precision by mitigating the potential for human error. Sophisticated algorithms are capable of scrutinizing enormous data sets, discerning patterns, and identifying anomalies that may elude human detection. As a result, not only are financial statements more accurate, but decision-making is also enhanced through the utilization of real-time insights.

Generative AI possesses the potential to exert a substantial influence within the domains of finance and accounting through the digitization and optimization of pivotal procedures encompassing accounts payable, accounts receivable, spend management, liquidity management, inventory control, cash flow management, and working capital management. The use of AI enhances the efficiency, cost-effectiveness, and flexibility of these processes in response to evolving business requirements.

Generative AI is transforming finance and accounting processes as follows:

- **Improved insights and decision-making:** Generative AI models can assist financial professionals in identifying anomalies, patterns, and trends in massive amounts of data, enabling them to make more precise predictions, risk assessments, and well-informed recommendations.

- **Increased efficiency and cost savings:** By automating repetitive tasks, streamlining processes, and decreasing manual errors, generative AI generates substantial efficiencies and cost savings in financial operations.

- **Targeted communications:** Generative AI models, empowered by vast data sets comprising textual content, categorical data, audio, video, and numerical data points, have the capability to generate customer responses in AI-powered chatbots or virtual assistants that are more organic and contextually pertinent.

- **Automation of repetitive tasks:** The implementation of automation for labor-intensive and repetitive tasks enhances precision and enables accountants to allocate their time toward more intricate assignments that demand human expertise and judgment. Additionally, automation increases efficiency, which permits accounting to expand in tandem with the workload.

- **Fraud detection:** Regenerative AI systems can assist in the identification of fraudulent activity or suspicious irregularities that may necessitate additional investigation through the analysis of vast quantities of financial data.

- **Document analysis:** Generative AI is capable of processing, summarizing, and extracting valuable information from substantial quantities of financial documents, including earnings calls, annual reports, and financial statements. This capability enables more streamlined analysis and informed decision-making.

- **Financial report generation:** Generative AI can assist finance teams in automating the creation of text, charts, and graphs and importing data from multiple sources more efficiently. These reports may include balance sheets, income statements, and cash flow statements.

- **Financial analysis and forecasting:** Generative AI models possess the capability to discern intricate patterns and interconnections within historical financial data, thereby facilitating the generation of predictive analytics pertaining to forthcoming trends, asset valuations, and economic indicators.
- **Improved compliance:** By automating the process of monitoring and reporting financial transactions, generative AI can aid organizations in adhering to accounting and financial regulations. This may assist in averting expensive fines and penalties.
- **Improved customer experience:** An enhanced customer experience can be achieved through the use of generative AI, which automates the resolution of disputes and provides customers with real-time updates on the status of their accounts. This may contribute to increased customer retention and satisfaction.

How Can Accounting Firms Leverage AI?

Here are a few ways accounting firms can leverage AI in their businesses:

1. **Client communications:** Generate initial drafts of client emails or newsletters using generative AI; subsequently, make revisions to ensure precision and incorporate personal insight.
2. **Client support:** Utilize chatbots enabled by AI to provide support and service to clients at any time.
3. **Audit automation:** Leverage artificial intelligence (AI) to detect discrepancies or anomalies in financial records automatically, gain insight from the broader audit community, and conduct audits with greater precision and efficiency.
4. **Compliance:** Predictive analytics enable artificial intelligence to identify prospective tax or noncompliance risks, offer suggestions to prevent legal consequences, and forecast violations in advance.
5. **Tax research and planning:** Utilize AI-driven tools to stay abreast of evolving tax laws and regulations and to systematically examine various tax planning scenarios on behalf of clients.
6. **Training:** Leverage AI for comprehensive industry research, timely trend analysis, and assistance with tax landscape evaluation.

Is Artificial Intelligence an Opportunity or a Threat to Accountants?

AI may empower professionals, augment human capabilities, and herald in an era of unprecedented productivity and value generation in the future. Generative AI serves as a catalyst for excellence and transformation in the accounting and finance industry, rather than a threat. AI does, nevertheless, present both opportunities and obstacles. Repetitive tasks, including data entry, invoice processing, and rudimentary recordkeeping, can be automated by AI applications. Although these developments have improved efficiency in operations, they appear to be eliminating the need for accounting professionals.

According to a recent research study, approximately 80% of the workforce perceives a 10% impact on work duties, whereas the remaining 20% observes a 50% impact. This creates a vulnerability for accountants, auditors, and tax preparers, necessitating that these professionals need to be updated with their technology skills set so that they adapt their expertise and collaborate with AI systems.

Students should be ready to learn new skills after graduating as required competencies will evolve within a few years, necessitating an adaptation of their daily duties.

`Financial Accounting` `Data` The macro record option in Excel illustrates the power of RPA for financial statement analysis. Try using it to analyze accounts receivable liquidity for a selection of leading outdoor gear companies.

APPLY IT 10.2

Use Process Automation to Analyze Financial Statements

You have developed an objective question: Which of the leading outdoor gear industry companies had the best liquidity with regards to accounts receivable? The following data is provided for each company for the years 2015–2020:

- Income statement: Net sales revenues, cost of goods sold, gross profit, and net income.
- Balance sheet: Year-end accounts receivable and inventory balances.

Record one macro routine on the first worksheet to calculate accounts receivable turnover, and then repeat the macro on the subsequent workbook sheets that contain the financial statement data from other companies.

SOLUTION

Ratio Values and Graph from the Comparison Worksheet

Comparison of Accounts Receivable Turnovers						
	2015	**2016**	**2017**	**2018**	**2019**	**2020**
Fenix	11.9	13.1	13.6	14.1	14.0	13.5
Clarus	5.7	5.9	5.8	5.9	5.9	4.9
Columbia	6.5	6.7	7.1	6.9	6.5	5.3
VF Corp	8.3	8.6	8.8	2.1	8.7	6.9

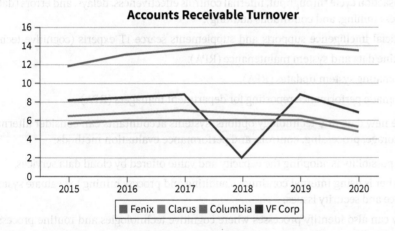

Fenix Outdoor has the best accounts receivable liquidity throughout this six-year period.

Building and Using the Excel Macro

1. Open the Apply It 10.2 data file. Your platform may ask you to enable macros and to make this file a trusted file. Select **Yes** for both.

2. Go to the first sheet for Fenix Outdoor and select the **View** tab. Select **Macro** (last option on right). Select **Record** and name your new macro "AccRecTurnover."

3. Place the cursor on cell C18. Type the formula "=C7/((sum(B13:C13))/2)" and click **Enter**.

4. Copy this formula to D18-H18. Remove the adjacent cell error by right clicking on the error icon to the left of this formula and select **Ignore error**.

5. Go back to **View Macro**, and stop recording.

6. Next, go into each remaining company data sheets and click Cell C18. Select **View > View Macros > AccRecTurnover > Run**. Watch as the macro performs the ratio calculations for each company, saving you from having to recreate the steps for each company. Remove the adjacent cell error on each sheet by right clicking on the error icon to the left of this formula and selecting **Ignore error**.

7. Now, open the Comparison worksheet. All the accounts receivable turnover results linked to this comparison sheet should be visible. Highlight all the data cells, B3:H7.

8. Under top menu, select **Insert**, and add a line chart.

9. Double click on the chart title and change it to "Accounts Receivable Turnover." Compare results.

10.3 How Are Data and Analyses Developments Impacting the Professional Practice Areas?

Emerging data, analyses, and technologies are significantly impacting each area of professional practice. Accounting tasks are more accurate and completed in less time, freeing accountants to focus on using critical thinking and creative ways to add value to their organizations.

Accounting Information Systems

Accounting information systems professionals manage the design, implementation, and evaluation of the accounting system transaction processing and business intelligence information. Many new data options are improving data volume, variety, veracity, and value for AIS users. New analysis tools discussed here help systems accountants improve their AIS data analyses:

- Detecting unauthorized intrusion (data mining and process mining).
- Transaction cycle throughput, internal controls effectiveness, delays, and errors (data mining, process mining, and continuous auditing).
- Artificial intelligence supports and supplements scarce IT experts (cognitive technologies).
- Routine data and system maintenance (RPA).
- Automating system updates (RPA).
- Automatic performance reporting for department managers (RPA).

With these new data and technology options, systems accountants can consider alternative data capture, storage, processing, controls, and performance evaluation methods:

- One possibility is adopting the capacity and value offered by cloud data services.
- Another is using internal continuous auditing and process mining to evaluate system performance and security issues.
- They can also identify processes where cognitive technologies and routine process automation can allow employees to spend more time interpreting information and adding value to their organizations.

For example, systems accountants can help marketing and sales departments by creating visualizations of the technologies being used by their key managers (**Illustration 10.21**).

Auditing

Both internal and external auditors also using many of the emerging data and technology options to increase the quality of audits while reducing their costs. RPA, cognitive technologies, process mining, and continuous auditing are improving analytical testing of controls and substantive testing since an entire population of transactions can be analyzed.

New combinations of data, information models, and graphics make it easier to understand a client's business and data (e.g., dashboard visualizations such as Illustration 10.15), and can be used to communicate and audit's "story" to management and boards of directors.

AIS audit trail log data (user ID, date, and time stamp) is helpful for verifying segregation of duties. Continuous auditing also has advantages:

- Reduced audit sample risk, as inferences from limited samples are reduced or eliminated from the process.

ILLUSTRATION 10.21   AIS Analytics Value for Marketing and Sales Functions

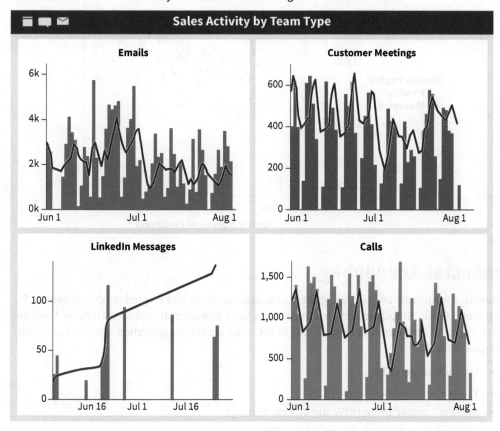

- Auditors can focus on prioritized risks in their clients' data, such as management's assertions and estimates, and increase their audit quality consistency across clients.
- Audits can be finished closer to the fiscal year end date, which will increase the value of the client's financial statement information in the capital markets.

Audit firms can also develop their own intellectual property intelligent assets as they create confidential tools for their firms. However, there may be audit risks associated with these emerging data analytics options, such as client AIS and auditor tool compatibility, and issues with data security and privacy. For example, audit risk is impacted if clients' systems are not compatible with new audit tools, if the client uses an integration of different systems patched together, or if the data integrity from the clients' system is low. In these cases, the tools may not retrieve enough data or the appropriate data for the auditors' evaluations.

Auditors are performing a variety of their tasks using the tools discussed in this chapter:

- Classifying unusual transactions (cognitive technologies).
- Performing risk-level assessments (continuous auditing and cognitive technologies).
- Selecting better samples for substantive testing (blockchain technologies and data mining).
- Performing analytics on selected data for substantive testing (process mining).
- Testing transactions for routine qualities (continuous auditing modules, cognitive technologies, and data mining).
- Monitoring and evaluating internal controls (process mining).
- Evaluating ongoing concerns (cognitive technologies).

Auditors often use analytics to improve judgments about whether recorded account balances are reasonable, which helps them improve their substantive test sample selections (**Illustration 10.22**).

ILLUSTRATION 10.22
Visualization Used by
Auditors for Reasonableness
of Payroll Expenses

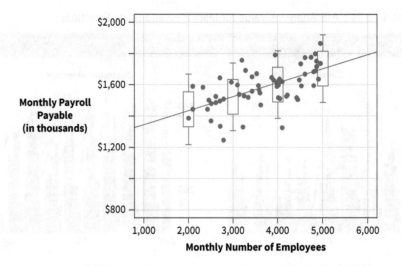

Financial Accounting

Financial accountants are also using these new data, analysis, and technology developments for both their GAAP compliance responsibilities and their assessments and predictions of business value, risk, and future capital needs. Some of the more common application areas of these technologies include:

- Reconciliations (RPA).
- Temporary account closures (RPA).
- Routine consolidations (RPA and process mining).
- Accounting period end closing entries (RPA).
- Footnote preparation (textual analysis).
- Statutory and regulatory report content generation (cognitive technologies).
- Proforma financial statement generation (data mining and pattern detection).
- Scanning of changes in external environment (textual analysis).
- Data patterns and relationships to explain stock market valuation changes (data mining, blockchain, and continuous auditing).

Routine process automations are a natural fit for financial accounting. Stable, iterative revenue, expenditure, payroll, production, and financial accounting processes can easily be captured and then reused with recorded macros. Additionally, process mining helps evaluate the efficiencies, effectiveness, and controls in each accounting step (see Illustration 10.16).

Cognitive technologies can be used to both predict financial outcomes and classify business option risks. Textual content is analyzed for regulatory implications and earnings expectations communication. Finally, many CFOs can now monitor their financial ratio performance real-time using live dashboards tied to their accounting systems (**Illustration 10.23**).

Managerial Accounting

Managerial accountants are not tied to the GAAP data restrictions or the IRS data rules, allowing them more freedom and creativity to solve problems and identify opportunities than the more regulated practice areas:

- Managerial accountants have traditionally used broad sets of operational and market data to find the most effective least expensive solutions for their organizations.
- As confidential advisors to the management team, they tend to quickly embrace new data analyses opportunities, for descriptive, diagnostic, predictive, and prescriptive objectives in budgeting, costing, pricing, investment, or controlling tasks.
- These new analysis tools are helping to improve the performance of functional departments, such as human resources, marketing, sales, and inventory management.

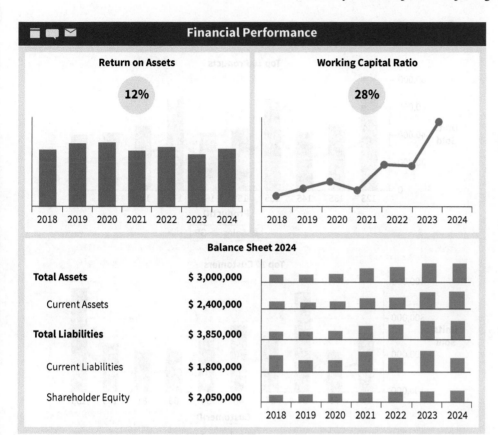

ILLUSTRATION 10.23
Sample Dashboard for
Financial Accountants

The new data options let managerial accountants add value by helping them ask better questions, accurately identify priority issues, and develop intelligence and solutions to support their management team's decision-making. Because smart devices and social media are increasingly used by organizations, managerial accountants are managing data with greater volume, variety, and velocity than before, and they must control data veracity by properly capturing, processing, and storing data.

Several new technologies are helping managerial accountants improve processes and add value to their organizations. RPAs can quickly create daily performance dashboards across organizational functions, cognitive technologies forecast sales and production levels, data and process mining help optimize operational control, and blockchain technologies are capturing resource transfers within the organization, such as inventory transfers across warehouses. Managerial accountants can keep track of their areas of responsibility using the tools discussed in this chapter to create visualizations for dashboards (**Illustration 10.24**).

Process mining is helping managerial accountants identify business process areas where costs can be reduced:

- Mining transactions for increased travel expense, miscellaneous expense, or overhead cost account to control costs.

- Cost savings in general, including reducing headcounts, are easier to identify with process mining.

Other technologies have applications, as well:

- Improving decision-making by making more types of data accessible for analysis.

- Discovering new business insights in revenue, expenditure, and operational processes (data mining, process mining, and cognitive technology).

- Increasing employee productivity with useful dashboards and automations of routine task completion (RPA).

- Enhancing product offerings through innovation desired by customers (textual analysis of social media postings).

ILLUSTRATION 10.24
Sample Dashboard for
Managerial Accountants

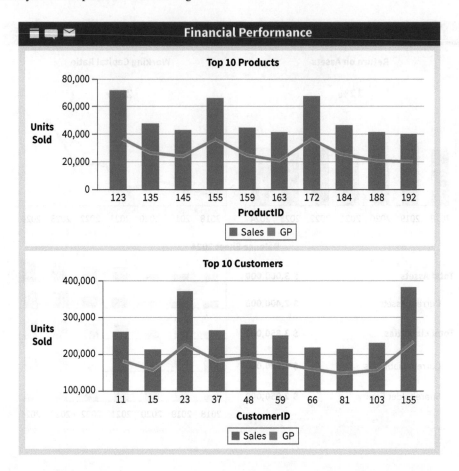

Managerial accountants are also faced with new challenges, many of which include ethical considerations about digital data privacy and security (see Illustration 10.7 and Applying Critical Thinking 10.5). Another challenge is data veracity, since dirty data can produce incorrect analysis results which can negatively impact decision-making. Properly preparing data catches and repairs corrupt, incomplete, inaccurate, or inappropriate data formats, which improves data analysis results' reliability.

Finally, managerial accountants might miss opportunities in data that they do not use in their analyses. Dark data refers to the available operational data that are not used by an organization. The related costs of data capture, management, and storage can be significant, and if the data are not being used, then the possible business intelligence value may be reduced.

Tax Accounting

While initially the slowest area of accounting practice to use data analytics, tax accountants are now moving quickly toward using many new data and analysis technologies:

- Cognitive technologies are heavily utilized for compliance testing and for the evaluation of multi-jurisdictional sales and use taxes.

- Textual analysis is increasingly used to better understand and interpret new tax law in the unstructured data posted on the internet.

- Process tools help tax accountants better understand which processes in an organization or client's portfolio are driving their tax liabilities, improving the value of tax planning significantly.

Data pattern documentation has been a long-held tradition for tax treatment choices. For example, consider when a tax accountant must explain the "tax shield" power of LIFO cost of goods sold valuation in inflationary periods to board members:

- If the tax accountant simply states that the LIFO tax shield defers income tax liabilities to a later taxable period without explaining why, the meaning of why this is the case may be lost.

- But, if that accountant additionally illustrates and explains how a LIFO adoption for inventory valuation on the balance sheet creates a stronger current cash flows relationship with cost of goods sold on the income statement, the board members can more easily follow how current tax liabilities and cash outflows would be reduced by the company's "tax shield."

Both tax planning and compliance practice areas are demanding more efficient processes, effective planning, accurate compliance, and increased tax intelligence. These new technologies are delivering this by analyzing greater data volume and data variety. RPA is providing efficiencies and decreasing tax function costs. Data mining visualizations can identify tax liability drivers. Cognitive technologies provide accurate tax liability predictions, as well as proper transfer pricing and tax treatment classifications, especially in assessing complex multi-entity and multi-jurisdictional tax liability contexts (**Illustration 10.25**).

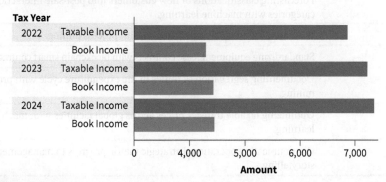

ILLUSTRATION 10.25 Tax Accountants Use Visualizations to Guide Their Judgments

PROFESSIONAL **INSIGHT**	**How Are New Technology Tools Used in Tax Accounting?**

Brandi recently graduated with a Master's in Accountancy and is working for a regional tax practice. She explained how she uses data analytics in her daily work.

Because different countries have different value-added, sales, and use tax policies and rates, companies have to be very strategic determining which parts of their operations are performed in which countries. Several new tools have helped me perform this work.

Transfer pricing refers to the prices at which we sell resources from our business units or subsidiaries in one tax jurisdiction to our companies in another tax jurisdiction for the purpose of minimizing tax liabilities. The different processing steps must be considered, from raw materials to finished goods, to determine where our company processes should be located.

I use a variety of advanced analysis tools in my daily tasks. I describe data with a data mining tool, and I gain insights about the risk in the data from process mining tools. I really enjoyed the freedom to help my company figure out the best country to create, further process, or assemble these resources. The objective is to operate legally while minimizing operational costs and tax liabilities. Before these process mapping technologies, such as Alteryx and Celonis, were available, we had to build individual Excel files for each possible operational combination between countries. Creating these spreadsheets was time consuming, they poorly documented the original purpose, and it was difficult to integrate and evaluate the information across these spreadsheets.

I used robotic process automation to retrieve and enter the data for the spreadsheets, which has saved me more than a dozen hours every week. A particular advantage of moving our work to newer technologies such as Power BI and Alteryx, is that automatic documentation is capturing each step of our workflows and our data manipulation processes alike.

Analyses that integrate data variety and data mining visualizations are helping tax accountants to better understand when their organizations or clients are approaching the boundaries of acceptable tax categories. The technology advances reviewed in this chapter are helping tax accountants drill down to supply chain events that are driving tax liabilities, advancing real-time tax advice potentially saving organizations and clients significant cash resources.

APPLY IT 10.3

Match Professional Practice Areas to Analyses and Technologies

Match how the following data analyses and technologies are used to at least one of the professional practice areas—accounting information systems (AIS), auditing, financial accounting, managerial accounting, and tax accounting.

Accounting Area	Data Analyses/Technology Uses
	Forecasting classifications of new customers into post-sale interaction categories with machine learning.
	Evaluating cloud data usage patterns with process mining.
	Standardizing equipment lease contracts with blockchain smart contracts.
	Documenting segregation of duties in the expenditure cycle with process mining.
	Optimizing taxable transfer prices across global facilities with machine learning.
	Communicating operational strategic metric progress to management with storytelling.
	Closing revenue, expense, gain, loss, and dividend accounts at year-end with RPA.
	Controlling unauthorized system access with process mining on login data.
	Verifying accounts receivable balances with fulfilled invoice data using process mining.

SOLUTION

Accounting Area	Data Analyses/Technology Uses
Managerial accounting	Forecasting classifications of new customers into post-sale interaction categories with machine learning.
AIS	Evaluating cloud data usage patterns with process mining.
Financial accounting	Standardizing equipment lease contracts with blockchain smart contracts.
Auditing	Documenting segregation of duties in the expenditure cycle with process mining.
Tax accounting	Optimizing taxable transfer prices across global facilities with machine learning.
Managerial accounting	Communicating operational strategic metric progress to management with storytelling.
Financial accounting	Closing revenue, expense, gain, loss, and dividend accounts at year-end with RPA.
AIS	Controlling unauthorized system access with process mining on login data.
Auditing	Verifying accounts receivable balances with fulfilled invoice data using process mining.

Chapter Review and Practice

Learning Objectives Review

❶ Describe data trends impacting the accounting profession.

Trends in data volume, variety, velocity, veracity, and value are creating both opportunities and challenges across accounting areas:

- Data volume refers to amount of data used in analyses. The increased volume of data generated and collected by organizations have led to new developments in data storage. Cloud data services offer organizations secure and easily expandable data storage, expert data management, hardware and software, and IT expertise. Private clouds serve a single organization or a set group of noncompeting organizations. Public clouds serve many different businesses. Hybrid cloud storage have both private and public virtual server sections.
- Data variety refers to the diversity of data structures and measurement scales in the data we want to analyze. Accountants have traditionally selected and analyzed structured data, but are now combining structured data with unstructured data for analysis, using pictures and text and GPS data, for example.
- Data velocity is the speed at which new data points are generated. The higher the data velocity, the faster data volume grows. High-velocity data can come from both internal or external sources.
- Data veracity is the reliability of data. Veracity depends on three things: if the data are expected to provide insights for the analysis, how accurate the data must be to generate useful insights, and how complete the data must be to generate useful insights.
- Data value refers to the additional benefits the data provides toward the objective of an analysis.
- There are also ethical considerations when considering the storage and use of data. Accountants must consider data privacy laws and regulations when working with, storing, and sharing data.

❷ Explain how technology developments are impacting data analysis in accounting.

Accountants can efficiently analyze more data than ever before using data analysis tools:

- Data analyses can produce new intelligence for improving how resources and processes can increase operational performance and competitiveness, and achieve financial objectives.
- Data mining is the systematic process of looking for issues or patterns occurring within or between data fields. Data mining is a common form of data analytics in accounting practice. Most data mining software automatically documents the mining steps, which is useful for data and analyses verification.
- Blockchain technologies create one shared, secure, and difficult to change record of transactions between parties. This technology creates smart contracts, which are secure online shared digital contracts.
- Robotic process automation software automates routine, stable processes that can then be easily repeated.
- Process mining tools measure the timing and flow of data captured as business events happen. These tools help accountants better evaluate business process control, efficiency, and effectiveness.
- Continuous auditing technologies are programmed modules embedded in the AIS that evaluate transactions as they occur throughout the year, reducing the year-end work.
- Textual analysis tools help accountants analyze word choices in footnotes, investor and management communications, and other documents, such as legal contracts.
- Cognitive technologies are artificial intelligence technologies that mimic human expert judgments.

❸ Demonstrate how data and technology developments are adding value to professional practice.

- Accounting information systems accountants can add value using AIS system log data and cognitive technologies, continuous auditing, data mining, process mining, and robotic process automation.
- New technologies can increase audit quality and reduce audit time and costs. RPA, cognitive technologies, process mining, and continuous auditing are improving analytical testing of controls and testing of entire populations of data, rather than just inferential samples, are creating new audit value.
- Financial accountants use new technologies in both their GAAP compliance responsibilities and for assessing and predicting business value, risk, and future capital needs. RPA, process mining, cognitive technologies, and textual analyses are all being used in the financial accounting function.
- New data options and technologies are helping managerial accountants better identify priority issues, ask better questions, use data with greater value, and develop intelligence solutions to support management decision-making.
- Tax accountants use cognitive technology for compliance testing, textual analysis to understand and interpret unstructured data, and process tools to better understand processes that affect tax liabilities.

Key Terms Review

Blockchain technologies 558
Cloud data services 546
Cognitive technologies 565
Continuous auditing technologies 563
Data mining 556
Data value 550

Data variety 548
Data velocity 549
Data veracity 550
Data volume 545
Hybrid clouds 547
Private clouds 546

Process mining tools 562
Public clouds 546
Robotic process automation (RPA) 560
Smart contracts 559
Textual analysis 564
Textual mining 564

How To Walk-Throughs

How To

HOW TO 10.1   Create a Comparative Income Statement in Excel

Illustration 10.6 demonstrated how considering the value of data can provide useful insights when deciding whether to drop a net loss-producing product line of computer keyboards (Product B). As a reminder, the segment contribution margin calculation was more valuable than the contribution margin calculation because it considered the traceable fixed costs which could be avoided if the product line were dropped.

What You Need: `Data` The How To 10.1 data file.

STEP 1: Open the Excel file and review the data field columns extracted from this company's AIS database. The retrieved data has summarized monthly totals for units sold, price, and cost information for the 2025 year for two product lines, A and B (**Illustration 10.26**).

ILLUSTRATION 10.26   Data Set Columns

	A	B	C	D	E	F	G	H	I	J	K	L
1	Year	Month	Product	SumUnits Sold	Price	VCunit	Traceable FCunit	Common FCunit	Total Revenues	Total DirectVC	TotalApplied TraceableFC	TotalApplied CommonFC
2	2025	January	A	600	$ 60.00	36.00	17.50	3.50	$ 36,000.00	$ 21,600.00	$ 10,500.00	$ 2,100.00
3	2025	January	B	1,710	$ 100.00	80.00	18.75	3.50	$ 171,000.00	$ 136,800.00	$ 32,062.50	$ 5,985.00
4	2025	February	A	700	$ 60.00	36.00	17.50	3.50	$ 42,000.00	$ 25,200.00	$ 12,250.00	$ 2,450.00
5	2025	February	B	1,640	$ 100.00	80.00	18.75	3.50	$ 164,000.00	$ 131,200.00	$ 30,750.00	$ 5,740.00
6	2025	March	A	760	$ 60.00	36.00	17.50	3.50	$ 45,600.00	$ 27,360.00	$ 13,300.00	$ 2,660.00
7	2025	March	B	1,360	$ 100.00	80.00	18.75	3.50	$ 136,000.00	$ 108,800.00	$ 25,500.00	$ 4,760.00
8	2025	April	A	740	$ 60.00	36.00	17.50	3.50	$ 44,400.00	$ 26,640.00	$ 12,950.00	$ 2,590.00
9	2025	April	B	1,270	$ 100.00	80.00	18.75	3.50	$ 127,000.00	$ 101,600.00	$ 23,812.50	$ 4,445.00
10	2025	May	A	820	$ 60.00	36.00	17.50	3.50	$ 49,200.00	$ 29,520.00	$ 14,350.00	$ 2,870.00
11	2025	May	B	1,200	$ 100.00	80.00	18.75	3.50	$ 120,000.00	$ 96,000.00	$ 22,500.00	$ 4,200.00
12	2025	June	A	900	$ 60.00	36.00	17.50	3.50	$ 54,000.00	$ 32,400.00	$ 15,750.00	$ 3,150.00
13	2025	June	B	940	$ 100.00	80.00	18.75	3.50	$ 94,000.00	$ 75,200.00	$ 17,625.00	$ 3,290.00
14	2025	July	A	980	$ 60.00	36.00	17.50	3.50	$ 58,800.00	$ 35,280.00	$ 17,150.00	$ 3,430.00
15	2025	July	B	860	$ 100.00	80.00	18.75	3.50	$ 86,000.00	$ 68,800.00	$ 16,125.00	$ 3,010.00
16	2025	August	A	1,040	$ 60.00	36.00	17.50	3.50	$ 62,400.00	$ 37,440.00	$ 18,200.00	$ 3,640.00
17	2025	August	B	720	$ 100.00	80.00	18.75	3.50	$ 72,000.00	$ 57,600.00	$ 13,500.00	$ 2,520.00
18	2025	September	A	1,220	$ 60.00	36.00	17.50	3.50	$ 73,200.00	$ 43,920.00	$ 21,350.00	$ 4,270.00
19	2025	September	B	650	$ 100.00	80.00	18.75	3.50	$ 65,000.00	$ 52,000.00	$ 12,187.50	$ 2,275.00
20	2025	October	A	1,300	$ 60.00	36.00	17.50	3.50	$ 78,000.00	$ 46,800.00	$ 22,750.00	$ 4,550.00
21	2025	October	B	600	$ 100.00	80.00	18.75	3.50	$ 60,000.00	$ 48,000.00	$ 11,250.00	$ 2,100.00
22	2025	November	A	1,380	$ 60.00	36.00	17.50	3.50	$ 82,800.00	$ 49,680.00	$ 24,150.00	$ 4,830.00
23	2025	November	B	550	$ 100.00	80.00	18.75	3.50	$ 55,000.00	$ 44,000.00	$ 10,312.50	$ 1,925.00
24	2025	December	A	1,560	$ 60.00	36.00	17.50	3.50	$ 93,600.00	$ 56,160.00	$ 27,300.00	$ 5,460.00
25	2025	December	B	500	$ 100.00	80.00	18.75	3.50	$ 50,000.00	$ 40,000.00	$ 9,375.00	$ 1,750.00

Sheet1

STEP 2: There are different ways to create comparative contribution margin income statements for 2025. Here is one option:

- Go to the **Data** tab and select **Sort**. A pop-up window will appear. Verify the default **My data has headers** has been checked. Select **Product** in the first drop-down list to ensure the data set is sorted properly.

- Insert two rows between Product A and Product B data to help separate this data (**Illustration 10.27**).

ILLUSTRATION 10.27 Results of Step 2

	A	B	C	D	E	F	G	H	I	J	K	L
1	Year	Month	Product	SumUnits Sold	Price	VCunit	Traceable FCunit	Common FCunit	Total Revenues	Total Direct VC	Total Applied TraceableFC	TotalApplied CommonFC
2	2025	January	A	600	$ 60.00	36.00	17.50	3.50	$ 36,000.00	$ 21,600.00	$ 10,500.00	$ 2,100.00
3	2025	February	A	700	$ 60.00	36.00	17.50	3.50	$ 42,000.00	$ 25,200.00	$ 12,250.00	$ 2,450.00
4	2025	March	A	760	$ 60.00	36.00	17.50	3.50	$ 45,600.00	$ 27,360.00	$ 13,300.00	$ 2,660.00
5	2025	April	A	740	$ 60.00	36.00	17.50	3.50	$ 44,400.00	$ 26,640.00	$ 12,950.00	$ 2,590.00
6	2025	May	A	820	$ 60.00	36.00	17.50	3.50	$ 49,200.00	$ 29,520.00	$ 14,350.00	$ 2,870.00
7	2025	June	A	900	$ 60.00	36.00	17.50	3.50	$ 54,000.00	$ 32,400.00	$ 15,750.00	$ 3,150.00
8	2025	July	A	980	$ 60.00	36.00	17.50	3.50	$ 58,800.00	$ 35,280.00	$ 17,150.00	$ 3,430.00
9	2025	August	A	1,040	$ 60.00	36.00	17.50	3.50	$ 62,400.00	$ 37,440.00	$ 18,200.00	$ 3,640.00
10	2025	September	A	1,220	$ 60.00	36.00	17.50	3.50	$ 73,200.00	$ 43,920.00	$ 21,350.00	$ 4,270.00
11	2025	October	A	1,300	$ 60.00	36.00	17.50	3.50	$ 78,000.00	$ 46,800.00	$ 22,750.00	$ 4,550.00
12	2025	November	A	1,380	$ 60.00	36.00	17.50	3.50	$ 82,800.00	$ 49,680.00	$ 24,150.00	$ 4,830.00
13	2025	December	A	1,560	$ 60.00	36.00	17.50	3.50	$ 93,600.00	$ 56,160.00	$ 27,300.00	$ 5,460.00
14												
15												
16	2025	January	B	1,710	$ 100.00	80.00	18.75	3.50	$ 171,000.00	$ 136,800.00	$ 32,062.50	$ 5,985.00
17	2025	February	B	1,640	$ 100.00	80.00	18.75	3.50	$ 164,000.00	$ 131,200.00	$ 30,750.00	$ 5,740.00
18	2025	March	B	1,360	$ 100.00	80.00	18.75	3.50	$ 136,000.00	$ 108,800.00	$ 25,500.00	$ 4,760.00
19	2025	April	B	1,270	$ 100.00	80.00	18.75	3.50	$ 127,000.00	$ 101,600.00	$ 23,812.50	$ 4,445.00
20	2025	May	B	1,200	$ 100.00	80.00	18.75	3.50	$ 120,000.00	$ 96,000.00	$ 22,500.00	$ 4,200.00
21	2025	June	B	940	$ 100.00	80.00	18.75	3.50	$ 94,000.00	$ 75,200.00	$ 17,625.00	$ 3,290.00
22	2025	July	B	860	$ 100.00	80.00	18.75	3.50	$ 86,000.00	$ 68,800.00	$ 16,125.00	$ 3,010.00
23	2025	August	B	720	$ 100.00	80.00	18.75	3.50	$ 72,000.00	$ 57,600.00	$ 13,500.00	$ 2,520.00
24	2025	September	B	650	$ 100.00	80.00	18.75	3.50	$ 65,000.00	$ 52,000.00	$ 12,187.50	$ 2,275.00
25	2025	October	B	600	$ 100.00	80.00	18.75	3.50	$ 60,000.00	$ 48,000.00	$ 11,250.00	$ 2,100.00
26	2025	November	B	550	$ 100.00	80.00	18.75	3.50	$ 55,000.00	$ 44,000.00	$ 10,312.50	$ 1,925.00
27	2025	December	B	500	$ 100.00	80.00	18.75	3.50	$ 50,000.00	$ 40,000.00	$ 9,375.00	$ 1,750.00

Sheet1

STEP 3: Enter a sum formula in cells D14 and D28 for total units sold for each product. The formula in the D14 cell is = sum(D2:D13). The other formulas follow the same pattern with their corresponding column letter name. The meaning of the calculated field in D14 = total Product A units sold and D28 = total Product B units sold. Then, in rows 14 and 28 enter similar sums for Columns I, J, K, and L (**Illustration 10.28**).

ILLUSTRATION 10.28 Results of Step 3

	A	B	C	D	E	F	G	H	I	J	K	L
1	Year	Month	Product	SumUnits Sold	Price	VCunit	Traceable FCunit	Common FCunit	Total Revenues	Total DirectVC	TotalApplied TraceableFC	TotalApplied CommonFC
2	2025	January	A	600	$ 60.00	36.00	17.50	3.50	$ 36,000.00	$ 21,600.00	$ 10,500.00	$ 2,100.00
3	2025	February	A	700	$ 60.00	36.00	17.50	3.50	$ 42,000.00	$ 25,200.00	$ 12,250.00	$ 2,450.00
4	2025	March	A	760	$ 60.00	36.00	17.50	3.50	$ 45,600.00	$ 27,360.00	$ 13,300.00	$ 2,660.00
5	2025	April	A	740	$ 60.00	36.00	17.50	3.50	$ 44,400.00	$ 26,640.00	$ 12,950.00	$ 2,590.00
6	2025	May	A	820	$ 60.00	36.00	17.50	3.50	$ 49,200.00	$ 29,520.00	$ 14,350.00	$ 2,870.00
7	2025	June	A	900	$ 60.00	36.00	17.50	3.50	$ 54,000.00	$ 32,400.00	$ 15,750.00	$ 3,150.00
8	2025	July	A	980	$ 60.00	36.00	17.50	3.50	$ 58,800.00	$ 35,280.00	$ 17,150.00	$ 3,430.00
9	2025	August	A	1,040	$ 60.00	36.00	17.50	3.50	$ 62,400.00	$ 37,440.00	$ 18,200.00	$ 3,640.00
10	2025	September	A	1,220	$ 60.00	36.00	17.50	3.50	$ 73,200.00	$ 43,920.00	$ 21,350.00	$ 4,270.00
11	2025	October	A	1,300	$ 60.00	36.00	17.50	3.50	$ 78,000.00	$ 46,800.00	$ 22,750.00	$ 4,550.00
12	2025	November	A	1,380	$ 60.00	36.00	17.50	3.50	$ 82,800.00	$ 49,680.00	$ 24,150.00	$ 4,830.00
13	2025	December	A	1,560	$ 60.00	36.00	17.50	3.50	$ 93,600.00	$ 56,160.00	$ 27,300.00	$ 5,460.00
14				12,000					$ 720,000.00	$ 432,000.00	$ 210,000.00	$ 42,000.00
15												
16	2025	January	B	1,710	$ 100.00	80.00	18.75	3.50	$ 171,000.00	$ 136,800.00	$ 32,062.50	$ 5,985.00
17	2025	February	B	1,640	$ 100.00	80.00	18.75	3.50	$ 164,000.00	$ 131,200.00	$ 30,750.00	$ 5,740.00
18	2025	March	B	1,360	$ 100.00	80.00	18.75	3.50	$ 136,000.00	$ 108,800.00	$ 25,500.00	$ 4,760.00
19	2025	April	B	1,270	$ 100.00	80.00	18.75	3.50	$ 127,000.00	$ 101,600.00	$ 23,812.50	$ 4,445.00
20	2025	May	B	1,200	$ 100.00	80.00	18.75	3.50	$ 120,000.00	$ 96,000.00	$ 22,500.00	$ 4,200.00
21	2025	June	B	940	$ 100.00	80.00	18.75	3.50	$ 94,000.00	$ 75,200.00	$ 17,625.00	$ 3,290.00
22	2025	July	B	860	$ 100.00	80.00	18.75	3.50	$ 86,000.00	$ 68,800.00	$ 16,125.00	$ 3,010.00
23	2025	August	B	720	$ 100.00	80.00	18.75	3.50	$ 72,000.00	$ 57,600.00	$ 13,500.00	$ 2,520.00
24	2025	September	B	650	$ 100.00	80.00	18.75	3.50	$ 65,000.00	$ 52,000.00	$ 12,187.50	$ 2,275.00
25	2025	October	B	600	$ 100.00	80.00	18.75	3.50	$ 60,000.00	$ 48,000.00	$ 11,250.00	$ 2,100.00
26	2025	November	B	550	$ 100.00	80.00	18.75	3.50	$ 55,000.00	$ 44,000.00	$ 10,312.50	$ 1,925.00
27	2025	December	B	500	$ 100.00	80.00	18.75	3.50	$ 50,000.00	$ 40,000.00	$ 9,375.00	$ 1,750.00
28				12,000					$ 1,200,000.00	$ 960,000.00	$ 225,000.00	$ 42,000.00

Sheet1

STEP 4: Starting in Column N row 3, enter the row descriptions and column titles from Illustration 10.6. Then, enter the cell address and formulas in each cell. Please note that column R has been removed. Adjust the column widths and properly format the data cells (**Illustration 10.29**).

ILLUSTRATION 10.29 Formatting the Table for Illustration 10.6 (With Cell Formulas)

	N	O	P	Q	S
4		2025 Income Statement			
5		ProductA	ProductB	Both Product Lines	Only ProductA
6	Sales Revenues	+I14	+I28	=O6+P6	+O6
7	Less: Variable Costs	+J14	+J28	=O7+P7	+O7
8	Contribution Margin	=O6−O7	=P6−P7	=Q6−Q7	+O8
9	Less: Avoidable Fixed				
10	Expenses	+K14	+K28	+O10+P10	+O10
11	Segment Margin	=O8−O10	=P8−P10	=Q8−Q10	+O11
12	Less: Unavoidable Common				
13	Fixed Expenses	+L14	+L28	=O13+P13	=O13+P13
14	Net Income	=O11−O13	=P11−P13	=Q11−Q13	=S11−S13

Sheet1

The completed Excel table should look equivalent to Illustration 10.6.

STEP 5: Consider how the analysis could contribute to the decision to keep or drop Product B. Are there any limitations to the analysis that should be considered?

- The results indicate this data has data veracity for the objective of deciding whether to drop Product B. By creating the comparative income statements in Illustration 10.6, we can analyze the contribution margin and segment margin, in addition to the net income generated by each product.

- Since many people are more proficient in Excel compared to other analysis tools, we may conclude that Excel was the best tool for efficiently building the income statement information models. We were able to calculate all totals quickly with cell references or easy formulas, and it is easy to format the table with both the text labels and the currency formatting in the table cells.

- It might be difficult for another employee or auditor to verify these calculations. They would have to examine each formula cell to determine if the calculations were appropriate or accurate. Since we cannot know what another person was thinking and deciding when creating this kind of information model spreadsheet, the finished spreadsheet does not provide the best documentation for someone else to understand, verify, or learn from. Additionally, the work we did for this spreadsheet could not be re-used with a new data set.

HOW TO 10.2 Use Process Automation to Analyze Product Contributions to Net Income

How To 10.1 demonstrated how to use Excel to create the analysis shown in Illustration 10.6. What if you wanted to create an automated process to generate the same illustration? An automated data analysis tool, Alteryx, can be used to create a comparative income statement.

What You Need: **Data** The How To 10.2 data file. (Ask your instructor how to access the Alteryx software and how to name the results files.)

STEP 1: Open Alteryx and select the **Favorites** tab at the top of the screen. This set of tool icons contains the tools necessary for recreating Illustration 10.6.

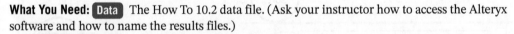

Illustration 10.30 is the completed, correct final Alteryx workflow. Use it as a guide as you work through the steps of this analysis.

ILLUSTRATION 10.30 Alteryx Workflow for Creating Comparative Income Statements

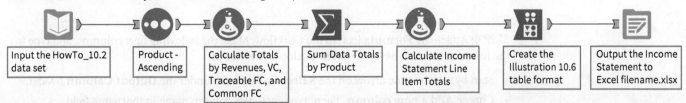

| Input the HowTo_10.2 data set | Product – Ascending | Calculate Totals by Revenues, VC, Traceable FC, and Common FC | Sum Data Totals by Product | Calculate Income Statement Line Item Totals | Create the Illustration 10.6 table format | Output the Income Statement to Excel filename.xlsx |

STEP 2: Add the **Input Data** tool to the workflow by dragging the icon into the biggest window on the Alteryx screen:

- Then, in the box under **Connect a File or Database**, select the down arrow. Import Sheet1 of the Excel data set.
- Run the input tool by clicking the blue **Run** button at the top right.

STEP 3: Add the **Sort** tool by dragging the icon into the workflow window to the right of the input icon.

- In the top-left window, sort on the **Product** column in ascending order.
- Add the annotation (a comment of your choice) by clicking on the small luggage tag icon, which is the third icon on the left of the screen.
- Run the sort (**Illustration 10.31**).

Notice the **Results** window at the bottom right. The second icon on the far left will allow you to look at the data being input into the Sort step. The third icon shows the data results after the Sort function has run. In this view, the Product column rows have been sorted, and the Product A rows are above the Product B rows. It is useful to remember these two icons, as they can be key for problem-solving.

ILLUSTRATION 10.31 Alteryx Workflow After Step 3

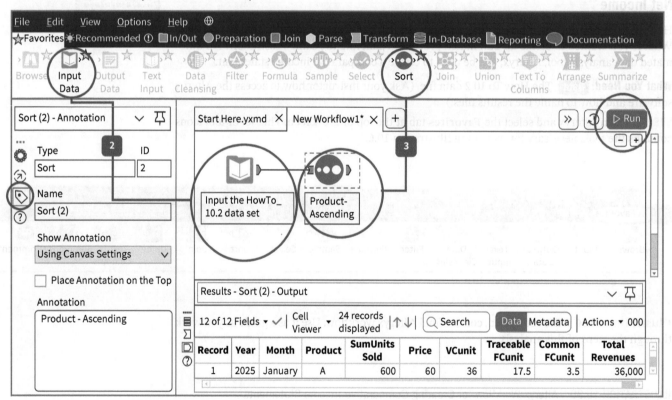

STEP 4: Attach the **Formula** icon to the workflow. Make the following new columns, and type in the formulas for each new column in the top-left window:

- Start by selecting the arrow on the **Select Column** tab under the **Output Column** header.
- Choose **Add a new column**. Then, type each new column name in that same field.
- Below that, type the formula in the expression space, and select the proper data type (for all the column fields you build in this exercise, select the type **Double**).

New Column	Formula for the New Column
RevenuesA	if [Product]="A" then [TotalRevenues] else 0 endif
RevenuesB	if [Product]="B" then [TotalRevenues] else 0 endif
VCforA	if [Product]="A" then [TotalDirectVC] else 0 endif
VCforB	if [Product]="B" then [TotalDirectVC] else 0 endif
TraceFCforA	if [Product]="A" then [TotalAppliedTraceableFC] else 0 endif
TraceFCforB	if [Product]="B" then [TotalAppliedTraceableFC] else 0 endif
CommonFCforA	if [Product]="A" then [TotalAppliedCommonFC] else 0 endif
CommonFCforB	if [Product]="B" then [TotalAppliedCommonFC] else 0 endif

- Add the annotation of your choice (small luggage tag icon) and run the formula tool (**Illustration 10.32**).

ILLUSTRATION 10.32 Alteryx Workflow After Step 4

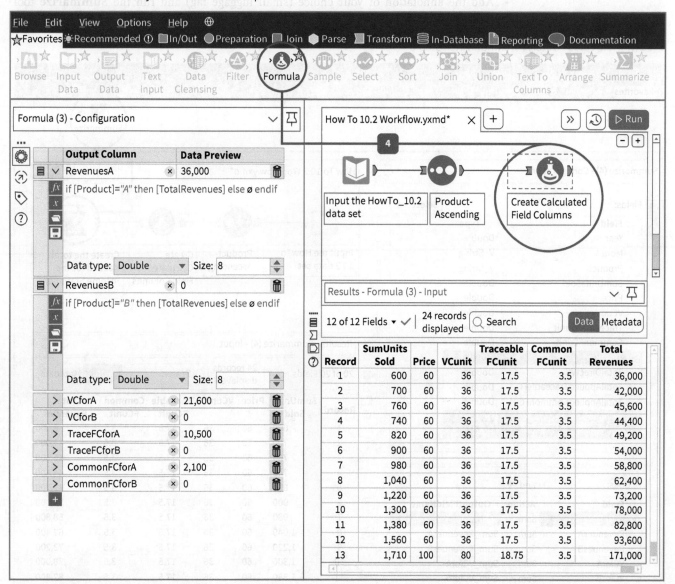

STEP 5: Attach the **Summarize** icon to the right end of the workflow:

- In the top-left window, select the fields listed in the left column of the table (you may have to scroll down to see them). Select a field by moving the cursor to the blank field to the left of the field name, hold down the control key, and left click on each field you want to select (you should select nine fields).

- Click **Add** and select **SUM**. These fields will automatically populate in the lower section, so you will not have to type the names (shown in the right column of the following table) in the Output field.

Field	Action	Output Field Name
TotalRevenues	Sum	Sum_TotalRevenues
RevenuesA	Sum	Sum_RevenuesA
RevenuesB	Sum	Sum_RevenuesB
VCforA	Sum	Sum_VCforA
VCforB	Sum	Sum_VCforB
TraceFCforA	Sum	Sum_TraceFCforA
TraceFCforB	Sum	Sum_TraceFCforB
CommonFCforA	Sum	Sum_CommonFCforA
CommonFCforB	Sum	Sum_CommonFCforB

- Add the annotation of your choice (small luggage tag) and run the **Summarize** tool (**Illustration 10.33**).

ILLUSTRATION 10.33 Alteryx Workflow After Step 5

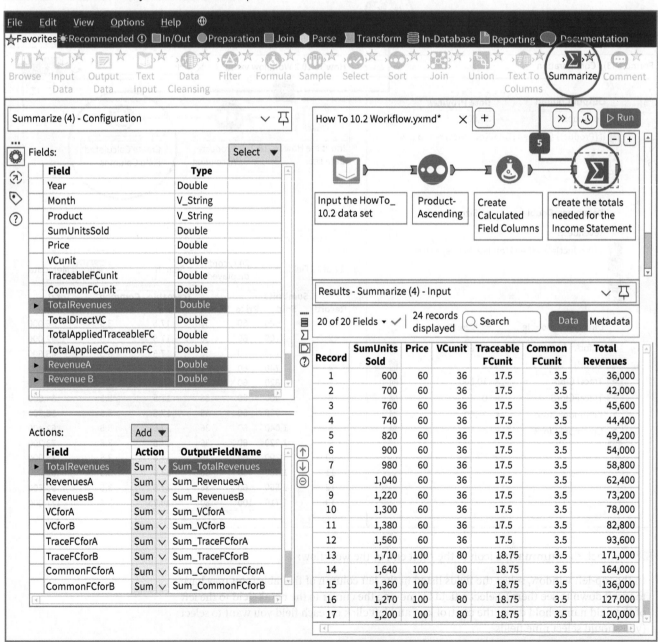

STEP 6: Attach the **Formula** icon to the right of the workflow:

- Make the following 13 new columns with their corresponding formulas. (*Hint*: Save time by selecting the field name from the dropdown list that appears when you type the bracket. This helps avoid typos, which could cause an error when you run the Formula function.) All new column types should be changed to **Double**.

New Column	Formula for the New Column
ContribMarginA	[Sum_RevenuesA]–[Sum_VCforA]
ContribMarginB	[Sum_RevenuesB]–[Sum_VCforB]
SegmentMarginA	[ContribMarginA]–[Sum_TraceFCforA]
SegmentMarginB	[ContribMarginB]–[Sum_TraceFCforB]
NetIncomeA	[SegmentMarginA]–[Sum_CommonFCforA]
NetIncomeB	[SegmentMarginB]–[Sum_CommonFCforB]
TotalVC	[Sum_VCforA]+[Sum_VCforB]
TotalContribMargin	[ContribMarginA]+[ContribMarginB]
TotalTraceFC	[Sum_TraceFCforA]+[Sum_TraceFCforB]
TotalSegmentMargin	[SegmentMarginA]+[SegmentMarginB]
TotalCommonFC	[SumCommonFCforA]+[Sum_CommonFCforB]
TotalNetIncome	[NetIncomeA]+[NetIncomeB]
NetIncomeOnlyA	[SegmentMarginA]–[TotalCommonFC]

- Add the annotation of your choice and run the formula tool (**Illustration 10.34**).

ILLUSTRATION 10.34 Alteryx Workflow After Step 6 (Showing Only the First Three Formulas)

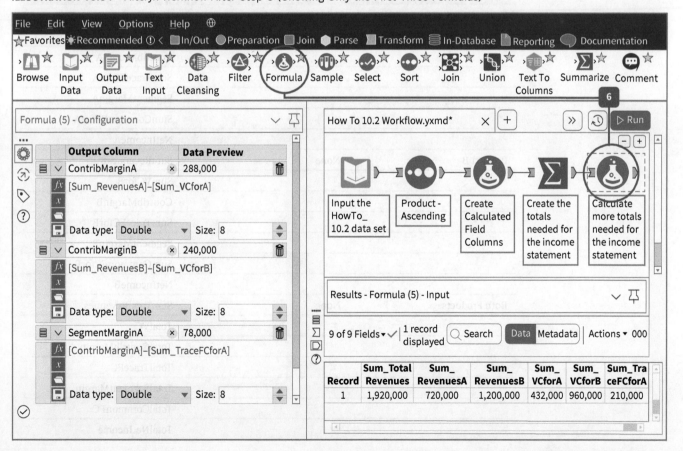

STEP 7: Attach the **Arrange** icon to the workflow (it can be found under the **Transform** menu, not the **Favorites** menu):

- In the **Key Fields** window at the top left, make sure all the key fields have been deselected, as those fields should not be columns in the income statement table (they should be deselected already, but ensuring they are deselected is a control).

- Below the section with these key fields, click the arrow to the right of **Columns**, and select **Add**. A new window will appear in the middle of the screen.

In this step, you will be adding the four income statement columns and the seven income statement rows (they are called Output fields in Alteryx):

	Product A	Product B	Both Products	Only Product A
Sales Revenues				
Variable Costs				
Contribution Margin				
Traceable Fixed Costs				
Segment Margin				
Common Fixed Costs				
Net Income				

Illustration 10.35 contains the information that should be entered for each income statement column.

ILLUSTRATION 10.35 Input Fields for Alteryx Arrange Step

Output Column Header	Description Field	Fields to Select
Product A	Add New Description	SumRevenuesA
		SumVCforA
		ContribMarginA
		SumTraceFCforA
		SegmentMarginA
		SumCommonFCforA
		NetIncomeA
Product B	None	SumRevenuesB
		SumVCforB
		ContribMarginB
		SumTraceFCforB
		SegmentMarginB
		SumCommonFCforB
		NetIncomeB
Both Products	None	SumTotalRevenues
		TotalVC
		TotalContribMargin
		TotalTraceFC
		TotalSegmentMargin
		TotalCommonFC
		TotalNetIncome

ILLUSTRATION 10.35 (*Continued*)

Output Column Header	Description Field	Fields to Select
Only Product A	None	SumRevenuesA
		SumVCforA
		ContribMarginA
		SumTraceFCforA
		SegmentMarginA
		TotalCommonFC
		NetIncomeOnlyA

- In the new window's **Column Header** field name, enter Product A. In the next field, select **Add New Description**. Note that the **Description** column only needs to be filled out for this first Product A column. For the other columns, select the Description option **None**.

- In the **Fields** section, select the fields indicated for this column and, subsequently, for each of the other columns needed for the income statement. Repeat this process by adding columns for Product B, Both Products, and Only Product A columns.

In the left window, find the **Output Fields** section, where the **Description** column has a blue highlight. In the Product A column to its left, examine the vertical order of the fields, and rearrange them in the correct vertical income statement order:

- Select the pull-down menu to the right of the field name and select the field that corresponds to the correct row order of the income statement.

- The correct order is listed in the left section of **Illustration 10.36** as a guide.

ILLUSTRATION 10.36 Alteryx Workflow Arrange Step 7 When Entering Product B Column

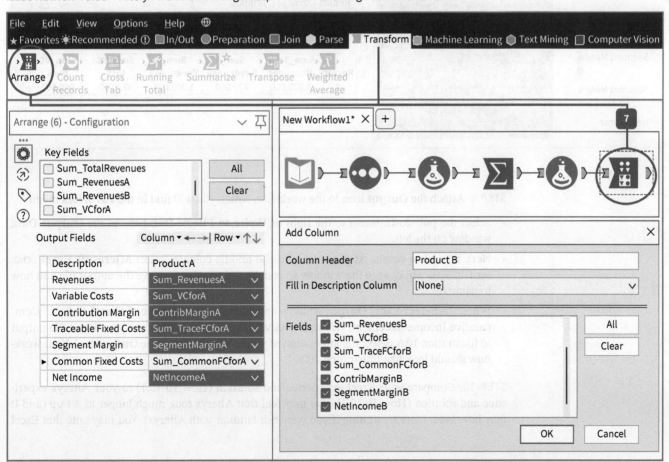

STEP 8: In the resulting table, use the arrows to move the fields in each column up and down as needed so they are in the proper income statement order from top (Sales Revenues) to bottom (Net Income). Annotate as you please (the luggage tag icon), and run the **Arrange** tool (**Illustration 10.37**).

ILLUSTRATION 10.37   Alteryx Workflow After Step 8

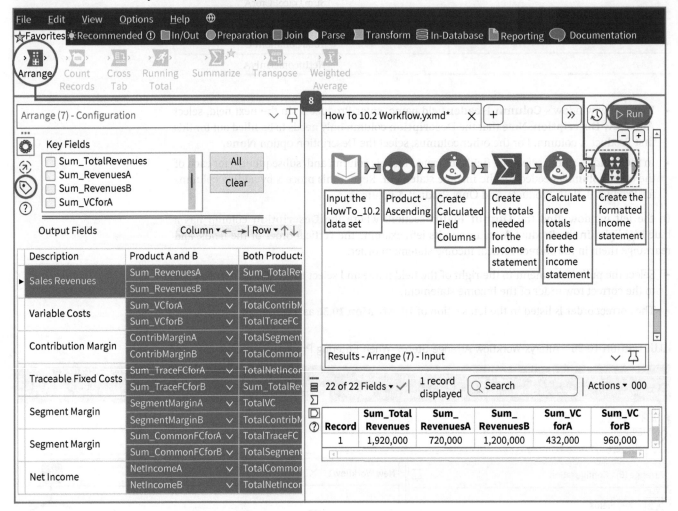

STEP 9: Attach the **Output** icon to the workflow, which you will find in the **Favorites** menu:

- Select the pull-down menu to the right of **Write to File** or **Database** in the **Output Data** window on the left.

- Next, a window opens. At the bottom of the middle column, select **Microsoft Excel .xlsx** format. This will change the window so you can select where to save the output file and how to name it.

- When the **Select Excel Output** window appears, change the name of Sheet1 to "2025 Comparative Income Statement." Do not specify a range of cells. Compare your Excel file output to Illustration 10.6. Select the annotation of your choice, and run the **Output** tool. Your workflow should look like Illustration 10.6.

STEP 10: Compare your Excel experience and solution (How To 10.1) to your Alteryx experience and solution (How To 10.2). You may feel that Alteryx took much longer to set up (and it may have been more frustrating if you were not familiar with Alteryx). You may note that Excel formatted the results as currency, while Alteryx did not. However, Alteryx provides valuable benefits over Excel:

- The Alteryx workflow documents and explains the data preparation and information modeling processes step by step. The steps and their order in Excel were not documented.
- Alteryx clearly names and defines the calculated data fields used as calculated field variables.
- Alteryx workflows are excellent documentation for auditors, and are effective training tools for employees. They also can be rerun with the same data or different data, such as the next period's inputs.
- New workflow icons can be easily added as branching off from any of the original workflow icons, and new icons can be added to the end of the existing workflow.
- Most accountants find it very easy to pick up, understand, and use another person's Alteryx workflows. This is not true of Excel.

Regardless of whether the comparative income statements were created with Excel or Alteryx, the resulting insights are valuable when deciding whether to drop a product line. We can conclude with confidence that this data have great data veracity and value for our objective.

Data The Data tag appears when the data required to answer a question or complete an exercise are available in the book's product page on www.wiley.com.

Multiple Choice Questions

1. (LO 1) Which of the following correctly lists the five data V's?

  a. Velocity, Value, Veracity, Vast, and Varied

  b. Velocity, Value, Veracity, Volume, and Variety

  c. Velocity, Value, Veracity, Volume, and Volatile

  d. Velocity, Value, Viable, Volume, and Variety

2. (LO 1) Navid is a financial accountant for a global company that daily processes millions of purchases from thousands of vendors. As he prepares the accounts payable records for the external auditors, he is interested in the ending accounts payable's data

  a. veracity.   **c.** variety.

  b. value.   **d.** velocity.

3. (LO 1) XYM, Inc. wants to change from in-house servers to using cloud service providers to increase their data storage capacity. This is likely due to high

  a. data value.   **c.** data volume.

  b. data veracity.   **d.** data variety.

4. (LO 1) Ziana was asked to analyze how many Instagram stories refer to her company. The unstructured textual data she will be analyzing has high

  a. data volume.   **c.** data velocity.

  b. data variety.   **d.** data value.

5. (LO 1) Which of the following is *not* likely a resource for a professional to stay up-to-date regarding data privacy regulation?

  a. The European Union's General Data Protection Regulation (GDPR)

  b. United States' Health Information Privacy Protection Act and the Health Insurance Portability and Accountability Act (HIPAA)

  c. California's Consumer Privacy Act (CCPA)

  d. The Sarbanes-Oxley Act of 2002 (SOX)

6. (LO 1) Data value describes the benefits data can provide, depending on the objective of the analysis. Accountants find data value very important when dealing with clients. As it pertains to tax accountants, which of the following most likely represents an instance of the best data value?

  a. Analyzing current stock prices by gathering data from a financial website

  b. Having a listing of all sales tax percentages within a state for a retail-based client

  c. Having a listing of average sales prices and associated sales taxes of apples available from a local produce provider

  d. Having a system error log produced by the tax preparation system

7. (LO 2) Which of the following presents the correct order of the data analyses value creation chain?

  a. Data analysis, new intelligence, strategy shifts, and value creation

  b. New intelligence, data analysis, strategy shifts, and value creation

  c. Value creation, strategy shifts, data analysis, and new intelligence

  d. Data analysis, data mining, data processing, data textual analysis, and value creation

8. (LO 2) The analysis stage of the data analytics process is currently enhanced by

  a. greater variety of data and combinations of data types.

  b. new accounting regulations.

c. financial statement totals.

d. comparison to last year's results.

9. (LO 2) Data mining techniques are being used by professionals to

a. determine the purpose of data analysis.

b. prepare the data for data analysis.

c. prepare the data and then explore the data further.

d. communicate the data analysis findings to stakeholders.

10. (LO 2) Different areas of the accounting profession use data analyses and related tools in varied ways. Depending on the accounting area, accountants are integrating data analysis tools into their tasks, affording them the opportunity to focus on other tasks. In auditing, which of the following are uses of cognitive technologies? Select all that apply.

a. Classifying unusual transactions

b. Diagnosing internal controls

c. Evaluating ongoing concerns

d. Performing risk-level assessments

e. Selecting better samples for yearly testing

11. (LO 2) Continuous auditing technologies have numerous benefits, including

a. allowing auditors to leave the majority of their testing for the end of the audit.

b. allowing audits to be more proactive than reactive.

c. allowing audits to be more reactive than proactive.

d. allowing issues to be evaluated at the conclusion of the audit.

12. (LO 2) Blockchain technologies are being heavily utilized for

a. smart contracts helping revenue recognition and lease documentation.

b. estimation of bad debts.

c. accumulated depreciation schedules.

d. performance dashboard metrics.

13. (LO 3) Data analysis tools are utilized in many areas of accounting. One of these ways is data mining within Accounting Information Systems (AIS) for which of the following purposes?

a. Artificial intelligence supports

b. Automated performance reporting for department managers

c. Automatic system updates

d. Detecting unauthorized intrusion

14. (LO 3) Auditors are embracing new data analyses options in all of the following areas except

a. classifying unusual transactions using cognitive technologies.

b. performing risk assessments with process mining technologies.

c. testing transactions with data mining technologies.

d. creating automatic performance reports for client management.

15. (LO 3) Which of the following summarizes why managerial accountants have quickly embraced new data and analyses options?

a. They are subject to regulatory restrictions.

b. They have a long, innovative tradition of using interdisciplinary data for problem-solving and to identify opportunities.

c. They are employees of the company.

d. They evaluate trends in financial balances over time.

16. (LO 3) Tax accountants are using emerging analysis technologies for which of the following?

a. Optimizing international transfer pricing choices

b. Determining applicable tax rates

c. Documenting property tax responsibilities

d. Outlining responsibilities in the engagement letter with their clients

Review Questions

1. (LO 1) Describe data variety, and give two examples of structured data and unstructured data.

2. (LO 1) Discuss why professionals are increasingly including unstructured data in their analyses. Provide an example of data analysis incorporating unstructured data.

3. (LO 1) Describe data veracity, and discuss why it is important for data analysis.

4. (LO 1) What is data velocity? Provide examples of sources that generate internal and external high-velocity data.

5. (LO 1) Explain the challenges organizations face due to the increasing rate of growth in organizational data. How are organizations responding to these challenges?

6. (LO 1) Discuss the importance of analyzing data with high data value.

7. (LO 1) Identify and describe the three types of data clouds.

8. (LO 2, 3) Explain the data analyses value creation chain. Provide an example highlighting the four aspects of the value creation chain.

9. (LO 2) What is the goal of process mining? Provide an example of how accountants are using process mining.

10. (LO 2) Describe the benefits of continuous auditing processes.

11. (LO 2) What are some of the benefits of blockchain technologies? What is an example of blockchain use in accounting?

12. (LO 3) Discuss how cognitive technologies are used by tax professionals to generate insights.

13. (LO 3) How have new data and technology options motivated systems accountants to consider alternative ways to evaluate AIS performance?

14. (LO 1, 3) Discuss the importance of managerial accountants considering data veracity as they perform data analysis for decision-making.

15. (LO 3) Identify examples of how new data and analyses technologies are adding value to professionals in financial accounting.

16. (LO 3) Describe the application of generative AI in accounting.

Brief Exercises

BE 10.1 (LO 1) `Accounting Information Systems` Yoshi is an accounting information systems accountant at a large medical facility where customers come from all over the country. As a medical facility, the company retains incredibly sensitive patient information, including social security numbers, dates of birth, and health insurance information. The company made an initiative to focus on data ethics in the coming year. Which would be a good first step for Yoshi to address the need for ethics in this environment?

BE 10.2 (LO 1) `Tax Accounting` Assume you are a senior tax accountant for U.S. Outdoor Adventures, a company with sales operations in 15 U.S. states. Your tax analyst has provided you with analysis results to support the company's annual sales tax compliance for each sales tax jurisdiction. You notice that the internal data used in the analysis only includes eight months of the year. With respect to data veracity, how can using eight months of data impact the conclusions reached in the analysis?

BE 10.3 (LO 1) For each statement, indicate which data characteristic it best describes: volume, variety, velocity, veracity, and value.

1. Josephine, an audit staff member, performed an analysis whereby she combined comments from customers' reviews with warranty expenses for the period. This analysis is an example of data _____.

2. Paolo verified that he had a complete download of all accounts receivable activity data before he calculated the AR aging at the end of the period. Having complete data is an example of considering data _____.

3. Rozik collected hourly temperature data outside his ice cream store to determine if there is a relationship between temperature and ice cream sales. Temperature data collected hourly each day is an example of data _____.

4. Janel's company has decided to move from in-house servers to cloud-based servers due to the amount of data that the company is collecting and storing. Movement to cloud-based data storage will address the company's concerns related to data _____.

BE 10.4 (LO 2) Match each statement to its related term. Each term can be used once, more than once, or not at all.

a. Data mining   c. Robotic process automation   e. Continuous auditing

b. Smart contracts   d. Process mining   f. Textual analysis

Statement	Term
1. When the client's weekly payroll journal entry value was outside the defined terms of normal authorized activity, the audit manager reviewed an automatically generated report.	
2. The financial accountant obtained an electronic file of the organization's press releases and related investor comments. The accountant analyzes the pessimistic and optimistic words to understand sentiment around the company's annual performance.	
3. The operations accounting manager reviewed an event log that documented how much time it takes to complete operational steps in sales, shipping, and sending invoices to customers.	
4. The tax accountant analyzed their client's online blog discussions to assess risk of tax evasion.	

BE 10.5 (LO 2) `Managerial Accounting` A managerial accountant analyzed production data to identify a product line that could realize cost savings if changes were made to its production strategies. The operations team implemented several changes to the product's production line, ultimately leading to costs savings for the manufacturing facility and product. Map these activities into the data analysis value chain for production efficiency. Link the following statements to the appropriate elements in the value chain:

a. Implement production modifications   c. Increase production efficiency

b. Analysis of production data   d. Identify production cost inefficiencies

1. Data Analysis	2. New Intelligence	3. Strategy Shifts	4. Value Creation

BE 10.6 (LO 2, 3) Match each statement to the most appropriate professional practice area. Each practice area can be used once, more than once, or not at all.

a. Accounting information systems
b. Auditing
c. Financial accounting
d. Managerial accounting
e. Tax accounting

Statement	Practice Area
1. Steven engaged in data mining as part of the risk assessment process to determine if there were concerning patterns in his client's sales cycle data.	
2. Chi used process mining to examine systems delays and errors. Her analysis results help identify new policies to optimize the system functionality.	
3. Lang used textual analysis tools to better classify his company's multi-jurisdictional transactions for compliance with new tax laws.	
4. Hemant employs smart contracts for all new leases made by his company. The smart contracts will improve GAAP lease classifications and revenue recognition.	
5. Bilal automated the process of calculating depreciation expense for his company's fixed assets by creating an Excel macro. He runs this macro at the end of each month to create his adjusting entry to record depreciation expense.	
6. Jasmine used textual analysis software to identify sentiment in her client's press releases. Her goal is to identify additional risks of material misstatements in her client's financial statements.	

BE 10.7 (LO 2, 3) Match each statement to the technology that the accounting professional will most likely choose to use. Each technology term can be used once, more than once, or not at all:

a. Data mining
b. Smart contracts
c. Robotic process automation
d. Process mining
e. Continuous auditing
f. Textual analysis
g. Cognitive technologies

Statement	Technology
1. A managerial accountant analyzes the comments made by customers when they return a product to identify where improvements can be made to return policy and procedures.	
2. An audit staff member examines sales returns data for the objective of discovering patterns among product type or delivery timing.	
3. To reduce processing time costs, the accounts payable (AP) manager wants the system to electronically match vendor invoices with their associated purchase orders and receiving reports instead of the current matching process performed by the AP clerk.	
4. An internal auditor examines patterns in employee reimbursements related to travel to identify unusual expenses.	

BE 10.8 (LO 3) **Accounting Information Systems** Different areas of the accounting profession use data analyses and related tools in varied ways. Depending on the accounting area, accountants are integrating data analysis tools into their tasks, affording them the opportunity to focus on other tasks. For accounting information systems, which robotic process automations (RPAs) are used?

Exercises

EX 10.1 (LO 1) **Accounting Information Systems** **Cloud-Based Data Storage** Assume you are an accounting information systems accountant at a healthcare company that prioritizes data ethics. Your company collects personally identifiable information about patients and providers, including data that is protected under The Health Insurance Portability and Accountability Act of 1996 (HIPAA). The company has grown recently due to acquisitions of physician practice groups, which increased the types and number of medical procedures performed. As a result, data volume has increased, and your company has decided that cloud-based storage will best serve the future data needs of the company.

Two vendors are finalists to provide that cloud-based storage. One vendor, PrivacyConcept, Inc. is offering a private cloud to host your company's data storage needs. A second vendor, SkyHighStorage, is offering a public cloud with appropriate internal controls to separate your company's data from its other customer's data. Write a memo to the CIO (Chief Information Officer) outlining the relevant data ethics considerations when using cloud services and for deciding between the two vendors.

EX 10.2 (LO 1) Data Managerial Accounting **Comparative Income Statement and Data Value** You are a managerial accountant for Water Sports, Inc., a manufacturer of inflatable and hard SUPS (stand up paddle boards). The VP of Operations is wondering whether Water Sports should drop an inflatable product line that has a net-loss performance. She has asked you to prepare a comparative income statement for two products—SUP Model SX (10'6" inflatable) and SUP Model FW (11' inflatable).

1. Create a comparative income statement for these two products.

2. Would eliminating one of the SUP models increase the company's profitability? Why or why not?

3. Consider the data value of the data set used in this analysis. What alternative analyses could you consider to address if you should drop a net-loss producing product?

EX 10.3 (LO 1) Auditing **Data Ethics** As an external auditor for a large public company client, your engagement team has implemented continuous audit modules into your client's AIS. These modules test and collect evidence of sales revenues transactions during the current year. Your engagement partner has asked you to draft a memo for the audit file to document the continuous auditing process steps, as well as the professional due care that will be taken, to keep the client's collected sales data confidential. An incomplete draft of the memo that is missing important components follows. Complete the memo when more information is needed.

March 15, 20XX

Memo for the Audit Files

RE: Continuous Audit of Revenue Data and Professional Due Care Considerations

This memo documents the engagement team's procedures to provide reasonable assurance regarding the client's revenue-cycle transactions and the engagement team's procedures to ensure that the client's data is kept confidential. First, we discuss the audit procedures and second, we discuss professional due care considerations.

Continuous Audit of Revenue Procedures
The client has provided us access to all sales transaction data in real time by allowing the audit firm to connect its proprietary analytics software to the company's relational database. As revenue transactions are recorded in the client's database, the auditor's software automatically tests and captures the audit data.

We performed audit procedures on this data throughout the year, including the following descriptive statistics and diagnostic tests:

1. _____

Based on these descriptive and diagnostic tests, and comparing our results to past years, abnormal transactions or anomaly transactions were identified and further investigated by collecting and reviewing their related source documents, such as contracts, invoices, and customer payments.

Professional Due Care Considerations
Since sales and collection transactions have a high data volume of personally identifiable data, great care must be taken to ensure that the client's data is kept private.

For example, **2.** _____

EX 10.4 (LO 1) Managerial Accounting **Data Characteristics** You are the managerial accountant for a national chain fitness company that owns several gyms and health food stores in populated locations. Your company also offers nutrition and personal training services. You have been asked to analyze sales revenues and cost of goods sold by comparing this year to the prior year. Your data strategy is to analyze the following data fields and measures. For each, discuss its data characteristics in terms of data volume, variety, velocity, veracity, and value.

1. The quantity of products sold in the health food stores.

2. The number of memberships sold each month.

3. The percentage of members who book appointments with nutrition or personal training professionals.

4. Member evaluations about experiences with nutritional or personal training professionals, including star ratings and comments.

EX 10.5 (LO 2) `Accounting Information Systems` **Robotic Process Automation** Your company asked you to automate the process of performing the three-way match control in the expenditure cycle. Currently, the AP clerk manually matches the vendor's name, quantity, and price between the vendor invoice, the purchase order, and the receiving report. This manual process takes the AP clerk all day, leaving no time to perform other tasks. Discuss how RPA can automate this internal control to reduce the hours engaged in this task.

EX 10.6 (LO 2) `Data` `Managerial Accounting` **Textual Analysis** You work in the corporate office of Sassy Seasonings, a large restaurant chain. The operations team has implemented new kitchen management policies at its most popular location. To understand whether these policies have improved customer satisfaction over time, the manager asks you to analyze data collected as part of the customer satisfaction survey. This data contains the date of the review and the customers' food and service ratings.

1. Classify the customer's food rating keywords into one of three groups: 1. Good, 2. Average, and 3. Poor.

   (*Hint*: First, sort the Customer Food Rating in alphabetical order by selecting all the data, not the headers, and checking the box for Headers in the Data. Then, create a new column for these food rating groups and manually code each row by typing one of the categories for each group: "1. Good," "2. Average," or "3. Poor" in the new column. Critical thinking tip: all coders have their own personal bias, so your coding may differ from others. A good control would be to have more than one coder and to analyze inter-coder reliability.)

2. Create a frequency distribution table using the COUNTIF function in Excel.

   (*Hint*: Starting in cell G3, use the COUNTIF function to total each food rating into one of the three categories, such as =COUNTIF(D3:D91,"1. Good"). Create a total row to show the total number of customer food ratings by category.)

3. Next, create another frequency distribution table by month for each of the customer food rating categories. Create a PivotTable on a new worksheet (name the worksheet "Frequency Table"), select the food rating groups as both rows and values, and then select Months as columns. Format the resulting table as necessary with column width changes.

4. Finally, create a line chart where months is on the *x*-axis and count of each rating is on the *y*-axis.

   (*Hint*: Create a PivotChart line graph using the frequency distribution table from question part 3. Select the PivotTable rows where the Jan, Feb, and March data resides for columns A–E. [Not the blue shaded header and Grand Total rows.] Then, create the line chart. You may need to switch the row/columns to present the months on the *x*-axis. Make any other formatting edits. Save the file.)

5. Based on your analyses, did the kitchen management policies implemented by your operations manager improve customer food ratings over these months?

EX 10.7 (LO 2) `Data` `Financial Accounting` **Process Automation** You are a financial accountant for Water Sports, Inc. Every month you create comparative income statements for your product lines in the GAAP format, a repeated process which consumes much of your time. You have decided to use process automation in Alteryx to generate comparative income statements faster and more efficiently.

1. Create a workflow in Alteryx to automate the process of creating comparative income statements with the following rows:

   - Sales Revenues
   - Less Cost of Goods Sold
   - = Gross Profit
   - Less Selling and Administrative Expenses
   - = Net Income

2. What is your interpretation of your analysis results? How would your interpretation be different if some of your production was not sold and still in ending inventory?

(*Hint*: Refer to How To 10.2 for the steps to create the workflow in Alteryx. Some of the Alteryx new columns and their formulas will be different from How To 10.2. For example, new columns include cost of goods sold rather than contribution margin, selling and administrative expenses rather than traceable fixed expenses, segment margin, and common fixed expenses. Assume that all variable costs and the traceable fixed costs are production costs that flow through inventory to cost of goods sold and that the common fixed costs are all selling and administrative expenses. Finally, assume that all products are sold in the period that they are produced and there are no ending inventory.)

EX 10.8 (LO 2) [Data] [Auditing] [Financial Accounting] **Robotic Process Automation** Your client, OneStopShop, Inc., is a public company with six independent business divisions: floor cleaning, lawn care, pest control, household cleaning, corporate office cleaning, and plumbing products. Your manager has asked you to calculate the following financial ratios for each of the divisions and compare their values between the current and previous years:

- Return on assets (net income/average total assets)
- Profit margin (net income/sales)
- Asset turnover (sales/average total assets)
- Current ratio (current assets/current liabilities)

The client has provided a data set with select income statement and balance sheet data for each division. Because this is a task that you are likely to perform for other engagements, you decide to build a macro in Excel to calculate these financial statement ratios. Record a macro for the floor cleaning division. Then, run this macro on each of the divisions to calculate the ratios for the remaining divisions.

EX 10.9 (LO 2) [Financial Accounting] **Blockchain Technologies** You are a financial accountant in a large retail company whose supply chain partners want to use blockchain technologies to record all transactions. Explain the financial reporting benefits from using blockchain technology and factors that need to be considered for this decision.

EX 10.10 (LO 2, 3) [Auditing] [Accounting Information Systems] **Technology Developments** You are a systems accountant working with your company's internal auditor to analyze the compliance of your company's authorized purchase credit card (e.g., "P-card") transactions with company policies. A new analysis technology helps you easily identify the spending transactions by several employees that do not comply with the policies. Explain which technology development described in the chapter would best help you find and document where controls in the P-card process either must be improved or added to prevent these unauthorized transactions.

EX 10.11 (LO 2, 3) [Financial Accounting] **Technology Developments** You work for an investment manager who asks you to retrieve a large portfolio of different companies' closing stock market prices each trading day. Which data analysis technology would make this daily task more efficient?

EX 10.12 (LO 2, 3) [Data] [Auditing] [Financial Accounting] **Textual Analysis** As the external auditor for a computer manufacturing client, you are asked to examine the company's warranty expense and related accrual adjusting entry for GAAP compliance in valuation calculations. The client provided the following summary of warranty expense related data from the prior year (audited) and the current year (unaudited):

F/S	AcctNo	AcctDescription	6/30/2025	6/30/2024	Difference	%Change
Income						
Statement		Warranty				
Account	32153	Expense	$ 347,954	$ 535,849	$ (187,895)	–35%
Balance Sheet		Warranty				
Account	23829	Liability	$ 121,784	$ 241,132	$ (119,348)	–49%

Both the warranty expense and warranty liability decreased significantly compared to the prior year. You asked your client's financial accountant why there was such a drastic decrease in the expense and liability. The accountant responded, "We have had significant increases in product quality and therefore we don't have a lot of warranty claims these days. Customers are happier."

The objective was finding evidence to support or deny this explanation, so you obtained customer satisfaction text data about the computers from social media postings. You planned to perform textual analysis regarding whether there was an increase in positive customer sentiment about the computer product quality.

1. Classify the customer comments into three groups: 1 = low quality, 2 = neutral, and 3 = high quality.

   (*Hint*: Sort the product ratings or customer comments in alphabetical order to make it easier to assign categories to each comment. Use the COUNTIF function to total each comment into one of the three groups. Critical thinking note: Your coding may disagree with other coders, and you might be inconsistent within your own coding.)

2. Create a frequency distribution table that shows the total number of customer comments by group, by month, and in total for each of the customer comment groups.

   (*Hint*: Transform the date column into months from the Home menu. In the Number section, select Custom formatting, then type "mmm" in the type (no quotes). This does not change the date data, just its presentation, preserving your original dates. Then, create a PivotTable using your groups as rows and values and months as columns.)

3. Create two time series visualizations to determine if customer sentiments about their computer products are improving or not. One visualization should use customer text comments and the other their product ratings.

4. Interpret these results and determine if any further audit steps are necessary to properly estimate the warranty expense and related accrual for the first six months. Suggest internal controls for the critical thinking risks mentioned in question 1.

Professional Application Case   SportsRFun

SportsRFun is a new chain of retail stores with both online and brick-and-mortar locations. They sell a variety of outdoor activity and sports products ranging from water sports to mountaineering and camping. The company is growing quickly, currently operating 10 stores across five states. These stores are supplied with products from a distribution center that receives all its purchased products from vendors. Online sales are processed out of SportsRFun's distribution center. The brick-and-mortar stores focus on high-quality customer service and offer classes for new outdoor sports enthusiasts. The company has developed strong relationships with its vendors and its customers. Customers tend to return to the stores, demonstrating significant customer loyalty.

Because SportsRFun is growing so quickly, they want to automate more inventory purchasing processes to make them more efficient and effective, with better internal controls. What follows is an entity-relationship diagram (ERD) showing the tables and variables involved in the process.

VendorMasterFile	PurchaseOrder	ReceivingReport	Invoices
VendorID	PONo	RECNO	InvoiceNO
VendorName	VendorID	PONo	PONo
VendorAddress	VendorName	VendorID	VendorID
VendorCity	PODate	VendorName	VendorName
VendorState	POItemID	ItemID	ItemID
VendorZip	POItemDescription	ItemDescription	ItemDescription
VendorPayterms	POItemCost	RecItemQty	InvoiceQty
	POItemQty	RecDate	InvoiceItemCost
	POExpectedPreceiptDate		InvoiceTotal

PAC 10.1 Accounting Information Systems: Use Process Automation for Accounts Payable

Data **Accounting Information Systems**   You are the systems accountant reviewing the accounts payable process to approve vendor invoices for payment. Currently, the process requires manual matching between the invoice, receiving report, and purchase order to approve the invoice for payment. You have interviewed the AP clerk and the financial accountant and noted that to approve an invoice for payment, the following conditions must be met:

- The invoice data must match the data included on the purchase order including, VendorID, ItemID, and Quantity.

- The invoice data must match the data included on the receiving report including VendorID, ItemID, and Quantity.

Use Alteryx to build a workflow that results in two outputs: a file that is "Okay to Pay" invoices and a file that is "Exceptions."

PAC 10.2 Auditing: Continuous Auditing of Company Purchases

Auditing   You are a senior auditor on the SportsRFun's annual audit. Your audit manager has asked you to develop a plan for the engagement team to use continuous audit methodologies to reduce the amount of audit work and testing performed at year-end. Your assigned audit area is the order-to-pay cycle. Draft a memo for the audit files discussing continuous auditing and outlining your plan for continuous monitoring of the purchasing data for your client.

PAC 10.3 Financial Accounting: Automate Procedures for Approving Vendor Payments

`Data` `Financial Accounting` `Accounting Information Systems` You are a financial accountant for SportsRFun. Currently, your process for approving vendor invoices for payment is matching the hardcopy invoice from the vendor to the relevant purchase order and receiving data in the AIS:

- Purchase orders are keyed into the AIS in the PurchaseOrder table by the purchasing group after they are sent to the vendor.
- Receiving report data is keyed into the AIS in the receiving department after items are received by the vendor.
- Upon receipt of a vendor invoice, the invoice is keyed into the AIS VendorInvoices table and filed by due date in the hardcopy file in the AP clerk's office.
- Daily, the AP clerk pulls the invoices that are due within the next few days and performs the following:

    Step 1: For each invoice, the AP clerk looks up the corresponding PO number to the PO in the PurchaseOrders table. The AP clerk verifies that the quantity purchased was the quantity invoiced. If the quantities agree within a 2% tolerance level, then the AP clerk moves to the next step.

    Step 2: For each invoice, the AP clerk looks up the PO number that corresponds to the PO number in the ReceivingReport table. The AP clerk verifies that the quantity received was the quantity invoiced. If the quantities agree within a 2% tolerance level, then the clerk moves to the next step.

    Step 3: For each invoice that passes steps 1 and 2, the AP clerk stamps "Okay to Pay" on the invoice and adds it to the Ok to Pay list, which is sent to the treasurer who prepares, signs, and sends checks.

1. Match and compare the quantities from the purchase orders, the receiving reports, and the vendor invoices. The matched invoice information within the 2% quantity deviation tolerance should be labeled as "Okay to Pay." Any invoices above the 2% quantity deviation should be labeled "Exception" so the AP clerk can follow up with the vendor.

2. Discuss the benefits of using Excel to increase efficiencies and potentially reduce errors in the approval of vendor invoices.

PAC 10.4 Managerial Accounting: Create a Vendor Performance Dashboard

`Data` `Managerial Accounting` `Accounting Information Systems` As a managerial accountant for SportsRFun, you want to know if there are patterns in the purchasing data. Create a visualization dashboard to measure the following metrics related to vendor purchases:

- The count of purchase orders for each vendor during this period.
- The percentage of purchase costs incurred during this period by vendor.
- The percentage of purchase costs incurred by product.

PAC 10.5 Tax Accounting: Explain Robotic Process Automation for Current Tax Rates

`Tax Accounting` Currently the data needed to complete the corporate tax return comes from several different data sources. Each month you download the data into Excel spreadsheets and use the Excel spreadsheet to complete the tax accrual analysis. Discuss how technology might be used to automate this process. Are there other technologies that SportsRFun should consider for use in the tax department?

Data Analytics and Decision-Making

Extract-Transform-Load (ETL) Process in AR Financial Services, Inc.

`Data` `Financial Accounting`

Introduction

AR Financial Services, Inc. operates across multiple geographies, offering a diverse range of financial products and services. With operations spanning banking, insurance, and investment management, the company generates substantial volumes of transactional and analytical data every day.

To streamline data management and mostly spreadsheet-based reporting processes, AR Financial Services adopted the extract-transform-load (ETL) framework powered by cutting-edge technology using SQL databases and data lakes. The ETL process involves the following three key stages:

1. **Extraction:** Raw data is sourced from various internal systems, including transaction databases, customer relationship management (CRM) platforms, and financial reporting tools. This data encompasses customer transactions, account balances, market data, and more.

2. **Transformation:** Extracted data undergoes rigorous transformation to ensure consistency, accuracy, and compliance with regulatory standards. This phase involves data cleansing, validation, normalization, and enrichment. Additionally, complex algorithms are applied for risk analysis, fraud detection, and performance measurement.

3. **Loading:** Transformed data is loaded into a centralized data warehouse or data lake, where it is organized into structured data sets for reporting and analysis purposes. This repository serves as a single source of truth for decision-making across the organization.

Data Extracts

Here are the partial data extracts from the customer transactions database of AR Financial Services, following both the extraction and transformation stages:

a. After-Extraction Stage

Base Transactions

Transaction ID	Customer ID	Transaction Date	Transaction Type	Amount	Currency	Account Type
1	C001	2025-02-15	Deposit	5,000.00	USD	Savings
2	C002	2025-02-16	Withdrawal	1,200.00	USD	Checking
3	C003	2025-02-17	Transfer	3,500.00	EUR	Savings
4	C001	2025-02-18	Deposit	2,500.00	USD	Investment
...	...	...	...	...	...	...

Additional Transactional Attributes

Transaction ID	Customer ID	Transaction Date	Dispute Flag
2	C002	2025-02-16	Yes
...	...	...	...

b. After-Transformation Stage

Transaction ID	Customer ID	Transaction Date	Transaction Type	Amount	Currency	Account Type	Country	Normalized Amount	Normalized Currency	Dispute Flag
1	C001	2025-02-15	Deposit	5,000.00	USD	Savings	USA	6,500,000.00	SKW	No
2	C002	2025-02-16	Withdrawal	1,200.00	USD	Checking	Canada	(1,560,000.00)	SKW	Yes
3	C003	2025-02-17	Transfer	3,500.00	EUR	Savings	France	5,075,000.00	SKW	No
4	C001	2025-02-18	Deposit	2,500.00	USD	Investment	USA	3,250,000.00	SKW	No
...	...	...	...	...	...	...	...	...	...	...

Despite the benefits of the ETL process, AR Financial Services encountered several challenges as follows during the implementation:

- **Data quality:** Ensuring data accuracy and consistency across different sources posed a significant challenge, requiring continuous monitoring and refinement of transformation rules.
- **Scalability:** As data volumes surged, scalability became a pressing concern. The ETL infrastructure had to be optimized to handle increasing workloads efficiently.
- **Regulatory compliance:** Compliance with stringent regulatory requirements, such as GDPR and Sarbanes-Oxley, necessitated robust data governance frameworks and security measures.

By effectively executing the ETL process, AR Financial Services gained the following valuable insights into its operational efficiency and performance metrics:

- **Financial reporting:** Timely and accurate financial reporting was facilitated, enabling stakeholders to monitor key performance indicators (KPIs) and make informed strategic decisions.
- **Risk management:** Advanced analytics and modeling techniques empowered the company to effectively mitigate risks, identify emerging threats, and optimize capital allocation.
- **Customer insights:** By integrating data from disparate sources, AR Financial Services gained a comprehensive understanding of customer behavior, preferences, and lifetime value, facilitating targeted marketing initiatives and personalized services.

Conclusion

ETL process has emerged as a cornerstone of data management and analytics in the realm of financial accounting. Through effective extraction, transformation, and loading of data, organizations like AR Financial Services can harness the power of data to drive innovation, mitigate risks, and enhance operational efficiency.

Case Questions

1. How does the ETL process contribute to improved financial reporting and decision-making within AR Financial Services, Inc.?
2. What are the key challenges associated with ensuring data quality and regulatory compliance in the context of the ETL process?
3. How has the scalability of the ETL infrastructure evolved to accommodate the growing volumes of data generated by AR Financial Services?
4. Can you provide examples of specific insights gained through data analysis facilitated by the ETL process, and clarify how they have impacted strategic initiatives within the organization?
5. What are your observations on data transformation in the data extracts? Do you see use of any external data in the transformation process?

Inventory Control Through ABC Analysis

Managerial Accounting **Data**

Introduction

Dongshan Spectrum Company is a manufacturing company that deals with a wide range of plastic products. Managing inventory efficiently is crucial for the company's operations and profitability. ABC classification categorizes inventory items based on their importance, allowing Dongshan Spectrum to prioritize resources and attention accordingly.

To optimize inventory management, the supply chain manager, Jeff Wang, decides to conduct an ABC classification analysis of its manufactured products with the help of Janine Chang who handles the inventory management system.

Jeff would also like to incorporate the requirements into the inventory management system, so that the system can provide the data for analysis in the future.

Data

The base data extract of products consists of the following columns:

- **Item ID:** Unique identifier for each inventory item.
- **Item Description:** Description of the inventory item.
- **Quantity Sold:** The quantity of the item sold over a specific period.
- **Cost per Item:** The cost associated with each inventory item in New Taiwan dollar (NT$).

Janine will extract base data from the inventory management system to a SQL database table named "InventoryData," and the structure of the table is as follows:

SQL

```
CREATE TABLE InventoryData (
    ItemID INT PRIMARY KEY,
    ItemDescription VARCHAR(255),
    QuantitySold INT,
    CostPerItem DECIMAL(10, 2)
);
```

Analysis

Jeff will classify inventory items into categories A, B, and C based on their importance in terms of cost and quantity sold.

Jeff advises Janine to adopt the following approaches:

1. Calculate the annual consumption value (ACV) for each item.
2. Rank items based on their ACV.
3. Assign categories (A, B, or C) to items based on their contribution to the total consumption value.

Step 1: Calculate Annual Consumption Value (ACV)

ACV represents the total value of an item consumed over a year. It is calculated by multiplying the quantity sold by the cost per item.

SQL

```
SELECT
    ItemID,
    ItemDescription,
    QuantitySold,
    CostPerItem,
    QuantitySold * CostPerItem AS AnnualConsumptionValue
FROM
    InventoryData;
```

Step 2: Rank Items Based on ACV

Sort the items in descending order of their ACV.

SQL

```
SELECT
    ItemID,
    ItemDescription,
    QuantitySold,
    CostPerItem,
    QuantitySold * CostPerItem AS AnnualConsumptionValue,
    ROW_NUMBER() OVER (ORDER BY QuantitySold * CostPerItem DESC) AS Rank
FROM
    InventoryData;
```

Step 3: Assign Categories (A, B, C)

ABC classification typically follows the Pareto principle, where a small percentage of items (A) account for a significant portion of the total consumption value, whereas a larger percentage of items (C) contribute less. Jeff has assumed the following ranges for ABC classification:

- **A:** Top 20% of items contributing to 80% of the total consumption value.
- **B:** Next 30% of items contributing to 15% of the total consumption value.
- **C:** Remaining 50% of items contributing to 5% of the total consumption value.

SQL

```
WITH RankedItems AS (
    SELECT
        ItemID,
        ItemDescription,
        QuantitySold,
        CostPerItem,
        QuantitySold * CostPerItem AS AnnualConsumptionValue,
        ROW_NUMBER() OVER (ORDER BY QuantitySold * CostPerItem DESC) AS Rank
    FROM
        InventoryData
)
SELECT
    ItemID,
    ItemDescription,
    QuantitySold,
```

```
CostPerItem,
AnnualConsumptionValue,
CASE
    WHEN Rank <= 0.2 * (SELECT COUNT(*) FROM RankedItems) THEN 'A'
    WHEN Rank <= 0.5 * (SELECT COUNT(*) FROM RankedItems) THEN 'B'
    ELSE 'C'
END AS Category
FROM
    RankedItems;
```

Create an Excel PivotTable

1. Export the result of the SQL query to Excel.

2. Create a pivot table using the exported data.

3. Arrange the data by ItemID, ItemDescription, QuantitySold, CostPerItem, AnnualConsumptionValue, and Category.

4. Use the pivot table to analyze and visualize the ABC classification of inventory items.

Conclusion

ABC classification analysis helped Dongshan Spectrum to identify the most critical inventory items (Category A) that require closer monitoring and control, enabling them to allocate resources efficiently and optimize inventory management strategies. By utilizing SQL queries and Excel pivot tables, the company can easily perform and visualize the ABC classification analysis based on the provided base data.

Data The base data for SQL is available in the BaseData Sheet of the InventoryData Excel File.

Case Questions

1. Why is it important for Jeff to conduct an ABC classification analysis on the inventory?

2. How is the annual consumption value (ACV) calculated in the provided SQL query? If Jeff wants to include raw materials, packing materials, and consumables in the analysis, what additional information is required in the analysis?

3. What is the significance of the Pareto principle in ABC classification analysis?

4. How can Excel pivot tables be utilized to visualize the results of the ABC classification analysis? What is the advantage of SQL over Excel for ABC classification analysis? How can Jeff and Janine take advantage of both the tools?

Leveraging Data Analytics for Business Growth

Managerial Accounting

Introduction

Anomax India manages an internet-based marketplace that provides an extensive range of merchandise, including apparel, electronics, household goods, and consumables. Anomax encountered obstacles in streamlining its supply chain, customizing customer interactions, and maintaining a competitive edge in the market due to its extensive product inventory and global customer base.

Data Analytics Implementation

Anomax allocated resources toward the implementation of sophisticated data analytics technologies and processes in order to tackle these obstacles. The following points depict an account of the manner in which they implemented data analytics in diverse facets of their enterprise:

- **Supply chain optimization:** Anomax effectively managed inventory levels, optimized logistic operations, and accurately predicted demand through the implementation of predictive analytics. It achieved these results by conducting an examination of historical sales data, market trends, external factors including economic indicators and seasonality, and thereby mitigating stock-outs, surplus inventory, and enhancing the overall efficacy of the supply chain.

- **Customer segmentation and personalization:** Anomax implemented machine learning algorithms and segmentation techniques to divide its customer base into discrete clusters according to demographic characteristics, browsing patterns, purchasing behaviors, and preferences. As a result, Anomax was capable of customizing promotional offers, marketing campaigns, and product recommendations, which increased consumer engagement and conversion rates.

- **Fraud detection and risk management:** Anomax implemented solutions based on data analytics to manage risk and detect misconduct. Through the examination of transactional data, user behavior patterns, and anomaly detection algorithms, Anomax has the capability to detect and alleviate fraudulent activities, safeguard customer data, and bolster platform trust and security.

- **Market intelligence and competitor analysis:** Anomax employed data analytics to conduct competitor analysis and market intelligence. Through the surveillance of social media sentiment, examination of competitor pricing strategies, and monitoring of industry trends, Anomax acquired significant knowledge regarding market dynamics, customer inclinations, and competitive positioning. This enabled the organization to formulate decisions based on data and maintain a competitive edge.

- **Operational efficiency and cost optimization:** The implementation of data analytics at Anomax was instrumental in enhancing operational efficiency and optimizing costs. Through the examination of operational data, identification of constraints, and implementation of process enhancements, Anomax successfully decreased operational costs, optimized resource allocation, and boosted departmental productivity.

Results

The implementation of data analytics initiatives yielded the following significant results and impact for Anomax:

- **Improvements in customer experiences:** The implementation of personalized product recommendations, targeted marketing campaigns, and streamlined user experiences resulted in increased customer retention rates, repeat purchases, and satisfaction.

- **Increased revenue and profitability:** Anomax achieved these results through the implementation of data-driven pricing strategies, optimized inventory management, and effective cross-selling and upselling initiatives.

- **Improved operational efficiency:** Cost savings, enhanced resource utilization, and streamlined supply chain operations led to improved resource allocation, decreased fulfillment times, and enhanced operational efficiency.

- **Improved risk management:** By implementing proactive risk management strategies, bolstered security measures, and sophisticated fraud detection capabilities, Anomax successfully reduced risks, safeguarded customer information, and maintained a dependable and secure online platform.

- **Strategic decision-making:** By providing actionable insights derived from data analytics, Anomax's leadership team was empowered to make well-informed decisions, efficiently allocate resources, and swiftly respond to dynamic market conditions.

Conclusion

To summarize, the utilization of data-driven insights to stimulate business expansion, enhance customer experiences, and streamline operations has had a profound and transformative effect on Anomax's experience with data analytics. Through the adoption of data analytics as a strategic facilitator, Anomax not only attained concrete outcomes including increased revenue, reduced expenses, and enhanced operational effectiveness, but it also established itself as a frontrunner in the digital age of electronic commerce. This case study highlights the significance of data analytics in the contemporary data-driven business environment as a key driver of innovation and competitive advantage.

Case Questions

1. What is the objective that Anomax is planning to achieve?
2. What were the primary challenges faced by Anomax before implementing data analytics solutions?
3. How did Anomax utilize data analytics to optimize its supply chain?
4. What techniques did Anomax employ for customer segmentation and personalization?
5. How did data analytics contribute to improved customer experiences at Anomax?
6. What were the benefits of implementing data analytics for risk management and fraud detection at Anomax?
7. How did data analytics help Anomax in making strategic decisions and staying competitive?

Time Series Model for Predicting Jute Yarn Demand

Introduction

Accurate sales forecasting in the appropriate quantity for upcoming periods is crucial in today's competitive landscape. This is essential for guaranteeing product availability and enhancing customer satisfaction. The accurate forecasting of product demand is important for mitigating inventory and streamlining operational challenges, ultimately leading to enhanced profitability. Ensuring timely and accurate fulfillment of customer demands in the appropriate quantity is the primary catalyst for profit generation. Therefore, in order to guarantee product availability at the most economical price, it is important to make predictions with the utmost precision. As prediction is an inherently ambiguous process, forecasting future events is not a simple task. Product diversification, brief product life cycles, and rapid technological advancements—among other factors—significantly complicate and block the accurate prediction of product demand. This case presents a model that determines the optimal prediction method according to the minimum values of forecasting errors. Sales data pertaining to jute yarn were obtained from Akij Jute Mills, Akij Group Ltd., a jute product manufacturer in Bangladesh, located in Noapara, Jessore. A time series depiction of demand data reveals that there are variations in demand over a given period of time. This study employed Minitab 17 software to implement eight distinct statistical forecasting techniques, including simple moving average (SMA), single exponential smoothing, trend analysis, Winter's method, and Holt's method. Eight forecasting methods were compared, with Winter's additive model emerging as the most accurate.

Forecasting Methods

Simple Moving Average Method

Simple moving average (SMA), also known as the rolling average, is calculated by averaging the observations in the entire data set. It predicts the subsequent period based on the arithmetic mean. By smoothing out short-term deviations in time series data, this technique identifies long-term cycles or trends.

Single Exponential Smoothing Method

Single exponential smoothing (SES) is an advanced technique and is a form of weighted averaging in which the future value is estimated by adding a percentage of the forecasted error to the previous forecast. It is straightforward to implement and calculate, as no history of previous input data is required. It eliminates the impact of unusual data uniformly.

Double Exponential Smoothing (Holt's Method)

Double exponential smoothing or Holt's method, introduced by Charles C. Holt in 1957, is employed to forecast data exhibiting a linear trend. It is built upon the principles of basic exponential filtering. Holt's method employs two distinct smoothing constants—alpha to represent the level and gamma to account for the trend—to smooth both the slope and trend in the time series.

Winter's Method

When a data set contains both trend and seasonality, this method may be applied. It is utilized to normalize data at each period by incorporating a trend component, a level component, and a seasonal component; it also offers forecasts for short to medium term. Models can be classified as either multiplicative or additive. When the quantity of the data affects the magnitude of the seasonal pattern, a multiplicative model is applied. The exact opposite of the multiplicative model is the additive model.

Trend Analysis

Trend analysis applies a general model to multiple time series data that exhibits a discernible trend pattern. It then offers traders insight into future events by utilizing historical data. There are S-curve, linear, and quadratic trends.

Decomposition

The decomposition technique is employed to partition time series data into seasonal and linear trend components. In accordance with the trend, seasonal components may be additive or multiplicative. The presence of a seasonal component in time series data is utilized to analyze the characteristics of the component elements.

Measures of Forecasting Accuracy

When comparing various forecasting alternatives, forecasting accuracy is a critical factor. In this context, accuracy pertains to forecasting error, which denotes the discrepancy between the predicted and actual value for a specified time period. This study employs the mean absolute deviation (MAD), the mean squared error (MSE), and the mean absolute percentage error (MAPE) as forecasting error determinants. MAD represents the mean absolute discrepancy between the predicted and actual value for a specified time period. MSE represents the mean of squared errors. MAPE signifies the mean absolute percent error.

Result Analysis

The analysis suggests that there are variations in demand from one period to another as depicted in **Illustration 1**. The demand trends for the years 2010, 2011, and 2012 exhibit minimal fluctuations. Demand remained constant for four weeks before increasing dramatically in week 5. It maintained a stable rate until week 9, when it abruptly declined. The highest trend of demand was observed during weeks 32–35 for each of the four years; seasonality was identified at this time. The mean demand has exhibited an upward trend from 2010 to 2012. Conversely, demand data pertaining to 2013 revealed substantial fluctuations in demand on a weekly basis, surpassing values observed in preceding years. The minimum demand value exceeded 1,000 tons, whereas the maximum demand occurred in 2010.

ILLUSTRATION 1   Time Series Plot of Jute Yarn Demand

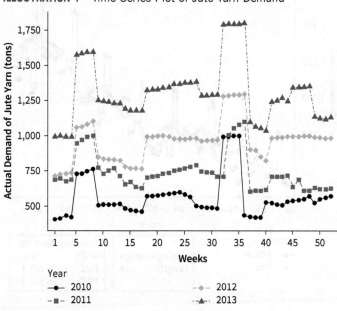

The forecasting errors for various forecasting periods using the SMA method are shown in **Illustration 2**. In the SMA method, 14 trials are taken through putting different values of n.

ILLUSTRATION 2   Forecasting Errors Under SMA Method

Length of Average in Weeks (n)	MAPE	MAD	MSD
2MA	8.3	70.5	19,431.2
3MA	10.8	91.4	24,473.3
4MA	13.2	112.1	29,783.9
5MA	14.1	121.9	32,376.7
6MA	14.7	127.5	33,504.7
7MA	15	131.1	33,920.3
8MA	15.1	133.2	33,976.4
9MA	15.3	135	33,949.8
10MA	15.1	134.7	33,797.7
11MA	15	133.5	33,577.2
12MA	14.7	131.4	33,334.6
13MA	14.4	129.6	33,163.5
14MA	14.2	128.9	33,243.4
15MA	14.3	129.8	33,645.2

On the basis of the measurement of 14 sets of error determinants, the minimum values of MAD, MAPE, and MSE are derived when the forecasting period (n) is set to 15 weeks. The 15-week range for the values of MAD, MAPE, and MSE is 70.5–135, 8.3–15.3, and 19,431.2–33,976.4, respectively. **Illustration 3** shows the relationship between actual demand and forecasted demand using the SMA method. Actual demand experiences abrupt increases and decreases, whereas forecasted demand fluctuates between its greatest and lowest values. The accuracy measures for MAPE, MAD, and MSD are 13.1, 117.4, and 26,912.1, respectively.

ILLUSTRATION 3 Comparison of Actual Sales with Forecasted Demand in SMA Method

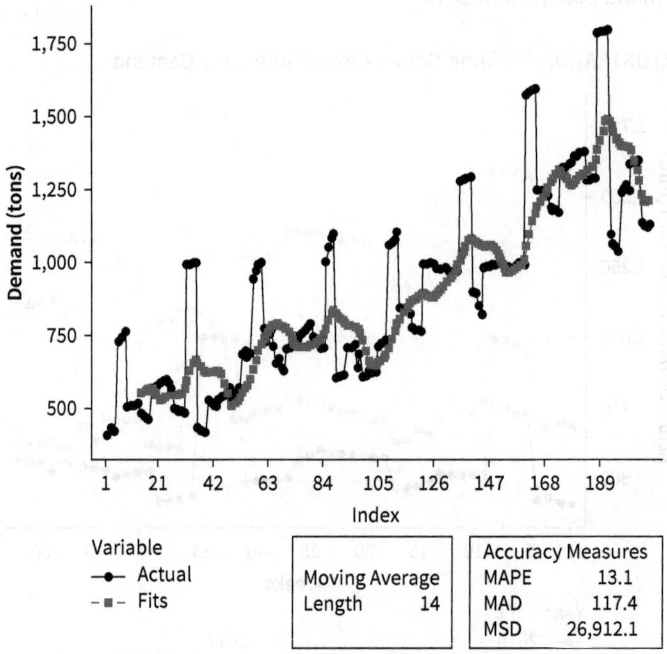

Variable		Accuracy Measures	
—•— Actual	Moving Average	MAPE	13.1
–■– Fits	Length 14	MAD	117.4
		MSD	26,912.1

On the other hand, in order to ascertain the optimal smoothing constant (i) for the singular exponential smoothing method, nine trials are conducted. It is observed that higher values of the smoothing constant result in the lowest forecasting errors. **Illustration 4** presents a range of forecasting error values corresponding to varying smoothing constants. The values of MAPE, MAD, and MSE are varied among 6.5–13.1, 53.6–116.8, and 15,457–29,939.5, respectively. It is evident from Illustration 4 that as the smoothing constant increases, the values of MAPE, MAD, and MSE decrease. As illustrated in **Illustration 5**, the volatility of actual and predicted demand is nearly identical when employing an SES method. The occurrence of minimum errors was observed at the optimal smoothing constant ($i = 0.9$). As shown in **Illustration 6**, nine trials are

ILLUSTRATION 4 Forecasting Errors Under SES Method

Value of Smoothing Constant (Alpha)	MAPE	MAD	MSD
0.1	13.1	116.8	29,939.5
0.2	12.6	109.1	26,144.4
0.3	11.8	101.1	23,576.3
0.4	10.8	92.2	21,390.4
0.5	9.8	82.7	19,528.3
0.6	8.7	73.6	18,003.7
0.7	7.8	65.7	16,822.2
0.8	7.1	59.1	15,977.1
0.9	6.5	53.6	15,457

conducted using varying smoothing constants (both level and trend) ranging from 0.1 to 0.3 in Holt's method. A comparison is presented in **Illustration 7** between the actual demand for jute yarn in tons and the demand forecasted using Holt's method at the most appropriate combination of smoothing constants for 2010–2013. The lowest values of errors are achieved at $\alpha = 0.3$ and $\gamma = 0.1$.

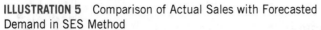

ILLUSTRATION 5   Comparison of Actual Sales with Forecasted Demand in SES Method

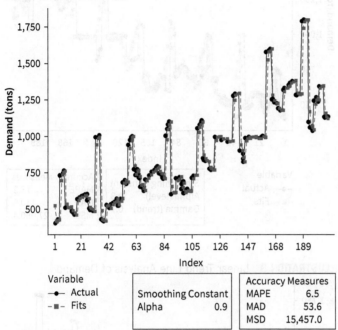

Variable	Smoothing Constant		Accuracy Measures	
—●— Actual	Alpha	0.9	MAPE	6.5
-■- Fits			MAD	53.6
			MSD	15,457.0

ILLUSTRATION 6   Forecasting Errors Under Holt's Method

Smoothing Constant Alpha (Level)	Smoothing Constant Gamma (Trend)	MAPE	MAD	MSD
0.1	0.1	15	128	32,880.4
0.1	0.2	15.9	136.7	36,354.1
0.1	0.3	18	152.1	42,391.8
0.2	0.1	14.2	119.8	29,969.1
0.2	0.2	16.3	135.5	34,575.1
0.2	0.3	17.8	147	38,415.1
0.3	0.1	13.2	110.6	27,050.4
0.3	0.2	14.5	120.4	30,592.1
0.3	0.3	15.1	125.9	33,875.7

From trend analysis on jute yarn demand data of 208 weeks, the obtained trend equation is $Y_t = 425.1 + 4.47 \times t$ which is shown in **Illustration 8**. In addition, the forecasting errors and forecasted values in relation to the actual demand are illustrated in Illustration 8. Furthermore, in order to ascertain the defects, two varieties of Winter's models—the multiplicative and additive models—are implemented. In total, 27 experiments were performed in which the values of three smoothing constants (α, γ, and δ) were varied in the range of 0.1 to 0.3. Seasonality for both

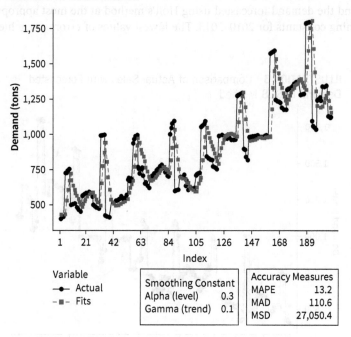

ILLUSTRATION 7 Comparison of Actual Sales with Forecasted Demand in Holt's Method

ILLUSTRATION 8 Linear Trend Line Analysis of Demand

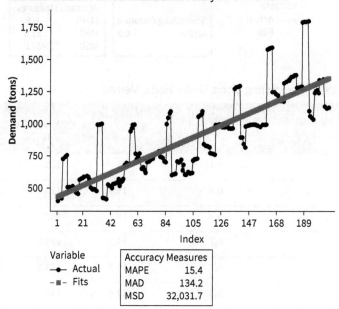

instances is approximately 52 weeks. **Illustration 9** displays 27 sets of forecasting errors derived from 27 trials using the multiplicative and additive Winter's model. The corresponding MAD, MAPE, and MSE, as well as the optimal smoothing constants for additive and multiplicative models, are displayed in **Illustrations 10** and **11**, respectively.

The figures show that minimum errors are obtained for both models at $\alpha = 0.3$, $\gamma = 0.1$, and $\delta = 0.1$. However, Winters' additive model yields more favorable outcomes in comparison to the multiplicative model. Measures of accuracy are determined using multiplicative and additive decomposition models that take into account both seasonal plus trend and seasonal pattern alone. The results of both models are summarized in **Illustration 12**, which reveals that the multiplicative decomposition model incorporating trend and seasonal effects exhibits the fewest errors.

ILLUSTRATION 9   Forecasting Errors Under Winters Method

Smoothing Constant Alpha (Level)	Smoothing Constant Gamma (Trend)	Smoothing Constant Delta (Seasonal)	Winters Additive Model			Winters Multiplicative Model		
			MAPE	MAD	MSD	MAPE	MAD	MSD
0.1	0.1	0.1	6.08	48.51	5,030.6	7.16	61.75	7,560.37
0.1	0.1	0.2	6.21	49.99	5,414.65	7.42	64.46	8,376.62
0.1	0.1	0.3	6.36	51.73	5,807.84	7.66	66.66	9,235.14
0.1	0.2	0.1	6.21	49.55	5,204.78	7.44	63.17	7,537.56
0.1	0.2	0.2	6.38	51.38	5,608.68	7.84	68.07	8,643.47
0.1	0.2	0.3	6.57	53.43	6,012.93	8.26	72.77	9,873.75
0.1	0.3	0.1	6.48	51.77	5,537.25	7.67	63.24	7,413.21
0.1	0.3	0.2	6.61	53.44	5,991.33	8.2	69.22	8,616.98
0.1	0.3	0.3	6.79	55.46	6,442.68	9	77.5	10,167.7
0.2	0.1	0.1	5.35	43.04	4,779.84	5.89	48.51	5,563.59
0.2	0.1	0.2	5.45	44.28	5,124.34	6.13	51.3	6,212.32
0.2	0.1	0.3	5.56	45.63	5,473.25	6.38	54.18	6,908.63
0.2	0.2	0.1	5.59	45.14	5,166.55	6.37	51.91	5,863.92
0.2	0.2	0.2	5.68	46.48	5,571.86	6.64	55.02	6,609.84
0.2	0.2	0.3	5.83	48.21	5,994.81	6.96	58.51	7,481.55
0.2	0.3	0.1	5.93	48.24	5,643.04	6.68	54.74	6,380.57
0.2	0.3	0.2	6.07	50.14	6,130.07	7.04	58.76	7,246.09
0.2	0.3	0.3	6.28	52.5	6,660.18	7.42	62.88	8,305.83
0.3	0.1	0.1	5.06	40.58	4,705.68	5.38	43.92	5,089.33
0.3	0.1	0.2	5.11	41.38	5,003.92	5.55	45.84	5,624.94
0.3	0.1	0.3	3.19	42.43	5,309.95	5.74	47.84	6,204.97
0.3	0.2	0.1	5.39	43.47	5,153.21	5.65	46.38	5,550.05
0.3	0.2	0.2	5.47	44.51	5,493.52	5.88	48.8	6,141.81
0.3	0.2	0.3	5.56	45.74	5,852.34	6.11	51.21	6,803.38
0.3	0.3	0.1	5.7	46.13	5,652.62	5.73	47.36	6,066.61
0.3	0.3	0.2	5.78	47.21	6,033.21	5.98	49.94	6,723.87
0.3	0.3	0.3	5.89	48.56	6,446.37	6.25	52.75	7,472.54

Additionally, the additive model with seasonal and trend effects yields the smallest error values. In **Illustration 13,** the comprehensive result of the calculations and analyses utilizing eight distinct forecasting methods is presented. The results demonstrate the existence of variations among the techniques that were implemented. MAD values range between 40.58 and 134.16, whereas MAPE values for various forecasting methods fall between 5.06 and 15.39. The moving average technique yields the highest value of MSD (33,243.4), whereas Winter's additive method contributes to the lowest value (4,705). When evaluating the performance of predicted methods, Winters' additive model exhibits the smallest forecasting error values, signifying the highest level of accuracy and suggesting that this method is appropriate.

ILLUSTRATION 10 Comparison of Actual Sales with Forecasted Demand in Winter's Additive Method

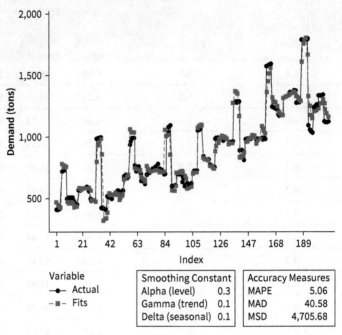

Variable	Smoothing Constant		Accuracy Measures	
—●— Actual	Alpha (level)	0.3	MAPE	5.06
– ■ – Fits	Gamma (trend)	0.1	MAD	40.58
	Delta (seasonal)	0.1	MSD	4,705.68

ILLUSTRATION 11 Comparison of Actual Sales with Forecasted Demand in Winter's Multiplicative Method

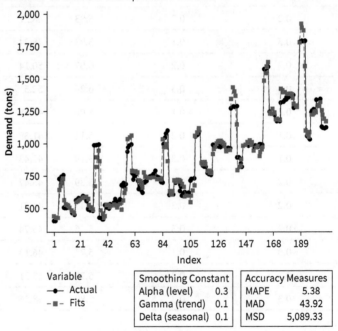

Variable	Smoothing Constant		Accuracy Measures	
—●— Actual	Alpha (level)	0.3	MAPE	5.38
– ■ – Fits	Gamma (trend)	0.1	MAD	43.92
	Delta (seasonal)	0.1	MSD	5,089.33

ILLUSTRATION 12 Summary of Decomposition Methods

	Decomposition			
	Multiplicative		**Additive**	
Measure	Trend and Seasonality	Only Seasonality	Trend and Seasonality	Only Seasonal
MAPE	8.35	31.8	8.16	31.8
MAD	67.66	252.6	65.93	252.4
MSD	7,573.78	86,107.7	7,467.41	86,446

ILLUSTRATION 13   Summary of All Forecasting Methods and Error Calculations

Forecasting Method	MAPE	MAD	MSD
Multiplicative decomposition model with trend and seasonality	8.35	67.66	7,573.78
Additive decomposition model with trend and seasonality	8.16	65.93	7,467.41
Moving average	14.2	128.9	33,243.4
Single exponential smoothing	6.5	53.6	15,457
Holt's method	13.2	110.6	27,050.4
Trend analysis	15.39	134.16	32,031.66
Winters multiplicative model	5.38	43.92	5,089.33
Winters additive model	5.06	40.58	4,705.68

Conclusion

The primary objective of this study is to ascertain the optimal forecasting methodology for forthcoming jute textile sales within the jute products manufacturing sector. The method of forecasting will be chosen according to the minimum values of forecasting errors, specifically MAPE, MAD, and MSD. In order to achieve this goal, various time series analyses are conducted on demand data spanning 208 weeks utilizing the Minitab 17 application, and accuracy metrics are computed. The results of an evaluation of the performance of eight forecasting methods indicate that Winter's additive model is the most appropriate method for predicting the actual demand.

Case Questions

1. What is the primary objective of accurate sales forecasting in the jute yarn industry?
2. What methods were employed in the study to forecast jute yarn demand?
3. What is the use of forecasting errors and how are they evaluated?
4. Why Winter's additive model is better than other forecasting methods?
5. Give insights into the key findings regarding demand trends and forecasting accuracy in the jute yarn industry.
6. How did the study contribute to the field of forecasting in the jute products manufacturing sector?
7. How did the study analyze and interpret time series data related to jute yarn demand?
8. What are some potential implications of the study's findings for the jute products manufacturing industry in Bangladesh?

Darwin Store Sales Analysis

Managerial Accounting

Introduction

Darwin, Inc. is a retail corporation that wants to analyze its sales data to identify trends, patterns, and insights that can help improve business performance. Chris, the data analyst, and Mahi, the managerial accountant, have set the following objectives:

- Explore sales data to understand sales trends over time.
- Identify top-performing products and categories.

- Analyze sales by geographic regions.
- Identify any seasonal patterns in sales.
- Explore correlations between sales and external factors like promotions or holidays.

Sales Data

Date	Region	Product ID	Units	Channels	Interval
02-Jan-23	North	BS-TEMP	3	Promotional	Seasonal
02-Jan-23	West	FS-EBK	2	Promotional	Seasonal
03-Jan-23	North	BMC-COURSE	1	Promotional	Seasonal
03-Jan-23	West	FFCHARTS-TEMP	4	Affiliate	Off-season
03-Jan-23	West	FS-EBK	5	Affiliate	Off-season
04-Jan-23	West	FS-EBK	6	Promotional	Seasonal
05-Jan-23	North	BS-TEMP	5	Organic	Off-season
05-Jan-23	West	CFM-COURSE	5	Promotional	Off-season
05-Jan-23	North	FFCHARTS-TEMP	1	Affiliate	Off-season
06-Jan-23	West	RE-TEMP	4	Promotional	Seasonal
06-Jan-23	North	RE-TEMP	2	Affiliate	Seasonal
07-Jan-23	West	RE-TEMP	3	Affiliate	Seasonal
08-Jan-23	West	CF-TEMP	4	Affiliate	Seasonal
09-Jan-23	West	PFSCH-TEMP	5	Promotional	Seasonal
10-Jan-23	North	FFCHATRS-TEMP	6	Affiliate	Seasonal
11-Jan-23	West	P&L-TEMP	1	Affiliate	Seasonal
12-Jan-23	North	CF TEMP	1	Promotional	Seasonal
13-Jan-23	North	R&M - EBK	2	Promotional	Seasonal
14-Jan-23	North	BS-TEMP	3	Affiliate	Seasonal
15-Jan-23	West	ES-EBK	5	Promotional	Seasonal
17-Jan-23	West	BS-TEMP	4	Organic	Seasonal
18-Jan-23	South	FFCHARTS-TEMP	6	Affiliate	Off-season
19-Jan-23	East	RE-TEMP	5	Affiliate	Off-season
20-Jan-23	West	BMC-COURSE	7	Promotional	Off-season
21-Jan-23	South	CF-TEMP	8	Promotional	Seasonal
22-Jan-23	East	PS-TEMP	9	Promotional	Seasonal
22-Jan-23	East	PS-TEMP	5	Organic	Seasonal
23-Jan-23	West	FFCHARTS-TEMP	5	Affiliate	Seasonal
23-Jan-23	West	RE-TEMP	2	Promotional	Off-season
24-Jan-23	North	BMC-COURSE	2	Promotional	Off-season
25-Jan-23	North	CF-TEMP	1	Organic	Seasonal
26-Jan-23	West	ES-EBK	8	Promotional	Off-season

The company has access to the data sources as mentioned in **Illustration 1**. Also, **Illustration 2** has been provided to analyze the impact of holidays and promotions on sales.

- **Sales data:** Includes information about sales transactions, such as product ID, date, quantity sold, revenue, and customer ID.
- **Product data:** Includes details about each product, such as category, price, and attributes.
- **Geographic data:** Includes information about store locations, regions, and demographics.
- **External factors data:** Includes data on promotions, holidays, and other events.

ILLUSTRATION 1   Data for Analysis

Transaction ID	Date	Product ID	Product Category	Quality Sold	Revenue	Customer ID	Price	Attributes	Store Location	Region
1	Jan-2023	1001	Electronics	2	500	101	250	High-tech	Store A	Urban
1	Jan-2023	1001	Electronics	2	500	101	250	High-tech	Store A	Urban
3	Jan-2023	1003	Home Appliances	3	300	103	250	Appliances	Store B	Suburban
4	May-2023	1002	Home Appliances	1	750	104	300	Appliances	Store A	Suburban
5	Oct-2023	1005	Electronics	1	300	104	250	High-tech	Store C	Urban
6	Oct-2023	1002	Home Appliances	3	750	101	150	Appliances	Store B	Rural
7	May-2023	1005	Home Appliances	1	300	103	150	High-tech	Store C	Rural
8	Feb-2023	1006	Electronics	2	400	103	180	Appliances	Store C	Suburban
9	Feb-2023	1003	Home Appliances	3	400	105	180	High-tech	Store B	Rural
9	Feb-2023	1003	Home Appliances	3	400	105	180	High-tech	Store B	Rural
10	Mar-2023	1006	Electronics	1	500	105	180	Appliances	Store A	Urban

ILLUSTRATION 2   External Factors Data Table

Event ID	Event Type	Event Date	Description
1	Promotion	Jan 2023	New year
2	Holiday	Feb 2023	Valentine's day
3	Promotion	March 2023	St. Patrick's Day Sale

Assume your role as Chris and implement the steps you have drawn to achieve the objectives for the aforementioned tables.

1. **Data Cleaning**
   - Remove duplicates and irrelevant columns.
   - Handle missing values (e.g., impute or drop as appropriate).
   - Ensure data consistency and integrity.

2. **Exploratory Data Analysis (EDA)**
   - Visualize sales trends over time using line charts or time series plots.
   - Identify top-selling products and categories using bar charts or pie charts.
   - Analyze sales by region using geographic maps or bar charts.
   - Explore seasonal patterns using seasonal decomposition or trend analysis.
   - Investigate correlations between sales and external factors using correlation matrices or scatter plots.

3. **Insights Generation**
   - Identify peak and low sales periods to optimize inventory management and marketing strategies.
   - Determine which products and categories contribute the most to overall sales and focus on promoting them.

- Analyze sales performance across different regions to customize marketing campaigns and promotions.
- Identify the impact of promotions, holidays, or other events on sales performance.

4. **Reporting and Visualization**

- Create interactive dashboards using data visualization tools, such as Tableau, Power BI, or Python libraries (Matplotlib, Seaborn).
- Present key findings, trends, and recommendations to stakeholders in a clear and concise manner.

Results

- Sales trends analysis revealed a steady increase in sales during the holiday season, with a significant spike during Black Friday and Cyber Monday.
- Top-performing products were found to be in the electronics category, with smartphones and laptops being the bestsellers.
- Sales were highest in urban regions compared to rural areas, indicating a need for targeted marketing strategies.
- Promotional campaigns during peak sales periods significantly boosted revenue, highlighting the importance of strategic promotions.

Conclusion

Through data exploration and analysis, the retail store chain gained valuable insights into sales trends, product performance, regional variations, and the impact of external factors on sales. These insights can be used to optimize inventory management, marketing strategies, and decision-making processes to drive business growth and profitability.

Case Questions

1. How can sales trends help a retail store chain plan inventory levels over time?
2. What are the benefits of identifying top-performing products and categories for a retail business?
3. How does analyzing sales by geographic region contribute to customized marketing campaigns?
4. Why is it important to identify seasonal patterns in sales for a retail store chain?
5. What role do external factors, such as promotions or holidays, play in influencing sales performance?
6. How can data cleaning ensure the accuracy and reliability of sales data for analysis?

Market Size and Share and Price Analysis for AutoX

Managerial Accounting

Introduction

In the competitive automobile industry, understanding market dynamics is essential for driving business growth and profitability. Market size variance and market share variance are two key metrics that help companies assess their performance relative to market conditions and competitors.

This case delves into the analysis of market size and market share for a Korean automobile company, AutoX. The company produces sedans, hatchbacks, and SUVs, targeting different segments of the market.

AutoX sets target sale prices for each car model based on market research, cost considerations, and competitive positioning. However, actual sale prices may deviate from the targets due to various factors, such as changes in consumer preferences, economic conditions, and competitive pressures. Analyzing market size and market share provides valuable insights into AutoX's performance and competitiveness in the automobile market.

George Lee, the head of marketing, and Lyn Jeong, the chief financial officer, want to discuss the sales growth and understand the influence of overall market growth, segment growth along with the marketing strategy, and the efforts of marketing team.

Data

They have considered year 2024 as the base for benchmarking current sales.

| Vehicle Category | Year 2024 | | | | | |
	Market Size	Units Sold	Market Share (%)	Mix (%)	Avg. Unit Rate (₩)	Total Sales (₩)
Sedan	13,500	4,050	30%	23%	32,500,000	131,625,000,000
Hatchback	17,500	7,875	45%	45%	39,000,000	307,125,000,000
SUV	9,000	5,400	60%	31%	52,000,000	280,800,000,000
	40,000	17,325	43%	100%		719,550,000,000

George made the following observations:

- Total market size in 2024 was 40,000 units out of which 17,325 units were sold by AutoX.
- Overall share in 40,000 units was approximately 43%.
- In case of individual segments, AutoX covered 30% market share of sedans, 45% market share of hatchbacks, and 60% market share of SUVs.
- Out of total 17,325 units sold by AutoX, sedans accounted for 23%, hatchbacks accounted for 45%, and SUVs accounted for 31%. In terms of volumes, AutoX has good share of hatchbacks in overall mix. However, SUV segment is close to hatchbacks in terms of sale value due to higher prices.
- The marketing agencies and sales teams are paid certain fees and commissions based on the sales value.

The current year 2025 reported the following sales numbers:

| Vehicle Category | Year 2025 | | | | | |
	Market Size	Units Sold	Market Share (%)	Mix (%)	Avg. Unit Rate (₩)	Total Sales (₩)
Sedan	14,850	3,713	25.00%	17%	31,200,000	115,845,600,000
Hatchback	20,300	10,150	50.00%	47%	41,600,000	422,240,000,000
SUV	14,400	7,920	55.00%	36%	53,300,000	422,136,000,000
	49,550	21,783	130.00%	100%		960,221,600,000

The overall growth in sales volume and value is reported at:

Vehicle Category	Year 2024			Year 2025			Growth	
	Units Sold	Avg. Unit Rate (₩)	Total Sales (₩)	Units Sold	Avg. Unit Rate (₩)	Total Sales (₩)	Market Share	Total Sales (₩)
Sedan	4,050	32,500,000	131,625,000,000	3,713	31,200,000	115,845,600,000	(337)	(15,779,400,000)
Hatchback	7,875	39,000,000	307,125,000,000	10,150	41,600,000	422,240,000,000	2,275	115,115,000,000
SUV	5,400	52,000,000	280,800,000,000	7,920	53,300,000	422,136,000,000	2,520	141,336,000,000
	17,325		719,550,000,000	21,783		960,221,600,000	4,458	240,671,600,000

Lyn wants to understand the following few implications:

- Is the individual segment growth influenced by the overall market growth?
- All types of selling fees and commissions are paid on total sales value. Does this mean that the efforts of marketing agencies and sales team facilitate each unit of sale?
- As part of the Korea Automobile Association, there are some joint efforts by all automobile manufacturers to push the growth of the industry. What are the implications of these shared efforts?

They have gathered some more insights from the sales team, which might be useful for financial analysis of the sales data:

- A few customers come with a specific segment in mind and these customers purchase the vehicle in the same segment.
- Majority of the customers have an open mindset and evaluate vehicles in all segments. They may decide in favor of any segment based on their budgets and personal preferences.
- Vehicles are offered at base price lists. Additional discounts or premiums are charged based on current market conditions on a case-to-case basis.

Analysis

Chua Li Yan, the management accountant, has also done some calculations based on the request of Lyn and George:

1. **Scenario 1: Individual segment growth is independent.** The estimated sale number, if we apply individual segment growth on base sale numbers of 2024:

Vehicle Category	2024 Market Size (A)	2025 Market Size (B)	Growth (C = B/A%)	Base Sales (D)	Expected Sales (E = D × C%)	Current Sale (F)	Variance (G = F − E)	Base Price (H) (in ₩)	Variance Value (I = G × H) (in ₩)
Sedan	13,500	14,850	110%	4,050	4,455	3,713	(742)	32,500,000	(24,115,000,000)
Hatchback	17,500	20,300	116%	7,875	9,135	10,150	1,015	39,000,000	39,585,000,000
SUV	9,000	14,400	160%	5,400	8,640	7,920	(720)	52,000,000	(37,440,000,000)
	40,000	49,550		17,325	22,230	21,783	(447)		(21,970,000,000)

2. **Scenario 2: Individual segment growth is largely dependent on overall market growth.** The estimated sale numbers, if we apply overall market growth percentage to the base number and assume that the company sustains the base sale mix:

Vehicle Category	2024 Market Size (A)	2025 Market Size (B)	Growth (C = B/A%)	Base Sales (D)	Expected Overall Sales (E = D × C%)	Mix 2024 (F)	Scenario 2 Expected Segment Sales (G = Total of E × F%)	Current Sale (H)	Variance (I = H − G)	Base Price (J) (in ₩)	Variance Value (K = I × J) (in ₩)
Sedan	13,500	14,850		4,050		23%	5,017	3,713	(1,304)	32,500,000	(42,380,000,000)
Hatchback	17,500	20,300		7,875		45%	9,755	10,150	395	39,000,000	15,405,000,000
SUV	9,000	14,400		5,400		31%	6,689	7,920	1,231	52,000,000	64,012,000,000
	40,000	49,550	124%	17,325	21,461	100%	21,461	21,783	322		37,037,000,000

3. Sales attributable to scenario 1 and scenario 2 as compared to actual sales:

Vehicle Category	Volumes Scenario 1 (A)	Scenario 2 (B)	Sales 2025 (C)	Base Price (D) (in ₩)	Sales Value Scenario 1 (E = A × D) (in ₩)	Scenario 2 (F = B × D) (in ₩)	Sales 2025 (G) (in ₩)
Sedan	4,455	5,017	3,713	32,500,000	144,787,500,000	163,052,500,000	115,845,600,000
Hatchback	9,135	9,755	10,150	39,000,000	356,265,000,000	380,445,000,000	422,240,000,000
SUV	8,640	6,689	7,920	52,000,000	449,280,000,000	347,828,000,000	422,136,000,000
	22,230	21,461	21,783		950,332,500,000	891,325,500,000	960,221,600,000

4. Effect of price element on current sales:

Vehicle Category	Volumes Sales 2025 (A)	Base Price (B) (in ₩)	Actual Price (C) (in ₩)	Sale Value 2025 At Base Price (D = A × B) (in ₩)	At Current Price (E = A × C) (in ₩)	Price Effect (F = E − D) (in ₩)
Sedan	3,713	32,500,000	31,200,000	120,672,500,000	115,845,600,000	(4,826,900,000)
Hatchback	10,150	39,000,000	41,600,000	395,850,000,000	422,240,000,000	26,390,000,000
SUV	7,920	52,000,000	53,300,000	411,840,000,000	422,136,000,000	10,296,000,000
	21,783			928,362,500,000	960,221,600,000	31,859,100,000

Additional information provided to Chua:

- Market size analysis can be done assuming the 2024 average prices as the base prices. These are also considered as the target price, subject to the discount and surcharge policies.
- Market share variance measures the difference between the actual market share captured by the company and the expected market share based on target sales volumes. George and Lyn agree that the 2024 volumes are the target sales volume for the purpose of market share analysis.

Conclusion

Analyzing market size variance and market share variance provides AutoX with valuable insights into its performance and competitiveness in the automobile market. Negative variances indicate areas where the company fell short of its targets, prompting further investigation into the underlying factors. By monitoring and addressing these variances, AutoX can refine its strategies, optimize pricing, and enhance its market position to drive sustainable growth and profitability in the dynamic automotive industry. While analyzing the sales data for AutoX, the effect of market size and market share provides useful insights into sales performance.

Case Questions

1. Which scenario seems more appropriate for analysis and why?
2. Is this analysis sufficient to explain the impact of efforts by the Korea Automobile Association to push the growth of the industry?
3. What is the contribution of the price element to the overall sales value growth?
4. Year 2024 has been taken as the benchmark to analyze the performance the current year. Is there a better way to analyze the current performance against a different benchmark?

Data Visualization of Financial Accounting Information

`Financial Accounting`

Introduction

The financial information from 10-K and proxy statements of Walmart is used in this case. The statements are retrieved from the Walmart website for the period from 2018 to 2023. Simplified statements from Stock-analysis-on.net are also used. We analyze income statements, balance sheets, and cash flow statements. From proxy statements, we collect salary and compensation information for CEOs, top non-CEO executives, and the board of directors. We must first effectively communicate the information before proceeding to develop dashboards in Tableau and create charts and graphs using Microsoft Excel. For the ratio analysis, we divide major income statement line items, such as cost of goods sold, gross profit, operating profit, net profit, and SG&A by net sales. We also divide major line items from the balance sheet by total assets to compute the ratios.

Data and Analysis

Our analysis focuses on key line items from Walmart's annual reports, highlighting the firm's value, short- and long-term financial health indicators, executive compensation, and shareholders' ownership percentage. **Illustration 1** presents a snapshot of Walmart's income statement from years 2018 to 2023, showcasing essential items, such as net sales, cost of sales, gross profit, selling, general, and administrative expenses (SG&A), operating income, and net income.

Illustration 2 presents the ratio analysis of the cost and income of Walmart from 2018 to 2023. As shown in the chart, the cost-to-sales ratio is constant from 2018 to 2023 at a slightly less

ILLUSTRATION 1 Key Line Items of the Income Statement of Walmart from 2018 to 2023

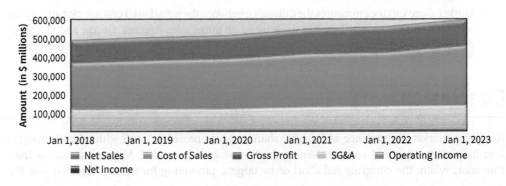

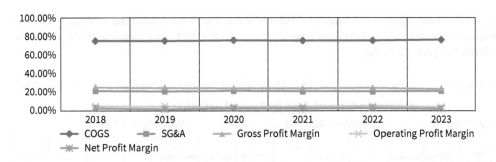

ILLUSTRATION 2 Profit Margin of Walmart from 2018 to 2023

80% level. SG&A expenses (22% of sales) do not change from 2018 to 2023. From 2018 to 2023, the gross profit margin showed no significant increase or decrease in sales. It only has a fixed rate of approximately 26% of sales throughout the years.

The operating profit margin shows a slight movement of increase from 2021 to 2022 and diminishes from 2022 to 2023. It had a sales rate of approximately 3% from 2018 through 2021, then increased from 3% to 4%, and eventually declined to 3% in 2023. The net profit margin shows a significant increase from 2019 to 2020, attaining a maximum with a constant sales rate of approximately 2%. Understanding the financial position and short-term capital management is key to the long-term success of a firm.

The analysis of Walmart's financial figures, as depicted in **Illustrations 3** and **4**, showcases the company's robust financial management strategies. Illustration 3 reveals a balanced approach to managing cash, accounts payable, short-term borrowings, inventories, and receivables, reflecting effective short-term liability management. This prudent approach contributes to the firm's stability and ability to maintain operations smoothly.

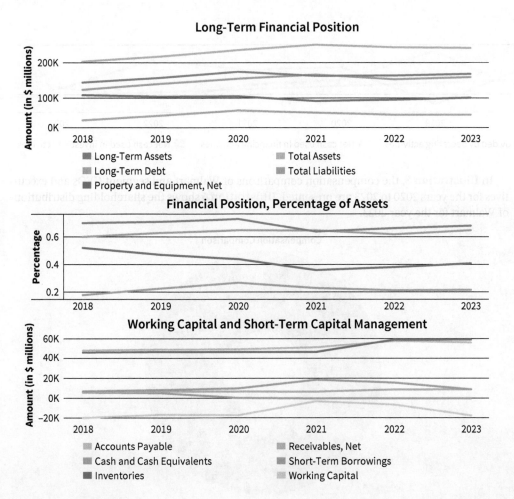

ILLUSTRATION 3 Long-Term Financial Position and Short-Term Working Capital Management of Walmart from 2018 to 2023

Overall, these figures demonstrate Walmart's excellence in generating consistent profits, building assets, managing short- and long-term capital effectively, and ensuring strong cash flow performance year after year.

ILLUSTRATION 4 Cash Flow Activities and Sources and Uses of Cash by Type of Activities of Walmart from 2018 to 2023

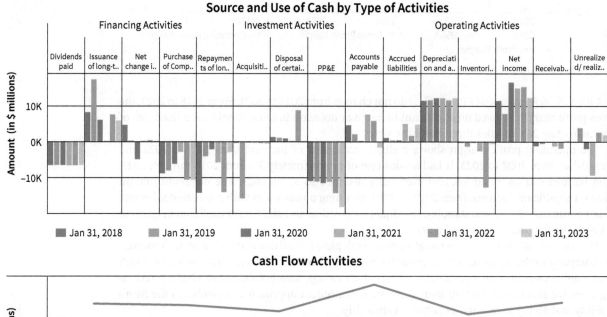

In **Illustration 5**, the compensation comparisons of Walmart and segment CEOs and executives for the years 2020 to 2023 are presented. **Illustration 6** shows the shareholding distribution of Walmart for the year 2023.

ILLUSTRATION 5 Executives' Compensation Comparison of Walmart from 2020 to 2023

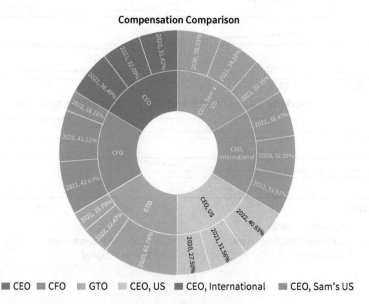

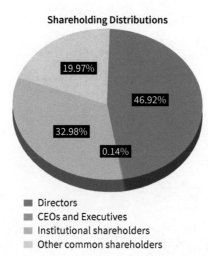

Shareholding Distributions

- Directors
- CEOs and Executives
- Institutional shareholders
- Other common shareholders

ILLUSTRATION 6   Percentage of Outstanding Shares Held by the Shareholders for the Year 2023

Conclusion

Incorporating visual aids such as graphs and charts in financial reporting, especially for nonprofessional stakeholders, enhances comprehension and facilitates informed decision-making for investors and other stakeholders. The analysis of Walmart's financial accounts and compensation structure showcases the effectiveness of visualization in conveying key financial insights.

Case Questions

1. What insights does the income statement visualization provide about Walmart's financial performance?

2. How is Illustration 1 visualization different from Illustration 2? Which is a better indicator?

3. How do you interpret Walmart's cash management strategy using Illustration 4?

4. How is the compensation distributed among various owners?

Glossary

A

Accurate In the context of data analysis, this means the measures used in the analysis are correct and free of errors.

Adjusted R square A regression statistic that explains how well the regression line fits the data.

Algorithms Sets of instructions that transform data into information.

Analytical database A clean, well-structured, integrated data set that can be used for analysis.

Anomaly An observation in the data that deviates from what is normal or expected.

Attributes The data fields that describe aspects of a resource, event, or agent of the object of interest. When the data source is a database, they are the columns in a data set.

B

Blockchain technologies Online technology that creates a single, shared record of transactions between parties.

C

Calculated columns A new data set column with values that are calculated based on the values in other columns.

Calculated data Discrete or continuous data that can be used for analysis purposes, these data are created when mathematical calculations are applied to one or more fields in a record/row.

Cardinality A constraint that defines how many times an instance of an entity may participate in a relationship.

Categorical data Labeled or named data that can be sorted into groups according to specific characteristics.

Cloud data services A popular solution for storing high-volume data, these services provide secure data storage using the organization's own resources or third-party resources.

Coefficient of determination Also called R square, it is a regression statistic that measures how well the regression line fits the data.

Coefficient of kurtosis (CK) A measure that describes how much data are in the ends of a distribution in a data set compared to the center.

Coefficient of skewness (CS) Measure of shape that describes the skewness of a distribution in a data set.

Cognitive technologies Artificial intelligence technologies that use algorithms that mimic the human thought process.

Composite column A column with cells that combines values for two or more characteristics.

Composite trend data relationship An integrated data relationship that shows the changes in a part-to-whole relationship over time.

Constraints In a linear optimization model, they are the limitations, requirements, or other restrictions that must be imposed on any solution.

Context When communicating data analysis results, the information that helps the audience better understand what is being communicated.

Continuous auditing technologies Programmed modules embedded in an organization's AIS that evaluate transactions as they occur.

Correlation analysis An analysis that shows relationships in data by measuring the linear relationship between two variables.

Correlation coefficient Also known as the Pearson product-moment correlation coefficient, it is a numerical value between -1 and $+1$ that measures the linear relationship of continuous variables.

Correlation data relationship A data relationship that indicates the degree to which two variables move in the same or the opposite direction.

Critical thinking Disciplined reasoning used to investigate, understand, and evaluate an event, opportunity, or issue.

Cross tabulation analysis An analysis that shows the number of observations in a data set for different subcategories of data.

D

Dashboard A graphical user interface that shows key performance indicators for an organization.

Data Raw figures and captured facts, such as categories, measures, and calculations.

Data analysis interpretation The process of evaluating an analysis to understand and explain its meaning.

Data analytics The process of analyzing raw data to answer questions or provide insights.

Data analytics mindset The habit of critically thinking through the planning, analysis, and reporting of data analysis results before

making and communicating a professional choice or decision.

Data connectors Intuitive software programs designed to extract data from spreadsheets, text files, and other data sources.

Data dictionary A chart of the data in a data set that indicates what data are available and where they can be found.

Data exploration Also called exploratory data analysis, it is the discovery process of looking for something new in the data.

Data extraction The first step in the ETL process, which involves transferring data from where they are stored to the platform where they will be transformed.

Data integration The process of connecting related data by defining relationships with primary and foreign keys or combining two or more tables with information from the same entity.

Data literacy The ability to understand and communicate data.

Data loading The process of making the analytical database available for use in software that performs the analysis.

Data matching A process that compares data and determines whether they describe the same entity.

Data mining The systematic process of looking for issues or patterns occurring within or between data fields.

Data model A data structure that shows the relationships among the different entities in a data set.

Data organization Rearranging data to make them easier to understand for analysis purposes.

Data preparation The process of transforming data into an analytical database by profiling, cleaning, restructuring, and integrating data prior to processing and analysis.

Data profiling The three-part process of investigating data quality, investigating data structure, and then deciding next steps for the analysis.

Data relationship A description of how data elements or values relate to each other.

Data restructuring Also known as data wrangling or data munging, this process changes how the data in a data set are organized, such as adding, deleting, and renaming columns or splitting and combining tables.

Data set A collection of data columns and rows available for analysis.

Data transformation In the ETL process, it involves improving the raw data for analysis through cleaning, restructuring, and integration.

Data value The benefits of certain data given in the objective of a data analysis project.

Data variety The diversity of data structures and measurement scales in data that are useful for analysis.

Data velocity The speed at which new data points are generated.

Data veracity The reliability of the data used for analysis.

Data visualization The graphical representation of data and information to provide meaning and insights during the data analysis process.

Data volume The amount of data selected for an analysis project.

Data warehouse Software, such as Power BI and Tableau, that stores and analyzes large data sets.

Decision variables In a linear optimization model, these are the unknown variables to be determined by the model.

Dependent variable In a statistical model, it is the outcome measure that is being predicted.

Descriptive analytics Data analysis designed to understand what is currently happening or what has happened in the past.

Descriptive questions Analysis questions designed to understand something that is currently happening or that has happened in the past.

Deviation data relationship A data relationship that shows how actual values deviate from their reference values.

Diagnostic analytics Data analysis designed to understand why something has happened.

Diagnostic questions Analysis questions designed to understand why an outcome occurred.

Dimensions In an accounting context, these are the data that provide context to analysis and give meaning to facts. They are the variables or fields that can be used to drill down or disaggregate (slice) analysis measures.

Dirty data Data that provide inaccurate or incomplete descriptions of a business' economic activities.

Distribution data relationship A data relationship that shows how the values of a numeric variable are distributed, or spread out, by providing the different values present in the data.

E

Explanatory data visualization The use of data visualization tools and techniques to communicate the results of an analysis.

Exploration structure A visual that describes the different data elements used in data exploration and how they are related.

Exploratory data visualization The use of data visualization tools and techniques to examine data to find insights.

External data Data that are acquired from outside an organization, such as weather or social media data.

External stakeholders Individuals or groups outside a company who may be impacted by and/or have an interest in the outcome of a data analysis project.

Extract-transform-load (ETL) The process of retrieving raw data from a source, cleaning, restructuring, and/or integrating them with other data, and then loading the data into software for analysis purposes.

F

Facts In an accounting context, the stored data that correspond to business transactions such as orders, sales, purchases, and payments.

Fields Separate columns representing the characteristics about each record stored in the columns of a data set.

Flows relationship The data relationship between resources and specific transactions.

Foreign key A column in a table that is a primary key in another table.

Frequency distribution A summary of activity in the observations within a given group or interval.

Functional relationship The effect of an independent variable on a dependent variable in a trendline.

Functions Predefined formulas built into analysis software that perform frequently used calculations.

G

Geospatial data relationship A data relationship in which numeric values are assigned to locations and encoded by color and size of the bubbles within the visualization.

Gestalt principles of visual perception Principles that describe how humans gain meaning from the stimuli around them.

H

Histogram A measure of shape that is a bar chart of a frequency distribution. The height of the bar reflects the frequency within the interval.

Hybrid clouds Data clouds that offer both private and public cloud data storage.

I

Independent variables Factors that influence the dependent variable.

Information Knowledge gained from data that is relevant for analysis purposes.

Information model An extension of the data model that includes calculated columns and measures.

Information modeling The process of generating additional knowledge from data that is relevant for analysis purposes.

Insight An observation that might significantly affect a business' decision-making.

Interactive data visualization A data visualization in which users can explore, manipulate, and interact with graphical representations of data.

Internal data Data found within an organization, such as sales and customer data.

Internal stakeholders Individuals or groups involved in a business' operations who may be impacted by and/or have an interest in the outcome of a data analysis project.

J

Join (See also Merge) The process of combining rows from two or more tables based on a related column between them.

K

Kurtosis A measure of shape that refers to how peaked or flat the data are in a histogram.

L

Law of continuity The Gestalt principle of visual perception which explains how people tend to perceive any line as continuing in its established direction and that objects aligned with each other are perceived as a single path or shape.

Law of focal point The Gestalt principle of visual perception that refers to how we are more attentive to whatever stands out visually.

Law of proximity The Gestalt principle of visual perception that states people will perceive visual elements based on how closely they are positioned to one another.

Law of similarity The Gestalt principle of visual perception that describes how similar elements tend to be perceived as a unified group.

Linear function A function that shows the steady increases or decreases over the range of the independent variable in a trendline.

Linear optimization The most common optimization model used in accounting, its output shows the optimal solution.

Linear regression A tool for building mathematical and statistical models to explain the relationship between a dependent variable and one or more independent variables.

M

Mean A measure of central tendency that is the sum of all observations in a data set divided by the total number of observations.

Measure An aggregated data information field that can be used for analytical purposes.

Measure of central tendency A single value that describes a set of data by identifying the central position within that data set.

Measured raw numeric data Discrete or continuous data created or captured by a controlled process that can be used in mathematical calculations for analysis purposes.

Measurement scale The type of information provided by a data field. Data can be categorical, ordinal, interval, or ratio measures.

Measures of dispersion Measures that describe the amount of variation in the data to help us understand what causes that disparity.

Measures of location Measures that determine the average or typical observation in the data set.

Measures of shape Measures that describe the distribution of the data in a data set.

Median A measure of central tendency that is the middle value when the data are arranged from smallest to largest in a data set.

Merge (See also Join) The process of combining rows from two or more tables based on a related column between them.

Mode A measure of central tendency that is the observation that occurs most frequently in the data.

Motivation The reason or stimulus for performing data analysis.

Multi-valued column A column with cells that contain multiple values of the same characteristic.

N

Nominal comparison data relationship A data relationship that compares the values of a categorical variable based on a second, numeric variable.

Nonmeasured raw data Typically categorical, discrete data fields, such as identification codes, that cannot be used in mathematical calculations.

Null value An unknown or missing value in a data set.

O

Objective The goal of a data analytics project.

Objective function In a linear optimization model, it is the mathematical equation that describes the output target to minimize or maximize.

Occurs relationship The data relationship that links the calendar to specific business transactions.

One measure, multiple analyses principle Refers to the fact that one measure can be broken down in many different ways.

Optimization The process of selecting values of variables that minimize or maximize some quantity of interest.

Outlier An extreme value in a data set, often defined as a data point that falls more than 1.5 times the interquartile range below the first quartile or above the third quartile.

P

Pareto analysis A statistical technique that visualizes the importance of different categories, ranks them, and shows how each category contributes to the cumulative percentage.

Participates relationship A data relationship that links agents to specific business transactions.

Part–to–whole data relationship A data relationship that compares parts to wholes and examines how the different parts compare to each other.

Pivot table An analysis tool that summarizes and reorganizes selected columns and rows of data.

Preattentive attributes Visual properties that people notice subconsciously.

Predictive analytics Data analysis that helps understand what is likely to happen in the future.

Predictive questions Analysis questions designed to help understand what is likely to happen in the future.

Prescriptive analytics Data analysis that determines the best course of action to achieve a goal in a specific scenario.

Prescriptive questions Analysis questions that determine the best course of action to achieve a goal in a specific scenario.

Primary key A unique value for each data row in a database table.

Private clouds Data clouds with restricted access that store the data for one organization or an agreed-upon group of organizations.

Process mining tools Tools that measure the timing and flow of data captured as business events occur.

Public clouds Data clouds that securely store data from multiple companies on shared servers using virtual server data separators.

Q

Query A request for data from a database so the data can be retrieved or manipulated.

R

Ranking data relationship A data relationship that orders the values of a variable sequentially based on the values of a second variable.

Reasoning The human process of logically forming conclusions, judgments, or inferences from facts.

Records Data in the rows of the data set representing instances of the phenomenon being captured.

Referential integrity A rule that states the values of a foreign key must be a subset of the values of its corresponding primary key.

Regression statistics Statistical measures used to evaluate the results of a regression model.

Relational database A collection of logically related data that can be retrieved, manipulated, and updated to meet users' needs.

Reliability In the context of data analysis, the data used are dependable and trustworthy.

Robotic process automation (RPA) Set of software technologies that record a specific order of human keystrokes and mouse activity steps within or across digital applications.

S

Scatterplot Visualization that shows the relationship between two numerical variables.

Self-service business intelligence software (SSBI) Easy-to-use, accessible software that can prepare data, analyze data, and report results.

Single-valued column A column in which each cell contains one value describing a single characteristic.

Skewness A measure of shape that describes the lack of symmetry of data in the distribution of the data.

Slicers An analysis tool that separates analysis measures per selected dimensions

Slicing The process of breaking data down into smaller parts.

Smart contracts Secure, online shared digital contracts.

Snowflake schema A data structure in which the information for a dimension is spread across multiple tables.

Stakeholders Individuals or groups who may be impacted by and/or have an interest in the outcome of a data analysis project.

Standard deviation A statistic that measures the dispersion of a data set relative to the mean. It is the square root of the variance.

Standard error A regression statistic that represents the variability of the observed dependent variable values from the values predicted by the regression model.

Star schema The recommended data structure for analytical databases. They consist of fact tables and dimension tables.

Structured Query Language (SQL) The standard query command language for database management.

T

Table How data related to an object of interest are stored in a relational database.

Technological agility An awareness of the latest technological developments and a willingness to work with new tools.

Textual analysis The process of analyzing word choice in footnotes, investor communications, blogs, social media postings, and other documentation.

Textual mining The process of transforming text into a format that can be used for analysis.

Time series data relationship A relationship that defines the values of a variable at sequential points in time.

Trend analysis A statistical tool that uses historical data to identify patterns.

Trendline In a trend analysis, it indicates the general course or tendency of the data and is created using historical data to estimate a line.

U

Union The process of combining different tables with the same data structure.

V

Validation rules An integral part of data profiling, these rules define what values are and are not acceptable for analysis when investigating the data quality.

Validity In the context of data analysis, it means that an analysis measures what it is supposed to measure and that it represents in reality.

Variable A data field used for analysis.

Variance A measure of dispersion that finds the average squared distance between the data points in the data set and the mean.

W

What table A dimension table that describes the resources involved in a business transaction.

What-if analysis A spreadsheet model that evaluates how changes to values and assumptions affect an outcome.

When table A dimension table that describes when the data from the business transaction occurred.

Who table A dimension table that describes agents involved in the business transaction data.

Index